TWELFTH CONFERENCE OF THE INTERNATIONAL BAR ASSOCIATION

INTERNATIONAL BAR ASSOCIATION

Twelfth Conference of the International Bar Association

Dublin, Ireland, July 11-15, 1968

Summary of Proceedings

Official Papers and Reports

List of Authors, Committee Members, Conferees, Patrons and Subscribers

Index to Topics discussed at Dublin and previous Conferences

SPRINGER-SCIENCE+BUSINESS MEDIA, B.V. 1968

Additional material to this book can be downloaded from http://extras.springer.com

ISBN 978-94-017-4549-9 ISBN 978-94-017-4694-6 (eBook)
DOI 10.1007/978-94-017-4694-6
Softcover reprint of the hardcover 1st edition 1968

TABLE OF CONTENTS

IV. Dublin Conference — Working Sessions

Topic No. 1

Plenary Session –

Topic No. 2

Plenary Session –

Topic No. 3

Plenary Session –

Topic No. 4

Plenary Session –

INTRODUCTION

This is a report of the International Bar Association's Twelfth Conference of the Legal Profession held in Dublin July 8–12, 1968 with the Incorporated Law Society of Ireland, in association with the General Council of the Bar of Ireland, as hosts.

Lawyers from every corner of the globe found in Ireland a country dedicated to the rule of law and a people who extended a warm and friendly welcome to their conferees and guests from overseas. The largest assembly of lawyers ever to attend an IBA conference participated actively in a well rounded program of professional topics. The outstanding social program was matched by the best Irish summer weather in decades. The final soireé at Castletown House was a fitting climax to a great conference.

The members of the legal profession listed in this volume have all contributed to the success of the Dublin Conference. To them are attributable the accomplishments of the International Bar Association over the twenty years which have passed since its birth in 1947. They are the heart and sinews of the IBA, professionally and financially.

This is principally a report on the Dublin Conference and especially the working program. Here will be found the reports on the topics discussed at the Conference in the language of the Rapporteurs' choice, a short summarization thereof, and a Summary of Discussions at the working sessions. In addition, the report includes a paper entitled "Report on Comparative Standards for the Determination of Eligibility for Legal Aid", presented to the General Meeting of the International Legal Aid Association, which was held in conjunction with the Conference; a brief description of the Origin and History of the Association in the four official languages of the International Bar Association; and various reports on organizational matters.

Information concerning the material on which combined reports were based and other language texts of some of the reports may be obtained from International Bar Association headquarters in New York and London.

The printed record of the Dublin Conference can reflect only in part the many hours of effort which made the Conference possible, both on the part of our Irish hosts and the Rapporteurs and National Correspondents who contributed to the working sessions. Special thanks are due to the various Conference committees of Irish lawyers and to the young law students whose contributions helped to make the Conference a model of administrative efficiency.

ORIGIN AND HISTORY OF THE INTERNATIONAL BAR ASSOCIATION

As early as 1932 the American Bar Association had appointed a committee to study the question of an international federation of national bar associations. During World War II, the conviction grew that the organized Bar of the world could make a substantial contribution to post-war reconstruction, stability and understanding. In 1944 a special committee was again established by the American Bar Association to investigate the feasibility and desirability of an international bar association. The need for such an organization was found to be great, and the likelihood of its appealing to the organized Bar throughout the world was far greater than a decade earlier. Therefore, in the spring of 1946 the committee sent to the various bar associations a draft plan of organization, together with a copy of the resolution of the American Bar Association's House of Delegates approving cooperation with the organized Bars of the nations of the world. The response was so encouraging that the House of Delegates on July 2, 1946 authorized the President of the American Bar Association to invite the associations to meet in New York. At that meeting, on October 8-9, 1946, representatives of national associations of more than twenty countries met. In addition national bar organizations from ten other countries sent their endorsement. The meeting resulted in the adoption of a revised draft of the constitution, and in February 1947 representatives of twenty-three national bar associations met again in New York to organize the International Bar Association.

The purposes of the IBA, "a non-political organization", as stated in Article I of the Constitution, are the following: –

To establish and maintain permanent relation and exchanges between Bar Associations throughout the world and their members.

To discuss problems of professional organization and status.

To advance the science of jurisprudence in all its phases.

By common study of practical legal problems to promote uniformity and definition in appropriate fields of law.

To promote the administration of justice under law among peoples of the world.

In execution of these objects to promote in their legal aspects the principles and aims of the United Nations and to co-operate with, and promote co-ordination among, international juridical organizations having similar purposes.

Provided that the Association is a non-political organization and as such shall not entertain any matter which is political in character.

The IBA is a federation of national bar associations. In countries where no national bar association exists, or where the national association itself is not a member of the IBA or where it is a member and approves, any other organization of members of the legal profession may be admitted to membership, provided that the voting power of the country is not thereby increased beyond the maximum allowed to its national organization or organizations. There are now 55 Member Organizations from 41 nations. Since the IBA is a federation, its Member Organizations are the source of its authority. The supreme governing body of the IBA is the General Meeting, which convenes at each biennial conference and is composed of delegates appointed by Member Organizations. Each Member Organization may appoint one delegate for each 1,000, or fraction of 1,000, of its own members, provided that no Member may have more than 10 delegates. The General Meeting elects officers of the Association, approves financial matters, passes resolutions of the Association, etc. There is no limit to the number of its members a Member Organization may accredit to attend biennial conferences as conferees – the limitation applies only to delegates appointed to the General Meeting, to make that body equitably representative of the legal profession of the world. Thus, when the IBA reaches a conclusion in its General Meeting, it speaks for the organized bar of most of the world.

When the Association is not convened in biennial conference, the governing body of the IBA is the Council, the members of which are nominated by Member Organizations. Each Member Organization is entitled to have one representative on the Council. In addition, officers of the Association are ex-officio members of the Council. The Council meets at least once each year and during a conference. There is also provided for Honorary Membership of the Council.

Individuals may be affiliated as Patrons or Subscribers if they are members of the legal profession and are approved by their respective national Bar associations. More than 1600 Subscribers and Patrons from all corners of the world are active in the IBA, and they constitute an important section of the Association – not only from the viewpoint of professional support, but from the financial angle as well. They attend biennial conferences – but they have no vote in the General Meeting, unless they are appointed by their own national bar associations to the General Meeting.

Twelve conferences have been held by the IBA. The first was the Inaugural Conference of October 1947, in New York. The Second Conference was held in The Hague in 1948 at the invitation of the Nederlandsche Advocaten Vereeniging; the Third Conference in London in 1950 as guests of The Law Society and the General Council of the Bar; the Fourth Conference in Madrid in 1952 under the auspices of the Consejo General de los Ilustres Colegios de Abogados de España; the Fifth Conference in Monaco in 1954; the Sixth Conference in 1956 at

Oslo at the invitation of Den Norske Sakførerforening; the Seventh Conference in Cologne in 1958 with the Deutscher Anwaltverein as Host Organization, assisted by the Kölner Anwaltverein; the Eighth Conference in Salzburg in 1960 under the auspices of Die Österreichischen Rechtsanwaltskammern with the Salzburg and Vienna Bars bearing the principal burden; the Ninth Conference in 1962 at Edinburgh, at the invitation of The Law Society of Scotland and the Faculty of Advocates; the Tenth Conference in Mexico City July 27-31, 1964, with the Barra Mexicana — Colegio de Abogados and the Ilustre y Nacional Colegio de Abogados de México serving as Host Organizations and the Eleventh Conference in Lausanne, Switzerland, July 11-15, 1966 upon the invitation of the Fédération Suisse des Avocats and the Avocats Vaudois (the Bar Association of the Canton of Vaud); the Twelfth Conference in Dublin, Ireland, July 8-12, 1968, with The Incorporated Law Society of Ireland as Host, in association with the General Council of the Bar of Ireland. The Thirteenth Conference is scheduled for Tokyo, Japan, August 24-28, 1970, upon invitation of the Japan Bar Association and the Japan Federation of Bar Associations.

One of the principal aims of the IBA is to provide an international meeting ground for practising lawyers. Although many topics on conference programs have been of interest to specialists, the trend is to emphasize in biennial conference questions which arise in every-day practice.

Reports have been published after each Conference. The Reports of the Third through the Eleventh Conference comprise bound volumes of papers. There is an ever-increasing interest in the published papers of International Bar Association conferences among the legal profession, related organizations, libraries and universities. Separate prints in the official languages of the IBA (English, French, German and Spanish) of many of the combined reports included in recent Conference books may be obtained from New York Headquarters.

Among the subjects discussed at various conference are "Restoration of the Law and Property Rights after World War II" at The Hague; "Coastal Waters and Appurtenant Subsoil" at London; "International Penal Law" at Madrid; "The Constitutional Structure of the United Nations" at Monaco; "International Shipbuilding Contracts — Particularly Legal Problems in connection with Finance and Security" at Oslo; "International Problems of Tort Liability and Financial Protection Arising from the Use of Atomic Energy" and "Protection of Investments Abroad in Time of Peace" at Cologne; "Continuing Education of the Profession" and "Foreign Subsidiaries" at Salzburg; "Anti-Trust Problems in Connection with Dealings with Common Market Countries" at Edinburgh; "World Habeas Corpus and International Extradition" at Mexico City; "The Practice of the Law by Persons Who Are Not

Lawyers" and "The Role of Lawyers in a Developing Country" at Lausanne, and "Warranties for the Protection of Consumers" at Dublin – and continuing discussions throughout several conferences of "Human Rights", "Fair Trial and Free Press", "International Judicial Cooperation", "Domestic Relations", "Immigration and Naturalization", "Air Law", "Economic Warfare", "Copyright", "International Economic Co-operation", "International Fiscal Law", "Prize Law", "Methods of Unifying the Law" and "Monopolies and Restrictive Trade Practices".

At the first five Conferences the topic of "An International Code of Ethics for Lawyers" was discussed, and the work culminated in the adoption by the General Meeting at Oslo of the Code published in the Oslo Conference Report. Rule 14 of the Code was amended by the General Meeting in 1964 at Mexico City, and the amended Code is printed in English, French, German and Spanish in the Tenth Conference Report. The Seventh Conference Report (Cologne 1958) includes committee reports on "International Shipbuilding Contracts" and "Administration of Foreign Estates" — both with Draft Conventions — which the IBA Council directed be sent to the United Nations and to other organizations working in the fields. Continuing work on the subject of "Legal Aid" resulted in establishment of the International Legal Aid Association under the auspices of the IBA. Work begun at earlier Conferences led to the adoption by the General Meeting at Salzburg of the Resolution on Sovereign Immunity printed in the Eighth Conference Report.

One of the purposes of the IBA is to promote in their legal aspects the principles and aims of the United Nations, and the Association has been granted Consultative Status with the U. N. in Category B.

Headquarters are located at 501 Fifth Avenue, New York, N. Y. 10017.

SUBSCRIBER and PATRONS

The major financial support of the IBA comes from Patrons in Canada and the United States of America who participate in the work of the Association either as Sustaining Patrons – $ 100 annually, Contributing Patrons – $ 50 annually, or Subscribing Patrons – $ 25 annually. Lawyers from other parts of the world may contribute as Patrons as specified above or as Subscribers with annual dues of $ 10. As noted above, applications for affiliation must be approved by the Member Organization in the applicant's country; and in the event that the respective national bar association is not affiliated as a Member Organization, the Council of the IBA will direct the method of approving and processing the application. Application forms may be obtained from Headquarters in New York. Patrons and Subscribers receive publications of the Association, including the "International Bar News" and the Books published after each of the biennial conferences. Of equal importance, however, to individuals now enrolled is the knowledge that they are assisting substantially in an important work.

THE INTERNATIONAL BAR ASSOCIATION INVITES THOSE MEMBERS OF THE LEGAL PROFESSION WHO SHARE ITS AIMS TO BECOME PATRONS OR SUBSCRIBERS. THERE CAN BE NO REAL WORLD ORDER UNLESS IT IS BASED ON JUSTICE AND THE RULE OF LAW, AND NO GROUP OF PEOPLE HAS GREATER RESPONSIBILITY TO FURTHER THIS IDEAL THAN MEMBERS OF THE LEGAL PROFESSION.

HISTORIQUE DE L'INTERNATIONAL BAR ASSOCIATION DEPUIS SES ORIGINES

Dès 1932, l'Association Américaine du Barreau avait désigné un comité chargé d'étudier la question d'une fédération internationale d'associations nationales du barreau. Les années de guerre virent se fortifier la conviction qu'une organisation mondiale du barreau pourrait apporter une contribution substantielle à la reconstruction, à la stabilité et à la compréhension mutuelle d'après-guerre. En 1944 un comité spécial fut à nouveau mis sur pied par l'Association Américaine du Barreau pour examiner la possibilité et l'opportunité de la création d'une association internationale du barreau. On constata/-que le besoin d'une telle organisation se faisait très fortement sentir; et les chances de voir une telle initiative favorablement accueillie des organisations du Barreau du monde entier parurent beaucoup plus fortes que dix ans auparavant. Dès le printemps 1946, le comité envoya donc aux diverses associations du barreau un premier projet d'organisation, accompagné d'un double de la résolution passée par la Chambre des Délégués de l'Association Américaine du Barreau, approuvant la coopération de cet organisme avec les organisations du Barreau de toutes les nations du monde. Cette démarche fut si bien accueillie que, le 2 juillet 1946, la Chambre des Délégués autorisa le Président de l'Association Américaine du Barreau à inviter les associations à se réunir à New-York. A cette réunion, tenue les 8 et 9 octobre 1946, assistèrent les représentants d'associations nationales de plus de vingt pays. En outre, les organisations nationales du barreau de dix autres pays s'associèrent par écrit à l'action entreprise par ce groupe. La réunion aboutit à l'adoption d'un projet révisé de constitution, et, en février 1947, les représentants de vingt-trois associations nationales du Barreau se réunirent à nouveau à New-York pour mettre sur pied l'Association Internationale du Barreau.

Les buts poursuivis par l'IBA, sont les suivants: —

- créer et maintenir des liens et des échanges entre les Associations du Barreau dans le monde entier et leurs membres.
- étudier les problèmes d'organisation et de statut professionnels.
- faire progresser la science juridique sur tous les plans.
- promouvoir l'uniformité et la précision dans les domaines appropriées du droit par une étude commune des problèmes légaux pratiques.
- promouvoir l'administration de la Justice selon le droit parmi les peuples du monde.
- promouvoir, dans l'accomplissement de ces buts, les principes et les buts des Nations Unies dans leurs implications juridiques et

coopérer avec les organisations juridiques internationales ayant de semblables objets et promouvoir la coordination entre elles.

"Sous réserve que l'Association soit une organisation non-politique, et en tant que telle ne traite aucun sujet ayant un caractère politique."

L'AIB est une fédération d'associations nationales du barreau. Dans les pays où il n'existe pas d'association nationale du barreau, ou dans les pays où l'association nationale elle-même n'est pas membre de l'AIB, ou dans les pays où elle est membre, et donne son assentiment, toute autre organisation de membres des professions juridiques peut être reçue au rang de membre, à condition que le pays en question ne voit pas par là son importance devant les urnes s'élever au-dessus du maximum de voix attribuées à son (ou ses) organisation(s) nationale(s). On compte à présent cinquante-cinq Organisations Membres appartenant à quarante et un Nation. L'AIB étant une fédération, la source de son autorité se trouve dans les Organisations Membres. La machine détentrice du pouvoir suprême de l'AIB est l'Assemblée Générale, qui se réunit à l'occasion de chaque conférence biennale et se compose de délégués désignés par les Organisations Membres. Chaque Organisation Membre peut désigner autant de délégués qu'elle compte de milliers de membres, plus un par fraction de mille membres. L'Assemblée Générale élit les responsables de l'Association, approuve la gestion financière, adopte les résolutions de l'Association etc. Aucune limite n'est fixée au nombre de membres qu'une Organisation Membre peut charger d'assister aux conférences biennales en qualité de congressistes — la limitation ne s'applique qu'aux délégués désignés pour l'Assemblée Générale, et a pour objet de rendre cette dernière équitablement représentative de la profession juridique mondiale dans son ensemble. Ainsi, lorsque l'AIB arrive à une conclusion au cours d'un débat de son Assemblée Générale, c'est au nom des organisations du barreau de la preque totalité du globe qu'elle s'exprime.

En dehors des réunions de l'Association à l'occasion des conférences biennales, l'AIB délègue ses pouvoirs au Conseil, dont les membres sont nommés par les Organisations Membres. La Constitution, telle qu'elle a été amendée à Cologne en 1958, prévoit que chaque Organisation Membre a le droit de se faire représenter au Conseil par un membre. En outre, les responsables de l'Association sont membres ex officio du Conseil. Le Conseil se réunit au moins une fois par an et au cours d'une conférence pour faire part de ses recommandations à l'Assemblée Générale. Il est également prévu que le Conseil puisse comprendre des Membres honoraires.

On peut s'affilier individuellement à titre de membre sociétaire si l'on est déjà membre de la profession juridique et si l'on a obtenu l'assentiment de l'association nationale du barreau de son propre pays. Plus de mille six cent membres sociétaires de tous les points du globe œuvrent au sein de l'AIB, et constituent une section importante de l'Association —

non seulement du point de vue du soutien professionnel qu'ils lui apportent, mais aussi du point de vue financier. Ils assistent aux conférences biennales — mais n'ont pas le droit de vote dans les délibérations de l'Assemblée Générale, à moins d'avoir été désignés comme membres de l'Assemblée Générale par leur propre association nationale du barreau. Un amendement a été également adopté à Cologne, grâce auquel le Conseil pourra modifier de pays à pays le montant de la cotisation versée à l'Association par les Membres Sociétaires, ce qui, espère-t-on, aura pour effet d'augmenter le nombre des membres des professions juridiques accordant leur soutien à l'œuvre de l'AIB.

Douze conférences de l'Association Internationale du Barreau ont déjà eu lieu: — la première fut la Conférence Inaugurale, qui se déroula à NEW-YORK en octobre 1947; — la seconde Conférence se tint à LA HAYE en 1948, sur l'invitation de la Nederlandsche Advocaten Vereeniging; — la troisième Conférence à LONDRES en 1950, la Law Society et le General Council of the Bar jouant le rôle d'hôtes; — la quatrième Conférence à MADRID en 1952, sous les auspices du Consejo General de los Ilustres Colegios de Abogados de España; — la cinquième Conférence à MONACO en 1954; — la sixième Conférence en 1956 à OSLO, sur l'invitation de Den Norske Sakførerforening; — la septième Conférence à COLOGNE en 1958, la Deutscher Anwaltverein jouant, avec la Kölner Anwaltverein, le rôle d'Organisations hôtesses; — la huitième Conférence a eu lieu à SALZBOURG en 1960, sous les auspices de Die Österreichischen Rechtsanwaltskammern; la neuvième Conférence se déroula à EDIMBOURG en 1962, sous l'égide de la Law Society of Scotland et de la Faculty of Advocates, la dixième Conférence s'est tenue à MEXICO du 27 au 31 juillet 1964, à l'invitation du Barra Mexicana, Colegio de Abogados, et de l'Ilustre y Nacional Colegio de Mexico; la onzième Conférence s'est tenue à LAUSANNE, Suisse, du 11 au 15 juillet 1965, à l'invitation de la Fédération Suisse et des Avocats du Barreau Vaudois; et la douxième à DUBLIN, Irlande, du 8 au 12 juillet 1968, à l'invitation de The Incorporated Law Society of Ireland, en association avec le General Council of the Bar of Ireland. Il est prévu que la treizième Conférence se tienne à TOKYO, Japon, du 24 au 28 août 1970, à l'invitation de la Japan Bar Association et de la Japan Federation of Bar Associations.

L'un des buts principaux de l'AIB est de fournir un terrain de rencontre international à l'homme de loi ordinaire actuellement engagé dans la poursuite de ses activités professionnelles. Bien que de nombreux sujets inscrits au programme des conférences aient pu revêtir un intérêt particulier pour le spécialiste, l'on tend de plus en plus, dans les conférences biennales, à mettre l'accent sur les problèmes posés par la pratique journalière de la profession.

Chaque conférence a été suivie de la publication d'un compte-rendu. Les conférences de Londres, Madrid, Monaco, Oslo, Cologne, Salzbourg, Edimbourg, Mexico et Lausanne ont donné lieu à la réunion sous forme de volumes de documents choisis. Les documents ayant fait l'objet de publication à la suite des conférences de l'Association Internationale du Barreau voient se porter sur eux l'intérêt sans cesse croissant du corps juridique du monde entier, des organisations annexes, des bibliothèques et des universités.

On peut se procurer au Siège de l'Association dans les quatre langues officielles de "l'International Bar Association" (anglais, français, allemand, espagnol) de nombreux rapports inclus dans les recueils publiés à la suite des conférences.

Les sujets discutés au cours des nombreuses conférences comprennent notamment: "Le Rétablissement de la Légalité et des Droits de Propriété après la Deuxième Guerre Mondiale" (La Haye); "Les Eaux Territoriales et les Fonds Sous-marins Accessoires" (Londres); "Droit International et Pénal" (Madrid); "La Structure Constitutionnelle des Nations Unies" (Monaco); "Les Contrats Internationaux de Construction de Navires — Problèmes Légaux Particuliers concernant les Finances et les Garanties" (Oslo); "Problèmes Internationaux de la Responsabilité Civile du fait des Dommages Extracontractuels et la Protection Financière dans le Domaine de l'Energie Atomique" et "Protection des Investissements à l'Etranger en temps de Paix" (Cologne); "Le Recyclage Permanent de la Profession" et "Les Filiales à l'Etranger" (Salzburg); "Problèmes de la Prohibition des Ententes par Rapport aux Transactions avec les Pays de Marché Commun" (Edimbourg); "Les Garanties de la Liberté Individuelle (Habeas Corpus) et l'Extradition" (Mexico City); "La Pratique du Droit par des Non Juristes" et "Le Rôle des Hommes de Loi dans les Pays en Voie de Développement" (Lausanne); et "Garanties pour la Protection des Consommateurs" (Dublin). Il a également été discuté, au cours de plusiers Conférences, des sujets suivants: "Les Droits de l'Homme"; "Impartialité des Débats et Liberté de la Presse"; "La Coopération Internationale dans le Domaine Juridique"; "Questions Nationales"; "Immigration et Naturalisation"; "La Juridiction Aérienne"; "La Guerre Economique"; "Les Droits d'Auteur"; "La Coopération Economique Internationale"; "Le Droit Fiscal International"; "La Règlementation des Prix"; "Méthodes d'Unification du Droit"; et "Pratiques Monopolistes et Restrictives des Echanges Commerciaux".

A chaque conférence, le sujet: "Un Code Ethique International à l'usage des Hommes de Loi" est également revenu en discussion, et ces travaux ont trouvé leur couronnement dans l'adoption par l'Assemblée Générale à OSLO du Code publié dans le Compte-Rendu de la Conférence d'OSLO.

Le recueil consacré à la septième conférence (COLOGNE 1958) comporte des rapports sur "les Contrats internationaux de Constructions Navales" et "le Règlement des Successions Etrangères", tous deux accompagnés du Projet de conventions que le Conseil fit adresser aux Nations-Unies et à d'autres organismes intéressés par ces questions.

Les travaux sur le sujet: "L'Assistance Juridique" ont abouti, à COLOGNE, au "Projet d'une Association Internationale d'Assistance Juridique", placée sous les auspices de l'AIB. Ce Projet a été publié dans le compte-rendu de la Conférence de COLOGNE.

L'art. 14 du Code a été amendé par l'Assemblée Générale en 1964 à Mexico et le Code amendé a été imprimé dans le rapport de la dixième Conférence en anglais, français, allemand et espagnol.

Les travaux entrepris au cours des conférences précédentes ont amené l'Assemblée-Générale réunie à SALZBOURG à approuver une résolution sur l'Immunité de Juridiction — figurant dans le recueil de la huitième conférence.

Le Siège de l'Association se trouve à 501, 5ème Avenue, NEW YORK, N.Y. 10017.

MEMBRES SOCIETAIRES ET ADHERENTS INDIVIDUELS

Le principal soutien financier de l'AIB lui vient d'adhérents individuels du Canada et des Etats-Unis qui participent aux efforts de l'Association — soit à titre de Membre bienfaiteur (cotisation annuelle $ 100), Membre actif (cotisation annuelle $ 50) ou Membre sociétaire (cotisation annuelle $ 25). Les avocats d'autres pays peuvent faire partie de l'Association, soit à titre d'adhérents individuels, ainsi qu'il est défini ci-dessus soit à titre de souscripteur (cotisation annuelle $ 10). Comme indique ci-dessus, les demandes d'adhésion au titre de Membre Sociétaire doivent avoir reçu la sanction de l'Organisation Membre du pays du postulant; et, dans le cas où l'association nationale du barreau intéressée ne serait pas elle-même Organisation Membre, le Conseil de l'AIB indiquera le mode de sanction que devra recevoir la demande et la marche à suivre pour l'examen de cette dernière. Les formulaires de demande peuvent s'obtenir en s'adressant au Siège de l'Association à New York ou aux Organisations Membres de l'AIB.

Les Membres Sociétaires reçoivent toutes les publications de l'Association, y compris les Nouvelles du Barreau International, dont la parution est trimestrielle, ainsi que les ouvrages publiés à la suite de chaque conférence biennale, dans la mesure où les disponibilités budgétaires le permettent. Mais non moins précieuse pour les Membres Sociétaires actuellement inscrits est l'assurance qu'ils ont d'apporter un concours substantiel à une entreprise des plus importantes.

L'ASSOCIATION INTERNATIONALE DU BARREAU INVITE CEUX DES MEMBRES DES PROFESSIONS JURIDIQUES QUI SE RECLAMENT DES MEMES IDEAUX QU'ELLE A DEVENIR MEMBRES SOCIETAIRES. IL NE PEUT Y AVOIR D'ORDRE MONDIAL VERITABLE QUE FONDE SUR LA JUSTICE ET LE RESPECT DU DROIT, ET A NUL GROUPE D'INDIVIDUS PLUS QU'AUX MEMBRES DES PROFESSIONS JURIDIQUES N'INCOMBE LA RESPONSABILITE DE PROMOUVOIR CES IDEAUX.

ORIGEN E HISTORIA DE LA INTERNATIONAL BAR ASSOCIATION

Ya en el año 1932 la American Bar Association había nombrado una comisión para el estudio de la cuestión relativa a una federación internacional de asociaciones forenses nacionales. Durante la segunda guerra mundial (II) fué adquiriendo ímpetu el convencimiento de que el foro del mundo podría contribuir de modo notable a la labor de reconstrucción y al fomento de la estabilidad y de la comprensión en la postguerra. En 1944 fué de nuevo establecida por la American Bar Association una comisión para investigar la conveniencia de una asociación forense internacional. Resultó haber gran necesidad de una organización de esta índole, y asimismo la probabilidad de que atraería al foro organizado en todas partes del mundo era mucho mayor de lo que lo fuera diez años antes. En consecuencia, en la primavera de 1946 la comisión dirigió a las diversas asociaciones del foro un proyecto de organización, junto con una copia de la resolución de la House of Delegates de la American Bar Association en que se aprobaba la cooperación con el foro organizado en las distintas naciones del mundo. La reacción fué tan entusiasta que la referida House of Delegates, con fecha 2 de Julio de 1946, autorizó al Presidente de la American Bar Association a que invitara a las asociaciones a una reunión en Nueva York. En dicha reunión, que se celebró el 8 y 9 de Octubre de 1946, se encontraron representantes de asociaciones nacionales de más de veinte países. Además, las asociaciones forenses nacionales de otros diez países enviaron su aprobación. De dicha reunión resultó la adopción de un proyecto de constitución revisado, y en Febrero de 1947 volvieron a reunirse en Nueva York representantes de veintitrés asociaciones forenses nacionales con objeto de organizar la International Bar Association.

Los fines para los que existe la IBA "una organización apolítica" como lo establece el artículo I de su Constitución, son los siguientes:

Establecer y mantener relaciones permanentes e intercambios entre las Asociaciones de Abogados del mundo entero y sus miembros.

Discutir problemas de organización profesional y de estado, legal.

Fomentar la ciencia de la jurisprudencia en todas sus fases.

Mediante un estudio común de los problemas jurídicos prácticos fomentar la uniformidad y definición en campos jurídicos adecuados.

Fomentar la administración de justicia bajo la ley, entre las gentes del mundo.

En ejecución de estos fines fomentar en sus aspectos jurídicos los principios y planes de las Naciones Unidas y colaborar y fomentar la coordinación con las organizaciones jurídicas internacionales que tengan propósitos similares.

Siempre que la Asociación sea apolítica y en consecuencia no se ocupe de asuntos de carácter político.

La IBA es una federación de asociaciones forenses nacionales. En los países en que no existe asociación forense nacional, o en que la asociación nacional no es afiliada a la IBA, o en que, siendo afiliada, lo apruebe, cualquiera otra organización de jurisconsultos puede ser admitida como afiliada, con la condición de que no vengan con ello incrementados los votos que tendrá el país correspondiente por encima del máximo concedido a su organización u organizaciones nacionales. Existen actualmente 55 Organizaciones Afiliadas pertencientes a 41 países. Como la IBA es una federación, la fuente de su autoridad reside en las Organizaciones Afiliadas. El supremo organismo dirigente de la IBA es la Asamblea General, la cual se reúne con ocasión de cada conferencia bienal y está compuesta de delegados nombrados por las Organizaciones Afiliadas. Cada Organización Afiliada puede nombrar un delegado por cada 1.000 miembros que tenga, o fracción de 1.000, y siempre que ningún miembro exceda de 10 delegados. La Asamblea General elige los dignatarios de la Asociación, aprueba las cuestiones financieras, aprueba resoluciones de la Asociación, etc. No existe límite para el número de miembros que una Organización Afiliada puede acreditar para que asistan a las conferencias bienales como participantes en la conferencia; la limitación es efectiva solamente con respecto a los delegados nombrados para la Asamblea General, siendo el objeto de dicha limitación el lograr que la Asamblea sea representativa de la profesión jurídica del mundo. Así, cuando la IBA adopta una conclusión en su Asamblea General, es la voz del foro organizado de la mayor parte del mundo la que habla.

Cuando la Asociación no se halla convocada en conferencia bienal, el organismo-dirigente de la IBA lo constituye el Consejo, cuyos miembros son designados por las Organizaciones Afiliadas. Cada Organización Afiliada está autorizada a tener un representante en el Consejo. Además los dignatarios de la Asociación son miembros del Consejo por derecho propio. El Consejo se reúne por lo menos una vez al año y durante las conferencias. También pueden nombrarse Miembros Honorarios del Consejo.

Pueden afiliarse a la IBA individuos en calidad de suscritores si son miembros de las profesiones jurídicas y son aprobados por sus respectivas asociaciones nacionales. Se los conoce como "Patrons" en Estados Unidos y Canadá y como "Subscribers" en el resto del mundo. Hay actualmente más de 1600 suscritores en las más diversas partes del mundo que actúan dentro de la IBA, constituyendo un importante elemento de la Asociación, no sólo desde el punto de vista de su apoyo profesional, sino también en el aspecto financiero. Asisten a las conferencias bienales, pero no tienen voto en la Asamblea General a menos que hayan sido designados para la misma por sus respectivas asociaciones forenses nacionales.

Hasta la fecha la International Bar Association ha celebrado ya doce conferencias. La primera fué la Conferencia Inaugural de Octubre de 1947, la cual tuvo lugar en Nueva York. La segunda conferencia se celebró en La Haya en 1948 a invitación de la Nederlandsche Advocaten Vereeniging; la tercera en Londres en 1950 por invitación de The Law Society y del General Council of the Bar; la cuarta en Madrid en 1952 bajo los auspicios del Consejo General de los Ilustres Colegios de Abogadas de España; la quinta en Mónaco en 1954; la sexta en 1956 en Oslo por invitación de Den Norske Sakførerforening; y la séptima conferencia tuvo lugar en Colonia en 1958, siendo la organización invitante el Deutscher Anwaltverein, asistido por el Kölner Anwaltverein. La octava conferencia se celebró en Salzburgo en 1960 bajo los auspicios de "Die Österreichischen Rechtsanwaltskammern", llevando el mayor peso en su organización las Asociaciones de Abogados de Viena y Salzburgo, la novena conferencia tuvo lugar en 1962 en Edimburgo a instancia de "The Law Society of Scotland" y "The Faculty of Advocates". La décima conferencia en la Ciudad de México del 27 al 31 de Julio de 1964, siendo las Organizaciones invitantes la Barra Mexicana y el Ilustre y Nacional Colegio de Abogados de México. La undécima conferencia se celebró en Lausana, Suiza, del 11 al 15 de Julio de 1966, siendo las Organizaciones invitantes la Fédération Suisse des Avocats y el Barreau Vaudois; la duodécima conferencia en Dublin, Irlanda, del 8 al 12 de julio de 1968, actuando como anfitriones The Incorporated Law Society of Ireland y el General Council of the Bar of Ireland. La décimotercera conferencia está programada para celebrarse en Tokio, Japón, del 24 al 28 de agosto de 1970, a invitación de la Japan Bar Association y de la Japan Federation of Bar Associations.

Uno de los objectivos de la IBA consiste en proporcionar un campo internacional donde puedan encontrarse y ponerse en relación quienes ejercen la profesión de abogado. Si por una parte han formado parte de los programas de las conferencias muchos temas que interesan a los especialistas, la tendencia que se ha manifestado en las conferencias bienales ha sido la de poner de relieve las cuestiones que se presentan en la práctica cotidiana del derecho.

A continuación de cada conferencia han sido publicados los Informes correspondientes. Los Informes de las Conferencias 3—11 constituyen unos volúmenes encuadernados que contienen una selección de documentos. Existe un interés cada vez mayor por los documentos que se publican sobre las conferencias de la IBA entre los miembros del foro de todas partes del mundo, las organizaciones relacionadas con el foro, bibliotecas y universidades. En las oficinas centrales de Nueva York pueden obtenerse ejemplares en los idiomas oficiales de la IBA (inglés, francés, alemán y español) de muchos de los informes que figuran en los libros de las recientes Conferencias.

Entre los asuntos que han sido discutidos en las diversas conferencias figuran los siguientes: "Restablecimiento de la Ley de los Derechos de

Propiedad después de la Segunda Guerra Mundial", en La Haya; "Las Aguas Costeras y el Subsuelo que les atañe", en Londres; "Ley Penal Internacional", en Madrid; "La Estructura Constitucional de las Naciones Unidas", en Mónaco; "Los Contratos Internacionales de Construcciones Navales", en especial los "Problemas Legales relativos a Finanzas y Garantías", en Oslo; "Problemas Internacionales de Responsabilidad por Daños y la Protección Financiera a Raiz del Uso de la Energía Atómica" y "Protección de Inversiones en el Extranjero en Tiempo de Paz", en Colonia; "Continuación de la formación profesional" y "Subsidiarios Extranjeros" en Salzburgo; "Problemas anti-trust en relación con las transacciones con los países del Mercado Común", en Edimburgo; y "Habeas Corpus mundial y Extradición Internacional", en México; "El Ejercicio de la Abogacía por Personas que Carecen de Título Legal para Ejercerla" y "El Papel de los Abogados en un País en Desarrollo", en Lausana; y "Garantías para la Protección de los Consumidores", en Dublín. Asimismo tuvieron lugar discusiones que han sido proseguidas en el curso de varias conferencias sobre los siguientes temas: "Los Derechos del Hombre", "Independencia en Los Juicios y Libertad de Prensa", "Cooperación Judicial Internacional", "Relaciones Domésticas", "Inmigración y Naturalización", "Derecho Aéreo", "La Guerra Económica", "La Propiedad Intelectual", "Cooperación Económica Internacional", "Derecho Fiscal Internacional", "Derecho de Presa", "Métodos para la Unificación del Derecho", y "Monopolios y Restricciones a Prácticas Comerciales".

En las cinco primeras Conferencias se ha discutido el tema de "Un Código Internacional de Etica para el Jurisconsulto", culminando dicha labor en la adopción, por la Asamblea General en Oslo, del Código que se publicó en el Informe de la Conferencia de Oslo. El informe sobre la séptima Conferencia (Colonia 1958) incluye informes del Comité sobre "Contratos Internacionales de Construcción Naval" y "Administración de Bienes Extranjeros" (ambos con Proyectos de Convención) que el Consejo de la IBA dispuso se enviaran a las Naciones Unidas y a otras Organizaciones dentro de ese mismo campo de acción. La regla 14 del Código ha sido enmendada durante la Asamblea General en 1964 en la ciudad de México, y el Código enmendado ha sido impreso (publicado) en inglés, francés, alemán y español en el informe de la décima conferencia. La labor emprendida en anteriores Conferencias ha dado como resultado el establecimiento de la International Legal Aid Association (Ayuda Legal), bajo los auspicios de la IBA; y condujo a la adopción por la Asamblea General en Salzburgo de la "Resolución sobre Inmunidad Soberana" que se incluye en el Informe sobre la octava conferencia.

Una de las finalidades de la IBA es la de fomentar en sus aspectos legales los principios y objetivos de las Naciones Unidas, organismo que ha concedido a la Asociación facultades de asesoría en la Categoría B.

La Sede de la IBA está situada en: 501 Fifth Avenue, New York, N. Y., 10017, E. U. A.

SUSCRITORES Y PATROCINADORES

Los Patrocinadores (Patrons) de Canadá y de los Estados Unidos de Norteamérica son los que aportan la mayor contribución económica a la IBA, y participan en el trabajo de la Asociación bien sea como "Sustaining Patrons", con la cantidad de $ 100.00 dólares anuales; "Contributing Patrons", $ 50.00 dólares anuales, o "Subscribing Patrons" $ 25.00 dólares anuales. Los abogados de otros países pueden inscribirse en cualquiera de las clasificaciones anteriores o como Suscritores con una cuota anual de $ 10.00 dólares. Como se ha indicado más arriba, las solicitudes para afiliación como suscritores tienen que ser aprobadas por la Organización Afiliada del país del solicitante; y en caso de que no esté constituída en Organización Afiliada la asociación forense nacional correspondiente, el Consejo de la IBA determinará el procedimiento de estudio y aprobación de las solicitudes. Los formularios de solicitud pueden obtenerse de la Sede Central de Nueva York. Los suscritores reciben cada una de las publicaciones de la Asociación, entre ellas la International Bar News y los libros publicados después de cada una de las conferencias bienales. De igual importancia para los suscritores inscritos es también el conocimiento de que aportan una ayuda indispensable a una labor muy valiosa.

LA INTERNATIONAL BAR ASSOCIATION INVITA A LOS MIEMBROS DE LAS PROFESIONES JURIDICAS QUE COMPARTEN LOS OBJETIVOS DE LA MISMA A QUE SE HAGAN SUSCRITORES. NO PUEDE EXISTIR VERDADERO ORDEN UNIVERSAL QUE NO ESTE BASADO EN LA JUSTICIA Y EL DOMINIO DE LA LEY, Y NINGUN GRUPO DE PERSONAS TIENE MAYOR RESPONSABILIDAD PARA EL FOMENTO DE ESTE IDEAL QUE LOS MIEMBROS DE LAS PROFESIONES JURIDICAS.

GRÜNDUNG UND ENTWICKLUNG DER INTERNATIONAL BAR ASSOCIATION

Schon im Jahre 1932 hatte die American Bar Association einen Ausschuß bestellt, um die Frage eines internationalen Zusammenschlusses der nationalen Anwaltsorganisationen zu untersuchen. Während der Kriegsjahre wuchs die Überzeugung, daß eine die Anwaltschaft der ganzen Welt umfassende Organisation einen bedeutsamen Beitrag für den Wiederaufbau nach dem Kriege, für Stetigkeit und gegenseitiges Verständnis leisten könne. 1944 setzte die American Bar Association einen Sonderausschuß ein, mit der Aufgabe, die Möglichkeiten und das Bedürfnis für eine internationale Anwaltsorganisation zu prüfen. Die Notwendigkeit einer solchen Organisation wurde bejaht und es wurde festgestellt, daß die Zustimmung der Anwaltsorganisationen in der ganzen Welt mit weit größerer Wahrscheinlichkeit zu erwarten sei als vor einem Jahrzehnt. Der Ausschuß versandte deshalb im Frühjahr 1946 an die nationalen Anwaltsorganisationen einen Organisationsplan mit dem Wortlaut der Entschließung der Vertreterversammlung der American Bar Association, die die Zusammenarbeit mit den Anwaltsorganisationen aller Nationen befürwortete. Der Widerhall war so ermutigend, daß die Vertreterversammlung am 2. Juli 1946 den Präsidenten der American Bar Association ersuchte, die Anwaltsorganisationen nach New York einzuladen. Dieses Treffen fand am 8. und 9. Oktober 1946 statt. Es nahmen daran die Vertreter von über 20 nationalen Anwaltsorganisationen teil. Außerdem hatten die Organisationen von 10 anderen Ländern schriftlich ihre Zustimmung erteilt. Auf dieser Zusammenkunft wurde der überarbeitete Satzungsentwurf angenommen und im Februar 1947 trafen sich erneut die Vertreter von 23 nationalen Anwaltsorganisationen in New York, um die International Bar Association zu gründen.

Die IBA hat sich folgende Aufgaben zum Ziel gesetzt:

Zwischen den Anwaltsvereinigungen (-organisationen) der ganzen Welt und ihrer Mitglieder dauernde Beziehungen zu schaffen und zu erhalten und unter ihnen Gedankenaustausch zu pflegen;

die Probleme der Anwaltsorganisationen und des Anwaltsstandes zu erörtern;

die Rechtswissenschaft auf allen Gebieten zu fördern;

die Rechtsvereinheitlichung und die Klarheit der Begriffe auf allen geeigneten Rechtsgebieten durch gemeinsame Untersuchungen praktischer juristischer Probleme zu fördern;

die Rechtspflege nach den Grundsätzen der Rechtsstaatlichkeit bei allen Völkern der Welt zu fördern;

bei der Durchführung dieser Aufgaben die Rechtsgrundsätze der Vereinten Nationen zu fördern und mit internationalen Juristenorganisationen mit ähnlicher Zielsetzung zusammenzuarbeiten;

unter Beachtung der Tatsache, daß die IBA eine „unpolitische" Organisation ist und sich nicht mit Fragen politischen Charakters befaßt.

Die IBA ist ein Zusammenschluß nationaler Anwaltsorganisationen. Soweit in einzelnen Ländern keine nationalen Anwaltsorganisationen bestehen oder die nationale Organisation selbst nicht Mitglied der IBA ist oder als Mitglied der IBA ihre Zustimmung erteilt, können auch andere Anwaltsorganisationen Mitglied der IBA werden. Doch darf in diesen Fällen die Stimmzahl des betreffenden Landes nicht die Höchstgrenze überschreiten, die seiner nationalen Anwaltsorganisation zusteht. Heute gehören der IBA 55 Mitgliedsorganisationen von 41 Nationen an. Da die IBA ein föderativer Verband ist, liegt die Entscheidungsgewalt bei den Mitgliedsorganisationen. Höchstes Organ der IBA ist die Generalversammlung, die aus den von den Mitgliedsorganisationen bestellten Delegierten besteht und alle 2 Jahre zusammentritt. Jede Mitgliedsorganisation kann für je 1000 ihrer Mitglieder einen Delegierten bestellen. Doch ist die Höchstzahl auf 10 Delegierte begrenzt. Die Generalversammlung wählt den Vorstand, beschließt über den Haushalt, faßt Beschlüsse der IBA usw. Die Zahl der Teilnehmer an den alle 2 Jahre stattfindenden Kongressen ist nicht beschränkt. Der Teilnehmer bedarf lediglich einer Bestätigung durch seine nationale Anwaltsorganisation. Jedoch ist die Zahl der für die Generalversammlung bestellten Delegierten beschränkt, damit die Generalversammlung als repräsentativ für die gesamte Anwaltschaft gelten kann. Wenn somit die Generalversammlung der IBA eine Resolution beschließt, dann spricht sie für die Anwaltsorganisationen der meisten Länder der Welt.

In den Zeiten zwischen den alle zwei Jahre stattfindenden Kongressen werden die laufenden Geschäfte der IBA vom Council erledigt. Die Mitglieder des Council werden von den Mitgliedsorganisationen bestellt. Die Satzung sieht vor, daß jede Mitgliedsorganisation einen Vertreter in den Council entsenden kann. Ehrenmitgliedschaft im Vorstand ist möglich. Die Vorstandsmitglieder der IBA gehören dem Council kraft Amts an. Der Council tritt mindestens einmal jährlich zusammen.

Einzelpersonen können sich der IBA als *Patrons* oder *Subscriber* anschließen, wenn sie der Anwaltschaft angehören und ihr Beitritt von der für sie zuständigen Anwaltsorganisation gebilligt worden ist. Zur Zeit wirken über *1600 Patrons* und *Subscriber* in allen Teilen der Welt in der IBA mit und stellen einen wichtigen Bestandteil der Vereinigung dar — nicht nur durch ihre fachliche Unterstützung, sondern auch durch ihre Beiträge. Sie nehmen an den alle zwei Jahre stattfindenden Kongressen teil, sind aber in der Generalversammlung nicht stimmberechtigt.

Bisher hat die International Bar Association zwölf Kongresse durchgeführt. Der erste war der Gründungskongreß im Oktober 1947 in New York. Der zweite Kongreß wurde 1948 auf Einladung der Niederländischen Advokatenvereinigung in Den Haag abgehalten; der dritte Kongreß fand auf Einladung der Law Society und des General Council of the Bar 1950 in London statt; der vierte Kongreß 1952 in Madrid unter der Schirmherrschaft des Consejo General de los Ilustres Colegios de Abogados de España; der fünfte Kongreß 1954 in Monako; der sechste Kongreß auf Einladung des Norske Sakførerforening 1956 in Oslo; der siebte Kongreß 1958 in Köln mit dem Deutschen Anwaltverein und dem Kölner Anwaltverein als Gastgeber. Der achte Kongreß fand 1960 in Salzburg unter der Schirmherrschaft der Österreichischen Rechtsanwaltskammern und der Federführung der Anwaltskammern Salzburg und Wien statt. Der neunte Kongreß wurde 1962 in Edinburgh auf Einladung der Law Society of Scotland und der Faculty of Advokates durchgeführt und der zehnte Kongreß in Mexico City vom 27. bis 31. Juli 1964, wobei die mexikanische Anwaltskammer, das Colegio de Abogados und das Ilustre y Nacional Colegio de Abogados de Mexico Gastgeber waren. Der elfte Kongreß fand auf Einladung des Schweizerischen Anwaltsverbandes und der Waadtlaendischen Anwaltskammer in Lausanne, Schweiz, vom 11. bis 15. Juli 1966 statt. Tagungsort des zwölften Kongresses vom 8. bis 12. Juli 1968 war Dublin in Ireland; gemeinsame Gastgeber waren die Law Society of Ireland und der General Council of the Bar of Ireland. Der dreizehnte Kongreß ist für Tokio vom 24. bis 28. August 1970 vorgesehen, zu dem die Japan Bar Association und die Japan Federation of Bar Associations eingeladen haben.

Es ist eine der wichtigsten Aufgaben der IBA, für den praktizierenden Rechtsanwalt einen internationalen Treffpunkt zu schaffen. Mögen auch manche der auf den Konferenzen behandelten Themen vorzugsweise das Interesse der Spezialisten gefunden haben, so geht die Entwicklung erkennbar dahin, Fragen in den Vordergrund zu stellen, die in der Tagespraxis des normalen Anwalts bedeutsam sind.

Im Anschluß an die Konferenzen ist stets ein Bericht veröffentlicht worden. Die Berichte der 3. bis 12. Konferenz sind in Buchform erschienen. Diese Berichte haben ein ständig steigendes Interesse bei allen Juristen, gleichartigen Organisationen, Bibliotheken und Universitäten gefunden. Sonderdrucke der Berichte in den offiziellen Sprachen (englisch, französisch, deutsch und spanisch) können von der Geschäftsstelle in New York angefordert werden.

Zu den Themen der verschiedenen Kongresse gehören u. a.: "Restoration of the Law and Property Rights after World War II" in Den Haag; "Coastal Waters and Appurtenant Subsoil" in London; "International Penal Law" in Madrid; "The Constitutional Structure of the United Nations" in Monako; "International Shipbuilding Contracts, Particularly Legal Problems in connection with Finance and Security" in Oslo; "International Problems of Tort Liability and Financial Protection Arising from the Use of Atomic Energy" und "Protection of Investments Abroad in Time of Peace" in Köln; "Continuing Education of the Profession" und "Foreign Subsidiaries" in Salzburg; "Anti-Trust Problems in Connection with Dealings with Common Market Countries" in Edinburg und "Welt-Habeas-Corpus und internationale Auslieferung" in Mexico-City; "Rechtsbesorgung durch Nichtanwälte" und "die Aufgaben des Anwalts in Entwicklungsländern" in Lausanne und "Produzentenhaftung" in Dublin – sowie auf mehreren Kongressen fortgesetzt die Themen "Human Rights", "Fair Trial and Free Press", "Internationale Rechtshilfe", "Domestic Relations", "Einwanderung und Einbürgerung", "Luftrecht", "Economic Warfare", "Copyright", "International Economic Cooperation", "Internationales Steuerrecht", "Prisenrecht", "Methoden der Rechtsvereinheitlichung" und "Monopolies and Restrictive Trade Practices".

Auf den ersten 5 Kongressen wurde das Thema „Internationaler Kodex des Standesrechts für Rechtsanwälte" erörtert. Diese Arbeit gelangte in Oslo durch Annahme des Entwurfs in der Generalversammlung zum Abschluß. Der Kodex ist im Oslo-Bericht veröffentlicht. Art. 14 des Kodex wurde von der Generalversammlung 1964 in Mexico-City revidiert (abgeändert) und der revidierte Kodex wurde im 10. (zehnten) Kongreßbericht in englischer, französischer, deutscher und spanischer Sprache gedruckt. Im 7. Kongreßbericht (Köln 1958) sind Ausschußberichte über "International Shipbuilding Contracts" und "Administration of Foreign Estates" — beide mit Konventionsentwürfen — enthalten, die auf Beschluß des Council der IBA der UN und anderen auf diesen Gebieten tätigen Institutionen zugeleitet worden sind. Die Arbeiten über das Thema „Rechtshilfe" führten zur Gründung der "International Legal Aid Association", die unter der Schirmherrschaft der IBA steht. Die auf früheren Kongressen geleisteten Vorarbeiten führten in Salzburg zur Annahme einer Resolution über "Sovereign Immunity" durch die Generalversammlung — veröffentlicht im 8. Kongreßbericht.

Der IBA ist von der UNO der Konsultativstatus in Kategorie B eingeräumt worden.

Das Büro der IBA befindet sich: 501 Fifth Avenue, New York, 10017, NY.

SUBSCRIBER und PATRONS

Einen wesentlichen finanziellen Beitrag zur IBA leisten die Patrons aus Canada und USA. Sie wirken mit als Sustaining Patrons (100 \$ jährlich), Contributing Patrons (50 \$) oder als Subscribing Patrons (25 \$). Anwälte aus anderen Ländern können als Patrons oder Subscriber mitwirken.

Subscriber zahlen jährlich 10 \$ an die IBA. Wie oben erwähnt, müssen Aufnahmeanträge die Zustimmung der für den Antragsteller zuständigen nationalen Anwaltsorganisation gefunden haben. Wenn diese nicht der IBA angehört, entscheidet der Council der IBA. Antragsformulare können vom IBA-Büro in New York und von den Mitgliedsorganisationen der IBA bezogen werden.

Die Subscriber erhalten alle Veröffentlichungen der IBA, einschließlich der *International Bar News*, die vierteljährlich erscheint, sowie die nach jedem Kongreß in Buchform veröffentlichten Berichte, soweit das die Finanzlage der IBA gestattet. Ebenso bedeutsam ist jedoch für die Subscriber die Kenntnis der Tatsache, daß sie durch ihre Zugehörigkeit einen wesentlichen Beitrag zu einer bedeutsamen Aufgabe leisten.

DIE INTERNATIONAL BAR ASSOCIATION BITTET ALLE RECHTSANWÄLTE, DIE IHRE ZIELE BILLIGEN, SUBSCRIBER ZU WERDEN. DIE WELTORDNUNG MUSS AUF RECHT UND GERECHTIGKEIT GEGRÜNDET SEIN. KEINEM BERUFSSTAND OBLIEGT EINE GRÖSSERE VERPFLICHTUNG, DIESES ZIEL ZU FÖRDERN, ALS DEN JURISTEN.

INTERNATIONAL BAR ASSOCIATION

Member Organizations

Australia	Law Council of Australia Temple Court, 75-85 Elizabeth Street Sydney, New South Wales 2000
Austria	Die Österreichischen Rechtsanwaltskammern Rotenturmstrasse 13, Wien I Österreichischer Juristentag Landesgerichtsstrasse 11, Wien VIII
Brazil	Instituto dos Advogados do Rio Grande do Sul Travessa Acilino Carvalho, 21 Pôrto Alegre, Rio Grande do Sul
Canada	The Canadian Bar Association 90 Sparks Street, Ottawa, Ontario
Denmark	Det Danske Advokatsamfund Ved Stranden 14, Copenhagen
England and Wales	General Council of the Bar Carpmael Building, Crown Office Row Temple, London E. C. 4 The Law Society The Law Society's Hall 113, Chancery Lane, London W. C. 2
Finland	Suomen Asianajajaliitto Simonkatu 12 A, Helsinki
France	Association Nationale des Avocats 30, Rue de Condé, Paris 6 e
Germany	Deutscher Anwaltverein e. V. Sievekingplatz 1, (2000) Hamburg 36
Guatemala	Colegio de Abogados de Guatemala Universidad de San Carlos de Guatemala
India	The Bar Council of India 40-43 Lawyers' Chambers, Supreme Court Bldg. New Delhi - 1
Iran	Kanoun Vokala Dadgostari, Teheran Palace of Justice, Teheran
Iraq	Naqabet Al-Muhamin Rashid Street, Baghdad
Ireland	The Incorporated Law Society of Ireland Solicitors' Buildings, Four Courts, Dublin 7 The General Council of the Bar of Ireland Four Courts, Dublin 7

Israel	Lishkat Orkhei Din B'Israel (The Israel Bar) 10, Daniel Frish St. (P. O. Box 1881), Tel-Aviv
Italy	Consiglio dell'Ordine degli Avvocati e Procuratori di Roma Palazzo di Giustizia, Roma
Jamaica	The Incorporated Law Society of Jamaica 5 Port Royal Street, Kingston
Japan	Japan Bar Association No. 1, 1-chome, Kasumigaseki, Chiyoda-ku, Tokyo Japan Federation of Bar Associations No. 1, 1-chome, Kasumigaseki, Chiyoda-ku, Tokyo
Korea	Korean Bar Association 38 Seosomoondong, Seodaimoongu, Seoul
Lebanon	Ordre des Avocats à Beyrouth Palais de Justice, Beyrouth
Liberia	Liberian National Bar Association Monrovia
Mexico	Barra Mexicana, Colegio de Abogados Varsovia Street No. 1, Mexico City, D. F. Ilustre y Nacional Colegio de Abogados de Mexico Liverpool 143, México 6, D. F.
Netherlands	Nederlandse Orde van Advocaten Frederik Hendrikplain 23, The Hague
New Zealand	New Zealand Law Society P. O. Box 5041, Wellington C. 1
Northern Ireland	The Incorporated Law Society of Northern Ireland Royal Courts of Justice (Ulster), Belfast 1 The Inn of Court of Northern Ireland Royal Courts of Justice (Ulster), Belfast 1
Norway	Den Norske Advokatforening Kirkegt. 26, Oslo 1
Pakistan	Pakistan Bar Association Second Floor, Dada Chambers, Bunder Road, Karachi 2
Peru	Colegio de Abogados de Lima Palacio de Justicia, 4^0 piso, Lima Federación Nacional de Colegios de Abogados Palacio de Justicia - 4 to. piso, Lima
Philippines	Philippine Bar Association P. O. Box 2084, Manila Philippine Lawyers' Association 406-408 Regina Building, Escolta, Manila

Portugal	Ordem dos Advogados, Conselho Geral Largo de S. Domingos, 14-D, 1, Lisbon
Puerto Rico	Colegio de Abogados de Puerto Rico Apartado de Correos 1900, San Juan
Scotland	Faculty of Advocates Advocates' Library, Parliament House, Edinburgh 1 The Law Society of Scotland Law Society's Hall, North Bank Street, Edinburgh 1
South Africa	The Association of Law Societies of the Republic of South Africa P. O. Box 1493 (8th Floor, J. B. S. Bldg., Church Square) Pretoria General Council of the Bar of South Africa 10th Floor, Innes Chambers, Pritchard Street Johannesburg
Spain	Consejo General de la Abogacía Española Palacio de Justicia, Madrid
Sweden	Sveriges Advokatsamfund Kammakargatan 10, Stockholm C
Switzerland	Fédération Suisse des Avocats Hirschengraben 11, Berne
Syria	Ordre des Avocats de Damas Ministry of Justice, Damascus
Thailand	The Thai Bar Bangkok
Turkey	Ankara Barosu Reisligi, Ankara Istanbul Barosu Baskanligi, Sirkeci Liman, Han No. 2/28, Istanbul
U. A. R. (Egypt)	Bar Association of the Egyptian Region, U. A. R. 51, Ramses Street, Cairo, Egypt
United States of America	American Bar Association American Bar Center, 1155 East 60 Street Chicago, Illinois 60637 The Association of the Customs Bar 80 Broad Street, New York, New York 10004 The Consular Law Society One Wall Street, New York, New York 10005 The Federal Bar Association 1815 H Street, N. W., Washington D. C. 20006

	National Association of Women Lawyers American Bar Center 1155 East 60 Street, Chicago, Illinois 60637
Uruguay	Colegio de Abogados del Uruguay Treinta y Tres 1359, Montevideo
Venezuela	Colegio de Abogados del Distrito Federal Apartado 347, Caracas
Zambia	The Law Society of Zambia P. O. Box 1094 Lusaka, Zambia

INTERNATIONAL BAR ASSOCIATION
OFFICERS

President

Patrick Noonan, LL. B., Ireland

Chairman

Sir Denys Hicks, O. B. E., England

Secretary General

Gerald J. McMahon, Esq., United States

Treasurer

Sir Thomas G. Lund, C. B. E., England

Assistant Secretaries General

RA Dr. Heinz Brangsch, Germany
Hr. Adv. Rolf Christophersen, Norway
Bert A. Early, Esq., United States
Maître Philippe Gastambide, France
Excmo. Sr. don Roberto Rayes, Spain

Assistant Treasurer

Paul B. DeWitt, Esq., United States

Honorary Life President

Loyd Wright, Esq., United States

Administrative Secretary

Hr. Adv. Arne Rikheim, Norway

INTERNATIONAL BAR ASSOCIATION
COUNCIL

Ex-Officio:

President: Patrick Noonan, Esquire, LL. B. (Ireland)
Chairman: Sir Denys T. Hicks, O. B. E., T. D., D. L. (England)
Secretary General: Gerald J. McMahon, Esquire (USA)
Treasurer: Sir Thomas Lund, C. B. E. (England)

Australia	H. E. Zelling, Esquire, Q. C.
Austria	RA Dr. Heinrich Foglar-Deinhardstein Dr. Dr. h. c. Hans Schima
Brazil	Sr. Dr. don Pedro Lairihoy
Canada	Everett Clayton Leslie, Esquire, Q. C., LL. D., D. C. L.
Denmark	H. r. sagfører Jon Palle Buhl
England	W. O. Carter, Esquire Alan de Piro, Esquire, Q. C.
Finland	Advokat Åke Roschier-Holmberg
France	Maître Henri Delmont
Germany	RA Dr. Walter Oppenhoff
Guatemala	Sr. Lic. don Edmundo Quiñones
Iran	Maître Abbass Naraghi
Iraq	Noel Rassam, Esquire
Ireland	Patrick Noonan, Esquire, L. L. B. Thomas A. Doyle, Esquire, S. C.
Israel	Yehuda Fraenkel, Esquire
Italy	On. Avv. Filippo Ungaro
Jamaica	Leslie E. Ashenheim, Esquire
Japan	Bengoshi Dr. Nobuo Naritomi
Korea	Byun Ho Sa Sungsoo Whang
Lebanon	Maître Youssef Alem
Liberia	Counsellor Clarence L. Simpson
Mexico	Sr. Lic. D. Manuel G. Escobedo Sr. Lic. D. F. Javier Gaxiola
Netherlands	Mr. Jan Reinier Voûte
New Zealand	R. Tonson Garlick, Esquire, LL. B.
Northern Ireland	Patrick Maxwell, Esquire William A. Campbell, Esquire, B. A.
Norway	H. r. advokat Rolf Christophersen
Pakistan	Md. Nurul Huda, Esquire

Peru	Sr. Dr. Javier Vargas
Philippines	The Hon. Arturo A. Alafriz Senator Lorenzo M. Tañada
Portugal	Prof. Dr. Adelino da Palma Carlos
Puerto Rico	Sr. Lic. D. William F. Santiago
Scotland	G. C. Emslie, Esquire, M. B. E., Q. C. W. A. Cook, Esquire, LL. B.
South Africa	D. J. Shaw, Esquire, Q. C. G. R. Ashman, Esquire
Spain	Excmo. Sr. D. Roberto Rayes y. Morales
Sweden	Advokat Arthur Boström
Switzerland	Maître Edmond Martin-Achard
Syria	Maître Dr. Moukarram Kouatli
Thailand	Nai Sansern Kraichitti
Turkey	Mrs. Güler Berkin Dr. Orhan Arsal
UAR (Egypt)	Dr. Gamal El Oteifi
United States of America	The Hon. Walter E. Craig Robert N. Anderson, Esquire Louis J. Paley, Esquire Bernard A. Grossman, Esquire Mrs. Mary Louise DeM. McLeod
Uruguay	Sr. Dr. don Armando R. Malet
Venezuela	Dr. Rafael Ruiz Carillo

Co-opted Members of the Council

Ireland	John Carrigan, Esquire
Switzerland	Maître Jean-Felix Paschoud

Honorary Life Presidents of the Council

Austria	RA Dr. Heinrich Foglar-Deinhardstein
Denmark	Dr. jur. Bernt Hjejle
United States of America	Loyd Wright, Esquire

INTERNATIONAL BAR ASSOCIATION
PAST OFFICERS

Chairmen

1947 – 1954	George Maurice Morris (U. S. A.) Deceased August 21, 1954
1955 – 1964	Loyd Wright, Esq. (U. S. A.)
1964 – 1966	Dr. jur. Bernt Hjejle (Denmark)

Presidents

1948 – 1950	Dr. Johannes Drost (Netherlands) Deceased September 18, 1954
1950 – 1952	Sir Leonard S. Holmes (England) Deceased March 9, 1961
1950 – 1952	Sir Godfrey Russel Vick (England) Deceased September 27, 1958
1952 – 1953	Excmo. Dr. Don Antonio de Goicoechea y Cosculluela (Spain) Deceased February 11, 1953
1953 – 1954	Illmo. Sr. D. Manuel Escobedo Duato (Spain)
1955 – 1957	Høyesterettsadvokat Finn Arnesen (Norway)
1957 – 1959	Dr. Dr. h. c. Emil von Sauer (Germany) Deceased January 25, 1967
1959 – 1961	RA Dr. Heinrich Foglar-Deinhardstein (Austria)
1961 – 1963	W. I. R. Fraser, Esq., Q. C. (Scotland)
1961 – 1963	Neil Watson, Esq., S. S. C. (Scotland)
1963 – 1965	Sr. Lic. D. Manuel G. Escobedo (Mexico)
1963 – 1965	Sr. Lic. D. F. Javier Gaxiola (Mexico)
1965 – 1967	Dr. Carlo Bonetti (Switzerland)

Secretary-General

1947 – 1952	Hon. Amos J. Peaslee (U. S. A.)

Treasurer

1947 – 1948	Henry F. Butler (Assistant) (U. S. A.)
1948 – 1950	Edward V. Saher (Netherlands)

COMMITTEES OF THE COUNCIL

Committee on Constitution and By-Laws

Chairman: Sir Thomas Lund, C. B. E. (U. K.)

Canada	D. Park Jamieson, Esq., M. B. E., Q. C., LL. D.
France	Maître Philippe Gastambide
Ireland	John Carrigan, Esq.
Mexico	Sr. Lic. don Manuel G. Escobedo
	Ex officio: Sir Denys T. Hicks, O. B. E., T. D., D. L.

Committee on "International Bar News"

Chairman: Sir Thomas Lund, C. B. E. (U. K.)

Germany	RA Dr. Walter Oppenhoff
	RA Dr. Heinz Brangsch
Ireland	John Nash, Esq.
U. S. A.	Gerald J. McMahon, Esq.
	Loyd Wright, Esq.
	Ex officio: Sir Denys T. Hicks, O. B. E., T. D., D. L.
	Editor: Mrs. Madeleine May (1965—1968)

International Bar Association
Union Internationale des Avocats Liaison Committee
IBA Members

Austria	RA Dr. Heinrich Foglar-Deinhardstein
U. K.	Sir Denys Hicks, O. B. E.
	Sir Thomas Lund, C. B. E.
U. S. A.	Gerald J. McMahon, Esq.

UIA Members

Luxembourg	Maître Ernest Arendt
France	Maître Albert Zurfluh
Switzerland	Dr. Hans Peter Schmid
U. K.	C. H. S. Blatch, Esq.

Membership Committee

Chairman: Robert N. Anderson, Esq. (U. S. A.)

Argentina	Sr. Dr. Policarpo A. Yurrebaso Viale
Germany	RA Dr. Heinz Brangsch
Mexico	Sr. Lic. D. Manuel G. Escobedo

Thailand	Nai Sansern Kraichitti
Zambia	R. G. Care, Esq.
	The Officers, ex officio

Patrons Committee

Chairman: Orison S. Marden, Esq. (U. S. A.)

U. S. A.	Robert E. Anderson, Esq.
	Hon. Walter E. Craig
	Loyd Wright, Esq.
	The Officers, ex officio

Committee on Topics for Future Conference Programs

Chairman: John Carrigan, Esq. (Ireland)

Denmark	Højesteretssagfører Jon Palle Buhl
England	William Oscar Carter, Esq.
Israel	Y. Fraenkel, Esq.
Mexico	Sr. Lic. don Manuel G. Escobedo
Philippines	Hon. Amelito R. Mutuc
Scotland	Neil Watson, Esq.
U. A. R.	El Ostaz Dr. Ahmed Z. El Chiati
	Ex officio: Sir Denys T. Hicks, O. B. E., T. D., D. L.

Standing Committees

Advisory Committee on Professional Ethics and Professional Privilege

The members of this Committee are listed hereinafter under the Dublin Conference Open Meeting of the Committee.

Committee on Monopolies and Restrictive Trade Practices

The members of this Committee are listed hereinafter under Dublin Conference Topic No. 1, "Procedure for the enforcement of laws regulating business transactions and particularly anti-monopoly, anti-cartel and anti-trust laws".

Committee of Secretaries

Australia

Stephen Charles — Victorian Bar Council
Miss B. K. Donkin — Queensland Inc. Law Society
J. N. D. Harrison — Law Society of Tasmania
Arthur Heymanson — Law Institute of Victoria
D. F. Jackson — Bar Association of Queensland
J. Angus Maitland — Law Society of South Australia Inc.

W. R. McComas – Law Council of Australia
T. Simos – Australian Bar Association
L. F. Osborne – The New South Wales Bar Association

Austria
RA Dr. Harald Foglar-Deinhardstein – Austrian Law Society

Antigua
C. O. R. Phillips – Antigua Bar Association

British Solomon Islands Protectorate
D. R. Davis – Attorney-General, British Solomon Islands

Canada
Ronald C. Merriam, QC – Canadian Bar Association
T. R. O'Donnell – The Law Society of Saskatchewan
H. St. Geo. Stubbs – The Law Society of Manitoba

Costa Rica
Lic. Oscar Bejarano Coto – Colegio de Abogados de Costa Rica

Denmark
P. Ostergaard – Det Danske Advokatsamfund

England & Wales
W. W. Boulton – General Council of the Bar
Sir Thomas Lund, CBE – The Law Society

Fiji
Faiz Sherani – Fiji Law Society

Finland
Klaus Lagus – Suomen Asianajajaliitto

Germany
RA Dr. Heinz Brangsch – Deutscher Anwaltverein e. V.

Ghana
N. Y. B. Adade – Ghana Bar Association

Hong Kong
Mrs. Shirley Woo – The Inc. Law Society of Hong Kong

India
Shri G. G. Kulkarni, BA, LL. B. – The Bar Council of Maharashtra
Sardar Bahadur Saharya – Supreme Court Bar Association, New Delhi
P. K. Thakor – Bombay Bar Association
Shri A. N. Veeraraghavan BABL – The Bar Council of India
N. Venkatarama Ayyar – The Madras Provincial Bar Federation

Ireland
G. D. Coyle – General Council of the Bar of Ireland
E. A. Plunkett – The Inc. Law Society of Ireland

Isle of Man
J. E. Crellin – The Isle of Man Law Society

Jamaica
J. C. Stone – The Inc. Law Society of Jamaica

Japan
Ryuichi Hirano – Japanese Bar Association

Kenya
A. D. Aitchison – The Law Society of Kenya

Malaya
K. A. Menon – Bar Council of the States of Malaya

Mauritius
V. J. P. Glover – Mauritius Bar Association

Netherlands
W. van der Meij – Nederlandse Orde van Advocaten

New Zealand
T. W. Ewing – The Law Society of the District of Auckland
J. H. Murray – Hamilton District Law Society
G. J. Seeman – New Zealand Law Society
The Honorary Secretary – The Gisborne District Law Society

Norway
Hr. Advokat Rolf Christophersen – Den Norske Advokatforening

Scotland
D. A. O. Edwards – Faculty of Advocates
R. B. Laurie – The Law Society of Scotland

Singapore
E. Albuquerque – Singapore Advocates & Solicitors Society

South Africa
C. Kinghorn – General Council of the Bar of South Africa
Eben Louw – The Ass. of Law Societies of the Republic of South Africa

Sweden
Advokat Holger Wiklund – Sveriges Advokatsamfund

Switzerland
G. Hochstrasser – Swiss Bar Association

Thailand
Nai Sansern Kraichitti – The Thai Bar

Trinidad
Senator the Hon. M. T. Inskip Julien – Trinidad Inc. Law Society

Uganda
The Honorary Secretary – The Uganda Law Society

United States of America
Bert H. Early – American Bar Association
M. Barry Levy – The Association of the Customs Bar

THE DUBLIN CONFERENCE

Dublin's fair city lived up to its name when it welcomed over 1500 lawyers and their guests to the Twelfth IBA Conference – July 8-12, 1968. This was a record attendance for an IBA Conference. But room was found for all and a warm and friendly welcome was extended. The conference was blessed with the most pleasant Irish summer in many years. The sun was shining brightly when Conferees and their guests were gaily piped into the opening session on Monday morning.

The capital city of Ireland with its charming mixture of bustling 20th century traffic and quiet side streets with rows of graceful Georgian houses, its elegant shops on Grafton Street and the wide expanse of O'Connel Street, provided an attractive setting for an international conference.

The working sessions of the Conference were held on the premises of the Royal Dublin Society, site of the famous Dublin Horse Show. Its Concert Hall was an ideal location for the Working and Plenary Sessions of the Conference. Simultaneous translation into English, French, German and Spanish was available at all Sessions.

The highlights of the Conference were the presence of Ireland's distinguished President, Eamon de Valera, at the Opening Session and the closing address on Friday morning by His Excellency U Thant, Secretary-General of the United Nations. At the end of the Conference the following telegram was sent to His Excellency Eamon de Valera:

"His Excellency Eamon De Valera

President of Ireland

At this, the conclusion of the IBA Conference, Dublin, 1968, we wish to convey our deep gratitude to you and to the people of Ireland for the warmth of your welcome and the open hospitality which we have encountered during our stay in Dublin.

Also, please accept our gratitude for lending grace to the Opening Session of the Conference, by honouring us with your presence.

INTERNATIONAL BAR ASSOCIATION

Signed: Patrick Noonan, Esq., President
Sir Denys Hicks, O. B. E.,
R. D., D. L., Chairman"

The Council met on Sunday afternoon, July 7, at the Royal Dublin Society Council Chamber and on Saturday morning, July 13, in the Council Chambers of the Incorporated Law Society of Ireland.

The General Meeting of the Association which speaks for the organized Bar of the world convened on Wednesday, July 10, with thirty-seven national Bar Associations and Law Societies represented by 101 Official Delegates.

Following the General Meeting, the International Legal Aid Association organized a discussion session at the Royal Dublin Society and Member Organizations of the International Bar Association and individual lawyers were urged to support the International Legal Aid Association by their affiliation and cooperation.

The Association is again indebted to its Assistant Secretary General RA Dr. Heinz Brangsch, Hauptgeschäftsführer of the Deutscher Anwaltverein (Germany) for his assistance with the production of the Conference Papers, and to all the Assistant Secretaries General for the cooperation in Conference work: H. r. advokat Rolf Christophersen (Norway), Bert H. Early, (United States), Maître Philippe Gastambide (France), and Excmo. Sr. don Roberto Reyes (Spain).

The advance work and preparation of Rapporteurs, Committee Chairmen, and Chairman and Vice Chairman of the Working Sessions of the Conference constituted the foundation for the productive Working Sessions of the Conference. The reports on all topics were available in English and on Topics No. 1 and 4 in German also. In addition, a summary of each report was available in French and Spanish, the other official languages of the International Bar Association. The Reports and Summaries are printed in this report.

OPENING PLENARY SESSION

The Formal Opening Session took place in the Concert Hall of the Royal Dublin Society on Monday morning, July 8. Conferees were welcomed to Ireland and to Dublin by Michael O'Morain, Esq., Minister for Justice, by The Lord Mayor of Dublin, Councillor Tom Stafford, and by Patrick Noonan, Esq., President of the Incorporated Law Society of Ireland. The President of Ireland, Eamon de Valera, and An Taoiseach (Prime Minister) Jack Lynch graced the session with their presence.

In welcoming conferees and their guests President Noonan said:

"It is my privilege and honour as President of the Incorporated Law Society of Ireland to be the first to address this 12th Conference of the International Bar Association. At the outset may I say, Mr. President, Sir, how pleased we are that you should have honoured us with your presence here today. We shall be greatly encouraged in our labours by the approval which your presence here this morning implies; and in this I speak not only for the Incorporated Law Society of Ireland but also for the International Bar Association.

I also greet the Taoiseach and the Minister for Justice. I am glad to have this opportunity of acknowledging the generous and whole-hearted cooperation which the Incorporated Law Society has received from the Taoiseach and his successive Ministers for Justice in the organization of this Conference since it was first projected.

If the number of registrations is a criterion then this Conference is already assured of success because they are equal to and possibly exceed the registrations of the previous conferences. Furthermore the conferees come from all parts of the world and there are no less than fifty-one countries represented here today. On behalf of the host organization I greet you and bid you welcome to our country and capital city and pray that you may have a most useful and enjoyable stay.

The Incorporated Law Society of Ireland were greatly pleased to have secured this important conference for Ireland and most happily during the year the General Council of the Bar of Ireland became a member of the IBA, and thereby enabled our Society to enjoy their cooperation and support. The organization of the conference fell on the shoulders of a small committee of lawyers assisted by their ladies and the Secretary of the Society. For twelve months now they have given themselves to this work with energy, enthusiasm and assiduous skill and a complete disregard of own interests and businesses. I acknowledge our debt to them the support and cooperation and assistance we have received from Bord Failte, the Royal Dublin Society, the transport authority, the hotels and catering establishments. To all of them I offer our sincere gratitude.

As this is Human Rights Year and as one of the objects of the Association as stated in its Constitution is "to promote in their legal aspects, the principles and aims of the United Nations", the Council thought it appropriate to invite U Thant, the Secretary of the United Nations to come to the Conference and he has very kindly consented to address the Conference on Friday. I am glad to say that during his visit he will be the recipient of an Honorary Degree from Dublin University.

All international conferences are good things because anything which brings people of different nations into personal contact and friendly discussion is helpful. Such meetings are as important as their subjects and law is a very important subject. It is law that distinguisher order from chaos and civilized society from anarchy, but order itself is not the ultimate purpose of law. If it were, tyranny would be the perfect achievement. The purpose of law is to create an ordered society in which the citizen can enjoy the maximum individual liberty and personal dignity, and thereby, be enabled to achieve personal fulfilment. Although principles may be immutable, law itself is not, indeed, it must be in a constant state of flux so as to adjust itself to the developing need of the society which it serves. It is unfortunately true that the development of law frequently falls behind. This defect must be combated vigorously. Particularly so since in the past twenty or thirty years the development of science, transport, communications and increase in population has been moving at a tremendous rate and appears likely to continue these trends at a progressively faster rate as time goes by. These developments have their own attendant problems. They tend to build up tensions between conflicting interests and to subject the law maker to pressures from recurrent crises of one kind or another arising from these conflicts. If legal research does not move at a sufficiently rapid pace to provide well thought out and philosophically sound solutions for these problems as they arise, the law maker will tend of necessity to meet his problems with ad hoc remedies and to think of the establishment and maintenance of order as an end in itself for society rather than society for the individual. I quote with approval a remark made by David A. Morse, a Director General of the International Labour Organization in a recent address when he said "preoccupation with economic development will make us forget that the aim of all human endeavor in whatever field must be to advance the freedom and dignity of man". Then he went on: "There is a serious risk that we shall be reduced to paying lip service to human rights, that we shall become so obsessed with material, economic and scientific progress that we shall be increasingly tempted to sacrifice the end to the means."

We must avoid these dangers and we can only do so by keeping our legal research moving at a pace equal to the tempo of development in other aspects of society, so that problems may be anticipated and met with well considered remedies as they arise.

One of the obvious ways of doing this is to borrow from one another. In particular we can learn from one another's experiences of successes or failures, especially as all states and countries are not in the same degree of economic, social and political development. That is why this Conference is so very important. I think you will agree that the programme of topics is suitably designed to achieve this end and I am sure we are going to have a most successful Conference and I pray God that much good may come to us all from its endeavours."

Responses to the addresses of welcome were made for the Continent of Africa by Michael H. Blackwood, Chairman of the Malawi Law Society (Malawi), for Asia by the Hon. Amelito Mutuc (Philippines), for Australasia by R. T. Garlick (New Zealand), for Europe by Me Henri Delmont, President of the Association Nationale des Avocats (France), for North America by A. Gordon Cooper, President of the Canadian Bar Association, and for South America and neighboring Islands by The Hon. Senator M. T. Inskip Julien (Trinidad), and for the International Bar Association by its Chairman, Sir Denys Hicks, O. B. E., T. D., D. L.

TEXT OF ADDRESS BY SECRETARY-GENERAL, U THANT, TO INTERNATIONAL BAR ASSOCIATION, DUBLIN, 12 JULY 1968

International Law and the United Nations

I am particularly happy to have an opportunity of addressing the International Bar Association in Dublin, the capital of a country which since its admission in 1955 has in all its United Nations activities consistently striven to make the rule of law prevail in international relations. As those who have followed the work of the General Assembly during those years are well aware, Ireland has taken a lead in endeavouring to strengthen the Organization and make it a more effective instrument for the achievement of the purposes of the Charter. The distinguished Foreign Minister, Mr. Frank Aiken, has had the satisfaction of seeing the General Assembly adopt only the other day a treaty on the non-proliferation of nuclear weapons, which sets the seal on a far-sighted initiative which he took ten years ago in the General Assembly and has continued to urge eloquently during the intervening years. He has also been responsible for focusing the attention of the Organization on the very vital problem of the financing of peace-keeping. In the United Nations Special Committee on Peace-Keeping Operations and in other forums I have had occasion to commend the steadfast efforts of the Irish Government in this matter, and I should like to do so again today.

It is also a very great pleasure for me to have this opportunity to speak to so distinguished a gathering of lawyers. By virtue of your participation in the International Bar Association, you have all demonstrated your devotion to the purposes of the Association, which, as stated in Article 1 of your Constitution, include the promotion of "the administration of justice under law among peoples of the world". It is the law, international law, that will form my main theme today, as I endeavour to sketch its increasing role in furthering international peace and co-operation.

First, however, I cannot fail to allude to 1968 as a very significant one in the history of the United Nations. It is the International Year for Human Rights. Four and a half years ago when the General Assembly designated 1968, the year of the twentieth anniversary of the adoption of the Universal Declaration of Human Rights, as the International Year for Human Rights, the Assembly decided that 1968 should be devoted to intensified national and international efforts and undertakings in the field of human rights. In these efforts and undertakings I am sure that the International Bar Association and its members will play an important role, for lawyers everywhere, and at all times, have demonstrated their close interest in, and desire for, acceptance of standards of fair treatment for all individuals and groups under a system of law binding on the national and international level. In the process of obtaining redress against violations of fundamental human rights, practising lawyers, whether judges or advocates, have obviously a very significant role to play.

That there may be differences of view on such matters as the precise role of legal process or the limitations in the jurisdiction of international organizations in matters concerning human rights needs no emphasis in a gathering of a body such as yours. But disagreements concerning these matters or doctrinal controversies should not blind us to the fact that barriers to co-operation such as those arising out of the difference in systems existing in many countries have not proved to be insurmountable obstacles to United Nations efforts in the field of human rights. As I had occasion to say in 1963, countries and peoples are increasingly recognizing that no country and no people has a monopoly on the rightness, liberty and human dignity, and our experience shows that the aspirations of peoples all over the world, whether in the civil or political field or the economic, social or cultural field, are basically the same although the approaches to their realization may be different. The developments in the United Nations and other international organizations abundantly show that any contemporary definition of international law which overlooks the individual not only fails to reflect the facts of international life today but also contributes to impeding the development of international law itself.

Over the years, substantial progress has been achieved through the United Nations and its family of organizations in setting international objectives and standards, often couched in the form of legal norms, in the area of human rights and fundamental freedoms. These objectives and standards underline in particular the essential interdependence of civil and political rights and economic, social and cultural rights, the right to self-determination of peoples, the rule of non-discrimination and that of the equality of men and women.

With the adoption in 1966 of the International Covenants on Human Rights — the vote of all 106 participating Member States was unanimous — and an Optional Protocol permitting consideration of complaints by individuals or private groups, the United Nations completed what is known as the International Bill of Rights, which consists of the Universal Declaration, the Covenants and the measures for their implementation. Thus the right of every individual, without distinction, to secure respect for his dignity as a human being, has been placed in an incontestable legal context. Besides the International Bill of Rights there have been many international instruments concluded under the auspices of the United Nations which have brought into the sphere of international law an ever increasing number of subjects connected with human rights and fundamental freedoms. It is hoped that very shortly the International

Convention on the Elimination of All Forms of Racial Discrimination will come into force — it requires only eight more ratifications or accessions to become effective — and thereby bring into operation for the first time in the United Nations a comprehensive machinery of implementation ranging from reports by States to fact-finding and conciliation bodies and procedures for dealing with individual petitions.

The International Conference on Human Rights convened by the United Nations recently in Teheran adopted a Proclamation of Teheran which is an eloquent statement of the objectives in the field of human rights. At the same Conference a number of resolutions were adopted — such as those concerning human rights and scientific and technological developments, economic development and human rights, human rights aspects of family planning, education of youth in the respect of human rights and fundamental freedoms, and human rights in armed conflicts — which demonstrate that the human rights programme of the United Nations is an integral part of its efforts to attain the Charter's objectives of peace and security, economic and social well-being and the harmonization of the actions of nations.

Bodies such as the International Bar Association can give a lead in informative consideration and deliberations, as well as in strengthening public understanding, of such matters both nationally and internationally. They can lay stress on the primary importance of respecting the intrinsic dignity of the human being, or what I frequently called the "human factor" in all national endeavours and undertakings. For important as international machinery is, we have to recognize and to stress that it is primarily within the countries and the communities that the promotion and protection of human rights has to be sought and achieved.

The International Bar Association can also give the lead in fostering and encouraging, on the national plane, the growth and development of international law as a whole, which, in the years ahead, must provide us with the backbone for peace, security and justice. The existing system of modern international law was built around the concepts of sovereignty and of independence. Yet while these may be called the roots of modern international law, they are also a hindrance in an age when we are moving from independence to interdependence. In national law the existence of and necessity for legislative, judicial and law enforcement organs are self-evident. In international law, because of the barrier of sovereignty, they have existed scarcely at all or only on an *ad hoc* basis. In the twentieth century, through custom, practice, treaty and judicial decision, the rules of international law have proliferated, but the development of means of truly enforcing those rules through compulsory adjudication and through collective action has been painfully slow. The horrors of two world wars, and the death and suffering of countless millions were the price mankind was forced to pay before that barrier of sovereignty was lowered sufficiently to permit international law, both on a regional and on a universal plane, to create or strengthen organizations designed to keep the peace and to settle disputes both through diplomacy and impartial adjudication. As a result we have today the Charter of the United Nations, the Statute of the International Court of Justice, and the regional organizations such as the Council of Europe, the Organization of American States, the League of Arab States and the Organization of African Unity.

Given this machinery and the principles upon which it is based – including, specifically, the principles of international law – what role does law play in keeping the peace today? At best it can be said that it can be likened to the candles which light the darkness. The Rann of Kutch dispute, which was a contributing factor leading to the war between India and Pakistan, has recently been settled by arbitration. A territorial dispute between Argentina and Chile has likewise been settled by the same means. The dispute between the Republic of Indonesia and the Kingdom of the Netherlands regarding West Irian, which had already broken out into armed clashes, was solved by an agreement negotiated by the parties in 1962. The more these examples are followed, the sooner the darkness will be dispelled.

Hope also lies along the road which has recently been followed in Antarctica and in Outer Space. A few years ago Antarctica was a possible source of friction and hostility by virtue of the numerous competing territorial claims by various States. With the conclusion of the Antarctic Treaty in Washington, on 1 December 1959, this potential source of strife and conflict was converted into an area of peace and co-operation. Principles were established for Antarctica, moreover, which were utilized as the foundation for the provisions which now govern man's exploration of the limitless realm of outer space. Through the instrumentality of the Legal Sub-Committee of the United Nations Committee on the Peaceful Uses of Outer Space, the Treaty on Principles Governing the Activities of States in the Exploration and Use of Outer Space, including the Moon and Other Celestial Bodies, was concluded in 1966. This Treaty affirms that the exploration and use of outer space shall be carried out for the benefit of all countries. It proclaims the freedom of outer space. It affirms that outer space and celestial bodies are not subject to national appropriation, and provides that outer space and celestial bodies shall not be used for any military purpose. It therefore establishes a broad and forward-looking regime for an area which might have become a source of strife and conflict. The process of law has neutralized this possible source of conflict, and has converted it into an area of peace and co-operation.

Within the framework of the regime established by the Outer Space Treaty, the United Nations continues work on more detailed aspects of the law of outer space. Only last December, the General Assembly commended to Governments the Agreement on the Rescue of Astronauts, the Return of Astronauts and the Return of Objects Launched into Outer Space. This constituted the culmination of five years of work by the Legal Sub-Committee of the United Nations Committee on the Peaceful Uses of Outer Space and yet another significant step in the development of international law relating to outer space. The text of the Agreement reflects a carefully designed balance between the legitimate interests of the party on whose territory search and rescue operations are conducted and those of the launching authority, and seeks to secure the safe and prompt return of astronauts and space objects to the launching authority. It is my hope that this Agreement will shortly be supplemented by an Agreement on liability for damage caused by objects launched into outer space, which was the principal item discussed by the Legal Committee of the United Nations Committee on the Peaceful Uses of Outer Space during a session in Geneva which ended a few days ago.

The law of outer space is therefore developing fast and along lines which promise much for the furtherance of peace and co-operation. There remains one other area for which a new regime may have to be created, and for which outer space should provide many fruitful analogies. This area is one of potentially vast significance in bettering the life of man in the generations immediately ahead, as it will, with improved technology, provide an almost limitless source of food and minerals. I speak of the sea-bed and ocean floor in areas now considered beyond the limits of national jurisdiction. On the initiative of Malta, the General Assembly, at its session last year, took up an item entitled "Examination of the question of the reservation exclusively for peaceful purposes of the sea-bed and the ocean floor, and the subsoil thereof, underlying the high seas beyond the limits of present national jurisdiction, and the use of their resources in the interests of mankind". The Assembly decided to establish a thirty-five member *Ad Hoc* Committee to Study the Peaceful Uses of the Sea-Bed and the Ocean Floor beyond the Limits of National Jurisdiction. This Committee has established a Working Group to consider the legal aspects of the item. Its task will not be either easy or short, in view of the many varying interests which are involved. However, if it proves to be as successful as the Legal Sub-Committee of the Committee on the Peaceful Uses of Outer Space we can rest assured that another potential area of friction between States will be converted, through law, into an area of peace and co-operation.

The role of international law is, of course, not confined to providing new regimes for new areas of man's endeavour. It also regulates existing relations between States. A very significant step was taken only a few weeks ago by the General Assembly of the United Nations, when it commended to States the Treaty on the Non-Proliferation of Nuclear Weapons. This treaty, taken together with the Moscow Test Ban Treaty of 1963, is the first really significant break-through in the field of global disarmament since the end of the Second World War. The nations of Latin America, on a regional plane, took a further significant step last year when, in Mexico, twenty-one of them signed the Treaty for the Prohibition of Nuclear Weapons in Latin America. This Treaty was welcomed with special satisfaction by the General Assembly of the United Nations last December as an event of historic significance in the efforts to prevent the proliferation of nuclear weapons and to promote international peace and security. If the treaties I have just mentioned can only serve as an inspiration and example for other measures of disarmament, we may be able to look forward to the end of the armaments race, and the release of enormous amounts of wealth and experience for peaceful development.

By way of parenthesis I may say that the U.N. and its family of specialised agencies are now studying the fact of the First Development Decade which was launched in 1961. We are studying methods and procedures and objectives for the 2nd Decade which is to be launched in 1971. One basic fact, the national interest of a country cannot be confined within the interests of a particular country. The national interests of many countries will depend primarily on international peace, international progress and international security. In launching the Second Development Decade, the international community through the medium of the United Nations and its family of agencies have to launch a global strategy and in making this global strategy we must recognize the fact that the world is divided into rich and poor countries. We have come to the crossroads of history. There are two courses open to them, either the rich and poor march together, work and strive together or the recent poor countries must wander aimlessly without any spirit of togetherness, without any direction and head to a chaotic future. These are the two choices open to mankind. If common sense prevails, both rich and poor will choose the first alternative with the very heartening development and the release of enormous amounts of wealth and experience for peaceful development. Only with this recognized can we march together, question our future together and then only will the world be a much happier place to live in.

These, then, are some of the bright places, where law has constituted the cornerstone of peace. However, there are still great areas of darkness and of strife in this world where force and power politics rule to the detriment of law and peace. In the ultimate analysis, law cannot prevail over force and power politics until mankind comes to regard the impartial adjudication of international law in disputes among States as the rule, not the exception.

If the record of the law in the history of keeping the peace is still a modest one, its record in the history of long-term international co-operation is a more brilliant one, less often discussed, perhaps, only because it relates to fields less spectacular than breaches of the peace. Here it may be said, at least in certain parts of the world, that through legal processes States are moving from independence to integration, particularly in the economic sphere. Indeed, there is already a fast-growing body of international norms which is beginning to be referred to as the "law of integration".

When we view the global picture of co-operation in economic and social questions, we see a world closely tied by thousands of treaties regulating matters as diverse as narcotics and commodity prices, slavery and atomic energy, road transportation and maintenance obligations. This co-operation is not limited to the economic and social needs of the day, but has also extended to the fabric of the law itself. In the twenty-twoyears of its existence, through codification in treaty form of the law of the sea, and of diplomatic and consular relations, the United Nations has achieved more progress in this field than was achieved in the previous three hundred years. The success earlier this year of the first part of the United Nations Conference on the Law of Treaties, has brought us to the threshold of a Convention, to be completed in Vienna next year, which progressively develops and codifies the entire law of treaties and which will, I hope, become one of the fundamentals of the constitutional law of the entire society of nations.

With the great success it has achieved in codifying and developing public international law in mind, the United Nations now seeks to achieve similar results in the field of private international law. An important step in this direction was the recent creation of the United Nations Commission on International Trade Law (UNCITRAL), which was established by the General Assembly in December 1966 and held its first session early this year.

The object of UNCITRAL is to deal with a concrete and practical problem.

Lawyers and persons engaged in international commerce are aware that conflicts and divergencies among the laws of different countries often constitute an obstacle to the flow of trade. The purpose of this new Commission is to help remove those obstacles by promoting the harmonization and unification of the law of international trade.

The different legal systems of the world and all stages of economic development are represented among the twenty-nine States elected by the General Assembly to membership in UNCITRAL. In addition to being spokesmen for their Governments the delegates are also eminent jurists. The combination of these elements gives me confidence that this new Commission will make a significant contribution to removing legal barriers to international trade.

It is true that the conclusion of international agreements on particular aspects of economic, social and legal matters is not as spectacular as the conclusion of agreements in the political field. However, through their sheer numbers and scope, and through their ultimate objectives of eliminating poverty and ignorance, the agreements themselves contribute to the stabilization and development of national societies, and thus contribute to the maintenance of international peace. The world will never be truly safe for peace until mankind has eradicated poverty, ignorance and injustice. The processes of international co-operation are simply the processes of ridding the world of these ancient evils.

As we look to the future we must realize that peace and co-operation are impossible without legal regulation. While international law does not yet carry the force or conviction of national law, even today it is the cornerstone of peace and co-operation on the international plane. As modern discoveries and technological progress bring growing interdependence, that interdependence must accelerate the further development of international law. The ultimate goal must be that fortunate day when international law will enjoy, in the society of nations, a place as important and as compelling as law in our present national societies. But to do so, it must be responsive to the realities of the world, to the needs of society, and to the temper of mankind. It cannot afford, any more than can national law, to refuse to meet the challenges with which it is confronted, or allow itself to become static. In the end, it is the confidence of peoples and of nations in the rule of law that can bring to international law its greatest strength, and to win this confidence it must be as dynamic as are the lives of peoples and nations themselves. Through international organizations means now exist for developing the law at an unprecedented rate, and, potentially at least, the means for enforcing that law also exists through those organizations. The cause of international law is a noble and a compelling one. It is a cause in which you all, as lawyers, have a part to play, and in which I wish you every success. We all live for the day when justice may be established in the hearts not only of men, but also of nations.

While this distinguished gathering comprises leaders of men and thoughts from many countries, I feel that it would be pertinent and appropriate to conclude my remarks with a brief observation on the role which leaders of men everywhere can play towards the achievement of the objectives of the United Nations. In the preamble of the League of Nations it started with the words "We the high contracting parties, will do this . . . do that . . . etc." In the Charter of the United Nations "We the peoples of the United Nations will do this . . . do this . . . "

In my view this is a very important difference. The League of Nations, which is now no more, started with the words "we the high contracting parties" — while in the Charter of the United Nations "we the peoples of the United Nations". So, although in the terms of the Charter, the Governments have to play a very important part, as equal members, whether large or small, I think it is very important that the peoples of the United Nations also be conscious of the problems facing the United Nations today; — not only in the economic field, but also in the political, legal, human rights and social fields. If the peoples of the United Nations are alert and if they are really dedicated to the ideals and ideas of the Charter, then the United Nations will really develop into an effective instrument for the development of all the functions outlined in the Charter. If this is our objective then, all of us, the peoples of the United Nations, should be more vigorous, more interested in the activities of the United Nations and then only we shall be able to contribute significantly towards the achievement of our objects, towards which the 24 member states are working with devotion and dedication.

THE SOCIAL PROGRAM

Our Irish hosts prepared a thoroughly enjoyable social program for Conferees and their guests. To round out the activities the Irish Ladies' Committee arranged a special program for the women guests, which included tours of Dublin and the surrounding countryside as well as several fashion shows. The program opened with receptions in the historic buildings of the Four Courts and the King's Inns. Later in the week, at the invitation of the Minister of Justice, Conferees attended an interesting soirée at historic Dublin Castle.

An "Irish Evening" was held on Tuesday which featured Irish folk music and dancing. On Wednesday the renowned Abbey Theatre of Dublin presented in its new and impressive building a play based on Brendan Behan's "Borstal Boy". For those who preferred lighter entertainment a program was available at the Gaiety Theatre. The climax of the social program was the closing banquet and dance at Castletown House, now newly restored and reputed to be one of the best examples of Georgian architecture in Ireland.

SUMMARY OF THE GENERAL MEETING

The Chairman, Sir Denys Hicks, called the General Meeting to order at 9:30 a. m., July 10th.

The Secretary General, Gerald J. McMahon, read the roll and announced that delegates from thirty-seven Member Organizations were in attendance.

He then summarized for the General Meeting his report as Secretary General, which is reproduced herein.

The report of the Treasurer, Sir Thomas Lund, was read and approved *).

The Chairman informed the General Meeting that at the Meeting of the Council held on July 7th the following members of the Committees of the General Meeting have been appointed:

Credentials Committee:

Chairman: Sr. Lic. Don Manuel G. Escobedo (Mexico)

Nominations Committee:

Chairman: RA Dr. Heinrich Foglar-Deinhardstein (Austria)
Members: All Heads of Delegations to the General Meeting

Committee to Draft Resolutions of Appreciation:

Chairman: Bert H. Early, Esq. (U. S. A.)
Members: John Carrigan, Esq. (Ireland)
Eric A. Plunkett, Esq. (Ireland)

The General Meeting confirmed the appointments.

The Chairman reported that since the last General Meeting the Council had elected to membership the General Council of the Bar of Ireland and the Law Society of Zambia. The General Meeting unanimously confirmed the elections.

The Chairman of the Committee on Constitution and Bye-Laws, Sir Thomas Lund, reported that the Council at its meeting in Amsterdam (22nd—23rd April 1967) had decided to bring before the General Meeting amendments to the Constitution to allow for co-option to the Council, to allow for membership of Regional Associations and to provide for new classes of Patrons; and at its Meeting at Dublin on 7th July 1968, to change Article V Section 4 (b) relating to payment of dues. Sir Thomas Lund read the proposed amendments.

*) See Page 364 for the Report of the Treasurer.

As discussion arose as to whether the provision allowing for membership of Regional Associations had been passed by the Council in Amsterdam the Chairman withdrew the proposed amendment.

Mr. Robert Mulky proposed a resolution, which was seconded by Mr. Jan Voûte, that co-opted members of the Council should not have the right to vote. The resolution was put to a vote and defeated by 51 votes to 17.

Me Jeantet proposed and Mr. Alan de Piro seconded motions:

(1) that the period of co-option be limited to 6 years but renewable, and

(2) that not more than two co-opted members from the same organization should serve on the Council at the same time.

The Chairman put these two motions to a vote and declared them carried by the required majority.

Finally, it was proposed by RA Dr. H. Burchard-Motz that co-option should be made by a two-thirds majority. This was seconded by a French delegate. The Chairman put this amendment to a vote and declared it carried by the required majority.

The Meeting left it to the Committee on Constitution and Bye-Laws to frame these amendments in the appropriate language.

The amendments to allow for new classes of membership and a variation in the payment of dues were put to a vote by the Chairman who declared them carried by the required majority.

The Chairman then submitted to the General Meeting his report concerning the progress of the Association since its inception and stressed the necessity for future planning. He urged an extension of the activities of the Association by establishing sections devoted to particular aspects of comparative law. He stressed the need for the organized Bar to assist bar associations, particularly those in developing countries. He emphasized the problem of finance and the need for additional funds to enable the IBA to expand its activities. He indicated that plans were in progress to extend the membership of the Association and to increase the number of Patrons and Subscribers.

The Chairman of the International Legal Aid Association, John S. Tennant, Esq., of the United States, reported on the activities of the I. L. A. A. over the past two years.

The report of the Nominating Committee was then presented which unanimously recommended the re-election of the following officers for a term of two years:

Chairman: Sir Denys Hicks, OBE, TD, DL (England)
Secretary-General: Gerald J. McMahon, Esq. (USA)
Treasurer: Sir Thomas Lund, CBE (England)

At the request of the Chairman, Philip Werner Amram, Esq., reported on the 1960 Hague Conference Convention on the Service of Documents in Foreign Countries and the 1968 Hague Meeting Draft Convention on Taking of Testimony in Foreign Countries noting that both conventions contained substantially all the basic conclusions which were reached by the IBA at the Cologne Conference upon recommendations from its Committee on International Judicial Co-operation.

Mr. Jan R. Voûte spoke at length of the need for the IBA to assist bar associations in developing countries and proposed a definitive programme for consideration by the IBA Council.

Me Edmond Martin Achard suggested that the IBA might in some way assist lawyers who are subjected to or threatened with punishment for their legitimate actions in the defense of their clients.

Bert H. Early, Esq., Chairman of the Committee to Draft Resolutions of Appreciation, then presented to the General Meeting the following draft resolution which was adopted by acclamation:

"The Officers, Delegates, Conferees and guests present at the Twelfth Conference of the International Bar Association in Dublin, Ireland, take this means to express officially and collectively their deep and earnest appreciation for the gracious hospitality and warm friendship which has been showered upon us by the members of the Incorporated Law Society of Ireland and of The General Council of the Bar of Ireland and by their families and fellow countrymen.

Measured by any standard, this Conference has been singularly successful. It has achieved new heights in meeting attendance and participation, and in the depth and breadth of program content. In no small way this is directly due to the widespread reputation of our Irish brothers for their hospitality, to the remarkable degree and amount of advance planning by the Irish Planning Committee, and to the finesse and effectiveness with which their plans have been so effectively executed. The attention to every detail of meeting arrangements at the Royal Dublin Society has made it possible to conduct the ceremonial, business and educational sessions of the Conference with dispatch and facility. The opportunities for social activity have been frequent and delightful. The receptions at the Great Hall of the Four Courts, the Library in the Solicitors' Buildings and the Great Hall of the King's Inns, the Irish Evening, the tours of the city and its many places of interest have all added immeasurably to the pleasure of our stay in this land and to our affection for the people of Ireland. Nowhere have we been accorded a higher degree of warmth and sincerity of friendship and hospitality.

We cannot individually thank all the persons and organizations who have contributed to the great success of this Conference, but there are those whom we would be remiss in our expression of appreciation if we were to fail to recognize. We desire to extend the warm thanks and appreciation of the International Bar Association to the following:

His Excellency Eamonn DeValera, President of the Republic of Ireland. An Taoiseach, Mr. Jack Lynch, and the Lord Mayor of Dublin for honouring us by their presence at our opening session;

Mr. Michael O'Morain, Minister of Justice of the Republic of Ireland, by his presence and for the reception which he has arranged for tomorrow evening;

The Chief Justice, the President of the High Court and the Judiciary for their presence and encouragement;

Patrick Noonan, Esq., President of the Incorporated Law Society of Ireland and Mrs. Noonan for his leadership and her graciousness;

The Benchers of the King's Inn, the General Council of the Bar of Ireland and the Incorporated Law Society of Ireland for their considerable help and generous assistance in ensuring the success of this Conference;

The Incorporated Law Society of Ireland and the General Council of the Bar for their hospitality throughout the week;

Eric Plunkett, Esq., as Secretary of the Incorporated Law Society of Ireland, and his wife Stella Plunkett, as Secretary of the Ladies' Committee, upon whom fell the main burden of planning and organizing this Conference and whose devoted work and energy have been responsible for its success; and their daughter Collette who served as a Steward;

The Carrigans all, John as Chairman of the Irish Committee, Shirley as Chairman of the Ladies' Committee and Janet and Michael as Conference Stewards;

The members of the Irish Committee, both Ladies and Gentlemen, who devoted so much of their time and so much enthusiasm to this Conference during the past two years and to whom the success of this Conference is essentially due;

And finally, the young – the Conference Stewards, including the Chief Stewards – who volunteered their services and who worked with such efficiency, dedication and courtesy at the Conference Centre and elsewhere."

On motion duly made, seconded and carried unanimously, these resolutions were approved.

The meeting adjourned at 12 : 15 a. m.

REPORT OF THE SECRETARY GENERAL

Gerald J. McMahon

To the General Meeting at the Dublin Conference, July 10th 1968

I. MEMBERSHIP:

The International Bar Association now has 58 member organizations in 43 countries. There are 5 member organizations in Africa, 14 in Asia, 2 in Australasia, 21 in Europe, 8 in North America and 8 in South and Central America and the neighbouring islands.

Since the last General Meeting in Lausanne, the following additions have been made to our roster of member organizations:

Ireland: The General Council of the Bar of Ireland was elected to membership by the members of the Council by mail vote in March 30, 1968.

Zambia: The Law Society of Zambia was elected to membership by the Council at its meeting in Dublin on July 7, 1968.

These applications will be submitted for confirmation by this session of the General Meeting.

The Council has invited to the Dublin Conference observers from present and former Commonwealth countries. Delegates are asked to assist in discussing and explaining IBA work to these observers and to other conferees. It is hoped that these observers will carry home a sufficiently favorable report of the IBA which will induce their associations to join the IBA.

II. COUNCIL:

Between the General Meeting at Lausanne July 13, 1966 and at Dublin July 10, 1968, the Council has met on four occasions — at Lausanne after the close of the Conference July 16, 1966, at Amsterdam, April 22-23, 1967, at Lisbon, March 2-3, 1968, and at Dublin, July 7, 1968 before the opening of the current Conference.

At the Council Meetings in Amsterdam and in Dublin, the Council has recommended that the amendment to the Constitution and By-Laws proposed by the Committee on Constitution and By-Laws be adopted by the General Meeting. Delegates are reminded that under the provisions of the Constitution and By-Laws, as amended at Cologne in 1958, each Member Organization is entitled to appoint one representative to the Council of the IBA. Delegates whose Member Organizations have not as yet named a Councillor are urged to request that such appointment be made, and to arrange for the Secretary General to be advised by written communication. It is also urged that any changes in the appointment of Councillors or in the elected Officiers of the Member Organizations be promptly conveyed to the Secretary General.

III. LAUSANNE CONFERENCE BOOK:

The "Eleventh Conference Report, Lausanne, July 1966" appeared in print in the Fall of 1967. Once again the publishing firm of Martinus Nijhoff in The Hague served as publisher, and the book was printed in Germany by Hans-Soldan-Stiftung, the firm responsible for the printing of the IBA Conference papers and reports since the Cologne Conference. The work was done under the direction of our Assistant Secretary General in Germany, Rechtsanwalt Dr. Heinz Brangsch. The book is available from Martinus Nijhoff or IBA New York headquarters in New York. The Price is $ 8.

IV. DUBLIN CONFERENCE 1968:

The President of the International Bar Association, Mr. Patrick Noonan, President of the Incorporated Law Society of Ireland, has assumed the principal responsibility for the arrangements for this year's Conference, with the able assistance of the Conference Committee, consisting of Members of the I. L. S. I. and in association with the General Council of the Bar of Ireland.

The success of their work is evident to all lawyers attending the Conference. The Secretary of the Incorporated Law Society of Ireland, Mr. Eric Plunkett, has carried the heavy burden of the day-to-day work preparing for the Conference, and no report would be complete without a gracious acknowledgement of the outstanding job done by the Ladies Committee.

Conference Papers and Reports:

The scores of individuals listed in the printed program, who have prepared the topics for discussion at this Conference, are deserving of our deep and sincere appreciation. Once again, the greatest burden has fallen upon the Rapporteurs and Chairmen of Committees, each of whom has worked closely with the Secretary General over the past year or more in an effort to meet difficult deadlines. It was possible to distribute by mail in the middle of June 1968, all the reports on the Conference topics in English, and with regard to two Topics also in German, to all conferees from Europe registered by the beginning of June.

Because of the expense involved and the pressure of time, no distribution of reports was made to conferees outside Europe. In addition to the reports in English and German, there has been made available a short summary of the reports in the official languages of the IBA, in which the report was not printed. The IBA Council is aware that Conference participation is improved when conferees have an opportunity to read the papers and reports before the opening of the Conference. Delegates, however, will also appreciate the burden borne by Rapporteurs and Committee Chairmen, by the Secretary General and the Assistant Secretaries General in the preparation and circulation of questionnaires and memoranda in four languages; in the assembly of information obtained in reply thereto, also in four languages, which must in some instances be reduced to the language of the Rapporteur; and, finally, in the preparation, translation and printing, again in four languages, of the report or summary thereof to be considered at the Conference.

Simultaneous Interpretation:

This is the sixth Conference of the IBA at which it has been possible to arrange to have simultaneous interpretation at the opening session and working sessions — and also at the plenary session at which His Excellency U Thant, Secretary General of the United Nations Organization will address the Conference. Simultaneous interpretation will be available at all the principal sessions of the working sessions. Any continuation meetings will be without simultaneous interpretation. It will be appreciated that the expenses involved are considerable — and that only well attended Conferences and maximum financial support by Member Organizations, Patrons and Subscribers make it possible to provide simultaneous interpretation.

The Dublin Conference Book:

The "Twelfth Conference Report, Dublin, July 1968" will be published as promptly as possible. It will be mailed to Member Organizations, Presidents of Member Organizations, Councillors, Rapporteurs, Patrons and Subscribers, and will also be available for sale.

V. RELATIONS WITH OTHER ORGANIZATIONS:

The International Bar Association has continued to co-operate with the following organizations:

United Nations: The attention of delegates is called to the regular reports submitted to the Council by the IBA Observer at the European Office of the United Nations in Geneva, Mr. Michael Brandon (U. K.). Mr. Brandon's current report is available at this Conference in mimeographed form.

Mr. Arne Rikheim, Administrative Secretary of the IBA, participated in the meeting of the United Nations Committee on Trade and Development's Committee on Invisibles and Financing related to Trade, second session in New York, July 4 - 19, 1967.

Mr. Alan C. L. Delgado of Jamaica participated on behalf of the IBA in the United Nations Seminar on "The Effective Realisation of Civil and Political Rights at National Level" in Kingston, Jamaica, April 25 - May 8, 1967.

Baron Erik Leijonhufvud of Sweden, participated on behalf of the IBA at a meeting of the United Nations Committee on Trade and Development, second session, in New Delhi, India, from February 1 - March 29, 1968.

Dr. Parviz Kazemi of Iran participated on behalf of the IBA in the "United Nations International Conference on Human Rights" in Teheran, Iran, April 22 - May 13, 1968.

International Commission of Jurists: Adv. Bertil Ahrnborg of Sweden represented the IBA at the I. C. J. Nordic Conference on the "Right of Privacy".

The IBA continues to keep in touch with other organizations in its field and its liason committee with the Union Internationale des Avocats is functioning smoothly.

VI. THE "INTERNATIONAL BAR NEWS":

The Editor of the "International Bar News", Mrs. Madeleine May, London, England, has retired and has been succeeded by Miss Jacqueline Auger of The Law Society. The "International Bar News" is now being published semi-annually, and the Editor is interested in receiving the publications of Member Organizations — marked to items of international interest. Delegates may be able to obtain copies of the various issues of "International Bar News" from their respective Member Organizations — but by becoming Patrons or Subscribers of the IBA they will be assured of receiving copies directly by mail, as well as all other publications of the IBA.

VII. COMMITTEES:

1. *Committees of the General Meeting:*

The Council appoints before the opening of the Conference, Committees on Nominations and Credentials, as well as a Committee to draft Resolutions of Appreciation to serve for the duration of the General Meeting.

2. *Standing Committees of the Council:*

So named to indicate that their work will continue from year to year, until such time as the Council directs their discontinuance.

The work of these committees is considered of such importance that the Council deems it desirable to have reports from time to time on each of the subjects:

a) Advisory Committee on Professional Ethics and Professional Privilege.

b) Monopolies and Restrictive Trade Practices.

c) U. I. A. Liason Committee. (Established to avoid conflicts and duplication of effort between the two organizations.)

3. Domestic Committee of the Council:

The membership of these Committees is to be reviewed at the Council meeting immediately following the close of each Conference. The members of the Committee to serve until the close of the next Conference:

Committee on Constitution and By-Laws.

Committee on Topics for Future Conference programs.

Membership Committee.

Committee on "International Bar News".

4. Committees for Specific Program Topics:

There are at present no such Committees, but specific Conference topics, not being handled by one of the standing Committees, are in effect handled by Committees made up of Rapporteurs and National Correspondents. Their work is complete at the close of the Conference, unless the Council directs otherwise.

5. Ad Hoc Committees of the Council:

These are appointed from time to time for specific Council assignments, their dissolution to be effected upon completion of their respective project. At its meeting in Amsterdam, the Council did establish five such Committees, each to explore a segment of the problems facing the IBA and its future course of work. These Committees are:

a) *Committee No. 1* – Bar Associataions – to enable them to give a more efficient and complete service to their members.

Committee No. 2 – The Profession collectively – advice on Public Relations and help in achieving a fair standard of remuneration.

Committee No. 3 – Individual lawyers – exchange of students, code of ethics, etc.

Committee No. 4 – Simplification of Problems arising from conflict of law and Practice.

Committee No. 5 – Outside ventures – assistance to developing countries; any other program that would appeal to foundations.

b) To increase revenues and individual membership:

Finance Committee.

Patrons Committee.

Membership of the Committee in categories 1, 2 (b), 3 and 5 above, is by Council appointment. However, it is the practice of the Council to request Member Organizations to nominate members for all the Committees in categories 2 (a) and 4. It is, in fact, important for Member Organizations to be represented on these Committees and it is also important for the work of the IBA that as many as possible of the Member Organizations are represented on the Committees or by National Correspondents, to ensure that the reports for the Conference cover as many of the various views of the IBA membership as possible. The assistance of delegates in the prompt appointment of Committee members will be appreciated.

VIII. COMMITTEE ON TOPICS FOR FUTURE CONFERENCE PROGRAMS:

This Committee will not hold open meetings at the Dublin Conference, but the Chairman of the Committee, Mr. John Carrigan (Ireland), will welcome suggestions from delegates and conferees with regard to topics for future conferences.

IX. MEMBERSHIP COMMITTEE:

The assistance of delegates in the work of the membership Committee will also be appreciated. The Chairman is Mr. Robert N. Anderson (U. S. A.), who is present at the Conference and will be most interested in furnishing the necessary information to any Organization interested in membership.

X. 1970 CONFERENCE:

At the Council meeting in Lausanne in July 16, 1966, it was decided that the 1970 Conference should be held in Tokyo, Japan, and the dates have been fixed for August 24 - 28, 1970.

XI. INDIVIDUAL PARTICIPATION IN THE WORK OF THE IBA:

One of the bulwarks for the International Bar Association is the individual lawyer affiliated as a Patron or a Subscriber of the Association. There are at present about 1600 Patrons and Subscribers from 56 countries. The professional assistance and financial support of these individuals make possible the work of the Association. All Delegates and Conferees attending the Dublin Conference who are not, as yet, Patrons or Subscribers are urged to join the IBA. A desk for this purpose has been set up in the Registration Centre.

XII. THE OFFICERS:

Delegates will wish to join in expressing appreciation to the elected and appointed Officers of the Association – all of whom serve without remuneration, and each of whom gives his time, efforts and resources to advance the work of the International Bar Association. The work of the Assistant Secretaries General is of the utmost importance – Rechtsanwalt Dr. Heinz Brangsch (Germany), høyesterettsadvokat Rolf Christophersen (Norway), Mr. Bert H. Early (U. S. A.), Maître Philippe Gastambide (France), and Excmo. Sr. D. Roberto Reyes (Spain). The support given by The Law Society in England and by its Secretary, Sir Thomas Lund, who serves also as our Treasurer, is greatly appreciated. The Assistant Treasurer of the Association is Mr. Paul B. DeWitt (U. S. A), the Executive Secretary of The Association of the Bar of the City of New York – who works closely on a day-to-day basis with the Secretary General. Due to the pressure of work on the IBA Officers and because of its growth over recent years, the Council has employed a full time Administrative Secretary, høyesterettsadvokat Arne Rikheim (Norway), who is working with the Secretary General at the IBA Headquarters in New York.

DELEGATES ACCREDITED BY MEMBER ORGANIZATIONS TO THE GENERAL MEETING AT DUBLIN

Australia:	*Law Council of Australia* H. E. Zelling, Esq., Q. C. K. Smithers, Esq. P. D. Connolly, Esq., Q. C. V. M. Corr, Esq. P. Atkins, Esq. T. Simos, Esq. K. Emerson, Esq. J. Nosworthy, Esq.
Austria:	*Die Österreichischen Rechtsanwaltskammern* RA Dr. Harald Foglar-Deinhardstein RA Dr. Ernst Jahoda RA Dr. Gustav Rinesch
Canada:	*Canadian Bar Association* A. Gordon Cooper, Esq., Q. C. E. C. Leslie, Esq., Q. C., LL. D., D. C. L. C. W. Brazier, Esq., Q. C. Charles Wolfson, Esq., Q. C. Ronald C. Merriam, Esq., Q. C.
Denmark:	*Det Danske Advokatsamfund* Advokat Axel Graff Højesteretssagfører Jon Palle Buhl Advokat Poul Ostergaard
England & Wales:	*General Council of the Bar* Sir Joseph Molony, Q. C. Alan de Piro, Esq., Q. C. *The Law Society* H. E. Sargant, Esq., M. A. R. F. Payne, Esq. William J. Brown, Esq., M. C. Sir John Burrows W. O. Carter, Esq. Sir Denys Hicks, O. B. E., T. D., D. L. Sir Thomas Lund, C. B. E. F. U. J. O'Brien, Esq. Sir Hilary Scott B. E. Toland, Esq.
Finland:	*Suomen Asianajajaliito* Asianajaja Klaus Lagus

France: *Association Nationale des Avocats*
Me Henri Delmont
Me Fernand Jeantet
Me Philippe Gastambide

Germany: *Deutscher Anwaltverein e. V.*
RA Dr. Walter Oppenhoff
RA Dr. Michael Oppenhoff
RA Dr. Kurt Ehlers
RA Dr. Hans Ehlers
RA Dr. Karl Marcetus
RA Dr. Heinrich Burchard-Motz
RA Dr. E. Gercke
RA Dr. Arved Deringer

Iran: *Kanoun Vokala Dadgostari, Teheran*
Dr. Ahmad Houman

Ireland: *The Incorporated Law Society of Ireland*
Eunan McCarron, Esq.
Brendan A. McGrath, Esq.

Israel: *The Israel Bar*
Yehuda Fraenkel, Esq.

Italy: *Consiglio dell'Ordine degli Avvocati e Procuratori de Roma*
Avv. Carlo Fornario
Prof. Avv. Fernando Della Rocca
Avv. Walter Prosperetti
Avv. Enrico Biamonti
Avv. Angelo Angelini-Roth

Japan: *Japan Bar Association*
Justice Toshio Irie
Japan Federation of Bar Associations
Bengoshi Dr. Nobuo Naritomi

Lebanon: *Ordre des Avocats a Beyrouth*
Mr. Mounir Shedadi
Mr. Jean Mobarak

Liberia: *Liberian National Bar Association*
Clarence L. Simpson, Esq.

Mexico: *Barra Mexicana*
Sr. Lic. don Licio Lagos
Sr. Lic. don Manuel G. Escobedo
Ilustre y Nacional Colegio de Abogados de Mexico
Sr. Lic. don Manuel G. Escobedo

Netherlands:	*Nederlandse Orde van Advocaten* Mr. Jan Reinier Voute Jhr. Mr. P. T. Beelaerts van Blokland
New Zealand:	*New Zealand Law Society* Russel T. Garlick, Esq. F. L. Parkin, Esq. J. B. O'Regan, Esq.
Northern Ireland:	*Incorporated Law Society of Northern Ireland* Patrick Maxwell, Esq. *The Inn of Court of Northern Ireland* Anthony Campbell, Esq.
Norway:	*Den Norske Advokatforening* Høyesterettsadvokat Georg Lous Høyesterettsadvokat Andreas Arntzen
Philippines:	*Philippine Bar Association* The Hon. Amelito Mutuc *Philippine Lawyers Association* Maurice C. Nubla, Esq.
Scotland:	*The Law Society of Scotland* J. Murray Wilkie, Esq. W. A. Cook, Esq. Joseph Mellick, Esq. R. B. Laurie, Esq.
South Africa:	*The Association of Law Societies of the Republic of South Africa* G. R. Ashman, Esq. J. V. Oosthuizen, Esq. P. Conradi, Esq., S. C. G. W. Cook, Esq.
Spain:	*Consejo General de la Abogacia Espanola* Sr. Lic. D. Jose Louis Del Valle Itturriaga
Sweden:	*Sveriges Advokatsamfund* Advokat Arthur Bostrøm Advokat Ove Wickman
Switzerland:	*Federation Suisse des Avocats* Dr. Max Büsser Dr. Giselher Hochstrasser
Syria:	*Ordre des Avocats de Damas* Robert Mulky, Esq.

Thailand:	*The Thai Bar* Nai Sansern Kraichitti
Turkey:	*Ankara Barosu* Avukat Erdogan Yesin
UAR-Egypt:	*The Bar Association of the Egyptian Region, UAR* Dr. Gamal El. Oteifi Maitre Kamal Halim Ibrahim Maitre Maher Mohamed Aly
United States of America:	*American Bar Association* Earl F. Morris, Esq. Bernard G. Segal, Esq. James D. Fellers, Esq. Hon. Walter E. Craig Victor C. Folsom, Esq. Gerald J. McMahon, Esq. Orison S. Marden, Esq. Loyd Wright, Esq. Robert G. Storey, Esq. John J. Goldberg, Esq. *Federal Bar Association* Robert N. Anderson, Esq. Philip Amran, Esq. Sigmund Timberg, Esq. Edward Karet, Esq. *National Association of Women Lawyers* Mrs. Dorothy G. Turkel
Also present:	*Young Lawyers International Association:* Eric Crowther, Esq. (England)

PLENARY SESSION

PROCEDURES FOR THE ENFORCEMENT OF LAWS REGULATING BUSINESS TRANSACTIONS AND PARTICULARLY ANTI-MONOPOLY, ANTI-CARTEL AND ANTI-TRUST LAWS

Chairman: George C. Seward, Esq. (USA) (American Bar Association)
Rapporteur: RA Arved Deringer (Germany)
Vice-Chairman: RA Dr. Otfried Lieberknecht (Germany)
Secretary: Michael O'Beirn, Esq. (Ireland)

Country	*Committee Members and National Correspondents*
Australia	C. L. D. Meares, Esq., Q. C.
Austria	RA Dr. Fritz Schönherr
Canada	C. W. Brazier, Esq., Q. C.
Denmark	Højesteretssagfører Gunnar Gersted
England	William J. Brown, Esq. (The Law Society) Jeremy Lever, Esq. (General Council of the Bar)
Finland	Advocat Åke Roschier-Holmberg
France	Me Fernand Charles Jeantet
Germany	RA Arved Deringer, M. d. B. RA Dr. Otfried Lieberknecht
Iran	Dr. Ali Khadem
Ireland	Ralph J. Walker, Esq.
Israel	Naftali Lipschütz, Esq.
Italy	Avv. Giuseppe Bisconti
Japan	Bengoshi Mr. Jyuzo Yamana
Korea	Byun Ho Sa Myong-Yun Kim
Lebanon	Faouzi Ghazi, Esq.
Liberia	Counsellor Clarence L. Simpson
Mexico	Sr. Lic. don Enrique Pérez Verdia
Netherlands	Mr. J. J. A. Ellis
New Zealand	G. S. Orr, Esq.
Norway	H. r. advokat Andreas Arntzen
Peru	Sr. Lic. Dr. Ulises Montoya Manfredi

Philippines	The Hon. Arturo A. Alafriz
Portugal	Dr. Fernando Pedroso Rodrigues
Puerto Rico	Sr. Lic. D. Rafael Buono Petrilli
Scotland	J. R. Fiddes, Esq. (Faculty of Advocates) K. J. A. Greig, Esq. (The Law Society of Scotland)
South Africa	D. J. Shaw, Esq., Q. C. (General Council of the Bar) G. C. Webster, Esq. (The Assn. of Law Societies)
Spain	Excmo. Sr. D. José Luís del Valle Iturriaga
Sweden	Advokat Per H. Osvald
Switzerland	Maître Pierre Jolidon
Thailand	Nai Sansern Kraichitti
Turkey	Mrs. Güler Berkin, Avukat
U. A. R. (Egypt)	Dr. Ahmed Zaki El Chiati
U. S. A.	George C. Seward, Esq. (American Bar Association) Sigmund Timberg, Esq. (Federal Bar Association)

Other Contributors

England	Dennis Thompson, Esq.
France	Me Jacques René Pascal Lassier Me Denis de Ricci Me Jean-Claude Goldsmith' Mr Jean Vadon
Ireland	Thomas Jackson, Esq.
Netherlands	J. A. Steinz, Esq.
Norway	Advokat Jonas W. Myhre
Portugal	Prof. Dra. Isabel de Magalhaes Colaço
Scotland	James Sutherland, Esq. (Law Society of Scotland)
Switzerland	Dr. Robert Steffen
U. S. A.	Edgar E. Barton, Esq. (American Bar Association) W. B. Comegys, Esq. (American Bar Association) T. B. Leary, Esq. (American Bar Association) T. M. Lofton, Esq. (American Bar Association) R. W. McLaren, Esq. (American Bar Association) B. G. A. Pasztory, Esq. (American Bar Association) W. Rowley, Esq. (American Bar Association) C. E. Stewart, Esq. (American Bar Association)

PROCEDURES FOR THE ENFORCEMENT OF LAWS REGULATING BUSINESS TRANSACTIONS AND PARTICULARLY ANTI-MONOPOLY, ANTI-CARTEL AND ANTITRUST LAWS

Report

submitted by ARVED DERINGER, Attorney, Bonn
Germany

After concerning itself with a comparative law presentation of national antitrust laws in Cologne (1958) and Salzburg (1960), the IBA's Committee on Monopolies and Restrictive Trade Practices turned its attention to specific antitrust questions arising in connection with supra-national bodies (Edinburgh, 1962) and international trade (Mexico City, 1964). This was continued with a discussion of international license agreements at the Lausanne Conference in 1966. To the foregoing the Twelfth Conference in Dublin (1968) will add a survey on the rules of procedure contained in the individual antitrust laws.

For the preparation of this report, a detailed questionnaire, attached as Exhibit A, was circulated. It was answered by the following committee members, to whom the writer is especially grateful:

Contributing Members of Committee

C. L. D. Meares (Australia), Fritz Schoenherr (Austria), C. W. Brazier (Canada), Gunnar Gersted (Denmark), Dennis Thompson (England), William J. Brown (England), A. Roschier-Holmberg (Finland) F. C. Jeantet and J. J. Lassier (France), Thomas Jackson (Ireland), Joseph J. A. Ellis (Netherlands), J. A. Steinz (Netherlands), G. S. Orr (New Zealand), Jonas W. Hyhre (Norway), K. J. A. Greig (Scotland), J. Sutherland (Scotland), D. J. Shaw (South Africa), Geoffrey C. Webster (South Africa), Per Hakan Osvald (Sweden), R. Steffen (Switzerland), Mrs. Guler Berkin (Turkey), George C. Seward wit hthe assistance of Edgar E. Barton, Walker B. Comegys, Thomas B. Leary, Thomas M. Lofton, Richard W. McLaren, Blaise G. A. Pasztory, Worth Rowley and Charles E. Stewart (United States).

I. INTRODUCTION

1. A discussion of the procedural rules of the individual antitrust and cartel laws was especially recommended at the Mexico City session for the reason that while the substantive law aspects of such laws have been made known or at least easily accessible to interested persons through previous efforts of the IBA and other organizations, this is not equally true for procedural regulations. In practice, on the other hand,

the procedural regulations play at least as important a role as the substantive law, inasmuch as companies and their advisers, in dealing with antitrust and cartel law questions of another country, must also be clear as to the appropriate agencies or courts, as to the form and content of necessary steps which may have to be taken and as to the more formal questions involved. Besides, the practical importance of substantive law depends largely on the procedural rules and their application by the competent authorities. It appeared useful therefore for the Committee to treat the questions of procedural law separately in a report devoted exclusively to that subject.

2. At any rate this report can only be an initial survey about the basic differences without being able to mention the connection of procedural law in this area with the general legal system (as a background) or to answer individual questions of specific law. The *connection between the special procedural rules* of the antitrust and cartel laws *and the general legal system* of a country is of special significance in the presentation of the special procedural rules for two reasons:

a) There is practically no country in which special procedure regulates all procedural questions arising in an antitrust or cartel case; even in countries with very detailed procedural rules one must still fall back on the general criminal, civil, procedural or administrative law in many questions. This is especially true in the more numerous countries in which the antitrust and cartel laws regulate procedure on a few basic points but leave everything else to the general law.

b) In addition, the particular procedural rules of the antitrust and cartel law can only, as a rule, be fully understood against the background of the particular general law. The reason is that the questions of whether for example certain duties and jurisdiction are delegated to government agencies or to the courts, whether the greater part of enforcement is carried out principally by civil, criminal or administrative process and other questions depend to a great extent on the role played by government agencies, courts and specific procedures in the general legal system of a country.

The questionnaire and this report should therefore properly have dealt with the general procedural law of the individual countries in considerable depth. That would however have far surpassed the framework of such a report. The questionnaire has thus only attempted through a very few questions in its first part to ascertain principles of the general law which are most important for the subject of this report.

3. The same difficulty arose to an even greater extent with respect to the *connection between the antitrust and cartel law* on the one hand *and general economic law as well as economic policy* on the other. It is

of decisive significance not only for the substantive law determinations of the antitrust and cartel law but even more so for the procedural determinations whether the economic policy of a country strives basically toward a system of private enterprise and free competition or whether it intervenes to a greater or lesser extent in the operation of the economy through governmental measures or even through the government's own participation.

For this reason the questionnaire has also attempted to ascertain these connections through a few questions at least in very rough outline.

4. In this connection it became clear that the direct or indirect *participation of the various states in* and their effect on *the economy*[1]) is very different in each case. In most countries the larger portion of enterprises are privately owned; it is only in the areas of power, water, transportation and communications that enterprises are managed in large part, although not exclusively, by the state or provinces, communities or other public entities. Beyond that, in many states the government participates in the ownership of individual enterprises in various industries as a result of historical developments. The government's participation in the economy is especially great in Austria (31 % of all employees), Great Britain and France (35 — 40 %), where entire industries or countless individual enterprises (France) were nationalized since World War II for political reasons. When in addition such key areas as large banks, insurance companies and press agencies are essentially state-owned and state enterprises enter into other fields through the formation of subsidiaries, as is the case in France, the laws for the protection of free competition lose most of their meaning. To be sure it must be noted that it is just in France that the distinction between the public and private sectors is losing significance as a result of the fact that on the one hand state enterprises operate increasingly on the basis of customary mercantile practices and on the other the private portion of the economy acts substantially in accordance with a state-influenced "concerted economy".

5. It is typical of current developments that the development of new industries or the solution of new problems (atomic energy) is promoted through state participation or state financing not only in countries with partly undeveloped fields such as South Africa and New Zealand but also in traditionally industrial countries such as the U. S. Add to this that as a result of World War II the influence of state regulations on the private economy has grown even in those countries where the economy is basically in the hands of private enterprise (e. g., perhaps surprisingly, Switzerland). This is especially true of a country like Turkey, where in the last decades industrialization and the fulfilment

1) Question 1

of certain of the state's obligations (defense!) was made possible only because the state itself became active in the iron and steel, textile, leather and countless other industries. In the first and second Five Year Plans, moreover, it is anticipated that the state will hereafter concern itself not only with the development of the infrastructure and the supplying of power and transportation but also with heavy industry as well as those areas in which private investment is not large enough. The aim is to make sure that the enterprises created by the state should later be gradually transferred into the private domain.

6. Thus, although, based on this survey, in most of the countries from which reports have been received the *greater part of economic activity is carried on by private enterprises*[2]) and accordingly the development of private enterprise as well as free competition belong to the essential goals of economic policy, this is not equally true for all countries. The laws for the promotion of free competition are quite distinguishable in outline and effectiveness (cf. for particulars heading II), and in particular countries (e. g., Finland) there is a tendency not only to promote certain less profitable branches of industry through state participation (as e. g., in Ireland, South Africa and New Zealand) but also to extend state influence generally in the economy.

7. More or less all states exert some influence on *private investments*[3]), most of them however only by promoting investments in particular regions or economic spheres through tax incentives, financial assistance and import licenses for investments (e. g., New Zealand and Turkey) or by making other investments more difficult. In some countries moreover there is government participation also in individual investment decisions. The influence of the public domain extends even further in the European Coal and Steel Community (ECSC) where the High Authority (since July 1967 the Commission of European Communities) can take a position with certain ensuing legal effects with respect to the investment programs of enterprises, as well as in France and Turkey where the government's "Plans" exert a substantial indirect influence on individual economic areas.

8. States generally exert no influence on *production planning of enterprises*[4]) except in the area of agriculture or indirectly through duties and tax incentives and burdens. An exception is again France where the "Plans" developed jointly by the public authority and private enterprise foresee specific growth rates based on given factors, the most important of which are productivity, population growth and investment. One procedure followed in this "économie concertée" (concerted

2) Question 2 a – c
3) Question 2 d
4) Question 2 e

economy) involves the "contrats de programme" (program contracts) under which an industry undertakes given development.

9. It is on the other hand quite common for states to influence the pricing practices of the economy through legislative or administrative measures. This is true at present generally for certain areas such as agriculture or public utilities and transportation, and also in times of shortages as for example particularly after World War II. Insofar as government price regulations [5]) are attributable to this last motive, the development has been generally regressive. On the other hand there are certain countries in which the price law still serves, often for political reasons, as an important tool of economic policy which may be used as may be considered necessary (this is especially true for Great Britain, France, Norway and also the Netherlands).

10. Similarly *state influence* is not infrequently exerted *on imports and exports* [6]) primarily through taxes and duties but also through quantitative restrictions on imports or through the promotion of exports. This influence however is being currently reduced not only as a result of the formation of supranational customs associations such as the EEC and EFTA but also of the increasing liberalization of international trade (e. g., Kennedy Round).

11. The following essential problems appear from the answers regarding the *basic principles for enforcement of general economic laws* [7]):

a) Jurisdictional problems arise in the federal states in which federal agencies and courts exist parallel to the agencies and courts of the individual states (U. S., Canada, Germany, Switzerland).

b) Is enforcement delegated to particular independent agencies with decisional and if possible enforcement powers (U. S.: Federal Trade Commission, Interstate Commerce Commission, etc.; Germany: Bundeskartellamt [Federal Cartel Office], Bundesaufsichtsamt für das Versicherungswesen [Federal Supervisory Office for Insurance], etc.), or to the competent ministries (France, Netherlands), or to the government in general?

c) Are the competent authorities empowered to make decisions (U. S., Germany, Netherlands), which are then as a rule subject to judicial review, or may they only initiate proceedings before the appropriate courts (U. S.: Antitrust Division; Great Britain, France, Denmark, Sweden, Norway)?

d) Is the power to review applications and agency decisions delegated to the general civil or administrative courts (U. S., Germany) or to special courts (Canada, Netherlands)?

5) Question 2 f
6) Question 2 g
7) Question 3

e) Is the decision in a given case reached principally on the basis of current economic policy (France, Netherlands) or does it take the form of an application of the law in which the agency has only limited discretion established by law (U. S., Germany)?

f) To what extent is the protection of the law afforded the affected enterprise through detailed procedural rules, through specific privileges or through the equal treatment of private persons appearing before the agencies and the representatives of the state?

g) May private parties compel the *institution of proceedings*[8]) in specified cases and under specified conditions (U.S., South Africa, Australia, Germany, France in certain cases, EEC, Switzerland, Sweden, Finland, Turkey) or does the agency and court decide in its own discretion whether or not to commence proceedings (Canada, New Zealand, Netherlands, Denmark, Norway)?

h) In almost all countries an opportunity is afforded private parties under specified conditions to obtain damages[9]) from the guilty parties for violations of economic regulatory laws.

II. THE ANTITRUST LAWS IN GENERAL

Aside from the general economic policy and legal system of the individual countries, the content and significance of the procedural rules for enforcement of antitrust and cartel laws naturally depend on the basic principles on which the antitrust and cartel law is founded. Dr. Mueller presented an excellent survey of these basic principles of antitrust and cartel legislation in the introduction to his report for the Tenth Conference in Mexico City (1964). For the purposes of this report it will therefore be sufficient to mention the following aspects:

12. In general the following *factual situations*[10]) may be discerned with respect to statutory regulation:

a) All laws encompass, in one way or another, restrictive arrangements and agreements among several persons and enterprises, while in only a few states, on the other hand, are concerted practices specifically included (e. g., U. S., Great Britain, South Africa, France, EEC Treaty, ECSC Treaty).

b) In none of the laws is a monopoly position or even a specific size for companies specifically prohibited; on the other hand, most laws provide against *misuse* (or abuse) *of a monopoly position* or domi-

8) Question 4
9) Question 5
10) Question 8

nant market position, although the definitions of a misuse are quite different.

c) *Mergers* as such, irrespective of their effect on the market, are only encompassed by Art. 66 of the ECSC Treaty, which imposes a requirement of approval; nevertheless the governing authority (of the ECSC) has by general regulation exempted all smaller mergers from this requirement. For the rest mergers fall under the antitrust prohibitions only if they result in a specified market position (notice requirement under § 22 of the German law) or in a specified effect on competition (§ 7 of the Clayton Act, sect 1 of the Netherlands Economic Competition Act), and in particular in the creation of a monopoly position (§ 1 of the Sherman Act, Great Britain, Canada, South Africa, New Zealand, Sweden, Norway).

13. Of greater materiality to the significance of the procedural rules are the *legal effects*[11]) provided for individual conduct by the antitrust laws: whether it is prohibited categorically and without exception, or whether though prohibited it is and may be permitted under specified conditions in individual cases, or whether it is permitted until and unless prohibited by an agency or court under specified conditions either categorically or in an individual case.

a) An *absolute prohibition*[12]) without specific rules relating to exemptions can only be found in the laws of Canada and Norway (for vertical agreements relating to unreasonable prices or conditions), also New Zealand (collective tendering or collective bidding at auction) and in Art. 86 of the EEC Treaty which treats misuse of monopoly as prohibitable. To be sure these three rules are characterized by the fact that prohibited act (e. g., unreasonable prices) is defined in such a way as to exclude the possibility of exceptions.

b) The only case in which *case law*[13]) has developed *an exemption* from a blanket prohibition is the "Rule of Reason" in the U. S. under which an act falling under the literal prohibition of the law may be found to be reasonable and therefore permissible.

c) In other cases the permitted *exemptions* to an effective blanket prohibition are *specified in the law* with the result that acts meeting the conditions of the exemption are permitted without any requirement of approval by an agency or court (legal exemption). This is true for the prohibition against collusive tendering in Australia and for Art. 59 bis of the French cartel decree.

d) Substantially greater is the number of instances in which the law, while establishing the conditions for *exemptions* from the general

11) Question 9
12) Question 9 a
13) Question 9 b

prohibitions, provides that the exemption is only available in the individual case if *permitted by a specific agency*[14]) or court (Germany, EEC Treaty, ECSC Treaty, Royal Decrees of 10/8/57 and 7/1/60 in Norway, resale price maintenance and tender cartels in Sweden and Finland) or at least if a proposed agreement is not objected to within a specified time (Germany). These cases are to be distinguished from the above-mentioned case of the legal exemption in that the exemption becomes effective only upon the decision of the agency (under the EEC Treaty, circumstances permitting, retroactively to a specified prior time assuming the conditions of the exemption have previously been met). In the case of the legal exemption on the other hand the act meeting the required conditions is ab initio permissible and effective even if this is only established later by an agency or court.

e) Of an entirely different nature are the laws in which restrictive conduct is basically permitted and only becomes unlawful if prohibited in the individual case by the competent agency or court (the *misuse laws,*[15]) e. g., in Great Britain, South Africa, Germany and ECSC Treaty in case of monopoly misuse, Netherlands, Switzerland, Austria, Denmark, Norway and Finland). The significance of these instances is distinguishable from that of those above-mentioned with respect to legal procedure in that in the latter the procedure leads either to an exemption or to ascertainment and, in a given case, punishment of the prohibited conduct, while in the former the prohibition is only the result of the procedure and a penalty is only considered after this prohibition has been violated. Even here there are two variations: in one the conduct in question must in any case be registered and is unlawful if and as long as it is not registered (thus e. g., Great Britain, Switzerland, Austria); in the other registration is not even required. If registration is conditioned on a definite if limited examinaton into whether specified statutory conditions have been met and whether any statutory objection to registration is present (Great Britain, Austria), such a system involves a mixture of prohibitory and misuse law – and whether it is more closely related to one or the other type of law depends in practice on the manner of enforcement. The Swedish antitrust law contains a peculiarity in that only a recommendation rather than a prohibition may be issued with respect to the undesirable practices.

f) It is true in the case of all the afore-mentioned legal systems that certain economic spheres (e. g., agriculture, transportation, insurance, banking) may be wholly or partly exempted by specific rules from general regulation. In this also one may again find, in addition to the previously listed alternatives, countless variations, which need not

14) Question 9 b
15) Question 9 c

here be discussed in detail since either they play no role in the treatment of procedural rules or since their many facets do not permit them to be considered. It is merely recommended therefore that in the case of activities or economic spheres which might possibly be exempted from the general antitrust law, examination should be made into whether special procedural as well as substantive rules governing such factual situations are in effect.

14. Regarding the possible legal consequences of antitrust violations, the following *categories of violations*[16]) must generally be distinguished:

a) The violation involves acts prohibited by the law and not exempted in the individual case. This situation arises under all the prohibitory laws but also under the misuse laws in which an unregistered agreement is made unlawful (e. g., Austria).

b) The violation involves acts declared unlawful under the applicable laws and hence specifically prohibited by the competent agency or court. This situation also arises under all the prohibitory laws as well as under the misuse laws containing the registration requirement.

c) The violation involves acts forbidden only by a decision reached in a specific case. This situation arises under the misuse laws if it is decided in the individual case that the situation constitutes a misuse and contravenes the public interest (e. g. the Netherlands).

d) The violation involves either (i) a violation of general procedural rules such as the registration requirement or (ii) a violation of specific order issued in individual cases by the competent agency or court (e. g., the giving of incomplete or false information).

15. As *legal consequences of a violation,*[17]) the following considerations arise:

a) The competent agency or court may determine the unlawfulness of conduct and prohibit its continuance (injunction, cease and desist order).

b) The agency or court may decree specific measures to correct the violation (injunctive relief).

c) The unlawful agreement may be invalid and unenforceable before the courts under the civil law.

d) The violation may entitle others to recover damages.

e) The agency or court may impose a fine or imprisonment.

---

16) Question 10
17) Question 10

16. In the case of conduct violating a general prohibition, all laws provide for a *money penalty or compensation;* it is not necessary that the conduct should previously have been specifically prohibited. If this has occurred and the conduct is nevertheless continued, this may be taken into consideration in the amount of the penalty. In addition in certain countries (e. g., U. S., France, Austria, Sweden, Finland) prison sentences may also be imposed. The same holds generally true in countries with misuse laws if certain conduct, which is determined to be a misuse or in contravention of the public interest and prohibited, is nevertheless continued. Additional exceptional penal measures are the seizure of the goods in question in the U. S., the confiscation of the purchase price in Sweden (a measure in practice never applied), the publication of decisions in the Netherlands and a prohibition against continuing a profession in Norway.

Besides penalties for substantive violations several antitrust laws also provide for penalties for violations of procedural rules, thus in Australia and Germany in case of failure to disclose or incomplete disclosure, and in addition in Germany, the EEC, the ECSC, Sweden and Finland for violation of the duty of disclosure after the agency has formally requested certain information or evidence. In addition the agency may compel the production of information required through the imposition of a fine which increases with every day of noncompliance.

17. More important in practice than the penal provisions, which have so far received widespread use in only a few countries, are the rights of the agency or court to *enjoin the continuation of specific conduct*[18]) prohibited generally or in an individual case or to order other additional steps to remedy the violation. This last possibility is available in the U. S. (equitable relief: divestiture, dissolution, compulsory license), Great Britain (divestiture), South Africa (withdrawal of tax or customs advantages, dissolution, etc.), Norway (order to enter into business relations with a specified customer), the Netherlands (Supply order, price rules, orders against tying clauses and related conditions of Supply and payment). It is noteworthy that the otherwise vastly detailed German law contains no provision for injunctions or similar measures.

18. The legal consequence of the *invalidity*[19]) under the civil law and consequently the unenforceability of an agreement appears primarily in all those instances in which the agreement violates an effective general prohibition. The same is true as a rule, although not in all countries, where an agreement is declared unlawful by a particular decision under a misuse law. For this reason e. g., the complaining party must first petition the civil court for dissolution of the cartel.

18) Question 10 b
19) Question 10 d

Until now it is only in the U. S. and Austria that it is clear that a party injured by the prohibited conduct may recover *compensation*[20]) for his damages from the guilty party. In the U. S. also the possibility of treble damages has proven to be an effective deterrent for antitrust violations. In Germany, the EEC and Norway the obligation to pay compensation has only been affirmed under specified conditions, while it remains in general quite restricted. For the rest, compensatory damages may only be recovered, if at all, under the rules of the general civil law.

III. PROCEDURES FOR ANTITRUST LAW ENFORCEMENT BY GOVERNMENT AGENCIES

19. The *distribution of responsibilities and jurisdictions*[21]) for enforcement of antitrust and cartel laws among the interested governmental authorities – government agencies, courts – is very different in individual countries. In Germany the Bundeskartellamt (Federal Cartel Office) combines in itself the preparatory activities of registration and examination as well as decisions concerning the granting of exemptions and the imposition of fines. Its decisions are subject to the review of a special appellate court and in the last instance the Bundesgerichtshof (Federal Court). The position of the Monopoly Control Authority in Denmark and the competent minister (Economy) in Holland as well as the Commission of the EEC is similar, in that all three have preliminary as well as decisional jurisdiction subject to court review. The position of the Federal Trade Commission in the U. S. is similar, in that it too can make decisions.

20. In other cases the preparation and commencement of proceedings rests with the competent minister or an agency subordinate to him, while the decision concerning the lawfulness or unlawfulness of specific acts is made by the courts, whose decisions are as a rule subject to the usual legal steps for appeal to the high courts. This is true first of all of the U. S. Antitrust Division, also of the Board of Trade in Great Britain in the prosecution of monopoly situations and of the Economy Department in Switzerland, each of which in turn initiates proceedings before the occasional courts of special jurisdiction or those of general jurisdiction. In the preparation of their decisions the courts in France, moreover, make use of the "Commission Technique des Ententes et des Positions Dominantes," and those in Switzerland of the Cartel Commission. Likewise, the actual findings of fact under the Restrictive Trade Practices Act of 1956 and the Resale Prices Act of 1964 (in Great Britain) are made by the Restrictive Practices Court,

20) Question 10 c
21) Question 12

while the registration of all restrictive agreements and the preparation and institution of proceedings are specifically assigned to the jurisdiction of the Registrar.

21. Even more complicated is the structure and relationship of the participating authorities, where registration and preparatory investigations rest with an agency which submits its reports either to a higher commission or to the competent minister who then proceed either to apply legally effective measures or to go before the courts. This structure may be found, with variations, in New Zealand, Sweden and Finland, that is, aside from Canada, in all the states which have wholly or principally misuse rules.

22. Insofar as courts participate in the enforcement, their *decisions* are generally *published*[22]). As for the decisions of the agencies involved, this is true as a rule only insofar as the decisions are of a certain conclusive nature, as in the case of the Federal Trade Commission in the U. S., the Registrar in Great Britain, the Federal Cartel Office in Germany, the Commission of the EEC, the Danish Monopoly Control Authority, but similarly also in the Netherlands, South Africa, Sweden, Norway and Finland. On the other hand, only the Federal Trade Commission in the U. S., the Commission of the EEC and the Danish Monopoly Control agency follow the practice of occasionally issuing guidelines or regulations of general application having a binding effect even on the agency in question. This is not true in the case of annual reports of various cartel agencies or commissions and even less so in the case of the speeches of individual employees. Although all these may offer to enterprises indications of the current policies of the agency in question, yet the enterprises may not rely on them as against the agency or before the courts — at least insofar as reliance on formal decisions is not involved.

23. As far as the decisions of the agencies or governmental branches are concerned, they have as a rule very *broad discretion in the construction and application of the laws*[23]). Naturally this is especially true in instances where the decision-making authority rests with politically responsible ministers. In all cases economic factors play a more or less important role, a fact that appears self-evident in the light of the nature of this area of the law. Of course it is particularly the politically independent agencies, such as the Federal Cartel Office in Germany, whose decisions are subject to thorough judicial review with respect to the interpretation of legal principles with economic significance and the evaluation of economic considerations. Nevertheless the legal interpretations of these agencies, as for example in the U. S., are quite meaning-

22) Question 13
23) Question 14

ful for enterprises, because there is only in very few instances a question of subjecting their decisions to judicial review.

24. The responsible agencies and also the courts naturally often fall back in their decisions on the *advice of independent experts and on the testimony of representatives of the particular industry involved*[24]). On the other hand only a few countries (France, Netherlands, EEC, Switzerland, Austria) have advisory bodies which are formally consulted by the deciding agency or minister or whose opinion is solicited.

25. The question of what *proceedings* are *instituted*[25]) and in what order is generally decided by the appropriate agencies in their discretion, which is not subject to review, unless the minister or the government is authorized to give instructions on this point. In most cases the agencies act by virtue of their office (ex officio) or at the instance of involved or affected enterprises. Only in a few cases does the law provide that the agency is obligated to institute proceedings at the instance of third parties (Germany, EEC). A special case is presented by Austria where the Cartel Court acquires jurisdiction if a cartel is reported.

26. To the extent that the agencies make binding decisions or even important preliminary findings, those who were party to the contract or conduct being reviewed ordinarily have the *right to be heard and to make motions*[26]). In most cases they can also take legal steps against such decisions, i. e. those of the Federal Trade Commission in the U. S., the minister in South Africa, the Commissioner for Trade Practices in Australia, the Trade Practices Commission in New Zealand, the Federal Cartel Office in Germany, the competent minister in Holland, the Commission of the EEC, the Danish Monopoly Control Authority and the Authority for Free Enterprises in Finland. Third persons or enterprises, whose interests were affected by the acts being examined, such as by a restrictive agreement, can in the same situations as a rule also be heard, although it is only in the U. S., South Africa, New Zealand, Germany, Holland (a limited group in certain cases) and Finland that they possess the right to obtain a legal remedy, while this question remains unresolved in the EEC.

Insofar as proceedings take place before the courts, the general rules naturally apply.

27. In general, the agencies have rather broad authority to *seek information* from the parties and to *take evidence* as well as to *initiate investigations*[27]). The authority of the Federal Trade Commission and

24) Question 15
25) Question 16
26) Question 17
27) Question 18 a

the grand jury in the U. S. have proven in practice to be extremely effective, since both can order the production of all documents and the giving of testimony under penalty of law. Similar although not as effective because of their complicated procedures is the authority of the Federal Cartel Office in Germany and of the Commission of the EEC. To the extent that agencies and their employees obtain *business secrets*[28]) through these rights, they are obligated to keep them secret. This is not equally true in countries where decisions are reached through public trials or where the essential results of the case are filed at what appears to be the conclusive stage of proceedings. Even in other cases, the duty of nondisclosure is limited, e. g. in Sweden and Finland, to 20 years.

28. An important practical question is whether and in what cases the parties involved may *refuse to answer certain questions*[29]). In court proceedings, the general rules of these courts usually govern. In proceedings conducted by agencies, the rules are different in the case of prohibitory and misuse laws. In countries with the former, information may be withheld if the parties were thereby to incriminate themselves or a closely related person. In any case this right is lost if not asserted at the proper time in the proceedings (U. S.). In addition the government can in the U. S., on the basis of a judicial decree (15 U. S. C. § 32), guarantee a witness in an antitrust case absolute immunity so that he may no longer rely on his right to refuse to give testimony. The role of a participant in an antitrust violation can thereby be changed from that of a defendant to that of a witness required to make full disclosure.

The right to withhold information on the basis of the privilege against self-incrimination is emphatically denied by the law in Australia, Denmark, Norway and Finland, all of them countries in which there are misuse laws and in which consequently the parties involved cannot be found guilty of an antitrust violation.

29. In the U. S. the case law (Hale v. Henkel, 201 U. S. 43 [1906]) has decided that the right to withhold information by reason of the privilege against self-incrimination is only available to natural persons and not to companies. The same result arises in other countries from the fact that, in the case of antitrust violations involving companies, only natural persons can give evidence. Insofar as these are parties to the violation, whether or not as agents for the company, they have the right to withhold information. If they are only witnesses, who may not themselves be made responsible for the violation (e. g. clerical workers), they can hardly refuse to give evidence on the grounds that they would thereby be charging their company with a violation. Even

28) Question 19 b
29) Question 19

companies on the other hand are given the right to withhold information on the grounds of self-incrimination in South Africa and New Zealand.

30. For several countries it is suggested that the parties may withhold information relating to trade secrets of a technical nature (U. S., Sweden, Finland). In the U. S. the disclosure of trade secrets may nevertheless be required if the benefits of disclosure for purposes of the proceedings outweigh the detriment to the enterprise involved.

31. In several countries it is pointed out that the right to withhold information, at least on the grounds of self-incrimination, does not at the same time give a person the right to refuse to produce documents.

32. A particular grounds for refusal to make disclosure is the *professional privilege*[30]). All countries affirm that the attorney may refuse to give information on such matters as were imparted to him in his capacity as attorney by his client. Such is not generally the case where the attorney at the same time belongs in some way, e. g. as director or employee, to the management of the enterprise, although the courts in the U. S. appear to be of different viewpoints on this question. In any case the attorney would in such situations have to convince the court or the agency that he obtained the information not as a member of management but as an attorney.

33. The difference between prohibitory and misuse laws and the nature of proceedings (civil, administrative or criminal) both play a role in determining whether the examining agency must obtain and produce *exonerating evidence*[31]) or whether this is left to the enterprises in question. In most countries with misuse laws the examining agency has the obligation of obtaining as clear a picture as possible as to whether or not specified conduct of enterprises runs counter to the public interest (thus e. g. specifically in South Africa, New Zealand, Netherlands, Switzerland, Sweden, Norway, Finland). But in case of prohibitory laws also (Germany, EEC) the duty of the agency in official proceedings to collect exonerating facts is at least theoretically recognized; even elsewhere, the agency may not conceal exonerating facts known to it (U. S., Great Britain). In practice however a party is ordinarily at a disadvantage if it cannot produce or prove facts favorable to its position. If the agency is unable to produce sufficient facts to establish that a violation of law is involved, then the principle of "in dubio pro reo" (in case of doubt for the defendant) comes into effect in criminal but also in administrative proceedings. If the company involved is unable on its part to rebut the agency's case as to the

30) Question 20
31) Question 21

existence of a violation or to present extenuating (exonerating) circumstances, then the violation is established.

34. If the examining agency comes to the conclusion that a violation of the antitrust or cartel laws is involved, this determination has *direct legal effect*[32]) in cases where the agency also has a decision making power. This is true e. g., in the case of the Federal Trade Commission in the U. S., whose determinations may not be rejected if supported by substantial evidence. It is moreover true in the case of the Commission of the EEC, which can both prohibit unlawful conduct and impose fines; of the German Federal Cartel Office, which can likewise prohibit some (though not all) types of (unlawful) conduct and impose fines; and of the Swedish Freedom of Commerce Board, which can order the cessation of an unreasonable refusal to deal.

In other cases legal effects ensue on the other hand only if the next forum to which the examining agency has submitted its own determination (government, minister, agency or court) so determines. Even this is not true if that forum's determination consists of a decision to initiate court proceedings. (Canada, France, Switzerland).

35. Insofar as the examining agency or the next forum can reach final decisions, such decision may also frequently consist of an *order* to companies *to stop engaging in certain conduct*[33]) (Federal Trade Commission and the courts in the U. S., Restrictive Practices Court in Great Britain, the criminal courts in Canada, the appropriate minister in South Africa, the Trade Practices Tribunal in Australia, the Federal Cartel Office in Germany but only in certain cases, the appropriate minister in Holland, the Commission of the EEC, the Monopoly Control Authority in Denmark, the Freedom of Commerce Board in Sweden in refusal to deal cases).

36. In criminal proceedings the decision of the preliminary forum is usually only binding where it has led to a prohibition, i. e. a cease and desist order. Similarly the courts are not bound in civil litigation by a determination of the examining agency that specific acts constituted a violation of the antitrust or cartel laws unless the agency has acted negatively by declaring a given contract to be void (thus e. g. in New Zealand and Netherlands) or has acted positively by granting an exemption from the prohibition (Germany, EEC). The only case in which the examining agency is competent to make a final determination, binding even on the courts, as to whether given acts violate the prohibition is under Art. 65 § 4 of the ECSC Treaty.

---

32) Question 22
33) Question 23

37. The procedural jurisdiction of the agencies extends as a rule also to *foreign firms*[34]) in the same manner as to domestic firms, assuming that foreign firms are substantially subject to the particular antitrust or cartel law. This depends in most laws on whether unlawful effects occur within the jurisdiction (e. g. U. S., Germany, Netherlands, EEC, Switzerland, Sweden) or whether the firms in question are in some way engaged in business within the jurisdiction (Great Britain, South Africa, New Zealand, Denmark, Finland). As a practical matter, the invoking of jurisdiction is naturally always conditioned on the agencies' ability to reach the foreign company within the jurisdiction. This question has till now apparently only been raised in the U. S. with any frequency, where there is a trend to expand the jurisdiction of antitrust authorities to the maximum possible extent.

38. In conclusion, the following may be remarked about the *distribution of emphasis as among the agencies and the courts*[35]) in the enforcement of antitrust and cartel laws, at least insofar as the individual countries have had any experience in this area:

a) In most countries the balance lies unequivocally on the side of the agencies. This is especially true in the U. S., although the Antitrust Division has no and the Federal Trade Commission has limited decision making authority. First it is of some significance that these agencies, as a result of their experience acquired over several decades, are able to decide what cases and what legal questions they will present to the courts for their decision. The main reason however is that only a fraction of all cases reaches the courts at all, while most proceedings are terminated by the agencies in the preliminary stage by a consent decree or in similar manner, as a result of which they have in practice considerable influence on the resolution of countless legal questions (Cf. the Report of the Committee to Study the Antitrust Laws, pp. 360—361). This holds true also for the German Federal Cartel Office and the Commission of the EEC, but also for a number of other countries such as Denmark, Sweden, Finland and Norway.

b) The same holds true to a differing degree for countries in which decisions concerning antitrust policy are substantially in the hands of the appropriate minister (South Africa, France, Netherlands). In such cases the attribution of greater importance to the politically responsible authorities stems from the fact that antitrust policy is regarded as a part of general economic policies.

c) The more important role is with the courts only in Great Britain and Canada, where the only task of the agencies is to prepare

34) Question 24
35) Questions 25 and 26

and initiate the proceedings, while all factual determinations rest with the special court or courts. The only exception to this in Great Britain relates to the duties of the Board of Trade within the framework of the Monopolies and Mergers Act of 1956.

d) Insofar as the agencies make final decisions in a case rather than merely presenting the case to the courts, the affected parties have the right to obtain judicial review.

IV. ADVANCE CLEARANCE AND EXEMPTION PROCEDURES [36])

39. In countries having prohibitory laws from which the agency may permit exemptions under specified conditions in individual cases, formal procedures are provided for the securing of such exemptions. In addition there is in most countries the possibility before the commencement of certain conduct (agreement, merger) of clarifying with the agency in advance whether such conduct is lawful. These procedures nevertheless are clearly distinguishable.

The *procedure for obtaining an exemption* finds its most detailed elaboration *in Germany*. This procedure provides that the cartel agency may give permission under certain conditions in the case of specified types of cartel agreements (structural crises cartels, rationalization cartels, export cartels affecting domestic commerce, import cartels, emergency cartels); other forms of cartels (conditions cartels, rebate cartels, specialization cartels) are permitted and effective if reported to the cartel agency and not opposed by the latter within 3 months; finally there are cases (standardization cartels, pure export cartels and the maintenance of resale prices of trademarked goods) in which simple reporting, though required, is sufficient to give effectiveness to the cartel. In all such cases reporting to the cartel agency is necessary and the reported agreement becomes effective, in the first group when the cartel agency grants the exemption and in the second when the period for rejection has expired. In the third group the cartel becomes effective when reported. On the other hand, even cartels falling into this category are prohibited and void if permission for them is not requested and they are not reported. In all cases the effectiveness as thus obtained is binding on the courts, since the decision of the cartel agency is constitutive, i. e., has specific legal effects and is not merely a factfinding one. Third parties whose interests are substantially affected may take part in the proceedings, make motions and under certain conditions prosecute appeals.

This procedure is of substantial significance since under the German legal system exemptions always require an action of the agency.

36) Questions 27 – 33

Note: This report will not deal with those exemptions which are specifically provided in Germany and in other countries for certain areas of the economy such as agriculture, transportation or public utilities.

40. The rules under the *EEC and ECSC Treaties* correspond to those in Germany with these exceptions:

a) Both treaties establish the conditions for an exemption in the form of a general rule without differentiating between different types of cartels.

b) While under the ECSC Treaty the legal effectiveness of the exemption commences when it is granted, the procedural rule under Arts. 85 and 86 of the EEC Treaty has created a complicated system of retroactivity under which the exemption may sometimes (depending on the Commission's decision) be made retroactive to the day of reporting or even to an earlier date.

c) Third parties, while they participate and are heard in the proceedings may not make formal motions or perfect appeals.

41. In addition, there are a few other cases providing for procedures for obtaining exemptions from the prohibitions contained in the statute or promulgated by the agency: in *the Netherlands* in case the minister has declared a group of contracts unenforceable; in *Sweden and Finland,* and similarly in *Norway,* for the generally prohibited acts involving resale price maintenance and submission cartels. In all these situations, however, no detailed procedural rules have as yet been developed, and they have all in practice been of little significance. If such an exemption is granted, it is binding on the courts. Third parties may not participate in the proceedings.

42. Art. 66 of the *ECSC Treaty* should still be noted as a special rule in that it provides for prior clearance of mergers. If the merger is effected without prior clearance, the governing authority and now the EEC Commission is authorized to impose a fine and, if the merger cannot be retroactively approved, to decree dissolution and take all necessary measures to make such dissolution retroactive.

43. As far as the possibility of *determining whether or not specific conduct violates the law is* concerned, only the ECSC and EEC Treaties contain appropriate provisions to this effect. The ECSC Treaty provides in Art. 65 § 4 that the governing authority and now the EEC Commission has exclusive jurisdiction to determine whether or not an agreement comes under the prohibition of Art. 65 § 1. Accordingly, the companies involved could also apply for a declaratory judgment which if granted would be binding on the courts.

EEC Order No. 17, the procedural rule relating to Arts. 85 and 86 of the Treaty, has taken over this procedure in a limited way: pursuant to Art. 2 of the Order the Commission may on request find that, according to the information it has obtained, there are under Art. 85, paragraph 1, or Art. 86 of the Treaty, no grounds for it to intervene with respect to an agreement, decision or practice. This so-called negative test is binding on the Commission insofar as it may only alter its decision upon learning of new facts; it is in no way formally binding on the courts of the member states. Nevertheless, this procedure in which by the way third parties may participate to the same extent as in exemption proceedings, has attained a certain practical significance since it enables the Commission through such decisions to clarify its views on the questions of law relating to the distinction between prohibited and permitted conduct. Since the Commission plays a decisive role in the development of the law of competition within the Common Market, the national courts ordinarily give substantial consideration to such views.

44. The legal effects are naturally different in situations in which companies, before embarking on certain activities, seek *informal clearance from an agency* as to whether the activities would violate the antitrust or cartel laws. This opportunity exists in all countries, but it is most frequently used in countries such as the U. S. and Germany which have very broad prohibitory cartel laws. Insofar as something more than an exchange of legal opinions is involved, the agencies customarily limit themselves to a declaration that they do not intend to institute proceedings with respect to the facts in question, as such facts were presented to them. The American agencies issue such declarations with respect to criminal and civil proceedings only in case of mergers; in other situations the declaration merely states that they will not institute criminal proceedings.

Naturally the courts are not bound by such declarations. Even the agencies are legally free to change their minds, at any rate if new facts appear. As a result, the opinions of companies are very much divided as to the practical value of this type of prior clearance. Kingman Brewster (*Antitrust and American Business Abroad,* p. 393) states on this point:

> "If there is no legal problem, why bother; the clearly illegal can be spotted quite easily by the counselor, the clearly legal gains nothing by official approval. If there is an evenly balanced doubt, then a favorable ruling cannot be expected. At best, an application will draw a time consuming investigation. A failure of approval, although formally without prejudice, will add greatly to the uneasiness. At worst, the application for approval may bring on dis-

approval and complaint, whereas otherwise the matter might have been passed over."

In practice this procedure involving prior clearance has in the U.S. and Great Britain only proved to be useful in case of mergers, in the case of which a clearance is made desirable by the definitive changes in position. In Germany, moreover, some favorable experiences have been made with this procedure in other cases.

V. PROCEDURES IN ANTITRUST CASES IN GENERAL

45. *Acts punishable*[37]) under the respective laws should be distinguished as between those which violate procedural regulations and those which violate substantive law. Among substantive law violations again there are some involving the effectuation of conduct prohibited by law and others involving continuation of conduct prohibited by a decision of the agency or court. To the first category also belong those situations in which conduct, which standing by itself would be lawful, is made unlawful until it is reported or registered. Finally some cartel laws (Germany, Austria) contain particular provisions against inducing or compelling others to engage in unlawful conduct.

46. Among punishable violations of procedural regulations of special significance are those involving the unauthorized withholding, or the submission of incomplete or false, information; some laws also penalize the failure to observe the duty to report (e. g. the Netherlands).

47. With respect to the *nature of the penalties*[38]) which may be imposed, all the laws down to the Swiss law provide an opportunity for monetary penalties or compensation, but till now widespread use of this has only been made in the U. S. Prison sentences are theoretically possible in the U.S., South Africa, Australia, France, the Netherlands, Austria, Denmark, Sweden and Norway, but have only been imposed till now in individual cases in the U. S. In most countries on the other hand there is a possibility (with such possibility being limited in Germany and Finland) for the issuance of injunctions which are also extensively utilized.

Compulsory divestiture in cases of unlawful mergers is only known in the U.S., Great Britain, South Africa and the ECSC; in practice this measure has likewise only been used in the U.S. Compulsory licenses based on the antitrust law (rather than on the patent law) exist in the U. S. and Great Britain.

---

37) Question 34
38) Question 35

Especially effective in the prevention of antitrust violations in the U. S. has been the right of injured parties to recover treble damages; elsewhere, the problem of compensatory damages has not played a significant role. Finally, the possibility of the confiscation of property or of overcharges on prices is known in the U. S., Denmark and Norway; nationalization as a penal measure is known in the Netherlands and Austria; and the loss of customs incentives is known in South Africa. Especially effective as against companies with dominant market power in the Netherlands has proved to be the possibility of the imposition of the duty to deliver, of setting prices and of prohibiting tying clauses.

48. In all countries, the responsible *representatives of a company*[39]) (directors, officers) may also be punished for violations incurred by their company. On the other hand, punishment of the owners (partners, stockholders) is nowhere provided.

49. In case companies *violate a regulation*[40]) which forbids them from engaging in certain conduct, in some countries contempt of court procedures are available (e. g., the U. S., Great Britain and Australia), in others a criminal proceeding ensues (South Africa, New Zealand, Netherlands), while in still others the agencies may impose fines or monetary penalties (e. g., Germany, the EEC, Sweden). In the Netherlands violation of a regulation of antitrust law constitutes an "Economic offense", implying liability to both criminal and civil sanctions. This is special criminal law.

50. On the subject of *jurisdiction*[41]) there are generally no special rules applicable to antitrust cases; instead the rules of general procedural law govern. This is likewise true of jurisdiction over foreign companies. Exceptions may be found in the U. S., where an action against a company may be commenced in each district in which it is engaged in business, and also in Germany and Austria, where cartel matters are handled by specified courts.

51. The same holds true for the *burden of proof*[42]). Here also the general rules apply, pursuant to which the agency or the prosecutor must present and prove the incriminating facts, and the company must present and prove the exonerating ones. (Cf. paragraph 30 supra).

52. The question of the *period of limitations*[43]) is only of significance where violations result in administrative or criminal proceedings, that is primarily in case of prohibited acts. Here a few laws have special rules providing mostly for not very long periods of limitations (e. g., in

39) Question 36
40) Question 37
41) Question 38
42) Question 39
43) Question 41

the U. S. 4 years; Austria 1 year except in certain cases in which there is no period of limitations; Germany 2 years; France 3 years; Sweden 2 years). In other cases, the general limitations rules of the criminal law apply. A particularity of the EEC: Neither the Treaty itself nor the hitherto published regulations contain any rule relating to the limitation of antitrust violations, so that it is disputed whether these actually are subject to limitation and if so after what period.

53. Insofar as administrative or criminal courts try antitrust violations, there is as a rule *opportunity for appeal*[44]) and in individual cases also for reversal. The rules, however, are too diverse to be set forth in this report.

VI. RIGHTS OF PRIVATE PARTIES TO COMMENCE ANTITRUST PROCEEDINGS

54. Only in a few cases do the antitrust laws contain specific provisions giving *private parties*[45]) damaged by an antitrust violation the right to sue for compensatory damages (U. S., Australia). In a number of other countries, such suits can be effectively pursued on the basis of general civil law rules requiring indemnification of damages arising from a violation of law (Canada, Germany within limits, France, Netherlands, Switzerland, Austria, Norway, Finland), while for the remaining countries there is no possibility for claims for compensatory damages arising out of antitrust violations. The amount of the damages to be compensated is determined on the basis of the general principles of the law relating to compensation, except in the U. S., where the injured party may sue for treble damages.

55. Similarly, only a few antitrust laws give private parties the opportunity to seek an injunction (only the U. S., Switzerland and the EEC), while in a few other cases decrees with prospective application may under certain conditions be applied for under the general rule (Canada, Germany, Austria).

56. Insofar as there is a possibility to institute proceedings of such type, the general procedural rules apply with respect to the recovery of the costs of the litigation, including attorneys' fees, with the one limitation that in the U. S. only the successful plaintiff and not the defendant may recover his costs. To the extent that such proceedings may be instituted at all, this right to recover court costs is in most cases available also to foreign companies. In fact some countries (e. g., France and Austria) require that foreign plaintiffs must deposit court costs in advance unless there is a reciprocity treaty in effect with their country.

44) Question 42
45) Questions 45 – 49

57. With regard to the legal effectiveness or *invalidity*[46]) of contracts violating the antitrust or cartel law, the following may be said: contracts in violation of a general prohibition are ab initio void. The same holds true for situations in which contracts require reporting as a condition of effectiveness but are not so reported. If, on the other hand, contracts become prohibited and unlawful only if prohibited by decision of the agency or court in individual case, then the invalidity commences with such decision. A certain exception from this rule holds true for Switzerland, where pursuant to Art. 6 of the cartel law, the court may determine the unlawfulness of a specified restraint on competition either with retroactive or prospective effect. Another exception arises in the case of the EEC, where as a result of a transitional rule the Commission may determine the time as of which the prohibition comes into effect with respect to preexisting cartels.

Insofar as a contract is void in accordance with these rules, the parties may not recover compensatory damages since they were participants in the violation.

58. The determination by the agency of the existence of a violation is as a rule not required to enable third parties to sue for damages (if this is permitted at all). This is, however, different in cases in which a particular violation must first be prohibited by the agency as constituting a misuse or being contrary to the public interest. In such cases, naturally the decision of the agency is a condition for the right to claim damages to be available.

59. The above-mentioned rule of the Swiss cartel law is the only one dealing with the question of when a private party may seek a *determination as to the existence of a violation*[47]) by way of a court decree. In all other countries this question depends on the procedural rules dealing with the question of when a determination as to a specific legal conclusion may be applied for.

60. Further procedural problems (referred to by Mr. Seward) not covered by the questionnaire:

a) The suspension of the statute of limitations during the pendency of antitrust proceedings; although private antitrust complaints must be made within four years after the violation, this period is suspended so long as a government civil or criminal case is pending (15 U. S. C. §§ 15 [b], 16 [b]).

b) Pursuant to the rule in 15 U. S. C. § 16 (a) a decision in a government antitrust case serves as prima facie evidence for all facts, with respect

46) Questions 50 – 52
47) Question 53

to which the parties are prohibited by the decision from presenting further evidence.

VII. TOPICS FOR DISCUSSION

Because of the great number of questions involved, the following topics will be specifically dealt with in the discussion:

A. Topics for representatives of countries which have antitrust laws:

1. Do the antitrust laws of your country have a significant effect on business practices?
2. With what frequency have the types of sanctions described below been imposed under the antitrust laws of your country:
   a) injunctions or cease and desist orders at the instance of public agencies,
   b) injunctions at the instance of private parties,
   c) fines, and
   d) imprisonment?
3. To what extent are advance clearance or exemption procedures of practical value under your country's legal system?

B. Topics for representatives of countries which do not have antitrust laws:

1. Do the procedural rules of your country's courts and administrative agencies give non-citizens and foreign owned business organizations sufficient opportunities to assert their rights when they are accused of violating your laws regulating business?

Exhibit A

I. *General information*

1. Comment on the extent to which your country's major industrial enterprises are owned privately or are owned or controlled by the government or by government controlled bodies.

2. Comment on the extent to which the objectives below stated have significance in the regulation of business in your country:

(a) The promotion of privately owned enterprise?

(b) The promotion of free competition among business enterprises?

(c) Governmental or quasi-governmental ownership of business enterprises?

(d) Governmental planning of private investments?

(e) Governmental planning of production?

(f) Governmental regulation of prices?

(g) Governmental regulation of exports or imports?

(h) Governmental aids for private enterprise?

3. Please give a general account of the court and other procedures used in your country to enforce your laws, and particularly laws regulating business entities and transactions if there are important differences in the enforcement procedures as to them. Differentiate between criminal and civil proceedings, and explain the function and responsibilities of public prosecutors and administrative agencies in such proceedings. The objective is to obtain a general account of your law enforcement procedures whether or not your country has "antitrust laws". You may exclude or merely mention currency regulation, tax regulation and procedures which affect only specified types of industries.

4. Do private parties have a right to initiate criminal proceedings for their own benefit? (This question relates to laws governing business transactions in general, not merely antitrust laws. The antitrust law aspects of the question may be explained under heading V below.)

5. Do private parties have a right to initiate civil proceedings to recover damages sustained by them as result of a violation of law by another person in a business transaction? Note that the antitrust law aspects of this subject may be explained under heading VI below.

II. *The antitrust laws in general*

6. Please describe very briefly any statute, treaty or other law effective in your country which regulates restraints on competition among businesses, monopolies, cartels and abuses of dominant position. For convenience, the term "antitrust laws" will be used to describe this type of regulation. Please list the official names, publication or effective dates and official citation of each of such antitrust laws.

7. Does the "Guide to Legislation on Restrictive Business Practices," published by the Organization for Economic Cooperation and Development in Paris, contain all of such antitrust laws? If not, please enclose with your answer a copy of all important provisions in English, French or German.

8. To what extent do the antitrust laws of your country regulate: (a) agreements which restrict competition, (b) abuse or misuse of a dominant position or monopoly power, (c) transactions which tend to create a monopoly such as mergers, combinations, etc.

9. Which of the following general types of restrictions are applicable to conduct prohibited by the antitrust laws of your country:

(a) General prohibition without specific provisions for exemption?

(b) Prohibition subject to exemption regulated in detail by statute, developed by the courts or left to the general discretion of the competent agency under prescribed conditions?

(c) General validity with the possibility of prohibition by the competent agency in the case of misuse?

10. Does violation of the antitrust laws of your country subject the violator to (a) criminal penalties? (b) injunction? (c) liability in a civil action to an injured party? (d) invalidity or unenforceability of offending contracts? Describe briefly the kinds of sanctions imposed against violators of your country's antitrust laws.

11. What rights of appeal does a defendant have?

III. *Procedures for Antitrust Law Enforcement by Governmental Agencies*

12. (a) What, if any, governmental officials or agencies are responsible, in whole or in part, for enforcement of your country's antitrust laws? (b) What are their respective functions? (c) What are their respective powers? (For convenience such officials or agencies will be referred to as the "agency.")

13. (a) Does the agency promulgate general regulations for the guidance of the public? (b) Does it publish its decisions for the guidance of persons in similar situations? (c) Does it in addition issue policy statements from time to time, and if so what is their legal effect?

14. (a) Comment on the discretion, if any, which the agency has in interpreting and enforcing the antitrust laws. (b) To what extent is economic analysis employed in its decisions?

15. (a) Is there any advisory or consultative body which includes non-official persons, such as independent experts or representatives of the industry? (b) If so, what are its functions and who appoints its members?

16. (a) Does the agency commence investigations or enforcement proceedings on its own initiative or on instructions from the government or only on complaints from private parties? (b) What is the extent of its discretion as to whether or not to commence proceedings after a complaint has been filed?

17. What parties are entitled to participate in the proceedings and what is the extent of their respective rights (a) to be heard, (b) to make motions and (c) to appeal from final determinations? (d) Do the answers to the questions in the last sentence apply equally to persons who were party to the restrictive conduct and to those who were merely affected by it?

18. (a) Please describe briefly the investigatory powers of the agency, including the power to compel testimony, to obtain documents, to inspect premises, etc. (b) Is there any obligation on the agency to keep secret any of the information obtained by it?

19. Under what circumstances, if any, does a private party have the right to refuse to disclose information requested by the agency? (b) Does a private party have a basic or constitutional right to refuse to give information which may incriminate him? (c) Does this also apply to a corporation?

20. (a) Is a lawyer entitled to refuse to disclose information about his client? (b) Is this still true if he is acting in a managerial capacity in addition to being a lawyer?

21. (a) Is the agency required to seek out evidence favorable to the defendant, or (b) does the defendant bear the entire burden to present the evidence in his favor?

22. What is the legal effect of a finding by the agency of a violation of the antitrust laws or a prohibition by it of a restrictive behavior as misuse?

(a) under administrative law;

(b) under criminal law;

(c) under civil law?

23. Is the agency entitled to issue a cease-and-desist-order (injunction) if it finds a violation of the antitrust laws? In what manner may such order be enforced?

24. To what extent are foreign firms, either within or outside your country, subject to the investigatory and enforcement powers of the agency?

25. Does a private party have a right of appeal against an adverse determination by the agency, and what is the extent of the courts' power to review its findings and decisions?

26. Please comment on the relative importance in your country of the agency and of the courts in the enforcement of the antitrust laws.

IV. *Advance Clearance and Exemption Procedures under the Antitrust Laws*

27. Are private parties (a) required to, or (b) may they at their option, seek clearance or approval from such officials or agencies (or any other governmental agency or bureau) for particular transactions or types of conduct either (c) before or (d) after effecting such transactions or engaging in such conduct? If so, summarize the procedures.

28. Does such procedure involve the filing or registration, either (a) mandatory or (b) permissive, of restrictive agreements or other conduct? When does the exemption become effective: is it (c) on filing, (d) on the failure of the agency to object or (e) on its making a favorable determination?

29. (a) What is the legal effect of a clearance or exemption obtained in accordance with the answers to Questions 27 and 28 above? (b) Is it binding on your courts?

30. What, if any, are the legal consequences to the parties of the failure to obtain the clearance or exemption referred to in the answers to Questions 27 and 28 above?

31. Are the clearance or exemption procedures available to foreign firms?

32. Please state your opinion as to the relative importance of the clearance or exemption procedure in the antitrust enforcement of your country.

33. (a) Under what circumstances, if any, are third parties entitled to participate in the exemption procedures? May they (b) make motions? (c) Appeal from exemptions?

V. *Procedures in Antitrust Cases in General*

34. Under which, if any, of your country's antitrust laws may criminal sanctions be invoked against private parties?

35. To what extent may the following penalties be imposed in antitrust proceedings? Please comment on the extent to which such penalties have in fact been imposed by the courts.

(a) Imprisonment?

(b) Fines?

(c) Indemnification of injured parties?

(d) Injunctions against future violations?

(e) Compulsory divestiture of interests in other companies?

(f) Compulsory licensing of industrial property rights?

(g) Other penalties?

36. To what extent are corporate officers, directors or stockholders responsible for antitrust law violations by their company?

37. (a) Describe briefly the procedures, if any, followed by the courts to secure compliance with antitrust decrees or injunctions. (b) Are criminal sanctions available in cases of noncompliance?

38. (a) Are there any special jurisdictional provisions applicable to antitrust proceedings? (b) Do the courts or enforcement tribunals of your country have jurisdiction over foreign enterprises within the jurisdiction?

39. (a) What are the rules relating to the burden of proof and the burden as to the production of evidence in antitrust proceedings? (b) Are there any grounds, such as privilege, on the basis of which a defendant is entitled to refuse to produce certain information or records in evidence?

40. What is the extent of the participation by the officials or agencies described in answer to Question 12 in antitrust cases?

41. Is there a statute of limitations which limits the time within which antitrust charges may be brought?

42. (a) Are there procedures for appeal from the decisions of the trial court in an antitrust proceeding? (b) To what extent may the appellate courts retry the factual issues in a case?

43. To what extent are attorneys' fees or expenses charged against a defendant who is found guilty of a violation?

44. Please describe any important aspects of procedures in antitrust proceedings in general not called for by the previous questions.

VI. *Rights of Private Parties to Commence Antitrust Proceedings*

45. Does a private party injured by a violation of an antitrust law have a cause of action enforceable through court proceedings either to restrain the violation or to obtain damages?

46. What is the measure of damages in such private antitrust actions?

47. Is injunctive relief available?

48. To what extent are attorney's fees or expenses awarded to the winning party?

49. Are there any restrictions applicable to foreign persons or foreign controlled corporations which would prevent their bringing an action to protect themselves against a violation of your country's antitrust laws?

50. Are agreements in violation of the antitrust laws void ab initio or are they subject to being declared void in futuro by a court or administrative agency?

51. If an agreement is void or voidable because it violates the antitrust laws, may a party to the agreement nevertheless be entitled to damages against the other party, and under what circumstances?

52. Is the determination of an administrative agency that an agreement is in violation of the antitrust law a prerequisite to a court decree awarding damages to an injured party?

53. Are the parties to an agreement entitled to obtain a declaratory judgment from the courts as to whether the agreement is in violation of the antitrust laws?

54. Please describe any important aspects of procedures in antitrust proceedings commenced by private parties not called for by the previous questions.

VII. *Addendum*

55. Please make any additional comments you may wish.

56. Please list the best books and articles published about the procedural aspects of your country's antitrust laws.

SUMMARY OF DISCUSSIONS

Chairman: George C. Seward (USA)

Vice Chairman: Otfried Lieberknecht (Germany)

Rapporteur: Arved Deringer (Germany)

Secretary: Michael O'Brien (Ireland)

The Chairman opened the meeting and outlined the matters to be discussed. He referred to the questions set out at page 25 of the Report and indicated that the speakers would address themselves either to topic A or topic B.

First the rapporteur gave a short summary of his report and discussed certain questions affecting the antitrust laws of the Common Market (EEC).

Other speakers from the Committee called by the Chairman listed by country were as follows:

Austria	Dr. Fritz Schoenherr (report read by Mr. Michael O'Brien)
Canada	C. W. Brazier
Denmark	Gunnar Gersted
England	Wm. J. Brown
France	Fernand Charles Jeantet
Germany	Dr. Otfried Lieberknecht
Ireland	Thomas Jackson
Italy	Giuseppe Bisconti
Netherlands	J. A. Steinz
Norway	Andreas Arntzen
Sweden	Per H. Osvald
Turkey	Mrs. Guler Berkin
USA	Sigmund Timberg Blaise Pasztory

The most important point to emerge from the discussion was that antitrust laws have had an effective impact on the behaviour of both business and industry, even in countries which have a misuse law such as the Netherlands. The approach in antitrust law appears to be different in certain countries. The USA, Canada and Germany have a highly developed system against restrictive trade practices and monopolies, while the French and Scandinavian antitrust laws have developed out of price control. They retain the price control features even to-day.

The discussion on measures against antitrust violations showed that fines are used in the USA, Germany and Austria and that most countries use injunctions as an effective sanction. The USA was alone in its use of treble damages although other countries use single damages as a remedy too.

In few countries only there is a formal procedure for advance clearance and excemptions but informal discussions with the authorities are often used although there was disagreement as to the benefit of such procedure.

New developments have been reported from England, France and Denmark.

The meeting was then thrown open for discussion from the house. Mr. Masterman of Australia delt with certain aspects of Australian law on antitrust and Sir Hilary Scott, England, dealt with regulations of professional ethics and whether a procedure for setting up a code of ethics might violate antitrust law. He thought it a matter that the International Bar Association might interest itself in.

Deringer

PLENARY SESSION

PROPOSED CODE OF CONDUCT TO INSURE FAIR TRIAL AND FREE PRESS

Chairman: H. E. Zelling, Esq., Q. C. (Australia)
Rapporteur: Dr. Jean-Flavien Lalive (Switzerland)
Vice-Chairman: Dr. Rudolf von Graffenried (Switzerland)

Country	*National Correspondents*
Australia	H. E. Zelling, Esq., Q. C.
Austria	RA Dr. Ernst Jahoda
Canada	Jules Deschenes, Esq., Q. C.
Denmark	Advokat Thomas Federspiel
England	William O. Carter, Esq. (The Law Society) Arthur C. Prothero, Esq. (The Law Society)
Finland	Asianajaja Klaus Lagus
Germany	RA Klaus Mathy
Iran	Mr. Mohamad Bagher Tajbakhsh
Ireland	Francis J. Lanigan, Esq. (The Incorporated Law Society of Ireland) Rory O'Connor, Esq. (The Incorporated Law Society of Ireland)
Israel	Mr. Avshalom Levy, Advocate Dr. J. Rotenstreich, Advocate
Lebanon	Mr. Amine Khoury
Netherlands	Mr. J. C. Hooftman
Norway	Advokat Torvald G. Løchen
Portugal	Dr. Francisco Salgado Zenha
Scotland	J. C. T. MacRobert, Esq. (The Law Society)
South Africa	Eben Louw, Esq.
Spain	Excmo. Sr. D. Sanchez Toves
Sweden	Advokat Ove Wickman
Switzerland	Dr. Jean-Flavien Lalive Dr. Rudolf von Graffenried
U. S. A.	The Hon. Paul C. Reardon Brigadier-General Lewis F. Schull (Federal Bar Association)

CODE OF CONDUCT TO INSURE FAIR TRIAL AND FREE PRESS

General Report

by Dr. JEAN-FLAVIEN LALIVE, Attorney-at-Law,
Geneva
Former Secretary General,
International Commission of Jurists

CODE OF CONDUCT TO INSURE FAIR TRIAL AND FREE PRESS

The International Bar Association chose as a subject to be debated during its Dublin Conference, the advisability of proposing the drafting of a "Code of conduct to insure fair trial and free press".

The choice of the subject followed upon the debate on the report submitted at the 11th Conference of the International Bar Association held at Lausanne in July 1966 concerning the "limits and restrictions of public reporting on criminal and civil Court proceedings". During the 1966 debates the question of reporting on judicial proceedings was widely discussed and a number of suggestions were explored as to the means for reconciling the generally accepted necessity of a free press with the equally important need of insuring proper administration of justice against infringement by those sections of the press and other news media, which are prone to attracting readers and clientele by means of sensational reporting on scandals etc.

Although the question as originally posed at the Lausanne Conference, concerned specifically the advisability of a Code imposing on the press rules of conduct in relation to reporting on Court trials, yet it soon appeared that the scope of the investigation should be widened so as to comprise rules of ethics and conduct of the press and other news media, in regard to other fields, overlapping strict judicial reporting. The conclusion arrived at was that the press constitutes a powerful tool of investigation and publicity, that can be and is directed to many subjects, of which judicial reporting forms a limited albeit important part. Therefore, if an enquiry were to be carried out concerning the advisability of formulating a Code of conduct for the press, such enquiry should embrace, in addition to judicial reporting, the effect of press reporting on matters pertaining to the right of individuals to privacy, a field in which the press has been active in recent times in a manner that has aroused sharp criticism from many quarters.

A further reason for including in this report the question of the protection of the individual's privacy from intrusions of the press, lies in the fact that in most legislations, the conduct of the press, in so far as juridical proceedings are concerned, is regulated in a more or less minute manner by statute or the common law, while individual privacy enjoys in practice a far looser legal protection; this, it is submitted, makes it the more important for a Code of conduct to substitute and complete legislation in this specific field.

In framing the questions under title V of the questionnaire circulated among members, account was taken of this requirement, and the answers received on this particular aspect of the problem, fully justified its inclusion in the investigation.

From the answers received, two guiding lines emerge:

i) Specific provisions contained in scattered statutory provisions or the common law, restrict the freedom of the press or other news media, in a number of limitatively defined cases relating to criminal and civil Court proceedings, mostly the former.

ii) In those countries where a Press Council or a Code of conduct has been set up or applies (such as Germany, Britain, Austria, Denmark, Massachusetts, U. S. A., Israel, Norway, South Africa, Switzerland) the powers conferred on the Bodies entrusted with the control of the press, consist of imposing upon offenders, sanctions such as reprimand, publication of rectification, exclusion from the press association, etc. all of which are sanctions of moral nature without entailing a penalisation in the strict sense of the word. It should be added that the answers received tend to show that generally the system of moral sanctions adopted in the countries concerned works quite satisfactorily.

From a theoretical point of view, however, the question could be posed whether moral sanctions would be sufficient to jugulate an unscrupulous press in other countries which would at some time in the future also set up Press Councils which might not enjoy the prestige and authority that have allowed their predecessors to exercise an effective control over the ethics of the press. The question, although theoretical, is worth while considering and possible solutions should be sought. Thus it could be envisaged, as is the case in some countries with regard to Councils representing certain professions, that a Press Council would be empowered by statute to apply penalisations (such as fines, suspension, damages, etc.) on journalists guilty of certain offences, the decision in this respect of the Press Council being subject to redress before a higher administrative or judicial Court. In such system, Press Councils would exercise a semi-judicial competence, and penalties (not merely recommendations) imposed by Councils for breach by members of the press of the rules of ethics applicable to the profession, could be submitted to, and finally decided upon by the ordinary Courts; the decisions of these would then serve to form a new corpus of judicial precedents specifically related to punishable press offences. In this manner, rules of ethics which hitherto remained deprived of any but a moral sanction would gradually penetrate the ambit of law and become mandatory as part of the law of the land.

The questions formulated in the questionnaire were divided under seven titles:

I) *Codes of conduct already in force*

The questions posed under this title tended to ascertain whether or not the countries concerned had established a Code of conduct and, in the affirmative, for how long such Code has been in force, whether it was particularly designed to ensure fair trial, whether it worked satisfactorily, etc. In short, under this title it was sought to elicit information as to the actual experience gained on the application of a Code of conduct, and to find out whether the ethical rules which the Codes intended to uphold were binding or merely served as recommendations.

II) *Content of such Codes of conduct*

Under this title it was sought to ascertain which are the guiding principles incorporated in the Codes of conduct in the countries which had one. A sample was given of principles which appeared to correspond to the basic ethical rules in this matter.

III) *Usefulness of such a Code of conduct with reference to the administration of justice and fair trial*

The questions posed under this title purport to find out whether the existence of a Code of conduct in relation to a proper administration of justice appeared necessary and, in the affirmative, the reasons militating in favour of a Code of conduct; such reasons could be the inadequacy of the statutory provisions aiming at preventing press abuses, or the belief that such abuses could be better prevented by means of ethical rules defined by representatives of the press itself, or the apprehension that a strict legal limitation of the press would hamper its freedom.

If the existence of a Code of conduct seemed unnecessary, it was sought to ascertain the reasons for this belief, such as the adequacy of the legal provisions in force in reconciling a proper administration of justice with a free press, or the opinion that a private Code of conduct did not stand a reasonable chance of being enforced, or because an amendment of existing legislation in the matter would be sufficient to attain the desired object.

IV) *Geographical scope: international or national Code of conduct*

The series of questions posed under this title aimed in the first place at ascertaining whether or not it was thought desirable that a universal Code of conduct should be drafted that would be applicable in all countries and, in the affirmative, whether it was thought advisable that such Code should be drafted under the auspices of international public bodies or agencies, or rather with the assistance of private organizations.

It was realized that at the present stage of international coordination and cooperation it would be extremely difficult to devise a uniform Code of conduct that could apply in numerous countries presenting a variety of legal systems with differing conceptions on the role of the press. Nevertheless, it was deemed useful to obtain answers to a precise question on the subject.

In case of a negative reply to the first question, it was sought to ascertain whether in the opinion of the national correspondents, a Code of conduct should be drafted in each country concerned, that would take account of local conditions and conceptions and whether such Code would entail a risk of conflict with existing legislation on the subject-matter or rather complement same.

V) *Subject matters and persons to be governed by such a Code*

It is under this title that answers were sought to the question whether the activity of the press should also be regulated by a Code in regard to fields other than reporting on judicial cases. Further questions on the subject of judicial reporting sought to ascertain whether it was thought desirable that a Code should impose restrictions on the press in regard to all or some of the phases of criminal proceedings, which of the persons participating in the publication of a newspaper should be under obligation to observe the rules of the Code, whether such Code should only apply to written press or to all news media and whether it was desirable to devise separate Codes in respect of each news medium.

VI) *Punishment*

Assuming the existence of a Code of conduct, it was sought to ascertain whether the national correspondents considered as being satisfactory in practice the results achieved by Press Councils in the exercise of their functions of supervision over the press in a number of countries such as Denmark, Germany, Israel, etc., or whether they deemed it preferable to entrust such supervision to mixed commissions comprising members of the press and jurists, with powers to sanction any offences with penalties in the strict sense of the word.

Here an attempt was made to elicit answers to the important question referred to above, whether moral sanctions on the press are to be considered sufficient, or more drastic measures are required to cope with press abuses in some limited cases.

In the same line of thought, questions were posed as to whether sanctions such as publication of rectification or excuses, exclusion from membership, etc. were deemed adequate, or whether it was thought proper to introduce more stringent measures of repression.

VII) *Proposals-Conclusion*

Under this final title questions were asked as to whether it was thought desirable to proceed with the drafting of a Code of conduct on the basis of replies received to the questionnaire or following a discussion of the subject at the Dublin Conference. The interest of this question is now behind us but the answers given may serve as a measure of the importance attached by members to the debates held by this Association.

Further questions dealt with the advisability of ascertaining the views of press representatives on the proposed Code of conduct, the outcome of any contacts members may have had with representatives of the press on the subject, and members' views on practical steps that could be taken by this Association in order to promote the adoption of a Code of conduct.

Sixteen National Correspondents sent replies to the questionnaire circulated, from which a number of conclusions can be drawn.

1. In regard to the questions formulated under title I of the questionnaire, the correspondents in nine out of the sixteen countries concerned, reported the existence in these countries of a Code of conduct or the equivalent thereto and of a Press Council entrusted with the supervision of the observance of the relevant rules by members of the press (Germany, Britain, Austria, Denmark, Israel, Massachusetts U. S. A., Norway, South Africa, Switzerland).

   In all cases, it was found that the rules issued by Councils to govern the conduct of members of the press are in the nature of recommendations, and that offences to such rules entail sanctions of a moral character varying between reprimand to exclusion from the press association. Further, the replies show that in eight of the nine countries above referred to (i. e. with the exception of Austria) 85 % — 100 % of the members of the press abide by the applicable rules and follow the recommendations of the Councils.

   In so far as Austria is concerned, it is reported that the Press Council formed in that country has not been able to exercise any restraining control over the press, and its recommendations and moral sanctions apparently go unheeded.

2. The principles laid down in title II met with a wide measure of approval with some qualifications and additions proposed by some countries; thus in so far as respect of privacy is concerned it was specified that there might be cases in which public interest must transcend the personal right of privacy (Massachusetts U. S. A.); the duty of being complete in reporting is admitted but doubts were expressed as to whether it is always possible; the protection of the right of personality can only be admitted to a certain extent (Israel); it should be emphasized that an accusation or attack should preferably not be reported unless the victim of such attack is allowed to present a reply (Norway); the freedom of the press should be emphasized (Portugal); no publication should be allowed which might prejudice the accused at his trial (Scotland); no reply was given to the questions under this title by the correspondent in Austria, as he considers that the regulations restraining the freedom of the press in his country are wholly inadequate and need complete reshuffling. In line with the old juridical tradition in Anglo-Saxon countries, which favours an empirical approach, the correspondents in Britain and Australia considered unnecessary to formulate guiding principles; the British Correspondent held that adequate rules could be evolved in time from the findings of the Press Council in each particular and concrete case.

3. In answer to the question under title III over the usefulness of a Code of conduct, correspondents from Germany, Austria, Denmark, Arizona U. S. A., Massachusetts U. S. A., Iran, Ireland, Israel, Norway, the Netherlands, Portugal, Scotland, South Africa and Switzerland, replied in the affirmative. Reasons given in so far as the interests of the press itself are concerned were generally that self-discipline resulting from the voluntary application of a Code of conduct would be preferable to legal regulations which are apt to harm freedom of press and expression (Germany, Arizona U. S. A.); and that it is in the interest of the press itself to obey voluntarily rules of ethics instead of being forced to do so by law (Norway). As regards the interest of a proper administration of justice and the right of the individual to privacy, the reasons given in favour of the adoption of a Code of conduct were that, although the statutory protection afforded is generally satisfactory, yet in some extreme cases it may be important to have the further safeguarding that a Code can provide (Denmark); that some abuses of the press could be better prevented by means of professional and ethical rules (Iran); that prior publication might influence the public from whom the jury is drawn, and fair trial must take precedence over freedom of press (Scotland); that it is essential to avoid informing the jury of previous bad character

of an accused before the latter has been tried (Ireland). Although the desirability of drafting a Code of conduct is admitted in principle, doubts were expressed as to its adoption due to the reluctance of the press to make binding commitments in this field (Massachusetts U. S. A.), and the absolute necessity of the adoption of a Code was also questioned by one correspondent (Switzerland).

The two correspondents from Britain and Australia replied in the negative to the question regarding the advisability of drafting of a Code of conduct, as they considered that the system prevailing in their respective countries works in a satisfactory manner. This view is of course in keeping with the traditional Anglo-Saxon approach which favours rules established by case law rather than a formal codification; it should be noted, however, that while a Press Council has been set up in Britain, Australia does not have a similar Body, which could evolve ethical rules applicable to some aspects of the activity of the press which are not regulated by statutory provisions.

4. In answer to the question under title IV whether an international Code of conduct would be desirable, correspondents from Britain, Austria, Denmark, Arizona U. S. A., Massachusetts U. S. A., Israel, Norway, Portugal and Switzerland replied in the affirmative, the general view being that the drafting of such Code could be better undertaken after a broad discussion of the subject at the I. B. A. Conference; however, many correspondents expressed the view that an international Code would rather serve as a model for national Codes to be drafted in each country to suit local conditions (Austria, Denmark, Arizona U. S. A., Norway), and that such an international Code should be drafted by professional bodies and jurists (Massachussets U. S. A., Portugal) or under the auspices of the I. B. A. and the International Press Institute (Israel, Norway) or under the auspices of the I. B. A., the U. N. and the Council of Europe (Austria, Switzerland).

Correspondents from Germany, Iran, Ireland, the Netherlands, Scotland and South Africa replied to this question in the negative, the reasons given being that each country should draft its own particular Code. The correspondent from Germany stated that if an international Code was to be drafted at all, this should only be done by the International Press Institute, and the correspondent from Australia denied the usefulness of establishing a Code of conduct, whether international or national.

Fourteen of the correspondents questioned replied that a Code of conduct could co-exist in their respective countries with legislation already in force on the subject, and that no conflict would arise between the two sets of rules if the Codes were properly drafted. However, the correspondents from Germany and Portugal voiced a different opinion stating that in their view conflicts would arise if a Code of conduct were added to the legislation in force in their countries.

5. To the questions asked under title V, fourteen correspondents answered that a Code of conduct should be applicable to all aspects of the professional activity of journalists, while the correspondents in Ireland and Israel held the view that the Code should only deal with reporting of Court proceedings.

   Fourteen correspondents expressed the opinion that no special rules of conduct are required in respect of each separate stage of the criminal proceedings, while a correspondent held that the general principles formulated in a Code of conduct should be the same as regards all stages of the criminal proceedings, but that there would be advantage to supplement such principles with special rules designed separately for each stage of the criminal proceedings (Norway) and another opinion was expressed to the effect that special rules of conduct should be drafted in respect of each stage of the criminal proceedings (Denmark, South Africa). To the question whether the rules of a Code of conduct should only apply to journalists or to all persons related to the publication of a newspaper, eight correspondents replied that the rules should be made applicable to all persons related to a newspaper; and the correspondent from Austria insisted that the rules should not apply solely to the responsible editor according to the legal system at present in force in Austria through the loopholes of which serious abuses are committed in practice. Other replies tended to exempt from responsibility for the application of the rules of a code, the owner and the printer of a paper (Iran), or the printer only (Ireland, Portugal) or to vary the degree of responsibility of the persons concerned with the proviso that the owner's responsibility should not be absolute (Israel), or to render responsible journalists only (the Netherlands) or to attribute the main responsibility for a breach of the Code to the editor-in-chief (Scotland).

   Twelve correspondents replied that a Code of conduct should be made applicable to all news media and no separate Code is needed in respect of each medium, while four of them were of opinion that special regulations should apply in regard to each communication medium concerned (Britain, Denmark, Norway, the Netherlands).

6. To the questions posed under title VI, correspondents in Germany, Britain, Denmark, Arizona U. S. A., Massachusetts U. S. A., Ireland, Israel, Norway, the Netherlands, South Africa, Portugal and Switzerland expressed themselves in favour of the functions of supervision of due observance of a Code, to be entrusted to a Press Council; however a number of correspondents seem also to favour the attribu-

tion of such functions of supervision to joint commissions of jurists and journalists empowered to impose certain administrative sanctions (Denmark, Arizona U. S. A., the Netherlands, South Africa).

The correspondents in Australia, Iran and Scotland did not favour the idea of a Press Council entrusted with the duty of sanctioning due observance of the Code of conduct though not for the same reasons: The Australian and Scottish correspondents consider the legal system in force in their respective countries as quite satisfactory and not requiring either a Code of conduct or a Press Council to enforce same; while the Iranian correspondent considers that a Code of conduct should be enforced by a joint commission of jurists and journalists and not by a Press Council.

Of particular interest is the answer of the correspondent in Israel who suggested that the Press Council be endowed with administrative repressive powers but that its decisions should be made subject to the control of the Supreme Court in the country; this system would imply the elaboration of rules and sanctions by the Press Council which would acquire legal force if and when approved by the High Court.

As to the penalties for breach of the rules incorporated in a Code of conduct, the suggestions range from the publishing of excuses to the suspension or exclusion from membership of the press organization. Correspondents in Arizona U. S. A., Ireland, Norway and the Netherlands considered advisable to include among the penalties envisaged, payment of damages to the victims of press abuses.

None of the correspondents favoured the idea of administrative sanctions applied by an independent administrative organization.

7. In answer to the questions set out under title VII, the correspondents from Austria, Arizona U. S. A., Norway, Portugal and Switzerland replied that they favoured the drawing up of a draft international Code of conduct on the basis of replies received to the questionnaire. Correspondents from Britain, Australia, Denmark, Iran, Ireland, Israel, Norway, the Netherlands, Scotland and South Africa, expressed the view that the drafting of a Code could be undertaken subsequent to the discussion to be held in the Dublin Conference, while the Portuguese and Swiss correspondents proposed that an already prepared draft Code should be discussed at the IBA Conference. The correspondent from Germany was of opinion that the drafting of a Code of conduct was undesirable since the instructions of the press council are generally observed by the press in his country.

To the question whether contacts were made with press people in order to ascertain their reaction to the proposal of an international

Code of conduct, answers showed that an extension of authority of the national Press Council seemed acceptable (Denmark), that the reaction of the press was unfavourable to a national Code of conduct and was bound to be more so in regard to an international Code (Arizona, Massachusetts U. S. A.), that newspaper people welcome the IBA's initiative provided any proposed rules should be drafted in cooperation with the professional bodies representing the press (Norway), that members of the press were opposed even to the rules at present enforced by law in the country (Australia, Scotland) and that newspaper people approve of the national Code of conduct devised by the local Press Council (South Africa).

The answers received to the question what are the practical steps proposed for promoting the adoption of an international Code of conduct, included suggestions that a special Committee of the IBA should contact press representatives (Britain), that the drafting of an international Code should be undertaken by the IBA and published under the auspices of the Council of Europe or the U. N. O. (Austria, Israel), that theIBA, national bar associations and jurists should press their views on national Press Councils and request the cooperation of national law Societies (Ireland), that information over the proposed international Code of conduct and the considerations which motivated its rules should be spread through contacts with press representatives so as to obtain their support in principle (Norway), that recommendations as to the proposed international Code should be published by means of circulars and articles and proposals be obtained from local press organizations (Switzerland).

In order to enable members to have a direct and detailed knowledge of the result of the enquiry carried out on Topic No. 2, we set out hereunder the questions circulated and the gist of the replies received from national correspondents. Of course, it has not been possible to include in this general report all the details and developments contained in the answers received, but members who so wish, may acquaint themselves directly with the reports mailed in response to the enquiry.

To designate countries, the correspondents in which replied to the questionnaire, abbreviations are used in manner following:

AUSTR	:	Law Council of Australia (Australia)
ÖSTER	:	Austria
DK	:	Det Danske Advokatsamfund (Denmark)
ENGL (L.S.)	:	The Law Society (England)
D	:	Germany
IRAN	:	Iran Bar Association (Iran)
IRE	:	Incorporated Law Society of Ireland (Ireland)

ISR	: Israel
NETHER	: Nederlandse Orde Van Advocaten (Netherlands)
NOR	: Den Norske Advokat forening (Norway)
PORT	: Portugal
SCOT	: The Law Society of Scotland (Scotland)
S. A.	: The Association of Law Societies of the Republic of South Africa (South Africa)
CH	: Fédération Suisse des avocats (Switzerland)
AR USA	: Arizona, U. S. A.
MASS USA	: Massachusetts, U. S. A.

I. CODES OF CONDUCT ALREADY IN FORCE

Question No. 1

– Do you have in your country a professional code of conduct governing the press? Yes – No.

Replies to Question No. 1

Yes: D, ENGL, DK, MASS USA, IRE, ISR, NOR, S. A., CH;

No: AUSTR, ÖSTER, AR USA, NETHER, PORT, SCOT, IRAN.

Question No. 2

If yes:

– Does such a code purport particularly to ensure fair trial?

Replies to Question No. 2

D	: The instructions of the press council of April 29, 1958 contain provisions governing the conduct of the press in relation to Court proceedings.
DK	: The code has a broader aim, but does also contain provisions to ensure fair trial.
IRE	: Yes.
ISR	: Yes.
NOR	: Yes.
S. A.	: No, because the principles designed to ensure fair trial are enshrined in the Statutes and Common Law.
CH	: No.

ENGL : No, the Code of Professional Ethics and Professional Usage and Practice relates to journalistic activity in general.

Question No. 3

– How long has such a Code been in force?

Replies to Question No. 3

D : Since 1958.

DK : The Code was adopted at a joint meeting of the Danish Press Organizations on 23rd November 1960.

NOR : Since 1952, last revised in 1965.

S. A. : The South African Press Board of Reference was constituted in March 1962 and the Code of conduct was adopted at the same time.

Question No. 4

– Does this system, as a whole, give full satisfaction?

Replies to Question No. 4

D : Yes.

DK : The Code is limited to press reporting on criminal cases. In this restricted field, the Code as a whole is considered as giving full satisfaction. But there is a general feeling that the Press Council's authority should be widened. The Council itself has submitted a proposal to the Press Organizations suggesting that its authority be extended to cases outside the field of criminal reporting to the extent necessary to protect people from unnecessary or serious offence. The Council does also suggest that it should be authorized to deal with any case in which it receives a complaint even if it is not from the offended person.

IRE : Yes.

ISR : Yes.

NOR : Yes.

ENGL : Yes.

S. A. : The system as a whole gives full satisfaction.

CH : Yes.

Question No. 5

– What is approximately the percentage of journalists who, in your country, respect the rules laid down in such a code?

Replies to Question No. 5

D : Although it is difficult to say, about 90% of the journalists respect the rules.

DK : Approximately 85% of the Danish Papers adhere to the Code and the Press Council's decisions.

ENGL : The great majority.

NOR : Approximately 100%.

S. A. : Judging by the very few occasions which the Board has had to investigate and adjudicate upon complaints, it is suggested that almost all journalists comply with the Code, though there are occasional transgressions.

ISR : Almost all.

CH : 90%.

Question No. 6

– Are these rules binding or do they only serve as recommendations?

Replies to Question No. 6

D : They only serve as recommendations.

ENGL : The Press Council has no power to enforce its rulings, but its authority has resulted in its findings being observed.

DK : The rules are binding on the papers which have adopted them, but many of the provisions of the Code are drafted in such a way that it is to some extent a discretionary question to be decided by the Press Council whether they have been violated.

MASS USA : The codes are not binding and serve only as recommendations and carry in general no sanctions for breaches.

ISR : Those rules that have the force of laws are binding and those that are part of the Press Council Rules are binding on the members in the same manner as in most voluntary organizations.

NOR	:	Recommendations, but in practice the journalists feel these rules to be binding.
S. A.	:	The rules are binding.
CH	:	Recommendations.

Question No. 7

– What are the sanctions provided for breaches of such a Code of conduct?

Replies to Question No. 7

D	:	In the form of criticism by the Press Council, which in case of an unequivocal breach of a known recommendation can be made in public by mentioning the name.
ENGL	:	Moral.
DK	:	In 1964 a Press Council was formed to consider alleged breaches of the Code. If the Press Council rules that the Code has been violated, the paper in question is under an obligation to publish the Press Council's decision.
MASS USA	:	Moral.
ISR	:	There are disciplinary sanctions within the Journalists' Organization and also penalties that may be imposed by the Courts of the State. The sanctions are: fine, imprisonment, suspension of publication, compensation and reprimand.
NOR	:	None. A special agency, "The Professional Press Committee", deals with breaches of the Code. This Committee is composed of three prominent press representatives. In some cases, the statements pronounced by this Committee are published together with the names of the implicated parties.
S. A.	:	In terms of Rule 3 (f) of the Constitution the Board may reprimand and may publish such reprimand and also cause a correction to be published where necessary.
CH	:	Exclusion from the association.

Question No. 8

– Please mention the elements and characteristics of this code which appear especially interesting and of such a nature as to serve as useful examples for similar codes of conduct in other countries.

Replies to Question No. 8

DK : The Code is only applicable on press reporting on criminal cases. The Press Council cannot on its own initiative take up a case. It can only deal with cases where it receives complaints from offended persons. The Press Council has no other sanctions than the one mentioned under 7 above. The following provisions of the Code may be of some interest.

The Papers shall refrain from "Trial by Newspapers". When reporting on criminal cases the journalists shall avoid inflicting unnecessary harm. The journalists should only use reliable sources. The Press should be careful not to obstruct the police investigations. The accused 's past should be omitted, especially previous sentences. The Papers should be especially careful when reporting cases involving young criminals or where suspended sentences are passed. The accused's nationality, race or political observation should be omitted if irrelevant to the case.

IRE : Quite apart from any specific rule, statutory or otherwise, the Press in this country have a very high ethical approach to reporting Court cases and usually insure that nothing appears in the newspapers which could unfairly affect a person before a Court charged with a criminal offence.

NOR : Details of special interests: *Before a charge is preferred in a criminal case:*

The *charge* should not be published until it has been served on the offender; the *name* of the suspect or accused and the names of witnesses should not be published unless the public interest so justifies.

Due consideration must be shown in *photographing* persons who have been arrested or are being questioned.

Reports on cases concerning *family matters* should be avoided and are permissible only under quite special circumstances.

Suicide or attempted suicide is usually not mentioned.

Any mention in the press of criminal proceedings which have not yet been concluded should be in the form of an *objective report.* As long as the question of guilt has not been decided, it is prohibited to use any formulation which implies a definite finding.

After the charge has been preferred:

Young offenders must be treated with particular consideration. If the prosecution can be expected to demand a suspended sentence or that the accused be placed in a labour school, and the case is not of general interest, it should be mentioned in a discreet manner and without name or photograph.

Reports on Court proceedings should be accurate and should present both sides of the case in *equal measures.*

If a newspaper has reported on the proceedings, it should also report the Court's *decision.*

If an *accusation or an attack* against a person or institution is reported, the answer given to the accusation or the attack should also be reported. The press should show particular care about mentioning such accusations or attacks against an outside party or a person who is not present, unless such person is allowed to reply.

In *civil cases,* the same principles apply. Divorce cases are not reported in the press, being considered as covered by the right of privacy.

In Norway, the ethical principles are contained in a small booklet entitled "BE CAREFUL" which all journalists have in their press card. This booklet emphasizes that the printed word is a powerful weapon and that the strictest requirements must be observed as regards the reliability and integrity of reports and comments.

Question No. 9

– Has the code of conduct in force in your country been drafted:

a) by journalists?

b) by lawyers and jurists?

c) by a joint body made of journalists and jurists?

d) any other group of people?

Replies to Question No. 9

D : It has been drafted by the Press Council which is constituted at a parity of ten publishers and ten journalists.

MASS USA : It has been drafted by joint bodies made up of journalists, lawyers and jurists.

ISR : The Rules of the Press Council were drafted by journalists.

NOR : The Norwegian Code of Conduct has been drawn up by the press organs (The Norwegian Press Federation) in consultation with the Chief Public Prosecutor, the Norwegian Association of Judges and the Norwegian Bar Association. The Code is recognized as adopted by the press itself.

S. A. : The code of conduct was drafted by a body of journalists with the assistance of lawyers.

CH : By a joint body made of journalists and jurists.

II. CONTENT OF SUCH CODES OF CONDUCT

Question No. 10

— Do you agree, with special reference to fair trial, that codes of conduct should contain the following principles:

a) rule of good faith;

b) duty of objectivity;

c) duty of being complete;

d) respect of privacy;

e) protection of the right of personality?

Replies to Question No. 10

D : Yes.

ENGL : It is unlikely in England that there could be an attempt to enunciate principles such as are mentioned in Question 10. All of those would be bound to play their part in the decisions of the Council, but the facts in each case would be considered, bearing in mind factors of public interest, private interest, and the need to maintain a free and fearless press. The laying down of rules would not be in accord with the English approach.

AUSTR : Do not think it is possible to answer this question in the way in which it is framed.

a) Do not understand what "a rule of good faith" means in this context.

b) Objectivity is a pure fantasy of the mind, there is no such thing.

c) If the trial is not reported completely and accurately, that of itself takes the report outside the protection of qualified privilege given by the statutory law of libel which makes most journalists see that their reports are reasonably complete and accurate.

d) There is no right to privacy as such under Australian law any more than under English law. The Courts have in all States the power by statute to forbid publication of evidence which is indecent, would reveal the identity of a victim of sex offences or relates to a juvenile.

e) Do not understand "protection of the right of personality". It is a meaningless phrase which could mean anything or nothing, depending on the Judge concerned.

DK : Yes.

AR USA : Yes.

MASS USA : Believe that the adoption of codes is salutary and that they should contain all the principles referred to on page 3 under 10, with the possible exception of "respect of privacy". There are sometimes reasons when the public right transcends the personal right of privacy.

IRAN : Yes, of course.

IRE : Agree with the points in this question.

ISR : a) Yes.

b) Yes.

c) Doubt whether this is possible.

d) Yes.

e) To a certain extent, yes.

NOR : Agree that codes of conduct should contain all the principles mentioned under this point.

NETHER : Certainly we agree.

PORT : Yes.

SCOT : Yes.

S. A. : It is agreed that codes of conduct should contain the principles mentioned.

Question No. 11

– Which other rules would you recommend?

Replies to Question No. 11

D : None.

AUSTR : The present law of contempt of Court and libel is a good law and does not need changing by code or in any other way.

ISR : It should be recommended that no name of an accused shall be published at any stage, before or during trial, until the person is convicted, unless the accused himself otherwise agrees.

NOR : The principles mentioned under point 10 are in our opinion the essential ones. It might in addition be desirable to emphasize that any accusation or attack against an individual or institution should preferably not be reported unless the victim is allowed to present his reply.

A person who is attacked must always be entitled to have his views and arguments published.

An important principle is the obligation to publish corrections of erroneous or misleading reports of importance to an individual or institution.

PORT : Freedom.

SCOT : No publication should be allowed which might prejudice the accused at his trial.

CH : None; we are generally in favour of clear and short rules.

III. USEFULNESS OF SUCH A CODE OF CONDUCT WITH REFERENCE TO THE ADMINISTRATION OF JUSTICE AND FAIR TRIAL

Question No. 12

– Does the existence of a code of conduct to ensure free trial appear necessary to you? Yes – No.

Replies to Question No. 12

D : Yes.

ENGL : No.

AUSTR : No.

ÖSTER : Yes.

DK : Yes, in some extreme cases.

AR USA : Yes.

MASS USA : Yes.

IRAN : Yes.

IRE : Yes.

ISR : Yes.

NOR : Yes.

NETHER : Yes.

PORT : Yes.

SCOT : Yes.

S. A. : Yes, it is in fact a sine qua non of a civilized country.

CH : Recommendable, but not yet necessary.

Question No. 13

— *If yes*, please state the reasons therefor. For example:

a) because there are no proper or adequate legal provisions governing the press;

b) because certain abuses of the press could, in your opinion, be better prevented by means of professional and ethical rules, such as a code of conduct for journalists, than by legal provisions;

c) because whenever ordinary laws are applied to prevent abuses, there is often the risk of a breach of the basic principle of the freedom of the press;

d) other reasons.

Replies to Question No. 13

D : All three reasons stated under a, b, c above.

ÖSTER : Such code should stress that all forms of abuse of the freedom of the press, which entail criminal penalties in Austria, are incompatible with the professional duties, the honour and the standing of journalism.

AR USA : A voluntary code of conduct would appear more desirable than statutory limitations on freedom of the press as a code would impress upon the members of the press the responsibility of accurate and fair reporting, with the further responsibility of assuring any person accused of crime a fair trial.

DK : In extreme cases it may be important to have the further safeguards which a code can provide.

MASS USA : Press-bar codes would be useful.

IRAN : Because there are not enough adequate legal provisions governing the press, and certain abuses of the press could better be prevented by means of professional and ethical rules.

IRE : It is essential in the interests of justice that (except for certain statutory provisions) the previous bad character of a person accused of a crime should not be known to the jury before which that accused is to be tried.

ISR : There are rules of conduct in the ordinary laws, and also professional and ethical rules that are an internal matter of the Journalists' Organization; although the Press Council has proved to be efficient in controlling the press, yet it is felt that a code would be better machinery and should also be more comprehensive in dealing with press regulations.

NOR : Rules of press responsibility can best be enforced by emphasizing the interests of the press itself in observing the rules and in doing so voluntarily.

NETHER : For the reasons stated under b) in question No. 13.

PORT : For the reasons stated under a) in question No. 13.

SCOT : Prior publication might influence the public from whom the jury is drawn.

S. A. : Because the various rules of the statute and common law of the Republic of South Africa ensuring free trial, are not consolidated into one statute.

CH : For the reasons stated under b) and c) in question No. 13.

Question No. 14

– *If no,* please state briefly the reasons therefor:

a) because the system in your country appears satisfactory to you;

b) because the moral standard of journalists and owners of newspapers in your country appears to you not to be high enough to hope that a private code of conduct could be respected and enforced (i. e. for commercial reasons; newspapers anxious to increase at any cost their circulation, etc.);

c) because only modifications in the legislation concerning the press appear to you as capable of preventing breaches of privacy committed by certain journalists;

d) other reasons.

Replies to Question No. 14

ENGL : A formal code of conduct would not serve a useful purpose in this country, nor would it be welcome, and indeed might well be less effective than the three factors which at present govern the position in England, namely the high standard of self-discipline of the English Press, the effect of the power of the Court in relation to matters detrimental to the administration of Justice, and the activities of the Press Council which deals with complaints. However, much can be learned by discussion of the different ways in which control is exercised in various countries, suggesting possibly improvement by adoption of methods proved elsewhere.

AUSTR : The system in the Commonwealth and the Australian States appears to be working satisfactorily.

IV. GEOGRAPHICAL SCOPE : INTERNATIONAL OR NATIONAL CODE OF CONDUCT

Question No. 15

– Is it desirable, in your opinion, that a standard code of conduct be drafted with the purpose of being applicable in all countries?
Yes – No.

Replies to Question No. 15

No: D, ENGL, AUSTR, IRAN, IRE, NETHER, SCOT, S. A.

Yes: ÖSTER, DK, AR USA, MASS USA, ISR, NOR, PORT, CH.

Question No. 16

– *If yes,* under which auspices and within which framework should such a draft be prepared?
  – United Nations?
  – Council of Europe?
  – Professional bodies (lawyers, i. e. I. B. A., journalists, i. e. Press Institute; professional associations of journalists, etc.?

Replies to Question No. 16

D : If a standard code should be drafted, the drafting should be entrusted to the International Press Institute.

ENGL : If it were thought desirable after full investigation of the position in all countries that an international code should be brought into being, this should be drafted by professional bodies in conjunction with journalists, the press, etc.

ÖSTER : Such international code should be drafted by the I. B. A. and published under the auspices of the Council of Europe or the United Nations.

DK : The basic principles of an international Code could be usefully discussed at the I. B. A. conferences.

MASS USA : The drafting of an international code could be entrusted to professional bodies.

ISR : The drafting of such code could be entrusted to a combined professional body formed by the I. B. A. and the Press Institute.

NOR : A draft code should be formulated in close cooperation with all the interested professional organizations (journalists, International Press Institute, lawyers, judges, I. B. A., etc.).

PORT : Such a code should be drafted by professional bodies (lawyers : I. B. A., journalists : Press Institute, professional associations of journalists).

CH : Such a code should be drafted by both the United Nations and the Council of Europe.

Question No. 17

– *If no,* is it preferable in your opinion that draft codes of conduct be prepared in each country, taking into account local conditions?

Replies to Question No. 17

D : Yes.

AUSTR : Yes, if codes were to be drafted at all, which is disapproved.

DK : Although an international code containing basic principles might serve a very useful purpose, it is suggested that only basic principles be agreed upon and that it be left to each country to draft its own code to suit local conditions.

AR USA : Yes, an international code could serve as a basis for national codes.

IRAN : It would be preferable that a draft code be prepared in each country taking into consideration certain local conditions and governing laws and customs.

IRE : Each country must have regard to local conditions.

NOR : Many countries would probably have to draft their own codes of conduct, but it might be of good help for them to have an international code as a model.

NETHER : Yes.

SCOT : Yes.

S. A. : It is preferable that draft codes of conduct should be prepared in each country taking into account local conditions.

Question No. 18

– Could such a code co-exist with legislation already in force in your country, complementing the latter?

Replies to Question No. 18

ENGL : Yes.

ÖSTER : Yes.

DK : Yes.

AR USA : Yes.

MASS USA : Yes.

IRAN : Yes.

IRE : Yes.

ISR : Yes.

NOR : Yes.

NETHER : Yes.

PORT : No.

SCOT : The common law rules do not need to be complemented.

S. A. : Yes.

CH : Yes.

Question No. 19

– Do you think that conflicts could arise with respect to the application of these two categories of rules?

Replies to Question No. 19

D : Yes.

ENGL : A code could co-exist with legislation already in force, because presumably such a code would simply represent the formalization of the conventions which have been established in the ways suggested, so that no conflicts would arise.

AUSTR : No.

ÖSTER : No.

DK : The Danish Press Council has so far had no difficulties with regard to the existing Danish legislation when applying the Code.

AR USA : No.

MASS USA : No.

IRAN : This depends on the governing political atmosphere and, for the time being, no.

IRE : No.

ISR : No.

NOR : Probably not. In Norway, there have been no conflicts of this kind.

NETHER : No.

CH : Not if the existing rules apply.

V. SUBJECT MATTERS AND PERSONS TO BE GOVERNED BY SUCH A CODE

Question No. 20

– Should such a code be applicable to all aspects of the professional activity of journalists or only to press reporting of Court proceedings (civil and criminal)?

Replies to Question No. 20

D	:	Such a code should be applicable to all aspects of the professional activity of journalists.
ENGL	:	Such a code should apply to press reporting and also to the means by which the material for reporting is obtained. It presumably needs to cover any matters not actually covered by the law.
AUSTR	:	"All aspects of the professional activities of journalists" are not understood. Journalists normally fall foul of the law of contempt not by their press reporting of Court proceedings but by reporting facts which might distort or hinder a proper trial. The only modification that could be made, would be to restrict the application of the Official Secrets Acts which are constantly misused as a cover-up for politicians.
ÖSTER	:	All aspects of the professional activity of journalists.
DK	:	All aspects of the professional activity of journalists.
AR USA	:	All aspects of the professional activity of journalists.
IRAN	:	All aspects of the professional activity of journalists.
IRE	:	Only concerned with reporting of Court proceedings.
ISR	:	Concern limited to a code in respect of press reporting on Court proceedings, civil and criminal.
NOR	:	All aspects of the professional activity of journalists.
NETHER	:	All aspects of the professional activity of journalists.
PORT	:	All aspects of the professional activity of journalists.
S. A.	:	All aspects of the professional activity of journalists.
CH	:	All aspects of the professional activity of journalists.

Question No. 21

– With respect to reporting of criminal proceedings, would it be proper to provide for special rules governing the various stages of the procedure?

a) pre-trial period: police and investigation

b) trial-judgment

c) after-trial period

Replies to Question No. 21

D	:	No.
ENGL	:	It is of interest to point out that the Criminal Justice Act 1967 has planned certain restrictions on the reporting of certain preliminary criminal proceedings and if publication takes place in contravention of the Act, any proprietor, editor or publisher of the newspaper, or person responsible for broadcasting etc. may be convicted of an offence.
AUSTR	:	No.
ÖSTER	:	No.
DK	:	Yes.
AR USA	:	Yes.
MASS USA	:	For a press-bar code to be practicable it must apply with equal force to the pre-trial period as well as to the trial period. Of less importance is the after-trial period prior to hearing before an appellate body.
IRAN	:	No.
IRE	:	Rules should apply in regard to the pre-trial period and during the trial until judgment. Reporting on after-trial period is not restricted.
ISR	:	No.
NOR	:	The general principles should be the same at all stages of the criminal proceedings, but it would no doubt be an advantage to supplement these principles with special rules for each stage mentioned.
NETHER	:	Yes.
PORT	:	Yes.
SCOT	:	Yes.
S. A.	:	Yes.
CH	:	No.

Question No. 22

– Should the rules contained in such a code be applicable only to journalists (court reporters, etc.) or to any person whose activity would relate to the publication of a newspaper (general manager, publisher, editor-in-chief, owner, printer, etc.)?

Replies to Question No. 22

D	:	The rules should be applicable to general managers, editors, publishers and journalists.
ENGL	:	Publishers, editors-in-chief and anyone responsible in the newspaper and periodical world is liable to the control of the Courts in relation to interference with the course of justice, and there is also control in relation to the law against obscenity.
AUSTR	:	Any person whose activity would relate to the publication of a newspaper or other periodical.
ÖSTER	:	All persons involved in reporting and publications in newspapers and periodicals.
DK	:	The Code should be drafted to cover not only the individual journalist, but also the editor-in-chief.
AR USA	:	The Code should be applicable to all persons engaged in news reporting services.
IRAN	:	Except owner and printer, to all those concerned in this field.
IRE	:	Rules should apply to all persons in the newspaper business, except perhaps the printer.
ISR	:	The rules should be applicable to any person whose activity would relate to publication of a newspaper, including: journalist, reporter, publisher, editor, owner, printer etc. except that the degree of responsibility should vary in respect of the persons mentioned, so that the responsibility of the owner, for example, should not be absolute.
NOR	:	Yes, any person whose activity would relate to the publication of a newspaper.
NETHER	:	Only to journalists.
PORT	:	All persons involved in the publication of a newspaper, with the exception of the printer.

SCOT : The main responsibility should fall on the editor-in-chief.

S. A. : The rules should be applicable to all persons connected with the publication of reports in a newspaper.

CH : All persons connected with the publication of reports in a newspaper.

Question No. 23

– Should such a Code of conduct relate only to written press or also to other communication media (radio, television, cinema news, etc.)?

Replies to Question No. 23

D : Such a Code of conduct should relate to all communication media.

ENGL : To all communication media.

AUSTR : All communication media.

DK : The Code of conduct should also be applicable to other communication media.

AR USA : It should relate to all persons engaged in any phase of news media functions.

MASS USA : It should apply to the publication of news in the press or in the other communication media.

IRAN : All communication media.

IRE : To all means of communication.

ISR : Such a code (one or several) should relate to all means of communications including radio, television, cinema news, books, pamphlets, etc.

NOR : Such a Code of conduct should relate to all communication media. Radio, television and cinema news have a great responsibility for the safeguarding of the rights of fair trial and rights of privacy. Precisely because these media have such great influence on public opinion, any infringement of the rules of fair reporting would entail widespread harm. Should be mentioned in particular problems related to programs involving hidden microphones, concealed cameras or the featuring of persons whose actions and words have been recorded without their knowledge.

NETHER : All communication media.

PORT : All communication media.

SCOT : All communication media.

S. A. : A Code of conduct should relate to all communication media.

CH : All communication media.

Question No. 24

– Would it be better to envisage separate Codes of conduct according to various communication media?

Replies to Question No. 24

D : No.

ENGL : Even if a common Code for all public communication were devised, its application would vary according to the media. Non objectionable matter in a book could be very objectionable in a film or on television.

AUSTR : No.

DK : Special provisions should deal with each communication medium.

AR USA : No.

IRAN : Not necessarily.

IRE : No.

ISR : It is in my opinion necessary to study this problem of the various means of communication before a decision is taken whether to have all the rules in one or separate codes.

NOR : The basic principles are the same for all media aimed at the general public and it is not necessary to let them be governed by separate Codes of conduct. It might be justified to restrict the rules concerning the professional and trade press.

NETHER : Yes, because every medium has its own needs (for example television-reporting of court sessions!)

PORT : No.

SCOT : No.

S. A. : No.

CH : No.

VI. PUNISHMENT

It is assumed that such a Code of conduct would involve the existence of a body entrusted with the supervision of its rules.

Question No. 25

– Do you think that such a function of supervision could be held by a Press Council, similar to those who appear to work satisfactorily in several countries (Denmark, Germany, Israel, Sweden, etc.)?
  Yes – No.

Replies to Question No. 25

D	:	Yes.
ENGL	:	Yes.
AUSTR	:	No, supervision should be left to the Courts of law.
DK	:	Yes.
AR USA	:	Yes.
MASS USA	:	Supervision through Press Councils except in certain limited situations.
IRAN	:	No.
IRE	:	Yes.
ISR	:	The immediate supervision should be held by a Press Council with a right of appeal to the Supreme Court of the country.
NOR	:	Yes.
NETHER	:	Yes.
PORT	:	Yes.
SCOT	:	No.
S. A.	:	No knowledge of the functioning of the Press Council in the countries mentioned but the Republic's Press Board of Reference fulfils a similar function satisfactorily.
CH	:	Yes.

Question No. 26

– Do you think it desirable to entrust with the supervision of such a Code of conduct a joint commission of jurists and journalists, whose powers would not only be ethical, but which would have the right to take certain administrative sanctions? Yes – No.

Replies to Question No. 26

No: D, ENGL, AUSTR, IRE, ISR, NOR, SCOT, CH.
Yes: DK, AR USA, MASS USA, IRAN, NETHER, S. A.

Question No. 27

– Please mention some examples of punishment which should be applied by the body entrusted with the supervision and observance of the rules stated in the Code of conduct.

For example:

a) publication of rectification or excuses by the newspaper which has published an article in breach of the rules laid down by the Code of conduct;

b) reparation to be paid by the newspaper involved to the person who has suffered damages as a consequence of the publication of an article;

c) in case of repetition, the journalist or the newspaper itself could be excluded from membership in the organization entrusted with the supervision and application of the Code of conduct, if it is a professional organization, such as the press council (such a sanction would, of course, only be effective if the press council were to enjoy a real prestige so that the exclusion would constitute a serious penalty of which all journalists and newspapers would be afraid).

Replies to Question No. 27

D : Publication of rectification and revocation of the statement objected to; publication of disapproval by the press council.

ENGL : Publication of apologies; possibly exclusion from membership of the organization.

AUSTR : Publication of rectification or excuses.

DK : Adequate sanctions would be publication of rectifications including the decisions of the Press Council.

AR USA : Punishment should include reparation to individuals injured, and suspension or expulsion from the news media organization of which the responsible individual is a member.

MASS USA : Sanctions might be imposed through Press Councils or through the Courts in certain limited situations.

IRAN : Agree with the examples of punishment given.

IRE : A Press Council could apply its own sanctions. Breach of legislative provisions are dealt with by the Courts.

Examples of Press Council sanctions: publication of rectification or apologies, reparation to be paid to the victim. Exclusion from membership of the professional organization is not very practical.

ISR : Reprimand, suspension of journalist or paper, fines, damages and publication of an apology.

NOR : In Norway, the rules are observed in a satisfactory manner without any provisions for punishment. Among the sanctions mentioned, the one given under a) is considered to be suitable.

NETHER : Publication of apology and payment of damages.

PORT : Agree with the three sanctions mentioned under a), b) and c).

SCOT : Fines and imprisonment.

S. A. : Reprimand, publication of the reprimand and correction to be published where necessary.

CH : Publication of rectification and apology; exclusion from membership of the professional organization.

Question No. 28

– Would you rather think that it would be better to find a means whereby breaches of this Code would be punished by administrative measures?

Replies to Question No. 28

D : No.

ENGL : No.

AUSTR : No.

DK : No, but the person who has been harmed should never be prevented from taking legal action.

AR USA : No.

IRAN : Not necessarily.

SCOT : No.

ISR : May be as a part of the penal means but not as a substitute.

NOR : This question is hard to answer. In Norway there has been no need for measures of this kind as long as the Code has existed.

NETHER : No.

PORT : No.

SCOT : No.

CH : No.

VII. PROPOSALS – CONCLUSION

Question No. 29

– Do you think it desirable to draw up such a Code of conduct prepared on the basis of replies received to this questionnaire?

Replies to Question No. 29

D : The instructions of the Press Council in connection with the jurisdiction of the law Courts lead to a sufficient and satisfactory arrangement. Further measures do not seem necessary.

ENGL : No.

AUSTR : No.

DK : No.

AR USA : A draft Code might be desirable for the purpose of starting intelligent discussions.

IRAN : No.

ÖSTER : Yes.

IRE : Not necessarily.

ISR : No.

NOR : Yes.

NETHER : No.

PORT : Yes.

SCOT : No.

S. A. : No.

CH : Yes.

Question No. 30

– Or, do you think that it would be better to wait for the results of the discussions which will take place in the Dublin Conference, before drafting such a Code?

Replies to Question No. 30

D : Inapplicable

ENGL : It might be better to wait for the results of the discussions which will take place at the Dublin Conference before drafting such a Code.

AUSTR : Interested to hear what the discussions reveal.

ÖSTER : A draft code drawn up on the basis of the answers to the questionnaire, could serve as a basis for discussion at the Dublin Conference.

DK : No draft code should be submitted to the IBA Conference in Dublin. It might, however, serve a useful purpose if the Conference could agree on basic principles for press reporting.

AR USA : Not necessarily. If replies to the questionnaire are adequate, it might be well to present a draft at the Dublin Conference. If replies are inadequate, it would be better to await the results of discussions at Dublin.

IRAN : Yes.

IRE : Yes.

ISR : Yes.

NOR : A draft should be submitted as a basis for further discussions in the Dublin Conference.

NETHER : Yes.

PORT : Yes.

SCOT : Yes.

S. A. : It would be better to wait for the results of the discussions which will take place in the Dublin Conference before drafting a Code of conduct.

CH : The draft should be made now, but discussed in Dublin.

Question No. 31

– Do you think it useful to contact representatives of the press in order to ascertain their position and reaction with respect to such a draft Code of conduct?

Replies to Question No. 31

D : Inapplicable

ENGL : If the Conference was in the main of the opinion that a Code should be drawn up, steps should be taken to implement that decision by the IBA setting up a special Committee which, among other things, would contact representatives of the Press, in order to obtain the reaction of the Press on such proposed Code of conduct.

AUSTR : Representatives of the press differ in their views much as any cross-section of the public will differ, except that they mostly think that they ought to have a right to publish more than the present contempt rules allow them to publish.

ÖSTER : Contacts with press representatives in order to ascertain their views on the proposed draft Code, are desirable.

AR USA : Yes.

MASS USA : Yes.

IRAN : It is a rather wise suggestion but not absolutely imperative or even necessary.

IRE : Not necessarily in this country.

ISR : Yes.

NOR : Yes.

NETHER : Yes.

PORT : Yes.

SCOT : Possibly no.

S. A. : Yes.

CH : Yes.

Question No. 32

– Have you already contacted newspaper people and do you have any idea as to their reaction with respect to this project?

Replies to Question No. 32

D : Inapplicable.

ENGL : No.

ÖSTER : No.

DK : An extension of the authority of the Danish Press Council seems to be acceptable to the majority of the Danish newspapers.

AR USA : No contact has been made with respect to an international Code; however, contact has been made with respect to national codes, and the general attitude seems to be that they are undesirable so far as newspaper people are concerned.

MASS USA : No contact made relative to the questionnaire, but consider that the reaction of the American press would be negative to such a project.

IRAN : No, have not had time to discuss the matter with the competent people; but will do it before the conference.

IRE : No.

ISR : No.

NOR : Yes. Newspaper people welcome IBA's initiative, but any proposed rules should be drafted in close cooperation with the professional bodies of the press and the journalists.

NETHER : No.

PORT : No.

SCOT : Newspaper people are opposed to the rules enforced in this country.

S. A. : Both lawyers and newspaper people in the Republic of South Africa approve of the South African Press Board of Reference's code of conduct.

CH : Yes, the association of the Swiss press.

Question No. 33

– What are, in your opinion, the practical measures which the IBA, National Bar Associations, and jurists in general could take in order to promote the adoption and respect of such a Code of conduct?

Replies to Question No. 33

D : Inapplicable.

ENGL : See reply to question No. 31 above.

AUSTR : None.

DK : See comments under questions 29 and 30.

AR USA : In the U.S. several joint discussions have been held between the news media and domestic bar associations with jurists participating. Generally the jurists and bar associations are in agreement that some form of code should be adopted. The news media people, while accepting the proposition that a code is desirable, have suggested draft codes which are generally innocuous, and which are so vague in scope that they would be generally unenforceable, and even if enforceable would not accomplish the desired end.

IRAN : All authorities concerned should exert their best efforts jointly to attain the desired aim, i. e. to promote the adoption and respect of such a code.

IRE : Press the view on the various press Councils and where same do not exist request the co-operation of the respective Law Societies in each country.

ISR : This is a very difficult question. It is thought that the IBA through the various international channels including the respective committees in the U. N. and the National Bar Associations, may promote the adoption of such a Code of conduct. The National Bar Associations, through the respective committees in their countries' Parliaments and through public opinion may achieve positive results in this respect.

NOR : First of all, it would be necessary to spread information about the Code of conduct and the principles and considerations that have dictated the rules. Representatives of the press should be contacted, the rules should be discussed with them and they should be encouraged to adopt such a Code of conduct. One cannot expect the rules to be generally accepted unless the press itself has cooperated in formulating them and the press organizations have agreed to support them in principle.

NETHER : Public relations contacts with journalists and their organizations.

CH : Recommendations, circulars, articles, local proposals.

SUMMARY OF DISCUSSIONS

The Chairman, *Mr. Zelling*, commenced the meeting at 11.30 a. m., and welcomed the delegates.

The Rapporteur, *Dr. Lalive*, then outlined the main features of his report. He said that fifteen national correspondents had replied to the questionnaire which had been sent to the respective countries prior to the Conference. Subsequently Sweden and Spain had also replied but too late to have their replies included in the printed report. He was anxious to thank the national rapporteurs for their most interesting and useful papers. The discussion today represented an extension of the discussion which arose at the Lausanne IBA Conference in 1966, on the topic "Limits and Restrictions of Public Reporting on Criminal and Civil Court Proceedings". He emphasized that today it was a code of *conduct*, and not a code of law, that was being discussed. The question of such a code of conduct was a controversial but important subject, since it related to three of the fundamental rights of men:

1. — Freedom of the Press and of Information, i. e. the right of the public to have information conveyed and opinions expressed freely;

2. — Fair Trial, that is the right of all men to receive an impartial and just trial without the creation of prejudice or popular or antagonistic emotions;

3. — The right of the individual to privacy, described in the report as the protection of the right of *personality*.

The European Convention for the Protection of Human Rights, representing the law now in force in many European countries, dealt with these freedoms. Freedom of the press was indispensable to any democratic community since, among other things, it was a defence against arbitrary Government. The protection of free speech and opinion was therefore in itself not to be questioned. With regard to fair trial, the Anglo-Saxon doctrine of "contempt of Court" was of great value to prevent some abuses of the free press, but it was perhaps not quite sufficient. It existed only partly in continental Europe; there was therefore room for extending and supplementing this concept and procedure in a number of countries. Furthermore, it was not sufficient to protect a third fundamental human right, less well-known but very important also: the right of privacy, i. e. the right of an individual to protect his private life from outside interference. There was therefore in this area a certain conflict of interests between these three rights, and this was growing more pressing. In countries where trials took place before a jury which should not be influenced beforehand, it was obvious that freedom of the press should be to some extent curtailed in the interest of fair trial. Contempt of Court as a means of controlling the press could be applied strictly or loosely in accordance with the prevailing ethos of the Court.

In civil matters such as divorce and also in relation to publication of matters affecting person's private life, there would appear to be a stronger case for restricting the freedom of the press, since there was no public interest to be protected and the publication of lurid details would serve no useful purpose.

Lawyers must learn to be less conservative in the face of developing technology, for example people's conversation can now be taped or recorded a hundred yards or more away and this sort of abuse should be sevenly punished. Excessive publicity by the press with regard to acts of violence also appeared to be weakening society's defences in this area.

Although some of these points seemed to fall outside the topic under consideration, they were all interlocked. There was therefore, according to a fast growing opinion, a pressing need for some form of legislation on a national or international basis for trying to deal with these problems and reconcile these rights with one another. Or better still, it appeared that a code of conduct should be adopted and that these rules could be upheld in observance by persuasion and possibly by some sanctions. In some countries, press councils exerted some pressure on offending newspapers and other news media. In other countries no restrictions whatever appeared to be placed on the freedom of the press. In other countries again the press was subject to severe restrictions. It did not appear likely at the present stage that a common denominator could be found which would be applicable to all countries.

However there appeared to be a strong case for making some attempt to achieve by a code acceptable standards in this area. Such a code could serve as a model. Its content would seek to ensure that good faith was exercised in reporting and that objectivity was observed in the matter of trials. Privacy should be respected where there was no public interest to divulge news concerning private people, even though this news resulted from a judgment delivered in public.

In short, the subject under review was of the gratest importance in modern society. It was not only a legal, but a social and psychological problem. But lawyers could contribute to its solution with a view to protecting our civilization from obvious abuses and trying to reconcile these three fundamental rights. The questionnaire sent to the national Bars had purported to examine the *lex lata* for the purpose of developing at a later stage a *lex ferenda*. In some countries, a press council had established a code of conduct which represented an interesting experience. But it was not certain that this solution could be extended to all countries.

Mr. Zelling asked the speakers, at the conclusion of Dr. Lalive's address, to direct their attention to the public and private aspects of a code of conduct and to state whether they considered that any abuses should be dealt with by a code or by some other method. With regard to the contents of a code, it would appear to be more a matter for committee work but their views generally on this aspect would be welcomed.

Speakers' Contributions

(for reasons of space not all speakers are included)

USA, Judge Reardon:

Judge Reardon stated that the problem of abuse of the freedom of the press was becoming more acute with the spread of international communication and the spread of international violence and turbulence. He was a member of a special committee dealing with the subject which was established following the assassination of President Kennedy. In America freedom of the press was governed by constitutional limits in many areas of human rights and in the matter of privacy the laws at present were not noticeably inadequate. The major problem in the U. S. was in relation to the conduct of criminal trials. It was the opinion of his committee that the primary responsibility rested with lawyers, officers of the Court and law enforcement agencies. The press in the United States was not enthusiastic about codes of control which deprived the press of sources of information. Freedom of the press was almost sacrosanct in the eyes of many publishers. The speaker considered that codes were good if they could be worked out by agreement as there was a reasonable chance of observance. He thought it would be better to have the code drafted by national agencies in conjunction with the press association.

As to the right of privacy, Judge Reardon said that it would be time enough to consider this aspect when the proper reporting of criminal matters was satisfactorily resolved.

Austria, Dr. Jahoda:

This speaker was of opinion that a code could be used to suit the circumstances of some countries but in Austria no code was necessary. There was complete freedom of the press and abuses could be controlled by law or by private complaint. With regard to private complaint however he was of opinion that it was a useless procedure and reliance should be placed on legal sanctions which were satisfactory in his country. The press was not permitted to intrude on the privacy of the individual. The judges, law officers and magistrates were deeply concerned to see that this right was observed. No comment was allowed by the press on the possibility of a law suit or on the value of any piece of evidence about to be offered in trial. A press council existed in Austria but it was pretty useless so-far as affording any better protection to the individual than that available in the law courts.

England, William O. Carter:

The English system was not perfect but it had many desirable features. There was no formal code of conduct but a press council existed which was established after a Royal Commission had looked into the subject of the freedom of the press in 1949. This press council was designed to raise standards and was in the main the outcome of the initiative of those editors and journalists who sought to ensure that the highest standards be observed in society. In 1953 Lord Devlin, then a Judge of the High Court, was made Chairman of the Council. While no formal code was drawn up by the Council a set of principles have evolved and recently the press council had brought out a book dealing with the history, procedure and cases dealt with by the council. After the Moors Murders Trial two basic principles were laid down by the council: (1) that no offer of payment should be made for the story of witnesses until the evidence was proven in Court: (2) that stories affecting the privacy of people in which there was no element of public interest should be avoided.

Ireland, T. A. Doyle, S. C.:

Mr. Doyle considered that a code was desirable but he drew the meeting's attention to the possibility that in certain circumstances mandatory provisions with regard to publication as well as non publication should be included in such a code. He instanced a case where an action against detergent manufacturers by a woman who had contracted dermatitis was before the High Court in Dublin for a period of nineteen days but no reporting whatsoever of the case took place by the public press. In his view this could have deprived many other victims of dermatitis of their lawful damages.

Rory O'Hanlon, S. C.:

Mr. O'Hanlon said that he was in favour of a code but pointed out that there was a distinction between the Anglo-Saxon countries and the continental position. In Ireland and in England all trials were public but recently legislation was introduced which prohibited preliminary press reports of criminal trials. On the continent however a distinction was made between public law and private law. Private law was generally concerned in the continent with litigation between two individuals. In Ireland the legal system did not offer relief against press reports of such litigation and in his view a code could eliminate this type of publicity. For example persons in the professions could be subjected to blackmail by unscrupulous litigation against them. A professional man who was not guilty of negligence would, as a result of adverse publicity of a case taken against him by a difficult client, be marked for the rest of his professional life with some suspicion. There would appear to be need to have a judicial discretion vested in the Court to prohibit publication at the request of one of the parties to a civil action. He felt that there was a case for drawing up an international press convention on the lines of the Conventions drafted by the Council of Europe to which nations could subscribe in accordance with their internal circumstances and as standards of behaviour impsoved.

Sweden, Ove Wickman:

Mr. Wickman said that freedom of the press was one of the four basic freedoms enshrined in Swedish legislation. In his country there existed a "Court of Honour" of the Swedish Press which was representative of the press and journalists with an impartial chairman who was generally a leading jurist and at present a Judge of the Supreme Court. The Board published from time to time pronouncements dealing with abuses of press conduct and this served as a salutary restraint on irresponsible press reporting.

Very recently the recommendation was made that the Board should have the right to sanction damages in certain circumstances. He approved this development.

Denmark, Thomas Federspiel:

The speaker considered that there was grave need to look at the right of privacy very closely. Generally more importance was attached to other rights but with the growth of modern technology the right of privacy was becoming a most important area. In his view abuses of the right of privacy should be resolved by appropriate legislation. Other problems however should be governed by codes on conduct to be observed by the press. He did not believe it realistic that a press code could be adopted by the IBA but recommendations might be made which might serve as a general code, to be amended and adapted to suit local conditions. In his country newspapers and the press council were negotiating with each other to broaden the role of the press council in many areas at present outside its scope.

South Africa, Mr. Switches:

He emphasized that some balance should be realized between the right of fair trial and the right of free expression of the organs of the press or other information. There was in South Africa a press council which had set up the highest standard of reportage. Lawyers should similarly establish higher standards of self-conduct and discipline. In his opinion, it would be sufficient to set up some general rules concerning these rights.

Netherlands, Pieter de Braun:

He wished to emphasize one point. The presence of the press at a trial could impede a fair trial. Witnesses, juries and other were influenced to a large or small extent by the fact that proceedings were published. He considered that some international organization should take the matter up to see how publicity could be controlled in this matter in the interests of fair trial.

Iran, Dr. Ahmad Houman:

Criminology research had shown that crimes tended to grow following publication of acts of violence and details of murders. The factors governing a code of conduct must differ in each country having regard to religious, moral, social and cultural differences. In Iran they had a conservative press council co-existing with a conservative judiciary with the result that many matters which progressive-minded people considered should not be made public were reported in the press without remedy. The press council believed for example that illicit relationships indulged in by women should be published in the interests of the religious code so as to prevent other members of the community from following their example and in effect to isolate such women, rather cruelly, in the interest of conservative standards of conduct. It was vital that teachers and the profession should begin to educate the public in the fields of modern, social science and to provide information about the contributions being made by psychology, criminology and sociology in matters affecting human behaviour. He was of opinion that the press council should comprise a judge of the High Court, a psychologist, a journalist and representatives of the publishers.

USA (Texas), Robert Storey:

Referring to the extensive work done by the American Bar Association on this topic, he expressed his preference for the drawing up of standards of conduct rather than legislation.

International Commission of Jurists,
Mr. Sean McBride, Secretary General:

Mr. McBride thanked the IBA for having initiated the discussion on this very important topic. The problem was a complex one and had been the subject of study by his organization. They would be pleased to work with the IBA on the problems involved. It was hard to reconcile a code of conduct governing both criminal trials and the right of privacy and possibly the two subject should be treated separately. The United Kingdom had done a lot of useful work. Possibly discussion with international press agents, the International Press Institute, and the International Union of Journalists (and also the International Association of

Democratic Journalists) could result in a draft code of conduct which would be of value to each country.

Dr. Lalive summed up and stated that a shift of emphasis had manifested itself at today's meeting in contrast with the discussion at the Lausanne Conference two years ago. He thought a gap had existed in the discussion, namely that nobody had developed what he thought should be included in a code of conduct. However today's discussion represented but one step in a much longer debate. He wished to see a steering committee of the IBA agree in principle to the drafting of a code which would not necessarily be a legally binding one. It was not desirable to proliferate legislation, although in some countries strong legislation might be necessary to deal with an unscrupulous press. The danger of any limitation of the freedom of the press and of information was of course to be taken into account. A code adopted by an international Conference in plenary session could set up a chain reaction which would have a profound influence for good in countries which required improvement in such matters. Such countries were numerous. If the abuse continued, governments and parliaments themselves might decide to take action, and this would give rise to another danger to the fundamental right of free press. In other words, the difficulty was to strike the right balance and to achieve co-ordination between the various rights. He wished to put it to the officers of the International Bar Association that they proceed with the work of drafting such a document. He agreed that as the question now arose, it had diverged from the question of fair trial only into the wider subject of the protection of individual privacy, but, as had been seen, to a large extent these rights were interconnected and it was best to look at such matters in a peaceful environment and in a dispassionate way rather than wait for discussion of the problem in turbulent times.

Dr. Lalive concluded by thanking the Chairman of the meeting for his assistance and support. The meeting conveyed their thanks to Dr. Lalive with acclamation.

Summary

This Working Session recommends as follows:

1. – That there is a demonstrated need for some form of code in relation to a fair trial and free press.

2. – That a Committee of the IBA be set up to draft recommendations for such a code and send the draft down to constituent bodies for consideration and report to the next general meeting of the IBA.

3. – That such committee consider (inter alia):
   (a) Whether the interest of the public is best served by a voluntary or compulsory code.

(b) Whether the enforcement of such a code should be by the Courts of Law, a press council, or in some other and if so what manner.

(c) Whether the preservation of the right to privacy should be dealt with in such a code or by legislation.

(d) Whether such a code would be national or international in operation.

PLENARY SESSION

THE LEGAL PROFESSION

(a) WHAT STEPS CAN BE TAKEN TO ENSURE THAT THE PROFESSION KEEPS UP TO DATE IN ITS KNOWLEDGE OF LEGISLATION

(b) THE ROLE OF THE BAR ASSOCIATION IN THE CHANGING WORLD AND ITS RESPONSIBILITIES IN THE DEVELOPING COUNTRIES

Chairman: Nai Sansern Kraichitti (Thailand)
Rapporteur: Sir Thomas Lund, C. B. E. (England)
Vice-Chairman: William Oscar Carter, Esq. (England)

Country	*National Correspondents*
Australia	W. B. Campbell, Esq., Q. C.
Austria	RA Dr. Harald Foglar-Deinhardstein
Canada	D. Donald Diplock, Esq., Q. C.
Denmark	Sec.-Gen. Poul Ostergaard
England	W. W. Boulton, Esq. (General Council of the Bar) William Oscar Carter, Esq. (The Law Society) Sir Thomas Lund, C. B. E. (The Law Society)
Finland	Asianajaja Mauri Hakapää
France	Maître Denis de Ricci
Germany	RA Dr. Heinz Brangsch
India	A. N. Veeraraghaven, Esq.
Iran	Dr. Ebrahim Taghvaii
Ireland	Brendan A. McGrath, Esq. (The Incorporated Law Society of Ireland) Dermot P. Shaw, Esq. (The Incorporated Law Society of Ireland)
Israel	Dr. A. Arazi, Advocate
Japan	Judge Keizo Kanno
Lebanon	Mr. Mounir Shehadi
Mexico	Sr. Lic. D. Salvador Compéan

Netherlands	Mr. W. van der Meij
New Zealand	G. J. Seeman, Esq.
Northern Ireland	A. Campbell, Esq.
Norway	H. r. advocat Rolf Christophersen
Philippines	Roman Ozaeta, Esq. (Philippine Bar Association)
	Dr. Tomás V. Barnes (Philippine Lawyers' Ass'n)
	Lorenzo M. Tañada, Esq. (Philippine Bar Association)
Portugal	Prof. Dr. Adelino da Palma Carlos
Scotland	D. A. O. Edward, Esq. (Faculty of Advocates)
	Robert Bertram Laurie, Esq., W. S. (The Law Society)
South Africa	Eben Louw, Esq.
Spain	Sr. Lic. D. Eugenio Mazon Verdejo
Sweden	Advokat Arthur Boström
Switzerland	Dr. G. Hochstrasser, Fürsprecher
Thailand	Nai Sansern Kraichitti
Turkey	Avukat Rahmi Magat
U. S. A.	Orison S. Marden, Esq. (American Bar Association)
	F. Trowbridge vom Baur, Esq. (Federal Bar Ass'n)

Answers from Non-Member Organizations

Australia	The Law Institute of Victoria
Canada	The Law Society of Alberta
	The Law Society of British Columbia
	The Bar of the Province of Quebec
Fiji	Fiji Law Society
Hong Kong	The Incorporated Law Society of Hong Kong
India	The Bar Association of India
Ireland	Tipperary Sessional Bar Association
Kenya	The Law Society of Kenya
Malaya	Bar Council (States of Malaya)
Malta	Camera degli Avvocati
Mauritius	Mauritius Bar Association
Nigeria	Nigeria Bar Association
Rhodesia	The Law Society of Rhodesia
Singapore	Singapore Advocates and Solicitors Society
Tanganyika	The Tanganyika Law Society
U. S. A.	The Association of the Bar of the City of New York
West Indies	The Trinidad Incorporated Law Society
Zambia	The Law Society of Zambia

THE LEGAL PROFESSION – WHAT STEPS CAN BE TAKEN TO ENSURE THAT THE PROFESSION KEEPS UP TO DATE IN ITS KNOWLEDGE OF LEGISLATION?

Report

submitted by THOMAS LUND,
Solicitor of the Supreme Court of Judicature, London,
England

INTRODUCTION

1. A detailed questionnaire was sent out to all member Bar Associations to obtain the data necessary for the preparation of this Report. Of the 56 organizations approached the 18 organizations listed in the Appendix to this Report responded before 1st May, 1968 when this Report was prepared. The information set out below relates solely to the associations from whom replies have been received.

2. The purposes of the enquiry are: –

i) to determine whether the provision of a continuing education programme is an accepted responsibility of Bar Associations;

ii) to determine what continuing education programmes are provided by Bar Associations;

iii) to obtain and discuss suggestions as to how the legal profession can best be kept up-to-date in its knowledge of law, practice, and procedure; and

iv) to ascertain whether, and if so what, research is undertaken to determine what is the present demand for legal services and whether the requirements are likely to alter in the future.

THE ACCEPTANCE OF RESPONSIBILITY BY BAR ASSOCIATIONS FOR PROVISION OF A CONTINUING EDUCATION PROGRAMME

3. It would appear that 14 of the 18 Bar Associations replying to the questionnaire generally accept this responsibility. In the Philippines the Bar Association accepts no responsibility for continuing education and the State University, supported mainly by Government funds, provides the programme through the Division of Continuing Legal Education of its Law Centre; in Scotland The Law Society of Scotland organizes lectures to keep members advised of the more important

changes in the law but considers it the responsibility of individual lawyers to keep up-to-date their knowledge of legislation by their own efforts. This view is shared by the General Council of the Bar in England

In Japan the Japan Bar Association has as its main objective the cultivation of mutual friendship among the profession and accepts no particular responsibility for keeping its members up-to-date with legislation. However, The Japan Federation of Bar Associations arranges special lecture courses throughout the country and judges and public prosecutors are specifically catered for by two specialist organizations. For judges the Supreme Court and the Legal Training and Research Institute arrange research conferences and discussion meetings and also distribute collections of judicial precedents and other data. The Ministry of Justice and the Research and Training Institute which is attached to it carry out a similar programme for public prosecutors.

Other bodies sometimes assist in the programme and offer facilities which complement those of the Bar Association. For instance, in New Zealand the New Zealand Council of Law Reporting assists the New Zealand Law Society; in Israel the Ministry of Justice shares the programme; in India the Indian Law Institute offers some facilities for lawyers.

4. Many countries have a system whereby there is a main (or Federal) Bar Association supported by numerous smaller regional Societies of lawyers in the provinces, districts, cantons, states. In the larger countries or those where lawyers are widespread and not concentrated in a few centres, these regional Societies must necessarily play an essential part in any continuing education programme if it is to be available on a country-wide basis. In such cases, although the Federal Organization accepts responsibility for providing a continuing education programme, it may be difficult or impossible for it to ensure that all regional societies provide a similar standard of education for members or even that any programme or a sufficiently complete programme is in being.

In fact, in most of the countries about which details are known the regional Societies do provide some continuing educational facilities for their members. This is done either on a "sub-contractual" basis with regional Societies arranging courses/meetings in their areas in the form and on topics suggested by the main or federal Bar Association or the regional Societies devise and arrange the meetings independently.

For example in Germany the Deutscher Anwaltverein as head organization of 180 local Societies itself provides courses of different types and duration and also assists the local organizations by suggesting topics for lectures, by preparing video-tapes for use by all, and by supplying outlines of lectures to the young lawyers. The local Associations arrange other courses regionally. The situation is similar in England, France, the Netherlands, New Zealand and Switzerland. In particular in the Netherlands, the implementation of the continuing education programme is almost entirely left to local societies.

5. The actual programme provided by each organization and its implementation are discussed later in this Report but it may be convenient at this point to consider whether the responsibility for providing such a programme should rest on the Bar Association or whether a more effective method of ensuring the continuing education of the legal profession would be for some other body e. g. a department of the Law Faculty of a University, to devote itself whole-time to the project. Is it necessary or desirable that the members of Bar Associations through payment of membership subscriptions should finance the programme? As the financing of Legal Aid Plans more and more becomes a responsibility of the State should the State assume also responsibility for financing the further education of lawyers?

The inherent difficulty in this proposal is not from the financial aspect but from the view point that the independence of lawyers is essential to the proper administration of any legal system and "state training" might be the first steps towards the nationalization of the legal profession: a prospect that is obviously unwelcome and undesirable in a free society.

THE CONTINUING EDUCATION PROGRAMMES CURRENTLY PROVIDED BY BAR ASSOCIATIONS

6. An analysis of the media employed by Bar Associations in their continuing education programmes is set out in the Appendix. Broadly speaking the continuing education programmes take the form of lectures or seminars on subjects of practical application, supplemented by various publications and reports of decided cases, changes in the Law and practice or procedure. The various media used are: —

(i) *Lectures and Lecture Courses*

All Bar Associations, with the exceptions of the Philippines Bar Association, The Japan Bar Association, the Bar Councils in England and Northern Ireland and the Faculty of Advocates in Scotland, arrange for lectures or talks either singly or as part of a course. In some cases the lectures given to one group of members are tape-recorded or prints of them are supplied for use by others after the first delivery of the talk.

Prints of lectures are widely used and distributed either free or at a small charge to cover printing costs. This is a means of ensuring that local societies which might not otherwise be in a position to afford their services have the opportunity of hearing learned and well-known speakers talking on specialised subjects, and enables the speaker who is only physically able to be present at a few centres, to deliver a number of talks over a period to reach a larger audience.

Residential courses, weekend courses or weekend "schools" and seminars are increasingly popular with legal professions in many countries, offering as they do an opportunity to study a topic in depth and to devote attention full-time to, for example, some complex new legislation hurriedly brought into effect (which appears to be the curse of lawyers in many countries). Such courses are held in varied surroundings – in University halls of residence, in hotels, in specialised conference centres. There are courses arranged by Bar Associations, local Societies, specialist membership "Groups" of Bar Associations or by commercial undertakings providing facilities for others as well as for lawyers.

Most courses are concerned only with a limited number of topics chosen for reasons of current interest or difficulty and specially prepared papers are delivered by the instructor. In most cases this is followed by discussion – in some cases by all those attending or (and this may be a more satisfactory way) by smaller groups of the delegates who later congregate again when a general discussion follows, which can be restricted more easily to the main issues rather than dealing with abstruse points which will have been dealt with in the smaller groups.

The Law Society (England) and the Norwegian Bar Association find it helpful to distribute in advance of a lecture a summary of points prepared by the lecturer which are a valuable aid to concentration during the course of the lecture. On occasions advance reading is also suggested.

All Bar Associations chiefly use practising lawyers as lecturers but academic lawyers from Universities and the Government administration and lawyers on the staff of Bar Associations are also used as are members of other professions, e. g. Accountants and Surveyors, where the topic chosen involves some other profession.

Although the topics discussed are generally confined to a particular branch of the law, both The Law Societies in England and Scotland and the American and German Bar Associations provide, or are considering providing lectures on office efficiency and management. The American Bar Association and the Law Society (England) have also organized lectures on Public Relations. In addition the German Bar Association includes topics which although not strictly concerned with the law are, nevertheless, of legal importance, e. g. ski law, wine law, art law. The Secretary of the Bar Association states that such lectures are extremely successful, one of their chief advantages being the value of bringing together lawyers with a common interest.

All Bar Associations state that lectures and lecture courses are extremely well supported and almost all appear to be considering some extension of their continuing education programme.

(ii) *Publications*

In addition to prints of lectures, another extensively used method of disseminating information is that of the Bar Association journal or newsletter containing notes and articles on current legal problems, new legislation, court decisions and procedural points. The Norwegian Bar Association publishes two reference books which give information on current legislation, literature, case law, and administrative regulations. These books are brought up-to-date bi-annually. Other facilities of this type include periodicals and text books available from law publishers and other sources, e. g. "Current Law" in England, the United States "Law Week" and the "Criminal Law Reporter" issued in the U. S. A. by the Bureau of National Affairs.

(iii) *Visual Aids*

The German and American Bar Associations alone make use of videotapes to supplement the information given and to add interest to lectures. The German Bar Association has, at present eight such lectures which are distributed to local organizations throughout the country. Lectures with films are in national use but in view of the expense of preparation and the speed with which they become out-of-date they tend to be prepared for the instruction not only of lawyers, but also of banks, commercial concerns, and other financial advisors, and may therefore be rather less detailed than if prepared for lawyers alone, although useful as a means of maintaining interest during the period of study. Videotapes have the advantages of being easily adapted to keep them up-to-date and of being cheaper to produce. The American Bar Association is in fact the only Association to make any real use of films which are prepared by the Association's own staff with the assistance of an educational film company. These films are hired out to other professions, as well as to State Bar Associations at a cost of $ 3 per viewer, with a minimum charge of $ 100 which includes a study outline for each viewer.

(iv) *Radio and Television*

These media are not used at all by any Bar Association for the education of their members. Various reasons are given, the main objection being the dangers of misleading the lay public or their misunderstanding of information intended for experts and the encouragement of "do it yourself" law. Another reason for not using television or radio is that the potential audience is too small to make the undertaking an economic proposal.

(v) *Programmes by Specialist Groups of Bar Associations*

Some Bar Associations have specialist groups meeting regularly to discuss and hear lectures on topics relating to a particular branch of the law. Membership is normally open to any member of the Bar Association specialising in that field of law. For example, company law, commercial law, matrimonial law, or taxation. Such lawyers need special facilities to assist them in keeping up-to-date in their particular fields and therefore require a programme which is restricted in scope but containing more precise details than the more general programme furnished for the "general practitioners of law".

In many countries there are also organizations open to membership by lawyers providing lectures and discussion groups on subjects of interest to lawyers, for example, in England there exists the British Academy of Forensic Sciences which is of particular interest to lawyers concerned with medical and scientific evidence involved in criminal or civil proceedings.

In many countries, for example the Netherlands, Ireland, the U. S. A. and England, Young Lawyers' Associations or Groups play a large part in any programme by arranging courses, lectures, conferences and discussions for their members specifically directed at the younger age groups. In some cases these courses take the form of "further" rather than "continuing" education in that the aim is to supplement the basic legal knowledge with subjects not specifically included in the syllabus of the Qualifying Examinations.

COST OF CONTINUING EDUCATION PROGRAMMES

7. From the information received it is impossible to give any comprehensive picture of the cost of such programmes nor is it possible to indicate the average charge made to participants other than to say that if any charge is made it is usually merely to cover administrative expense so that no Bar Association receives large profits from these activities. Indeed in some cases the costing of the programme is such that little if any profit ever results and sometimes a deficit is made. Examples of the cost of attending part of the programme in various countries are set out in the Appendix.

THE RESEARCH CURRENTLY BEING UNDERTAKEN BY BAR ASSOCIATIONS TO ASCERTAIN THE PRESENT DEMAND FOR LEGAL SERVICES AND POSSIBLE FUTURE REQUIREMENTS

8. It appears that very little if any research is being undertaken by Bar Associations apart from the setting up of Committees to look into certain aspects of future practice. An example of this are the Special

Committees on The Future of the Profession set up by The Law Societies in England and Scotland to consider what changes are necessary in the training of lawyers in the light of a forecast of what the future demands on the profession for legal services are likely to be. The Danish and Netherlands Bar Associations have set up Special Committees to examine ways in which their continuing education programmes can be extended and the Israel Bar Association is planning an extension of their programme to aid new immigrants, who are often lawyers of long standing, to enable them to acclimatize themselves as quickly as possible to the laws and structure in Israel. The Law Society (England) is considering the problem created by new legislation which frequently affects members of the public in ways of which they have no knowledge unless its implication is specifically brought to their attention. Some lawyers' firms in England already circularise their existing clients with details of legislation which affects them, without first having been asked for advice on the point in question. The Law Society is considering making available to legal firms at their request an information service for the benefit of their clients.

However, in the U.S.A. considerable work has been done and the American Bar Foundation, an independent legal research organization with an annual budget of $ 445,000, conducts research at the request of the American Bar Association. In 1965 this Association set up a Special Committee on Availability of Legal Services 'with authority to study and make recommendations with respect to the adequacy and availability of legal services to all who need such services'. The Committee considers among other things:

i) the extent of unfilled needs for legal services;

ii) the adequacy of existing methods and institutions for providing legal services;

iii) means of improving such methods and institutions;

iv) whether new methods and institutions are required; and

v) whether group legal service plans are needed and may be established with appropriate safeguards to preserve ethical values of the profession and protect the public.

A legal research foundation has recently been formed in Auckland, New Zealand, who publish a current legislation service and undertake the organization of two or three-day conferences on specialist topics, particularly business law.

9. Other than in America and England no research appears to have been undertaken into the use of computers as a means of assisting lawyers to keep up-to-date with their knowledge of legislation although the German Bar Association have set up a Special Committee to watch

developments. Possibilities that have been discussed are a centralised computer system for storing the legal knowledge of experts for the use of less specialised lawyers when the need arises. Reports of decided cases might be fed into 'memory banks' and categorised together with all legislation concerning that point so that a lawyer with a particular problem to solve would be saved the trouble of research and could be supplied with the necessary data which had been sifted to a certain extent by the computer. It is not suggested that such a system could ever replace the lawyer but it could at a cost save valuable time which would enable the lawyer to devote his thoughts to the most appropriate remedies rather than spend long periods in searching through his library.

HOW CAN THE LEGAL PROFESSION BEST BE KEPT UP-TO-DATE IN ITS KNOWLEDGE OF LAW, PRACTICE AND PROCEDURE?

10. The majority of programmes at present in being concentrate on courses or single lectures that provide for the lawyer who requires a precis of new law correlated to existing legislation, designed to fill the gaps in his knowledge and to call to his attention new points of procedure and practice so that he can, at a later time, study the relevant provisions in detail. The more developed programmes also provide for a regular review of the law and any changes over a period e. g. the annual "Autumn Refresher Course" of six lectures arranged by The Law Society (England) spread over a period of about six weeks. The Law Society's College of Law also provides annual "Crash Courses" viz. these are ten lectures on selected practical subjects concentrated into a period of two days requiring full-time attendance by the participants. The German and American Bar Associations similarly arrange courses of lengths varying from two to fourteen days on a residential basis.

11. In all the countries concerned the most extensively used form of teaching is that of the lecture where a number of lawyers sit in a room and listen to an address by one man. If the lecturer is a good speaker and teacher, the interest of his audience is maintained and something is learned; but if the speaker, although an acknowledged expert in his field, is not a good lecturer and does not possess those skills so vital to maintain interest, the attention of his audience will wander to other matters like office problems, clients' affairs, the golf course.

12. One of the most important considerations to be taken into account to ensure successful teaching is the means by which the audience can be assisted in concentrating its mind on the theme of the study session.

It is here that audio-visual aids such as video-tapes and films are useful as the pictorial illustration of points involved eases concentration. In addition the human memory frequently is more able to retain information in picture form than in merely words or written material. Thus the use of video-tapes should be encouraged. It is surprising that only the German and American Bar Associations make any use of this medium although the Federal Swiss Bar Association is showing a film at a Conference to be held this summer.

13. Residential courses have many advantages not the least of which is complete separation from office worries and interruptions so that the participants may devote their whole attention to study. Another advantage is the opportunity of meeting and exchanging information with lawyers from other districts with similar interests. It is debatable whether only one theme or topic should be studied. If a single theme is the subject of the course it can be considered in detail but there is a danger of the conferees becoming bored. The study of a number of topics offers an opportunity to assimilate greater knowledge and may well make the course attractive to an increased number of lawyers. However, conferees may attend only those sessions in which they are personally interested so that the rest of the course is of no help to them.

14. In selecting the subject it is necessary to give attention to general practical information, to new legislation and to a review of particular topics in the light of new laws affecting them. It is also becoming increasingly necessary that lawyers should have knowledge of matters other than those of a strictly legal nature. As office units become larger a new science evolves — that of office administration and management techniques. This applies not only to lawyers' offices but also to the running of other concerns. Many lawyers are employed full-time in the legal departments of commercial business undertakings and in Government Departments and the lawyer should be equipped to play his part in the administration of the whole concern.

Such skills are partly instinctive and may be developed during legal training but as the need for persons capable of administration in large organizations grows so does the need for specialists and specialist training in this field.

In addition, in order to be able to advise clients in all walks of life, a lawyer must have as wide a general knowledge as possible and to develop this he needs to be offered opportunities of learning something of other subjects. To advise an engineer whose machine has caused injury he needs to understand how the mechanical device works; to help a businessman arrange a partnership with another he may need to know the pitfalls to be guarded against in the particular trade.

It is notable that only The Law Societies in England and Scotland and the German and American Bar Associations include any non-legal subjects in their continuing education programmes. For the most part Bar Associations appear to rely on other organizations in their countries assisting lawyers in this respect.

TENTATIVE CONCLUSIONS

1. It appears that the majority of Bar Associations accept responsibility for providing a continuing education programme, often assisted by outside local societies, specialist groups of members and outside bodies.

2. The programmes are mainly directed towards considering important changes in case law or legislation. Attempts to add to the knowledge of lawyers gained in their qualifying examinations by providing lectures on non-legal subjects such as office management and efficiency are confined to the Law Societies in England and Scotland and the German and American Bar Associations. In this modern day and age lawyers must of necessity become also men of affairs and it is surprising that so few continuing education programmes help to equip them to play a part in commercial life.

3. In no country are lawyers required to participate in a continuing education programme and it would appear that no Bar Association is considering whether for example it would be desirable to impose a compulsory course after, possibly, 10 years of practice leading to the award of a diploma without which lawyers would be precluded from further practice.

4. In the absence of such compulsion it is left to Bar Associations to try to make their continuing education programmes as attractive as possible. It is all the more surprising that only the German and American Bar Associations use visual aids to add interest to their lectures.

5. Research into the use of computers as an aid to keeping lawyers up-to-date with new case laws and legislation is entirely neglected in all countries other than America, England and Germany. The developments in this field should be watched closely as, if it is found that computers can be successfully used for this purpose, Bar Associations must know how to take advantage of this development in modern science.

The Appendix to this Report is published on the last pages of this book.

THE ROLE OF THE BAR ASSOCIATION IN A CHANGING WORLD AND ITS RESPONSIBILITIES TO THE DEVELOPING COUNTRIES

Report

of the Rapporteur THOMAS LUND, Solicitor of the Supreme Court
of Judicature, London
England

INTRODUCTION

1. The objects of including this subject for discussion by members of the International Bar Association are —:

1) To enable such members each to take stock of their own position in the light of: —

(a) the role being played by other Law Societies and Bar Associations across the world, and

(b) any trends which on enquiry are shown to have developed over recent years; and

2) To enable the Law Societies and Bar Associations in the developing countries to consider: —

(a) the steps which they might take and in what order to produce a strong body of lawyers in the light of: —

(i) a knowledge of what others are doing or are thinking of doing, and

(ii) the opinions of others as regards the relative importance of the functions which they discharge; and

(b) possible ways of obtaining practical assistance from the better organized and more experienced associations which may be able and willing to assist.

2. With these objectives in mind, a questionnaire was sent to the President and Secretary of 180 Law Societies and Bar Associations throughout the world, whether or not they were members of the I. B. A.

This questionnaire is in very general terms. It groups a number of broadly defined topics under one or other general headings inviting a 'yes' or 'no' answer and therefore needs a great deal of detailed development before a really full picture can be obtained of the parts played by the organized Bar in the world today.

3. No question is included on the subject of "Continuing Education" (i. e. post-graduate education for the practising lawyer) as this topic is the subject of a separate session at the Conference and another very detailed questionnaire has been circulated in respect of it. The subject must, however, be borne in mind in connection with the present topic.

4. This Report is divided into two parts dealing respectively with the two parts of the topic under consideration. In Appendix I, there is set out an analysis of the number of Law Societies and Bar Associations undertaking the various activities listed, the number of such Societies which have undertaken each within the last five years, and the number which are considering further extension of their work.

The last column shows the extent to which the Societies regard their several functions as being of fundamental importance to the profession.

5. The direct answers to the Questionnaire received before 1st May, 1968 when this Report was completed are set out in summary form in Appendix II. Although 43 Law Societies and Bar Associations responded, unfortunately no replies were received from several of the leading members of the I. B. A., as will be apparent. Of those which replied, 5 are local, State or Provincial Law Societies or Bar Associations and are from countries which are not represented amongst the member organizations of the I. B. A. The information set out below relates solely to the associations from whom replies have been received.

Part II of this Report contains an examination of the responsibility of Bar Associations to the developing countries and raises certain points for discussion at the Conference.

PART I

6. Before attempting an analysis of the functions at present performed it may be convenient to consider the respects in which Bar Associations have recently extended their activities and what further extensions are now under consideration.

7. Ten societies have embarked upon promulgating rules of professional conduct within the last five years, 9 societies have started to engage in Law Reform activities and of the various societies concerned with (i) enquiries into character of new entrants to the profession (ii) control of education, training and examination (iii) admission (iv) fixing of fees (v) protection of the profession against encroachment (vi) arbitration between members (vii) library facilities (viii) publication of annual reports and legal journals (ix) administration of legal aid (x) arranging conferences for members and (xi) encouraging formation of

Affiliated or Regional Groups of the profession — at least 6 have started upon each of these activities within the same period of five years.

PRESENTLY UNDER CONSIDERATION

8. A significant clue to one present trend affecting the profession lies in the fact that although only associations have made arrangements for special rates of insurance against professional negligence, 6 other associations have this matter under active consideration. Again, 5 associations are considering the provision of bursaries for students (7 only already provide them) and another 5 are considering the establishment of a reference library.

In addition to a current 25 societies administering legal aid in Civil matters, a further 4 are now in the process of undertaking this work. An extension into each of the following fields of activity is now in contemplation by at least 3 societies: —

I Office efficiency
II Training unqualified staff
III An appointments registry
IV Office accommodation for members
V Catering facilities
VI Protection against encroachment
VII Employment of Public Relations Consultants
VIII Creating Sectional or Regional groups of lawyers

WORK CURRENTLY PERFORMED

9. SELECTION, EDUCATION, TRAINING AND EXAMINATION OF LAW STUDENTS

57 per cent of the Bar Associations conduct enquiries into the suitability and fitness of proposed entrants to the profession, 50 per cent supervise the training of law students, whilst 48 per cent conduct or lay down the standards of the qualifying examinations. Approximately 39 per cent consider these three activities as being of fundamental importance.

The Israeli Bar Association, in addition to undertaking these functions, also organizes special professional courses for immigrant advocates.

In Kenya, Malaysia, Singapore, Tanzania and the State of Victoria, Australia the Bar Associtions nominate representatives on to a Government appointed Council of Legal Education which is responsible for the selection, education, and training of law students. In the State of Queensland, Australia, the control of entry into the profession is within the province of a Solicitors' Board on which The Law Society of Queensland is represented.

Although in the United States the local Bar Associations conduct examinations and make enquiries into the suitability of entrants into the profession, the American Bar Association recommends the general standards of all examinations and approves law schools and establishes their standards.

In India the Bar Associations of the several States control the training and examinations for admission in their own State subject to the over-riding control and supervision of the Bar Council of India.

Only the Thai Bar, The Law Institute of Victoria, (Australia), the American Bar Association and the Law Societies of Alberta (Canada) Ireland, England and New Zealand administer bursaries or scholarships for law students and, surprisingly, only 21 per cent encourage or assist in the running of law students societies.

10. CONTROL OVER PRACTISING LAWYERS

76 per cent of Bar Associations lay down rules of professional ethics and 50 per cent regard this activity as being of fundamental importance. In the majority of countries the task of enforcing these rules rests with the Courts as opposed to the Bar Association itself.

55 per cent control the admission to the profession but in a number of countries this is done by the Minister for Justice or some other Government official, usually after seeking the views of the Bar Association on the suitability of the applicant.

Of the Bar Associations replying from the developing countries only the Bar Associations in India, Malta, Singapore and Thailand and the Law Societies in Fiji, Tanzania, and Trinidad admit to the profession.

II. EDUCATION OF UNQUALIFIED STAFF IN LAWYERS' OFFICES

Only 10 per cent of the Bar Associations are concerned in any way with the training or education of unqualified staff in lawyer's offices and only 4 per cent regard this as an important function of Bar Associations. In England, The Law Society is concerned in an advisory capacity with the examinations for unqualified staff conducted by a separate institute formed with the assistance of the Society in 1960 to promote the interests of such staff. The Law Society of Scotland itself conducts examinations for unqualified staff, whilst the Danish Bar Association has supported the formation of a company which runs a school for lawyers' secretarial staff.

In Switzerland secretarial staff in lawyers' offices are required to serve a three-year apprenticeship and to pass an examination. During this period the apprentice attends a course one day a week for instruction in law and commercial matters. These courses are financially supported by the Bar Association.

12. PROFESSIONAL BUSINESS

Both the fixing (or being instrumental in fixing) scales of fees and the protection of the profession from encroachment by other organizations or persons undertaking legal work is carried out by approximately 67 per cent of the Bar Associations. About 35 per cent consider these to be among the most important functions of a Bar Association. Efforts to improve the business efficiency of the profession are only made by 18 per cent of the Bar Associations. This service is provided by most of the European Associations including The Law Society in England (which has a special department trained for the purpose) and by the American, Australian, Canadian, and New Zealand Associations. Apart from these only the Hong Kong Law Society, the Bar Council of Malaya and the Bar Association of Malta provide this service.

13. THE PROVISION OF SERVICES FOR MEMBERS

The services provided for members by Bar Associations vary widely, the most common being the provision of an Appointments Registry (34%) and a reference Library (41%), the arrangement of various insurances at reduced rates (37 %), the organizing of social events (39 %) and the production and sale of legal forms (32%).

A wide range of services are provided by Bar Associations in Australia, Austria, Canada, Germany, Iran, Israel, the United Kingdom and the United States of America. Out of those Bar Associations replying from the Continent of Africa, the only service given, other than the provision of a reference library and arrangements for reduced insurance, is by the Law Society of Rhodesia which has an Appointments Registry. Excluding Associations in Australia and New Zealand, it appears that very few Bar Associations in the Far East provide services for members other than the arrangement of occasional social events and, in the case of the Bar Council of Malaya the Phillipine Lawyers' Association and the Thai Bar Association, arranging for the publication of legal forms and textbooks.

Of the services listed (see Appendix II), the majority of Bar Associations consider the provision of a reference library as the most important service to be offered to members (it is notable that the Library of the Faculty of Advocates in Scotland is open on a twenty-four basis) followed by the provision of an Appointments Registry, a photocopying service, the production of legal forms and promoting the publication of legal text books. Examples of unusual services offered to members are: —

(i) Arrangements made by the Austrian Bar Association to provide old age, disability, widows' and orphans' pensions to lawyers' dependants.

(ii) The insurance scheme organized by the Association of Law Societies of South Africa run in conjunction with other professions, thereby obtaining more advantageous rates.

(iii) A scheme for members for private treatment in cases of illness run by the Law Society of Scotland.

(iv) The bulk purchase of stationery, goods and furniture by the Bar Association of Sweden to enable these goods to be available to members at reduced prices. The Law Society of Alberta (Canada) arranges with publishers to offer, to members certain law reports and periodicals at a discount if orders are placed through the Society.

(v) The Law Society of New Zealand has recently set up a Travel Committee to organize bulk travel at reduced rates to overseas conferences and possibly holiday travel for members. This service is also provided by The Law Society in England.

(vi) Extensive publishing activities carried out by the Norwegian Bar Association which include the publication of books containing judgments and decrees of the Courts and indices to legal literature, case law, statute law and administrative regulations. The Society also publishes "Check Lists", which are lists indicating the work a lawyer should or must do for the performance of a particular job, for instance acting on the sale or purchase of property or forming a company.

(vii) The Danish Bar has established a scheme and employed staff for supplying a "locum tenens" for its members in the event of long illness, serious accident or death.

14. PUBLIC RELATIONS

67% of the Bar Associations publish an Annual Report although in the case of some Associations, such as The Law Society of Trinidad, these Reports are only sent to members at three-yearly intervals. However, only seven of the Associations employ a full or part-time Public

Relations Consultant — The Law Societies in England and Scotland, the Bar Council in England, the American Bar Association, the Bar Associations of Quebec (Canada) and the Netherlands and the Phillippines Lawyers' Association. Three other Bar Associations are considering employing a Consultant. The Secretary of the Tipperary Sessional Bar Association comments "In my opinion the lack of communication between the profession and the public is extremely serious. An enlightened communication service — or Public Relations service — to prevent the profession being constantly misrepresented to the general public is a fundamental necessity for every Bar Association." If this opinion is accepted it is difficult to understand why so few Bar Associations employ even part-time Public Relations Consultants.

39% of Bar Associations have established a Compensation (or Guarantee) Fund to compensate losses which clients suffer through dishonesty by a lawyer or his staff. The Law Society (England) regards its compensation Fund as being the most important single step towards the maintenance of good relations with the public and it is surprising that only 31% of Bar Associations think the establishment of such a Fund to be of great importance. Amongst the developing countries only Associations in Malaysia, Singapore and Rhodesia have a Compensation Fund.

15. ADMINISTRATION OF LEGAL AID

Just over 50% of Bar Associations are responsible for or assist in the administration of a civil legal aid plan in their country, whilst 41% undertake a similar responsibility in respect of a criminal legal aid plan. 29% regard this as being one of the most important functions of a Bar Association. This responsibility is accepted by the professional organizations in all British Commonwealth countries with the exception of Kenya, Malta, and Singapore. In Europe, only the member bodies in England, Northern Ireland, Scotland, Sweden and Portugal and Austria (both civil legal aid only) undertake the function.

It is not known to what extent those replying are actually concerned with the day-to-day administration of the legal aid plans or merely encourage their members to assist in their administration.

16. CONFERENCES AND OVERSEAS RELATIONS

The majority of all Bar Associations (57%) organize Conferences for their own members; whilst 41% organize Conferences of their members with members of other legal organizations in their country and 43% with those in other countries. 54% have some special link, such as joint committees with other legal associations both in their own and other countries.

All Bar Associations in Europe other than the Bar Council in England and the Bar Associations in Austria and Northern Ireland, organize conferences of their own members and all have some form of contact with other legal Associations in their own or other countries. Of the Bar Associations in the developing countries, the Law Societies of Hong Kong, Fiji, Kenya, Rhodesia and Trinidad and the Bar Associations of Malta, Singapore and Thailand do not organize conferences for their own members and the Law Societies of Fiji, Kenya and Trinidad and the Bar Associations in Malta, Mauritius and Singapore have no contact with other associations either in or outside their own countries.

Many of the links with Bar Associations in other countries are through membership of international bodies such as the I. B. A. or of regional groups, for example the Law Association for Asia and the Western Pacific, the Inter-American Bar Association, the Arab Lawyers' Union or the Association of Law Societies of Southern Africa. The Bar Associations of the five Scandinavian countries meet every three years and once in every five years there is a Conference of Law Societies and Bar Associations of the British Commonwealth countries.

17. PROMOTION OF SECTIONAL OR REGIONAL GROUPS OF LAWYERS

46% of the Bar Associations encourage or assist in the running of affiliated regional Law Societies but only 24 % organize Young Lawyers or sectional groups. 17 % consider that the organization of affiliated regional Law Societies is of fundamental importance to a Bar Association as compared with 21% in respect of Young Lawyers' Groups and only 16% for sectional groups. Of the Associations in the developing countries only the Law Societies of Fiji and Rhodesia and the Philippine Lawyers' Association have affiliated regional societies and none have any sectional or Young Lawyers' Groups, other than the Bar Association of Nigeria which organizes a Young Lawyers' Group.

The majority of Associations in Australia, Canada, Europe, New Zealand and the United States undertake these functions.

18. LAW REFORM

67% of the Bar Associations undertake research into the reform of existing laws or make recommendations for new laws on their own initiative and 71% following a request to do so from the Government. 74% submit recommendations for the making of new, or the amendement of existing rules of practice and procedure and 62 % for the amendment of Parliamentary Bills. 41% regard these functions as being of fundamental importance to Bar Associations.

Without exception the Commonwealth Associations replying all undertake these functions as do all those in the United States. The same is true of those in Europe, with the exception of Portugal.

19. IMPROVING THE SERVICES OFFERED BY THE PROFESSION TO THE PUBLIC

Closely connected with the undertaking of research into law reform is the carrying out of research to ascertain how legal services to the public can be improved. Many Bar Associations through their Councils and Committees keep this question under constant review; for example in many instances standing committees have been set up to consider rules of practice and procedure and statutes with the aim of preventing undesirable time lags between the initiation and completion of contentious and non-contentious matters and the provision of the most efficient and economical service to the public. The majority of Bar Associations also give information and assistance to Government Departments concerned with the improvement of the administration of justice.

It appears, however, that very few Bar Associations undertake specific research to ascertain how an improvement in the services offered to the public can be effected, although the Bar Association of Quebec (Canada) has arranged for a social-economic survey of the profession in Quebec by an independent research team and a similar economic survey was undertaken by The Law Society (England) in 1965. In 1966 The Law Society set up a Special Committee to consider the future of the profession over the next 20 years and, in the light of the probable demand for the services of the legal profession, to devise a suitable system of training and education for lawyers to equip them to meet these probable future demands. The Law Society of Scotland has set up a similar committee.

The Association of Swiss Lawyers considers it impossible to meet future demands for legal services unless the legal profession remains free and independent and its status is protected and enhanced. An alliance of all liberal professions in Switzerland has been formed with the aim of awakening the public's appreciation of the importance of the free practice of the professions.

20. IMPROVING THE SERVICES OFFERED BY BAR ASSOCIATIONS TO THEIR MEMBERS

Bar Associations can and should play a vital role in helping their members to provide an improved service. At another Plenary Session this conference is discussing the problem of how Bar Associations can assist their members to keep up-to-date with the increasing spate of complex new legislation. This is only one of the ways in which positive help can be given. The majority of Bar Associations, through their Councils and Committees, constantly review the services they provide for their members and consider how these could be improved. No separate research is undertaken amongst members specifically for this purpose although, through the media of their annual reports and journals, suggestions are invited from members and their opinions are sought at meetings and social functions. Many Bar Associations find contacts with other Associations through international and regional legal organizations particularly helpful in ascertaining what services others provide.

PART II

21. THE RESPONSIBILITY OF BAR ASSOCIATIONS TO THE DEVELOPING COUNTRIES

The Questionnaire asked Bar Associations to give particulars of the assistance which they give to Bar Associations in developing countries. From the answers received it is clear that little assistance is given other than information and advice in response to requests regarding the constitution of a projected Bar Association or on problems of conduct and etiquette. Practical help appears to be confined to explaining to visiting lawyers from developing countries how the profession in the developed countries is organized and to the presentation of duplicate or otherwise unwanted law books by wealthier Bar Associations to those Associations with ill-equipped libraries.

The older-established Bar Associations in developing areas such as those in Australia, New Zealand, and the Republic of South Africa can give particular assistance to the newer Associations in those areas from their own experience of the problems to be faced. Membership of international legal organizations or regional groups such as The Law Association for Asia and the Western Pacific plays a very important part in helping new Bar Associations as the conferences of such bodies enable their representatives to meet and discuss problems with representatives of the older-established Associations. The Law Societies of Rhodesia and South West Africa are affiliated to the Association of Law Societies of South Africa who can therefore enjoy the benefits arising from the Association's activities.

One of the problems facing Bar Associations in developing countries is highlighted by the position in the Phillippines where there exist no less than six national and 80 local Bar Associations. This proliferation of Bar Associations has in their view prevented the emergence of an organized national legal fraternity of sufficient strength to give lawyers an effective voice on matters of judicial reform, law revision and other major problems in the administration of justice. As a result of this there is no really effective Bar Association. Practically all the groups are without premises, law journals or a law library and they are so weak that the Government ignores their views whenever expressed.

In other developing countries the problem is that there is no Bar Association at all thus preventing the profession achieving through united efforts an improvement in their own capabilities, an increase in the effectiveness of their service to the public and the maintenance of the standards of the profession. The legal professions in developing countries face particular problems in education and training. Often legal faculties have only recently been established in the Universities and difficulties are encountered in setting and maintaining standards and recruiting experienced law tutors. Again in many countries there are too few established legal firms able to offer practical training and experience to newly qualified lawyers.

CONCLUSIONS

22. The services now offered by Bar Associations to their members vary widely. In general Bar Associations in the more developed countries provide a wider range of services and this is no doubt governed largely by the availability of finance. Although the majority of Bar Associations have some responsibility for the selection, training and examination of law students very few are engaged in research into the probable future demands by the public for legal services. Unless research is undertaken it is difficult to see how a system of education and training can be adapted to equip the profession to meet these demands.

23. Although technological advances have produced a wide range of new office equipment designed to improve efficiency, few Bar Associations offer any advice to members on the selection and use of such equipment. This is a field in which Bar Associations can surely help lawyers to improve their service to the public and that this is increasingly realised, is borne out by the fact that there are at present under consideration by a number of Associations the subjects of office efficiency and, the training of unqualified staff. Only the American Bar Association and The Law Society (England) appear to have undertaken any research into how the use of computers might improve efficiency.

24. Public Relations activities in the majority of Bar Associations are confined to publishing journals and annual reports. This vital function of Bar Associations appears to have been very much neglected, but is actively under consideration at the present time by three further Bar Associations.

25. The importance of contacts with the legal profession in other countries is increasingly recognised and almost all national Bar Associations now belong to some international legal organization or regional group.

26. To a growing extent the profession has accepted its responsibility to ensure that legal services are available to all persons regardless of means.

27. In the light of the views of Bar Associations as to the relative importance of the functions which they perform, it should now be possible for the Bar Associations in the developing countries who wish for assistance to plan their own programme of expansion and to seek the help of those with experience in the particular fields.

The Appendix to this Report is published on the last pages of this book.

Summary of Discussions

Mr. *Nai Sansern Kraichitti* took the chair when the first part of Topic Nr. 3 was discussed. There was a large audience present and the panel consisted of Dr. Harald Foglar-Deinhardstein (Austria); Mr. W. O. Carter (England); Judge Keizo Kanno (Japan); Mr. Brendan McGrath (Ireland); Mr. Orison Marden (USA) and

Sir *Thomas Lund,* the Rapporteur, opened the discussion by reference to the report which he had submitted on the subject and which had been circulated. He suggested that information concerning the work that individual Bar Associations were carrying out in the sphere of post-graduate education could be used to advantage by other Bar Associations who were contemplating activity in the same field.

He drew particular attention to Paragraph 5 of his report and he emphasised that if the responsibility of the continuing education of lawyers was taken over by the State, that this could interfere with the independence of the profession.

He felt that there was a greater realisation amongst lawyers to-day of the necessity of keeping up to date, so far as this was possible, with new legislation. The attitude that when one qualified one's studies were at an end, no longer persisted. Indeed, courses in office management and efficiency were matters which should be dealt with more generally. Only three or four Bar associations provided lectures which dealt with this subject. He mentioned that the German Bar Association conducted a course of lectures dealing with such divers subjects as steel law, art law and wine law.

The Rapporteur expressed the view that one of the steps which the International Bar Association could take is to build up a dossier on the steps being taken by member associations in the field of post-graduate education. Then the experience of the various member associations could be used to advantage by those wishing to avail themselves of it, or to enlarge the scope of their own activities in this sector.

Dr. Foglar-Deinhardstein (Austria) pointed out that a lawyer who is not up to date is unable to give good advice to his clients and, indeed, can be a disgrace to the profession. He disagreed with the Rapporteur in the importance which he placed on the role of the Bar Association in legal education. In Austria, he believed that there were sufficient opportunities for keeping up to date by reference to professional journals, reports, etc. He did not believe that very much could be gained by a discussion at seminars, unless the meeting was justified by the discussion of some vitally important topic.

Mr. *W. W. Boulton* (England) said that he formed part of a very small professional body because the Bar of England and Wales comprised something over two thousand members. When you have a small professional body such as this, the question of priorities arises, and then one has to ask oneself whether continuing legal education is high enough up on the list of priorities. He felt that it was up to the individual barrister to see that he was up to date, because if he made a mistake this would be reflected in his reputation, which would suffer. He felt that as a general rule barristers always, as a matter of course, referred to the various law journals and were sufficiently up to date as a result of this, and the fact that their practice was specialized.

Mr. *Brendan McGrath* (Ireland) thought, from listening to the speakers from Austria and England, that there was a certain amount of complacency with reference to this vitally important subject.

In the first instance we should identify the problem. We should ask ourselves what is the service that we should provide, and what is the criterion of that service? Quality and cost was the answer to this question. To-day there is a radical change in social conditions, and the law must be seen in a changing society. The shift is from private to state law. In administration the shift is from the courts to specialized tribunals. So, of necessity, the type of lawyer is changing, and must change. The clients used to ask for implementation and he now asks for guidance. The non-lawyer is competing with the lawyer. In the United States this is called 'private ordering'. Not all rights are capable of indication in a court of law, so we have the growth of administrative tribunals. We must have an eye to the consumer, because he regards the product we provide — at the moment — as complex, and the manpower that provides it as resistant to change.

He believed that we must not go backwards into the future, but that we must relize the task ahead of us and tackle it so that we could be up to date with the changing conditions, and so provide the service that was expected.

Me. Enrico Biamonti of Italy expressed the view that members of the legal profession ought more and more to make their views heard because the common legal principles which they all shared made them the best foreign ministers for their countries. He thought that this could be achieved in two directions which were of particular importance, first by the preparation and submission to Governments of legal subjects which could be the subject of international agreement and secondly by the exchange of law students under the guidance of various Bar Associations.

In connection with the first of these proposals he thought that it was in the interest of the free world to be as united as possible in the field of law. The lawyers themselves could well take the initiative in this respect. As regards his second proposal the future of the world would be in the hands of the young who would have to know the legal systems of other countries besides their own. It should therefore be made very easy for them to cross national frontiers. He thought that the Bar Associations of different countries ought to organize exchanges of law students particularly with students in underdeveloped countries and try to resolve the different material and economic problems with which the countries were faced. Several European Bar Associations, he pointed out, had already reached agreement in this connection.

In conclusion he directed attention to the principle that in all countries the whole basis of the legal profession must be upon professional competence and strict ethical rules.

Judge Kaizo Kanno pointed out that in Japan there was a course for judges who had been appointed, and this enabled them to be trained and to avail themselves of the experience of their more senior colleagues.

Mr. Orison S. Marden (USA) said that in America every lawyer is presumed to know all the law, but that this, of course, is not possible. However, they do try to have continuing education courses, and recent experience has shown that their members are increasingly ready to pay the cost of week-end seminars and courses of lectures.

The Chairman then opened the discussion to the audience and a number of speakers expressed their views, one of whom suggested that the International Bar Association should consider sponsoring Summer courses in different countries, which would be open to the members of other Bar Associations. The Rapporteur, in summarising the views of the various speakers, said that his impression was that the greater number present thought that the Bar Associations should try to give continuing legal education to its members. He did not feel that the idea of a Summer school was workable, amongst other things because of the difficulty of selecting topics which would be wide enough to be of interest to the citizens of a number of different countries. The discussion was indeed fruitful because it had stimulated considerable thought on the subject, and this was demonstrated by the variety of the views that had been expressed.

SUMMARY OF DISCUSSIONS

Mr. Nai Sansern Kraichitti (Thailand) took the chair for the afternoon session, when this topic was discussed. On the panel there were Dr. Harald Foglar-Deinhardstein (Austria); Mr. W. O. Carter (England); Mr. Dermot P. Shaw (Ireland).

The Rapporteur, *Sir Thomas Lund,* commenced by asking the question "What can the International Bar Association do in this field?".

In the first place he felt that one should ask what were individual Bar Associations doing for their own members. The questionnaire that had been circulated was the first attempt that had been made to get an overall picture of what the different Bar Associations throughout the world were doing for their own members. He pointed out that it is great help for any association taking on a new project to have the benefit of the experience of others by reference to the trial and error of others in the same field.

The Rapporteur, in referring to the second part of his paper said that we should ask ourselves what can we do to create a strong and independent Bar in developing countries.

Mr. Dermot P. Shaw (Ireland) suggested that the Bar Association had seven main functions, as follows: —

1. To ensure the maintenance of integrity, competence, etc., of the profession.
2. To promote facilities for a satisfactory legal service at a reasonable cost.
3. To appreciate the problems of its own members, with a view to ready assistance.
4. To act as a public relations platform for the profession.
5. To liaise with Government Departments as much as possible.
6. To make and maintain contacts with other professional bodies.
7. To create social relations between its members.

As he saw it, the following difficulties faced the practitioner to-day: —

1. Lack of competent staff.
2. The necessity of keeping up to date, particularly with statutory regulations.
3. The particular difficulty in Ireland of collecting in costs, because of the antiquated system where an itemised bill has still to be furnished if requested.

He suggested that the work of the Courts could be streamlined and that this would help to solve the problem of lack of competent staff. The Courts should be on a business footing. He also suggested that the International Bar Association should get each member association to keep a register of all members, which would be furnished to the Headquarters Association so that it could, upon request, furnish the names and addresses to a lawyer in one country seeking a practitioner in another, perhaps, who is engaged in a specialized field. He felt that there was a case for regional conferences.

When the subject was opened for discussion, *Mr. Beelaerts van Blockland* (Netherlands) pointed out that in his country a local bar association had the right to oppose the application of a practitioner who wished to practise. If they do oppose, the judge will refuse the application. An appeal then lies to a tribunal which consists of the representatives of the local Bar Association and judicial representatives, the latter being in the majority.

Mr. George Cook (South Africa) stated that it was essential that the Bar Association should be a completely independent body and that it must ensure that the ethics education, and quality of the service by its members to the public should always be of the highest degree. Freedom of action was always desirable, but might appear difficult to justify on the grounds that non-qualified persons were not free to practise law. However, this could be justified because of the necessity of the protection of the interests of the public.

The best form of public relations was to make sure that the standards of your own members were sufficiently high so that the public would have no cause of complaint. If standards were only mediocre, the aim should be to raise them. He felt that Bar Associations should consider operating a provident fund to help members in their old age. In South Africa they had a large one which was operated by a number of professions, including doctors and architects.

Dr. Harald Foglar-Deinhardstein (Austria) emphasised the necessity for the constant availability of training courses for staff. Qualified staff should not waste their time doing work which unqualified people could do. Ordinary run-of-the-mill tasks should be dealt with by unqualified staff, which would allow proper concentration by qualified staff on the complex problems. In Austria there are courses for training staff which enables them to attend Court on the practitioner's responsibility.

Mr. *Henri Delmont (France)* pointed out that the French Bar Associations role is to control discipline. He felt that regional meetings were desirable providing that they were held at a university level.

Mr. *Julian Doyle* (Australia) said that in this changing world he sensed a change in attitude towards the following: —

(a) Moral values.

(b) Between generations.

(c) In relation to individual freedom.

As a member of parliament he felt that each Bar Association should keep the closest possible liaison with the legislature, and that discreet pressure should be applied to the legislature from time to time to ensure that basic rights were not eroded. In developing countries he felt that the need of close co-operation with the legislator was very great to protect the individual's freedom which had often been won at great sacrifice.

The Rapporteur, in concluding, mentioned that a note had been made of the various suggestions which had been made at the meeting and that he would put these before the Council in due course.

PLENARY SESSION

WARRANTIES FOR THE PROTECTION OF CONSUMERS

Chairman: RA Dr. Heinrich Foglar-Deinhardstein (Austria)
Rapporteur: RA Dr. Gustav Rinesch (Austria)
Vice-Chairman: RA Michael Oppenhoff (Germany)

Country	*National Correspondents*
Australia	V. M. Corr, Esq.
Austria	RA Dr. Fritz Czerwenka RA Dr. Heinrich Foglar-Deinhardstein RA Dr. Gustav Rinesch
Canada	Irwin Dorfman, Esq., Q. C. Charles Wolfson, Esq., Q. C.
Denmark	Advokat Erik Rasmussen
England	Anthony Evans, Esq. (General Council of the Bar) Denis A. Marshall, Esq. (The Law Society) John May, Esq., Q. C. (General Council of the Bar)
Finland	Advokat Olof Hernberg
France	Me J. L. Delvolvé
Germany	RA Michael Oppenhoff
Iran	Dr. A. Farman-Farmayan
Ireland	Gerald J. Moloney, Esq. (The Incorporated Law Society of Ireland)
Israel	Mr. I. Ganon, Advocate Mr. A. Shomar, Advocate
Japan	Judge Keizo Kanno
Lebanon	Mounir Shehadi, Esq.
Netherlands	Mr. H. B. A. Verhagen
New Zealand	Colin I. Patterson, Esq.
Norway	Mrs. Inger Valle, LL. B.
Philippines	Ambassador Marcial P. Lichauco
Portugal	Dr. Angelo de Almeida Ribeiro
Scotland	Peter Maxwell, Esq., Q. C.
South Africa	G. W. Cook, Esq.
Sweden	Advokat Nils Kärrlander
Switzerland	Maître Edmond Martin-Achard
Turkey	Nurkut Inan, Esq.
U. S. A.	John T. Chadwell, Esq. (American Bar Association) Mark R. Joelson, Esq. (Federal Bar Association)

PRODUZENTENHAFTUNG

Report

vorgelegt von Rechtsanwalt DR. GUSTAV RINESCH, Wien
Österreich

Alle Zivilrechts-Systeme wurzeln, soweit es sich um die Erfassung und Regelung wirtschaftlicher Beziehungen der Bürger handelt, im Wirtschaftsleben des 19. Jahrhunderts. Der Konsument deckte seinen Bedarf an Konsumgütern im allgemeinen beim Erzeuger oder im Kleinhandel, das *allgemeine Vertragsrecht* der Zivilgesetzgebung regelte in großen Umrissen die Möglichkeiten des Käufers, wenn er nicht zufriedengestellt war. War der Konsument aber durch das gekaufte Gut zu Schaden gekommen, so enthielten diese Zivilgesetze *allgemeine Schadenersatzgrundsätze* (im anglo-sächsischen Rechtsbereich Law of Torts), in der Regel kannte der geschädigte Konsument auch seinen Vertragspartner und wußte daher, an wen er sich als Verantwortlichen zu halten hatte.

Diese Zivilgesetze der Wende des 18. zum 19. Jahrhundert sind in allen westlichen Ländern in Geltung, jüngere Staatsgebilde haben sie meist von ihren Vorbildern übernommen.

Als eine Folge der gigantischen industriellen und gesellschaftlichen Revolution der Welt, die dem 20. Jahrhundert sein Gepräge gibt, werden auch die wirtschaftlichen Beziehungen innerhalb der Gesellschaft komplizierter und für den einzelnen immer schwerer überschaubar. Der Massenbedarf erfordert Massenproduktion, die technische Entwicklung bringt neue Gefahren für jeden einzelnen, der Kleinhandel entwickelt sich zum Welthandel, das erwachte Sozialbewußtsein verlangt den Schutz des sozial Schwachen.

Damit sind wir auch schon bei dem Thema „Warranties for the Protection of Consumers", welches die IBA auf diesem Kongreß zur Diskussion stellt.

Dieser zusammenfassende Bericht verarbeitet Beiträge folgender Ländervertreter: C. M. Corr, Australien; I. Dorfman, Kanada; Ch. Wolfson, Kanada; E. Rasmussen, Dänemark; A. Evans, Großbritannien; D. A. Marshall, Großbritannien; J. May, Großbritannien; K. Lagus, Finnland; M. Oppenhoff, Westdeutschland; M. Shehadi, Libanon; C. I. Patterson, Neuseeland; I. Valle, Norwegen; F. Czerwenka, Österreich; M. P. Lichauco, Philippinen; P. Maxwell, Schottland; G. W. Cook, Südafrika; E. Martin Achard, Schweiz; N. Inan, Türkei; J. T. Chadwell, USA; M. R. Joelson, USA.

I.

Die allgemeine Vertragshaftung des Produzenten, auch die auf Vertragsgrundlage beruhende Schadenersatzpflicht – bei Verschulden verschiedener Grade – besteht in fast allen Zivilrechtssystemen nur gegenüber der anderen Vertragspartei. Dieser Grundsatz als Ausgangspunkt für Versuche zur Erweiterung in Rechtsprechung und Lehre (Privity of Contract) ist universell anerkannt, er hat drei Gesichtspunkte:

1. Wofür haftet der Produzent ohne – oder ohne nachgewiesenes Verschulden?
2. Wann und
3. in welchem Umfang tritt Verschuldenshaftung ex contractu ein?

Zu 1): Die Verpflichtung zur Rückgängigmachung des Vertrages, Kaufpreisminderung, verbesserten Nachlieferungen, bei Fehlen einer ausdrücklich zugesicherten Eigenschaft der Ware, Ersatz entgangenen Gewinnes, – in Deutschland, Schweiz und Österreich unter dem Begriff der Gewährleistung verstanden – sind die direkten Folgen der Verletzung eines Lieferungsvertrages infolge von Sachmängeln, z. B. mangelhafter oder vertragswidriger Qualität der Ware. Für Folgeschäden, das sind jene, die erst durch den Gebrauch der schadhaften Ware beim Käufer entstehen, haftet der Produzent ohne Verschulden nach Deutschem, Österreichischem und Schweizer Recht nicht. – Bloß in Norwegen und Dänemark (für Gattungswaren) und Libanon scheint eine allgemeine Erfolgshaftung des Produzenten ex contractu zu bestehen.

a) Das Recht von Großbritannien hat schon 1893 im „Sale of Goods Act" die Vertragsmerkmale im Warenhandel eingehend geregelt und gewisse Bedingungen und Garantien zum stillschweigenden Vertragsinhalt (implied warranties) gemacht, auch wenn solche in die Lieferungsverträge nicht ausdrücklich aufgenommen waren. Die wichtigsten Vertragsmerkmale nach diesem Gesetz sind: Ware nach Muster oder bestimmter Beschreibung muß diesem Muster oder dieser Beschreibung entsprechen: Solche Ware muß von guter handelsüblicher Qualität (merchantable quality) sein, wenn sie nicht vor Übernahme vom Käufer geprüft werden konnte; die Ware muß dann auch besonderen Erfordernissen des Käufers entsprechen, wenn dieser bei Bestellung ausdrücklich darauf hingewiesen hat und der Verkäufer durch die bekannte Eignung seines Betriebes auch in der Lage war, solche besonderen Bedingungen zu erfüllen.

Vertragsbedingungen und stillschweigender Vertragsinhalt nach dem „Sale of Goods Act" wirken in allen Fällen nur inter partes! Sie können durch Vereinbarung ausgeschlossen werden. Allerdings kennt der „Sale of Goods Act" aber auch der viel spätere „Hire Purchase Act" auch die einschränkende Regel, daß essentielle Vertragsmerkmale auch durch Vereinbarung nicht wirksam ausgeschlossen werden können (Statutory warranties).

Für den Letztverbraucher sind die Regeln des Sale of Goods Act, die längst Bestandteil des Common Law geworden sind, nicht gültig. Neuseeland 1908, Süd-Afrika und Australien haben den Britischen Sale of Goods Act unverändert übernommen, etwas abgeändert Kanada.

b) die USA, deren Gesetzgebung in den einzelnen Staaten oft unterschiedlich ist, immer aber durch die richtungweisende Rechtsprechung befruchtet wird, haben erst in neuester Zeit ein ähnliches Gesetzeswerk, wie den Sale of Goods Act in Großbritannien geschaffen, der in der überwiegenden Mehrheit der Staaten angenommen wurde. Der „Uniform Commercial Code" ist stillschweigender – jedoch vertraglich meist abänderbarer – Vertragsinhalt für aller Art Handelsgeschäfte und schafft gewisse Rechts- und Sach-Vermutungen, grundsätzlich inter partes. Er regelt Rechts- und Sachmängel, ausdrückliche und stillschweigende Garantien im Waren- und sonstigem Verkehr, Milderung der Garantie bei Ausverkäufen, Kennzeichnungspflicht, Musterkauf, Handelsbräuche, Prüfungspflicht des Käufers, etc. Keine Qualitätshaftung für Ware aus zweiter Hand. Auch wird dort der Versuch gemacht, die Schutzwirkungen bei Verletzung der „express or implied warranties" auf einen engeren oder weiteren Personenkreis, vom Konsumenten aus betrachtet, zu erweitern. Meines Wissens ist diese Erweiterung vom Kongreß der USA noch nicht gebilligt worden.

Wörtlich nahezu gleichlautende Bestimmungen sind in den Civil Code der Philippinen aufgenommen.

Das Libanesische Recht läßt den Produzenten auch gegenüber dem Letztverbraucher haften, wenn die Ware so fehlerhaft ist, daß sie zum gewünschten Gebrauch ungeeignet ist. Die Reklamationsfristen sind dort kurz und verwirken bei Versäumnis den Haftungsanspruch.

In der Deutschen Rechtslehre wird der Versuch unternommen, die vertragliche Haftung auch auf Dritte, die nicht Vertragspartei sind, auszudehnen:

i) Ausdehnung des vertraglichen Haftungsanspruches auf die Familie, Haushaltsangehörige und Dienstnehmer des Käufers, also einen vom Produzenten überschaubaren Personenkreis. Die Rechtssprechung ist dieser Erweiterung jedoch nur dann gefolgt, wenn es sich um Personenschäden, nicht Vermögensschäden handelte.

ii) Zulässigkeit der Erhebung des zivilrechtlichen Haftungsanspruches gegen den Produzenten durch den Zwischenhändler, und zwar nicht in dessen eigenem Namen, sondern im Interesse des geschädigten Letztverbraudhers. (Eine Ausdehnung des Instituts eines „Vertrages zugunsten Dritter"). Auch in dieser Richtung haben die Gerichte nur in seltenen Ausnahmefällen entschieden.

d) Aus dem Vertrag haftet der Produzent grundsätzlich auch für das – schuldhafte oder nicht schuldhafte – Verhalten seiner Angestellten oder jener Personen, deren er sich zur Vertragserfüllung bedient. Die Frage des vorliegenden eigenen Verschuldens des Unternehmers bleibt in diesem Zusammenhang unerörtert. So im Deutschen, Österreichischem, Schweizerischem und Türkischem Recht. Das ist also ein Fall echter Erfolgshaftung zwischen den Vertragspartnern.

Zu 2) Der Produzent haftet zwar grundsätzlich ohne Rücksicht auf Vertragsbeziehungen *für Verschulden* = negligence. Die zivilrechtliche Deliktshaftung verlangt also keine „privity of contract", die anfänglich im USA-Schadenersatzrecht Haftungsvoraussetzung war. In den deutschen, schweizerischen, österreichischen, türkischen und libanesischen Zivilgesetzen, sowie in allen Ländern des ehemaligen britischen Empire, in denen das Law of Torts gilt, steht der deliktische Haftungsanspruch *jedermann*, der durch ein Produkt zu Schaden gekommen ist, gegen jeden Vormann, jedes Glied der Kette zwischen Produzenten und Letztverbraucher, nach seiner Wahl zu, dem ein Verschulden bei Erzeugung oder Verteilung des fehlerhaften Produktes nachgewiesen werden kann.

Die Hauptaufgabe dieser Untersuchung ist es, festzustellen, ob die Gesetzgebung und Rechtsprechung in dieser Beziehung dem letzten Konsumenten ausreichend Schutz gewährt:

a) Im Recht der *USA* hat eine lange Reihe von Entscheidungen der staatlichen und Bundes-Gerichte der Haftung des Produzenten für Verschulden (negligence) und breach of warranty gegenüber dem Letztverbraucher zum Durchbruch verholfen. Die Rechtsprechung verlangt vom Produzenten – (in ähnlicher Weise auch vom Händler) – alle vernünftigen Vorsichtsmaßnahmen im Produktionsablauf zu beobachten, die vorhersehbaren Schaden vermeiden. Dies gilt in erhöhtem Maß von Produkten, die das Leben und die Gesundheit des Verbrauchers beeinflussen, also von Nahrungsmitteln, Heilmitteln, Kosmetika, Giften, Explosivstoffen; daraus entwickelten sich auch Regeln bei an sich gesundheits- und lebensgefährlichen Produkten zur ausreichenden Warnung, Beschriftung und Gebrauchsanweisung, besonderer Verpackung, deren Nichteinhaltung schon *an sich* negligence bedeutet.

Die Beweispflicht des verletzten Verbrauchers – ohne jede Vertragsbeziehung, – erstreckt sich auf die Fahrlässigkeit des Erzeugers und auf den Causalzusammenhang zwischen Ware und erlittenem Schaden.

Der rechtspolitische Grund der Haftung ist der öffentlich-rechtliche Schutzanspruch des Verbrauchers, die „public policy". In weiterer Entwicklung dieses Schutzanspruches geht ein beachtenswerter Trend der Gerichte in bisher 15 amerikanischen Bundesstaaten seit 1963 soweit, daß er den Grundsatz der „strict liability in tort" aufstellt für Konsumgüter, die infolge ihrer gesundheitsgefährlichen Beschaffenheit oder fehlerhaften Herstellung tatsächlich gesundheitlichen Schaden herbeigeführt haben. Es bedarf dann gar nicht des Beweises des Verschuldens mehr, wenn der Kläger nur den entstandenen Schaden und den Zusammenhang zwischen Produkt und Schaden nachweist. Die Fahrlässigkeit wird einfach als gegeben angenommen, bildet also eine „presumption of facts", in Wahrheit schon einen reinen Fall der *Erfolgshaftung*.

b) Die Gerichte Großbritanniens gehen bei Beurteilung der Produzentenhaftung wohl von der Präsumption aus, daß im Zweifel keine Haftung des Produzenten für Fahrlässigkeit besteht, vorausgesetzt, daß er die normale Sorgfaltspflicht, „reasonable duty of care", eingehalten hat. Es haben sich da ähnliche Regeln, wie unter a) aufgezählt, bezüglich Verpackung, Beschreibung, Beschriftung und Warnung vor gefährlichen Eigenschaften gebildet, die den Begriff der „duty of care" ausmachen.

Ebenfalls in die Nähe der reinen Erfolgshaftung kommen die Vorschriften des „Consumers Protection Act 1961", welcher die Regierung ermächtigt, für ganz bestimmte Erzeugnisse, die Leben und Gesundheit gefährden können, Schutzvorschriften zu erlassen, deren Verletzung den Erzeuger für den Gesundheitsschaden, den wer immer erlitten hat, ohne Verschuldensnachweis haftbar macht. Die britische Regierung hat allerdings von dieser Ermächtigung erst sehr beschränkt Gebrauch gemacht und solche Schutzvorschriften nur für elektrische und Gas-Heizgeräte und Kinderbekleidung erlassen.

c) Kanada hat die Haftungsprinzipien des Produzenten von Großbritannien aus dessen Rechtsprechung übernommen. Als grundlegend wird dort die Entscheidung des House of Lords Donoghue v. Stevenson (1932) angesehen, deren Hauptsätze lauten:

> "A manufacturer of products which he sells in such a form as to show that he intends them to reach the ultimate consumer in the form in which they left him with no reasonable possibility of intermediate examination, and with the knowledge that the absence of reasonable care in the preparation of putting up products will result in an injury to the consumer's life or property, owes a duty to the consumer to take that reasonable care."

Der Beweis der Nichtbeobachtung der „duty of reasonable care" obliegt immer dem klagenden Verbraucher, jedoch kehren die Kanadischen Gerichte in Schadensfällen aus verdorbenen Lebensmitteln die Beweislast um und verlangen den Entlastungsbeweis vom Produzenten.

In diesem Zusammenhang verweise ich auf die wichtige in allen anglosächsischen Ländern gültige Beweisregel „res ipsa loquitur", die in dem Kapitel über „Beweislast", Nr. II näher erörtert werden soll.

Die Entwicklung in Australien, Neuseeland und Süd-Afrika folgt ebenfalls den in Großbritannien entwickelten Grundsätzen, ohne daß Besonderheiten zu vermerken wären.

d) Die Verschuldenshaftung des Herstellers ist in der Deutschen Bundesrepublik im Bürgerlichen Gesetzbuch § 823 ff kodifiziert, dessen Schutzbereich immer weiter ausgedehnt wird, u. a. über die Haftung für fahrlässige Handlungen hinaus auf Haftung wegen Unterlassung. In diesem Zusammenhang entwickelte die Rechtsprechung einen ganzen Katalog von Verhaltenspflichten des Herstellers, deren Vernachlässigung an sich schon Ansprüche für dadurch eingetretene Schäden auslöst. Die Sorgfaltspflichten des Produzenten entsprechen dem, was im anglosächsischen Rechtsbereich unter „duty of reasonable care" verstanden wird, (siehe Abs. b, c). Diese „Verkehrssicherungspflichten" sind in ihrer Wurzel — über die private deliktische Haftung hinaus — ebenso öffentlich-rechtlichen Charakters, entsprechend dem in USA entwickelten Grundsatz der „public policy" (siehe Abs. a). Die weitere Entwicklung hat dazu geführt, daß heute jede der möglichen Fehlergruppen „Konstruktions- und Fabrikationsfehler, mangelnde Prüfung, mangelnde Aufklärung", Schadenersatzansprüche begründet, ausgenommen höchstens solche, die bei aller Vorsicht und Erfahrung nicht voraussehbar waren.

Begünstigt wird der Produzent andererseits durch das Bestehen einer Vorschrift, die einem Anspruch ex delicto gegen ihn vielfach seine Durchschlagskraft nimmt: Da sich der Fabrikant regelmäßig einer Anzahl von Hilfskräften bedient, kann er sich von der Haftung entlasten, wenn er nachweist, daß er den schuldtragenden Angestellten, dessen Fehler den Schaden verursacht hat, sorgfältig ausgewählt, überwacht oder daß der Schaden auch bei Einhaltung aller Sorgfalt eingetreten wäre. Dieser Exculpierungsgrund ist für den Konsumenten unbefriedigend, weil er dann mit seinen Ansprüchen allein auf den meist finanziell schwachen Angestellten verwiesen wird. Hierin liegt ein Grund, weshalb die Lehre immer versucht hat, zwischen Letztverbraucher und Produzenten eine Vertragsbeziehung zu konstruieren, innerhalb welcher der Unternehmer für den Erfüllungsgehilfen haftet. Die Gerichte sind dieser Tendenz in Deutschland zögernd gefolgt, wenn sie auch die Organisationspflicht = Überwachungspflicht des Unternehmers immer mehr verschärft haben.

Unter anderem wird in Deutschland auch aus obigem Grund der Konsumentenschutz als unzureichend angesehen, weil sich die zivilrechtliche Verschuldenshaftung doch vom Verschuldens*nachweis* nicht vollständig loslösen kann. Der Gesetzgeber bereitet deshalb eine Ergänzung der schadensersatzrechtlichen Vorschriften in der Art vor, daß der Unternehmer für alle Schäden haftet, die seine Erfüllungsgehilfen fahrlässig herbeigeführt haben, ohne daß ihm die Exculpierung möglich ist. Diese Verschärfung, die eine Lücke des Konsumentenschutzes schließt, ist deshalb vertretbar, weil sich der Produzent gegen diese Risiken leicht durch Versicherung abdecken kann. — Ein Übergang zu einer zivilrechtlichen Haftung ohne Verschulden ist in Deutschland, wenn auch vielfach diskutiert, nicht geplant.

Wohl besteht, — wie in den meisten Staaten — die öffentlich-rechtlich begründete *Haftung ohne Verschulden* in der Form der Gefährdungshaftung entstehend aus *dem Betrieb* von Eisenbahnen, Luft- und Kraftfahrzeugen, Energieleitungen. Derartige Schadenshaftungen bestehen nicht dem Einzel-Verbraucher gegenüber, sondern gegenüber der Allgemeinheit. (In Großbritannien „Consumer Protection Act 1961").

e) Das Schweizerische Obligationsrecht regelt die Haftung aus unerlaubter Handlung in Art. 40 CO, der auch für den Warenverkehr gilt. Auf diese allgemeine Haftungsbestimmung, die nach dem Schweizerischen Landesbeitrag, der mir vorliegt, noch niemals in einem Schadensfall zwischen Produzenten und Letztverbraucher vor einem Schweizerischen Gericht judiziert wurde, ist im Prozeßfall die Beweisregel „respondeat venditor" anzuwenden, also die Umkehrung der Beweislast auf den beklagten Produzenten. — Nach § 197 CO haftet der Produzent auch bei unverschuldeter Unkenntnis für das Fehlen solcher Eigenschaften der verkauften Ware, die ihr normalerweise zukommen. Das ist eine Art Qualitätsgarantie, die dem englischen Begriff „Good merchantable quality" nach dem Sale of Goods Act gleichkommt.

f) Das Österreichische Recht kennt eine besondere über die allgemeinen Schadenersatzgrundsätze des Allgemeinen Bürgerlichen Gesetzbuches hinausgehende Haftung des Produzenten gegenüber dem letzten Verbraucher nicht. Jeder Beschädigte kann vom Erzeuger bei Schadensnachweis und Nachweis der Causalität Ersatz verlangen.

g) Das Dänische Recht, enthalten im Sale of Goods Act 1906, kennt die Produzentenhaftung auf Vertragsgrundlage, nicht aber gegenüber dem Letztverbraucher ohne Vertragsbeziehung.

Der Norwegische Purchase Act enthält keine Produzentenhaftung, die über Vertragshaftung hinauswirkt, über Verschuldenshaftung und einen etwa erweiterten Kreis der Anspruchsberechtigten liegen keine Details vor.

Das Finnische Recht läßt den Produzenten umfassend für Schäden des Verbrauchers haften ohne Rücksicht auf Vertragsbeziehungen, verlangt aber vom Kläger den Beweis.

h) Der Türkische Code of Obligations enthält in seinen Schadenersatzbestimmungen die Haftung des Produzenten bis zum Letztverbraucher bei Verschuldens- und Causalitätsnachweis, er haftet – was für den Unternehmer auf eine Erfolgshaftung hinauskommt – für jedes Verschulden seines Angestellten wie für sein eigenes.

i) Nach dem Civil Code der Philippinen ist hingegen ohne Vertragsbeziehung zwischen Partnern keine Haftung für Schäden vorgesehen, es scheint aber doch generell Verschuldenshaftung zu bestehen.

Zu 3) *Umfang des Schadenersatzes:*

Während sich in einigen Ländern die Ansprüche des Verbrauchers wegen Nicht- oder fehlerhafter Erfüllung eines Vertrages gegen seinen Vertragspartner (Produzenten) *ohne Vorliegen eines Verschuldens* auf Wandlung (Rückgängigmachung) und Kaufpreisminderung, allenfalls Verbesserung, nicht aber auf sog. Folgeschäden, beschränken (Deutsche Bundesrepublik, Österreich) machen andere Länder keinen Unterschied im Umfang der Ersatzmöglichkeiten zwischen Schaden ex contractu und Schaden ex delicto, u. zw.:

In Großbritannien, Süd-Afrika, Kanada, Australien, Neuseeland wird die allgemeine Regel umschrieben mit: . . . "that the claimant may recover damages in respect of any loss which is reasonably foreseeable as the natural and probable consequence of the breach of contract or tort as the case may be." – Dem richterlichen Ermessen wird also viel Spielraum gelassen, wobei das Schwergewicht auf dem Beweis der Causalität des erlittenen Schadens liegt. Finnland und Norwegen überlassen die Bestimmung der Schadenshöhe kurzerhand dem Richter.

Die USA haben im „Uniform Commercial Code" (der bereits unter 1 b erwähnt, auch auf den Philippinen eingeführt ist) den Schadensumfang in allen Vertragsverletzungen einheitlich geregelt und genau definiert, jedoch in keiner Weise eingeschränkt, wenn das Prinzip des „proximate damage", der Causalität beobachtet wird.

Anscheinend bloß das Deutsche (und Österreichische) Recht machen den *Verschuldensnachweis* zur Voraussetzung für den Zuspruch von Schadenersatz für sog. Folgeschäden, entgangenen Gewinn, auch Schmerzensgeld. Unter besonderen Umständen haben auch Dritte, zu deren Unterhalt der Geschädigte beitrug oder in deren Haushalt oder Gewerbe er tätig war, einen direkten Schadenersatzanspruch. All dies ohne ziffernmäßige Begrenzung, jedoch hat die Rechtsprechung die Maxime der „adäquaten Causalität" entwickelt. Wenn der Eintritt und die Höhe des Schadens außerhalb jeder Wahrscheinlichkeit liegt, ist Causalität nicht mehr gegeben und insoweit kein Schadenszuspruch.

II.

Die bisherige Untersuchung hat die Voraussetzungen für die Haftungstatbestände erfaßt, ohne Beweisbarkeit sind sie aber für kein Gericht existent. Deshalb die gesetzlichen *Beweisregeln*, die *Beweislast*-Verteilung, das Bestehen von Rechts- und Tatsachen-Vermutungen *(Präsumptionen)*. Die Länderbeiträge haben auch da neben der Erkenntnis des Common Sense, daß, wer einen Anspruch vor Gericht erhebt, ihn auch zu beweisen hat, einiges Interessante gebracht; vor allem muß es der noch nicht betriebsblinde Jurist mit Vergnügen erfahren, daß in Norwegen der Idealfall herrscht: Dort entscheidet über die Verteilung der Beweislast in jedem Fall der Richter!

a) Die allgemeine Regel, daß den geschädigten Konsumenten die Beweislast trifft, wird für diesen durch die in Großbritannien entwickelte Maxime „res ipsa loquitur" für Schadensansprüche aus Massen-Konsumgütern industrieller Erzeugung, z. B. fabriksverpackten Markenartikeln wesentlich erleichtert.

Diese Maxime besagt, daß eine Ware, die sich in allen Erzeugungsphasen unter der Kontrolle des Produzenten befand, die verpackt und unverändert durch Zwischenhandel beim Konsumenten ankommt und dort Schaden erzeugt, durch Verschulden des Produzenten defekt war. Diese Tatsachen zu beweisen, wird in der Regel leicht gelingen, der Richter hat es dann mit einer Tatsachen-Vermutung (presumption of fact) zu tun, die letzten Endes wieder zu einer Erfolgshaftung im Einzelfall führen kann. In solchen Fällen findet also nach Erbringung des prima facie Beweises eine Umkehrung der Beweislast statt. Der Produzent ist es dann, der das Nichtvorliegen der Maxime „res ipsa loquitur" beweisen oder andere Exculpierungsgründe, wie Abwälzung auf Erfüllungsgehilfen, force majeure, Mißbrauch durch den Konsumenten, etc., suchen muß.

Alle Länder anglosächsischen Rechts handhaben die Beweisregel „res ipsa loquitur" in analoger Weise. Es scheint jedoch, daß die Abwälzung der deliktischen Haftung des Produzenten auf den Erfüllungsgehilfen in USA nicht angenommen wird.

b) In der Deutschen Bundesrepublik hat sich eine der vorerwähnten ähnlichen Beweisregel durchgesetzt, der sogenannte Anscheinsbeweis, eine auf Erfahrung beruhende Vermutung in Fällen von typischen Produktions- oder Lieferungs-Abläufen, in denen ein typischer Tatbestand auf einen bestimmten Erfolg hinweist.

Von vornherein ist der Produzent dann beweispflichtig, wenn die Lieferung einer Ware oder Erbringung einer Leistung an sich eine Rechtsguts-Verletzung darstellt. Es obliegt dann dem beklagten Produzenten, den Entlastungsbeweis als Rechtfertigungsgrund zu führen.

Der Schweizerische Code d'Obligations schließlich kennt zu der Regel der klägerischen Beweispflicht keine Rechtsvermutungen oder Ausnahmen. In Art. 55 CO ist die Möglichkeit der Entlastung des Produzenten durch Abwälzung auf den schuldigen Erfüllungsgehilfen, was nicht nur für die deliktische, sondern auch für die vertragliche Haftung zu gelten scheint.

III.

Qualitätsgarantien:

Neben den bereits untersuchten zivilrechtlichen allgemeinen und besonderen Haftungsgrundsätzen zum Schutz des Verbrauchers haben viele Staaten Schutzgesetze und Garantiebestimmungen erlassen, die an sich öffentlich-rechtlichen und strafrechtlichen Charakter tragen, von Behörden überwacht und erzwungen werden können, deren Nichteinhaltung aber keine direkten Garantieansprüche des Konsumenten gegen den Produzenten auslöst. Zwischen den Vertragspartnern, bzw. im Verhältnis zwischen Produzenten und Letztverbraucher hat ein Verstoß gegen solche Gesetze gewöhnlich den Erfolg einer Beweiserleichterung im Zusammenhang mit der Haftung des Produzenten ex delicto.

Zu unterscheiden ist zwischen *freiwillig* gegebenen Garantien des Erzeugers und *gesetzlichen* Qualitäts- und Zulassungsvorschriften.

1) *Freiwillige* Garantieerklärungen werden von Erzeugern in weitem Umfang gegeben, sie bestimmen meist selbst den Umfang und die Art der Garantie und verpflichten sich zum Umtausch der Ware, zur kostenlosen Verbesserung, meist innerhalb einer selbst gesetzten Frist (z. B. Automobile, Uhren). Rechtlich gesehen handelt es sich um eine zusätzliche Gewährleistungsverpflichtung, bzw. deren Beschränkung in einer meist genau umschriebenen Form, eine Haftung aus dem Vertrag, der privity of contract, die keine zusätzlichen Probleme bietet. Folgeschäden, auch solche, deren Causalität mit einer freiwillig gegebenen Garantie unbestritten ist, werden niemals mitumfaßt. Im allgemeinen wirken derartige Garantien bis zum Letztverbraucher.

2) *Gesetzliche* Qualitätsvorschriften und Zulassungsvorschriften gibt es in allen Staaten in großer unüberschaubarer Zahl. Sie haben als Schutzgesetze des Konsumenten gesehen überwiegend strafrechtlichen Charakter und Straf-Sanktionen, ihr Sinn ist Sicherung des Lebens und der Gesundheit der Menschen. Deshalb ist der Verkehr mit Lebensmitteln, Medikamenten, Giften, Explosivstoffen mehr oder weniger genau reglementiert und unterliegt auch bestimmten Qualitätsvorschriften.

Auch die Sicherheitsvorschriften für den Verkehr zu Lande, zur See und in der Luft dienen dem Schutz desjenigen, der solche Leistungen in Anspruch nimmt, wobei immer noch davon ausgegangen wird, daß der Betrieb dieser Verkehrsmittel unter besonders gefährlichen Verhältnissen erfolgt. Die zivilrechtlichen Ansprüche des Verletzten sind da meist unabhängig vom Verschuldensnachweis, aber oft umfangmäßig beschränkt, weil sie gewöhnlich durch Versicherung, teilweise auch durch Pflichtversicherung abgeschirmt sind.

Ich glaube, daß eine Aufzählung auch nur der wichtigsten in diesem Kapitel allgemein erwähnten Qualitätsgarantie-Gesetze überflüssig ist, da sie zivilrechtlich keine Sonderprobleme bieten.

IV.

Am Schluß soll darauf hingewiesen werden, daß seit 1930 im Institut für Internationales Privatrecht daran gearbeitet wird, das Recht des Kaufes beweglicher Gegenstände international zu vereinheitlichen. Nach längerer Unterbrechung der Vorarbeiten, auch infolge des 2. Weltkrieges, kam es im April 1964 in Den Haag zu einer internationalen Konvention über Kaufverträge für bewegliche Sachen, die von 28 Nationen unterzeichnet wurde, darunter alle Staaten Europas, USA, Japan. Die Ratifizierung ist allerdings erst durch 12 Staaten, darunter Großbritannien, Frankreich, Deutschland, erfolgt.

Die Konvention beschränkt sich auf Rechte zwischen Verkäufer und Käufer, ohne auf Haftung für Verschulden und Rechte des Letztverbrauchers einzugehen.

SUMMARY OF DISCUSSIONS

The report given by the Rapporteur, *Dr. Gustav Rinesch* (Austria), was followed by a discussion in which ten National Correspondents took part.

Mr. Gerald J. Moloney (Ireland) initially stated that the legal situation in Ireland is basically similar to the U.K. concerning consumers' protection and accordingly decisions of the U.K. Courts have a persuasive effect in Ireland. He then set out a far-reaching program on the subject, the main points being:

1) Warranties on goods should be mandatory. The present law in Ireland which makes the warranty available only to the purchaser should be broadened to cover anyone who might reasonably be expected to use such goods.

2) The right of action should be available for the consumer against the last vendor. The vendor in turn should have the right to join as a co-defendant anyone who has given him a warranty on the same — defective — goods.

3) The burden of proof should be shifted to the defendant. Mr. Moloney suggested a practical system of classifying the goods and services offered with guarantees and warranties. He further suggested that relatively expensive goods and goods that are either intrinsically dangerous, or possibly dangerous if defective, should carry a very high degree of warranty. For less costly items the warranty would not be so wide and, at the other end of the scale, throw-away-goods would carry either a minimal guarantee, or none at all. He admitted that this sort of quality-consciousness could be costly but still would satisfy the customer by increased protection.

Mr. Moloney's suggestions were well received as a practical contribution both at the meeting and in the Irish press.

Mr. Charles Wolfson (Quebec, Canada) added to his written contribution and again stated that Canada adopted the legal principles of the United Kingdom governing the sale of goods. However, in the Province of Quebec the approach is different. There exists an inherent warranty for a latent defect, and the seller is obliged by law to warn the buyer against such latent defects, both known and unknown. The seller can contract out of liability for simple negligence, but not for gross negligence, not only for the manufacturers' fault, but also for the fault of his employees and persons, or things under his care.

The determination of what is a defect is left to the Court. A consumer buying immovable property has to engage an architect to prove the defect. In the case of the sale of used cars, if there is even a slight defect in the vehicle, this is taken seriously. The consumer is entitled to return the vehicle and get a refund of the money paid.

In the case of DeLange, decided in 1954, a consumer bought a bottle of lemonade with a "foreign" body in it. He sued the manufacturer and recovered damages.

Mr. Vernon M. Corr (Australia) dealt with the problem of "strict liability". There should be an obligation imposed on the manufacturer for personal injuries sustained by the consumer. The USA has developed this aspect of the Law. Mr. Corr admitted that insurance could become very expensive and the cost would probably have to be passed on to the consumer. He also stated that warranties of merchantable quality should not be excluded.

Sir Joseph Maloney Q.C. (United Kingdom) related that he was Chairman of the "Committee for Consumer Protection" established in 1962 in England. This Committee recommended:

1) The creation of a Consumer Council which already exists in some countries. It is created to watch out for consumers' interests, and to press for new legislation for the protection of the consumer. Three Acts of Parliament have been passed since the Report of the Council for Consumer Protection.

2) The Hire Purchase Act: The purchase price limit was raised from £ 300 to £ 2,000 and applies to all consumer purchases. Under the Hire Purchase Act, the consumer has now four days in which to return the goods if he does not wish to keep them. This provision was designed to protect the consumer who buys goods from the door-to-door salesman and is rushed into making a quick decision.

3) The Trade Description Act was also passed and comes into force in 1969. When operative, it will be an offence to describe any goods in such a way as to deceive the public into thinking it is getting goods which are better than they in fact are. This will also apply to all advertisements of goods. The law also requires that goods be clearly labelled.

4) Finally, there are alterations in the Sale of Goods Act, which are covered by the Report of Dr. Rinesch.

Dr. Jorgen Hansen (Denmark) stated that the Scandinavian Courts accepted the imposition of strict liability on the manufacturer, particularly in the sales of feedstuffs and fertilizers. These countries have a system under which the manufacturer and vendor are both held liable for the product, with a strict liability on the part of the manufacturer for all mass-produced goods.

Me J. L. Delvolvé (France) noted that the Law of France was similar to the Law of the Province of Quebec. French Jurisprudence has managed to modernize Article 22 of the Canadian code: "Seller not liable for defects in goods unless they are apparent at the time of sale." The consumer is now protected almost completely, but the manufacturer is not liable for obvious defects.

Mr. James Fellers (USA) also dealt with the subject under the heading of "strict liability". In Oklahoma and forty-nine other States of America there is no special statutory law. However, the consumer does receive protection. Dangerous goods sold to the consumer which cause injury create liability in tort for the manufacturer. In a California case the doctrine of strict liability was enunciated that the manufacturer is liable for personal injury caused by a product placed on the market by him.

Judge Keizo Kanno (Japan), among general observations about the the legal situation in Japan on the subject, dealt with the question of latent defects. In his country the manufacturer would be liable for damages caused by such defects, even if there is no negligence on his part. General liability of manufacturer and employer depends on the consumer's proving negligence on their part. Voluntary warranties are widespread and need no proof of negligence if shown to exist within a fixed period. (Sale of cars.)

Mr. H. B. A. Verhagen (Netherlands) reviewed the problem where proceedings should be instituted if manufacturer, seller and consumer all reside in different countries.

Finally *Mr. Erdogen Yesin* (Turkey) stated that in Turkey there is no specific legislation dealing with the protection of consumers. However the Turkish Code of Obligations and the Code of Commerce — under the subject of privity of contract — establish a principle that there is liability of seller to purchaser, even if the seller has no knowledge of the defect.

Conclusion

The rather condensed Report of extensive and valuable contributions of 21 countries and this Summary show a clear tendency to increase the protection available to consumers. Privity of contract, initially essential for contractual liability, is gradually losing its importance. Public policy induces the legislator to follow progressive Court decisions, pace-makers of consumer protection in all countries.

This development, not favorable to the manufacturer, leads us to examine also principles of procedure, chiefly the rules governing the burden of proof. And also here we see the same progressive tendency in favour of the consumer. In the opinion of the Rapporteur the philosophers' stone for a simple, and in most cases satisfactory, solution of problems of "Consumers' protection" lies in shifting the burden of proof from plaintiff to defendant. To promote endeavours in this direction seems an appropriate project for the International Bar Association.

PLENARY SESSION

THE LAW RELATING TO THE SUPPORT AND CUSTODY OF CHILDREN IN ITS INTERNATIONAL AND COMPARATIVE ASPECTS

Chairman: Counsellor Clarence L. Simpson (Liberia)
Rapporteur: The Hon. Jacob T. Zukerman (American Bar Association)
Vice-Chairman: Prof. Henry H. Foster, Jr. (American Bar Association)
Secretary: Dr. Doris J. Freed (American Bar Association)

Country	*National Correspondents*
Australia	The Hon. Justice Roma Mitchell
Austria	RA Dr. Walter Schuppich
Canada	James C. MacDonald, Esq.
Denmark	Advokat Aage Spang-Hanssen
England	Bryan Anns, Esq. (General Council of the Bar) Bruce Campbell, Esq., Q. C. (Gen. Council of the Bar) George A. MacDonald, Esq. (The Law Society)
Finland	Mars. Helvi Sipilä
France	Maître Jean B. Vadon
Germany	Dr. Dieter Ahlers RA Heinrich Wölper
Iran	Mr. A. Ehteshami
Ireland	Patrick C. Moore, Esq. (The Incorporated Law Society of Ireland)
Israel	Mr. Justice Y. Kister
Italy	Professor Avv. Fernando Della Rocca
Lebanon	Faouzi Ghazi, Esq.
Liberia	Counsellor Clarence L. Simpson
Mexico	Sr. Lic. D. Benjamin Flores Barroeta
Netherlands	Miss S. Boekman Mr. H. Jonker
New Zealand	Dr. B. D. Inglis, Esq.

Northern Ireland	E. Alan Camerton, Esq., B. A., LL. M.
Norway	H. r. advocat Signe Marie Stray Ryssdal
Portugal	Dra. Elina Guimaraes
Scotland	Mr. John Horsburgh, Advocate (Faculty of Advocates) Sheriff Hamilton Lyons (The Law Society) Dr. S. N. Harris (Association of Law Societies)
South Africa	Professor J. N. R. van Rhyn (Assn. of Law Societies)
Spain	Excmo. Sr. D. Sanchez Toves
Sweden	Advokat Valborg Lundgren
Switzerland	Dr. Max Büsser
Turkey	Avukat Atilâ Sav
U. S. A.	Prof. Henry H. Foster, Jr. (American Bar Association) Dr. Doris J. Freed (American Bar Association) R. Lee Newton, Esq. (Federal Bar Association) The Hon. Jacob T. Zukerman (American Bar Assn.)

SUPPORT AND CUSTODY OF CHILDREN – INTERNATIONAL AND COMPARATIVE ASPECTS

Report

submitted by the Honorable JACOB T. ZUKERMAN
USA

INTRODUCTION

1. This report has been prepared on the basis of the replies furnished to the questionnaire sent in connection with this topic (Questionnaire attached)

2. We have generally followed the sequence in the questionnaire and have attempted to summarize the reported information. Where we have given illustrative jurisdictions, these are not intended to be exclusive. There may be others.

3. We have used the following code abbreviations to designate the various nations which have replied:

ASLA	– Australia	– Roma Mitchell
AST	– Austria	– Walter Schuppich
C	– Canada	– James C. McDonald, Henry L. Cartwright, Douglas Fitch, J. Stuart Clyne, William E. McDonald
D	– Denmark	– Aage Spang-Hanssen
E	– England	– George A. MacDonald
FD	– Finland	– Helvi Sipilä
FR	– France	– Jean B. Vadon
G	– Germany	– Dr. Ahlers, Heinrich Wölper
H	– Holland (Netherlands)	– H. Jonker, S. Boekman
IR	– Iran	– Abdullah Ehteshami
ISR	– Israel	– Y. Kister
IT	– Italy	– Fernando Della Rocca
MEX	– Mexico	– B. F. Barroeta
NZ	– New Zealand	– B. D. Inglis
NI	– Northern Ireland	– E. A. Comerton
NY	– Norway	– Signe Maria Stray Ryssdal
P	– Portugal	– Elina Guimaraes
SCT	– Scotland	– John Horsburgh, Hamilton Lyons

SA	– South Africa	– J. M. R. van Rhyn, S. N. Harris
SZ	– Switzerland	– Max Büsser
T	– Turkey	– Atila Sav
US	– United States	– Henry H. Foster, Jr., Doris J. Freed

I *Support of Children*

A. *The Laws Relating to Responsibility in Each Country*

The top age of children for whom parents are responsible is fixed in most countries. In 9, it is age 21 (ASLA, E, FD, H, IT, MEX, P, SCT, US [mostly]). In 6, it is 18 (D, IR, ISR, NY, SA, T). It varies from 16 to 20 in 6 others. There is no limit in 3 (AST, FR, G). In most instances, responsibility continues beyond the age limit if the child is unable to work due to disability. There are a few exceptions (D, and in US, the State of New York).

In practically all cases, both parents are liable although the father carries the primary obligation; if the father is missing or unable to do so fully, the mother must support in part or in whole. In some countries, if the obligation is enforced against only one parent, the other can obtain reimbursement in proportion to respective assets (FR, some states in US, SZ).

While in most countries both the mother and the acknowledged or adjudicated father of an out-of-wedlock child are liable, there are many exceptions in the ages up to which support is required, particularly by the father (e. g. FD up to 17 only instead of 21, unless child is disabled; In SZ, up to 18 instead of 20; in H the father is secondarily liable to a limited extent only, depending on his obligations to other children an the ability to work of the out-of-wedlock child).

In some countries, the child's marriage or full-time employment even at an earlier age, relieves the parents completely (NI, IR, US). In many others, they become secondarily liable (ASLA, AST, G, ISR, MEX, SZ, SA). SCT continues primary liability for the son, even after marriage, but it is secondary for a married daughter. A number of countries hold the parents liable even after the age limit, while child completes college or professional school (ASLA – 2 years additional; in C, even though married, upon age 21; D – to age 24; G; MEX – to age 21, even if married; NZ; NY; P; SCT; SZ; SA; some states of US).

In Mexico, parents remain responsible for "food, clothing, lodging and assistance" in cases of illness and generally there is no age limit when children are in need. Parents also must provide support by will (1) to male descendants less than 21, and (2) to unmarried daughters.

Grandparents in many countries are secondarily responsible (ASLA, AST, E, FR, G, H, IR, ISR, MEX, NZ, P, SCT, SA, US [some states]). In Mexico, grandparents (and ascendants nearest in degree) are held liable. There is no liability of grandparents in D, FD, NY, T, SZ.

In every country reporting orders for support are subject to modification because of changed circumstances.

B. *Standards Applied in Determining Responsibility and Need*

Generally the amount of support for children is determined in accordance with the ability of the parent to support and with the standard of living of the parents and, of course, considering the needs of the child. However, in some jurisdictions, if support is being sought by the welfare authorities, only the child's minimum needs are considered (Some courts in Ontario, Canada, in some states of US; NI).

In most countries the following standards are taken into consideration in arriving at the actual amount:

(1) Salary or income from business or profession

(2) Other income or assets

(3) Parents' expenses and obligations, including those to children of other relationships, as well as to other relatives, where required by law or custom

(4) Potential earnings (*not* so in AST, FR, NI, SCT, Some states in US).

If the father is remarried with children in both families, most countries feel that neither group has a priority over the other (In most states of the US there is a tendency to favor the children of the earlier marriage). However, most of the correspondents pointed out that realistically the children of the present relationship must be considered in determining ability to support. In Iran the children in the present group are considered first. In T, allocation is fixed in the order of rights of inheritance.

If the father has out-of-wedlock children, by and large the children of the marriage have a preferred status, for even if there has been an adjudication of paternity and a court order for support, the ability to support is affected by the father's expenses in caring for his family. Thus, while many countries do not distinguish legally, there is a practical preference for the child of the present marriage. This may however be reversed if the father is now living with out-of-wedlock child. Note that in P, an out-of-wedlock child cannot be placed in the parent's home without permission of the other spouse: Iran comments that "This, 'out-of-wedlock', is not a practice . . . because, as soon as the girl is found expectant, the easiest way is to marry and then the child shall not be considered 'out-of-wedlock'; bigamy and polygamy allowed except it is not practiced among Christians."

In fixing the sum for out-of-wedlock children, some countries appear to make no distinctions (AST, D, E, FD, G, H, IR, MEX, NZ, NY, SZ, SA, some states in US). In FR, offspring of adulterous relationships receive less. In ASLA, on a needs basis only. In T, less favored if there are children of a marriage.

Some countries provide some financial aid to parents even without proof of need. For example: ASLA – Social Security benefits – first child under 16, 50 c per week; second child under 16, $ 1 per week; third child under 16, $ 1.50 per week; each subsequent child an increase of 25 c per week; for every child between 16 and 21 in school or college, full-time, $ 18 per quarter; also C, G (beginning with third child); ISR, NI, SCT, SA.

C. *Enforcement of Support*

The determination of the responsibility for and the amount of support and the enforcement of the order are generally in the hands of courts. There are some exceptions. In British Columbia (C) the Superintendent of Child Welfare has discretion to increase payments required by agreements made under the Children of Unmarried Parents Act and to enforce. In Ireland, administrative bodies (Sheriffs, Bailiffs, Province Boards, Bench of Magistrates). Also, D, Mex, NY (in all of which handled by administrative body, except if incidental to a matrimonial action).

In general, these matters are handled in the civil courts. In 7 countries there are family or children's courts. In most of these, support of children is also ordered by the courts dealing with divorce and separation.

By and large the parties must apply to the court or administrative body for enforcement of orders already made. In most countries, the public prosecutor will assist, since non-support is a crime or offense. In Iran the ecclesiastical courts may assist.

In practically every country wilful failure to obey an order is punishable by either fine or imprisonment. Statutes vary: up to 3 months – Ontario (Can.), NI; up to 6 months – AST; MEX; NY; most states in US; up to 1 year – FR; SA; up to 2 years – H; up to 3 years – SZ; up to 5 years – G.

In some jurisdictions, there is the right to demand security, pledges, guarantees, bonds or deposits (MEX, US). Sometimes wage assignments are used (D, US).

There is less and less of a tendency to employ criminal enforcement if it is possible to use civil procedures.

In most countries the national government does the enforcing. Exceptions are ASLA, (State), C (Province or City), D (Local counties), E (Local courts), FD (Administrative Board), G (States), MEX (Local), US (Local courts).

Where agreements have been entered into for support of children, generally they are subject to court review and revision. In some cases, a change of circumstances is required (E, FR, NI) although in most the court may choose to not approve the agreement itself (ASLA, AST, C, D, FD, G, H, ISR, MEX, NZ, NY, P, SA, T, US). In IR, the court may intercede only if agreement is illegal. In SZ, only if the right to modify has been reserved.

D. *Extent of Problem of Non-Support*

It is interesting to note that very little in the way of statistics is available as to the extent of non-support or desertions. Finland reported that in 1966, 31,937 children were being paid for by the government and that in 1965, 2,155 parents who had been in default had been sentenced to the workhouse. Holland reports that 10 years ago the Courts for Child Protection collected about 65% of amounts due and that they estimate the same for now. Mexico shows a total of 346 non-support trials in 1966.

As to desertions, Finland reported 1,126 children deserted in 1965 by both parents. In the US in 1963, it was estimated that there were more than 10,000,000 women and children who had been deserted in some 2,600,000 family units.

Efforts to locate missing parents are the responsibility mainly of the deserted families themselves, although with the increase of governmental assistance, these agencies have been assuming greater roles in this area. State police, and prosecuting officials have assumed varying responsibilities in ASLA, C, D, E, FD, FR, G, H, IR, ISR, MEX, SA, US and SZ. Welfare officials assist in ASLA, D, FD, FR, H, ISR, SCT, SZ, US. In AST, universal registration exists. In NY, the Collector of Contributions helps in location.

E. *International Support*

(1) The following countries have signed the Convention on the Recovery Abroad of Maintenance (in force since May 25, 1967).

Of the countries reporting: AST, D, FD, FR, G, H, ISR, IT, MEX, NY, P. *Other countries not reporting:* Belgium, Bolivia, Brazil, Cambodia, Central Africa Republic, Ceylon, Chile, China, Colombia, Cuba, Czechoslovakia, Dominican Republic, Ecuador, El Salvador, Greece, Guatemala, Haiti, Holy See, Hungary, Monaco, Morocco, Niger, Pakistan, Phillipines, Poland, Spain, Sweden, Upper Volta, and Yugoslavia.

(2) The following countries have signed the Hague Convention of October 24, 1956 re: Child Support; AST, H, SZ.

(3) The following countries have signed the Hague Convention of April 15, 1957 re: recognition and enforcements of judgments for child support: AST, D, H, NY, SZ, US.

(4) In addition

ASLA – reports bilateral arrangements between states and territories and with British Commonwealth countries.

C – Reciprocal Enforcement of Maintenance Orders Act (all provinces of C, ASLA, England, nine other countries and State of Michigan (U. S.).

D – Scandinavian Treaty with FD, NY, Sweden and Iceland – Foreign order filed with county court which fixes amount of support.

E – Reciprocal statutes with other Commonwealth nations.

FD – See D – a new action must be brought. Foreign decree not binding but will be considered.

FR – Foreign court order enforceable under French rules of private international law – by exequator (order for enforcement) obtained from French Court.

G – Parents may be sued for support of children abroad – regardless of treaty. Foreign order considered but not binding.

H – Foreign order cannot be enforced unless there is a special treaty. If child abroad and parent in H, order of support possible.

ISR – Even if no treaty, Attorney-General of ISR, may dispense and request enforcement by ISR, court.

NZ – Reciprocal statutes with other British Commonwealth nations.

NY – See D.

NI — See NZ.

MEX — Reciprocity principles permit enforcement, code provides for (1) Letters requisitional, (2) personal summons on Defendant, (3) enforcement formalities according to law of foreign country.

SA — Reciprocal Recognition with British Commonwealth nations and territories, as well as many other countries. (Matrimonial Causes Jurisdiction Act of 1939, amended 1953). Also Maintenance Orders Act of 1923.

SCT — Reciprocal arrangements with Bahamas, Ghana, Gibraltar, Malta, Newfoundland (C), New Zealand, Nigeria, Saskatchewan (C), Kenya, Tanzania, Singapore and other dominions and protectorates. Also FR, Belgium, India, Pakistan, ASLA, NY, AST, and H.
If foreign order subject to review and modification not enforceable (except of English court).

SZ — Each canton decides separately. Generally enforced if non-appealable, proper jurisdiction in rendering country, if reciprocal, and if not against Swiss public policy.

T — Several treaties with countries where T citizens live or work. (Countries not specified).

US — If support obligation has been reduced to final judgment. Some states will extend comity. In a few cases in Pennsylvania and New York, orders for support of child have been made. New York has recently adopted a reciprocal act with any province of Canada.

F. *Recommendations For Action*

1. *Within each country* —
   a) In Federal states, uniform reciprocal laws as in ASLA, C, and US.
   b) Creation of public youth welfare official or other service (AST, MEX, SA).
   c) Treatment as a social rather than primary legal problem. (AST, D).
   d) Governmental guarantees — with action against parent for reimbursement (FD, IR).
   e) Creation of location services (ISR).
   d) No orders without social agency report (SA).

2. *Intercountry*
   a) New International Reciprocal Act (ASLA, E, FR, G, MEX, SA, and US).

b) Adoption of existing conventions (SZ).
c) International Marriage Convention (FD).
d) International Treaty under U. N. (T).

G. *Suggested Topics For Discussion In Dublin*

1. Reciprocal International Support (ASLA, E, FD, FR, IT, US).
2. Support to out-of-wedlock children (AST, E).
3. Governmental Guarantees of Support (FD).
4. Methods of Enforcement (MEX).
5. Public or private insurance against contingency of child support (US).
6. Standard setting in awards (MEX, US).
7. Should courts be used only as a last resort? (US).

II. *Custody of Children*

A. *The Laws and Practices in Each Country*

1. *Determination*

In the main, decisions as to custody and the enforcement of awards are the responsibility of the courts. When a matrimonial cause is being heard, the same court generally determines custody. Otherwise, other civil or family or juvenile courts deal with this. In many countries, the enforcement, while remaining under court authority, is turned over to welfare departments or other agencies (FD, ISR, MEX, NY, SZ, T).

In some countries, administrative bodies, such as the Department of Social Welfare, determine child custody, particularly where they are wards of the state, but generally subject to appeal to the courts. (ASLA, AST, D, MEX, NY, SZ. [Juvenile offenders and illegitimates]).

2. *Standards*

The overriding principle in all countries is that of "the best interests of the child," although interpretations vary considerably. Most jurisdictions state that the parents have equal rights, certainly when children are born in wedlock. Yet, the majority tendency seems to be in favor of the mother for all children of tender years, the exceptions being those in which the mother is very, very, unfit. (Possible differences occur in FR, in NI, where father has paramount right even against the mother, except where he forfeits it by his conduct), in Scotland and Portugal. In Israel there is a rebuttable presumption that a child up to six needs to be with its mother, also under Jewish religious law, that a daughter should remain with the mother. (Similarly in England – up to four; in Mexico – under five; in British Columbia (Canada) up to twelve. In NZ, father generally gets a growing boy. A SA survey shows 63% to the mother.

In some countries, grandparents or other relatives are granted custody if the parents are unavailable or unfit. But seldom do they get preference over the parent. It is not possible in D, FD, NY.

The preferences of the child are considered in most countries (ASLA, AST, C, D, E, FD, H, ISR, IT, NZ, NY, NI, P, SCT, SZ, US). However, great concern is expressed as to whether it is really the child's preference or the result of influence. Greater weight is given to older children, 14 and over.

In determining custody, fitness of the parent is an important factor in every country. Yet custody generally may be awarded under the "best interests of the child" rule to a mother living with a man to whom she has not been ceremonially married, or even to an adjudged adulterous parent. Also to a father who has not remarried. Each of these cases is decided on an individual basis and the determination often is affected by the attitudes of the judge or jury. If there is any danger that the child may be adversely affected by the situation, the decision might be otherwise.

In every jurisdiction, agreements covering custody are subject to court review and revision. In some, the agreement must be approved (AST, MEX).

Custody of an out-of-wedlock child is generally granted to the mother, although in most states the father may request it. (ASLA, AST, ISR, MEX, NZ, P, SCT, US).

In Austria, the father must care for child, if the mother fails to do so. In France, the parent who first recognized the child as his or hers, gets custody. In Germany, a special welfare authority, JUGENDAMT, gets custody but courts may award to unwed mother. In NZ, the mother has a "slightly better claim."

3. *Visitation*

Generally visitation is not dependent upon the payment of support obligations, but in some countries a flagrant violation may be taken into consideration in determining its continuance (ASLA, C – reasonable access also considered, NI, SCT, US – where order expressly conditioned on visitation rights. In some nations, there is no right to visitation – (H, T).

As a rule, visitation is not granted to grandparents or other relatives. Exceptions for grandparents; FR, IR, ISR, NZ, SCT, SA, SZ, US (some states).

The wishes of the child are generally taken into consideration, if old enough and apparently not unduly influenced (Exceptions – G).

Visitation may generally be enforced through the same court or administrative body which makes the determination. A wilful defaulter may generally be punished by imprisonment or fine. It is not enforced in H, MEX or NZ. In England, they have found the threat of change in custody to be an effective tool.

B. *Recognition of Orders of Other Countries*

All jurisdictions agree that each will make the determination based upon the presence of the child within the jurisdiction. Most will give consideration to the order of the other country, particularly if the child and parents were within that country's jurisdiction when the order was made, but no country will be completely bound by it. Austria recognizes determination of state of origin of the father, and if he is deceased, that of mother.

The Scandinavian countries have reciprocal treaties. (Convention of February 6, 1931). Yet the "best interest of the child" is determined by the country in which the child is located. The same countries are now considering a new convention for the mutual enforcement of custody determinations.

France will not recognize custody determinations of other countries regarding children within its borders but the German courts will do so.

In Holland, which is a signatory to the Hague Convention of June 12, 1902, the national law of the child is applicable.

The British Commonwealth also have reciprocal treaties.

Switzerland has treaties with Belgium, Germany, France, Italy, Austria, Sweden, Spain and Czechoslovakia as to certain cantons: Bern with Roumania; Lucerne with Lichtenstein; St. Gallen with Austria; Zurich with Austria. It is considering the draft of the International Convention on Recognition and Enforcement of Child Custody Decisions (49th Conference of International Law Association).

There is also pending the Hague Convention of October 5, 1961 on guardianship matters.

C. *Inter-State or Inter-Province Enforcement Within the Country*

Where the child lives in a state or province other than that of the suing parent, problems arise as to which court has jurisdiction. In most cases the court where the child resides will assume jurisdiction over custody. If the law under which it operates is a federal law, then there is less of a problem. But questions do arise when the laws are different in each of the states or provinces involved.

In some cases the court from which an abduction took place (as in Canada) or which granted the divorce or separation (as in France) or of the child's domicile (as in Holland or P) or of the marital home (as in Mexico or Norway) may take jurisdiction. But there is a limit to what it can do about enforcement in the absence of the child or offending parent.

In the US there is great confusion among the states as to the basis for exercising custody jurisdiction. It may be (1) that defendant is domiciled, resident or present in the forum (2) that child is domiciled in, although absent from, the forum (3) that child is physically present in forum (4) combination of two of the above. There is also a serious problem because under American law, a parent who abducts a child may do so to relitigate the merits in the new state in an attempt to secure a change of custody.

D. *Recommendations for action or legislation in each Country*

1. Appointment by court of counsel for the child to protect his interests (C).
2. International enforcement of decrees or agreements (E, FD, FR, ISR, NY).
3. Uniform Minor's Code (MEX).
4. Jurisdiction should be based on ordinary residence of the child (SCT).
5. Proper arrangements for custody as condition precedent to granting divorce (SA).
6. Greater use of specialized agencies for reports (SA).
7. All divorce and custody matters to be handled more informally, perhaps in Family Court with assistance of social worker, psychologist and psychiatrist (SA).
8. Steps to discourage abductions in violation of custody and visitation orders. Courts should decline to change other country's decree at request of violating party unless children are dependent or neglected (US).

E. *Suggested topics for discussion at Dublin*

1. Problems arising from intercountry removal of children in violation of court order (ASLA, US).
2. Control of passport issuance where custody or access order in existence (ASLA).
3. International Enforcement of Orders or Agreements (E, FD, FR, ISR, IT, MEX, SA).
4. Uniform Custody Laws (NY).
5. Determination of child's domicile (SCT, SA).
6. Children of polygamous unions (SA).
7. Should parent always prevail over non-parent in custody proceedings? (US).

8. May custody be awarded to an adulterous or alcoholic mother? (US).
9. What are the evidentary rules as to admissibility of investigations and reports on family background and psychiatric and social needs of the child? What court facilities are needed for investigation of custody disputes? Should other governmental or welfare agencies make investigations and reports? (US).
10. Should custody disputes be handled in a non-adversary proceeding?

III. *Interprofessional Co-operation in Dealing with Problems of Support and Custody of Children*

A. *Whose responsibility to establish the facts?*

There is a difference of opinion as to who should do the marshalling of the evidence. Most countries say the parties themselves (ASLA, AST, C, FD, FR, G, IR, ISR, MEX, NZ, NY, NI, SCT, SA, SZ, US). Yet it is clear that in most disputed proceedings, additional help is required. In some countries, welfare agencies provide this (ASLA, C-Ontario, FD, FR, G, H, ISR, MEX, NY, NI, SA, US [some states]). In many jurisdictions the court has a responsibility for getting information (AST, FR, G, IR, IT, MEX, NY, SZ). The court does not do so in others (C, NZ, NI, SCT).

B. *Use by courts of other professions in arriving at decisions*

1. Court welfare officers, psychologists or psychiatrists on staff (ASLA, AST, C, FR, FD, G, ISR, IR, IT, MEX, P, US).
2. Referrals to non-court professionals for recommendations (D [on consent], E, FD [on consent], FR, G, H, ISR, IR, MEX, NZ, NY, SCT, SA, SZ, US).
3. Referrals to non-court professionals or other agencies for determinations (AST, FD [on consent], IR).

C. *Handling by Agencies or Organizations other than the courts*

1. No country felt that decisions should be removed from the courts, although some felt that this should be handled by specialized family courts.
2. Great stress was laid on proper utilization by the courts of trained workers and specialized agencies to make investigations, reports and recommendations.

APPENDIX

REPLIES TO QUESTIONNAIRE

Received from National Correspondents

I. *As to Support of Children*

A. *What are the laws in your country relating to responsibility of parents to children?*

1. To what age?

Australia	– *Federal* – Matrimonial Causes Act – 21 years. *State* – Maintenance Act (South Australian Act basis) 18 years or self-supporting. (May be extended 2 years if child training for profession or trade).
Austria	– No age limit – until self-supporting.
Canada	– Criminal responsibility up to 16 years. *Ontario:* Maintenance orders in Juvenile and Family Courts, age 16; in Surrogate and Supreme Courts, no limitation – ordinarily age 16, may extend to age 21; *Alberta:* Maintenance orders to age 21; *British Columbia:* The Court of Summary Process has jurisdiction to age 18.
Denmark	– 18 years.
England	– Generally 16 but may be continued to 21 or over. Liability of parent ends at age 16 if child committed or placed.
Finland	– Age 21 unless self-supporting before that age.
France	– No age limit.
Germany	– No age limit.
Iran	– Boys, 18 years (or when recognized as adult by law). Girls, 18 or sooner (15 if recognized as adults).
Israel	– 18 years. (Under Jewish law, 15 years).
Mexico	– Responsibility of parents for food, clothing, lodging and assistance in cases of illness has generally no age limit when children in need and parents have resources. Also parents must provide support by will (1) to male descendants less than 21, and (2) to unmarried daughters.

Netherlands	– 21 years or marriage if that occurs first.
New Zealand	– 16 years.
Norway	– 18 years or later if child incapable of supporting himself. In special cases may cease when child 15 years.
North. Ireland	– Varies according to particular statutes. *Common law,* no legal obligation on parent; *Criminal law,* neglect up to 17 years; *Summary Jurisdiction Act,* 16 years; *Maintenance and Affiliation Orders Act,* up to 16 years.
Portugal	– 21 years.
Scotland	– No age limit. Obligation subsists until child self-supporting; normally until child 21 years.
South Africa	– 18 is usual age at which parental obligation ceases, but it is not a rigid rule.
Switzerland	– Normally until the 20th birthday of the child.
Turkey	– 18 years.
United States	– Usually 21 years although the legislatures of the various states may fix different age (i. e. Hawaii, 20 years; in 8 states, 21 for males and 18 for females; Kentucky, 18 for both males and females).

1. (a) Any exceptions for physical or mental disability beyond the age? What are these exceptions?

Australia	– *Federal* – Matrimonial Causes Act – exception in discretion of court in special circumstances. *State* – Maintenance Act – yes – if child over 18 unable to earn his own living because of physical disability or mental incapacity.
Austria	– Yes – if child becomes unable to support itself, whatever the reason, parents again responsible.
Canada	– *Ontario:* Possible for order beyond age of 21 in any circumstances; *Alberta:* Court has discretion; *British Columbia:* No special provision for exceptional circumstances.

Denmark	– No.
England	– See 1.
Finland	– In case of illness or inability.
France	– In case of need.
Germany	– Yes.
Iran	– Yes – if children become ill or insane. The court determines the date when this is over.
Israel	– Yes. In case of disability (no restriction or limitation as to causes of disability) this responsibility on parents under the Maintenance Act and under Jewish Religious Law.
Mexico	– Yes. Parents are responsible for children with disabilities even when over 21 (not as exception but in accord with Mexican legal system), unless they are married or have children of 21 or over of their own. Then responsibility belongs to spouse or to their adult children.
Netherlands	– Not as to parents but anyone who lacks sufficient means of support (no reason given) is entitled to receive aid from Government funds. If mother unwed and father has not "recognized" child, father only responsible after child's majority if child unable to support itself because of mental or physical disabilities. Same limitation as to liability of mother for out-of-wedlock child after its majority.
New Zealand	– Yes – where child suffers from some physical or mental disability.
Norway	– Yes. If child has such poor health or small ability that it is incapable of supporting itself.
North. Ireland	– Yes. Under the *Inheritance Act* a son or daughter who is, by reason of mental or physical disability, incapable of maintaining himself or herself. Yes. Under *Maintenance* and *Affiliation Orders Act* if earning capacity of child is impaired through illness or disability of mind or body.
Portugal	– Yes. Deaf and mute or blind children can be declared incapable in last year of their minority. Also prodigals, i. e. alcoholics or drug addicts.

Scotland	– Yes – if child is physically or mentally unable to support himself.
South Africa	– Yes. If child, for some reason, such as physical or mental disability is unable to support himself after 18, then parental obligation continues.
Switzerland	– When child is permanently incapable of earning a living due to infirmity or necessity of child's being cared for in an educational establishment, supplemental obligation of support (necessary support) replaces obligation of support (means basis).
Turkey	– After majority, support only in issue in cases of guardianship (insanity or feeble mindedness; wastefulness; drunkenness; misconduct and mismanagement of affairs).
United States	– Yes, in some states, if child is handicapped, dependent and unable to support itself. General rule is that once a parent's liability has terminated, it will not be revived by subsequent incapacitation of the child.

2. Are both parents responsible or only the father?

Australia	– *Federal* – Matrimonial Causes Act – Both parents responsible. *State* – Maintenance Act – Both parents and if child is legitimate, stepfather, stepmother and grandparents also responsible.
Austria	– Both parents, but father is *primarily* responsible. If father is without means or dead, mother is responsible.
Canada	– *Criminal Code:* Either parent but father is *primarily* responsible. (Mother may be responsible if she is head of the household); *Ontario:* No legislation requiring mother to support unless divorced for her adultery; *Alberta:* Only the father; *British Columbia:* Mother may be liable. (If separated, under separation agreement or possessed of property, her liability may be up to one-half).
Denmark	– Both parents.
England	– Both parents.

Finland	– Both parents.
France	– Both parents. Father *primarily* responsible. If father is dead or without means, mother is liable.
Germany	– Generally both but father *primarily* responsible.
Iran	– Both parents.
Israel	– *Maintenance Act* – apparently both. *Jewish Law* – both parents primarily and equally responsible.
Mexico	– 1. Minor children of undissolved marriage, father is primarily responsible; 2. Minor children of annulled marriage or of divorced parents, both parents responsible; 3. If divorce is voluntary, both parents decide who is responsible; they must present agreement. They may decide both will be responsible.
Netherlands	– Both parents according to their means and ability to pay.
New Zealand	– Both parents according to their financial means.
Norway	– Both parents according to his or her financial ability.
North. Ireland	– Both parents.
Portugal	– Both parents are responsible, but if father is dead, absent or incapacitated, the mother takes over.
Scotland	– Both parents, father primarily, mother if father is dead or not able to support the child. If children illegitimate, both parents equally liable.
South Africa	– Both parents.
Switzerland	– The support obligation is primarily that of the father.
Turkey	– Father and mother, if they work together, share a common responsibility.
United States	– Usual American rule – father has *primary* duty but mother, in exceptional circumstances, may have a secondary liability.

2. (a) If the mother may be held liable, under what conditions?

Australia	– *Federal* – Matrimonial Causes Act – In discretion of court; having regard to means, earning capacity and conduct of parents and all other relevant circumstances. Maintenance may be ordered paid by either party. *State* – Maintenance Act – Maintenance may be ordered paid by either party. If child illegitimate, father, mother's husband and mother responsible in that order.
Austria	– If father is without means or dead, the mother is responsible.
Canada	– *Criminal Code:* Either parent may be held, but in practice, the mother normally only if she is the actual head of the household.
Denmark	– Both parents must provide for the child.
England	– If in receipt of income.
Finland	– Parents responsible according to their abilities either by financial means or work at home or by other means.
France	– The mother is liable if the father is dead or has not the means.
Germany	– The mother is obliged to earn money outside the household only if the income of the father is insufficient for proper support.
Iran	– Mother may be liable when the father is "unfit, physically, mentally, morally or financially" and the wife accepts such responsibility.
Israel	– *Maintenance Act* – Both parents primarily and equally responsible. *Jewish Law* – Mother responsible if the father fails to support or maintenance by the father is inadequate and the mother has sufficient means to support.
Mexico	– If marriage undissolved, mother may be held liable if she has property of her own or does any work, or practices any profession, trade or business. Her contribution should never exceed one-half of family expenses unless husband is incapacitated for work and has no property; then all expenses are wife's, payable from her property.

If marriage dissolved by annulment or "necessary" divorce, mother is responsible. Also if it is so agreed in agreement of Voluntary divorce.

Netherlands – Both parents are responsible according to their means and ability to pay. Unwed mother is fully responsible during child's minority; the father only to a limited extent.

New Zealand – The degree of responsibility will depend normally upon the financial means of both parents.

Norway – Both parents liable according to his or her financial ability.

North. Ireland – *Maintenance and Affiliation Orders Act* – If wife petitions for divorce on ground of her husband's insanity.

Portugal – Both parents responsible, but if father is dead, absent or incapacitated, the mother takes over.

Scotland – Mother liable if father is dead or unable to support child. (With illegitimate children both parents equally liable until child is 16).

South Africa – If the mother possesses sufficient means, and the father is without means, the mother will be solely liable.

Switzerland – Insofar as the father does not or cannot furnish support, the mother must do so and can seek recourse against the father if he is capable of working but fails to do so.

Turkey – If parents work together, they exercise a common responsibility.

United States – Mother, in some states, may be held secondarily liable where the father is incapacitated or has abandoned the family and the mother has means or potential or actual income. In some states, if father fails to support and children in need, mother may be held liable. Welfare laws often stipulate mother's secondary liability after father's primary obligation. "Family allowance" statutes may impose liability for necessaries on a mother.

2. (b) If both are liable, is the father primarily responsible?

Australia — *Federal Act* — Discretion of the court.
State Act — Maintenance may be ordered paid by either party.

Austria — Yes. If father is without means or dead, mother is responsible.

Canada — Under *Criminal Code,* either parent may be held responsible; in practice the father is held to be primarily responsible.

Denmark — Apparently both parents equally responsible.

England — Both primarily liable.

Finland — Both equally responsible.

France — Yes.

Germany — As a rule both, but there is some sort of primary responsibility of the father as he is primarily responsible for support. As to children of unwed parents, father is primarily responsible in relation to the mother.

Iran — Father is considered primarily liable.

Israel — *The Maintenance Act* — Yes. The court may allocate support between them or adjudge them liable, jointly and severally.
Jewish Law. — Yes.

Mexico — If marriage undissolved, father is primarily responsible.
In case of an annulled marriage or one dissolved by "necessary" divorce, father not always primarily responsible; both parents responsible in proportion to their property to supply maintenance and education of their sons until 21 and of daughters (who live "honorably") until they marry. In the case of "voluntary" divorce, a greater responsibility may be placed on the father or on the mother.

Netherlands — Both parents are responsible according to their means and ability to pay.

New Zealand — Both parents responsible; degree depends upon their financial means.

Norway — Both parents liable according to financial ability.

North. Ireland — *Maintenance and Affiliation Act — Welfare Securities Act* — Both liable.

Portugal — Both responsible but father is the family leader.

Scotland — Yes.

South Africa — Generally speaking, both parents are liable.

Switzerland — The support-obligation is primarily that of the father.

Turkey — If parents work together, they share a common responsibility.

United States — General American rule is that father has primary duty regardless of mother's resources. In a few states by statute, mother is equally liable.

2. (c) If both are liable, how is responsibility allocated?

Australia — *Federal Act* — Court allocates in its discretion having regard to the means, earning capacity and conduct of the spouses and all other relevant circumstances.
State Act — Father, mother, stepfather, stepmother and grandparents are liable to contribute according to their several abilities and in above order.

Austria — The father provides the subsistence and the mother has the care of "the body and health".

Canada — See answers to I. A. 2. (a) and I. A. 2. (b).

Denmark — Apparently both parents are responsible; both directly to the children and to the public. If children removed from home for parental neglect both parents are obliged in principle to refund to public all expenses. If parents do not live together and child is with mother she can obtain child support from father and vice versa.

England — Discretionary.

Finland — According to their abilities and either by financial means or work at home or by other means.

France — Where the obligation to support a child has been enforced against one parent only, this parent can in turn obtain contribution from the other in proportion to respective assets.

Germany — See answer to I. A. 2. (b).

Iran — "The support and custody of the children" up to 2 years for sons and 7 years for daughters must be provided by father (living accommodations and support) "and the wife is to maintain and practice this at home and also while she is taking care of them especially in the absence of father".

Israel — *Maintenance Act* — The court may allocate support between the parents or adjudge them jointly or severally liable. (The Act contains no directions).
Jewish Law — If the father fails to support or maintenance by the father is inadequate, the mother is liable if she has sufficient means.

Mexico — 1. Legitimate children — 1/2 of liability may be allocated to the mother.
2. Children of annulled marriage or one dissolved by necessary divorce, when both parents have means, the court allocates according to their assets, but if only one has resources, he alone must support.
3. Agreements of voluntary divorce, both parents determine manner of allocation.

Netherlands — Both parents are responsible according to their means and ability to pay.

New Zealand — The financial means of the parents determines the degree of their responsibility.

Norway — According to the financial ability of each parent.

North. Ireland — Depends on particular statute.
Matrimonial Causes Act — Husband or wife (if she petitions for divorce on ground of husband's insanity) may be ordered to secure such gross or annual sum as court deems reasonable.

Portugal — No answer given. See I. A. 2. (a).

Scotland — Both parents are not liable at same time. With illegitimate children, both parents liable.

South Africa — Responsibility is allocated according to relative means of parents.

Switzerland — The charge is divided ultimately according to the property regime of the parents. The statutory and most common type is the "community" regime where the assets of the spouses are combined into an economic unity and the husband administers the wife's assets without her consent if necessary. If the mother has to consume her own assets to support the child because of the father's neglect of duty, at the end of the marriage, she has an indemnification claim against her husband.

Turkey – If parents work together, they share a common responsibility.

United States – Responsibility is allocated by equitable principles with regard to condition and means of each parent and the needs of the children. Usually where mother is liable under Welfare laws, if she must pay creditors or provide support, she will have a cause of action to recoup such payments from father.

3. Is the parent responsible if the child is married, working, studying in college or professional school?

Australia – If child is married, husband or wife of child is primarily responsible, but parents may be secondarily responsible. If child is working, normally parents not responsible but if child's wages insufficient to maintain child, parents are responsible. If child is studying in college or professional school, under *State Act*, parental responsibility may be extended for 2 years beyond child's reaching age 18.

Austria – If daughter married, duty of parents becomes secondary.

Canada – *Ontario:* Unlikely parent would be found responsible if child married or working. If child under 21 and in college or professional school – order made until 21. Not likely thereafter.
Alberta: Child under 21 and attending institution of learning, judge has discretion to order support.
British Columbia: Same rule would apply.

Denmark – Contribution to a daughter ceases when she is married unless county authorities decide otherwise. If child studying, support obligation may continue until 24 years.

England – Yes, if an order has been made.

Finland	– If child continues studies and is in need of support, parents are responsible until child is 21. Marital status is not a decisive factor.
France	– Question of liability only arises when child in need of support, which is a question for the court.
Germany	– Yes, if child is studying in college or professional school and needs support and parents able financially. If a child is married, husband responsible primarily and parents only if financially able.
Iran	– No. If child elopes or commits rape and is forced by Office of District Attorney to marry, child remains under support of the parent who voluntarily undertakes the responsibility of their support. If child elopes, parent only responsible for support if parent's fault.
Israel	– Under *Maintenance Act*, if daughter under 18, her marriage would have little bearing as to liability of parents; if married daughter (over 18) cannot obtain support from her husband, parents may be liable. Question of children studying is governed by above principles.
Mexico	– If the child is married, no liability on parent; in case of need, duty on child's spouse, but if spouse incapacitated and parent can afford obligation, parent is again responsible. Parent's obligation, if child studies (in college or professional school), only until child 21 years.
Netherlands	– The only criterion is the minority of the child, or its need, if it is of age.
New Zealand	– If child is engaging in full-time training or study, responsibility of parents for support may continue after 16.
Norway	– No special rules for married children but it is generally assumed that married child must be responsible for its own support. Parents can be ordered to contribute to education of child over 18 if this is reasonable according to parents' finances, child's abilities and situation in general.
North. Ireland	– *Maintenance and Affiliation Act* – Child in education or training after age 16 – court may direct support for 2 years or up to 21 years. If a female child is married, no order will be made.

Portugal – A married child ceases to be a minor. The parent is responsible for a child studying, and as a general rule for one working.

Scotland – Father of married female child liable secondarily (primary responsibility on husband). Father of married male child responsible (but not for his daughter-in-law). Parent is responsible if child is studying in college or professional school and unable to support itself.

South Africa – If daughter marries, duty of support in first instance, falls upon her husband. If her husband is unable to support her, parents again become responsible, if she is unable to support herself. Same rule applies to married son. A child who can maintain himself through income from employment, is not entitled to support from parents.

A child studying in college or professional school, and who cannot support himself, is entitled to support from parents. Whether child can request parents to send him to college or professional school depends on standard of living and station in life of the parents.

Switzerland – If parents or the child chooses, with their consent, a training that is not finished when child reaches majority, parents remain liable for child's support up to time when it is reasonable for the child to have finished such training. (Parents have duty to have child trained "according to their economic situation", taking into consideration the child's talents and inclinations).

If child marries, this effects majority and parental support obligation ceases. (But eventual supplemental support obligation remains).

Turkey – Marriage effects majority. If child in need after majority, parents responsible.

United States – Marriage of a minor child effects its emancipation as a general rule and there is no longer parental responsibility for support. (Few states – marriage of minor must be with parental consent). If child working and parent emancipates it, no parental support obligation. In some states, parent must pay for child's college education and under older rule, father does not have this duty unless he had agreed to send child to college.

4. Is there a difference as to children of unwed parents?

Australia	– *Federal* – Matrimonial Causes Act – Applies only where a purported marriage and a nullity suit or an adopted child. Even though child is of unwed parents, such child may receive support. *State* – Maintenance Act – If child illegitimate the father, the mother's husband and mother are responsible (in this order).
Austria	– No difference as to children of unwed parents.
Canada	– *Ontario:* No obligation to support illegitimate child in absence of agreement or affiliation order. (Order limited to age 16). *Alberta and British Columbia:* Putative father has similar liability as in Ontario.
Denmark	– No difference.
England	– Yes.
Finland	– Putative father liable until age 17 (if special reason he can be made liable until 21 – if child ill or unable to support itself or has special talents).
France	– If the father has both legitimate and illegitimate children, the legitimate children have a preferred status. If no legitimates, no difference in the rules as to support.
Germany	– If children are sound and healthy; there is a difference in case of children of unwed parents, since the father's obligation ends with 18th year.
Iran	– When court determines child of unwed parents, belongs to either parent, no difference "Except for the stipulated terms and conditions provided for the unwed parents, all the ordinary terms and conditions for the support of the different children shall be the same."
Israel	– No difference as to children of unwed parents. (Under the Act or under Jewish Law).
Mexico	– Yes. Duty to support only as a result of filiation acknowledgment, whether voluntary or judicial. The obligation falls on both parents if they made such acknowledgment, or only on the one who made it.

Netherlands – Unwed mother is fully responsible during child's minority. The father only to a limited extent (depending on his responsibility to other dependents. After child's majority father is only responsible for its support if child unable to support itself because of physical or mental disabilities. Same with mother (if child conceived in adultery or incest).

New Zealand – In theory, no. In practice, yes – particularly as to father's financial responsibility.

Norway – No difference.

North. Ireland – As to provisions for children of unwed parents, it makes a difference as to whether the claim is by a mother for maintenance or a claim in relation to payment by the state under some family allowance plan. Moral obligation extends to illegitimate children.

Portugal – Children of unwed parents are ruled as legitimates, i. e. "according to the situation". But parents only have paternal authority over illegitimates if they recognized them willingly or if the court granted them this power at their request.

Scotland – Yes. Obligation is joint as to children of unwed parents. Both parents are equally liable to maintain the child until age 16. (At common law if child physically or mentally incapable or not self-supporting, the obligation continues).

South Africa – No difference.

Switzerland – There is a difference. Father is only obliged to contribute to child's support until child is 18. When father legitimates such child by marrying the mother or adopting the child or if court awards him the child, the father has the same responsibility as for a child born in wedlock.

Turkey – Guardianship of children of unwed parents is with mother. In the event of a paternity suit, the court determines which parent is to exercise the authority.

United States – Yes. Mother of illegitimate child (aside from certain statutes which impose liability upon the father whose paternity has been established) has support duty. Some states hold that support duty is owed to every child by parents whether they are married or not. Sometimes duty is statutory. In most states statutes provide for proceedings to establish illegitimate child's paternity and to compel support. This duty continues generally until child reaches majority. A putative father may obligate himself for support by agreement.

5. Are grandparents responsible for grandchildren?
If so, under what conditions?

Australia	– *Federal* – Matrimonial Causes Act – No. *State* – Maintenance Act – Yes, for maintenance of legitimate grandchildren, after father, mother, stepfather, stepmother.
Austria	– Yes, if mother is dead, or has no means, paternal grandparents are responsible, then maternal grandparents.
Canada	– *Ontario* – No. *Alberta* – Statute provides responsibility in case of "need" but is never enforced. *British Columbia* – No.
Denmark	– No.
England	– Yes, if child has been committed to care of local authority.
Finland	– No.
France	– Yes, if parents are dead or without the necessary means.
Germany	– Grandparents might be responsible if parents unable to give the needed support.
Iran	– If minor's father dies or becomes insane, grandfather becomes legal guardian and must provide support except when he does not want "the responsibility and exhibits reasonable evidence acceptable to the court for refusing or when he is found unfit" . . . then he shall be excused from such responsibility."
Israel	– Yes, both under the Act and under Jewish Law if parents fail or their means are inadequate.
Mexico	– Yes, and so are ascendants nearest in degree. The court distributes amount due from grandparents (i. e., if both maternal and paternal), in proportion to their assets and if only one has resources, "he alone shall comply with the obligation").

Netherlands – Yes, in case of lack of means of support of parents.

New Zealand – In theory, yes. In practice, to a limited extent and only if financial support cannot be derived from parent or parents.

Norway – No.

North. Ireland – No reply.

Portugal – Grandparents are only responsible when the parents are dead or incapacitated and they are chosen as guardians. But grandchildren can claim *support* from them ("alimony").

Scotland – Yes, where both parents are dead or without means; paternal grandparents being primarily liable and maternal grandparents secondarily liable.

South Africa – If both parents are unable to support their children, the duty passes to the grandparents (both paternal and maternal).

Switzerland – No, not strictly in a legal sense, but in a moral sense, yes. However, they must assist grandchildren in case of emergency; also where grandparents, not parents, are appointed as guardians of the children. The moral duty may rise to the legal obligation of supplemental support when the parents are unable to support or neglect their duty and children are in need. Responsibility of grandparents, then, is for the living expenses of the grandchild according to the standards of those liable. If grandparents die, then this duty of supplemental support, would devolve upon surviving great-grandparents.

Turkey – Not in principle, but in certain cases, a court can name them as guardians.

United States – No, in absence of statutes. In some states, welfare laws impose such a duty on grandparents of indigent children under certain circumstances; usually where grandparents have sufficient means and parents unable to support child, or where father is dead. Duty of grandparents under such laws is secondary.

6. Are orders for support subject to modification because of changed circumstances?

Australia – Yes, both under the Federal and State Acts.

Austria – All orders for support are submitted to the "clausula rebus sic stantibus".

Canada	– Yes, in Ontario, Alberta and British Columbia.
Denmark	– Yes.
England	– Yes.
Finland	– Yes, if essential changes take place, either concerning the need or the ability to support.
France	– Yes.
Germany	– Yes.
Iran	– Yes, by petition of the beneficiary and/or the minor himself or anybody who reports the changes to the Surrogate's Court and/or the District Attorney.
Israel	– Yes, both under the Act and under Jewish Law.
Mexico	– Yes. "Court resolutions . . . in connection with support . . . may be changed and modified because of changed circumstances."
Netherlands	– Yes.
New Zealand	– Yes.
Norway	– Yes.
North. Ireland	– Yes – Maintenance and Affiliation Orders Act (1966).
Portugal	– Yes.
Scotland	– Yes.
South Africa	– Yes.
Switzerland	– Yes, when conditions change, judicial and administrative arrangements for support may be modified or suspended.
Turkey	– Yes. Agreements as to support are subject to review by the court. The authority of the court is not limited by the agreement of the parties.
United States	– Yes, generally. The power to modify may be reserved in the original order. Statutes providing for courts to order child support in matrimonial cases usually authorize modification.

B. *What standards are applied in the determination of responsibility and need?*

1. Is the amount determined on the basis of minimum needs or in accordance with the ability or means or social standing of the parents?

Australia	– In accordance with the ability, means and social standing of the parent as well as the needs of the child.
Austria	– On the income, means and social standing of the parent, and on the needs of the child.
Canada	– *Ontario:* Station in life or social position of the parent. The means of the mother are also taken into account. Some judges will assess on minimum needs. Matter is in court's discretion. In Juvenile and Family courts, statute limits amount to $ 20 a week for each child. *Alberta:* Basis is need relative to social standing of parent. *British Columbia:* Basis is father's financial ability.
Denmark	– In accordance with the interests of the child and the social standing of the parents.
England	– In accordance with financial ability of parent.
Finland	– In accordance with the ability, means and social standing of the parent.
France	– Both the needs of the children and the financial position of the parents.
Germany	– Social and financial position of the child but the ability, means and social standing of the parents are also taken into account.
Iran	– The ability and means or social standing of the parent is the main factor.
Israel	– *The Act* contains no provisions; the courts have full discretion. *Jewish Law* – the minimum in any case, but able parents may be compelled to pay more according to their means.
Mexico	– On the basis of needs of the child and resources of the parent; not only minimum needs but according to parents' resources.
Netherlands	– Means and ability to pay of the parent.

New Zealand – All relevant circumstances including ability, means and social standing are taken into account.

Norway – Amounts are fixed in accordance with the parents' financial ability and the costs of the child's upbringing.

North. Ireland – Depends on who brings the application. If wife sues for child support, the courts will take all factors into account, including the parents' assets and income, and the standard of living to which they should be accustomed.
Under *Welfare Services* or *Supplementary Benefits Act* – minimum needs.

Portugal – Amount is based both on ability and means of parent and needs of the child.

Scotland – Amount is assessed by reference to financial and social standing of parent.

South Africa – On the basis of the ability, means and social standing of the parents.

Switzerland – The amount of support is apportioned to the parents' capacity to earn a living and to the needs of the child; it must at least conform to the parents' standard of living.

Turkey – The court exercises a broad discretion; fixes the amount according to child's minimum needs, parents' ability to pay and their station in life.

United States – Disagreement among American statutes. Some cases hold children entitled to support according to father's financial standing rather than on basis of child's actual needs. Most state statutes fix measure on basis of childrens' minimum needs, but current consensus is that father must do what he is financially able to do despite state expressing duty in terms of child's minimum needs.
Under Welfare laws, measure is minimum needs of child.

2. How do you determine ability to support?
   (a) Do you consider (1) Salary or income from business or profession? (2) Other income or assets? (3) Parents' expenses and obligations? (4) Parents' potential earnings?

Australia – (1), (2), (3) and (4) are all considered.

Austria – Consideration is given to income through work; income through personal fortune; taxes and unavoidable expenses are deducted, potential earning not considered by leading case.

Canada – *Ontario:* (1), (2), (3), (4) all considered but little weight given to potential earnings.
Alberta and *British Columbia:* Potential earnings not considered.

Denmark – All four points are taken into consideration.

England – (1), (2), (3), Yes. (4) Rarely, except if parents wilfully refrain from earning.

Finland – In case of (4), consideration given to fact that parent purposely earning less than his potential; i. e., continuing studies after a degree to avoid support obligation.

France – Liability to support is determined solely on parents' actual income.

Germany – All income and assets are taken into account, as well as expenses and other obligations, especially for support of other persons. All four factors taken into consideration.

Israel – All circumstances are considered.

Mexico – Resources are determined in accordance with (1) salary, commercial or professional income of one or both parents, (2) other income or assets, (3) parents' legitimate expenses and obligations, (4) any other possible income of any kind that parents may have.

Netherlands – All four factors taken into consideration.

New Zealand – All four matters considered.

Norway – The parents' financial situation as a whole is taken into account, their capital and present income and also potential earnings.

North. Ireland – Actual income considered, but not potential earnings. Parents' expenses and obligations considered – court has wide discretion.

Portugal – All assets are considered. Roughly 1/3 of total income is outside limit.

Scotland – All sources of income considered and also expenses and obligations, but not potential earnings.

South Africa — All factors mentioned are taken into consideration.

Switzerland — The ability of the parents to support is measured by: (1) their own income and assets, (2) the resources allowed to them from the assets of the child and the child's earnings from work, if any, (3) the support-obligation towards the other spouse or spouses, and other children, and the obligation of supplemental support towards their own parents and adult children (which has a preference against other claims against parents), (4) Parents' potential earnings. (Children's support claim exists without regard to parents' minimum needs).

Turkey — Salary or income and resources of parents considered.

United States — Usually consideration given to income, resources, ability to pay of the parent, the needs of the child, and the social standing and standard of living of parents, as well as physical condition of parent and child. Except where statute stipulates, no fixed formula. But in ascertaining ability to support primary emphasis is on economic circumstances of parents and children, parents' salary, wages, earning capacity or prospective earnings and frequently parent's assets and liabilities are considered and their nature. Parents' expenses are also considered. In some states potential earnings are considered.

2. (b) If the father is remarried with children in both families, which children have a prior claim, if any?

Australia — No difference between children of two families.

Austria — Children of several marriages have the same rights.

Canada — *Ontario:* Whether priority created depends on each case.
Alberta: The first family has prior claim but in practice, second families' need ranks ahead.
British Columbia: Father is equally responsible for children of both families.

Denmark — Legally, none of the children have a prior claim. Practically, where children of 1st marriage are with their mother, father's obligation is to pay amount fixed by county authorities. His obligation to children of second marriage is an obligation to support.

England	– No priority.
Finland	– All children are equal.
France	– Children of both families have equal claim.
Germany	– No priority of claim.
Iran	The priority is with the children who are living with the father except in those cases where the wife has custody and the father is obliged to pay alimony and living expenses. Then, when "there be a source of income known to the court . . . , the court shall indicate the monthly expenses to be paid to the child living with the mother". In cases where the court does not know of such a source of income and the mother must "demand and beg for it at intervals, the bureaucracy and legal process is so long that it is cheaper to dispense with the demand". Where children of different marriages are in same house as the father, no difference.
Israel	– No difference.
Mexico	– No difference. All children have the same support rights.
Netherlands	– Theoretically none, but in practice the children of the second family will usually be given priority, because their presence is taken into consideration in determining father's ability to pay.
New Zealand	– All circumstances are considered but other things being equal one would start from the proposition that all children had an equal claim.
Norway	– The father has the same support obligation to the children of both marriages but the larger the number of children, the smaller the amount payable to each group of children.
North. Ireland	– No direct answer to this.
Portugal	– There is no priority of claims.
Scotland	– There is no priority as between children of a prior and of a subsisting marriage.
South Africa	– Both sets of children have an equal claim.
Switzerland	– There is no priority of claims by children born of different marriages.

Turkey — The allocation of support is fixed in the order of the children's rights of inheritance.

United States — Father's obligation to support new wife and children may be a factor in determining amount of support payable for children of prior marriage. Usually father's obligation to his first family is regarded as a prior claim.

2. (c) If the father has out-of-wedlock children, do the children of his marriage have a preferred status?

Australia — Children of the marriage do have a preferred status over out-of-wedlock children. Support of illegitimate children is ordered only on the basis of need.

Austria — Illegitimate children are not inferior to legitimate children.

Canada — *Ontario:* No preferred status as to amount of support but the right of illegitimate children to support must be established by agreement or affiliation proceedings.

Denmark — No. In practice, the father's duty to out-of-wedlock children who live with their mother is to pay an annual sum.

England — Yes. Tendency to equate needs of illegitimate children with social status of mother. Legitimate children take social status of father, frequently better. But minimal requirements of each group are in parity.

Finland — Not necessarily. Only if child is recognized and registered as father's child. Same for children who are conceived during parents' engagement or when they later become engaged.

France — No. Out-of-wedlock children have same status as children born in wedlock (except when adulterine bastards).

Germany — Children of father's marriage do not have a preferred status; under certain circumstances the rights of out-of-wedlock children might be stronger.

Iran — "This, out-of-wedlock, it is not a practice in Iran, because as soon as the girl friend is found expectant, the easiest way is to marry and then the child shall

	not be considered out-of-wedlock." Bigamy and polygamy allowed except not practiced among Christians. The out-of-wedlock children do not inherit from their father but from their mother.
Israel	– No, neither under the Act, nor under Jewish Law.
Mexico	– No, because general rule that parents must support their children applies. The only problem lies in the voluntary or judicial acknowledgment of filiation; once the relationship is established the out-of-wedlock child must be supported by the father exactly as if he were a legitimate child.
Netherlands	– Theoretically, none. In practice the present family will usually be given priority because their presence is taken into consideration in determining parents' ability to pay.
New Zealand	– Yes, in practice.
Norway	– No.
North. Ireland	– Yes. An illegitimate child is not treated as its father's issue; but illegitimate children must be maintained by putative father who has been adjudged the father. (Court order provides for his weekly payments up to £ 2.10.0 until child is 16, Maintenance and Affiliation Orders Act, 1966).
Portugal	– Yes. An out-of-wedlock child cannot be placed in the parent's home without permission of the spouse.
Scotland	– Yes. Legitimate children have priority over illegitimate ones in Scotland.
South Africa	– Not as regards the right and obligation to maintenance and support.
Switzerland	– The children of the father's marriage have a preferred status insofar as they have a claim for complete support, while the out-of-wedlock children, if not recognized, can only claim a contribution to their support. In principle (not in degree), however, the support-obligation and the obligation to contribute have the same priority.
Turkey	– Yes. Legitimate children have a preferred status.

United States — Yes. In the majority of states, natural child does not have equal rights to support or inheritance with children born in wedlock. (In Arizona and Oregon statutes equalize status of out-of-wedlock children except under Federal Welfare Laws.) Illegitimate children excluded from coverage of Workmen's Compensation and Wrongful Death Acts as well as some Federal social legislation.

3. Does your government provide financial aid to children when the parent is in a position to provide support? If so, what kind?

Australia — Yes. Child endowment is paid by the Commonwealth as part of the Social Service Benefits, irrespective of financial position of parents. For a first child under 16, 50 cents per week; for a second child under 16, $ 1.00 per week; for a third under 16, $ 1.50 per week; for each subsequent child an increase of 25 cents; for every child between 16 and 21 receiving full-time education (and not employed), $ 18 per quarter.

Austria — No answer given.

Canada — The Federal Government maintains a universal system of family allowances. Small monthly amounts paid for each child under 16.
Ontario: Payments to mother by Municipal and Provincial Governments in case of need.
Alberta: If father is not paying, Welfare Dept. pays on basis of "need".

Denmark — If parents able to support, but cannot be persuaded to do so by county authorities, they will be removed to an infant home and parents will be obliged to refund a portion of expenses.

England — Yes. (a) Monetary allowancy from Ministry of Social Security who press mother to proceed against father to obtain monetary order; (b) if child in local authority home or foster care, local authority proceeds against father.

France — Not when the parent is in a position to provide support.

Germany — Yes. The Government pays a stipend beginning with the third child if parents are able to pay support. If parents are in need, they might get stipend beginning with second child.

Iran	– Apparently not. No official organization or special budget to provide help even to persons in need. Then there are some governmental as well as private charitable organizations to help. If parents have income and fail to support their children, there must be a good reason. Court decides whether reason is acceptable.
Israel	– Yes. By the Social Welfare Service, and by National Insurance. Support is given in money, release from school fees, placement of children and their maintenance in institutions, and with foster parents, if necessary.
Mexico	– No, not when the parent is in a position to provide support. In the case of helpless minors the Government provides certain social services, not financial, such as those of the National Institute for Childhood Protection and other institutions of the Department of Health and Assistance.
Netherlands	– Yes, in case of need. The Governmental agency will try to obtain reimbursement from a parent. The aid will usually consist of payment of an amount (sufficient to support the child) to the parent or person caring for the child. In exceptional cases, payment in kind may be given.
New Zealand	– This is done particularly in the case of separated parents, where the father is not supporting the children. The Government provides financial aid and recovers it or a portion of it from the father.
Norway	– By statute. The State prepays contributions (in the amount of Kr. 100. per month) if the parent who is ordered to pay support, fails to do so.
North. Ireland	– *Welfare Services Act* provides residential accommodations (this may include board and other items). The State may claim repayment from the father. *Supplementary Benefits Act* (1966) provides for benefits for those in need and recovery from responsible parent. *Family Allowance Act* (1966). The Ministry pays, for every family having 2 or more children, an allowance for each child (except the oldest) at the rate of 2 shillings per week for the first child (excepting the oldest) and 10 shillings per week for all the others.

National Insurance Act (1966) provides maternity benefits; allowances to child's guardian; to divorced women in certain circumstances and may allow increased grants to children.

Portugal – No. If a child is destitute, it can be placed in an orphanage.

Scotland – Yes. Even where parent in position to provide support. Family allowances paid to the mother for each child after the first.
National Assistance provides for payments to custodian when parents not providing support. A grant is given to expenses of senior school education which is provided free. Also, all university students are entitled to a minimum grant related to parent's circumstances.

South Africa – All children are entitled to free medical aid in municipal clinics; there is a school feeding scheme in some of the provinces; in all the provinces, free medical and dental examinations by governmental medical officials (regardless of ability of parents to pay).

Switzerland – No. Nevertheless the Government (State, Canton, Municipality) contributes in many ways to the well-being and education of children with nursery-schools, vacation homes, student-insurance, sports subsidies, etc. The Cantons furnish free tuition and free books and other assistance in the public secondary schools and grant children's allowances to employees up to a certain income and age level. The Confederation gives limited family allowances to rural employees and independent small farmers. In some Cantons there are also scholarships and student-loans.

Turkey – No. But governmental aid is given by means of scholarships to students and also aid is given by corporations and foundations.

United States – No. But there are meals and/or milk provided in some schools and scholarships provided by state as well as private institutions of higher learning; system of free college education in process of legislation.

4. Is there a difference in support as to out-of-wedlock children?

Australia – The only difference is the basis upon which the parent is ordered to support. In the case of out-of-wedlock children the basis would be need.

Austria	– Apparently no difference.
Canada	– *Ontario:* Support limited normally on a nominal basis. *Alberta:* No difference in theory but in practice smaller amounts awarded in affiliation cases. *British Columbia:* Generally awards based to greater extent on need than on ability to pay and social standing and standard of living of mother more important.
Denmark	– No difference.
England	– No.
Finland	– Normally support is based on means, ability and social standing of mother but condition of father considered if better. If father has recognized and registered child as provided by law, child has right to support in accordance with father's ability, means and social standing. Same as to children conceived when parents engaged to marry or when parents become engaged later.
France	– No difference unless children offspring of adulterous relationship.
Germany	– Legal rights of out-of-wedlock children might be stronger. Support determined by social and financial position of mother primarily. Also, father cannot claim inability to support.
Iran	– A psychological difference but no material difference.
Israel	– No.
Mexico	– None, when determining resources and needs. See answer to I. A. 4, for the differences in the allocation of the parents' responsibility.
Netherlands	– No.
New Zealand	– In theory, no. In practice, probably some difference.
Norway	– No.
North. Ireland	– Depends upon applicable statute – in some, no.
Portugal	– Yes. Only legitimate children can claim support from uncles.

Scotland — Yes. (1) Obligation between father and mother is joint and not joint and several; (2) By statute the obligation of support continues until child is 16, but without prejudice to common law obligation of support until child able to earn a subsistence; (3) Obligation does not extend to ascendants.

South Africa — Although the parental power of a child born out-of-wedlock vests solely in the mother, both the natural father and the mother have the legal duty of support. The child's position is similar to that of a legitimate child of divorced parents whose custody is given to the mother.

Switzerland — As far as the mother and her family, the out-of-wedlock child has the same legal position as a legitimate child. It remains with the mother and she must care for it. The father need provide only an adequate contribution toward its support and education until it reaches age 18. An obligation of supplemental support does not exist.

Turkey — No difference when there are no legitimate children. When there are, legitimate children are less favored.

United States — See answer to I. B. 2. (c).

C. *How do you enforce support?*

1. Who decides as to the amount of support and who does the enforcing?

(a) Administrative bodies? Which?

Australia — No.

Austria — No.

Canada — *Alberta:* No.
Ontario: No
British Columbia: No, except that in certain cases the Supt. of Child Welfare has discretion to increase payments required by agreements made under the children of Unmarried Parents Act; for enforcement of amended agreement, Family Court.

Denmark — The local counties (administrative bodies) decide on the amount and do the enforcing.

England	– No.
Finland	– Administrative bodies of first instance enforce (sheriffs, bailiffs, Province Boards and Bench of Magistrates. Judgments are usually enforced by authorities of first instance).
France	– No.
Germany	– No.
Iran	– No.
Israel	– No.
Mexico	– The amount to be paid could be determined by (1) the parents liable, (2) the other parent or ascendant exercising the parental authority, or (3) the Department of Public Prosecution. In voluntary divorce, parents agree and Court determines procedure. The Department of Public Prosecution (an administrative body) may be in charge of enforcing support.
Netherlands	– Councils for child protection in every Court district, advise the Courts as to the amount of support and whenever the Court so decrees, enforce the Court orders.
New Zealand	– No.
Norway	– The County Governor decides the amount of support of children born out-of-wedlock. In connection with separation or divorce, if parties agree to let him decide, he can stipulate the amount of child support.
North. Ireland	– No.
Portugal	– No.
Scotland	– No.
South Africa	– No.
Switzerland	– Not administrative bodies. Civil Court determines the amount of support and enforcement is had according to normal legal executional procedures.
Turkey	– No.
United States	– No. A Court determines the amount of child support and enforcement is by Court order.

1. (b) Courts? Which type of courts handle these cases? Those dealing with criminal matters? With civil actions? Others?

Australia — Courts. Under *Federal* (Matrimonial Causes Act) the Supreme Courts of the States. Under *State* legislation, Courts of Summary Jurisdiction or Supreme Courts.

Austria — Courts. The Civil Courts are competent where claims of minor children established through non-disputed procedure. The Criminal Court prosecutes violations of support duty.

Canada — *Ontario:* Juvenile and Family Courts; if none, Magistrate's Courts; Surrogate Court or Supreme Court. Juvenile and Family Court is a quasi-criminal court, uses criminal sanctions. Magistrate's Court is a criminal court. Surrogate Court is a civil court (only sanction, contempt or execution against property). Supreme Court has both civil and criminal jurisdiction, enforces orders for maintenance as does Surrogate Court.

Alberta: Supreme Court decides where matter is incidental to divorce actions. Family Courts (divisions of Magistrate's Court) decide where maintenance orders are main relief. Supreme Court judges rotate and handle all varieties of litigation.

British Columbia: Family and Children's Court has only municipal jurisdiction. Occasionally, when there is a divorce or separation decree, Supreme Court will enforce payment. (But court in which application made enforces).

Denmark — One must differentiate between the obligation to support owed the family and that owed the public (i. e., loans or subsidies to deserted wives and children and public's expenses for child's stay at an infant home). The support owed to family members might be fixed by the Court in matrimonial cases but in any other case (and in the judgment cases too), the amounts are fixed by administrative bodies (i. e., the local counties).

England — Yes. Magistrate's Court sitting as Domestic Court, exercising civil jurisdiction (90%). High Court in others.

Finland	– Courts decide as to amount of support – Common Courts; Circuit Courts in rural areas; in towns, those dealing with civil matters.
France	– Civil Courts in France determine amount and enforce payment.
Germany	– Lower courts decide as to amount. Enforcement by officials of civil courts.
Iran	– Usually a petition and claim which is filed for child support is sent to the district attorney. Every such claim is adjudged by the Trial Court. But recently, special courts (called Family Protection Courts) deal with such cases. If an offense has been perpetrated, the case is referred to the Penal Court.
Israel	– Civil and Religious Courts decide as to the amount of support and the ordinary execution offices enforce.
Mexico	– Civil Courts, at the request of persons mentioned in answer to C. 1. (a), decide on the amount. These courts have the necessary means of enforcement.
Netherlands	– The Civil Court decides as to the amount of support. The Juvenile Judge must be one of the three judges in session.
New Zealand	– These matters fall within a special jurisdiction of both the Summary Proceedings Court and the Supreme Court.
Norway	– In cases other than those in C. 1. (a), the amount of support is determined by the ordinary civil courts of law in connection with separation or divorce.
North. Ireland	– The courts normally decide the amount except as maximum is specified by statute. Then the special statutory bodies, such as the welfare authorities or Supplementary Benefits Commission have a certain discretion as to amount. Courts of Summary Jurisdiction deal with these matters except where High Court will do so in connection with divorce or nullity proceedings. Criminal Courts do not enforce payments but by threat of punishment for statutory non-support, provide a sanction. Court of Summary Jurisdiction may order attachment against property, imprisonment up to 3 years or attachment against pension or income.

Portugal – The "Minor Courts", special ("Central") courts in Lisboa, Porta and Coimbra. Elsewhere they are sections of ordinary courts.

Scotland – Decisions as to amount of support are made by the Civil Courts, and enforced by the parties in the first instance. These courts are Court of Session-Sheriff Courts. Wages may be attached or personal property may be sold or imprisonment may be had unless defaulter can establish failure to pay not wilful.

South Africa – The amount of support is decided by the courts dealing with civil actions: (a) Supreme Court (custody and support of minors in matrimonial actions); (b) Children's Court (in respect to certain categories of children).

Enforcement may be by a civil action (at instance of child or other spouse) but usually, the statutory criminal remedies are used. (Children's Act provides that one who is legally liable for child support and fails to support child despite ability to do so, is guilty of an offense and is liable to prosecution in Magistrate's Court).

Enforcement may be had either by ordinary execution or by commitment for contempt or by prosecution under Children's Act.

Switzerland – As long as parents are married the Civil Court will, if necessary and on petition of one of the parties, determine the children's support claim. The court can instruct the husband's debtors (or the wife's debtors) to pay directly to the wife. In case of divorce and in case of out-of-wedlock children, the court fixed the amount (in hearing in divorce or paternity case). The father of the illegitimate child may bind himself contractually to pay support. The claim of support can be enforced in all these cases according to the normal execution procedures.

Turkey – The amount of support is enforced by the Civil Courts dealing with civil actions. Generally, the justices of the peace (lower court magistrates are in charge of these matters).

United States – A court determines the amount of support and enforcement is by court order. Enforcement is in various ways depending on statutes of the various states;

e. g., by law actions in civil courts; by creditors for necessaries furnished children; in an equity proceeding; in matrimonial proceedings – enforceable by contempt. Most actions for child support are statutory actions of a civil or quasi-criminal nature.

	Supreme Court	Civil	Crim-inal	Juv. or Family	Magis-trate	Surro-gate	Relig.	Admin.
Australia	x							
Austria		x	x					
Canada:								
Ontario				x				
Alberta	x			x				
Brit. Col.	x			x				
Denmark	x (matri.)							x
England					x			
Finland		x						
France		x						
Germany		x						
Iran				x				
Israel		x					x	
Mexico		x						
Netherlands		x (incl. Juv. Judge)						
New Zealand		x						
Norway	x (matri.)							x
North. Ireland	x	x						
Portugal		x						
Scotland		x						
South Africa	x			x				
Switzerland		x						
Turkey		x						
United States	x			x				

1. (c) Other methods?

Australia	– No.
Austria	– The Criminal Court prosecutes violations regarding support duty.
Canada	– No other methods in Ontario, Alberta or British Columbia.
Denmark	– No.
England	– No.
Finland	– No.
France	– No answer.
Germany	– No.
Iran	– Mostly such cases are dealt with and settled in the ecclesiastical courts if and when ecclesiastical issues are involved. Sometimes the court makes a reference and the referee suggests a settlement. Recently they have "courts of equities, and most of the sheriffs and elders in the villages settle such issues . . . in the peaceful manner they deem advisable and reasonable."
Israel	– No.
Mexico	– There is the right to demand security (such as a mortgage, pledge, guaranty bond or deposit). Also the judge may fix (on demand and without a hearing), a "provisional pension", and judge may employ such means as he considers advisable to enforce payment of this "provisional pension".
Netherlands	– No.
New Zealand	– No.
Norway	– The spouses can also agree between themselves on the amount of child support.
North. Ireland	– No.
Portugal	– No.
Scotland	– There are other indirect methods of enforcement such as imprisoning a parent who wilfully fails to comply with a court order for support. The national government may institute criminal proceedings against a

parent who fails to support his children (if able) and he may be fined or imprisoned.

South Africa – Spouses may agree as to child support and this may be incorporated into divorce decree if court approves it but court may always vary this in interests of child.

Switzerland – The father of an illegitimate child may bind himself contractually to pay support.

Turkey – No.

United States – See I. C. 1. (b).

2. Are agreements concerning support subject to court review and revision?

Australia – *Federal* – Unless court sanctions agreement, the court may always make its own order.
State – An agreement does not oust court of jurisdiction to make its own order.

Austria – All agreements regarding child support must have consent of the court.

Canada – *Ontario:* Yes, despite agreement of parent.
Alberta: Yes. Agreement does not oust court's jurisdiction.
British Columbia: Yes.

Denmark – Agreements as to child support are never binding on the children and can be reviewed by the local counties at any time.

England – Yes, if change of circumstances.

Finland – Only in case one of the parents demands it.

France – Yes, because of changed circumstances.

Germany – Yes.

Iran – No, not unless arrangement is found to be illegal. But if both parties demand ratification of their agreement by the court, "the court shall ratify the same after the respective ceremonies are practical and adhered to."

Israel – Yes.

Mexico – Yes. Agreement in divorces *must* be approved by the judge during a hearing with the Department of Public Prosecution; this implies review and revision; court may even reject it.

Netherlands – Yes.

New Zealand – Yes.

Norway – Yes, even though the amount has been agreed to by spouses.

North. Ireland – Yes, because of change of circumstances.

Portugal – Yes.

Scotland – Agreements concerning support as well as court decisions may be reviewed and changed because of change of circumstances.

South Africa – Yes. Agreement cannot deprive court of right to modify in interests of child. In divorce action, court will incorporate agreement only if it approves it; such an agreement can always be varied by court on application in best interests of child.

Switzerland – In case of a support-settlement agreement, the court may not change the support unless the right to modify has been reserved.

Turkey – Yes. The court's authority is not limited by the agreement of the parties.

United States – Yes. The parents by private contract may not foreclose court jurisdiction to review and revise. However, a court gives great weight to amount agreed upon by the parties. The power to modify child support is regarded as inherent in the proper court.

3. If the parent fails to support, may he be imprisoned or punished in any way? Please describe.

Australia – *Federal Act* – Yes. Person in default may be punished by imprisonment for failure to comply with court order.

State Act – Father, but not mother, may be imprisoned. Court may order suspension of order on condition of paying arrears (as ordered) plus current support.

Austria	– Yes. If parent's failure endangers the support or education of the child, the criminal court can punish him with imprisonment up to six months.
Canada	– *Ontario:* Juvenile and Family Court or Magistrate's Court may imprison defaulter for period up to 3 months, after hearing, if default not due to inability to pay. Surrogate and Supreme Courts will only imprison for contempt of court; i. e., if failure to pay amount ordered was deliberate. *Alberta:* Yes. Father may be imprisoned for default. (This rarely occurs). *British Columbia:* Family Court can commit a defaulting father, to common jail (proceeding by way of show cause summons). Similar procedure in Supreme and County Courts if judgment was their order. (Rarely done as wife is required to pay costs).
Denmark	– First, if parent fails to pay attempt will be made to have amount withheld from his salary; as a last attempt he may be imprisoned for a certain time (but the imprisonment does not diminish his obligation for payment).
England	– Yes. Abandonment is criminal offense punishable by imprisonment up to 5 years. Non-payment of maintenance orders may result in imprisonment for contempt.
Finland	– Father may be placed in workhouse.
France	– If parent fails to comply with court order, he is guilty of offense "abandonment of family", punishable by fine of 300–600 francs or imprisonment from 3–12 months, or both.
Germany	– Yes. If failure is wilful and support of person entitled endangered, defaulter may be punished in Germany by imprisonment from 1 day to 5 years. (Very rarely done).
Iran	– Only when a complaint is filed with the district attorney against the parent responsible. Failure is not an offense unless it is proven to have been done with malice which makes it a penal case. Then the Penal Courts decide as to the punishment. Otherwise it is considered a civil case.

Israel	– Yes. The parent may be imprisoned in the course of execution to enforce payment; in the case of neglect, he may be punished under the criminal law.
Mexico	– Yes. In addition to civil sanction (loss of parental authority), parent subject to criminal sanction for offense of "abandonment of persons", of 1 to 6 months imprisonment, and parent is also deprived of "family rights".
Netherlands	– If a parent wilfully leaves a child destitute, he may be punished by imprisonment for up to 2 years or by a fine of up to 600 guilders. (Rarely done and maximum punishment is never given).
New Zealand	– Yes. Failure to support is a quasi-criminal offense for which parent may be imprisoned or fined. If he fails to obey court order, usually he is ordered to pay off arrears in installments, subject to imprisonment for failure to do so.
Norway	– If failure to support is wilful and parent has financial means or ability, he may be punished by fines or imprisonment up to 6 months. Under Criminal Code (rarely used) punishment may be for up to 2 years.
North. Ireland	– Yes, may be imprisoned (by court of summary jurisdiction) for up to 3 months if no sufficient distress against defaulter's goods, or attachment against pension or income.
Portugal	– If parent wilfully fails to support, he or she will be considered guilty of crime of "family desertion" and punished by imprisonment.
Scotland	– Yes, parent who wilfully fails to comply with court order may be imprisoned.
South Africa	– Yes. A parent wilfully failing to support child (despite ability to do so), may be fined up to £100 and/or sentenced to imprisonment for up to 1 year. Often fine and/or sentence suspended on payment of amount court orders.
Switzerland	– Deliberate neglect of support obligation because of aversion to work or debauchery is, upon complaint, punishable with imprisonment from 3 days to 3 years. Municipal or Cantonal child welfare agencies may bring complaint.

Turkey — No, not unless default results in a criminal offense (death, for example); he may be imprisoned.

United States — Yes, since child support orders emanate from courts, there is an inherent power to punish a wilful violation of a support order by civil or criminal contempt. Theoretically, in civil contempt, a father may be committed to prison until willing to comply with court's order. Statutes in many states place a time limit on period of commitment (usually 6 months). A father may be subject to criminal prosecution for desertion or non-support.

4. Is such enforcement done by the national (or federal) government? Or by local government (state, province, town, city)?

Australia — Enforcement is done by the State Court at the instance of the State Welfare Department. In the case of orders under the Federal (Matrimonial Causes Act), the powers of enforcement are in the State Courts.

Austria — Enforcement is done by the national government.

Canada — In general, enforcement is carried out by the province or by the city police forces established under provincial legislation.

Denmark — Enforcement is done through the local counties.

England — Abandonment-national; Maintenance-local.

Finland — Enforcement can be requested by the administrative board dealing with questions of maintenance in the community where the child resides, and the decision is made by the Province Board.

France — By the national government.

Germany — The enforcement is under federal law. The actual enforcement, however, is by people employed by the different German states.

Iran — Iran does not have different governments. All courts are but one court.

Israel — Such problems do not arise in Israel. The Attorney General or his representatives as well as Social Welfare Officers have some powers to prosecute actions for child support.

Mexico — Enforcement is by the local judicial authorities; civil or criminal courts, depending on the case.

Netherlands — By the national government.

New Zealand — Enforcement may be by complainant or complainant's lawyer or by officers of the court. The latter are government officials. Such an officer is attached to every Court of Summary Jurisdiction in New Zealand.

Norway — The national government but criminal proceedings are rarely instituted.

North. Ireland — In the case of neglect under the Children and Young Persons Act, the prosecutor will be the Crown; under the other specific statutes, the statutory bodies themselves can prosecute.

Portugal — By courts of place of child's residence if child and parent do not live in same place.

Scotland — The national government (not local), assists in enforcement by instituting criminal proceedings against defaulting parent who fails (although able) to pay child support.

South Africa — The enforcement is by the national government through the Magistrate's Court.

Switzerland — The criminal case is tried by the ordinary criminal courts of the place where the support is payable.

Turkey — Report does not specify.

United States — Enforcement is usually secured in the county of the state where the action was originally brought. Generally only the court which entered the support order has the power and authority to enforce it directly by contempt procedure. The federal government generally is not concerned with the enforcement of state child support orders. If a father who is subject to a court order flees the jurisdiction, it is possible to secure support through uniform support law enforcement (see IC 5).

5. Is there a problem when the parent lives in a city or province other than that in which the child resides? If so, how is it handled?

Australia — *Federal Act* — All courts having jurisdiction under the Act act in aid of and are auxiliary to each other,

so that the orders of one state court can be enforced in another state court.
State Act — Orders in other states may be enforced upon their registration in the state in which enforcement is sought.

Austria — The claims of support, their prosecution and enforcement are guaranteed in the whole country.

Canada — *Ontario:* If the cities are within the province but in different counties, the mother must either bring proceedings in the Supreme Court having jurisdiction throughout the province or in the appropriate Surrogate or Juvenile and Family Court. Under the legislation administered by Juvenile and Family Courts, where proceedings are commenced in one jurisdictional area, and the father lives in another and does not appear, the court makes a provisional order which must be confirmed in father's jurisdiction after he has an opportunity to be heard.
Similar procedure exists between courts of different provinces. There is also statutory recognition of maintenance orders made in other provinces and procedures prescribed for their enforcement and similar reciprocity exists with many foreign countries.

Denmark — No problem.

England — No.

Finland — The request comes from the community where the child resides and the decision as to enforcement is made by the Province Board where the parent resides.

France — There is no problem.

Germany — No problem since the entire procedure is governed by federal law.

Iran — There has never been such a problem. When the issue is once decided by the court, that is all.

Israel — Problem does not arise.

Mexico — The only problem is to determine the competence of the judge who is to try the case. In principle, it is the judge of the residence of the defendant parent; if the case deals with minor legitimate children living with their mother who has been abandoned by their father, the competent judge is that of the mother's residence. Supreme Court of Justice has established rule that "The competent court is that of the presumptive abandoned spouse." (Because of similarity among local laws of various states). Almost all the states, give reciprocity to judgments of courts of the other Mexican states.

Netherlands — No problem as long as both are in the Netherlands.

New Zealand — No problem.

Norway — No special problem.

North. Ireland — Procedure exists to take care of this by registration of order.

Portugal — Competent court is that of children's residence.

Scotland — No legal (as distinct from practical) problem because in general (a) proceedings for court order may be brought in appropriate court where child resides, and (b) court order may be enforced in any part of the United Kingdom.

South Africa — No particular problem is experienced, except insofar as that of tracing a defaulting party which is a serious problem.

Switzerland — The court of the place where the support is payable has jurisdiction. That place is usually easy to determine. Procedural difficulties are unlikely to arise.

Turkey — No problem.

United States — Yes. Ordinarily the initial support order will be made against a father in the courts of the state where he is found. However, the Uniform Reciprocal Enforcement of Support Law, provides that the support action may be commenced in the state where the wife and children live and when the father is located in another state supplemental proceedings may be brought there with the record being forwarded from the first state and the eventual order being entered in the receiving state. Collection of arrearages reduced to judgment *must* be recognized and enforced in all states. However, a state may collect sums past due even if not reduced to judgment in original state, if it wishes to do so. The Uniform Registration of Foreign Judgment Act (adopted in a few states) makes possible treatment of sister state decrees as if entered by local courts.

D. *How great is the problem of non-support of children in your country?*

1. Do you have any statistics for the last five years? (If so, please give details).

   (a) As to extent of non-support – how many cases, number of children involved?

Australia	– No statistics able to be obtained.
Austria	– No adequate records, but according to Youth Authorities, in about 20% of cases, public welfare must interfere or contribute to child support; 80% of parents provide support.
Canada	– No reliable available statistics.
Denmark	– No statistics.
England	– No. Not available at time of writing. Enquiries proceeding.
Finland	– Number of children paid for by Government: 1964 (26,274), 1965 (29,512), 1966 (31,937). Parents in default and sentenced to workhouse (excludes Helsinki): 1962 (2,075); 1963 (2,128); 1964 (2,462); 1965 (2,155).
France	– Information not reported. Within province of Ministry of Justice.
Germany	– No statistics. Local authorities in area of Bremen said that as far as out-of-wedlock children, few cases, and even fewer as to children of divorced parents.
Iran	– Not at present.
Israel	– No up-to-date statistics with exception of cases supported by Social Welfare Offices.
Mexico	– Non-support trials: 1961 (608); 1962 (336); 1963 (306); 1964 (234); 1965 (325); 1966 (346).
Netherlands	– No recent statistics. About 10 years ago the Councils for Child Protection collected about 65% of amounts due and it is believed that currently the record is at least as good. No available data as to number of cases involved.
New Zealand	– No present statistics are available.
Norway	– No statistics, but problem is not a serious one.

North. Ireland – No answer given in report.

Portugal – Not answered in report.

Scotland – Statistics showing extent of problem not readily available, but the coverage provided in default of the parents by the national government meets the problem so far as the children are concerned.

South Africa – Exact figures not available, but the majority of prosecutions under the Children's Act (for ill-treatment, neglect, abandonment and non-support of children) were for non-support. Those for ill-treatment, neglect or abandonment were only 1.8% and 2.8% of total number of prosecutions for 1963/64 and 1964/65 respectively. The total number of prosecutions for 1964/65 dropped by more than half as compared with those for 1963/64. Totals in number of prosecutions for 4 provinces (re offenses against white children) were 1452 for 1964; 601 for 1965. Contribution Orders against white parents during 1964 and 1965:
1964 – 639 (2,225 children involved);
1965 – 661 (3,001 children involved).

Switzerland – There are no general and regular statistics on this subject.

Turkey – Not answered in report.

United States – A 1955 sample study of aid to dependent children reported that child support payments (averaging $ 67.63 per month) had been ordered or agreed upon in 42% of the 162,440 families where father had left the home but that in only 1/2 of these cases did he pay anything. Total contribution by these fathers was estimated at $ 20 million. Problem of non-support is a major social and legal problem.

1. (b) As to number of desertions by fathers and/or mothers.

Australia – No statistics available.

Austria – No problem.

Canada – No reliable available statistics.

Denmark – No statistics.

England – No statistics.

Finland	– Number of children deserted by both parents: 1961 (1,444); 1962 (1,361); 1963 (1,259); 1964 (1,180); 1965 (1,126).
France	– Information may be obtainable from Ministry of Justice.
Germany	– Number of parental desertions extremely low. Hardly any case known in Bremen area.
Iran	– Not at present.
Israel	– No statistics given.
Mexico	– No statistics given. Generally fathers are the ones who desert; exceptionally mothers.
Netherlands	– Nothing known about number of desertions.
New Zealand	– No available statistics.
Norway	– Problem not a serious one.
North. Ireland	– No statistics furnished.
Portugal	– No information furnished.
Scotland	– No available statistics which would provide reliable estimate.
South Africa	– See answer to D. 1. (a).
Switzerland	– No information furnished.
Turkey	– No information furnished.
United States	– Current desertion figure between 400,000 and 500,000 a year and in 50–60 % of these cases there are children. In 1963, estimate is that more than 10 million women and children were deserted by husband-father and 2.6 million family units were involved. Numbers probably have increased substantially since then.

2. What methods are employed for locating missing parents? Whose responsibility is this? The Courts? The family's? Other? Agencies? If so, which.

Australia	– Attempts to locate missing parents are made by: (a) State police departments; (b) State Social Welfare Department; (c) Commonwealth Social Services Department.

Austria	– In Austria everyone must register with police. Missing persons can be sought through police.
Canada	– In Ontario, Alberta and British Columbia, responsibility to locate missing persons in order to serve them in support proceedings is on party seeking maintenance. The Family Courts use the local police to effect service but they must be given an address.
Denmark	– The local counties will ask the police for assistance.
England	– On abandonment – police. In non-support – Ministry of Social Security, local authority or other parent seek missing parent. Welfare bodies often try to assist. If court orders arrest, police do try to trace. If no court order for arrest, "by private enquiry agents or through employment exchange records or hearsay".
Finland	– The Social Officers and the police.
France	– Responsibility is that of police authorities and of administrative bodies.
Germany	– Usually the Public Prosecutor has an order of arrest issued and sent to all police stations.
Iran	– Ordinary means is to publish notice in newspapers, radio, television and/or sending data to the branches of the Ministry of Justice, police, gendarmerie, town managers, mayor, etc., with orders to report results. This is the responsibility of the children's court and/or the district attorney. The court decides which authorities to send notice to.
Israel	– At the instance of the family or Social Welfare Officers, the Police Forces and Social Service Workers Act.
Mexico	– The responsibility belongs (when family fails and situation implies a delinquent attitude of missing parent) to Department of Public Prosecution, under whose orders Judicial Police act. Where situation is that of civil judicial status of "absence", summons may be sent even to foreign countries. Also a parent might be summoned to a civil trial for non-support (where domicile unknown) and publication is had in legal and principal newspapers. Court might attach real estate or withhold personal property. Court asks police to investigate.

Netherlands	– Missing parents are located primarily through the register of inhabitants of each town; otherwise through police. There is no direct responsibility. The other parent or the family will usually take steps or sometimes the Welfare Agencies.
New Zealand	– No specific methods. The basic responsibility is that of the family and police aid may be invoked.
Norway	– The collector of contributions examines the population records, the seamen's office and other institutions.
North. Ireland	– No information supplied.
Portugal	– There are no special ways of locating missing parents.
Scotland	– The Ministry of Social Security will supply information as to whereabouts of a defaulting parent to any person having a legitimate interest. The responsibility rests on the party instituting the action. Often the solicitors of such party make inquiries through the departments offering state benefits.
South Africa	– Failure to comply with court order is a criminal offense, therefore, criminal investigation department has responsibility. The family often are able to supply information.
Switzerland	– Various methods used. Boards supervising guardianships in some cases can demand assistance from police (if failure to support is criminal). Also non-profit social organizations and child welfare agencies try to locate person liable for child support. In general, there is no clear legal demarcation line between competence of state and private aid institutions.
Turkey	– No information supplied.
United States	– If deserted family is destitute, ultimate responsibility is on public welfare agencies or on wife and mother if she wishes to make father pay support. Uniform Reciprocal Enforcement of Support Law in effect in each state and non-support cases may be processed across state lines. Wife/mother begins action at her home and decree handed down at place where husband/father is found. Difficulties in enforcement. Sheriffs or prosecutors may be uncooperative. Father may disappear in large cities. They are usually located

by local police or sheriffs; there are also a few private agencies which assist and private investigators may be employed.

E. *Is it possible for children in another country to secure support from a parent in yours?*

1. Does your country have any treaty with any other country or is it a signatory to any convention as to support? If so, with which? Has it been enforced? What has been your experience?

Australia – Australia has many bi-lateral arrangements for enforcement of maintenance orders between Australian states and territories and British Commonwealth countries, colonies, protectorates and trust territories. The recent Uniform Maintenance Act in Australia will supply a good basis for reciprocal enforcement in States of Australia of orders made in other countries and vice versa.

Austria – Austria is a member of Hague Convention of October 24, 1956 re child support and of Hague Convention of April 15, 1957 re recognition and enforcement of judgments for child support.

Canada – No treaties or conventions with other countries. *Ontario:* Reciprocal Enforcement of Maintenance Orders Act (Reciprocating states – all provinces of Canada, Australia, England, 9 other countries and State of Michigan) provides means for 2 reciprocating states to cooperate and if plaintiff's case is successful, a provisional order is obtained which is either confirmed or not in defendant's jurisdiction.

Denmark – Denmark has treaties with the other Scandinavian countries (Finland, Norway, Sweden and Iceland). Denmark ratified the Convention on the Recovery Abroad of Maintenance. Also (in Jan. 1966) Denmark ratified the Hague Convention of April 15, 1958 on Recognition and Enforcement of Decisions relating to maintenance obligations toward children.

England – With other commonwealth countries. Expensive. Long delays.

Finland – 1932 Convention (applicable to Denmark, Ireland, Norway, Sweden and Finland), providing that a judgment of a court of these countries is recognized and enforceable in any other of these countries. This works well. Also ratified the Convention of the Recovery Abroad of Maintenance (Sept. 13, 1962).

France – Ratified Convention on Recovery Abroad of Maintenance (June 24, 1960). Children living abroad may obtain support from parents who live in France if there is an order of the foreign court enforceable in France under French rules of private international law.

Germany – Ratified Convention on Recovery Abroad of Maintenance (July 20, 1959). Unimportant as regardless of where children live, parents living in Germany may be sued for support.

Iran – No.

Israel – Ratified Convention on Recovery of Maintenance Abroad (June 20, 1956). It has been acted on with success in cases where its machinery was invoked.

Mexico – Yes, according to Mexico's laws on international judicial cooperation. Mexico has signed Convention on Recovery Abroad of Maintenance (June 20, 1956). It has not recognized the Convention on Enforcement of Foreign Judgments nor the International Private Law Convention held in Havana in 1928, accepting the Bustamente Code.

Netherlands – Holland is a signatory to Convention of June 20, 1956 on Recovery Abroad of Maintenance (July 31, 1962) and to Hague Convention of April 15, 1958 re Recognition and Enforcement of Foreign Child Support Orders. Both Conventions have been enforced, but not many cases in which their machinery has been used.

New Zealand – Within British Commonwealth a series of reciprocal statutes, but no treaty; re enforcement of orders outside Commonwealth, New Zealand provides that some of these orders be enforced as if New Zealand orders.

Norway – Norway has decided (by August 20, 1965 Royal Decree) to ratify Hague Convention of April 15, 1958 re Recognition and Enforcement of Child Support Decrees. Norway is a party to New York Convention of June 20, 1956 re collection of support abroad. (No obligation imposed to enforce on members but it helps). Since 1931, Norway has had conventions with the other Scandinavian countries for collection of support payments. (The last one is Convention of March 23, 1962, between Norway, Denmark, Finland, Iceland and Sweden). This is of great practical importance.

North. Ireland — No treaty as to child support but two statutes dealing with enforcement of foreign court orders. Maintenance Orders Act provides for registration and enforcement of orders between Dominions and Northern Ireland.

Portugal — Ratified Convention on Recovery Abroad of Maintenance (Jan. 25, 1965).

Scotland — If Scotland is father's domicile, any order by a Scottish court for child wherever resident is enforceable. Reciprocal arrangements exist for enforcing decrees of courts of the Bahamas, Ghana, Gibraltar, Malta, Newfoundland, New Zealand, Nigeria, Saskatchewan, Kenya, Tanzania, Singapore and other Dominions and protectorates and of France, Belgium, India, Pakistan, Australia, Norway, Austria and the Netherlands. If a foreign support award is subject to review and modification, it will not be enforced in Scotland — exception is that of an English court where reciprocal rights of registration of decrees exist. If support decree is unalterable, it may be enforced if defendant was a party to foreign action.

South Africa — The Republic of South Africa is not a party to any treaty with any other country, nor is it a signatory as to any Convention as to support.

Switzerland — On July 4, 1963 (eff. date, Jan. 17, 1965), became a party to Hague Treaty of April 15, 1958, on Recognition and Enforcement of Judgments for Child Support. (Also parties to such Treaty are Belgium, Denmark, Western Germany, Finland, France, Italy, The Netherlands, Austria). Switzerland is also a party to the Hague Convention of October 24, 1956 on the applicable law in cases of child support obligations (eff. date for Switzerland Jan. 17, 1965). Practical value of these treaties depends on number of states which are a party to these treaties. For Switzerland the ratification by neighboring states is valuable

because formerly their domestic laws (especially those of Italy) opposed enforcement of Swiss paternity judgments.
Welfare agreements with France (Sept. 9, 1931); West Germany (July 14, 1952); Italy (October 15, 1875); Austria and Hungary (December 7, 1875); Portugal (May 16, 1898); Turkey (December 13, 1930).

Turkey — Turkey has several treaties with countries where Turkish citizens live and work (countries not specified).

United States — Hague Convention concerning the Enforcement of Decisions relating to Maintenance Obligations toward Children (open for signatures April 15, 1957).

2. Are you contemplating any such new treaty or convention?

Australia — Recent Uniform Maintenance Act of Australia will make it possible for reciprocal enforcement of support with foreign countries.

Austria — No.

Canada — Not as far as is known.

Denmark — No.

England — None known.

Finland — No information supplied.

France — Yes.

Germany — Not as far as is known.

Iran — No.

Israel — No information about this.

Mexico — Not for the moment.

Netherlands — Not as far as is known.

New Zealand — No.

Norway — No.

North. Ireland — No knowledge as to this.

Portugal — No information supplied.

Scotland	– No.
South Africa	– No.
Switzerland	– No.
Turkey	– No information supplied.
United States	– No knowledge as to this.

3. If there is no treaty how can foreign orders for support be enforced?

Australia	– New Uniform Maintenance legislation provides for enforcement on basis of reciprocity.
Austria	– See answer to E. 1. and 2.
Canada	– Through provincial statutes providing for the reciprocal enforcement of maintenance orders.
Denmark	– Normal procedure is that the foreign support order is given to the County Authorities of the county where the father or mother lives and these authorities fix the amount to be paid by the parent in Denmark to the child who lives abroad.
England	– By obtaining order in British courts based on order of foreign court.
Finland	– New action must be brought in Finland. (If foreign country affords due process of law and legal safeguards, foreign judgment not binding, but significance will be attached to it). A number of bilateral arrangements exist.
France	– By exequatur (order for enforcement) obtained from French court.
Germany	– Depends on reciprocity where no treaty exists and if reciprocity exists, foreign order may be enforced. There are treaties with a number of countries.
Iran	– As far as records show, there have been no demands of such nature as yet. If and when such order is ever issued, in order to be enforced in Iran it would have to be ratified by Iranian courts as well. It would have to be demanded by a country which has a reciprocal treaty with Iran. Then after a petition filed with the Probate Court, that Court would ratify it.

Israel	– Israeli Act for Enforcement of Foreign Judgments; generally reciprocity is required but Attorney General of Israel may dispense with this and request enforcement by Israeli court.
Mexico	– By reciprocity principle which permits enforcement of foreign support orders. (Code provides for letters requisitional; personal summons on defendant; enforcement of formalities according to laws of foreign country, etc.)
Netherlands	– Foreign orders cannot be enforced unless there is a special treaty. However, where children live abroad and domicile of parent is in The Netherlands, legal aid (because of legal aid treaty) may obtain order of support from court of parent's domicile.
New Zealand	– Specific provision in New Zealand law that some of such orders may be enforced in New Zealand as if they were New Zealand orders.
Norway	– A new action for support must be brought in Norway in absence of any Convention for collection of foreign support orders.
North. Ireland	– Maintenance Orders Act of 1920 provides for enforcement in England and Ireland of maintenance orders of the Dominions. Act of 1950 makes similar provision for enforcement of orders made in any part of United Kingdom.
Portugal	– No information supplied.
Scotland	– The holder of a foreign judgment for support may bring an action for "decree conform". (Foreign order duly certified is submitted to Scottish court and subsequent decree will validate foreign order for enforcement in Scotland).
South Africa	– The Matrimonial Causes Jurisdiction Act of 1939 (as amended in 1953), provides for reciprocal recognition of certain divorce and separation decrees and covers ancillary orders for child support. The Maintenance Orders Act of 1923 provides for the direct enforcement in South Africa of Maintenance Orders for a wife and dependents made in certain countries or territories on a reciprocal basis (England, N. Ireland, Guernsey, Isle of Man, Rhodesia, Zambia, Malawi, S. W. Africa, Nesotho, Bostswana, Swaziland, Kenya,

Nigeria, Australian Capital Territory, New S. Wales, N. Territory of Australia, Queensland, S. Australia, Victoria, W. Australia, Norfold Islands, Cocos [Keeling] Isl., New Zealand, Ontario, Canada, Cyprus, Fiji, Mauritius, Sarawak, Singapore, St. Helena, Island of Jersey, British Columbia).

Switzerland — If no international treaty, the general national law on enforcement of foreign judgments comes into play and the Cantons determine this in varying ways. (Majority require that foreign judgment be non-appealable and that the rendering country had jurisdiction and had given reciprocity and that judgment is not against Swiss public policy).

Turkey — Problem resolved according to general law.

United States — Where support obligation has been reduced to final judgment, American courts may extend comity to the decree. In a few cases, in Pennsylvania and New York, orders have been made in this type of case.

F. *What suggestions do you have for possible action in each country for dealing with problems of non-support? For international enforcement?*

Australia — Uniform Maintenance Act of Australia can provide a good basis for enforcement of foreign orders in Australia and for domestic orders in foreign countries.

Austria — Suggests creation of a public youth welfare office where parents not able to furnish support. These offices can count on cooperation and legal aid among countries.

Canada — No suggestions made.

Denmark — Problem social one; generally one of broken homes, alcoholism, bad apartments. Children more and more rarely removed from homes.

England — Inter-country registration of orders of other country or certificate. Collecting court to use own powers of enforcement.

Finland — 1. Re dealing with problem of non-support, advance payment by government and government then to deal with parent.

2. Re international enforcement, suggests international marriage conventions similar to one among Scandinavian countries.

France	– Suggests international treaties for this purpose.
Germany	– Suggests no method but aim which should be that child, regardless of its domicile, should be able to obtain support from parents, wherever they live.
Iran	– A law should be passed in Iran to enforce the support of needy children by a governmental or private organization financed by the government. Such body should support needy children – reimburse itself from the property of the parent, if any. These children should be supported, educated, etc., as deemed necessary or advisable.
Israel	– Suggests facilities and aid to locate deserting fathers or generally parents who neglect child support; to ascertain their means and enforce any judgments against them.
Mexico	– Suggests a minor's code: to establish rules to allocate responsibility of child support for minors; to establish means of enforcement; specialized courts and procedures; protection institutions; penalties and other measures; interstate and international cooperation systems, etc.
Netherlands	– No special suggestions. In Netherlands, because of many welfare facilities, child support is not a serious problem.
New Zealand	– See E. 1., 2. and 3.
Norway	– No suggestions made.
North. Ireland	– No suggestions made.
Portugal	– No suggestions given.
Scotland	– Problems of non-support not so serious or widespread as to call for action for international enforcement.
South Africa	– 1. The perennial problem of international enforcement of maintenance should be considered and a combined international effort should be made. 2. Courts should not make orders on matters of support until full reports have been obtained from suitable specialized agencies.

3. Government departments directly concerned with family welfare should become more directly interested in problem of non-support and senior experienced officials should deal with these matters.
4. Mass media should be used to educate the country.

Switzerland — Suggest countries becoming a party to the two Hague treaties (April 15, 1958 treaty on Recognition and Enforcement of Child Support Obligations and October 24, 1956 treaty on applicable law in cases of child support obligations) or to the New York Convention (June 20, 1956) on enforcement of support claims.

Turkey — Suggests international treaty under United Nations auspices.

United States — A study should be made of Uniform Reciprocal Enforcement of Support with a view to adapting it to international enforcement of wife and child obligations.

G. *What special questions on child support do you suggest for our discussion in Dublin?*

Australia — Reciprocal enforcement of maintenance orders, efficacy of present legislation, necessity for further legislative or other action, difficulties and hardships caused by enforcement or non-enforcement of foreign support orders.

Austria — Support awarded to out-of-wedlock children and its inadequacy which places main burden on mother. Improvement of position of out-of-wedlock children. Increase in support for legitimate children.

Canada — No questions suggested.

Denmark — No special questions.

England — 1. What are criteria for fixing amount of support? Ability to pay? Minimum need of child? Social status of child or parent?
2. Should state or local authority undertake support of all illegitimate children? Of all children of broken marriages? On request only? As act of discretion by the state?

Finland — 1. Responsibility of government to pay support in advance on behalf of parent. Are there similar systems in other countries? How do they work?

2. Method of deciding "ability" to pay and "need". What standards are used?

3. Enforcement of child support judgment in other countries.

France — The international enforcement of support orders.

Germany — No questions suggested.

Iran — No answer.

Israel — No questions suggested.

Mexico — The formulation of a minor's code for each country and discussion of fundamental standards in the support chapter of such code, or if this is too extensive, discussion of "measures to assure support and preference to be given to support of children", i. e., enforcement of child support against assets of parents.

Netherlands — No suggestions since non-support of children is not a serious problem in The Netherlands because the State assures child support by means of its many welfare facilities.

New Zealand — No questions suggested.

Norway — No questions suggested.

North. Ireland — No questions suggested.

Portugal — No questions suggested.

Scotland — No questions suggested.

South Africa — No questions suggested.

Switzerland — No questions suggested.

Turkey — No questions suggested.

United States — 1. Are there any systems of private or public insurance against contingency of child support?

2. May a percentage of wages be set as a ceiling for child and wife support in order to confine judicial discretion in making "realistic" awards?

3. To what extent should wife/mother be made equally responsible for child support (if she has assets or is employable?)

4. Should courts be encouraged to handle support matters by conference and conciliation and impose orders only as a last resort?
5. Should Uniform Reciprocal Enforcement of Support Act be adapted for international acceptance?

II. *As to Custody of Children*

A. *What are the laws and practices in your country relating to custody of minor children?*

1. Who decides and enforces custody?
   (a) Administrative bodies? Which?

Australia — Only where child is made a ward of the State because in need of protection, etc.; then question as to the child's custody is decided by the Department of Social Welfare.

Austria — Administrative bodies as part of the public youth welfare program cooperate if the "corporeal, mental, psychic or moral development" of the child requires it.

Canada — No.

Denmark — In matrimonial cases — no. If parents do not live together but no matrimonial action, the County Authorities determine custody.

England — No.

Finland — Custody is decided by the courts, and enforced by the administrative bodies which are the same as those which enforce support judgments. (See I. C. 1 [a]).

France — No.

Germany — No.

Iran — Details of laws translated will be handed in at Conference or if desired, before.
Not administrative bodies — Supervisory and Guardianship Departments are courts. In the Civil Code, Family Protection Act, Marriage Act and Penal Code laws provide:

(a) Violation and status or condition must be reported to District Attorney and to Guardianship Department of Surrogate's Court;

(b) Bill or petition must be filed;

(c) Bill or petition referred to appropriate court;

(d) Bailiff and/or District Attorney, etc., are the authorities who enforce the order.

Israel — The courts (Civil Courts, Religious Courts and in cases within Juvenile Act, Juvenile Courts) decide custody disputes. Enforcement is by execution officers of the courts or by the court in contempt proceedings and in some cases by social workers.

Mexico — Custody is decided by agreement or by civil, criminal and judicial authorities, and even administrative bodies, depending on the case (due to lack of an agreement or to enforce an agreement). The administrative bodies which act in appropriate cases are Social Prevention Department; Minors' Board of Trustees and Juvenile Courts (acting in an administrative capacity).

Netherlands — The Court (Justice of the Peace) decides custody disputes and the enforcement is the same as with any other judgment – if necessary the Police assist.

New Zealand — No.

Norway — If the parents disagree as to which one is to have custody, they can agree to let county governor decide. (His decision may be appealed to Ministry of Justice).

North. Ireland — No – by courts.

Portugal — No.

Scotland — No – by courts.

South Africa — No.

Switzerland —

1. In cases dealing with illegitimate children, the Board supervising guardianships decides custody;
2. In divorce cases the ordinary Civil Court decides custody.
3. In the juvenile offenders law, partly the courts and partly the administration (schools and Boards supervising guardianships, child-welfare agencies) decide custody. This Board also decides custody of illegitimate children.

Turkey – The court determines custody and a Board called "The Union for the Protection of Children" enforces the court decision. (There is one Board in each department).

United States – No. The courts make and enforce custody awards – either courts of general jurisdiction sitting in equity, or in some states concurrent or exclusive jurisdictions given to the family, juvenile or domestic relations courts.

1. (b) Courts? Which type of courts handle these cases? Those dealing with criminal matters? With civil actions? Other?

Australia – Yes. 1. In matrimonial causes by the Supreme Courts of the States exercising Federal jurisdiction;

2. Apart from matrimonial causes, by the Supreme Courts of the States under their Guardianship of Infants Acts;

3. In South Australia, by a Court of Summary Jurisdiction who can grant wife an order in nature of a judicial separation;

4. The Supreme Courts dealing with custody do so in the exercise either of their Matrimonial Causes jurisdiction, or of their jurisdiction over infants.

Austria – If the parents live separately without being divorced, the court decides question of custody. The Civil Courts are competent in non-disputed procedures.

Canada – *Ontario:* The determination as to custody and the enforcement of custody orders are handled by the Juvenile and Family Courts; by the Magistrates' Courts; by the Surrogate's Court (where no Family Courts), or by the Supreme Court. (The Juvenile and Family Court is a quasi-criminal court employing criminal sanctions to enforce its orders; the Magistrate's Court is a criminal court; the Surrogate's Court is a civil court; the Supreme Court has both civil and criminal jurisdiction, but these proceedings are on civil side).

Alberta: By either the Family Courts (a division of the Magistrate's Court) or by the Supreme Court.

British Columbia: By the Family and Children's Court or the Supreme Court.

Denmark	– In matrimonial cases, the ordinary civil courts.
England	– Civil Courts – Magistrates (90%); High Court (10%).
Finland	– Custody is decided by the courts; enforced by the administrative bodies. The courts are the same as in 1. C. 1 (b).
France	– Civil courts determine and enforce custody.
Germany	– There is a special department of the Lower Courts which decides custody (not criminal).
Iran	– It depends on the nature of the offense; desertion, abandonment, etc. as decided and resolved by the District Attorney. If it falls under the civil code, the Civil Courts, Surrogate's Court or Probate Court; if offenses fall under Penal Code, the Court of Felony.
Israel	– See II. A. 1 (a).
Mexico	– When there is no agreement or to enforce an agreement, and in divorces, etc., civil courts determine and enforce custody. Criminal courts may handle such matters and also Juvenile courts (in case of juvenile delinquency).
Netherlands	– The Justice of the Peace decides on custody except in divorce or separation cases. Enforcement is the same as with any other judgment. (Police will assist if necessary).
New Zealand	– The courts. The Supreme Court has inherent and statutory jurisdiction in divorces. The Courts of Summary Proceedings have limited statutory jurisdiction.
Norway	– If parents fail to agree to leave custody decision to the County Governor, the ordinary civil courts decide.
North. Ireland	– This is dealt with by the High Court as a civil matter in the Chancery Division. (Statutes provide for decisions being made in certain instances by the court of summary jurisdiction).
Portugal	– Custody of children is fixed by agreement between the parents or by the Courts for Minors.
Scotland	– The civil courts make the decisions and the parties (in the first instance) enforce them.

South Africa — Matters of custody are determined solely by the civil courts. In divorce, Supreme Court; under Children's Act, Children's Court.

Switzerland — See II. A. 1 (a).

Turkey — The courts dealing with civil matters determine custody. After a court decision, a Board, "The Union for the Protection of Children", enforces the court decision.

United States — See A. 1 (a). Custody issues arise in matrimonial actions, in habeas corpus proceedings, proceedings instituted by petition, and in family or juvenile court actions (where dependency or neglect is alleged or a petition for termination of parental rights is filed). Custody determinations are always made and enforced by courts. Usually the judge is the trier of fact (in a few states a jury may be required or demanded).

1. (c) Other methods?

Australia — None.

Austria — None.

Canada — None.

Denmark — No.

England — No.

Finland — Apparently not.

France — Apparently not.

Germany — None.

Iran — It depends upon the District Attorney and the Referee and/or ecclesiastical courts.

Israel — See II. A. 1 (a) and (b).

Mexico — Agreements between parents or various judicial or administrative bodies. See II. A. 1 (a).

Netherlands — Apparently not.

New Zealand — Apparently not.

Norway — Agreements between parents; either parent may have agreement reviewed by the court.

North. Ireland — Apparently not.

Portugal — Apparently not.

Scotland — A person failing to comply with a court order for custody may be imprisoned.

South Africa — Apparently not.

Switzerland — Apparently not.

Turkey — Apparently not.

United States — No.

2. What standards are applied in custody determinations?

(a) What are the relative rights of the parents?
Does the mother always get the preference?
If not, when?

Australia — In law the rights of the parents are equal and neither parent is to be preferred, though the "best interests of the child" rule does require that more frequently children of tender years are placed with the mother.

Austria — Parents are equally entitled to custody, but mother is in first place responsible for physical care of the child, but otherwise she has no preferred right over father.

Canada — *Ontario:* By statute — both parents have equal rights to custody.

Alberta: Mother receives preference unless "unfit".

British Columbia: By statute, parents have equal rights; where child under 12 years, custody is generally given to mother (in absence of evidence she is unfit or unable to care for children).

Denmark — If parents agree, decision is made in accord with their agreement if not against interests of children. If parents cannot agree, decision based upon what is fair and reasonable in accordance with interests of children. If parents equally fit to care for children but one is to blame for marriage failure, custody to innocent party. Children under 2 will only be taken from mother in exceptional cases.

England — Equal. In law — mother, if child illegitimate. In practice, mother gets preference if child 4 or under, or if a young girl.

Finland — Rights of parents are equal. Interest of child paramount. If both parents suitable but one is considered responsible for family breakdown, the other parent receives preference.

France — Parents have equal rights. Often (but not always) mother receives the preference.

Germany — Where parents married, they are jointly entitled to custody. In case of divorce, innocent party should get custody but custody of young children generally given to mother.

Iran — The mother has custody of all infants up to 2 years, if a daughter up to 7. If parents are separated and father is proven unfit or mother applies and father approves, mother gets custody until child (boy or girl) is legally an adult. If mother is proven unfit, she *never* is awarded custody.

Israel — There is a rebuttable presumption in the Act and in Jewish law that a child up to 6 needs to be with its mother. Also in the Jewish law there is a rebuttable presumption that it is for a daughter's benefit to remain with her mother. The Act of 1960 does not contain this presumption but it is followed as a matter of practice. Under the Civil Capacity and Guardianship Act of 1962 both parents are natural guardians of their children.

Mexico — (a) Children of undissolved marriages — both parents have joint right to custody.

(b) Children of dissolved marriage by mutual consent divorce, custody is given to parent as agreed upon by them in their agreement.

(c) Children of dissolved marriage by necessary divorce, if cause is adultery, parental authority is in innocent spouse; if cause is serious physical cruelty and innocent spouse died, guilty spouse recovers parental authority; if cause is incurable impotence, custody given to healthy spouse but other spouse preserves rights of parental authority.

(d) Children of annulled marriage, custody goes to good faith spouse but other spouse retains parental authority.
If child less than 5 years, Code provides that custody shall be in mother; in some other instances (wife sues husband with respect to "judicial deposit") custody of children under 7 to mother unless she is a prostitute, panderer, habitually intoxicated or has a contagious disease or her conduct presents a serious danger to health or morality of the children.

Netherlands — A certain preference is given the mother as the person most directly concerned with the care and upbringing of children. But no question of the right of a parent to custody. Child's best interest controlling.

New Zealand — Relative rights of parents are supposedly equal but usually considered appropriate for mother to have custody of girls or very young children; father is usually considered as more suitable person to have custody of boys or children past infancy. (These are rules of thumb — often varied).

Norway — Child's custody in mother when young (unless mother is unfit). Parents' wishes should be taken into account. Thus mother does not always get preference but usually she will be awarded custody of young children.

North. Ireland — Father has permanent right even against mother except where father forfeits it by his conduct. (Other things being equal, it is preferable that a child of tender years should be with its mother).

Portugal — Custody fixed by agreement between parents or by the courts. Courts may give custody to one of the parents or to a third person or to an educational establishment.

Scotland — Rights of parents equal; no preference in favor of father or mother.

South Africa — As a rule, the custody of young children or girls is given to mother (unless her character or conduct make this undesirable or where home and circumstances of father are more satisfactory). Sometimes custody of some children given to mother; others to father. In a survey, it was found that custody was given to mother in about 63% of the cases.

Switzerland — If possible, custody of small children and daughters given to mother if she is in a position to take personal care of them; sons who are nearly grown up to father; siblings not separated unless strong reasons for doing so.

Turkey — Not directly answered.

United States — Although avowed rule (by statute or court decision), is that each parent has equal rights and that between them the "best interests" of the child determines which is to have custody, it is generally assumed that "best interests" of child require that custody be given to mother, especially in the case of children of "tender years" and daughters. In reality father's interests are usually regarded as subordinate to mother's except in case of a teenage son. Thus, only an "unfit" mother (when she is guilty of immoral conduct, especially in presence of children, drunkenness, violence and other egregious misbehavior, or mentally or emotionally ill) will be deprived of custody.

2. (b) Are grandparents or other relatives ever given custody when a parent is available? If so, when?

Australia — Yes. 1. The Matrimonial Causes Act specifically provides that the court may, if it deems it desirable, give custody to a person other than party to the marriage. (This would include grandparents or other relatives.)

2. The court in the exercise of its inherent jurisdiction may give custody to a person other than parents.

Austria — Relatives do not generally have the right to custody. If they take over the care of a child they don't need permission of the court.

Canada — *Ontario:* Might be that grandparents could bring action for custody. As incidental to divorce action, court has wide discretion and could award custody to the grandparents or other relatives.
Alberta: Court may award custody to any person.
British Columbia: Such an award would only be made if both parents unfit.

Denmark — No. The court must choose between the parents.

England — Yes. At request or with consent of parents, or if parents unsuitable.

Finland	— No.
France	— Custody may be given to grandparents or other relatives where parents are unfit.
Germany	— Only under the rule of the "best interest of the child".
Iran	— A grandparent is a legal custodian; where it is contended he is not fit, the Surrogate's Court or District Attorney may indicate a Supervising Adviser to act jointly.
Israel	— Yes. Sometimes, especially where mother died leaving young children and court concluded custody in maternal grandparents would be for welfare of children.
Mexico	— Yes. When both parents have lost parental authority or have been deprived of it. In case of necessary divorce where grounds were adultery or serious damage — custody may be given to grandparents or to other relatives if no grandparents.
Netherlands	— If the parent not qualified (i. e., a minor or insane), another relative may be given custody (or a stranger). Grandparents do not have a special preference except perhaps where an unwed mother is a minor herself.
New Zealand	— Yes, if in best interests of child.
Norway	— No.
North. Ireland	— Not answered.
Portugal	— Yes.
Scotland	— Yes.
South Africa	— In very special circumstances, i. e., as where neither of spouses is able to make suitable arrangements for the child and where its interests would be better served by placing child with third party, the court may award custody to a third person (grandparent or other relative).
Switzerland	— Parents are required to place child away from home for certain reasons; i. e., where parents live in a politically or climatically dangerous place or are not in a position to raise child because of their work. In such cases it is advisable to place child with grandparents or other relatives.
Turkey	— If parents are dead or in prison.

United States	– The usual rule is that natural parents prevail over grandparents or other relatives, unless it is found that the parent is "unfit" (abandoned the child, otherwise forfeited parental rights, or would be an immoral or unwholesome influence).

2. (c) Are the preferences of the children considered? If so, when?

Australia	– Yes, if they are of sufficient age. Custody order not ordinarily made in opposition to wishes of boy 14 or over or girl 16 or over.
Austria	– Wishes of children taken into consideration only if in their interest.
Canada	– *Ontario:* Yes. Weight depends on child's age. Order will usually not be made against preference of child 14 (sometimes younger). *Alberta:* Child's preference considered if court is satisfied that child not unduly influenced by either parent and is old enough. *British Columbia:* Preferences of children over 12 considered.
Denmark	– Yes. If it can be proved that the children's expressed preference is not due to undue influence of parent with whom they live; it will be considered, especially for children over a certain age. The older the child the more weight its preference will be given.
England	– Yes, if old enough – but preference slight.
Finland	– Yes, where they are above 15.
France	– Usually, no.
Germany	– Usually not, but it might be when considering "the best interests of the child".
Iran	– Preferences of the children is one of the factors to be considered in determining the best interests of the children.
Israel	– Yes.
Mexico	– No. But minors over 16 years have right to designate their guardian when there is no person to exercise guardianship over them.

Netherlands – Yes, in appropriate cases. Council for Child Protection investigates in almost all cases where parents do not agree (by trained social worker) and tries to ascertain real preference of child (by psychological tests, psychologist, psychiatrist, etc.). Child is never asked its preference by the court.

New Zealand – Yes. Greater weight is given to preferences of children over 14.

Norway – Courts can question children if either parent requests it. (Not done with younger children). If child is 14 or more, child's preference important element.

North. Ireland – Yes, where the child is of an age to make a choice. (Held that a boy of 14 was old enough). Court cannot make an order against wishes of child of 16 or over.

Portugal – Yes, unofficially.

Scotland – Yes, if children are of sufficient age.

South Africa – Yes, where child has reached the age of discretion its preference will be considered.

Switzerland – In principle, no. If children are of sufficient age, yes.

Turkey – Yes, if they are old enough.

United States – Although most American courts profess to consider child's wishes as to custody (if child of sufficient age), the cases indicate that the child's preferences not considered as significant as parental equities or court's preference for a mother or natural parent. But some statutes give a child over a certain age the right to select parent. (This is not binding on court, if court finds parent is "unfit").

2. (d) Do you have a "Best interests of the child" rule?

Australia – Yes. In Matrimonial Causes Act the interests of the children are stated to be "the paramount consideration".

Austria – Yes. The court takes child's interests into consideration.

Canada – *Ontario, Alberta* and *British Columbia:* "Welfare of child" is given paramount consideration.

Denmark – Yes. See II. A. 2.

England — Yes.

Finland — Yes, the interests of the child are paramount.

France — Yes.

Germany — Yes.

Iran — Yes.

Israel — Yes.

Mexico — Social Prevention Department, Juvenile Courts, Minors' Board of Trustees, the National Institute for Childhood Protection, all look out for the interests of the child. The Department of Public Prosecution is heard by the courts in all matters relating to minors (agreements by spouses as to custody or guardianship of children in voluntary divorces).

Netherlands — The best interest of the child is the guiding principle in all cases.

New Zealand — Yes.

Norway — Yes.

North. Ireland — Yes.

Portugal — Yes.

Scotland — Yes. The welfare of the child is declared (by statute) to be the first and paramount consideration.

South Africa — Yes. This is the main consideration to which all other considerations (such as guilt or innocence of the spouses, etc.), must yield.

Switzerland — The law is impregnated with the principle of the "best interests" of the child (physical and mental well being).

Turkey — Yes.

United States — Yes. See A. 2. 1.

2. (e) Do you consider whether the parent is a "fit and proper person"?

(1) Is custody ever awarded to a mother living with a man to whom she has not been ceremonially married?

(2) Is custody ever awarded to an adjudged adulterous parent?

(3) Is custody ever awarded to a father who is not remarried?

Australia	– Consideration is given to whether the parent is a "fit and proper person" but court's discretion is not limited and custody may be awarded to: (1) a mother living with a man to whom she has not been ceremonially married; (2) to an adjudged adulterous parent; (3) to a father who has not remarried.
Austria	– Yes. If conduct of parent is liable to endanger child's interests custody may be awarded: (1) to a mother living with a man to whom she is not married; (2) to an adjudged adulterous parent; (3) fact of father's remarriage is not decisive; important to know if he is in a position to undertake the child's education which is usually not the case if he is single and has a profession.
Canada	– In *Ontario, Alberta* and *British Columbia,* the question of parental fitness is considered: (1) custody may be awarded to a mother living with a man to whom she is not ceremonially married if it is in best interests of the child; (2) custody may be awarded to an adjudged adulterous parent; (3) custody may be awarded to a father not remarried.
Denmark	– Yes. (1) If the mother is not "fit" and the father is even less "fit", the mother may be awarded custody; (2) No; (3) Yes, often.
England	– (1) Yes; (2) Yes; (3) Yes, but rarely of a young baby.
Finland	– Yes. (1) Yes, in interests of child, if mother is more suitable than father; (2) Yes, depends on interests of the child; (3) Yes as in (2) above.
France	– Yes. (1) Yes in special circumstances, in particular if child is very young or if there is a favorable report to the court on the home by a Welfare Officer; (2) Yes; (3) Yes.
Germany	– Yes; insane persons, drunkards, minors and bankrupts, and those who have lost their rights as a German citizen are excluded by law. (1) This might happen under the rule of best interests of the child; (2) same answer as (1); (3) same answer as (1).
Iran	– (1) This would be a rare situation, but if in best interests of minor, court would award mother custody; (2) Very rare in Iran as polygamy is practiced and the divorce of "such concubinage is also popular"; (3) Yes, if he demands it and the courts approve.

Israel — Yes. (3) Yes.

Mexico — Yes. (1) Yes unless the Department of Public Prosecution or the court disapproves as endangering the morality of the children or because of mother's depraved habits; (2) no, not if adultery was cause of the divorce; (3) possibly.

Netherlands — No, this is not important in itself. (1) Yes; (2) Yes; (3) Yes.

New Zealand — Yes, a vital consideration. (1) Yes; (2) Yes; (3) Yes.

Norway — Yes. Parent's conduct and mode of life important in deciding which could best raise child. (1) Yes; (2) Yes; (3) Yes.

North. Ireland — Yes. Court has regard to conduct of a parent. (1) Yes; (2) Yes; (3) Yes.

Portugal — Not answered specifically.

Scotland — Yes. (1) Yes, if in interest of child's welfare; (2) Yes, if in interest of child's welfare; (3) Yes, if in interest of child's welfare.

South Africa — In determining what is in best interests of a child, one consideration is whether parent is fit and proper person to have custody. (1) Mother's living in adultery is a consideration against her being awarded custody, but no absolute bar; depends on nature of the association, its stability, etc. and relative merits of placing child with father; (2) Yes, depending on circumstances — if not promiscuous, not an absolute bar (3) Yes, depending on criterion of best interests of child.

Switzerland — Yes. (1) No; (2) No; (3) Yes, if mother dies, father retains custody.

Turkey — Yes. (1) Mother living with a man to whom she is not ceremonially married may lose custody; (2) Mother who has been found guilty of adultery may lose custody.

United States — Yes, "fitness" of parent considered, especially if contest between a parent and a third person. (1) Ordinarily, no, since such a mother is deemed "unfit": occasionally, yes. (2) Courts differ as to whether or not a mother's adultery characterizes her as "unfit".

Courts require adulterous mother to make a strong showing to overcome presumption of unfitness. More recent cases more willing to conclude a mother's adultery may be counterbalanced by other factors. (3) Yes, in exceptional cases, if father can provide a suitable home (i. e., if he lives with his parents or has an efficient housekeeper). Much depends on "fitness" of mother, home she can provide and whether she works or not. Generally a mother not remarried will be preferred over father not remarried, except in case of teenage boys.

2. (f) Are agreements concerning custody subject to court review and revision?

Australia	– Yes.
Austria	– All agreements by parents re custody need consent of the court.
Canada	– In Ontario, Alberta and British Columbia – Yes.
Denmark	– Yes, but where child has lived with one parent several years, agreement is seldom changed.
England	– Yes.
Finland	– If parents have agreed re custody, it is normally confirmed by the court unless against best interests of child or if change in conditions has occurred.
France	– Yes.
Germany	– Yes, but only under the general rule of the "best interest of the child".
Iran	– Yes, if there are legal reasons and "protests made to the District Attorney".
Israel	– Yes.
Mexico	– All agreements must be reviewed, revised and approved by courts in presence of Department of Public Prosecution.
Netherlands	– Agreements re custody are not binding on the court but court will usually follow wishes of parents. Any decision re custody is subject to court review and revision on ground of changed circumstances.
New Zealand	– Yes.

Norway	– Yes, if special interests so indicate and it is in interests of the child.
North. Ireland	– Yes, if agreement is against best interests of the child.
Portugal	– Yes.
Scotland	– Yes, agreements and court decisions subject to review and revision.
South Africa	– Yes, for good cause in interests of the child.
Switzerland	– Agreements re custody do not need court approval and they can be modified or suspended by those who exercise the parental authority, "provided that claims, if any, of the other party to the arrangement are respected".
Turkey	– Decisions re child custody are made by the court and may be modified by the court.
United States	– Yes, in theory but in practice courts generally accept custodial arrangement agreed to by parents. Courts generally may modify custody award on proof of substantial change in circumstances.

2. (g) Who gets custody of out-of-wedlock children?

Australia	– The mother is the natural guardian but the father may apply to the court for custody.
Austria	– The mother in the first instance. If the child is not well cared for, the father is obliged to keep it, and if this is not possible, he must provide a secure and proper home for it.
Canada	– The mother generally. In *Ontario,* the father has no statutory right to the child but may have a right based on the welfare of the child and court's inherent jurisdiction.
Denmark	– The mother.
England	– The mother.
Finland	– The mother.
France	– The custody belongs to the parent who exercises parental control, i. e., the parent who first recognized it as his or her child.

Germany	– Generally, the custody is with the special Dept. of Welfare authorities (the "Jugendamt"). Upon request, the custody might be granted by the Dept. of the Lower Courts which decides custody (the "Vormundschaftsgericht") to the unmarried mother.
Iran	– The court decides if the parents do not agree. If neither parent accepts the child, the mother must care for it until the court decides if an agency is to take custody.
Israel	– Practically the mother (father generally not interested) but no legal objection to the father's having custody.
Mexico	– When both parents have acknowledged an out-of-wedlock child and live together, both have parental authority. In case of disagreement, court decides. Where both parents acknowledge out-of-wedlock child at same time, but do not live together, they may agree as to custody; if not, court decides. If acknowledgment is not at same time, parental authority is in the parent who first acknowledged but they may agree otherwise. In default of parents where child was acknowledged, parental authority in paternal and maternal grandparents.
Netherlands	– Not answered.
New Zealand	– Usually the mother will be regarded as having a slightly better claim.
Norway	– The mother.
North. Ireland	– The mother.
Portugal	– No set rule. Interests of child prevail. Custody is given to one of the parents, to a third person or to an educational institution.
Scotland	– The mother has the legal right but if question is raised, the courts decide according to child's best interests.
South Africa	– The mother.
Switzerland	– Generally to the mother. If she in unfit, a guardian is appointed.
Turkey	– Unions established by law for the protection of children.

United States — Generally the mother but in some states courts have awarded custody to the father in the child's best interests, if mother egregiously "unfit". Natural father has a secondary claim and is preferred over "strangers".

3. What general rules are applied in allowing visitation?

(a) Is visitation ever contingent on receipt of support payments?

(b) Is visitation allowed to grandparents or other relatives?

(c) Are the child's wishes taken into consideration?

Australia — *General Rules:*

(a) Normally access is not contingent on receipt of support payments, but probably no order for access would be made in favor of a parent who flagrantly disobeyed an order for maintenance.

(b) Ordinarily orders for access are not made in favor of grandparents or other relatives, nor is there specific power in the court to do so. An order for custody in favor of a parent could be made contingently upon access being allowed to grandparents or other relatives.

(c) The wishes of the child are taken into consideration on matters of access if the child is of sufficiently mature years.

Austria — (a) No connection between obligation to furnish support and visitation.

(b) Wishes of the children only taken into consideration if "objectively justified".

(c) No answer.

Canada — *General Rules:*

Orders awarding custody are usually made subject to "reasonable access" by other parent. The usual order provides for access on Sunday afternoons.

Ontario: Access is usually exercised outside the custodial parent's residence — generous access allowed.

(a) Visitation is never expressly so conditioned but on application to the court to enforce visitation rights, the court may consider failure to make payments.

(b) Would be extremely rare that grandparents or other relatives would apply for visitation. Either parent when exercising custody or visitation could bring children to grandparents or relatives.

(c) *Ontario:* Child's wishes considered; wishes of older children may be decisive.
Alberta: Court is loath to believe that a child should not visit the other parent.
British Columbia: Child's wishes considered but generally not as significant as in custody.

Denmark — (a) No.
(b) No. (Unless parties agree).
(c) Yes, if they are really considered to be children's wishes.

England — (a) No.
(b) No, except in rare cases.
(c) Yes, but not decisive.

Finland — *General Rule* — Visitation is always allowed; namely twice a month if practicable. Non-custodial parent normally also allowed to have child for a month or two weeks during child's vacation.
(a) No.
(b) No.
(c) Yes, especially in the enforcement, child's wishes are considered.

France — (a) Visitation is never contingent on support payments.
(b) Visitation is allowed to grandparents; not to other relatives.
(c) Wishes of child normally taken into consideration after age 16.

Germany — (a) As a rule, no.
(b) As a rule, no.
(c) As a rule, no; but if there is a reason, the judge of the court determining custody (Vormundschaftsgericht) might hear the child.

Iran — (a) No. Visitation is as court originally desides.
(b) Yes.
(c) Not answered.

Israel — No general rules in Israeli law. Practically, the court considers the importance of the natural ties between children and parents and sometimes of other relatives, not only as a parental right but as a matter of benefit to the child.

(a) No.

(b) Sometimes.

(c) Yes.

Mexico — No special rules. Visitation is a matter of agreement by parents or court decision.

(a) Not exactly. The non-payment of support might result in the loss of parental authority.

(b) No law governing this; it is not usually included in the agreement.

(c) No law but perhaps children's wishes are considered.

Netherlands — The court does not decide on visitation. It is left to the custodian of the child. There is never a *right* to visitation, not even for the other parent. General feeling is that visitation is not in all cases desirable. Whenever problems arise as to other parent seeing child, the Council of Child Protection will generally offer to mediate.

New Zealand — Rules re visitation are extremely flexible and (a), (b) and (c) are "regarded as relevant factors".

Norway — Law provides that non-custodial parent may obtain an order as to whether he or she is to have visitation and extent thereof.

(a) Visitation is not contingent on support payments.

(b) No — only parents are granted visitation.

(c) Child's wishes may influence court's decision.

North. Ireland — In visitation orders (as in custody), the court considers conduct of parents and their wishes. It will exercise its jurisdiction in interests of child. Court exercises wide discretion as to visitation; only affects parents.

(a) Terms of an order not contingent on support, although breach of order to support will be taken into account.

Portugal — No set rules. Visitation rights of non-custodial parent fixed by agreement of parents or by courts for minors.

If child is placed with another person or at school, visitation rights of both parents fixed.

(c) Children's wishes are unofficially considered.

Scotland — General rules re visitation are similar to those re custody.

(a) Access is not directly contingent on support payments but a wilful failure to make such payments would be relevant as to defaulter's fitness to have access.

(b) Visitation has been allowed to grandparents recently but not to other relatives.

(c) Child's wishes taken into consideration if child of sufficient age.

South Africa — Non-custodial spouse has a right of reasonable access whether order says so or not. Court may refuse visitation to non-custodial parent in interests of child. Non-custodial parent must be a "fit" person. Aim is to preserve a degree of parent-child relationship in non-custodial parent.

(a) No.

(b) Depending on interests of the child, and court order, yes.

(c) Yes.

Switzerland — Extent of visitation rights of non-custodial parent is determined by the court (generally for not more than 1/2 or 1 day a month. Exceptionally, in interests of child, visitation is denied or suspended.

(a) Visitation right is completely independent of support-obligation. It cannot be waived.

(b) No provision in law for visitation right of grandparents; but today a delegated right can be given to them, when the parent who has the visitation right cannot exercise it.

(c) Children have no right to be heard by the court but the child may have the court's decision revised through the Board supervising guardianships, in the child's interest.

Turkey — No general law concerning visitation rights. Rules re visitation are formulated and regulated by the Boards of "The Union for the Protection of Children".

United States — (a) Generally no, but opposite has been held. If agreement or court order expressly conditions father's visitation rights upon payment of child support, non-payment of child support may forfeit visitation privileges.

(b) Obligation to permit visitation with grandparents a moral, not a legal duty, but in some cases grandparents or other relatives have been allowed to demand and receive visitation privileges.

(c) Ordinarily child's wishes as to visitation will not prevail over wishes of legal custodian, parent unless in child's "best interests". Court may consider child's wishes but this is not conclusive on court.

4. What methods, if any, do you have for enforcing visitation?

Australia — No answer given.

Austria — The court which ordered visitation may enforce it by coercive measures.

Canada — Procedures available are criminal sanctions in the Juvenile and Family Court or Magistrate's Courts and citation for contempt in the higher courts.

Denmark — Enforcement available by execution of the sheriff but he is not supposed to enforce visitation if he considers this to be harmful to the child (but no fixed rules and common view that rules of visitation are unsatisfactory). (Proposed that enforcement through local Welfare Society and/or no enforcement).

England — Threat to transfer custody to other parent.

Finland — Enforcement by same authorities who enforce custody judgments.

France — Parent who fails to comply with order of Civil Court for visitation is guilty of a criminal offense.

Germany — If necessary, order will be enforced by an official ("Gerichtsvollzieher") similar to a sheriff or court marshall whose task is to enforce all judgments, especially those ordering a payment.

Iran — Visitation shall be as originally provided by the court, or as mutually agreed.

Israel	– The same as in custody orders.
Mexico	– No method for enforcing visitation.
Netherlands	– Visitation is not enforced.
New Zealand	– No particular methods for enforcing visitation.
Norway	– It can be enforced against parent who refuses to allow visitation by a current daily fine imposed by the court.
North. Ireland	– No statutory methods. Court would, where necessary, use its contempt power.
Portugal	– Enforcement by courts.
Scotland	– A person failing to comply with a court order may be imprisoned and the failure to comply might also jeopardize the right to custody.
South Africa	– Depends on terms of order; bad faith, failure to comply normally amounts to contempt of court. Failure of spouse who has sole custody to grant the other spouse access without reasonable cause, constitutes a criminal offense, as does failure to notify other spouse of any change of address.
Switzerland	– Cantonal Procedural Laws regulate enforcement. Generally no enforcement by police but in some places it is granted or used as a threat. Normally only psychological means are used. Court issues an order to the defendant to guarantee other parent visitation right with threat of jail (1 day to 3 months) or a fine (maximum 2000 f. s.). If failure continues, he may, according to various Cantonal rules, be punished again.
Turkey	– Rules concerning visitation are regulated by a Board called "The Union for the Protection of Children".
United States	– In most states, enforcement by exercise of court's contempt powers. If violator out of state or country, a restraining order or injunction may issue to order party in question to comply with prior court order. Theoretically it is possible for the party who has been deprived of custody or visitation rights pursuant to a prior court order to have such rights confirmed (by writ of habeas corpus or petition in equity), at place where children or other party are found but

practically the local resident (who is the defendant in the habeas corpus or petition in equity proceeding) is favored by local court.

B. *Do your courts recognize the custody determinations of other countries as to children in your country?*

1. Does your country have any treaty with any other country or is it a signatory to any convention as to custody? If so, with which? Has it been enforced? What has been your experience?
2. Are you contemplating any such new treaty or convention?

Australia — The courts "pay regard" to the orders of any foreign court properly having jurisdiction, but if the child was within the jurisdiction of an Australian court, that court would decide custody.

(1) No.

(2) Not known.

Austria — The court recognizes the determination of the state of origin of the father, and if he is dead, that of the mother.

(1) Not answered.

(2) No.

Canada — Decision of a foreign court (including that of another province, is a circumstance which is considered (and given a great deal of weight in a subsequent custody proceeding), but is not conclusive. The whole question is reopened and all circumstances considered. Normally a Canadian court has jurisdiction where child resides within its territory.

(1) No treaty or convention.

(2) No information re any intended treaty or convention.

Denmark — Foreign determinations not binding unless so stated in a treaty.

(1) Yes. Denmark has treaties with other Scandinavian countries but with no other countries. Scandinavian decisions are therefore respected in Denmark; decisions of other countries will not be binding; Danish court will rule according to child's best interests.

(2) No other treaties contemplated as far as is known.

England – (1) Reciprocal with Commonwealth countries.
(2) Not known.

Finland – (1) The convention between the Scandinavian countries.
(2) No answer given.

France – French courts do not recognize custody determinations of other countries as to children in France.
(1) No treaty or convention with other countries.
(2) Answer ambiguous.

Germany – German courts recognize the custody determinations of other countries as to children living in Germany.
(1) No treaties.
(2) No.

Iran – If approach of other countries is similar to Iran's and result is not contrary to Iranian law and is found to be the best solution, Iran's courts will ratify and enforce foreign rulings.
(1) No.
(2) Study of issue of reciprocity going on.

Israel – Yes. Provided foreign court had jurisdiction according to Israeli concepts (order made in foreign court while parents and child were resident there) and provided that enforcement would not be contrary to interest of child.
(1) No.
(2) Not answered.

Mexico – Doubtful whether Mexico recognizes custody decisions of other countries of child residing in Mexico.
(1) No.
(2) No.

Netherlands – (1) Netherlands is a signatory to Hague Convention of June 12, 1902 which has been enforced. National law of child is applicable.
(2) No.

New Zealand – Custody determination of court of another country is regarded as a factor to be taken into account in assessing the minor's best interests. If minor likely

to be returned to country which made the decision, New Zealand courts may refuse to deal with case.
(1) No.
(2) No.

Norway — (1) Convention of February 6, 1931 between Norway, Denmark, Finland, Iceland and Sweden re guardianship matters.
(2) Same countries planning a convention for mutual enforcement of custody decisions. Norway has not decided whether to sign Hague Convention of October 5, 1961 re guardianship matters.

North. Ireland — Court will give weight to decision of foreign court, but considers infant's welfare as first and paramount consideration.
(1) No answer.
(2) No answer.

Portugal — Competent court is that of child's residence.
(1) Not answered.
(2) Not answered.

Scotland — Courts of Scotland will recognize custody decisions of other countries if validly made. Person who obtained decision raises action for "decree conform", certified copy of foreign order submitted to Scottish court and subsequent decree validates it.
(1) No.
(2) No.

South Africa — If South African court approves of foreign order, it will give practical effect to it by order stating applicant is entitled to custody or that respondent hand over child; if South African court disapproves, it will make its own decision. Section 6 of the Matrimonial Causes Jurisdiction Act of 1939 (dealing with recognition of certain divorce and separation decrees) extends to custody orders.
(1) No.
(2) No.

Switzerland — If a foreign decree is recognized as valid in Switzerland, custody decisions made in connection therewith are also recognized.
(1) Treaties on recognition and enforcement of court decisions with Belgium, Germany, France, Italy, Austria, Sweden, Spain, Czechoslovakia.

Reciprocal agreements of certain cantons with foreign countries: Bern with Roumania, Lucerne with Lichtenstein, St. Gallen with Austria, Zurich with Austria.

(2) Yes. Draft of international convention has been prepared on recognition and enforcement of decisions on child custody (49th Conference of International Law Association).

Turkey — Foreign decrees not controlling.
(1) Not answered.
(2) Not answered.

United States — (1) No.
(2) No information.

C. *Do you have any problems within your country as to children living in another city or province?*

Which court determines custody? Where the children reside? Where the father lives? Where the mother lives? What other considerations?

Australia — (a) *Matrimonial Causes Act.* No difficulty since state courts administer Federal Jurisdiction Act and a question of custody can be removed from one State Supreme Court to another.
(b) *State Supreme Courts exercising State Jurisdiction.* Court within whose jurisdiction child resides will make determination. Also possible that a court may exercise jurisdiction even though child is not residing in its jurisdiction, on application of a father or mother. There may be problems of enforcement if child remains outside its jurisdiction.
(c) South Australian Court (by virtue of State Maintenance Act), can exercise jurisdiction only if mother is granted separation and child is within state when order is made.

Austria — No problems.

Canada — In each province the court governing the district or territory where the child resides determines custody. Exceptionally, where an abduction has occurred, the court where the applicant parent resides will deal with the case. (The court is competent even though the child is not present but court has discretion as to exercise of its jurisdiction and may not do so because its order reaching beyond its boundaries may be unenforceable).

Denmark	– No.
England	– No. Residence of child or of father or mother. In some cases, domicile.
Finland	– No. Depends on where defendant resides.
France	– No. Competent court is that which granted the decree of divorce or judicial separation; normally that where husband was domiciled at commencement of action.
Germany	– No.
Iran	– Not much. All courts are similar. The court where the case is "preferred" is competent and such court observes all considerations. Its rulings are subject to protest and revision by District Attorney, either on a report to him or by filing a petition.
Israel	– No.
Mexico	– In a trial for annulment or divorce, the competent court would be that of the marital home; if abandonment is ground, the court of the abandoned spouse's residence; if controversy is only over custody court of minor's residence, enforcement through "letters requisitorial" to court of defendant's domicile.
Netherlands	– No. In general, the Court of the child's domicile decides. If no domicile in The Netherlands, the court of the child's residence decides or if no official residence, the Amsterdam Court where custody decision is an incident of divorce or separation, then that court decides.
New Zealand	– No. Question of venue generally decided by such matters as convenience of witnesses, etc.
Norway	– Question of custody initially decided in connection with separation or divorce. If transfer of custody is desired, action must be brought against parent having custody in district where he or she permanently resides.
North. Ireland	– No. Jurisdiction based on presence of infant within jurisdiction. But courts also claim jurisdiction if infant is a subject of their country regardless of where

he is. In "exceptional circumstances", court may take jurisdiction where children are outside the jurisdiction.

Portugal — If child and parent do not live in the same place, competent court is that of child's residence.

Scotland — Yes. Problems arise through conflicts of jurisdiction between courts in different parts of the United Kingdom (Scotland, England and Northern Ireland), from a difference of view as to whether child's domicile (as determined by father's) controls or child's residence.

South Africa — *Custody and guardianship orders* (no matrimonial suit), domicilary court, irrespective of residence or physical presence of parties or child. If child "in need of care" under Children's Act of 1960, it is that where child resides or happens to be.

Matrimonial action pending — Interim Custody Orders, appropriate court is that of matrimonial domicile irrespective of physical presence of parties or child.

Custody and guardianship orders ancillary to matrimonial action — Court of the domicile (irrespective of residence or physical presence of parties or child) (in a separation suit, court of common residence). After divorce or separation (if no custody order made therein, court of present domicile of the father.

Modification of custody or guardianship order — if court (Supreme Court) that pronounced the order was that of the domicile and still is, it has jurisdiction (continuing jurisdiction). Competency also in the court of the domicile of the child; (when foreign order is concerned, court is that of residence or presence of the minor).

Switzerland — In divorce or paternity proceeding, court which has jurisdiction, determines custody. If a guardian must be appointed for the child, jurisdiction in child's domicile (parents' residence or residence of parent who has parental authority or if child has no legal representative he has domicile of his own.) For preventive measures, the authorities of the place where child lives.

Turkey — No. Custody of children may be determined by all justices of the peace (custody is a matter of public policy).

United States — Yes. There is confusion among states as to basis for exercise of custody jurisdiction. May be:

1. That defendant is domiciled, resident or present at the forum; 2. child is domiciled (although absent) from forum; 3. child is physically present at forum; 4. combination of any one of above three bases at forum. Also a serious problem due to the encouragement given unwittingly by American law to parent abducting a child in order to relitigate merits of custody in another place to obtain an order changing custody.

D. *What suggestions do you have for possible legislative or other action in each country for dealing with problems of custody?*

Australia — None.

Austria — Not answered.

Canada — Legislation is necessary in all provinces to enable the court to appoint counsel for the child in all custody cases and especially where there is a demonstrable conflict of interest between the child and both parents.

Denmark — None.

England — Reciprocal international provisions between countries with comparable legal systems — to control unauthorized removal.

Finland — The international enforcement of the judgment or agreement on custody.

France — International treaties for the automatic enforcement of custody orders of foreign courts.

Germany — None.

Iran — Iran's legal system is unique. However, after hearing others, Iran may suggest comparative solutions.

Israel — To give more weight to interests of children and to regulate international cooperation in cases where one of the parents removes a child from the jurisdiction without the other's consent or when jurisdiction of two or more countries is involved.

Mexico — Each country should consider joining in a Minor's Code which would include regulations as to custody and protection of minors' interests. (See answer to 2. F.).

Netherlands — None.

New Zealand — None.

Norway — A form of international cooperation on conventions under which custody determinations of other countries would be recognized and enforced in any participation. Before this, it would be necessary to introduce more uniform legislation re which parent gets custody in separations and divorces.

North. Ireland — None.

Portugal — None.

Scotland — It has been suggested that jurisdiction should be based on the ordinary residence of the child.

South Africa — (a) Proper arrangements for child custody should be a condition precedent to the granting of a divorce decree.

(b) More use should be made of services of specialized agencies for full reports to the court on custody matters.

(c) All matters re divorce, custody, etc. should be conducted more informally (perhaps in a special family court, with judge assisted by social worker, psychologist and psychiatrist).

Switzerland — None.

Turkey — None.

United States — Steps could be taken to discourage abduction of children in violation of prior custody and visitation orders. Many cases where children taken to a foreign country in violation of custody or visitation order and then new custody proceedings brought to change legal custody. Courts of any country should decline to change foreign custody decrees at request of party who has violated a prior order unless children are dependent or neglected.

E. *What special questions on Child Custody do you suggest for our discussion in Dublin?*

Australia	– Problems arising from the removal of children from the jurisdiction of a court which has made an order for custody. Might include a discussion of issuance of passports where orders for custody or access are in existence.
Austria	– Not answered.
Canada	– Not answered.
Denmark	– No suggestions.
England	– (1) International treaties. (2) Help of police on international basis.
Finland	– The international enforcement of custody orders or agreements.
France	– The international enforcement of custody orders.
Germany	– No suggestions.
Iran	– None at this time.
Israel	– To regulate international cooperation where one parent without consent of the other, removes child out of court's jurisdiction or where two or more countries are involved.
Mexico	– A Minor's Code in each country and general standards as to child custody. If this is too broad a topic, "Practical Judicial Measures To Enforce Custody Agreements and Orders."
Netherlands	– No special suggestions though there are a number of problems as to custody.
New Zealand	– No suggestions.
Norway	– Uniform legislation in European countries as to which parent should have custody.
North. Ireland	– Not answered.
Portugal	– No suggestions.
Scotland	– Matters referred to in C. and D.
South Africa	– (a) Problems arising out of custody of children out of polygamous unions and out of polygamous unions by natural law and custom.

(b) Question of matrimonial jurisdiction in cases mentioned in (a).

(c) Ways and means to arrange custody matters on an international basis or by conventions. Recommendation – South African practice to grant maintenance grants to all foreign nationals irrespective of their period of residence.

Switzerland – No suggestions.

Turkey – No suggestions.

United States – 1. In a custody dispute between parent and non-parent, does former invariably prevail even though best interests of child favor giving custody to non-parent?

2. If petitioner has violated the terms of a custody or visitation order, under what circumstances will prior orders be modified?

3. May custody be awarded to an adulterous or alcoholic mother?

4. What are evidentiary rules as to admissibility of investigations and reports on family background and the psychiatric and social needs of the children? What are the court facilities for investigation of custody disputes? Do governmental or welfare agencies make investigations and reports?

5. Should custody disputes be resolved by adversary process or should such issues be handled in some other way? If so, how?

III. *Interprofessional Cooperation in Dealing with Problems of Support and Custody of Children*

A. *Whose responsibility is it to establish the facts and provide the evidence?*

1. The parties themselves?
2. The courts?
3. Others?

Australia – Ordinarily the responsibility is on the parties, not the courts. Departments of Social Welfare seeking maintenance orders provide their own offices to establish facts and provide evidence.

Austria — 1. In civil proceedings, the parties must establish the facts and provide the allegations (to establish paternity and to fix support of "full aged" children).

2. In non-disputed proceedings the court must take the necessary measures and decide facts. (In determining visitation, support; right of child re education, care and professional training). Anyone may inform the court about facts bearing on welfare of the child.

Canada — 1. Generally, it is the parties themselves who have the responsibility. With minor exceptions, the issues are developed and proved according to the rules of the adversary system.

2. No (not the courts).

3. *Ontario:* In all actions for marriage dissolution where there are children under 16, the pleadings must be served on the Official Guardian (office under Attorney General's Dept.), whether or not custody is at issue. This official, through a social worker of one of the Children's Aid Societies makes an investigation and report to the court "upon all matters of custody, maintenance and education of the children". In practice, the investigation is usually a home visit and an interview with each parent. Report reflects what parents say; contains background information on parents and children and each parent's plans and home to be provided for child; also statement by parties as to their financial circumstances, and any other "relevant information". Report does not contain a recommendation re custody. By statute, the report is evidence. Parents may dispute any statement and cross-examine investigator. In Surrogate and Supreme Court (where custody only is at issue), investigation is not a matter of course but may be ordered by court in its discretion. (Usually not requested by parties nor ordered by court.)

Denmark — 1. No.

2. The courts — often assisted by parents' attorneys.

England — 1. Yes.

2. Yes, if dissatisfied with information provided by parties.

3. Local authorities and welfare departments, including children's officers. Certain voluntary organizations.

Finland — 1. The parties.

2. Where the parents are in disagreement, the administrative authorities in charge of matters re custody and child care, will be asked to study the case and give their opinion.

3. See 2.

France — 1. The parties themselves.

2. When the evidence of the parent applying for custody is not conclusive or is disputed by other party, the court will appoint a Welfare officer to investigate and report to the court with recommendations as to custody.

Germany — 1. 2. & 3. First the parties try to prove the facts. The courts also may order evidence taken and appoint experts to give opinions and recommendations.

Iran — 1. 2. & 3. The claimant. The court may demand from the parents and other parties, witnesses or others, answers to any question.

Israel — 1. Yes.

2. Generally not, but the court may on its own motion request a report from the Public Welfare Officer which will be evidence. The court may also give notice of the proceeding to the Attorney General's representative who may intervene and supply evidence.

3. As above, the Attorney General's representatives in cases of care and protection before the Juvenile Court — the proper welfare officer.

Mexico — 1. In civil cases in which support and custody is principal issue, parties establish the facts and provide the evidence.

2. Civil and criminal courts may investigate, call witnesses, etc.; Juvenile courts have even broader powers and may, through their investigation department, "study the minor's social surroundings" and his conduct.

3. In civil actions, the Department of Public Prosecution usually requires verification as to income of

person obliged to provide support. In criminal prosecutions, this Department handles the action and must establish the facts and provide the evidence.

Netherlands — 1. 2. & 3. In the first place the parties present the facts. If there is any question, the Council of Child Protection, on order of the court, will investigate and try to establish the evidence.

New Zealand — 1. Yes.
2. No.
3. No.

Norway — 1. In practice, it is usually the parties themselves who provide the necessary evidence.
2. The courts can also on their own initiative obtain the necessary evidence. In questions of custody, the law provides that whenever necessary the child care committee or other experts should be called to express an opinion before custody is decided.

North. Ireland — 1. The parties themselves. If social workers, psychologists, etc., are called by the parties, the court will take account of their evidence.

Portugal — Not answered.

Scotland — 1. The parties themselves.
2. No.
3. When it comes to the attention of a local authority that a child is neglected or ill treated, etc., it may institute proceedings before the courts to have child committed to care of local authority or a fit person.

South Africa — 1. 2. & 3. Primary responsibility rests upon applicant. Use is made of reports of social welfare workers, etc. If criminal aspects, Police Dept. investigates and obtains evidence. Attorney General has responsibility to decide if a prosecution is to be instituted and in lower courts, public prosecutor has this responsibility.

Switzerland — 1. Plaintiff must in first instance establish the facts and provide the evidence.
2. In a divorce proceeding, in questions of child custody, the court may assemble evidence to assist it in determining custody, support, visitation.

Several cantons permit court to assemble evidence in paternity proceedings.

3. Child in paternity proceedings is represented by his counsel who can charge a lawyer with representation in court. Large cities have a professional guardian to represent child.

Turkey — Not answered.

United States — Custody cases are presented in American courts within the adversary framework. In custody cases many American courts will not consider investigations and reports in the absence of stipulation by the parties, and the judge may not have authority to confer with the child unless the parties agree. Thus there are serious limitations on the court's authority. In practice, the court hears and sees the evidence presented by opposing counsel according to the rules of practice and procedure. In some states, masters or referees may be used for the fact-finding function. Typical situation is that the parties have the responsibility (within framework of the adversary process) of providing the evidence. It is their responsibility to procure and present the evidence; it is the responsibility of the court to determine the facts.

B. *What use do your courts make of other professions in arriving at decisions regarding non-support and custody determinations?*

1. Do the courts have social workers, psychologists, psychiatrists or other professionals on staff?
2. Do your courts refer to non-court professionals for recommendations?
3. Do your courts refer such questions for determination by other agencies or workers?

Australia — *Matrimonial Causes Act* provides for appointment of Welfare officers and for receipt by the court of reports from them on questions of custody. Supreme Court of South Australia has such an officer permanently employed and his services are available for such reports.

1. Not on staff. (Evidence tendered on behalf of the parties may be received from social workers and psychologists and psychiatrists).
3. No.

Austria — 1. Juvenile court makes use of psychologists and psychiatrists.
2. The courts can make use of the so-called juvenile courts assistance in cases where the interests of the children are concerned.
3. Corporations, societies and willing persons can be active in this juvenile court assistance.

Canada — 1. *Ontario:* Juvenile and Family Courts and the *British Columbia* Family and Children's Courts have clinical facilities staffed by social workers who function in custody cases to bring out dispositions by agreement. If there is a contest which cannot be resolved in this way, a court referral is made and adversary proceedings take place. Superior courts do not have such facilities.
2. No, courts do not have the power to do this without consent of parties.
3. No.

Denmark — 1. No.
2. In matrimonial cases the parents often agree upon a solution after which a psychiatrist examines the children, etc. and gives his opinion. Otherwise the courts have no assistance from other authorities except that the court might ask the local child welfare authority for a closer examination of the home.
3. No.

England — 1. Yes, probation services. No psychological or psychiatric service on staff.
2. Yes. National Health Service and professional witnesses provided by parties.
3. No.

Finland — 1. Yes.
2. If parents agree, administrative authorities in charge of custody and child care will study case and give an opinion.
3. See 2.

France — 1. Yes.
2. Yes.

Germany — 1. Not on staff, but the court might employ psychologists, psychiatrists or other professionals (who are civil servants with Government Health Authorities).

2. Yes.

3. No.

Iran — 1. Some are governmental staffed and sometimes they use university professors.

2. Often.

3. Courts may indicate referees or use the agencies concerned.

Israel — 1. 2. & 3. The social welfare workers are employed by Minister of Social Welfare, not by the court. When they make inquiries and prepare recommendations for the court or enforce court orders, they act as if officers of the court. When courts request a report from such officer, he consults psychologists, psychiatrists, physicians and teachers and includes their opinions in his report. Also, any party may bring in such a professional expert as witness.

Mexico — 1. Juvenile courts have such experts. Other courts may order testimony by such experts.

2. Yes; they may also refer to relatives.

3. Not specifically, except as explained above.

Netherlands — 1. No.

2. In practice, no.

3. Yes. The Council of Child Protection may delegate part of the investigation to one or more specialists. The court may also order such an investigation by specialists.

New Zealand — 1. No.

2. Yes. A Government Department known as the Child Welfare Division is often asked by the court to report on such matters.

3. In general, no.

Norway — 1. & 2. Not on staff. The courts, however, can take statements from the Child Care Committees (which have social workers on their staffs in larger towns). They meet with parents and often with the child and visit the home.

3. The court.

North. Ireland — 1. No.
2. No.
3. No.

Portugal — 1. Courts have special social workers.

Scotland — 1. No.
2. Yes.
3. No.

South Africa — 1. Not on staff, although all professional officers of the Department of Social Welfare are regarded as officers of the court. All the other agencies and professions are also at the disposal of the court either through the parties when called as witnesses or on the initiative of the court.
2. Yes, but not to the extent it should do.
3. Not for a final determination (which rests with the court) but to investigate and report.

Switzerland — 1. No.
2. Where judge has insufficient knowledge to evaluate the facts, he is required to call in experts for their opinion. He is not bound by their opinions and may order another expert opinion.

Turkey — Not answered.

United States — 1. 2. & 3. The use of evidence as to the psychiatric condition of the contesting parties and of the child is increasing. Some states provide for this by statute. Some states' courts refer cases to outside agencies for investigation and report. In most states, however, there is a lack of confidence in such reports and obstacles are placed in the way of getting background reports and case histories before the court. A number of Family Courts and Juvenile Courts in various states have a professional staff of trained social workers, probation officers, psychologists and psychiatrists who prepare reports for these courts and other courts handling custody cases. (These in larger cities). This is the exception, not the rule. Vast majority of custody disputes are solved in adversary contests heard by judges who are not specialists and who do not have the benefit of investigations, reports and recommendations by professionally trained personnel.

C. *Do you feel that these matters might be handled by agencies or organizations other than courts? If so, which?*

Australia	– No.
Austria	– Juvenile courts – assistance supported by the courts.
Canada	– These matters should be decided by courts. But the courts should have the power to seek recommendations from qualified workers who can make a complete investigation.
Denmark	– No.
England	– No. Domestic Courts are specialized.
Finland	– No. Courts should decide but opinions of other authorities should be heard.
France	– No. Courts alone should have power to decide custody issues but assistance from social workers or psychiatrists is advisable.
Germany	– No.
Iran	– Courts must decide; if and when power is vested elsewhere, the "enforcement must necessarily be governmental".
Israel	– No. Courts but they should accept advice of properly qualified professional people.
Mexico	– Matters should be regulated by a "Minor's Code"; judicial and administrative bodies with investigators and assistance would be responsible for decisions.
Netherlands	– No.
New Zealand	– No. However, much might be said for an independent body to collect the evidence in custody and other cases involving minors.
Norway	– No.
North. Ireland	– Not answered.
Portugal	– Not answered.
Scotland	– No reason to believe present arrangements are not satisfactory but agencies or organizations other than courts (existing Children's Committees of the local authorities or new specifically constituted bodies) might handle these matters.

South Africa — In South Africa, there is a strong feeling that these matters should be handled by a special family court. An alternative proposal is to have part of the Supreme Court deal exclusively with these matters (assisted by social workers, psychologists and psychiatrists as assessors).

Switzerland — Support cases — no. Custody cases — more reason to have these handled by non-judicial agencies but courts preferable.

Turkey — Not answered.

United States — No, access to the courts in such cases cannot be foreclosed and constitutional issues would be raised if there were a legislative attempt to cede custody jurisdiction to administrative tribunal or other governmental agencies. This might be a denial of due process of law under the federal Constitution. It is not politically feasible and probably would be impractical.

SUPPORT AND CUSTODY OF CHILDREN INTERNATIONAL AND COMPARATIVE ASPECTS

National Paper

submitted by HENRY H. FOSTER, Jr. and DORIS JONAS FREED,
USA

I. AS TO SUPPORT OF CHILDREN

Introduction

At common law, the parental obligation to support children presented a curious lacuna between moral and legal duties. Blackstone said that the duty to provide maintenance for children was "a principle of natural law" (1 Bl. Comm. 667). If it was such a principle it was a moral right without adequate legal remedy, although ecclesiastical courts perhaps lent their authority as a matter of conscience to force fathers to discharge their natural duty, and in chancery a quasi-contractual duty of support eventually became a matter of equity. (See *Greenspan v. Slate*, 97 A 2d 390 [N. J. 1953]).

Unlike the situation where the wife was permitted to pledge her husband's credit for necessaries, a child had no such privilege, except where there was an express or implied authorization from the father according to agency principles. Otherwise, neither the child nor any creditor who had provided him with necessaries had any cause of action against the parent. An infant could not sue a parent, with or without a guardian ad litem. No action in assumpsit was maintainable. However, in the nineteenth century it was held that a wife justifiably living separate and apart from her husband due to his misconduct and having legal custody of the children could pledge the husband's credit and he was liable for necessaries received by the wife, including clothes for the child. (*Bazeley v. Forder*, [1868] L. R. 3 Q. B. 559).

The only common law remedy provided by civil law was due to the operation of the Elizabethan Poor Laws of the early seventeenth century (43 Eliz. c. 2) which permitted the parish to recoup for alms or assistance given to the family. Under certain circumstances, the father might be compelled to support his children according to his ability if they became destitute and the parish provided for their maintenance. (See *Mortimore v. Wright*, 6 Mees. & W. 482, and *Shelton v. Springett*, 11 C. B. 452). Even the duty of wife support likewise depended upon application of the Poor Laws, until a doubtful decision, misconstruing supposed precedents, itself became a precedent for non-support suits. (See *Manby & Richards v. Scott,* 83 E. R. 268).

Insofar as the criminal law was concerned, a father's abandonment and non-support of children eventually became a common law misdemeanor, if such neglect occasioned injury. (9 Halsbury's Laws of England [2 d ed.] 443). Today, in the United States, every state has enacted criminal statutes that make desertion and non-support an offense, generally a misdemeanor. Such criminal statutes are strictly construed and today are rarely used in most jurisdictions because there are better alternative and more effective remedies. The word "parent" in such statutes has been construed not to cover a stepfather or the father of an illegitimate child. If the statute makes failure to support a crime, then one may be found guilty by failure to furnish things suitable to his station in life, though bare necessities are provided, but if the statute speaks of a failure to furnish necessities, it may be interpreted as requiring the provision of only bare necessities. (Madden, PERSONS AND DOMESTIC RELATIONS [112, 1931]). Generally, however it is no defense that others have provided necessities to the children, although the father's inability to provide is a good defense. Abandonment as a crime requires both separation from the child and neglect to provide for its needs, and mere absence from the child is not sufficient.

Because of the paucity of legal remedies to enforce the parental obligation of child support, a hodge podge of statutes have been passed to make up for that deficiency. In addition to a civil action by a creditor who has supplied necessaries and the statutory crime of abandonment, usually there are four or five civil or quasi-criminal remedies also provided by state law. Federal law does not concern itself directly with the problem of non-support. Moreover, it sometimes has been held that notwithstanding the uncertainty of the common law, a legal duty of child support may be imposed in the absence of statute as "a matter of natural right and justice". (See *Campbell v. Campbell,* 20 S. E. 2 d 237 [S. C. 1942]).

Where the duty of child support emanates from a statute derived from the Elizabethan Poor Laws, the measure of the duty is apt to be minimal and to be contingent upon the father having "sufficient means". Such duty generally is enforced in family or juvenile courts. When, however, the father's duty of support is reflected in a court order incident to divorce, where possible the measure of the duty is apt to be maximal and in accord with the father's standard of living and station in life. In addition, ordinarily the parental duty of support ceases when a minor achieves emancipation or majority, but under American welfare statutes a duty of minimal support may continue after majority, if the parent is of "sufficient means" and the adult child is destitute or otherwise handicapped. Thus, in effect, there are two systems of family or support law existing side by side, the older being a welfare measure to reduce public assistance and usually entailing the joint and equal liability of both parents, and the larger non-welfare duty of support involving the primary liability of the father and usually a secondary liability on the part of the mother. In the latter instance, a child in New York may be entitled to support "according to the father's means and the child's needs" (*Farrah v. Farrah*, 102 N.Y.S. 2d 147 [1951]); in California "in a manner suitable to the father's circumstances" (*Schumm v. Berg*, 224 P. 2d 56 [Cal. App. 1951]); and in Pennsylvania such a child is entitled to "proper and reasonable support" (*Commonwealth v. Horner*, 77 A. 2d 641 [Pa. Super. 1951]). The difference between the two tests is illustrated by the disagreement as to whether or not a father is obligated to pay for the college education of a talented minor.

With reference to illegitimate children, at common law the natural father was not required to support his illegitimate child, and such remains the rule in Texas and Idaho. Statutes providing for paternity or filiation proceedings in some states may be construed so as to entitle the illegitimate child to the same right of support as a legitimate child (for example, in Arizona, California, New York, and North Carolina), but more often, in practice, the amount ordered is apt to be minimal rather than maximal.

The obligation for child support is viewed as a continuing one and orders for child support usually are regarded as not final and subject to modification due to changed circumstances. A substantial change in the financial circumstances of the father or in the needs of the child may warrant modification. In Georgia, however, a father may be ordered to pay a lump sum in complete discharge of his support duty, and if he does so, he no longer is liable for child support. (See *Yarborough v. Yarborough*, 290 U.S. 22 [1933], sustaining the Georgia support statute which still is in effect, even though the child had moved to another state and a grandfather had been forced to maintain him).

Since the father's duty to support his legitimate children is imposed by law, there are only a few exceptional situations where he may be relieved of such duty. In addition to emancipation of the child which terminates the parental obligation to support, at least unless the child becomes destitute, in some states the mother by contract may assume the primary support obligation, or it may be imposed where she wrongfully obtains custody of the child and voluntarily supports it. (See *Broemmer v. Broemmer*, 219 S.W. 2d 300 [Mo. App. 1949]; and *Central Manufacturers, etc. v. Friedman*, 209 S.W. 2d 102 [Ark. 1948], 1 A.L.R. 2d 557). Depending upon statutes and terms of the decree, a father's estate may or may not be liable for child support until a child reaches majority. Usually his estate is not so liable. In some rare instances where visitation rights and child support are deemed to be interdependent, a violation of the father's visitation rights by the mother, as where without court permission she moves with the child out of the jurisdiction, may suspend the father's duty to continue to pay child support.

Enforcement of child support orders is a difficult problem which has been alleviated only to some extent by uniform laws that permit the interstate rendition of support cases. Greater emphasis should be placed upon the informal processing of support cases and every effort should be made to get the father to agree to pay a specified sum so that there is a moral as well as legal commitment to do so.

A *Laws of American jurisdictions relating to parental responsibility for child support*

1 *To what age?*

Legal rights and duties between parent and child are governed by the law of the respective states in the United States, and only incidentally or indirectly by federal law. The legal obligations of parenthood include the duty to support and maintain minor children and such duty is imposed by various statutes. Generally, the states provide that there is parental responsibility for child support during the child's minority, which usually is until the child reaches the age of 21 years, although the legislatures of the various states may fix different ages after which a parent is no longer liable for child support. For example, in Hawaii, it is 20 years for both males and females, and in about eight states the age is fixed at 21 for males and 18 for females. In Kentucky, it is 18, for both males and females. In the remaining 42 American jurisdictions the duty persists until the son or daughter reaches 21.

In the majority of states, a valid marriage emancipates minors of both sexes, and parents thereafter are not legally responsible for child support. The reason advanced is that the marriage of a minor child creates relations inconsistent with the child's subjection to the control and care of the parent.

In some states, marriage emancipates a minor child only where the parents consented to the marriage and the minor who elopes is not thereby emancipated. Emancipation also may be by agreement between parents and the minor, and such agreement may be implied from circumstances and conduct, as for example where the minor leaves the family home, takes a job, and maintains his own home. In a few cases, it has been held that parental abuse or serious mistreatment of a minor effects an emancipation.

The legal consequence of emancipation is that mutual rights and duties between parent and child are extinguished. On the one hand the parental duty to support may be terminated, on the other, the parent no longer has a legal right to the services and earnings of the minor. Regardless of emancipation, however, welfare laws may require parents, according to their means, to support minor or adult children who are in danger of becoming public charges. Such duty under welfare laws is to be distinguished from the ordinary duty of parental support that is measured by different standards and generally is larger in amount.

In order to understand the parental duty of child support, it is necessary to note not only the multiplicity of remedies imposed to enforce that duty but also the fact that the duty is enforced in different courts employing different measures and standards. Child support, when an adjunct to divorce, tends to be related to alimony and the amount set for child support may be relatively small when alimony is proportionately high. This may be due to the fact that although the husband or former husband can deduct alimony from his income tax and make it taxable to the wife or former wife, the tax laws do not permit him to deduct child support. Hence it is to his tax advantage to have the sum he may have to pay upon divorce listed as alimony rather than child support. The court where divorces are obtained also is accustomed to awarding larger amounts as alimony or support than that ordered by a family or juvenile court, and its clientele may be more prosperous than that of the latter court. The usual standard for the divorce court is that where possible the male bread winner will be required to maintain his family in the style and manner they were accustomed to while the family was intact. Of course, such is impossible except in the case of a prosperous male.

The criminal, quasi-criminal, or civil court that handles the great bulk of wife and child support cases where an action is brought for that specific purpose, rather than as an adjunct to divorce, is apt to draw its clientele from the middle and lower income brackets. At least in metropolitan areas, such courts are swamped with cases and perforce such matters are quickly disposed of, some courts handling 50-100 support cases a day. The defendants in such cases frequently are embittered because of the summary character of the proceedings and because they are being ordered to pay support when from their point of view they receive nothing in return. For this reason such men often leave the state, refuse or fail to pay at all or to pay on time, and it is difficult to enforce court orders.

In most states it is a misdemeanor to be guilty of desertion and non-support and a husband or father who deliberately fails to provide for his family may be fined or sentenced to prison. Such statutes today are rarely enforced, in part because the family may have to go on public assistance while the man languishes in jail. Wage attachment commonly is regarded as a more effective remedy. In addition, juvenile court acts often contain an express provision authorizing the trial in such courts of cases of non-support.

The welfare laws in most states and the federal Social Security Act, adopt the premise that before a wife or family is entitled to public assistance an effort must be made to force a separated husband or father to contribute according to his means. This duty stems from the Elizabethan Poor Laws and the man is regarded as a resource that must be tapped before public welfare may be granted to the family. The duty is imposed as a matter of economics, to cut down on the expenditure of public funds, and it may be no defense that his separation from the family was not his fault or due to the fault of the wife. In the ordinary support case, however, the wife may have to prove that the separation is due to the fault of the husband, although in a few states such as New York, the husband may be obligated to support the wife where they live apart by mutual consent.

There also are many different sanctions for the enforcement of the duty to support. The obligor who willfully violates a court order may be cited for contempt and sentenced to jail. His property is subject to attachment. He may be required to post security in advance to insure the payment of the sums ordered. And perhaps most effective, his wages may be attached.

(For a discussion of the inter-relationship between alimony and support actions, see Foster & Freed, LAW AND THE FAMILY, New York, Introduction to Vol. II [1966]. For an outstanding article on the history and economics of support, see ten Broek, *California's Dual System of Family Law*, 16 Stanford L. Rev. 257, 900 [1964], and 17 Stanford L. Rev. 614 [1965]).

(a) *Exceptions as to termination of duty of child support for physical or mental disability beyond age of child's minority*

In some jurisdictions, state constitutions or statutes impose upon a parent the duty to support his adult child, as where the child is handicapped and dependent and unable to support itself. Some courts (e. g., *Breuer v. Dowden*, 268 S.W. 541 [Ky. 1925]) have held that in order for a parent to be liable for an incapacitated adult child, the child must have remained in the family home. However the majority rule rejects such a qualification. A parent thus may continue to be liable for the support of a child who, as a result of some mental or physical disability, is incompetent to take care of himself at the time he reaches majority, although once a parent's liability has terminated, the general rule is that it will not be revived by the subsequent incapacitation of the adult child.

The Medical Assistance Program or Title XIX of the federal Social Security Act (P.L. 89-97) limits the support obligation to the duty to support a spouse or a child under 21 years of age. This provision of but one of the social security programs was seized upon by the State of New York as the basis for changing its entire policy as to the legal obligation to support indigent relatives. In 1966 the New York legislature eliminated the reciprocal support obligation running between grandparents and grandchildren, and more important, it repealed the duty to contribute to the support of indigent adult children and that of children to support indigent parents. (See Laws of 1966, Chaps. 256 and 257; Laws of 1967, Ch. 184.) In most other states, however, there remains a legal duty to support indigent adult children or indigent parents insofar as other welfare programs are concerned. Thus, in New York parents no longer are legally obligated to support adult children, even though the latter are indigent or handicapped, but in most states such obligation remains except as to the Medical Assistance Program.

2 *Are both parents responsible or only the father?*

(a) *If the mother is liable, under what conditions?*

The usual American rule is that the father has the primary duty to provide child support but that the mother, in exceptional circumstances, may have a secondary obligation in that regard. Usually the mother's secondary duty of child support is imposed by statute where the father is incapacitated or has abandoned the family and the mother has means or the potential of earning income. In some states, however, the mother's secondary duty of child support may arise if the father fails to discharge his primary duty and the children are without means. In addition, if a mother assumes the care and maintenance of her children, she may thereafter be liable for their support.

It generally has been held that the father's duty of child support ceases where the mother takes the children with her and abandons the home without cause. Other cases hold that in such a situation the father remains liable for the maintenance of his children, but not for wife support, especially where he permits the children to remain in the custody of the mother. Unless he contracts otherwise, the father's duty of child support ceases on his death, but this rule has been changed in some jurisdictions so as to obligate his estate for a family allowance.

Welfare laws frequently stipulate the primary duty of the father and the secondary obligation of the mother for child support. The economic measure of such obligations is the "means" of the obligor and the sum ordered usually is minimal as compared with the amount ordered in ordinary support actions. It is intended to keep the recipient off of public assistance, not to maintain him according to the style and standard of living enjoyed when the family was a unit.

So-called "family expense" statutes have changed the common law immunity of a wife or mother to suits for necessaries and the exclusive liability of the husband-father. Such statutes make the wife or her property jointly liable with the husband for necessaries furnished to the family or for family expenses. Family expense statutes vary in scope and application, although the great majority make the wife liable regardless of which spouse contracts the obligation, and a small minority make her liable only where she contracts herself.

A typical family expense statute is that of Illinois (Ill. Smith Hurd Ann. ch. 68, § 15) which provides: "The expenses of the family and of the education of the children shall be chargeable upon the property of both husband and wife, or of either of them, in favor of creditors therefor, and in relation thereto they may be sued jointly or separately." Similar statutes have been enacted in at least 23 states for the benefit of creditors. In 5 of the 23 states the wife has no right of indemnification from the husband for the purchase of necessaries unless he agreed to repay. (See *Truax v. Ellett,* 15 N.W. 2d 361 [Iowa 1944]). In the remaining states, and in those states not having family expense statutes, the wife has a right of indemnification against the husband for her expenditures for family necessaries while they were separated.

Since the modern American mother more often than not is employable and has an earning potential, and a substantial percentage of mothers are employed, it is to be anticipated that her legal liability for child support will be further extended by case law and statute. It might be in better accord with the economic facts to impose upon her primary as well as secondary duties of child support in some situations. Thus, there is authority to the effect that the mother is liable for child support when the father fails in his duty and the children are without means. (See *Boerger v. American Gen. Ins. Co.,* 100 N.W. 133 [Minn. 1959]; *Haslett v. Haslett,* 268 N.Y.S. 2d 809, 25 A.D. 2d 256 [N.Y. 1966]; and *Bachtel v. Bachtel,* 127 N.E. 2d 761 [Ohio 1954]). The mother also has been held liable where she voluntarily assumed the care and maintenance of the children. (See *Jeacock v. Schorb,* 39 N.Y.S. 2d 51, 265 App. Div. 147 [N.Y. 1942]; *Commonwealth v. Cameron,* 179 A. 2d 270 [Pa. 1962]). Moreover, it is sometimes held that the mother is primarily liable for child support where she leaves the home without justification, taking the children with her. (*Stillmunkes v. Stillmunkes,* 65 N.W. 2d 366 [Iowa 1954]; *McDaniel v. McDaniel,* 15 P. 2d 229 [N.M. 1932]; *Butler v. Commonwealth,* 110 S.E. 2d 686 [Va. 1922]). There also are cases to the contrary. (See *Addy v. Addy,* 36 N.W. 2d 352 [Iowa 1949]; *Russell v. Russell,* 154 So. 2d 881 [Miss. 1934]).

(b) *If both are liable is the father primarily responsible?*

The father, as a general rule has the primary duty to support, maintain and educate his children. The father's primary duty of support exists, regardless of the mother's financial resources. (See *McQuade v. McQuade,* 358 P. 2d 470 [Colo. 1960]; *Libby v. Arnold,* 161 N.Y.S. 2d 798 [N.Y. 1957]; and *Schade v. Schade,* 80 N.W. 2d 416 [Wis. 1957]).

However, in a few states due to statutes the mother is equally liable with the father. Under such statutes it has been held that the obligation of the father and mother is joint and several, and not primary and secondary, but it has also been held that such statutes do not relieve the father of his primary obligation.

(c) *If both are liable, how is responsibility allocated?*

Joint responsibility, where it exists, is allocated by equitable principles with regard to the condition and means of each parent. In determining the amount to be paid by each parent, courts will inquire as to the needs of the child or children, and the ability of each parent to furnish means for child support. (See *Stillmunkes v. Stillmunkes,* 65 N.W. 2d 366 [Iowa 1954]).

Joint and equal liability was unknown to the common law and usually is imposed by "family expense" statutes in order to enable creditors to recover from either parent for "necessaries" provided to the family, or, as previously noted, the mother may be liable under welfare laws which are concerned with tapping all family resources before public assistance is provided. Even where the mother is liable under such laws, and her obligation is referred to as "joint and equal", if she is forced to pay creditors or to provide support, usually she will have a cause of action to recoup such payments from the father and a right to be indemnified, at least if the separation was due to his fault, or in some states even where the separation was by mutual consent.

A distinction is made between the situation where the husband-father is living in the home and where the parties are separated, especially due to the husband-father's fault. In the former situation, expenditures by the wife from her own funds may be regarded as a gift and not a debt owed to her by the husband.

3 *Is the parent responsible if the child is married, working, studying in college or professional school?*

If a child is emancipated, the child is entitled to his own earnings and the parent's legal obligation of support ceases.

As a general rule, the marriage of a minor child effects an emancipation and there no longer is parental responsibility for the child's support. It is settled law that marriage of a minor with parental consent effects emancipation but in a few states there is no emancipation if the marriage was without parental consent.

The fact that a child is working does not relieve the parent from support liability since the parent legally is entitled to the child's earnings. However if a parent totally emancipates a child, conferring on the child the right to his own earnings, such action terminates the parental support obligation. The parent may emancipate the child for the balance of his minority or for a shorter period.

In recent years, some cases have forced a father to pay for his child's college education. This trend continues and the duty has been reiterated in court decisions. The reasoning in such cases is that college education is a necessity, not a luxury, for young people of ability. An order, therefore, may be made against a father of sufficient means to defray the costs of an education beyond high school when the child is talented and eager for such training. The older cases, and a few of recent date, do not impose such a duty on the father unless he had agreed to send the child to college. (See Inker & McGrath, *College Education of Minors*, 6 J. Family Law 230 [1966]).

4 *Is there a difference as to children of unwed parents?*

Although in the case of legitimate children, either the father is primarily liable for child support, or the father and mother are both responsible; a distinction is made in most states when support of illegitimates is at issue. For example, general statutes, which impose on a parent the duty to support a minor child, are uniformly held to apply only to legitimate children. The mother of an illegitimate child is, (aside from certain statutes which impose liability upon the father once paternity is established), charged with liability to support her illegitimate child. (See 98 A.L.R. 2d 445). However, some jurisdictions such as Arizona and Kansas hold that a duty of support is owed to every child by its parents whether they are married or not. Sometimes this duty is statutory, whereas in other cases, the courts have held that under present-day conditions, there should be no distinction between legitimate and illegitimate children insofar as the parental duty of support is concerned, even in the absence of statute. (See *Barrett v. Barrett*, 39 P.2d 621 [Ariz. 1934], and *Doughty v. Engler*, 211 Pac. 619 [Kansas 1923]).

In most states, statutes have been passed providing for filiation or bastardy proceedings to determine the paternity of an illegitimate child and to compel the support of the child by the person found to be its father. These statutory provisions are generally the exclusive basis of liability, and the non-adjudicated father of an illegitimate child is not within the purview of a law which punishes a parent who neglects or refuses to support his minor child. A statute providing for inheritance by an illegitimate child who has been recognized by its father, does not obligate the father to support the child.

However, where a statute imposes a support duty upon a defendant found to be the father of an illegitimate child, this duty generally continues until the child reaches his majority, and when an order has been entered obligating the father to support the child, under some statutes the duty continues as a charge upon the father's estate after his death.

Although the mother of an illegitimate child is primarily liable for its support, the majority of jurisdictions recognize that the putative father may obligate himself to support the child by express or implied contract. Such contracts have been held to be in accord with the policy of the law, especially where a putative father is obligated by statute to support his illegitimate child, and the fact that the contract is given on condition that a bastardy proceeding shall not be instituted, or shall be discontinued, does not make it void. In most jurisdictions, the courts hold that such a contract need not be in writing since it is not within the statute of frauds, although some courts have held to the contrary.

The problem of support for illegitimate children is a matter of considerable economic consequence. In 1965, about two per cent of the unmarried women in the United States gave birth to 291,200 illegitimate children, the illegitimacy ratio (illegitimate births per 1,000 live births) was 77.4, and the illegitimacy rate (the number of illegitimate births per 1,000 unmarried women) was 23.4. [See Vital Statistics of the United States, 1965, vol. I, Natality table 1–25]. In New York City in 1967, out of a total of 145,342 live births, there were 24,074 illegitimate children, or an illegitimacy rate of 16.6 per cent. [Vital Statistics of New York, 1967]. Of course, the illegitimacy problem is related to poverty, restrictive divorce laws, and the economic fact that the expense of divorce may price it out of the market since in larger cities it may cost $ 500 to $ 1,000 dollars. Legal Aid services for matrimonial problems, and legal services provided under poverty programs, may mitigate somewhat the incidence of illegitimacy, as may the pharmaceutical discoveries of recent years. A substantial proportion of the funds expended for Aid for Dependent Children under the public assistance program go to maintain and support illegitimate children whose fathers cannot be located or are unable or unwilling to support them.

5 *Are grandparents responsible for grandchildren? If so, under what conditions?*

In the absence of statute, grandparents are not bound to support their grandchildren. In some states, however, welfare statutes impose such a duty on grandparents to support indigent grandchildren under certain circumstances. (See *Nations v. Nations,* 128 So. 2d 228 [La. 1961]; *In re Allen's Estate,* 25 N. W. 2d 757 [Neb. 1947]). The fact that the parents of the child are living does not relieve the grandparents from their statutory liability. Such a duty usually is imposed only where the grandparents are of sufficient ability to furnish support, where the parents are unable to do so, where there is no nearer relative who is able to support them, or where the father is dead. Under such statutes the liability of the parents is primary and that of the grandparents only secondary. The grandparent is not liable to support illegitimate grandchildren under statutes requiring a grandparent to support his grandchildren. New York recently repealed its statute imposing support duties on grandparents.

6 *Are orders for support subject to modification because of changed circumstances?*

The judgment, order, or decree in an action for support and maintenance of children, generally may be modified in a proper case because of changed circumstances of the parties, and the power to make such modification may be reserved in the original order or decree. Statutes in divorce or separation cases which authorize the courts to provide for the support of the parties' minor children, usually authorize the modification of an order or decree with respect to child support from time to time as shall be reasonable and proper. In Georgia, however, by statute the father's obligation of child support may be permanently discharged by the payment of a lump sum therefor.

B *What standards are applied in the determination of responsibility and need?*

1 *Is the amount determined on the basis of minimum needs or in accordance with the ability or means or social standing of the parent?*

The parental duty of child support is perhaps the most extensively enforced obligation arising out of the family relationship. To make up for the uncertain antecedents of the common law in this regard, most states have adopted an assortment of statutes, procedures and remedies to shore up the obligation, particularly that of the father (See Foster, *Dependent Children and the Law,* 18 U. Pitt. L. Rev. 579 [1957], and *Strange v. Strange,* 148 So. 2d 494 [Ga. 1966], for a recent discussion of the father's common law duty to support his children). As we have seen, although the primary duty rests upon the father, the mother by statute frequently is made secondarily liable for family necessities. Moreover, in addition to the liability of the father of legitimate children for child support, a natural father may be held accountable, and a stepfather, a foster father or one standing in loco parentis, may also be held accountable. (See Katz, *Foster Parents Versus Agencies,* 65 Mich. L. Rev. 145, 160 [1966]).

There is disagreement in the American jurisdictions as to the measure of the duty of child support and as to what (if any) circumstances other than emancipation of the child may relieve the father. The problem as to measure involves the question of whether the father must support his children according to his financial means – a test roughly comparable to his obligation to pay alimony – or according to their needs. A few recent decisions have held that children were entitled to be supported according to their father's financial standing rather than according to their actual needs. (See *Schwartz v. Schwartz,* 265 N. Y. S. 2d 820 [N. Y.

Family Ct. 1966]). However, perhaps the statutes of most states in imposing the obligation of child support express such duty in terms of the minimum needs of children, although in computing that amount many courts also consider the financial ability and social standing of the father. Certainly, the current consensus is that a father financially able to do so should support his children in accustomed style even though the statutory standard is expressed in terms of minimum needs.

When the duty of child support is imposed under welfare laws because the recipient is or is about to become a public charge, the "needs" test rather than the "station in life" test is most apt to be used. In such cases, as we have seen, the obligor is viewed as a resource to be tapped before public assistance such as Aid for Dependent Children may be provided by the government. In the United States, the A. D. C. program costs almost two billion dollars annually and is the largest item in the public assistance budget, hence to keep down costs efforts are made to force mothers to seek child support orders from fathers before the former may qualify for A. D. C.

The disagreement in American statutes and decisions as to the appropriate measure of child support becomes apparent where the issue is whether or not a father, in the absence of agreement, is obligated to provide a college education for a gifted child. The earlier cases uniformly held there was no such obligation, but more recent decisions have reasoned that college education is more of a necessity than a luxury and that even where the statutory measure is "minimum need" a father who has the financial means may be required to provide a college education for a minor child who deserves such an opportunity. (See Foster and Freed, *Children and the Law*, 1966 Annual Survey of American Law, 649, 658, and Inker & McGrath, *College Education of Minors*, 6 J. Family Law 230 [1966]).

2 *How do you determine ability to support?*

(a) Do you consider

1 *Salary or income from business or profession?*

2 *Other income or assets?*

3 *Parents expenses and obligations?*

4 *Potential earnings?*

In making a determination as to a parent's ability to support a minor child, usually consideration is given to a number of factors such as the income, resources and ability to pay of the parent, the needs of the child, and the social status and standard of living of the parents, as well as the age, health, and physical condition of the parent and the child. Except where prescribed in detail by statute there is no fixed formula for determining the amount to be awarded; the amount rests within the discretion of the trial court whose decision will not be reversed unless there is a clear showing of abuse of discretion.

In ascertaining the ability to support, primary emphasis is given to the economic circumstances of the parent and children. The courts give substantial consideration to salary and wages as well as earning capacity or prospective earnings. Thus, besides considering past and present earnings, courts often inquire into how much the parent is likely to earn or is capable of earning at present or during the immediate future, and frequently conclude that a parent's earning capacity is far greater or far less than his previous earnings might indicate, and that the amount of an award should be based upon such earning capacity rather than prior earnings.

The courts, besides considering a parent's earnings and earning capacity, also frequently take into consideration the parents' assets and liabilities and income from other sources. Also, where a wife is considered at least partially responsible for supporting the minor children, her assets or the income she may derive from sources other than her income, have been considered. Not only is the extent of a parent's assets considered, but also their nature, as for example, whether they are likely to yield a significant amount of income and whether they are capable of being readily liquidated and whether they have been acquired through gift or inheritance as well as through the party's own efforts.

A parent's expenses and obligations are also considered and in determining ability to pay child support, consideration is also given to expenses on behalf of others for whom he is legally or morally obligated. For example, if a man has been married more than once, his obligations to support a prior wife and children is a prior obligation. In addition he may be under an obligation to help support his own parents, especially if they are of advanced age, and he may feel morally obligated to support other relatives. (However, New York in 1967 eliminated the responsibility of parents to support adult children and the liability of adult children for indigent parents. N. Y. Laws of 1967, ch. 184. In *Matter of Dabbs v. Burrell,* 53 Misc. 2d 349 [N. Y. Family Ct., Ulster County 1967], it was held that due to the change in the New York law a New York parent would not be required to support his adult child living in another state even though under such state's law local parents might be required to contribute to the support of adult indigent or handicapped children).

The courts have also devoted attention to the issue of necessary expenses, especially living expenses of the parent and child. In ascertaining living expenses, consideration is given to such items as food, clothing, shelter, transportation and medical care.

In some states it is assumed that where possible children are entitled to the same economic advantages and standard of living as their parents had enjoyed before their separation. However, a father should not be required to pay for his children's expenses which are unnecessary or unduly extravagant.

The age, health, or physical condition of a husband, wife, or child may be of substantial importance. For example a child who is very young, usually has less expenses than those expended for an older child.

It should be noted that in many jurisdictions child support is ordered in proceedings which are of summary character and that frequently the basis for the sum ordered is not set forth in an order or opinion. In such instances, there is no sure way of knowing what prompted the order or the factors considered by the court. In courts where fifty or more non-support cases are heard each day, it appears that judges on an *ad hoc* basis arrive at what they regard to be a realistic sum, that is the amount that seems fair and that probably will be paid by the father. Where several judges hear non-support cases, there is apt to be a substantial variation between orders and the individual attitudes of the several judges becomes apparent. (See Foster, *Dependent Children and the Law,* 18 U. Pitt. L. Rev. 579 [1957]).

(b) *If the father is remarried with children in both families, which children have a prior claim, if any?*

Where, after a divorce, a father remarries, his remarriage does not in itself constitute a ground for reducing his obligation to provide support for the children of a prior marriage, but his obligation to support his new wife and the children of the new marriage may be a factor to be considered in determining the amount of support he should pay for the children of his prior marriage. [See Annot., 89 A. L. R. 2d 106].

Thus, reduction or termination of child support payments has been sustained in a number of cases where it was shown that the father was unable to meet the required payments and at the same time to properly maintain his new family.

Also, where after a remarriage, the father's financial condition has worsened, courts have considered this to be a factor in reducing payments for the children of his first marriage, although the contrary also has been held.

Usually, the father's obligation to his first family is regarded as a prior claim and that of his second family is subordinate. As a practical matter, this view makes for difficulties where the father does not earn enough to support both families. The second wife is likely to bitterly resent anything paid to the first family and this places a strain on the second marriage. Wisconsin requires a divorced father who is under a support order to obtain court permission for remarriage and the court may insist that the prospective second wife appear with the man so that she may be fully informed about his prior obligation and that support for her will have to come from what is left over. The economic dilemma in such cases is that neither family may be able to live at a decent standard, and perhaps some form of insurance under Social Security or from a private insurer should be devised to remedy the situation.

(c) *If the father has out-of-wedlock children, do the children of his marriage have a preferred status?*

Since the common law gave little if any protection to children born out of wedlock and did not provide for legitimation, American law in this regard is purely statutory. All states provide for some form of statutory legitimation, the most common being the subsequent marriage of natural parents. In a substantial number of states recognition and acknowledgement of paternity similarly effects a legitimation, and in a few states there is a combination of the two types of legitimation. In all states, except Texas and Idaho, there also are statutory procedures of a criminal, quasi-criminal, or civil nature to force putative fathers to pay minimal child support for their illegitimate children and maternity expenses for the mother.

Where the putative father is married and has a legal family, his natural child ordinarily does not have equal rights to support or to inheritance along with children born in lawful wedlock. In two or three states, however, the status of illegitimacy has been abolished and natural children for most purposes are treated the same as children born in wedlock. Arizona and Oregon have tried to abolish the status of illegitimacy or to substantially reduce its consequences, and in a number of states the children of a marriage later annulled and held to be void or voidable are declared legitimate by statute and are treated as if born in lawful wedlock. However, in a state such as New York, the court in annulment actions may have discretion to limit the effect of legitimatization to rights other than succession to real and personal property of a deceased parent. [See N. Y. Domestic Relations Law § 145].

With reference to the inheritance rights of illegitimate children, at common law the illegitimate inherited from no one, but nearly all states now provide by statute that an illegitimate child occupies the same position with respect to his mother as does a legitimate child. However, in most states an illegitimate child does not inherit from his father, other than by will or where the father has legitimated the child. In only a few states does a judgment in a paternity or filiation proceeding confer inheritance rights against the father. Not all intestacy laws provide that the illegitimate inherits from the mother's family and only a few make provision for his inheritance from his father's family. Inheritance laws generally designate only the legitimate child as heir of his father, his mother, his ancestors, and collaterals. Illegitimate children, except in Arizona and Oregon, are not accorded such treatment. (See Krause, *The Non-Marital Child,* 1 Family Law Quarterly 1, 2 [1967], and other articles by Krause in 44 Tex. L. Rev. 829 [1966], and 65 Mich. L. Rev. 477 [1967]).

Such discrimination as to inheritance rights between legitimate and illegitimate children also carries over to support and custody problems. Quite often the mother of an illegitimate child will be expected to work and contribute to its support where such would not be the case if the child were legitimate. Usually the legitimate child has broader rights to support in terms of the level of support and its duration. In the past, most courts have held that a natural father has no custody or visitation rights, nor parental authority, over his illegitimate children. More recently, however, a few cases have concluded that a natural father should be accorded limited visitation and custody rights.

Among the economic disadvantages of illegitimacy is the exclusion of illegitimate children from the coverage of workmen's compensation and wrongful death acts, as well as some federal social legislation, so that such children may receive no benefits or pension rights if their father is killed or injured. There is a current awareness that such discrimination is difficult to justify and it is to be anticipated that in the near future questions will be raised as to the constitutionality (under equal protection or due process principles) of such discrimination. Since currently one in sixteen children born in the United States is illegitimate, and in some urban centers perhaps 40 per cent of live births are illegitimate, there are substantial problems of economic policy as well as justice for illegitimate children. The cost of placing illegitimate children on a parity with legitimate children is a factor that makes it politically difficult to abolish the status of illegitimacy.

Regretfully, we must report that only in Arizona and Oregon does the illegitimate child have equal status with legitimate children, and even in those states discriminations may occur under federal welfare laws or due to private contract. The illegitimate child almost invariably gets a lower sum ordered for his support than would be true if he were legitimate; his mother has a greater duty of support; his father a lesser duty. In all but a few states he is at a substantial disadvantage insofar as inheritance rights are concerned, at least with regard to inheritance from or through his father. He is not legally entitled to assume the name of his father. All of this is a cruel inheritance from the common law and the result of timid statutory reform that has not dared to recognize the fact that although parents may be illegitimate, their children are not unless one adopts the heartless dogma that the sins of the father (and mother) are to be visited upon the progeny.

3 *Does your government provide financial aid to children when the parent is in a position to provide support? If so, what kind?*

As a general proposition, neither federal, state nor local governments provide financial aid to the children of parents who are able to maintain them. However, government subsidy may be received in the form of scholarships for education, social security benefits as for blind or handicapped children, and special training or care as for mentally retarded or emotionally ill children. In addition, the government may pay for "hot lunch" programs for school children from lower income homes.

In recent years there has been considerable discussion of the feasibility of having the federal government pay out „family allowances" or reducing the income tax on large families. As yet, no such laws have been enacted, although a father obtains a $ 600 exemption on his federal income tax for each dependent he provides for, and there have been proposals that substantial deductions be allowed to fathers who are sending children to college.

Subject to the above and similar exceptions, government does not provide financial aid to families where parents are willing and able to support their children. There are, however, a host of educational, recreational, and other programs that are paid for out of local, state, or federal tax funds.

4 *Is there a difference in support as to out-of-wedlock children?*

This question is answered in greater detail by the answer to question A 2 (c).

Generally, illegitimate children are apt to receive a smaller amount as child support than legitimate children in comparable economic circumstances, and the amount awarded in paternity or filiation proceedings usually is a minimal amount based on the means of the natural father. As previously stated, the mother of an illegitimate child has a primary support obligation, whereas the mother of a legitimate child ordinarily has only a secondary support obligation.

C *How do you enforce support?*

1 *Who decides as to amount of support and who does the enforcing?*

a) *Administrative bodies?*

b) *Courts? Which types of courts? Criminal? Civil?*

c) *Other methods?*

A court determines the amount of child support and enforcement is by court order. The parental obligation is enforceable in various ways, depending upon the statutory remedies provided in particular jurisdictions.

For example, the obligation may be enforced by common law actions in the civil courts by creditors for necessaries furnished to the children. A parent, in a proper case, and sometimes as a result of express statutory provision, may be liable for necessaries furnished to his minor unemancipated child by a third person, whether procured by the child or by the mother. Where necessaries are provided solely on the credit of the child, the parent is not liable, nor is the parent liable for necessaries furnished to a child who is fully emancipated, unless the parent made an express promise to pay.

The obligation alternatively may be enforced in an independent proceeding brought by a child (or in its behalf by a guardian ad litem) in a civil court or in an equity proceeding (even in the absence of a statute authorizing such action), in which event the amount of the allowance is within the discretion of the trial court.

Most actions for child support are statutory proceedings of a civil or quasi-criminal nature and usually the statute sets forth vague standards for determining amount and provides various sanctions for enforcement of the order. In New York, where the support action is brought in the Family Court, the father "is chargeable with the support of his child and, if possessed of sufficient means, may be required to pay for his support *a fair and reasonable sum according to his means,* as the court may determine." (N. Y. Family Ct. Act § 413). When the father's child support obligation is imposed by the court of general jurisdiction in conjunction with a matrimonial action, however, the court in its discretion may order the payment of such maintenance "*as justice requires,* having regard to the circumstances of the case and of the respective parties and to the best interests of the child." (N. Y. Domestic Relations Law § 240).

As illustrated by the New York standards above, statutory criteria for determining the amount of support are exceedingly vague and provide little guidance other than admonitions that the award should be fair and equitable. This is true of most support statutes. Various welfare and public assistance programs, however, employ rather detailed criteria in determining the amount of assistance to be awarded in particular cases. Hence, it would be possible to devise guidelines that would reduce the arbitrary character of many support orders. Such should be done because judges and courts tend to lack consistency in computing support and the order may serve punitive purposes. It is sometimes said that there is a tradition that courts will award up to one-third of a man's income as alimony or wife support and up to half his income where also there are children to be provided for, but such ceilings are rarely written into statutes.

In many, if not all American jurisdictions, it is made a criminal offense by statute for a parent to desert, abandon, or fail to support a minor child. The offense is purely statutory. Under some of those statutes the child must be destitute or in necessitous circumstances and the parent must know of such condition. Under such statutes, a parent may be compelled to support his child by action in a criminal, juvenile or family court, pursuant to the statute. The general purpose of such statutes is to punish a parent for failure to fulfill his legal duty of supporting and protecting his minor children and thereby preventing them from becoming public charges, and punishment of the parent is one of the statutory purposes. Such statutes are not a substitute for civil proceedings to compel a parent to contribute a reasonable sum for the support of his children. In some jurisdictions, statutes provide for the sequestration or seizure and impounding of the property of an absconding parent, for the support of necessitous children.

In proper cases, support for the children may be ordered in suits for annulment, separation or divorce by the court hearing the matrimonial action, The practice and procedure for the enforcement of an order or decree requiring a father to make payments for the support of his minor children may be by contempt proceedings, and as in the case of an ordinary judgment, by execution. In most states, the court rendering a matrimonial decree is given the contempt power by statute, sometimes with express provisions for other types of enforcement proceedings as well as by the exercise of the contempt power. Such power would seem to be inherent even in the absence of specific statutory authority.

Courts possess a considerable range of discretion in their enforcement of orders. According to the great weight of authority, contempt proceedings to enforce support payments are deemed to be civil, not criminal, in nature.

2 *Are agreements concerning support subject to court review and revision?*

The parents by private contract may not foreclose court jurisdiction to order child support. Such agreements always are subject to review and revision in appropriate proceedings. However, a court hearing a child support action may give great weight to the amount agreed upon by the parties and ordinarily it will be accepted by the court unless it is clearly inadequate.

It is important to remember that the issue of child support frequently arises as a collateral issue in matrimonial actions and that in the United States ten per cent or less of divorce actions are contested. In the uncontested divorce case, where the parties have signed a separation agreement, usually the terms agreed upon for alimony and child support are accepted by the court and incorporated into its decree. In this sense the parties set the amount, although whatever sum they stipulate may be rejected by the court, or if accepted in the initial decree, usually may be modified later if application is made.

As distinguished from alimony, the power to modify orders for child support is regarded as inherent in the appropriate court and with or without statutory authority a change of circumstances may be the basis for modification of a prior order, even though as to alimony the usual rule is that either a statute must authorize modification or the original decree must reserve such power. Perhaps in most jurisdictions a court which ordered child support has authority to cancel or reduce arrears due on prior orders. The Uniform Reciprocal Enforcement of Support Law or its equivalent exists in all states and permits enforcement of child and wife support orders on an inter-state basis when the father has left and gone to another state.

3 *If the parent fails to support, may he be imprisoned or punished in any way?*

Since child support orders emanate from courts there is inherent power to punish a willful violation of a support order by civil (or possibly criminal) contempt procedures. Theoretically, in the case of civil contempt, a court may commit a contumacious father to prison until he is willing to comply with the court's order and such is not regarded as being unconstitutional as imprisonment for debt. Statutes in many if not most states, however, set a time limit on the period of commitment for civil contempt by a contumacious father or husband, six months being the usual period.

In addition, even though no support order has been made, a father guilty of desertion and non-support may be subject to criminal prosecution for a misdemeanor or may be subject to proceedings in a family or juvenile court.

Many judges feel that the exercise of contempt powers is unwise or not warranted except in extreme cases. Those who share that belief feel that wage attachment is a more effective and socially desirable alternative since imprisonment ordinarily stops the father's income and his family may have to go on public assistance. Other judges assume that the threat of imprisonment is a great deterrent to non-compliance with support orders and are more willing to employ contempt citation as the ultimate sanction.

4 *Is such enforcement done by the national (or federal) government? Or by local government (state, province, town, city?)*

Enforcement of child support orders usually is secured in the county of the state where the action was originally brought. Generally, only the court which entered the support order has the power and authority to enforce it directly by contempt procedure. The enforcement proceedings are a step in the original action and incidental thereto, and no other court, even if it had power to do so, would interfere or take cognizance, but would refrain from doing so out of comity. Once the court of a particular *county* has obtained jurisdiction, removal of the husband to another county does not terminate its powers and jurisdiction. His removal from the state, however, may affect the power of the court, as its process will not ordinarily run beyond the territorial limits of the *state* wherein it sits. The court can hold a defaulting husband in contempt, even where he is out of the state, but it cannot punish him unless it can "catch" him. Because each state now has the Uniform Reciprocal Enforcement of Support Law, or its equivalent, it is possible to have an interstate enforcement where the father has fled to another state and it no longer is necessary to extradite and return him to the original state.

The federal government generally is not concerned with the enforcement of state child support orders, but if a father who is subject to a court order flees the jurisdiction, there is federal authority to arrest and detain him as a fugitive across state lines.

5 *Is there a problem when the parent lives in a city or province other than that in which the child resides? If so, how is it handled?*

The duty of child support is a personal one and for jurisdiction to be exercised by American courts there must be personal jurisdiction over the parent charged with the duty or quasi in rem jurisdiction over his local property. This means that ordinarily the initial support order will be made against a father in the courts of the state where he is found. However, as previously mentioned, under the Uniform Reciprocal Enforcement of Support Law, the support action may be commenced in the state where the wife and children live and when the father is located in another state supplemental proceedings may be brought there with the record being forwarded from the first state and the eventual order being entered in the receiving state.

It also has been held in a recent New York decision that a Canadian mother might follow her husband to New York and there sue for child support in the New York courts. The same privilege is accorded to citizens of other states.

With reference to enforcement of prior child support orders and the collection of arrearages, the several states are required by the federal Constitution to give full faith and credit to past amounts due that have been reduced to judgment but not to sums not vested because subject to modification. However, if a second state cares to, it may lend its enforcement machinery to collect sums past due even though subject to modification and not reduced to judgment in the state of rendition. Under the Uniform Registration of Foreign Judgment Act, which has been adopted in a few states, it is possible to treat sister state decrees the same as if they had been entered by local courts. This latter approach is to be commended, especially in view of the fact that each year one American family in seven moves its home, in many instances across state lines, and such mobility is on the increase.

D *How great is the problem of non-support in your country?*

1 *Statistics*

It is difficult if not impossible to isolate cases of willful non-support from those attributable to poverty or unemployment. Such statistics as are available, from government sources or otherwise, may not stand up under critical evaluation and analysis.

If we start with the problem of desertion, the common estimate is that the number of desertions each year is approximately the same as the number of divorces. If such is the case, the current desertion figure would be somewhere between 400,000 and 500,000 annually, and in at least 50—60 per cent of those cases, there are children in the family. In rare instances it is the wife rather than the husband who deserts; and although desertions by the wife are not unknown, perhaps she is the deserter in something less than ten per cent of the cases.

It also is difficult to distinguish between abandonment or desertion as a legal matter and estrangement by mutual consent. The cases show that there often is marked conflict as to the facts regarding separation, what precipitated it, and whether or not it was by mutual consent.

It has been estimated that in 1963 more than 10 million women and children in the United States were affected by desertion of the husband-father and that 2.6 million families units were involved. These numbers must have grown substantially since 1963. In 1958, out of 25.8 million families with children under 18 years of age, 11 per cent or 2.8 million lived in homes broken by death or desertion. (See *Children in the Changing World,* The White House Conference on Children and Youth, Washington, D.C. [1960] p. 21; and the article by Hon. Jacob T. Zukerman, in the ENCYCLOPEDIA OF SOCIAL WORK p. 305).

In 1962, approximately 870 million dollars were spent in aid to dependent children for some 573,000 families in which the father was estranged. Currently, the cost of the Aid for Dependent Children program has risen to between 1½ and 2 billion dollars annually. In New York City, alone, there are 800,000 citizens receiving some form of public assistance at an estimated cost of a billion dollars for 1968. It is estimated that there are about 1.2 million poor families now receiving A.D.C., although there are at least 2 million who deserve and need it. In the United States, there are about 70 million persons under the age of 18, of whom approximately 17 million are in poor families.

With reference to the amount of assistance paid to A. D. C. families, the sum is fixed by the states, within broad federal guidelines. The southern states, in particular, present a shocking picture of the inadequacy of the A. D. C. program. In Texas a family of four on A. D. C. is said to require a minimum of $ 154 per month to exist above bare subsistance, but receives only $ 98; Albama says $ 177, and pays $ 81; Mississippi says $ 194, and will give no more than $ 50 and actually gives less. In northern industrial states, larger sums are given as assistance due to higher living costs, but in no state does the amount given enable families to live in dignity and comfort.

The statistics for New York for the month of December 1967, show that four-fifths of the relief expenditures in the welfare budget represented aid to dependent children and to adults taking care of them. In that month there were 196,938 families in New York (of which 146,237 were in New York City) receiving A. D. C. There were 793,399 persons in the state of which 582,871 were in New York City, who were involved in A. D. C., and there were 575,075 children in the state of which 422,044 were in New York City who were the basis for A. D. C. payments. The average payment for the family was $ 242.51 in the state and $ 254.58 in New York City, and the average payment per person was $ 60.20 and $ 63.87, respectively. (*New York Times*, March 7, 1968, p. 58, col. 4).

A 1955 sample study of A. D. C. cases in one locale reported that child support payments, averaging $ 67.63 per month, had been ordered or agreed upon in 42 per cent of the 162,440 families where the husband-father had left home, but that only in about half of these cases (18.3 per cent of the total A. D. C. cases), did he pay anything pursuant to the order. The total contribution by these fathers was estimated at $ 20 million dollars, which amount per cent of A. D. C. expenditures, and almost one out of ten fathers was either in prison or in the past has been imprisioned for contempt or criminal non-support. In 54.5 per cent of the cases the whereabouts of the father was unknown. In other words, efforts to force fathers to meet their legal obligation of child support, and thus to reduce A. D. C. costs, have not been very successful. (See Foote, Levy, & Sander, FAMILY LAW 938 [1967]).

One of the few detailed studies on a local level, disclosed that there were arrearages in 89 per cent of the cases where the husband-father had been ordered to pay alimony or support directly to the court, and that in 47 per cent of the cases, no payment at all was made by the obligor. (Steininger, *Study of Divorce and Support Orders in Lake County, Indiana,* 1956—57). It is a conservative estimate to say that well over half the support orders entered by courts are disobeyed.

There are a number of reasons why support orders are violated and why various techniques have failed to secure enforcement. For one thing, many of the men subject to such orders are victims of poverty and unemployment. Although over-all unemployment in the United States has averaged 3.8 per cent for the past two years, for Negroes it has averaged 7 per cent, and for Negroes between 16 and 21 years old, it has been close to 25 per cent. In New York City, 80 per cent of those receiving public assistance are Negroes and Puerto Ricans. Thus, there is an obvious correlation between poverty, unemployment, racial discrimination, broken homes, and public assistance including A. D. C.

Despite the tremendous cost of welfare programs, it could be noted that not only are assistance payments inadequate for a minimal existence, but in addition many families deserving and needing assistance, do not get it. Less than 8 million out of 30 million low-income American families get any public assistance. As we have seen, although there currently are at least 2 million poor families headed by females who are entitled to A. D. C., only 1.2 million receive it.

In addition to the factors of poverty and unemployment, there are other reasons why support orders are chronically violated. Despite all of the elaborate statutory machinery for enforcement, an ingenious and determined man, who is not anchored to a particular locality, may successfully escape compliance. By losing himself in a large city, or moving to another state, he may evade his obligation of child support and flaunt the court order. It is the middle class man who has an investment in his job and locality, and who cannot readily move to another place or disappear, who is caught by the enforcement machinery of the law.

It should not be assumed that all men who disobey support orders are lawless or bad citizens. The ineffectiveness of many court orders may be due to the unrealistic amount the man was ordered to pay, for in many instances he is left without sufficient means to live in dignity. He may not have been accorded an opportunity to tell his side of the story, the order may have been jammed down his throat, and his resentment at being so treated may be justified.

In a few scattered cities or counties, an effort has been made to give the potential obligor a hearing before imposing an order. This is done by calling him in for an informal conference before the matter is set for trial. At the conference a skilled member of the staff listens to his grievances, explores the economics of the situation, and then ascertains what the man would regard as a fair and reasonable sum for the support of his family. If the sum is realistic, and the man agrees to pay it on time, generally it is accepted by the court. The obligor participates, in the determination of the economic future of the family. Experience has shown that in at least 90 per cent of the cases where the support order is arrived at in this manner, there is full compliance. Psychologically, the man has made a moral commitment, has "shaken hands on it," and in good faith intends to discharge his obligation. (See Foster, *Dependent Children and the Law*, 18 U. Pitt. L. Rev. 579 [1957]).

It is not an exaggeration to say that the problem of non-support is a major social and legal problem in the United States. It is related to poverty, unemployment, family breakdown, social alienation, racial discrimination, and a whole host of other larger problems. Nonetheless, whether viewed as an aspect or facet of a larger problem, or looked at by itself, it is clear that the economics of family failure warrants greater attention and concern. Upon reflection, it might be found that a program of social or private insurance against the support and alimony obligation would best serve the social and economic interests of the public. As things now stand, American law as to support, alimony, and enforcement, does not meet the needs and the problems of our industrialized, mobile, and individualistic society. Much more important, however, is the urgent need to overhaul the welfare system and to replace it with one that has the objective of bringing the poor and the handicapped into the mainstream of our affluent society.

2 *What methods are employed for locating missing parents? Whose responsibility is this? The courts? The family's? Other agencies? If so, which?*

Formerly, it was necessary to locate a missing father and then to extradite him back to his home state to face criminal charges for non-support. Such procedure was expensive, inefficient, and time comsuming. Today, each state has the Uniform Reciprocal Enforcement of Support Law (or its equivalent) and non-support cases may by processed across state lines or in different counties of the same state. One portion of the action is commenced by the wife-mother at her home, the decree eventually is handed down at the place where the husband-father is located. The constitutionality of such procedure has been sustained and it is a great improvement over the former law.

There remain, however, substantial difficulties in enforcement. It is not too difficult for an estranged man to disappear in metropolitan areas. There may be few if any leads as to his whereabouts. Sheriffs or prosecutors at his new place of residence, for any one of a number of reasons, may be uncooperative. Although the Social Security Act requires that a mother in order to qualify for A. D. C. must report a deserting father to law enforcement officials, and the federal government has agreed to make available to state or local officials any information it has acquired as to the deserter's whereabouts (see Pub. Law 89—97, § 340, amending 42 U. S. C. A. § 1306), only recently has the

Social Security Administration begun to make its files available so that a man may be traced through his social security number to his new place of employment.

Absconding husbands or fathers sometimes are located, if at all through the intercession of local police or sheriffs. Federal authorities ordinarily are not involved unless the man is a fugitive from a more important charge. Employers in a particular industry, usually do not care to get involved in the domestic problems of their employees. There are a few private agencies, such as the Family Location Service agency of New York City, which undertake to assist wives in tracking down errant husbands. Private investigators also may be employed by middle class clients.

In a sense, the ultimate responsibility for locating absconding husbands or fathers is that of public welfare agencies if the deserted family is destitute, or on the wife-mother if she cares to enforce the support obligation rather than to maintain the family out of her own earnings.

E *Is it possible for children in another country to secure support from a parent in yours?*

1 *Does your country have any treaty with any other country which is a signatory to any convention as to support?*

The United States although not a signatory to the Convention on the Recovery Abroad of Maintenance (in force since May 25, 1957), nor to the New York Convention of 1956, nonetheless is a party to the Hague Convention Concerning the Enforcement of Decisions Relating to Maintenance and Obligations Towards Children (open for signatures April 15, 1957). Hence it may be necessary to reduce a support order to final judgment before an action may be brought in the United States to collect thereon.

Recently, however, New York has held that a Canadian wife might maintain an action for wife and child support in the New York Family Court having jurisdiction over the person of her husband. (See *Rohonezy v. Rohenezy*, 273 N. Y. S. 2d 409 [1967]). There appears to be little authority as to whether or not a foreign wife may sue for child or wife support in an American court but it is to be hoped that the New York decision will establish a precedent for future cases. If the arrearages or amount due is reduced to final judgment in her country, presumably comity will be accorded to the judgment. Such is the rule as between sister states in the case of alimony, where the federal Constitution requires full faith and credit only where the sister state judgment is final and has fixed a specific sum as due and vested.

2 *Are you contemplating any such new treaty or convention?*

It is not known whether or not the United States presently is contemplating any new treaty or convention dealing with child support. It is hoped that the Dublin Conference of the International Bar Association may precipitate an interest in the problem of international enforcement of support obligations. The International Association of Penal Law likewise has manifested an interest in the international enforcement of support obligations and American representatives are concerned about the matter.

3 *If there is no treaty how can foreign orders for support be enforced?*

As previously stated, where the support obligation has been reduced to final judgment, American courts may extend comity to the decree. Moreover, New York has permitted an action to be maintained in its Family Court by a Canadian wife seeking wife and child support from her husband who then was living in New York. (See *Rohonezy v. Rohonezy*, 273 N. Y. S. 2d 409 [1967]).

F *What suggestions do you have for possible action in each country for dealing with problems of non-support? For international enforcement?*

It is recommended that a study be made of the Uniform Reciprocal Enforcement of Support Act with a view of adapting it to the international enforcement of wife and child support obligations. This statute, drafted by the Commissioners on Uniform State Laws, has had an unparalleled success in achieving acceptance by divers state legislatures. Only New York, and one other American jurisdiction, both of which had previously adopted a substantially identical act, do not have the Uniform law, but the results are the same. This uniform law, although not always literally complied with in its application, is a great improvement over the former chaotic situation.

The Uniform Act makes it possible to initiate the action at the place where the wife and children are located, then to forward the record to the place where the husband is found. He is entitled to interpose defenses but if it is found that he is legally obligated to pay support, an order is entered against him and enforced at his domicile. One difficulty in the practical application of the act is that local police or prosecutors differ in their diligence and enthusiasm in picking up the man, processing the case, and enforcing the order. With experience as to the reciprocal benefits to be derived, cooperation has improved.

In the interim, while an adaptation of the Uniform Act is considered, perhaps efforts should be made to bring some test cases in order to determine the extent to which comity will be accorded to support judgments and if original support actions may be commenced by foreign nationals. It should be noted that the American Uniform Act requires that the plaintiff be a legal dependent, that is a wife or child, and it is not available to collect alimony for a former wife who is divorced from the obligor. Consideration should be given to the policy issue of excluding the alimony decrees of former wives from the purview of any international compact or accord. Perhaps, with such an exclusion, it might be easier to reach agreement, even though logically such cases should be covered. Where there is divorce, however, logic seldom is compelling.

G *What special questions on child support do you suggest for our discussion in Dublin?*

The following questions as to child support may be of interest and concern:

1. Are there any systems of private or public insurance against the contingency of child support? Is it possible to devise a system whereby premiums may be paid, or payroll deductions made, to establish a fund to insure against the financial hardships of family breakdown? If feasible, would such a system be economically and socially desirable? Is there any evidence that such a system itself would precipitate family breakdown?

2. Is it practicable to set a percentage of wages or a ceiling as to child and/or wife support in order to confine judicial discretion in making "realistic" awards? Regardless of who is to blame for family breakdown, does it do more harm than good to impose a support order on a man with a marginal income? For example, should the husband-father's support duty be tied into and limited by the local public assistance or welfare measure of support and not be greater?

3. To what extent should the wife-mother be made equally responsible for child support, assuming she has assets or is employable? Is it anachronistic to impose a primary duty on the husband-father and only a secondary if any duty upon the wife-mother who has means or employment potential?

4. By education and otherwise, should courts be encouraged to handle support matters by conference and conciliation and to impose orders only as a last resort?

5. Should the Uniform Reciprocal Enforcement of Support Act be adapted for international acceptance?

II. AS TO CUSTODY OF CHILDREN

Introduction

The proverbial wisdom of Solomon, at least in some measure, was vouchsafed by the manner in which he handled a disputed custody case. Through the ages contests over children have been a burden to judicial conscience and a source of anxiety. A distinguished American judge has observed that "A judge agonizes more about reaching the right result in a contested custody issue than about any other type of decision he renders." (Botein, TRIAL JUDGE 273 [1952]).

In the United States, the law relative to custody and visitation rights is largely based upon state statutes as construed by state courts. There is no direct federal law on the subject, although issues may arise under the federal Constitution where a parent contends that he or she was deprived of custody or visitation rights without due process of law, or where a second state refuses to give full faith and credit to the custody decree of a sister state. Most of the state law on the subject has evolved in this century, although basic principles were formulated during the latter half of the last century.

It was necessary to enact statutes in America because the common law was feudalistic as to the relationships between parent and child and husband and wife. In feudal England, custody automatically was an incident of guardianship of lands and only gradually came to be regarded as a trusteeship with responsibilities toward the child. Wardship and marriage rights of feudal lords were a lucrative business. It was not until the Court of Wards and Liveries was established during the reign of Henry VIII that some legal protection was accorded children. A 1600 statute transferred such jurisdiction to Chancery which developed the theory of *parens patriae,* largely to protect the property of children. Although Chancery came to recognize the mother as the natural guardian of her children upon the death of their father, it was not until 1839 that the Chancellor by statute was given power to award the custody of infants under seven years to her rather than to the father when the family was separated. This change on the equity side eventually carried over to the law courts where the writ of habeas corpus was used to determine custody issues.

Today, in many if not most states, parents by statute stand on a parity as to custody and visitation rights. A typical statute declares that "In all cases there shall be no prima facie right as to the custody of the child in either parent." (N. Y. Dom. Rel. Law §§ 70, 240). Thus, in legal theory parents have equal claims to the custody of their children and there has been an abrogation of the common law patriarchial doctrine that the father had the exclusive or paramount right to his child's custody.

The American statutes declaring an equality of rights as between parents should not be taken at face value. In practice, the mother almost always prevails unless she is egregiously unfit or had abandoned or relinquished her children. This is especially true as to children of "tender years" (meaning pre-adolescent), and daughters. Only as to teen age sons does the father have anything like an equal claim to custody. However, courts are solicitous in according him visitation rights.

The standard tests, usually applied, for the determination of custody disputes are "the best interests of the child" test, and the "unfit parent" test. The prevailing view is that in custody disputes between parents, the best interests of the child controls the custody award, but in disputes between a parent and a "stranger" (meaning any non-parent), the parent is entitled to custody unless he or she is an "unfit" parent. Of course the two tests do not necessarily conflict and often overlap, but in practical application the result is that the mother ordinarily wins custody as against the father or a stranger, and the father usually is awarded custody where the dispute is between him and a non-relative.

The American cases indicate some awareness of changing social values. The moral judgment as to what constitutes parental "unfitness" varies somewhat between urban and rural areas and may not be the same today as it was in the last century. Lord Eldon deprived the poet Percy Shelley of the custody of his children because he regarded him as vicious, immoral, and atheistic. (See *Shelley v. Westbrooke*, 37 E. R. 850). Some years later, a mother who had advocated birth control and who had been prosecuted for distributing birth control information, was deprived of the custody of her son and daughter. (*Re Besant*, LR 11 Ch. Div. 508). By today's standards, neither the poet nor the pamphleteer would be regarded as "unfit."

As we shall see, the problem areas in the American law of custody are (1) the automatic preference given a mother or parent when such is contrary to the best interests of the child, and (2) the enforcement of custody and visitation awards. In addition, there is a further problem as to the admissibility of investigations and reports in custody proceedings.

The American law as to custody is summarized in Foster and Freed, *Child Custody*, 39 N. Y. U. L. Rev. 423, 615 (1964). See also, Foster & Freed, LAW AND THE FAMILY Chap. 29 (1966). Also of interest are Simpson, *The Unfit Parent*, 39 U. Det. L. J. 347 (1962), and Oster, *Custody Proceeding*, 5 J. Family Law 21 (1965). For a discussion of legal and psychiatric problems, see: Ackerman, THE PSYCHODYNAMICS OF FAMILY LIFE (1958); Despert, CHILDREN OF DIVORCE (1962); NEUROTIC INTERACTION IN MARRIAGE (Eisenstein ed. 1956);

Fluegel, THE PSYCHOANALYTIC STUDY OF THE FAMILY (1945); Levy & Monroe, THE HAPPY FAMILY (1938); Note, 73 Yale L. J. 151 (1963); and Drinan, *The Rights of Children Whose Parents Are Divorced*, U. of Ill. Law Forum 618 (1962).

A – *What are the laws and practices in your country relating to custody of minor children?*

1 *Who decides and enforces custody?*

a) *Administrative bodies? Which?*

Administrative tribunals do not make nor enforce custody awards. Jurisdiction to hear disputes as to custody usually is vested in courts of general jurisdiction sitting in equity but in some states concurrent or exclusive jurisdiction is given to family, juvenile or domestic relations courts. Usually, the facts regarding the custody dispute are heard by a judge although a few states permit or require a jury determination. Perhaps most awards of custody and visitation rights are made incident to divorce or judicial separation, although every American jurisdiction also provides for independent custody proceedings, usually being heard on a writ of habeas corpus or by petition in the court of general jurisdiction or in some cases in the family or juvenile court where statutes permit. Such jurisdiction over custody matters applies to both original jurisdiction and to requests for enforcement or for a modification of prior awards.

(For a general discussion of the law pertaining to custody, see Foster & Freed, LAW AND THE FAMILY – New York, Vol. II, Chap. 29 [1966]. The following articles are of general interest: Simpson, *The Unfit Parent*, 39 U. Det. L. Rev. 347 [1962]; Stansbury, *Custody and Maintenance Across State Lines*, 10 Law & Contemp. Prob. 819 [1944]; *Symposium on Custody*, 10 Law & Contemp. Prob. 697–866 [1944]; Ratner, *Legislative Resolution of the Interstate Child Custody Problem*, 38 So. Cal. L. Rev. 183 [1965]; Ratner, *Child Custody in a Federal System*, 62 Mich. L. Rev. 795 [1964]; Oster, *Custody Proceeding: A Study of Vague & Indefinite Standards*, 5 J. Family Law 21 [1965]; Drinan, *The Rights of Children in Modern American Family Law*, 2 J. Family Law 101 [1962]; and Foster & Freed, *Child Custody*, 39 N. Y. U. L. Rev. 423, 615 [1964]).

1 b) *Courts? Which type of courts handle these cases? Those dealing with criminal matters? With civil actions? Other?*

In the United States, custody issues arise in matrimonial actions (divorce and judicial separation), in habeas corpus proceedings, proceedings instituted by petitions, and in family or juvenile court actions where dependency or neglect is alleged or a petition for termination of parental rights is filed. Custody determinations are always made and enforced by courts. Usually the judge is the trier of fact although in a few states a jury may be required or demanded to pass upon the issue.

Moreover, even in the absence of statute, equity principles govern custody cases and the main objective is said to be the protection of the child and the promotion of his welfare, rather than the punishment of unworthy parents.

The prevailing American views as to jurisdiction to grant an initial custody award may be grouped into four categories: (1) The state where the defendant is domiciled, resident, or is personally served, (i. e., is subject to personal jurisdiction of the court), has personal jurisdiction over both parties to the custody dispute. (2) The state of the child's domicile, the status of the child being regarded as a "res" present there, and such domicile of the child either being that of its father, where the child is legitimate, or of its mother, if illegitimate, or the domicile of the parent with whom it is then living, has jurisdiction. (3) The state where the child is physically present has jurisdiction because such state has immediate access to the child and a concern as to its welfare. (4) Initial custody jurisdiction may be exercised by a state on the basis of any one of the above bases of jurisdiction, and there may be concurrent jurisdiction when the child's domicile, the child, and the defendant are in different states, but one state may abstain from the exercise of jurisdiction in favor of another state that has a greater interest in the child. Jurisdiction to enforce or to modify a prior custody award requires the presence of the child and/or personal jurisdiction over the defendant at the forum.

There is considerable conflict and uncertainty in the United States as to whether or not the federal Constitution permits any or all of the above four bases of custody jurisdiction to be exercised in particular circumstances and as to whether or not the Full Faith and Credit Clause of the federal Constitution requires recognition of prior custody awards of sister states. It has been held that recognition need not be given to a custody award to the father in a divorce case where the mother and the children were absent from the forum and present in another state. (*May v. Anderson*, 345 U. S. 528 [1953]). Since custody awards are not deemed to be final because they are modifiable due to changed circumstances, other states readily assume jurisdiction for the purposes of modification and reject prior determinations as to custody. This whole matter urgently needs clarification and at the present time efforts are being made to draft a model law for the several states which would set the rules as to both initial jurisdiction to award custody and jurisdiction to modify a prior award. Such a uniform law, if enacted by most states, would discourage the current inducement the law unwittingly gives to violate the terms of a prior custody award and to flee to another state in the hope of obtaining a new and more favorable award. A few states, applying equitable principles, refuse to hear a request for modification of a prior custody award made by a party who has violated the prior order.

Ordinarily, parents who violate custody orders are not subjected to criminal prosecution for such serious crimes as kidnapping or abduction, although they may be adjudged to be in contempt of court if they ever return to the jurisdiction, or there may be a forfeiture of any security posted in order to assure compliance with the order.

American courts agree that if a child within the court's jurisdiction has become dependent or neglected, there may be an assumption of control and custody and the child will be deemed to be a ward of the state. This is true regardless of the whereabouts of the parents. A more questionable assumption, sometimes encountered, is that once a court has custody jurisdiction it continues indefinitely regardless of the removal of both parties and the child from that state.

The greatest shortcoming of American law regarding custody is the failure as yet to devise workable rules that insure good faith compliance with custody orders. The lack of such rules encourages self-help and utilization of children as pawns in a bitter struggle between divorced parents. (See Foster & Freed, LAW AND THE FAMILY – New York, Vol. II, Chap. 29 [1966]).

c) *Other methods?*

Custody awards are made only by courts. However, there are many social agencies, public and private, that deal with dependent or neglected children and it is not uncommon for such agencies to secure an informal placement of children in foster homes or institutions by securing an agreement to such action from the mother or parents. The volume of such placements may exceed the number of official court cases.

In addition, since custody orders are not regarded as final and are subject to modification in the same or another state, de facto custody sometimes is secured in defiance of prior court orders. In short, legal custody emanates from a court order or agency placement, de facto custody may derive from agreement or a taking of the child.

2 *What standards are applied in custody determinations?*

a) *What are the relative rights of the parent? Does the mother always get the preference? If not, when?*

At least in modern times, American courts reject the feudal notion of the common law that the father had an exclusive or preferred natural right to the custody of his children that was paramount to the interests of the mother. The avowed or ostensible rule, established by American statutes and decisions, is that each parent has an equal claim to custody and that as between them the "best interests" of the child determines placement. However, in application, it generally is assumed that the child's "best interests" invariably require that custody be awarded to the mother, especially in the cases of children of "tender years" (pre-adolescents) and daughters. In reality, the father's interests usually are regarded as subordinate to the mother's, except perhaps where the dispute is over the custody of a teen age son, and this is true even though statutes purport to give both parents an equal right to custody. Thus, save under exceptional circumstances only an "unfit" mother will lose a child's custody to the father.

Where it is clearly established that the mother is "unfit," the court may award custody of children to the father or to a "stranger" such as some other relative. The strongest case for depriving a mother of custody is where she abandoned or deliberately relinquished her parental rights, as for example, where she left the home to move in with a lover and had no further or limited contact with her children, is guilty of immoral conduct (especially in the presence of children); drunkenness, violence, and other egregious misbehavior, may justify a finding of maternal "unfitness." In addition, mental or emotional illness may be deemed to make a mother "unfit" for custodial purposes. It should be noted that in many instances there is an overlap between the "unfitness" and "best interests" tests in that ordinarily it is not to the best interests of a child to be awarded to the custody of an "unfit" mother, although presumably it sometimes may be to his best interests to be awarded to a fit father instead of a fit mother, even though our courts usually refuse to do so. (See Simpson, *The Unfit Parent*, 39 Det. L. J. 347 [1962]).

b) *Are grandparents or other relatives ever given custody when a parent is available? If so, when?*

By statute and decision natural parents have a preferred or natural right to custody of their children and prevail over "strangers" such as grandparents or other relatives. "Strangers", as a term of art, includes all persons other than natural parents. The general rules applied by American Courts are: (1) In most states a natural parent may be deprived of custody only where he or she is deemed to be "unfit" or the award is made to the other natural parent. (2) Where the dispute as to custody is between natural parents, it is said that the best interests of the child determines custody; (3) but where the dispute is between a natural parent and a stranger, including a grandparent, the "best interests" rule is inapplicable in most states and it must be found that the parent is "unfit" before an award may be made to the stranger. Generally, parental "unfitness" covers a variety of situations including where the parent abandoned the child, otherwise forfeited parental rights, or would be an immoral or unwholesome influence.

The usual rule that natural parents prevail over other relatives in custody disputes often is applied even where the relatives have had de facto custody for an appreciable length of time and have become parent substitutes. An inflexible application of the rule in such cases may work hardship upon the child, especially where there has been little or no contact with the natural parent whose home includes a step-parent who is unknown to the child. In one case, the Nebraska court awarded custody of an 11 year old daughter to the remarried natural father after the death of the child's mother. The latter, after a divorce and an award of the baby's custody to her, had moved in with her parents and had let them take care of the child while she worked. The divorced father had no meaningful contact with his daughter for ten years. The mother was killed in an automobile accident and the natural father sought to reclaim his child. The court ignored the stated preference of the 11 year old daughter that she remain with the grandparents whom she regarded as her real "parents," and found that since the father had not been shown to be "unfit" he was entitled to custody. (*Raymond v. Cotner*, 120 N. W. 2d 892 [Neb. 1963]).

An Iowa decision which attracted national concern and interest is the case of *Painter v. Bannister* (140 N. W. 2d 151 [Iowa 1966]). There the Iowa court purported to apply the "best interests" rather than the "unfitness" test and awarded custody of a four year old boy to his maternal grandparents in preference to the natural father who had placed him with the grandparents temporarily after the deaths of the mother and another child, on the understanding that the son would be returned as soon as the father re-established a suitable home. The case was shocking because the court in rationalizing its result said that a small town in Iowa was a more wholesome environment than the "bohemian atmosphere" of the San Francisco bay area. The decision is ironic because in the past the questionable decisions have been those where an automatic preference was given to the natural parent at the expense of the child's best interests while in *Painter v. Bannister* the "best interests" test is misused to reflect local prejudice and in disregard of the understanding and circumstances of the placement with the grandparents. In most states, the natural father would have succeeded in obtaining the return of his son, and such would be automatic unless the father was proved to be "unfit". Unfortunately, strong reaction to the Iowa rule may perpetuate the automatic application of the "unfitness" test in other states. Neither rule or test should receive automatic or inflexible application.

(For a discussion of this problem, see Foster & Freed, *Child Custody,* 39 N.Y.U.L.Rev. 423, 615 [1964]; Simpson, *The Unfit Parent,* 39 Det. L.J. 347 [1962]; and Oster, *Custody Proceedings: A Study of Vague and Indefinite Standards,* 5 J. Family Law 21 [1965]).

c) *Are the preferences of the children considered? If so, when?*

The preference or wishes of the children are rarely decisive. However, most if not all American courts profess to consider the child's wishes regarding custody and visitation rights, at least if the child is deemed old enough to reason in that regard. The cases, however, indicate that the child's preference is not considered as significant as parental equities or the court's almost automatic preference for a mother or a natural parent over strangers. However some states by statute give the child who is over a certain age the right to select the parent he desires to live with. (For example, see *Smith v. Smith,* 386 P. 2d 900 [Utah 1963]). Even so, such a selection is not binding if the court finds the parent chosen to be unfit. Utah, however, has held that if the parent the child prefers is fit, the selection is binding.

At least where the pertinent factors are evenly balanced, the child's wishes should be decisive unless the person chosen by the child is obviously unfit or the child's choice is the result of coercion or bribery. Where the child's attachment to one parent is intense, severe damage may result from awarding custody or excessive visitation rights to the other. Whenever a child indicates a strong preference, the court should thoroughly study not only what is best for the child's psychological welfare but also what effect custody and visitation rights will have on his emotional and mental health. (See Goldstein and Katz, THE FAMILY AND THE LAW 256 et seq [1965]).

d) *Do you have a "Best interests of the Child" rule?*

As previously stated, in legal theory the "best interests of the child" rule applies where the custody dispute is between natural parents, although in practice the mother usually prevails. Where the custody dispute is between a parent and a "stranger" (any non-parent), the "best interests" test is replaced or superceded by the requirement that for a parent to be deprived of custody there must be proof of parental "unfitness". Some of the older American decisions speak of a natural or property right of a parent in a child.

The impact of modern behavioral science has been such that a few courts have come to doubt the wisdom of hard and fast rules which dictate an automatic preference. There is some tendency to give equal emphasis to the best interests of the child even where the dispute is between a parent and a "stranger", especially where the "stranger" has had de facto custody for a long period of time and a substitute parent-child relationship has developed. Where psychiatric evidence or other proof is adduced to show that a child would be emotionally or otherwise harmed by being forced to return to a parent he hardly knows, modern courts may favor maintenance of the status quo regarding custody.

It must be conceded, however, that probably most American courts continue to require proof of parental unfitness in order to (1) terminate the parental rights of a parent having custody, and (2) to permit a "stranger" having de facto custody to prevail over a parent seeking to regain custody. In the latter situation, where the child has identified with the substitute parents and perhaps has been in the home for several years since infancy, the older cases seem to express the shibboleth that "blood is thicker than water" and to arbitrarily disregard the best interests of the child and the love which has developed between the child and the substitute parents.

Another factor that should be weighed but which usually is disregarded, is the social and psychological fact that the real alternative in custody disputes is not so much that between placement with individuals but the choice to be made between two homes. Where the divorced father seeks to regain custody from maternal grandparents following the death of the working mother, and the 11 year old daughter since infancy really was raised by the grandparents and identified with them as her parents, it was unfortunate that the Nebraska court did not take into account that the home of the father included a second wife who was a complete stranger to the child. Such was a factor to be considered along with the attachment between the child and the grandparents and her adjustment to their home. (See *Raymond v. Cotner*, 120 N.W. 2d 892 [Neb. 1963]). To date, however, there is only one lower court opinion that stresses the "step-parent element" and holds that it is a decisive factor in weighing and balancing all relevant considerations. (See *Custody of Hampton*, 5 Adams Co. L.J. 84 [Pa. Orphans' Ct. 1963], discussed in 1963 ANNUAL SURVEY OF AMERICAN LAW at 429).

What is needed is a weighing and balancing approach. The best interests of the child although always a factor to be considered, should not be regarded as the sole factor. The same is true of the parental "unfitness" test. All relevant circumstances should be taken into account and due regard should be given to the emotional needs of the child, the legitimate interests of contending parties, and the inter-relationships which have existed with the child in the past. The circumstances and reasons for past placements of the child and the potential for his future development in the alternative environments also should be considered. It has been the judicial tendency to indulge in absolutes and to automatically apply fixed rules, rather than to weigh and balance all relevant factors, that has led to many unfortunate decisions. An eclectic approach plus the greater use of background and psychiatric reports would permit courts to do a more adequate job in determining custody, but even the wisdom of Solomon would not suffice to resolve some of the custody disputes committed to the conscience of our courts.

e) *Do you consider whether the parent is a "fit and proper person"?*

1 *Is custody ever awarded to a mother living with a man to whom she has not been ceremonially married?*

Ordinarily, an American court will not award custody to a mother living with a man to whom she is not married and she is deemed to be an "unfit" parent. Judicial attitudes, however, may differ somewhat between urban and rural areas and most courts today profess a more sophisticated attitude than would have been true a generation or two in the past. Moreover, the alternatives available for placement may be so poor as to offset the presumed immorality of the mother. Thus, a Louisiana case held that the fact that a divorced mother lived for a few months with a paramour until she realized that he would not keep his promise to marry her, did not warrant a change of custody from her to the father of their four year old child. (*Fletcher v. Fletcher*, 170 So. 2 d 144 [1964]). Another Louisiana case held that the unconcealed dating of an unmarried man by the divorced mother, and his helping with household chores and looking after the child, did not justify a change in custody. (*Trawick v. Trawick*, 173 So. 2 d 341 [1965]). Perhaps today most enlightened courts would make distinctions between immorality which has a direct effect upon child rearing and that which does not, and perhaps between promiscuity and relative stable relationships. (See *Bunin v. Bunin*, 298 N. Y. 391, 83 N. E. 2 d 848 [1949]).

As previously stated, the prevailing rule is that for a "stranger" to be awarded custody in preference to a natural parent, it is necessary to prove the parent "unfit", but in a custody dispute between parents the "best interests" of the child rule controls in theory although the mother usually is awarded custody unless she is "unfit".

2 *Is custody ever awarded to an adjudged adulterous parent?*

As indicated in response to the last question, American courts differ as to whether or not adultery by the mother ipso facto characterizes her as an "unfit parent". Nebraska appears to adopt the rule that the adulterous mother is disqualified as a matter of law from legal custody. (See *Morrissey v. Morrissey*, 154 N. W. 2 d 66 [Neb. 1967]). Maryland requires an adulterous mother to make a strong showing to overcome the presumption of unfitness for custody, and has held that her subsequent marriage to the paramour was insufficient evidence that she had reformed and become fit. (*Mason v. Mason*, 179 A. 2 d 897 [1962]). Other states give different weight, depending upon all the circumstances, to proof of her adultery.

The more recent cases appear to be more willing to conclude that proof of a mother's adultery may be counter-balanced by other factors involving the best interests of the child, although in some cases the mother's adultery tips the scales against a custody award that otherwise would have been made to her. (See Foster & Freed, LAW AND THE FAMILY – New York, Vol. II, Chap. 29 [1966]).

3 *Is custody ever awarded to a father who is not remarried?*

In exceptional cases, courts do award the custody of children to a father who remains single after his divorce from the mother. As previously pointed out, American courts show a marked tendency to favor the mother over the father even though in legal theory their claims to custody are equal, and in the case of children of "tender years" and daughters, usually it must be shown that the mother is egregiously unfit for the father to prevail. However, a few courts favor the parent who obtains the divorce, and in such case, a plaintiff-husband may be awarded custody of the children, especially where the mother was guilty of serious misconduct. Such an approach is punitive, may be contrary to the welfare of the children, and ignores the fact that the dynamics of family breakdown may not be accurately reflected in the court record, especially in uncontested cases.

If the father, although he does not remarry after divorce, nonetheless provides a suitable home and proper care, as for example where he lives with his parents, or retains an efficient housekeeper, such may be a suitable environment and a reasonable alternative to awarding custody elsewhere. Much will depend, in the judicial reckoning, upon the fitness of the mother, the home she intends to provide, and whether or not she must work or will devote her time to the care and upbringing of the children. It may be a safe generalization, however, to say that ordinarily a mother who has not remarried is to be preferred over a father who has not remarried and custody will be awarded to her except possibly in the case of teen age boys. Of course, the absence of a mother or a mother substitute in the home, is a substantial factor against awarding custody to an unmarried father.

f) *Are agreements concerning custody subject to court review and revision?*

Most if not all American jurisdictions accept the theory of *parens patriae* and view children as wards of the court. The assumption is that the state has an interest and concern regarding the welfare of children that is superior to that of any private parties, including parents. It follows from this theory that parents may not by private contract foreclose such public concern and that any agreement or stipulation regarding custody and visitation rights always is subject to overriding public policy.

In practice, however, courts usually accept the custodial and visitation arrangements agreed to by parents unless it clearly appears that the terms are unreasonable and contrary to the best interests of children. In the usual uncontested divorce case where the parties have entered into a separation agreement, the terms as to custody and visitation spelled out in the agreement are accepted and adopted by the court and incorporated into its order. Hence, although the terms agreed upon are not binding on the court, it usually accepts the stipulation of the parents when they can agree as to custody and visitation. However, if such terms should prove to be unworkable or to the detriment of the children, they always are subject to modification by the court which retains final authority.

Until recently, there was considerable controversy concerning arbitration clauses in agreements regarding custody. Although there is a division of judicial authority, and some early decisions held such arbitration clauses to be void, the definite trend in American cases is to enforce the agreement for arbitration, subject, however, to the court's discretion to accept or reject the arbitration award as justice dictates.

In effect, courts having responsibility concerning the welfare of children may not be ousted of such jurisdiction, by private agreement or otherwise. The court which renders the initial order concerning custody and visitation rights invariably retains inherent jurisdiction to alter or modify such orders upon proof of a substantial change in circumstances even though such authority is not expressly reserved in the initial order. In addition, such authority to alter or modify upon proof of changed circumstances, frequently is conferred by statute.

Judicial authority to modify or alter custody awards usually is dependent upon proof of a substantial change in circumstances which make provisions of the prior decree inadequate or not to the best interests of the children. Courts differ as to what constitutes a "substantial" change in circumstances and a few cases seem to assume that the mere passage of time in itself is a "substantial" change. Due to the human propensity to try to obtain more favorable advantage, and sometimes to use children as pawns in a power struggle between divorced parents, it is an abuse of authority to alter or change custody without proof of a change of circumstances beyond the contemplation of the original order, unless detriment to the children on the one hand, or their obvious advantage on the other, warrants the modification. In some states the custom or practice is to refer modification petitions to the judge who first heard the matter and thus to avoid a "shopping around" for a more favorable decision and needless duplication of evidence.

Although courts of original jurisdiction in making or modifying custody and visitation orders are free to disregard the terms agreed upon by parents, it is rare for appellate courts to reverse the decision of the trial judge who heard the evidence and observed the parties. Such orders will not be disturbed upon appeal except for a clear abuse of discretion or error in the application of law.

Thus, private agreements concerning custody always are subject to court review and revision, but in uncontested cases courts ordinarily accept the stipulations of the parties. Due to the fact that in America over ninety per cent of divorce cases are uncontested, and there is no dispute over custody in the original proceedings, the danger is that courts may rubber stamp agreements or terms that are not actually in the best interests of children and that no independent investigation will be made as to what is for their welfare.

g) *Who gets custody of out-of-wedlock children?*

The mother, unless egregiously unfit, has the prior claim to the custody of children born out of wedlock. Her right to custody is superior to that of the natural father or any other person. In some states there are statutes expressly recognizing the common law right of a mother to the custody of illegitimate children.

The natural father, however, has a secondary claim to his illegitimate child, and is entitled to custody in preference to "strangers", although his rights are subordinate to those of the mother. If it is shown to be to the best interests of the child, the natural father may be awarded custody. In addition, even though legal custody is awarded to the mother, a few recent cases have held that visitation rights may be awarded to the natural father where he is not obviously unfit and such visitation is conducive to the child's welfare.

The mother may forfeit her right to the custody of her illegitimate children by ill treatment, abandonment, non-support, or where they become dependent or neglected. She also may consent to the placement of the child for adoption or foster home care.

Controversies over the custody of illegitimate children generally arise in habeas corpus proceedings or in the family or juvenile court when dependency or neglect is alleged or it is sought to terminate her parental rights. Courts usually apply the "best interests of the child" test in such cases, but the mother of an illegitimate child ordinarily will not be deprived of her child merely because it was born out of wedlock. Of course, if she is otherwise an "unfit" mother, she may lose legal custody of her child.

There is a recent tendency in American cases to recognize and extend the legal rights of a putative father. Since he has a duty and may be ordered to provide support for his natural child, there should be some reciprocal privileges or rights. For example, it has been held that on the mother's death the natural father, if a fit person, is entitled to custody of his illegitimate child, and his legal right to custody may be superior to that of any person other than the mother. He even may prevail over the mother where she neglects the child. In one case it was held that a putative father has a right to appear in juvenile court proceedings regarding his illegitimate child (*In re Aronson*, 58 N.W. 2d 553 [Wis. 1953]), although perhaps that decision is not in accord with the general rule. Where the mother abandons or relinquishes her illegitimate child, the putative father may have a prior right to custody if he promptly asserts his claim. (See *In re Brennan*, 134 N.W. 2d 126 [Minn. 1965]).

Perhaps most important, visitation rights are being accorded to putative fathers seeking such a privilege, as long as such is in accord with the best interests of the child. (See *Baker v. Baker*, 85 A. 2d 816 [N.J. 1913]; *Commonwealth v. Rozanski*, 213 A. 2d 155 [Pa. Super. 1965]; *Stong v. Owens*, 205 P. 2d 48 [Cal. App. 1949]; *Ex parte Hendrix*, 100 P. 2d 444 [Okla. 1940]; *Hixson v. Hixson*, 263 P. 2d 597 [Ore. 1953]). Such privilege of visitation, however, may be conditioned upon his continuing support (See *In re Anonymous*, 172 N.Y.S. 2d 186 [1958], and *Mixon v. Mize*, 198 So. 2d 373 [Fla. App. 1967]), although it also has been held that unless there is a failure or refusal to so provide for the child upon demand, visitation privileges would be granted to the putative father. (See *Bagwell v. Powell*, 99 So. 2d 195 [Ala. 1957]).

With reference to adoption, the general rule is that the putative father has no privilege of giving or withholding his consent to his child's adoption and that only the consent of the mother is required. Statutes frequently so provide. (See for example, N. Y. Dom. Rel. Law § 111 [3]). Nonetheless, a few cases have raised exceptions to this general rule, as for example, where the natural mother dies pending adoption of her child and the putative father may be given the right to revoke the mother's consent. (See *Ex Parte Schwartzkopf*, 31 N.W. 2d 294 [Neb. 1948], and *In re McGrew*, 190 P. 2d 804 [Cal. 1920]). In addition, if after the mother has placed the child for adoption, the natural parents marry and hence legitimate the child, his consent may be essential for the completion of the adoption. Although this is the usual rule, California has held to the contrary. (See *In re Laws' Adoption*, 201 Cal. App. 2d 494 [1962]). Moreover, an Arkansas statute requires consent of the father to adoption where paternity has been established by court order, and in the District of Columbia such consent also is necessary where he has acknowledged the child or voluntarily contributed to its support. (See Ark. Stat. § 56–106 [c] [1947]; and D.C. Code § 16–202

[1940]). In the state of Washington, if the natural father has some right of custody or visitation, his consent is essential to the adoption of his illegitimate child. (See *In Re Hope's Adoption*, 191 P. 2d 289 [Wash. 1948]). As for the right to be notified of a pending adoption proceeding, the usual rule is that notice need be given only to those whose consent is required. However, a recent decision of the United States Supreme Court (*Armstrong v. Manzo*, 380 U. S. 545 [1965]) held that due process of law requires notification of pending adoption proceedings to a divorced father and the language of the decision may be broad enough to include a putative father, at least where he has acknowledged or has contributed to the support of his child. In a few states, such already is the current practice. (See *Mixon v. Mize*, 198 So. 2d 373 [Fla. App. 1967], and North Dakota Cent. Code § 14–11–10 [1959]).

It should be noted that just as the putative father's consent generally is not necessary for the adoption of his child, save for the exceptions and trends noted above, so too the mother's consent appears not to be required if the putative father desires to legitimate his natural child by recognition and acknowledgement. (See *Fladung v. Sanford*, 75 P. 2d 685 [Ariz. 1938]).

It would seem that as a matter of justice and logic, if a putative father is to be subject to the duty of child support he should be accorded parental rights and privileges that do not conflict with his child's best interests. However, Illinois in construing its statutes has held that the putative father must bear the onus without correlative rights. (See *Wallace v. Wallace*, 210 N. E. 2d 4 [Ill. App. 1965]). It is one thing to hold that the putative father has no custody or visitation rights if (as in Texas and Idaho) he has no legal duty to support illegitimate children, it is another matter to foreclose him from association with his child where such is to the best interests of both. Due to the prevalence of illegitimacy in America, perhaps courts should adopt the perspective of what is to the best interests of the "putative family" and allocate duties and rights accordingly.

3 *What general rules are applied in allowing visitation?*

a) *Is visitation ever contingent on receipt of support payments?*

Generally, the mother's violation of a court order entitling the father to visitation rights does not relieve the father of his duty to provide child support in accordance with the order. However, it has been held that a court may suspend the father's duty temporarily pending the mother's compliance with the visitation terms of the order. (See *Beddini v. Beddini*, 117 N. Y. S. 2d 511).

If a separation agreement or a court order expressly conditions the father's visitation rights upon his payment of child support, the right and the duty may be deemed inter-dependent, and his non-payment may forfeit visitation privileges. Likewise, a mother's violation of the father's visitation rights may justify discontinuance of support where the agreement or order for support is dependent upon her compliance with his visitation rights. Ordinarily, unless the agreement or order *expressly* make visitation rights and the duty of child support dependent, they will be construed as independent clauses or terms. In some states, however, it is customary to condition the father's visitation rights upon his regular payment of child support. In such states he must apply to the court for modification in order to be relieved from his duty of child support, as where his circumstances have changed so that he no longer is able to pay the amount originally ordered but desires to continue visitation with his child.

Difficult problems are presented where the mother desires or is forced to move and take the child with her to another state or country and such move interferes with the father's rights as to visitation. Such may occur due to her remarriage, career opportunities, or because of health reasons. In such cases the mother may seek and obtain modification of the prior custody and visitation order if the court agrees that she is reasonable in leaving the jurisdiction. In some instances, courts have modified prior orders and have required her to pay the cost of periodic returns of the children to the father's home.

b) *Is visitation allowed to grandparents or other relatives?*

The obligation of a parent to permit children to visit grandparents and other relatives generally is a moral but not a legal duty. In some cases, however, grandparents or other relatives may be able to demand and receive legal rights of visitation. For example, the maternal grandparents of an orphaned child who was placed in the custody of paternal grandparents, were successful in demanding visitation rights. (See *In re Lippincott*, 124 A. 2d 532, affirmed 128 A. 2d 254 [N.J. 1924] and see also *Anonymous v. Anonymous*, 269 N.Y.S. 2d 500 [1966]).

The rationale for denying visitation orders to grandparents or other relatives is that only persons who have a legal right to custody may claim visitation privileges, and that the latter derives from the former. (See *Jackson v. Fitzgerald*, 185 A. 2d 724 [D.C. 1962]). Thus, where a child is in the legal custody of his father, who is a fit person, grandparents or other relatives may be denied visitation rights.

Agreements by parents that grandparents or other relatives will receive visitation privileges may be unenforceable and deemed to be contrary to public policy. (*Ex parte Windell*, 107 P. 2 d 708 [Kan. 1940]). The best interests of the child is the controlling issue as to whether or not visitation rights will be ordered, subject to the limitation that ordinarily only one who has some valid or contingent claim to custody has a legal right to visitation.

c) *Are the child's wishes taken into consideration?*

Statutes permitting, the wishes of the child have the same limited effect upon visitation rights as they do upon custody matters. In other words, ordinarily the child's preference as to visitation will not prevail over that of the parent who has legal custody, except perhaps where the child's welfare clearly coincides with his wishes. However, the court may ascertain the desires and wishes of the child and consider such factor even though it is not a conclusive basis for decision. In some instances the extent of visitation privileges has been based upon the stated preferences of children. (See *People ex rel Baird v. Baird*, 67 N. Y. S. 2d 758 [1947]).

From the standpoint of the best interests and welfare of children, greater heed should be given to their stated preferences because psychological and other harm may be occasioned to them if their wishes are treated as a negligible factor. In this regard, of course the age of the child is important in determining how much weight should be given to stated preferences, but the strong feelings of young children also should receive more consideration than is customarily given to them by our courts. (See Goldstein and Katz, THE FAMILY AND THE LAW 256 et seq [1965]).

4 *What methods, if any, do you have for enforcing visitation?*

In most states, orders and decrees regarding visitation and custody are enforced by the excercise of contempt powers to punish violations. Thus, one who stands in deliberate violation of a custody or visitation decree may be subject to an order to show cause why he should not be found in contempt of court. If he does not purge himself of contempt, he may be committed to prison until he is willing to abide by the order.

Of course, if the violator of a custody or visitation order is in another state or country, and not subject to the personal jurisdiction of the court, he cannot be punished for contempt unless he returns to the original place. However, on the basis of the original personal jurisdiction over the party, a restraining order or injunction may issue to order the party in question to comply with the prior court order. Such continuing jurisdiction has been exercised and sustained in many cases. The state or country where the party enjoined may be sometimes respects the restraining order or injunction in collateral proceedings. It must be conceded, however, that there is a marked propensity to favor the local resident in such cases even though he or she has violated the decree of another state.

A frequent example is where a mother frustrates the visitation rights of a father by removing the children from the state or country without the court's knowledge or permission. Belated injunctions or the instigation of contempt proceedings are of limited practical value. To some extent, the danger of removal of the children from the jurisdiction, may be guarded against by requiring a bond or security to be posted to ensure compliance with the court order, and in some states such practice is adopted.

In the United States there are a few court decisions which have applied the equity doctrine of "clean hands" against a party who has violated a prior custody or visitation order and seeks a new determination of his rights in that regard. Although the "clean hands" doctrine is purely discretionary and its application is not required by fixed rule or statute, a decent respect for and deference to, prior decrees commends its application except where the child has been abused, or is dependent or neglected, and for that reason the court should intervene.

Theoretically, it is possible for the party who has been deprived of legal rights to custody or visitation pursuant to a prior court order to have such rights confirmed and restored at the place where the children and the other party are found. Such actions proceed on the basis of a writ of habeas corpus, or by petition, in equity. As pointed out, the practical difficulty in such cases is that American courts generally have paid inadequate attention to the fact of violation of court orders and tend to favor the local resident who is the defendant in the habeas corpus or equity proceeding.

B *Do your courts recognize the custody determinations of other countries as to children in your country?*

1 *Does your country have any treaty with any other country or is it a signatory to any convention as to custody?*

The United States does not have any treaty with any other country as to child custody it also is not a signatory to any convention in that regard.

are not final in the sense that they remain subject to modification due
Since the custody and visitation decrees of sister states customarily
to a substantial change in circumstances, American courts usually are

open for a reconsideration of such matters. There is uncertainty as to whether or not the Full Faith and Credit Clause of the federal Constitution (Art. IV, § 1) has any application to the custody decrees of sister states. (See *Ford v. Ford,* 371 U. S. 187 [1963]; *Kovacs v. Brewer,* 356 U. S. 605 [1958]; *May v. Anderson,* 345 U. S. 528 [1953];*New York ex rel Halvey v. Halvey,* 3330 U. S. 610 [1947]; and Comment, *Full Faith and Credit to Custody Decrees,* 73 Yale L. J. 134 [1963]).

There also is uncertainty and confusion as to whether or not and to what extent principles of res judicata or collateral estoppel are applicable to prior custody awards where modification is sought. Some states, such as New York, seem to deny any res judicata effect to prior custody proceedings. (See *Bachman v. Mejias,* 136 N. E. 2d 903 [N. Y. 1956]). Other states hold the prior order conclusive as to facts and circumstances up to the date of the decree, and still other states insist upon a real and substantial change of circumstances and hold that unless such new circumstances are shown the parties are bound by the original decree. (See Foster and Freed, LAW AND THE FAMILY – New York, §§ 29:35 [1966]).

Moreover, states where the children are found or where they have their domicile frequently assume *parens patriae* power to protect children or to further their interests. In such cases, courts may intervene not only where children are dependent and neglected, but also to further their best interests by modifying prior custody and visitation awards.

It is not surprising, with so much uncertainty as to the stability of domestic decrees, that American courts may not extend comity to foreign custody and visitation orders. However, New York has recognized and refused to modify a Swiss custody award where the party seeking modification in New York had violated the Swiss decree, thus applying the "clean hands" doctrine to sustain the effect of a foreign country custody decree. (See *Application of Lang,* 7 N. E. 2d 1029 [N. Y. [19]; and see also *Ex parte Dawson,* 3 Bradf. 130 [N. Y. 18], the earliest known international custody case to arise in America). Thus, although comity may be accorded to a foreign country custody decree or equitable principles may preclude its modification, as a practical matter a slight showing of change in circumstances may suffice for the assumption of jurisdiction by an American court where the children and one party to the custody dispute are subject to its personal jurisdiction.

2 *Are you contemplating any such new treaty or convention?*

No new treaties or conventions are in prospect regarding child custody. Until the Supreme Court of the United States clarifies the existing law regarding custody jurisdictions, both original and for modification, it is unlikely that agreement can be reached as to the controlling principles. However, it might be possible to reach an accord as to the desirability of refusing to exercise jurisdiction to modify foreign (or sister state) custody and visitation decrees at the petition or request of a party who has violated a prior order, unless there is a clear showing that the child in question is dependent or neglected. As we have seen above, there is New York precedent for such a policy.

Further, it should be noted that the Commissioners on Uniform State Laws currently are engaged in the project of drafting a model law concerning jurisdiction to make or modify custody awards. When this task is completed, it may be enacted in at least some states and it might influence the Supreme Court if another inter-state custody problem is presented.

C. *Do you have any problems within your country as to children living in another city or province?*

There is substantial disagreement in the American statutes and decisions as to the appropriate basis for an assumption of original jurisdiction to issue custody and visitation orders. In part, the confusion arises because such questions may come before the court as an incident to divorce, annulment, or judicial separation, or in independent proceedings by petition or writ of habeas corpus. Obviously, where the custody dispute is a part of a larger dispute in a contested divorce case, the tendency is to assume comprehensive jurisdiction over all matters including custody, if the court has jurisdiction over the subject matter of divorce. Divorce jurisdiction in the United States usually has been regarded as resting upon domicile of one or both parties, and hence it sometimes is assumed that the divorce court at the domicile of the plaintiff also has jurisdiction to award custody even if the children and the other party are absent from the state. *May v. Anderson* (345 U. S. 528 [1953]), however, casts doubt upon such an assumption of custody jurisdiction.

The American cases indicate that initial jurisdiction to award custody may be assumed where (1) the defendant is domiciled, resident, or present at the forum so that there is personal jurisdiction over both parties; (2) where the child is domiciled at the forum, perhaps, even though absent therefrom, such domicile being that of its father or possibly that of the parent with whom he is living; (3) the child is physically present at the forum; and (4) where any one or a combination of the above three bases exists at the forum. (See Foster and Freed, LAW AND THE FAMILY §§ 29:2 [1966]). The decisions of one state, such as New York, may give examples of an exercise of custody jurisdiction on the basis of all of the above bases of jurisdiction.

It is not clear whether or not the Due Process Clause of the federal Constitution permits an exercise of custody jurisdiction except where both parties are subject to the court's jurisdiction, as in (1) above. *May v. Anderson*, supra, held that Ohio need not give full faith and credit to a Wisconsin custody order incident to a valid divorce decree. The domicile of the father, the matrimonial domicile of the parties, and perhaps the domicile of the children were in Wisconsin. The parties had separated, the mother taking the children with her back to her old home in Ohio, hence the mother and children were not physically present in Wisconsin at the time of the divorce. Probably, the mother had acquired a new domicile of choice in Ohio. The principal opinion of the Supreme Court stressed the personal rights of the mother to custody, and held that such rights could not be cut off without personal jurisdiction over her. However, if the mother had stayed in Wisconsin, the husband had left, and the mother had sought and obtained a Wisconsin divorce without personal jurisdiction over the husband, it may be doubted that the Supreme Court would hold that there was a violation of due process in the custody award or that the decree was not entitled to such full faith and credit as custody decrees generally may be entitled to receive. Although not stressed in the main opinion, it may be that absence of the children was as significant a factor as the lack of personal jurisdiction over the mother.

In addition to the confusion over custody jurisdiction, there also is a serious social problem due to the encouragement American law unwittingly gives to abducting the child in violation of a custody and visitation decree in order to relitigate the merits in the hope of obtaining a change of custody. This critical problem has been previously discussed and does not require further elaboration.

D *What suggestions do you have for possible legislative or other action in each country dealing with problems of custody?*

Steps could be taken to discourage the abduction of children in violation of prior custody and visitation orders. There are many cases where children have been taken to a foreign country in violation of the terms of the original custody or visitation order and then new custody proceedings brought to change legal custody. At a minimum, the courts of any country should decline to change foreign custody decrees at the request of a party who has violated the prior order, unless the children are dependent or neglected.

It would seem that the criteria or tests applied for determining custody awards probably are a matter of local concern.

E *What special questions on child custody do you suggest for our discussion in Dublin?*

The following questions as to child custody may be of interest and concern:

1. In a custody dispute between a parent and non-parent, does the former invariably prevail even where the best interests of the child clearly favor placing custody with the non-parent? Suppose, for example, the parents were divorced when their child was a few months old and the court awarded custody to the mother who moved in with her parents. The mother worked and the grandparents raised the child, and became substitute parents. When the child was 11 years old, the mother was killed, and the father who has remarried now seeks to regain custody from the grandparents. Moreover, for the past eleven years, the father has not seen or communicated with his daughter. What result would be reached? (*Cf. Raymond v. Cotner*, 120 N. W. 2d 892 [Neb. 1963]; *Commonwealth v. Gard*, 66 A. 2d 300 [Pa. 1949]; and *Chapsky v. Wood*, 26 Kan. 650 [1881]).

2. If the petitioner has violated the terms of a custody or visitation order, under what circumstances will prior orders be modified?

3. May custody be awarded to an adulterous or alcoholic mother?

4. What are the evidentiary rules as to the admissibility of investigations and reports on family background and the psychiatric and social needs of children? What court facilities are there for investigation of custody disputes? Do governmental or welfare agencies make investigations and reports?

5. Should custody disputes be resolved by the adversary process or should such issues be handled in some other way? If so, how?

III INTERPROFESSIONAL COOPERATION IN DEALING WITH PROBLEMS OF SUPPORT AND CUSTODY OF CHILDREN

A *Whose responsibility is it to establish the facts and provide the evidence?*

Custody cases are presented within the adversary framework in American Courts. In the last century, courts by analogy referred to a "property interest" of a parent in a child. In this century, the phraseology may be that a parent has a "natural right" to custody or visitation. The result of either the "property interest" or "natural right" approach is that only an unfit parent loses in a custody dispute, even though the best interests of the child clearly dictate placement elsewhere.

It should be noted that in other actions where child placement is at issue court proceedings may be more informal. For example, adoptions and proceedings in juvenile or family court tend towards informality and usually are not comparable to the adversary process as it exists in custody cases. Investigations and reports as to history and background are more readily admitted and considered by the court where the procedure is informal, and the "hearsay" exclusionary rule is mitigated or not applied. In custody cases, however, many American courts will not consider investigations and reports in the absence of stipulation by the parties, and the judge may not have authority to confer with the child to ascertain the child's preference as to custody and visitation unless the parties agree to such procedure. Such is not usually the case in adoption or other proceedings involving child placement. (See Foster and Freed, *Child Custody*, 39 N. Y. L. Rev. 615 [1964]).

Thus, although the court may have a broad equitable discretion in determining what is to the best interests of the child, there are serious limitations on the court's authority to order or to receive investigations and reports. In practice, the court hears and sees the evidence presented by opposing counsel according to the rules of practice and procedure. In some states, masters or referees may be used for the fact finding function and to report back to the court for its decision.

The opinion of the trial judge although subject to review by appellate courts, rests upon a broad discretion and it is rather rare for an appellate court to reverse on the facts a trial judge's decision. When the trial court is reversed, usually it is for an error of law, or because inadmissible and prejudicial evidence was considered.

In some states, courts hearing custody disputes are authorized by statute to order investigations and reports by the court's staff or other agencies. Where received, such reports are advisory only, and the trial judge may disregard any recommendation which may have been made.

Thus, the typical situation in American custody cases is that the parties have the responsibility, within the framework of the adversary process, of providing the evidence for judicial determination on the merits. It is the responsibility of the parties through counsel to procure and present the evidence; it is the responsibility of the court to determine the facts, to resolve the dispute, and to award custody. In such cases, the adversary system may be a great handicap to arriving at a just and proper disposition and reform is needed so that social, phychological, and economic facts may be brought to the court's attention where such information or data is relevant and a fair opportunity for cross-examination or rebuttal is accorded.

B *What use do your courts make of other professions in arriving at decisions regarding non-support and custody determinations?*

1. *Do the courts have social workers, psychologists, psychiatrists and other professionals on staff?*

2. *Do your courts refer to non-court professionals for recommendation?*

3. *Do your courts refer to such questions for determination by other agencies or workers?*

Investigations and reports of social workers, preferably those attached to the staff of the court, and the evaluations of psychiatrists and behavioral scientists are the two most important kinds of professional assistance available in custody cases.

The use of evidence as to the psychiatric condition of the contesting parties and of the child appears to be increasing. Some states by statute provide for social investigations, reports and recommendations when child custody is at issue. (See Cal. Civ. Proceed. Code § 263, N. Y. Family Court Act § 653; and Children's Bureau, Social Security Adm., U. S. Dept. of H. E. W., "Legislative Guides for the Termination of Parental Rights and Responsibilities and the Adoption of Children"). Some state courts refer cases to outside agencies for investigation and report. In most states, however, there is a lack of confidence in the reports of social workers, psychologists and psychiatrists, and obstacles are placed in the way of getting background reports and case histories before the court.

A number of Family Courts and Juvenile Courts in various states have a professional staff of social workers, probabtion officers, psychologists and psychiatrists. The social work profession supplies case workers and probation officers who prepare reports for juvenile courts, family courts, and for other courts handling custody cases. Such courts generally are located in metropolitan areas and do not exist in smaller communities. Thus, it is the exception, rather than the rule, to have a juvenile or family court with a trained professional staff. Unfortunately, the vast majority of custody disputes are solved in adversary contests heard by judges who are not specialists as to such issues and who do not have the benefit of investigations, reports, and recommendations by professionally trained personnel.

C *Do you feel that these matters might be handled by agencies or organizations other than courts? If so, which?*

Under the American constitutional theory of checks and balances and judicial review, courts have the responsibility for the ultimate resolution of such matters as disputes regarding custody. Access to the courts in such cases cannot be foreclosed, particularly since the writ of habeas corpus is a traditional means for raising such an issue. The adversary system, however, permits the use of masters or referees who hear the evidence and report and recommend to the trial court for its decision. Practical reform could be achieved by the employment of specialized masters who are learned in law and the behavioral sciences and assigning disputed custody cases to them.

Constitutional issues would be raised if there were a legislative attempt to cede custody jurisdiction to administrative tribunals or other government agencies. Such might be a denial of due process of law under the federal Constitution. Moreover, it is not politically feasible and probably would be impractical. Thus, the hope for improvement in the processing of custody disputes lies with court reform, specialized family courts, and providing professional staffs. Although such reform is expensive, it is well worth the price if in fact we believe the platitude that our youth are our greatest national resource.

SUMMARY OF DISCUSSIONS

The law relating to the support and custody of children in its international and comparative aspects.

The Rapporteur, Judge Zukerman, explained that the report had been prepared on the basis of 22 answers to questionnaires sent to some 50 countries. Reports from Ireland, Lebanon, Liberia, and Spain were received too late for inclusion in the Rapporteur's summary. Italy's answers were included in the report but not in the appendix since it had already gone to press.

Printed copies of the national reports from the United States and Ireland were distributed to those in attendance at the session.

The Rapporteur summarized the similarities and differences disclosed by the national reports. With reference to custody, all countries reported that they apply the „best interest of the child" test. In the case of child support, all countries impose a primary obligation upon the father but differ as to whether or not the mother's child support obligation is primary or secondary. The standards applied for child support are generally based on the ability of the parent to support and the parent's standard of living.

In the majority of the countries reporting, support is generally enforced by the courts and in practically all countries a willful failure to obey a court order for support is punishable by fine or imprisonment. The Rapporteur then noted the international conventions on child support that are in force and the countries which are signatories thereto.

The recommendations for action made by the various countries were as follows: in federal states, uniform reciprocal state laws; creation of public youth welfare officials; governmental guarantees of support with restitution from the parent.

The Rapporteur also stressed the importance of deference to child custody awards of other countries and the discouragement of child abduction in order to modify a child custody award. He also noted that the Scandinavian countries, the members of the British Commonwealth, and many other countries, have reciprocal treaties in this area.

The Rapporteur reported that the reporting countries have recommended the following:

1. international enforcement of decrees and agreements;
2. a uniform minor's code;
3. greater use of specialist agencies;
4. appointment by the court of counsel for the child.

There were three skits written by Professor Foster illustrating problems of custody, desertion, and non-support. Acting in these skits were Elizabeth Plunkett, Susan Goldman, and Doris Jonas Freed with Professor Foster in the role of attorney.

The national Correspondents then spoke briefly. Mr. Moore (Ireland) stressed the fact that maintenance in the international area was of vital importance. He recommended further study by the International Bar Association in the field of international custody problems.

Judge Mitchell (Australia) spoke of international enforcement of support orders by commonwealth treaties.

Mr. Vadon (France) noted that French courts do not recognize custody orders of foreign countries but try the case de novo.

Mr. MacDonald (England) gave an eloquent summary of the policy issues involved in child support and custody cases and plead for reciprocal cooperation and assistance in such cases.

Mrs. Berkin (Turkey) advocated special children's courts staffed by expert personnel and deplored the fact that children are used as pawns in custody struggles between parents.

Mr. Pablo-Blanco (Spain) noted that Spain was a signatory to the October 24, 1956 Hague convention on child support, as were a number of other countries.

Professor Della Rocca (Italy) mentioned that at present a reform of Italian law in these areas is being contemplated. He further spoke of the importance of the problems raised by non-support.

Mr. Conradie (South Africa) spoke of important changes made by the Maintenance act of 1963 and noted that now the inferior courts may alter or rescind orders of the Supreme Court.

Mr. Seligman (Israel) spoke in favor of legal aid services on a reciprocal basis.

Upon the conclusion of the brief remarks of the Correspondents, statements were made by interested persons in the audience.

Dr. Doris Jonas Freed summarized the American report.

The Chairman, Vice-chairman, and Rapporteur received extremely valuable assistance from Anthony Collins (Ireland) who served as secretary for the session.

The Rapporteur summarized the session and made the following observations:

1. that those in attendance were agreed upon the need to develop international machinery for support cases, whether by the adoption of treaties or by a uniform support of dependents law;

2. the need to approach child support and custody in terms of social and human values rather than in a purely legalistic way;
3. the urgent need for further study of the international aspects of child support and custody problems; and
4. the urgent need for effective enforcement machinery for court orders including the provision of legal assistance by legal aid or otherwise to poor families.

OPEN MEETING OF THE ADVISORY COMMITTEE ON PROFESSIONAL ETHICS AND PROFESSIONAL PRIVILEGES

(1) THE FORMS OF CO-OPERATION BETWEEN QUALIFIED LOCAL LAWYERS AND FOREIGN LAWYERS PRACTISING IN THE SAME COUNTRY AND

(2) THE FORMS OF CO-OPERATION BETWEEN QUALIFIED LAWYERS IN DIFFERENT COUNTRIES

Chairman: Mr. Jan Voûte (Netherlands)
Secretary: Mr. L. Hardenberg (Netherlands)

Country	*Committee Members*
Australia	J. B. Piggott, Esq., C. B. E.
Austria	RA Dr. Harald Foglar-Deinhardstein
Canada	Everett Clayton Leslie, Esq.
Denmark	Højesteretssagfører Jon Palle Buhl
England	Harry Kirk, Esq. (The Law Society) Kenneth Jones, Esq., Q. C. (Gen. Council of the Bar)
Finland	Asianajaja Mauri Hakapää
France	Me Gabrielle Faber Me Eliane Walrafen
Germany	RA Dr. Heinrich Ackermann
Iran	Maître Mehdi Maleki Maître Abbas Naraghi
Ireland	Dermot P. Shaw, Esq. (Inc. Law Society of Ireland)
Israel	Dr. Joshua Rotenstreich, Adv.
Italy	On. Avv. Filippo Ungaro
Japan	Bengoshi Mr. Fuji Nomura (Japan Bar Association) Bengoshi Mr. Noboru Toichi (Jap. Fed. of Bar Assns.)
Mexico	Sr. Lic. D. Manuel G. Escobedo
New Zealand	E. D. Blundell, Esq.
Northern Ireland	Captain Norman Murray (Inc. Law Society)

Norway	H. r. advokat Erik M. Martens
Peru	Sr. Lic. Dr. Felix Navarro Irvine
Philippines	Dean José M. Aruego (Philippine Lawyers' Assn.) Senator José W. Diokno (Philippine Bar Assn.)
Portugal	Dr. Angelo de Almeida Ribeiro
Scotland	Professor R. D. Ireland (Faculty of Advocates) Neil Watson, Esq., S. S. C. (The Law Society of Scotl.)
South Africa	C. M. Venter, Esq.
Spain	Illmo. Sr. D. Rafael Pastor Botija
Sweden	Advokat Holger Wiklund
Switzerland	Prof. Dr. Conrad Fehr
Turkey	Maître Saffet Nezihi Bölukbasi
U. A. R. (Egypt)	Maître Kamal Tewfick
U. S. A.	John P. Bracken, Esq. (American Bar Association) Irving Jaffe, Esq. (Federal Bar Association) Theodore R. Kupferman, Esq. (Consular Law Society) Miss Mildred Bixby (Nat. Assn. of Women Lawyers)

INTERIM REPORT

to the

ADVISORY COMMITTEE ON PROFESSIONAL ETHICS AND PROFESSIONAL PRIVILEGE

of the

INTERNATIONAL BAR ASSOCIATION

Chairman: Mr. Jan R. Voûte (Netherlands)
Secretary: Mr. L. Hardenberg (Netherlands)

1. At the plenary session, Lausanne 1966, the Chairman said that the development of modern trade, the increasing number of international transactions, the formation of groups of nations (in Europe, America, Africa) will lead to forms of co-operation between lawyers in different countries, and asked the meeting: is it desirable that the advisory committee takes up the study of this point for a future conference of the IBA? The question was answered in the affirmative (Lausanne Conference Book p. 90, 94) and the committee has been invited to organize an open meeting on the following topics:

a) the forms of co-operation between qualified local lawyers and foreign lawyers practising in the same country;
b) the forms of co-operation between qualified lawyers in different countries.

Subsequently, as an immediate result of the first exchange of ideas between the members of the committee, the following additional questions have been formulated:

> should the IBA recommend to the several national bar associations that the national associations recognize the right of a non-national lawyer to engage in the practice of law in foreign jurisdictions to the bars of which he has not been formally admitted?
>
> to what qualifications, if any, should this recognition be subject?
>
> should the recognition be limited to individual practitioners or extended to law partnerships and if so, only to law partnerships limited in their membership to lawyers of but one nation or even to international law partnerships?

This interim report is based on the ample material assembled for the Lausanne Conference and the additional information supplied since then.

2. The problems indicated above arise whenever a client needs legal assistance in a foreign country or on a point of foreign law, which almost always renders it inevitable to call in a foreign lawyer. This is not so easy as it might seem. In the first place, the selection of a lawyer, which is often difficult enough at home, is a most hazardous adventure abroad. (Incidentally, the conferences of the IBA offer a very good opportunity to become acquainted with colleagues from other countries and their special problems). In the second place, even if an honest and capable lawyer is available, he may not be accustomed to deal with the usually very special problems of a foreign client, who by language and also by many legal aspects of his business, usually keeps at least one foot firmly in his home country and is not or at least insufficiently aware that his own law does not follow him wherever his trade may take him.

Consequently as the local bar is less equipped to meet with the foreign clients' demands, the need for a specialized intermediary, who speaks the clients' language and undertakes the burden of translating and solving both linguistic and legal puzzles increases accordingly. Undoubtedly a thorough education of the local bar will keep foreign competition in check – in many countries obviously with good results – but presumably will never wholly eliminate it.

3. In this respect the difference between a lawyer, who from time to time, perhaps even frequently, goes abroad to assist his clients and the one, who sets up a permanent office in a foreign jurisdiction either independent or as a branch office, seems only a gradual one. The very interesting problems which accompany a lawyer travelling abroad have been discussed at the Mexico Conference, especially as regards his professional secrecy (Mexico Conference Book p. 322) and at Lausanne it became clear that this activity is allowed practically everywhere (Lausanne Conference Book p. 19). The more, however, becomes clear also the necessity of an enquiry into the motives, which are opposed to the establishment of permanent foreign offices. It is remarkable that many countries, which have objections to the establishment of such offices, permit their own bar to set them up in other countries freely. Although this report is by no means intended to criticize any national legislation it is suggested that this attitude seems as illogical as it is understandable.

4. An important factor in the legislation of almost all countries is the protection of the public against incompetent legal advisers. This justified the question at the Lausanne meeting (Lausanne Conference Book p. 30), whether or not in modern countries with their highly complicated social and legal structure it would be advisable to reserve in the public interest the legal practice exclusively to those qualified, as is already generally the case with the medical profession. Roughly speaking, however, the

scope of national protective measures ends where the special problems of very many foreign clients begin, so, in other words, a parallel may be drawn between this protection and the general competency of a national bar.

5. Therefore, even if the first additional question ("should the IBA recommend to the several national bar associations etc.") may be framed too widely – which in view of the answers received seems to be the case – it might be useful to distinguish between a foreign lawyer who

a) engages in legal practice as a whole and e. g. also represents his clients in the courts of the country in which he is a guest; this would be possible only when he is also formally admitted to the local bar or fulfils any other requirements of the local laws and rules;

b) limits his activities to those of an expert intermediary in international affairs between subjects of his home country and of the country where he has his office. No doubt this latter activity can hardly be defined more narrowly and here much will depend upon the tact and wisdom of those involved especially in their dealings with the local bar.

6. This leads to the main questions: the forms of co-operation between local lawyers and their foreign colleagues, residing either in the same country or staying abroad. Leaving aside for the moment those countries where partnerships between members of the legal profession are not permitted at all, and assuming that special problems can only arise when the foreign colleague has not been admitted to the local bar, there are two separate questions here: is such a co-operation allowed at all and if so, only ad hoc or more closely, perhaps even in partnership?

The answer to the first question depends upon whom the national bar is prepared to treat on an equal basis as its own members. A certain minimum of requirements seems only justified. The same difficulties appear whenever a foreigner claims a right to professional secrecy.

Both parts of the last question can be answered in the affirmative: co-operation ad hoc with foreign colleagues has become almost a routine business in an increasing number of law offices all over the world, and partnerships between members of at least two different bars exist also, albeit that this does not imply that the partners are qualified in both countries, so that this happens even in countries, where the establishment of foreign law offices it not permitted. In such cases the partners have their own offices in their home countries which co-operate on a contractual basis.

7. Nothing contained in this report should be considered as more than a very tentative conclusion. It is for the meeting to decide, how the questions should be answered and which recommendations, if any, should be made to the national bar associations.

L. Hardenberg, Secretary

Amsterdam, May 1968

SUMMARY OF DISCUSSIONS

On July 12, 1968 the Advisory Committee on Professional Ethics and Professional Privilege organized an open meeting where the above printed interim report was discussed. The conferees showed an overwhelming interest. In fact the conference room could hardly contain them all, about eighty lawyers from very different countries.

The Chairman said that already during a preparatory meeting of the Committee it was felt that today's topics might easily lead to an even more general discussion of the position of the lawyers in the near future, which would be a very interesting topic for the 1970 Tokyo Conference to deal with.

Dr. Robert Briner (Switzerland) agreed and pointed out that the position of the lawyers in that country had already undergone considerable changes in their relations with banks, chartered accountants, trust companies and others. He foresaw the necessity of new adequate forms of co-operation.

This was also the view of Mr. John P. Bracken (USA), who strongly advocated consideration of this problems at Tokyo.

Mr. Richard P. Brown (USA) added the suggestion that the incorporation of law firms be considered too.

Mr. Dermot P. Shaw (Ireland) said that this might involve the alternation of existing statutes but was of the opinion that there was no reason why this should not be done if it was felt that it was an advantage to the legal profession and to the public to do so.

These views largely concurred with those of the Rapporteur, who said that also in the Netherlands the co-operation with other professions and the incorporation of a law firm were under discussion. The Rapporteur referred to the new French law on "Sociétés civiles professionelles" and recalled that during yesterday's meeting Sir Hilary Scott (England) had raised the very interesting question of the lawyers' ethical codes and professional rules as seen through the eyes of the monopolies commissions.

At the conclusion of the meeting, during which many other participants expressed their views, it was unanimously decided to recommend to the Council that the following topics which in several countries are already of an increasing practical importance, be investigated further, if possible in co-operation with the Union International des Avocats, and prepared for discussion in a general meeting at the Tokyo conference:

a) the forms of co-operation between lawyers and members of other professions;

b) the organization of a lawyer's practice in the form of a limited liability company;

c) the necessity – as a matter of public interest – to distinguish the ethical codes and professional rules from other "restrictive practices";

d) the position of lawyers in future years in general.

Several speakers emphasized the urgent need of their national organizations for ample information and if possible support and guidance from the IBA.

INTERNATIONAL LEGAL AID ASSOCIATION

COMPARATIVE STANDARDS FOR THE DETERMINATION OF ELIGIBILITY FOR LEGAL AID

Chairman: John S. Tennant, Esq.,
President, International Legal Aid Association (USA)
Secretary General: Sir Thomas Lund, C. B. E. (England)
Rapporteur: Frances Madeleine May, Solicitor (England)

INTRODUCTION

1. In 1966 the International Legal Aid Association published a Directory containing details of the Legal Aid and Advice plans in 357 countries, provinces, and states across the world. The Directory is a result of three years research by the I. L. A. A., which gathered the information from practising and academic lawyers, Law Societies, Bar Associations, and Embassies in the countries concerned. It is believed to be the first survey in this field since one undertaken by the League of Nations in 1922.

2. A study of the many Legal Aid plans summarized in the Directory discloses a noticeable variation in the standards applied to determine whether a person is entitled to Legal Aid. The financial limitations vary from a figure involving almost total destitution to sums of quite substantial amounts as regards both income and capital, e. g. a person with an annual income of up to £ 1,600 ($ 3,740) a year may be eligible for Legal Aid in proceedings in England and Wales, Scotland or Northern Ireland. It has accordingly been thought that it would be both interesting and instructive to analyse the eligibility standards applied.

3. The information contained in this report is based solely on the information contained in the International Legal Aid Directory, and a first supplement published in 1967.

4. Set out in the appendix to this report is an analysis of the Means Tests applied in 177 countries, provinces, and states to applications both for civil and criminal Legal Aid.

HOW FREQUENTLY IS A MEANS TEST APPLIED TO APPLICATIONS IN (a) CIVIL, AND (b) CRIMINAL PROCEEDINGS

(a) *Civil Proceedings*

5. Generally, Legal Aid is only granted in civil claims if the applicant can properly be considered "a poor person", that is to say of very modest means. However, in certain classes of cases (e. g. those concerning children and lunatics and workers' claims for compensation arising out of accidents at work), Legal Aid is granted without regard to the financial circumstances of the applicant in Bulgaria, the Central African Republic, Chad, Denmark, France, Gaboon, and Poland. In the South American Republics of Costa Rica and Venezuela, there is no means limit for minors, (i. e. those under the age of 21) and in the U. S. S. R., Czechoslovakia and New Hebrides, it would appear that Legal Aid is provided without reference being made to any applicant's financial means.

(b) *Criminal Proceedings*

6. In criminal cases, Legal Aid is again normally only available if the applicant can be considered "a poor person". However, in 48 countries, including almost all the South American countries, Legal Aid may be given without reference to the applicant's means in all classes of criminal cases. No means test is applied in Liechtenstein and Poland in cases in which a defence lawyer is compulsory under the national law; in Scotland, where the accused is in custody at the initial pleading diet; in the former French African colonies of Dahomey, Guinea, the Ivory Coast, Mauritania, Niger, Senegal and Togo for minors, those accused before the Assize Courts and those liable on conviction to transportation; in Israel for those under the age of 16, for those who are blind, deaf, or dumb, and for those accused of a capital offence or one punishable with a minimum sentence of ten years imprisonment; and in the United Arab Republic for those accused of a "felony".

7. In the few countries, in which a definite financial limit is imposed the limits as regards both capital and income, are normally so low as to involve indigence.

ARE THE CAPITAL AND INCOME LIMITS FIXED OR AT THE DISCRETION OF THE AUTHORITY CONCERNED?

8. In the majority of countries no definite means limits are set. It is left to the discretion of the competent authority to decide in each case whether the applicant's means are such that he or she should be

granted Legal Aid. The test generally applied is whether the applicant has sufficient means to enable him to obtain the services of a lawyer to represent him and to pay the other costs of the proceedings without detriment to the support of himself and his dependants. In some countries, an additional test applied is whether or not the applicant pays any local or national taxes.

9. In the Cayman Islands, Cyprus, Costa Rica, Ecuador, England and Wales, the Falkland Islands, Gibraltar, Guatemala, Guiana, Hungary, the Isle of Man, Mauritius, Malta, Northern Ireland, Roumania, Scotland, Singapore, Spain, South Georgia, Trinidad and Tobago and St. Vincent, the maximum limits are laid down as regards both income and capital, usually arrived at after deduction of such necessary expenses as those of maintenance of the applicant and his family, wearing apparel and tools of trade. The maximum limits vary between the more generous fixed in England and Wales, New Zealand, Northern Ireland, Scotland, a number of the Canadian Provinces, and of the States of Australia and USA, to the requirement that the applicant be destitute and without any income or capital in Roumania, the Philippines and Indonesia.

10. In a number of countries a limit on capital only is applied, although the applicant's income must normally be insufficient to enable him to be able to afford to pay the legal costs. These countries are the Bahamas, British Honduras, Fiji, Hong Kong, India, Jamaica, Malaysia, Malta, Puerto Rico, Rhodesia, Seychelles and Swaziland. This capital limit may, however, be as low as £ 6.5 s. Od. in British Honduras, or as high as 500 Malaysian dollars in Malaysia. In the Canadian Provinces of Nova Scotia, Ontario, and Manitoba, in Ceylon, the East Cameroons, many of the Indian States, the Netherlands Antilles, and many of the South American Republics, only an income limit is prescribed, but here again the applicant's capital must normally be insufficient to enable him to meet the legal costs.

11. In Cuba, Spain, the Australian State of New South Wales, and several of the South American Republics, the limits are fixed according to the national or state basic wage. In 1966, in New South Wales the limit was fixed at Australian £ 100 above the basic wage, while in Spain and the South American Republics the limit is based on the basic wage. In South Africa and certain of the Indian States, different limits are applied according to the tribe or caste of the applicant, and in some Indian States, this limit varies according to whether the applicant comes from the town or country. In Rhodesia, Malaysia, and Mauritius the limits vary according to the Court before which the proceedings are to be heard, while in the Netherland's Antilles, the income limit is considerably higher for cases concerning a contract of employment as well as for females in matrimonial cases. In

contrast, in Swaziland, a lower capital limit is fixed for matrimonial cases.

WHAT DEDUCTIONS ARE USUALLY PERMITTED BEFORE CAPITAL AND INCOME ARE ASSESSED?

12. The usual deductions permitted are the necessary expenses of the applicant and his dependants, wearing apparel, household furniture, and tools of trade. In some cases a specific sum is deductable for each dependant and in Singapore a set sum of 1000 Malaysian dollars is deductable for living expenses and 500 dollars for rent, before calculating the maximum allowable income of 3 500 dollars. The subject matter of the proceedings is also generally excluded in assessing the capital. Except in matrimonial cases, an applicant's income and capital normally must include the income and capital of the spouse.

13. In England and Wales, New Zealand, the Australian State of New South Wales, Northern Ireland and Scotland, the value of the applicant's house is excluded up to the value of £ 3 000 after deducting any mortgage. The deductions and allowances which are made from the gross income, which include allowances for rent, rates, income tax, and other outgoings, in England and Wales, Northern Ireland, and Scotland are such that persons with an annual income of £ 1 600 may be eligible for Legal Aid in proceedings.

WHAT AUTHORITY IS RESPONSIBLE FOR ASSESSING THE APPLICANT'S CAPITAL AND INCOME?

14. When Legal Aid is provided by the State it is usually for the judge before whom the proceedings are to be heard, or some court official or official in the Government Office responsible for the administration of the Legal Aid Plan to decide whether an applicant's financial position is such as to entitle him to Legal Aid. In countries where a professional organization administers the Legal Aid plan, either with voluntary funds or with financial assistance from the State, it is normally left to the committee of the Bar Association or Law Society to determine the applicant's financial standing. In yet other countries the responsibility lies with the Income Tax Office or the Municipal Authority in the applicant's place of residence, or some Government Department responsible for the distribution of Government funds to persons in need.

15. If the assessment of the applicant's capital and income is left to some authority or committee other than the Court or professional organization responsible for the administration of the Legal Aid plan, that authority is usually required to make a full report of their findings either orally or in writing to the responsible Court or organization to whom is left the ultimate decision whether or not to grant Legal Aid.

WHAT ARE THE REQUIREMENTS AS TO PROOF OF LACK OF MEANS?

16. Normally the applicant must state his financial position, liabilities, number of dependants etc., usually in the form of an oral or written statement to the court or other authority responsible for determining his means. In many cases, he will be required to swear an affidavit as to his means and in Rhodesia he is required to produce supporting affidavits of two householders. The applicant's written statement must normally be supported by one or more of the following documents: —

a) A certificate from the Income Tax Authority showing amount of tax paid.

b) A certificate from the Municipal Authorities in the applicant's place of residence, or from a Government Office responsible for distributing Government funds to persons in need.

c) A certificate from the applicant's employer showing the amount of salary paid.

IS THE APPLICANT REQUIRED TO MAKE ANY CONTRIBUTION TOWARDS THE COST OF THE PROCEEDINGS?

17. The financial aid provided under Legal Aid plans varies so greatly from country to country that without a very detailed study it is impossible to state accurately the degree of contribution the applicant has to make in each country towards his legal costs. In almost all countries, the grant of Legal Aid covers court fees but often other disbursements, such as stamp duties, fees of expert witnesses and witnesses' expenses are not included, nor are the fees of the lawyer who represents the applicant. In the majority of countries, however, an assisted person is not required to make any contribution towards the cost of the court proceedings, or his lawyer's fees. In other countries the assisted person may be required to make a contribution

which is assessed either by the court or the legal profession according to a fixed scale or determined solely according to the individual financial circumstances of the assisted person. In criminal cases in Denmark, Hungary and Sweden the assisted person is required to repay all costs incurred in the proceedings, including his lawyer's fees, if he is found guilty of the crime of which he is accused. So far as it has been possible to ascertain in civil proceedings in almost every country an assisted person will be required to repay all fees paid out on his behalf out of monies recovered in the proceedings. In addition, in a number of countries, an assisted person will be required to pay all such fees at any time in the future if there is an improvement in his financial circumstances. It is not known whether there exists any system for following up such cases where payment of fees has been "suspended" and for ascertaining whether the assisted person improves his financial circumstances. Nor does there appear to be any legal definition of the expression „improvement of financial circumstances" so as to determine whether and, if so, when a person's means have increased to such an extent as to make him liable to pay the fees incurred.

CONCLUSIONS

18. A means test is imposed in every country other than the U. S. S. R., Czechoslovakia and New Hebrides, except that in certain other countries there is no means test in criminal proceedings.

19. In England and Wales, New Zealand, Northern Ireland, Scotland and a number of the Canadian Provinces and of the States of Australia and the USA, the financial limits are so generous that a person with quite substantial capital and income may be eligible for Legal Aid, although it is likely that he may be required to make a contribution towards the cost of the proceedings. In the majority of other countries, however, the limits are at the discretion of the court or authority concerned, and are so low as to be equivalent to indigence. It follows therefore that in the countries named above a large proportion of the population may be eligible for Legal Aid whereas in the majority of other countries, the advantages of Legal Aid are confined to the truly indigent or pauper.

20. Economically many countries would appear to be in a position to provide a comprehensive Legal Aid system, with the aid of contributions from assisted persons on a graduated scale, but in far too many countries, assistance is denied to all but the destitute.

21. It may be that it is the duty of the legal profession to embue their governments with a far greater sense of urgency to consider these problems than they have hitherto.

APPENDIX

ADEN

Civil	No specific limit but applicant must show inability to pay Court fees.
Criminal	No means limit.

AFGHANISTAN

Civil	No specific limit but applicant must show he is a pauper.
Criminal	Same as civil.

ANGOLA

Civil	No specific limit but applicant must show insufficient means to pay legal costs.
Criminal	Same as civil.

ANTIGUA

Civil	No provisions.
Criminal	No specific limit but applicant must show insufficient means to pay legal costs.

ARGENTINA

Civil	No specific limit but applicant's income must be barely sufficient to maintain himself and dependents.
Criminal	Same as civil.

AUSTRALIA, The States of:

NEW SOUTH WALES

Civil	Capital — A£ 200 excluding personal belongings, tools of trade and a A£ 3,000 equity in a house. Income — A£ 100 above State basic wage (A£ 921 in 1966) + A£ 150 for each dependent.
Criminal	No specific limit but applicant must be unable to pay legal costs.

NORTHERN TERRITORIES

Civil	No provisions.
Criminal	No specific limit but applicant must show insufficient means to pay legal costs.

SOUTH AUSTRALIA

Civil	No specific limit but must show insufficient means to pay legal costs. Proof — State dec.
Criminal	Same as civil.

TASMANIA

Civil	No specific limit but applicant must show insufficient means to pay legal costs.
Criminal	Same as civil.

WESTERN AUSTRALIA

Civil	No specific limit but applicant must show insufficient means to pay legal costs.
Criminal	Same as civil.

VICTORIA

Civil	*State Scheme* — Capital and Income limit of A£ 250. *Professions' Scheme* — no specific limit but applicant must show insufficient means to pay legal costs.
Criminal	Same as civil.

AUSTRIA

Civil	No specific limit but applicant must show insufficient means to pay legal costs without detriment to his own and independent means of subsidence.
Criminal	Same as civil.

BAHAMAS

Civil	Capital limit of £100 excluding sum in dispute. No income limit but Government must be satisfied of need for legal aid.
Criminal	Same as civil.

BAHRAIN, Qatas and Trucial States

Civil	No provisions.
Criminal	No specific limit. Grant in discretion of Court.

BARBADOS

Civil	No provisions.
Criminal	No specific limit but applicant must show insufficient means to pay legal costs.

BARBUDA

Civil	No provisions.
Criminal	No specific limit but applicant must show insufficient means to pay legal costs.

BELGIUM

Civil	No specific limit. Grant in discretion of Court of 'Bureau de Consultation Gratuite'.
Criminal	Same as civil.

BERMUDA

Civil	No provisions.
Criminal	No specific limit but applicant must show insufficient means to pay legal costs.

BOLIVIA

Civil	No specific limit but applicant must show insufficient means to pay legal costs.
Criminal	No means limit.

BOTSWANA

Civil	No provisions.
Criminal	No specific limit but applicant must show insufficient means to pay legal costs.

BRAZIL

Civil	No specific limit but applicant must show insufficient means to pay legal costs.
Criminal	Same as civil.

BRITISH HONDURAS

Civil Capital limit of £6. 5. Od. No income limit but applicant must show insufficient means to pay legal costs.

Criminal No specific limit but applicant must show insufficient means to pay legal costs.

BRITISH SOLOMON ISLANDS PROTECTORATE

Civil No provisions.

Criminal No means limit.

BRITISH VIRGIN ISLANDS

Civil No provisions.

Criminal No means limit. Grant in discretion of Court.

BRUNEI

Civil No provisions.

Criminal No means limit.

BULGARIA

Civil No specific limit but applicant must prove 'low Income'. No means limit in some classes of proceedings.

Criminal No specific limit but applicant must prove 'low Income'.

BURMA

Civil No provisions.

Criminal No means limit.

BURUNDI

Civil No specific limit. Grant in discretion of Court President or Public Prosecutor.

Criminal Same as civil.

CAMBODIA

Civil No specific limit but applicant must show insufficient means to pay legal costs.

Criminal No means limit.

EAST CAMEROUN

Civil No Capital limit. Income limit usually £250 p. a. single person, £500 p.ba. married person.

Criminal No means limit.

WEST CAMEROUN

Civil No provisions.

Criminal No means limit.

CANADA, The Provinces of:

ALBERTA

Civil No specific limit but applicant to show indigence.

Criminal Applicant must show insufficient capital to pay legal costs. Income limit usually $2,000 p. a. single person; $2,500 p. a. married person plus $300 each dependent.

BRITISH COLUMBIA

Civil	No specific limit and each application considered on own merit.
Criminal	Same as civil.

MANITOBA

Civil	No specific capital limit but applicant must not own property alone or jointly. Income limit flexible of $ 125 per month single man; $ 150 per month married man.
Criminal	Same as civil.

NOVA SCOTIA

Civil	No specific limit on capital. Usual income limit of $ 2000 — $ 3000 per annum.
Criminal	Same as civil.

ONTARIO

Civil	No specific limit on Capital. Income limit of $ 1,700 p. a. single person; $ 2,500 p. a. married person plus $ 300 for each dependent.
Criminal	Same as civil.

SASKATCHEWAN

Civil	No organized plan.
Criminal	Magistrates Courts — each Local Bar Association has own regulations. High Court — No specific limit but applicant must show insufficient means to pay legal costs.

THE YUKON AND NORTHWEST TERRITORIES

Civil	No provisions.
Criminal	No specific limit but applicant must show insufficient means to pay legal costs.

CAYMAN ISLANDS

Civil	Limit — Capital £ 300; Income — £ 4 per week.
Criminal	Same as civil.

CENTRAL AFRICAN REPUBLIC

Civil	No specific limit but applicant must show he pays no taxes and has insufficient means to pay legal costs. In certain cases legal aid available without means test.
Criminal	No means limit.

CEYLON

Civil	No specific capital limit, but applicant must own nothing to make a grant unreasonable. Income limit — gross income of applicant and family not exceeding Rs. 150/ — per month.
Criminal	No means limit.

CHAD

Civil	No specific limit but applicant must show he pays no taxes and has insufficient means to pay legal costs. In certain cases legal aid available without means test.
Criminal	No means limit.

CHANNEL ISLANDS JERSEY

Civil No specific limit. Grant at discretion of Batonnier.

Criminal Same as civil.

CHILE

Civil No specific limit but applicant must show he is a 'poor person'.

Criminal Same as civil.

REPUBLIC OF CHINA (Taiwan)

Civil No specific limit but applicant must show insufficient means to pay legal costs.

Criminal Same as civil.

COLUMBIA

Civil No specific limit but applicant must prove income is scarcely sufficient to maintain himself and his family.

Criminal No means limit.

THE CONGO

Civil No specific limit but applicant must show he pays no taxes.

Criminal No means limit.

COSTA RICA

Civil Minors (under 21 years) — No means limit. Others — must obtain declaration of Poverty from Court showing capital and income less than 250 C. p. a.

Criminal Same as civil.

CUBA

Civil Applicant must obtain declaration of poverty from Court showing income not exceeding twice the wages of day labourer in his place of residence or no income.

Criminal No means limit.

CYPRUS

Civil Capital — £ 10, Income — £ 10/ — per week.

Criminal Same as civil.

CZECHOSLOVAKIA

Civil No means limit.

Criminal No means limit.

DAHOMEY

Civil No specific limit but applicant must show insufficient means to pay legal costs.

Criminal Same as civil but no means limit for minors and those accused in Assize Courts or liable to transportation.

DENMARK

Civil Generally no specific limit but applicant's income should not exceed a worker's (e. g. 20,000 — 25,000 dakr) and he should have no liquid capital.

Criminal No means limit.

DOMINICA

Civil No provisions.

Criminal No means limit.

DOMINICAN REPUBLIC

Civil No specific limit but applicant must show income scarcely sufficient to maintain himself and his family.

Criminal Same as civil.

ECUADOR

Civil Capital — no real estate over 1,000 sucres in value. Income — not exceeding 500 sucres p. a.

Criminal Same as civil.

ENGLAND AND WALES

Civil Legal Aid for Proceedings — Disposable Capital of £ 500. Disposable income under £ 700 p. a. Legal Aid for a Claim — Disposable income under £ 325 p. a.

Criminal No specific limit but applicant must show insufficient means to pay whole of legal costs.

FALKLAND ISLANDS

Civil Capital — £ 50, income — over £ 2 per week.

Criminal Same as civil.

FIJI

Civil Capital — £ 20, Income — no specific limit.

Criminal No specific limit. Grant in discretion of Court or Attorney-General but always given for capital offences.

FINLAND

Civil No specific limit but applicant required to show insufficient means to pay legal costs.

Criminal Same as civil.

FRANCE

Civil No specific limit but applicant must show he pays no taxes and has insufficient means to pay legal costs. No means limit in certain exceptional cases.

Criminal No means limit.

GABOON

Civil No specific limit but applicant must show he pays no taxes and has insufficient means to pay legal costs. No means limit in certain exceptional cases.

Criminal No means limit.

GAMBIA

Civil No provisions.

Criminal No specific limits. Grant in discretion of Court.

FEDERAL REPUBLIC OF GERMANY

Civil No specific limit but applicant must show insufficient means to pay legal costs.

Criminal No means limit.

GHANA

Civil	No provisions.
Criminal	No specific limit but applicant must show insufficient means to pay legal costs.

GIBRALTAR

Civil	Capital — £200, Income — £4. 1. 6d.
Criminal	No specific limit but applicant must show insufficient means to pay legal costs.

GILBERT AND ELLICE ISLANDS COLONY

Civil	No provisions.
Criminal	No specific limit but applicant must show insufficient means to pay legal costs without hardship.

GREECE

Civil	No specific limit but aid only available to truly indigent.
Criminal	Same as civil.

GREENLAND

Civil	No organized plan.
Criminal	No means limit.

GRENADA

Civil	No provisions.
Criminal	No specific limit but applicant must show insufficient means to pay legal costs.

GUATEMALA

Civil	Real property must not exceed 500 Kuetzales. Daily income must not exceed 1 Kuetzale.
Criminal	Same as civil.

GUINEA

Civil	No specific limit but applicant must show insufficient means to pay legal costs.
Criminal	Same as civil but no means limit for minors or accused in Assize Court or liable to transportation.

BRITISH GUIANA

Civil	$1.25 (B. W. I.) Capital. $5 (B. W. I.) per week Income.
Criminal	Same as civil.

HAITI

Civil	No provisions.
Criminal	No means limit.

HONDURAS

Civil	No specific limit but applicant must show he is a 'poor person'.
Criminal	Same as civil.

HONG KONG

Civil	Not more than H. K. 500 worth of property. Income — no specific limit.
Criminal	No specific limit but applicant must show insufficient means to pay legal costs.

HUNGARY

Civil No Capital other than household furniture and wearing apparel. Income limit of $ 20 per month.

Criminal No means limit.

ICELAND

Civil No specific limit but applicant must show insufficient means to pay legal costs.

Criminal No means limit.

INDIA GENERAL PROVISIONS

Civil No property worth Rs. 100 other than necessary wearing apparel or unable to pay legal costs.

Criminal No specific limit but applicant must show insufficient means to pay legal costs.

STATES OF: ANDHRA PRADESH

Civil Capital — no specific limit. Income — Rs. 1,500 in the mofussil or Rs. 2000 in the twin cities of Hyderabad and Secunderabad.

Criminal Same as civil.

BIHAR

Civil Applicant must show he is a pauper and possesses less than 10 acres of cultivable land.

Criminal Same as civil.

GUJARAT

Civil No specific limit but applicant must show insufficient means to pay legal costs.

Criminal Scheduled Castes/Scheduled Tribes — no limit. Accused persons in Sessions Cases — Income of less than Rs. 1800/ — p. a. Accused of Capital Offence applicant must show insufficient means to pay legal costs.

KERALA

Civil Capital — no specific limit. Income — Rs. 100 per month.

Criminal Same as civil.

MAHARASHTRA

Civil Capital — no specific limit. Income Rs. 1,800/ — p. a.

Criminal Capital — no specific limit. Income — Rs. 1,800/ — p. a. in mofussil and in respect of Backward Classes; Rs. 2,500/ — p. a. in Greater Bombay Area.

MYSORE

Civil No provisions.

Criminal No specific limit but applicant must show insufficient means to pay legal costs.

THE PUNJAB

Civil Capital — no specific limit. Income — usually under Rs. 100 per month.

Civil No organized plan.

WEST BENGAL

Civil	Capital — no specific limit. Income — Rs. 250 per month.
Criminal	Same as civil.

INDONESIA

Civil	Income — no income whatsoever. Capital — no specific limit.
Criminal	No means limit.

IRAN

Civil	No specific limit but applicant must show insufficient means to pay legal costs.
Criminal	No means limit.

IRAQ

Civil	No specific limit but applicant must show insufficient means to pay legal costs.
Criminal	No means limit.

REPUBLIC OF IRELAND

Civil	No specific limit but applicant must show insufficient means to pay legal costs.
Criminal	No means limit.

ISRAEL

Civil	No specific limit but applicant must show insufficient means to pay legal costs.
Criminal	Same as civil. No means limit for accused charged with capital offence or one punishable by ten years imprisonment; an accused under 16 years or an accused who is blind, deaf and dumb.

ITALY

Civil	No specific limit but applicant must show insufficient means to pay legal costs.
Criminal	Same as civil.

THE IVORY COAST

Civil	No specific limit but applicant must show insufficient means to pay legal costs.
Criminal	Same as civil. No means limit for accused in Assize Courts, minors and accused liable to transportation.

JAMAICA

Civil	Capital — £25. Income — no specific limit. Grant in discretion of Court.
Criminal	Insufficient means to pay legal costs.

JAPAN

Civil	No specific limit but applicant must show insufficient means to pay legal costs.
Criminal	No means limit.

JORDAN

Civil	No provisions.
Criminal	No specific limit but applicant must show insufficient means to pay legal costs.

KOREA

Civil No provisions.

Criminal Same as civil.

LAOS

Civil No provisions.

Criminal No means limit.

LEBANON

Civil No provisions.

Criminal Same as civil.

LESOTHO

Civil No provisions.

Criminal No specific limit but applicant must show insufficient means to pay legal costs.

LIBERIA

Civil No provisions.

Criminal No specific limit but applicant must show insufficient means to pay legal costs.

LIBYA

Civil No provisions.

Criminal Same as civil.

LIECHTENSTEIN

Civil No provisions.

Criminal Same as civil. No means limit where minimum sentence for crime is 5 years imprisonment.

LUXEMBOURG

Civil No specific limits. Grant in discretion of Court.

Criminal Same as civil.

MADAGASCAR

Civil No specific limits. Applicant may possess moderate means.

Criminal Same as civil.

MALAYSIA

Civil High Court — no property of value exceeding $ 500 Malayan currency. Lower Courts — applicant must show insufficient means to pay Court fees.

Criminal No means limit.

MALAWI

Civil No provisions.

Criminal Same as civil.

MALI

Civil No specific limit. Grant in discretion of Court.

Criminal No means limit.

MALTA G. C.

Civil Capital £25. Income — no specific limit.

Criminal No means limit.

ISLE OF MAN

Civil Discretionary limit of Capital — £100. Income — £8 per week.

Criminal No specific limit. Grant in discretion of Court.

MARTINIQUE

Civil No specific limit but applicant must show he pays no taxes and has no income.

Criminal No means limit.

MAURITANIA

Civil No specific limit but applicant must show insufficient means to pay legal costs.

Criminal Same as civil. No means limit for accused in Assize Court, Minors and accuseds liable to transportation.

MAURITIUS

Civil Applicant must not possess more than Rs. 300 — Supreme Court, Rs. 150 — District Court.

Criminal Applicant must not possess more than Rs. 300 unless an Appeal Case where limit is — Rs. 400.

MEXICO

Civil Applicant must not possess more than Rs. 300 — Supreme Court, Rs. 150 — District Court.

Criminal Same as civil.

MONTSERRAT

Civil No provisions.

Criminal Same as civil.

MOROCCO

Civil Applicant must not possess more than Rs. 300 — Supreme Court, Rs. 150 — District Court.

Criminal Same as civil.

MOZAMBIQUE

Civil Applicant must not possess more than Rs. 300 — Supreme Court, Rs. 150 — District Court.

Criminal Same as civil.

NEPAL

Civil Applicant must not possess more than Rs. 300 — Supreme Court, Rs. 150 — District Court.

Criminal Same as civil.

NETHERLANDS

Civil Applicant must not possess more than Rs. 300 — Supreme Court, Rs. 150 — District Court.

Criminal Same as civil.

NETHERLANDS ANTILLES

Civil Usual limits Capital — no specific limit. Income — fls. 2,000 p. a. for single person; fls. 2,600 for married person; fls. 7,500 for case concerning a contract of employment; fls. 10,000 for female applicant in matrimonial case.

Criminal Usual limits Capital — no specific limit. Income — fls. 2,000 p. a. for single person; fls. 2,600 for married person.

NEW HEBRIDES

Civil No means limit.

Criminal No means limit.

NEW ZEALAND

Civil Capital — £ 50, Income — applicant must show insufficient means to pay legal costs.

Criminal Same as civil but no capital limit.

NICARAGUA

Civil Capital — no specific limit. Income — daily income of less than 500 pesos.

Criminal No means limit.

NIGER

Civil Applicant must not possess more than Rs. 300 — Supreme Court, Rs. 150 — District Court.

Criminal Same as civil. No means limit for accused in Assize Court, Minors and accuseds liable to transportation.

NIGERIA

Civil No specific limit but applicant must show he is a pauper and has insufficient means to pay legal costs.

Criminal No means limit.

NORTHERN IRELAND

Civil Usually 'disposable' Capital of £ 500. 'Disposable' Aid Income — excluding applicant's house unless value, after deducting mortgage, exceeds £ 3,000 — for proceedings — £ 700 p. a. Aid for a claim — £ 325 p. a.

Criminal No specific limit but applicant must show insufficient means to pay legal costs.

NORWAY

Civil No specific limit but applicant must show insufficient means to pay legal costs.

Criminal No means limit.

PAKISTAN

Civil No specific limit but applicant must show insufficient means to pay legal costs.

Criminal Same as civil.

PANAMA

Civil Capital — no specific limit. Income — less than 200 balboas p. a.

Criminal Same as civil.

PAPUA AND NEW GUINEA

Civil	No specific limit but applicant must show insufficient means to pay legal costs.
Criminal	Same as civil.

PARAGUAY

Civil	No specific limit but applicant must show insufficient means to pay legal costs.
Criminal	No means limit.

PERU

Civil	Capital — applicant must show insufficient means to pay legal costs. Income — £ 50 p. a.
Criminal	Same as civil.

PHILIPPINES

Civil	Applicant must be without means.
Criminal	No means limit.

POLAND

Civil	No specific limit but applicant must show insufficient means to pay legal costs. No means limit in certain exceptional cases.
Criminal	Same as civil.

PORTUGAL AND PORTUGUESE TERRITORIES

Civil	No specific limit but applicant must show insufficient means to pay legal costs.
Criminal	Same as civil.

PUERTO RICO

Civil	Capital $ 305,100.00. Income — no specific limit.
Criminal	No specific limit but applicant must show insufficient means to pay legal costs.

REUNION

Civil	No specific limits. Applicant to show insufficient means to pay legal costs.
Criminal	Same as civil.

RHODESIA

Civil	No specific limits; applicant to show insufficient means to pay legal costs. High Court limit on capital — £ 50.
Criminal	No specific limits, applicant to show insufficient means to pay the legal costs.

ROUMANIA

Civil	Capital assets or income.
Criminal	Same as civil.

ST. KITTS-NEVIS-ANQUILLA (THE LEEWARD ISLANDS)

Civil	No provisions.
Criminal	No specific limits; applicant to show insufficient means to pay legal costs.

ST. LUCIA (WINDWARD ISLANDS)

Civil	No provisions.
Criminal	There is no means limit.

ST. VINCENT (WINDWARD ISLANDS)

Civil	Capital and Income limit of £5 excluding wearing apparel and the subject matter of the proceedings.
Criminal	No specific limits; applicant to show insufficient means to pay legal costs. Legal Aid is available irrespective of means to an accused charged with the crime of murder.

EL SALVADOR

Civil	Capital — no specific limit. Yearly income must not exceed 400 pesos.
Criminal	There is no means limit.

SAN MARINO

Civil	There is no specific limit. Applicant must show he is unable to pay the legal costs.
Criminal	Same as civil.

SCOTLAND

Civil	'Disposable' capital — £500 plus £75 for a first dependent, £50 for a second dependent and £25 for each further dependent. 'Disposable' income — £700 per annum.
Criminal	There is no means limit if accused in custody at initial pleading diet. If not in custody the grant in discretion of the Court.

SENEGAL

Civil	No specific limit; applicant to show insufficient means to pay legal costs.
Criminal	No specific limits; applicant to show insufficient means to pay legal costs. No means limit for an Accused in Assize Courts or Liable to transportation or Minors.

SEYCHELLES

Civil	Capital — Rs. 300 (£22.10 s) excluding applicant's wearing apparel. Income — no specific limit.
Criminal	No means limit.

SINGAPORE

Civil	Capital — $3500/ — (Malayan) per annum including wearing apparel, applicant's tools of trade, dwelling house and furniture. Income — $3000/ — per annum deducting $200 for each dependant, $1000 for the living expenses of the applicant and $500 for rent.
Criminal	There is no means limit.

SOUTH AFRICA

Civil There are specific limits fixed for each Magisterial District, regard being had to local conditions. Example of income limits fixed in Durban (Province of Natal) are:
White persons: Single person R. 50 per month.
Married R. 100 per month, plus R. 10 per child.
Coloured and Asiatic Persons: Single person R. 30 per month.
Married person R. 50 per month plus R. 8 per child.
Bantu Persons: Single person R. 20 per month.
Married person R. 30 per month plus R. 6 per child.

Criminal Same as civil.

SOUTH GEORGIA

Civil Capital — £ 50. Income — over £ 2 per week.

Criminal Same as civil.

SPAIN

Civil Capital — twice the average minimum wage of 120 ptas per day. Income — 120 ptas per day.

Criminal Same as civil.

SUDAN

Civil No provisions.

Criminal Capital — no specific limit; applicant to show insufficient means to pay legal costs.

SWAZILAND

Civil Capital — not exceeding £ 25 excluding household goods, wearing apparel and tools of trade. In matrimonial cases the limit is £ 15.

Criminal There is no means limit.

SWEDEN

Civil No specific limit; applicant to show insufficient means to pay legal costs.

Criminal There is no means limit.

SWITZERLAND

Civil There are no specific limits but applicant must show that he cannot pay legal costs and that his income and capital do not exceed an amount necessary to support himself and his dependents.

Criminal No specific limits; applicant to show insufficient means to pay legal costs.

SYRIA

Civil No specific limit; applicant to show insufficient means to pay legal costs.

Criminal Same as civil.

TANZANIA

Civil No specific limit; applicant to show insufficient means to pay legal costs.

Criminal No provisions.

THAILAND

Civil	No specific limit; applicant to show insufficient means to pay legal costs.
Criminal	There is no means limit. The only requirement is that the accused shall be unrepresented by a lawyer.

TOGO

Civil	No specific limit; applicant to show insufficient means to pay legal costs.
Criminal	No specific limits; applicant to show insufficient means to pay legal costs. No means limit for accused before the Assize Court, those accused of a crime, the maximum penalty for which is life imprisonment or minors.

TRINIDAD AND TOBAGO

Civil	Capital — £ 50 ($ 240 T & T currency) Income — £ 2.10 s ($ 12 T & T currency) per week from all sources.
Criminal	There is no means limit.

TUNISIA

Civil	There are no specific limits. The grant is in the discretion of the Breau d'Assistance Judiciaire.
Criminal	There is no means limit.

TURKEY

Civil	No specific limit; applicant to show insufficient means to pay legal costs.
Criminal	Same as civil.

UGANDA

Civil	No specific limit; applicant to show insufficient means to pay legal costs.
Criminal	There is no means limit.

U. S. S. R.

Civil	There is no means limit.
Criminal	There is no means limit.

UNITED ARAB REPUBLIC

Civil	No specific limit; applicant to show insufficient means to pay legal costs.
Criminal	No specific limits. Applicant to prove inability to pay legal costs. No means limit where accused is charged with having committed a felony.

UNITED STATES OF AMERICA

Civil	Criminal legal aid is provided by numerous State and private organizations. Each of these organizations determines the means limits to be applied and the practice therefore varies considerably as between legal aid offices in the same State and even within the same city.

URUGUAY

Civil	No specific limit; applicant to show insufficient means to pay legal costs.
Criminal	There is no means limit.

VENEZUELA

Civil	There are no specific limits but an applicant must obtain a declaration of poverty from the Court showing he is unable to pay the legal costs. In workmen's compensation cases the applicant will be considered poor if his wages do not exceed 20 bolivares. No means limit for minors.
Criminal	There is no means limit.

VIETNAM

Civil	No specific limit; applicant to show insufficient means to pay legal costs.
Criminal	Same as civil.

YUGOSLAVIA

Civil	No specific limit but applicant to show insufficient means to pay the legal costs 'without damage to the necessary support of himself and family'.
Criminal	Same as civil.

REPORT OF THE TREASURER

At the Council Meeting in Amsterdam April 22-23, 1967 it was decided for practical reasons to change the International Bar Association's Fiscal year to run from October 1 to September 30, instead of the Calendar year.

Accordingly, due to the change of Fiscal year, the Report of the Association's Certified Public Accountant printed herein covers the first nine months of 1967 and is submitted as the Report of the Treasurer.

To the Council, International Bar Association:

We have made an examination, as outlined below, of the statement of cash receipts and disbursements of the New York bank accounts of the INTERNATIONAL BAR ASSOCIATION for the nine months ended September 30, 1967. Our examination was limited to the cash transactions which were handled in New York and recorded in the Association's New York cash records. We did not make an examination of receipts and disbursements passing through the books of The Law Society on behalf of the Association's Treasurer in London, England, which have been reflected in the statement of the New York current (commercial) account. These transactions for the nine months ended September 30, 1967 were certified as correct by the Assistant Secretary, Finance, of The Law Society, and are summarized below:

Receipts	$ 1,286.28
Disbursements	4,903.01
Net disbursements	$ 3,616.73

We traced the totals of collections recorded in the Association's cash records to deposits in the New York current (commercial) account and examined paid checks, bank advices, and vouchers in substantiation of the recorded disbursements. Interest earned on reserve (savings) accounts was agreed with related deposits in such accounts. The amounts on deposit in the New York bank accounts at the beginning and end of the period were confirmed directly to us by the depositaries and were reconciled with the balances or book overdraft shown in the Association's records.

As we did not examine the records pertaining to the cash receipts and disbursements reported by the Treasurer in London, England, we can form no opinion regarding such transactions. In other respects, in our opinion, the afore-mentioned statement fairly summarizes the recorded cash receipts and disbursements of the New York bank accounts of the International Bar Association for the nine months ended September 30, 1967 on a basis consistent with that of the preceding year.

We transcribed the information in the accompanying statement of cash receipts and disbursements of the Amsterdam and Hamburg bank accounts of the Association, but we did not verify the information shown. Accordingly, our opinion expressed above is not applicable to this statement.

LYBRAND, ROSS BROS. & MONTGOMERY

New York, October 18, 1967.

INTERNATIONAL BAR ASSOCIATION

STATEMENT of CASH RECEIPTS and DISBURSEMENTS
NEW YORK BANK ACCOUNTS

for the nine monts endet September 30, 1967

CURRENT (Commercial) ACCOUNT:

	Year 1967 Budget	Nine Months Ended September 30, 1967 Budget	Nine Months Ended September 30, 1967 Actual
Operations other than conferences:			
Receipts:			
Member organizations' dues . . .	$ 9,000.00	$ 8,000.00	$ 7,395.55
Patrons' and subscribers' contributions	24,000.00	22,500.00	24,985.89
Subscribing libraries			75.00
Miscellaneous	100.00	75.00	152.35
	$ 33,000.00	$ 30,575.00	$ 32,608.79
Disbursements:			
Headquarters:			
Office facilities	$ 5,000.00	$ 3,750.00	$ 4,005.28
Salaries and payroll taxes . . .	25,000.00	18,750.00	20,646.28
Stationery and supplies	1,000.00	750.00	1,638.53
Telephone, cables and postage .	1,700.00	1,225.00	1,031.62
Services, repairs, rentals, etc. .	1,000.00	750.00	660.00
Audit of accounts	750.00	750.00	800.00
Equipment	800.00	600.00	774.00
Miscellaneous	1,000.00	750.00	66.25
Lausanne Conference book . . .	7,500.00		90.00
International Bar News	7,000.00	3,500.00	3,324.99
Chairman of Association	350.00	300.00	100.00
Treasurer and Assistant Treasurer	1,000.00	750.00	284.26
Assistant Secretaries General . .	500.00	375.00	
Membership Committee	25.00		
Council of Association and contingencies	3,500.00	3,000.00	2,301.57
	$ 56,125.00	$ 35,250.00	$ 35,722.78
Excess of disbursements over receipts from operations other than conferences			$ 3,113.99

STATEMENT of CASH RECEIPTS and DISBURSEMENTS
NEW YORK BANK ACCOUNTS, Continued

	Year 1967 Budget	Nine Months Ended September 30, 1967 Budget	Nine Months Ended September 30, 1967 Actual
Conferences:			
Receipts, Lausanne Conference . . .	$ 2,100.00	$ 2,100.00	$ 2,570.88
Disbursements:			
Dublin Conference	6,500.00	1,000.00	523.84
Lausanne Conference			807.93
	$ 6,500.00	$ 1,000.00	$ 1,331.77
Excess of receipts over disbursements from conferences . . .			$ 1,239.11
Net excess of disbursements over receipts			$ 1,874.88
Transfers from reserve (savings) account			35,500.00
			$ 33,625.12
Book overdraft, January 1, 1967 . . .			11,815.06
Balance on deposit, September 30, 1967			$ 21,810.06

RESERVE (Savings) ACCOUNTS:

Balance on deposit, January 1, 1967	$ 76,163.86
Interest earned	2,589.09
	$ 78,752.95
Transfers to New York current (commercial) account	35,500.00
Balance on deposit, September 30, 1967	$ 43,252.95

STATEMENT of CASH RECEIPTS and DISBURSEMENTS
AMSTERDAM and HAMBURG BANK ACCOUNTS

for the nine months ended September 30, 1967

Firma E. Lemberger, Amsterdam, the Netherlands:		
Balance on deposit, January 1, 1967		Fl. 4.207,00
Receipts from Association's book publisher in The Hague, representing sales of publications in 1965 and 1966		2.669,50
		Fl. 6.876,50
Disbursements:		
Council and contingencies	Fl. 1.916,35	
Bank charges	5,15	1.921,50
Balance on deposit, September 30, 1967 .		Fl. 4.955,00
Vereinsbank, Hamburg, Germany:		
Balance on deposit, January 1, 1967		DM 3.335,91
Receipts from subscribers' contributions . . .		558,13
		DM 3.894,04
Disbursements:		
Reprints of conference books	DM 232,85	
Bank charges	3,60	236,45
Balance on deposit, September 30, 1967 .		DM 3.657,59

Note: The above statement is unaudited. See comment in auditors' report.

INDEX TO TOPICS DISCUSSED AT DUBLIN AND PREVIOUS CONFERENCES

Many of the papers written on the topics listed below will be found in the Reports published by the International Bar Association after each Conference. The Summary of the Second Conference at The Hague is a small brochure (now out of print); but beginning with the "Third Conference Report (London, July 1950)", books have been published containing selected papers and committee reports; and beginning with the "Seventh Conference Report (Cologne, 1958)", the books have included in their original language all official national papers and all combined reports. The books may be ordered from the International Bar Association's publisher at The Hague, Martinus Nijhoff; and the prices range from 22.50 guilders to 28.50 guilders. In addition, separate publication has been made of the papers prepared by committee members on the 1954 Monte Carlo Conference topic "International Aspects of Nationalization" (now out of print); and of the Rapporteur's Report and all of the national papers prepared for the 1956 Oslo Conference on "International Shipbuilding Contracts – Particularly Legal Problems in Connection with Finance and Security" (now out of print).

1948 – Second Conference – The Hague
1950 – Third Conference – London
1952 – Fourth Conference – Madrid
1954 – Fifth Conference – Monte Carlo
1956 – Sixth Conference – Oslo
1958 – Seventh Conference – Cologne
1960 – Eighth Conference – Salzburg
1962 – Ninth Conference – Edinburgh
1964 – Tenth Conference – Mexico City
1966 – Eleventh Conference – Lausanne
1968 – Twelfth Conference – Dublin

ADMINISTRATION OF JUSTICE

ADMIRALTY AND PRIZE LAW

1948 Admiralty and Prize Law.
1952 Prize Law.

AIR LAW

1948 International Air Law.
1950 Air Law (under "Conflicts of Laws").
1952 Air Law.

ATOMIC ENERGY

1958 International Problems of Tort Liability and Financial Protection Arising out of the Use of Atomic Energy.
1960 Atomic Energy.

BUSINESS AND CORPORATION LAW

(See also "Monopolies and Restrictive Trade Practices" and negotiable and commercial instruments)

1948 Business and Social Law.
(Note: Papers covered oil, gas and petroleum legislation.)
1952 Subsidiary corporations under the civil and common law.
(Discussed in Symposium on Miscellaneous Topics.)
1958 The American Close Corporation and its Equivalent, and the Status of Wholly-Owned Subsidiaries in Other Countries.
1958 Insurance Protection against any and all Types of Lawsuits.
1960 The Formation and Operation of Foreign Subsidiaries and Branches, including the Extent to Which Foreign Subsidiaries are Entitled to Special Treatment under the Law of Their Incorporation or under International Law.
1966 The consideration of Powers of Attorney given by Foreigners to Local Lawyers; the Condition of Their Validity and of Their Termination.
1968 Warranties for the Protection of consumers.

COASTAL WATERS AND APPURTENANT SUBSOIL

1950 The Character and the Scope of the Rights Asserted or Exercised by States in the Western Hemisphere over Coastal Waters and Appurtenant Subsoil.
1952 Coastal Waters and Appurtenant Subsoil.

COMPARATIVE LAW (See also "Unification of the Law")

1948 Comparative Law.
1948 Principles to be Followed in Recognizing Foreign Instruments.
1948 Renvoi.
1950 Statute of Tangiers. (Sub-topic under "Conflicts of Laws".)
1950 Egypt's Historical Role. (Sub-topic under "Conflicts of Laws".)
1950 Women's Rights. (Sub-topic under "Conflicts of Laws".)

1952 A report on legal terminology and comparative law; Catalogue des sources de documentation en matière juridique; and Projet de loi des femmes. (Discussed in a Symposium on Miscellaneous Topics.)
1968 The law Relating to the Support and Custody of Children in its International and Comparative Aspects.

CONFLICTS OF LAWS
1950 Air Law.
1950 Statute of Tangiers.
1950 Egypt's Historical Role.
1950 Women's Rights.
1950 Law of Divorce.
1950 Judicial Assistance.
1950 Negotiable Instruments.
1950 Law of Succession.
1950 Law of Trusts.

DOMESTIC RELATIONS
1950 Law of Divorce. (Sub-topic under "Conflicts of Laws".)
1952 Domestic Relations.
1954 Extra-Territorial Effects of Divorces and Separations.
1956 Foreign Divorces – Problems Arising and Possible Solutions.
1968 The law relating to the Support and custody of Childrens in its International and Comparative aspects.

ECONOMIC CO-OPERATION (See also "Property Rights")
1948 The European Recovery Program.
1950 Legal Problems in Connection with International Economic Co-operation.
1952 International Economic Co-operation.
1954 International Economic Co-operation.
1956 International Economic Co-operation.

ETHICS (See also "The Legal Profession")
1948 An International Code of Ethics for Lawyers.
1950 The Legal Profession (Ethics Committee Report).
1952 Code of Ethics Committee Report. (Discussed in Symposium on Miscellaneous Topics.)
1954 International Code of Ethics for Lawyers.
1956 (*Note:* The "International Code of Ethics for the Legal Profession, Adopted by the General Meeting of the International Bar Association at Oslo on July 25, 1956" appears in the Sixth Conference Report, pp. 13-16. The text as amended at Mexico City in July 1964 appears in English, French, German and Spanish in the Tenth Conference Report, p. 23.)

1960 Professional Conduct

(a) The Client's Privilege of Secrecy in his Communications with his Attorney.

(b) The Propriety of Attorneys Using Wire Recorders and Film Cameras for Evidence, etc.

1962 Sub-topic under "Protection of the Individual":

(b) (i) The Recognition in Courts Abroad of the Lawyer's Confidentiality; (ii) The Attorney's Duty to Protect the Interests of his Clients against Demands by Fiscal and Other Governmental Authorities for the Disclosure of Information.

1964 The Client's Right to Secrecy in his Dealings with the Legal Profession:

(a) A comparison of the inroads made in each country whether by statute or otherwise, and

(b) Consideration of the need for and of ways of protecting the client and the legal profession against such inroads.

FISCAL LAW

1948 International Fiscal Law.
1950 International Fiscal Law.
1952 International Fiscal Law.
1954 Experience with Treaties to Avoid Double Taxation.
1956 Suggestions for Improvement of International Treaties to Avoid Double Taxation.

HUMAN RIGHTS (See also "Protection of the Individual" and "World Habeas Corpus")

1948
1950
1952 } Human Rights. (In 1952, discussed in Symposium on Miscellaneous Topics.)
1954
1956

1966 Limits and Restrictions of Public Reporting by The Press of Criminal, Civil and Administrative Court Proceedings.
1968 Proposed Code of Conduct to Insure Fair Trial and Free Press.

IMMIGRATION AND NATURALIZATION

1948 Nationality, Naturalization and Immigration.
1950 Immigration and Naturalization Laws.
1952 Facultad de libre elección de nacionalidad en los casos en que por la legislación de más de un país se otorgue al individuo el derecho a pertenecer a los mismos. (Discussed in Symposium on Miscellaneous Topics.)

1954 Immigration and Naturalization.
1956 Immigration and Naturalization.

JUDICIAL CO-OPERATION

1950 Judicial Assistance. (Sub-topic under "Conflicts of Laws".)
1952 International Judicial Co-operation.
1954 International Judicial Co-operation — Taking Evidence Abroad.
1956 International Judicial Co-operation:
(a) Difficulties arising in connection with taking evidence abroad,
(b) Serving Judicial documents abroad.
1958 International Judicial Co-operation: Bases for Agreement between Civil Law and Common Law Countries.
1960 International Judicial Co-operation — Draft Convention for Taking Evidence and Serving Documents Abroad.
1962 Report of the Committee on International Judicial Co-operation: Draft Convention on International Judicial Assistance in Civil and Commercial Matters.

LEGAL AID (See also "The Legal Profession")

1948 The Status of Lawyers and of their Organizations and Legal Aid.
1950
1952 Legal Aid. (In 1952, discussed in Symposium on Miscellaneous Topics.)
1954
1958 Legal Aid (Plan for an International Legal Aid Association).
1960 (Note: Organizational meeting of the International Legal Aid Association was held at Salzburg, July 7, 1960.)
1962 The essential requirements for a national Legal Aid and Advice Plan, and the practical possibilities of establishing such a plan, or part of it, in the various countries.
1966 Legal Aid Facilities in Europe.
1968 Comparative Standards for the Determination of Eligibility for Legal Aid.

THE LEGAL PROFESSION (See also "Ethics" and "Legal Aid")

1948 Legal Education and Admission to the Profession.
1948 (See topic under "Legal Aid": The Status of Lawyers and of their Organizations and Legal Aid.)
1950 The Legal Profession.
1956 The Legal Profession — The Work of the Organized Bar in Furthering the Legal Profession and its Public Services.
1958 Qualifications to Practice Law in the Foreign and International Field.

1958 Consideration of the Various Plans for Providing Retirement Income for Members of the Legal Profession.

1960 The Function of a Bar Association in Providing Services to the Profession and the Public: Continuing Education of the Profession.

1962 Organization of a Lawyer's Office.

1962 Explaining to the Public the Services of the Legal Profession:
(a) Methods of bringing to the public notice the advantages of a lawyer's services, e. g., via books, pamphlets, speaking programs, radio and television, institutional advertising; and the individual lawyer's duty to explain matters which may lead to adverse criticism of the profession.
(b) Explaining the basis for lawyers' fees.
(c) Explaining the security of clients' moneys; i. e., fidelity, guarantee or compensation funds.

1966 (a) Restrictions on Lawyers Qualified in Foreign Countries and Practising Elsewhere; and
(b) Establishment of a Law Office in a Foreign Jurisdiction and Problems Related Thereto.

1966 The Practice of the Law by Persons Who are Not Lawyers.

1966 The Role of Lawyers in a Developing country.

1968 Steps that can be Taken to Ensure that the Profession Keeps up to date in its Knowledge of Legislation.

1968 Role of the Bar Association in the Changing World and its Responsibilities in the Developing Countries.

1968 The Forms of Co-operation between Qualified Local Lawyers and Foreign Lawyers Practicing in the Same Country.

1968 The Forms of Co-operation between Qualified Lawyers in Different Countries.

MONOPOLIES AND RESTRICTIVE TRADE PRACTICES

(See also "Business and Corporation Law")

1958 Monopolies and Restrictive Trade Practices.

1960 Monopolies and Restrictive Trade Practices.

1962 Monopolies and Restrictive Trade Practices: Anti-Trust Problems in Connection with Dealings with Common Market Countries.

1964 Anti-Trust Problems in International Trade.

1966 Anti-Trust Aspects of International License Agreements Relating to Patents, Trademarks and Knowhow.

1968 Procedure for the Enforcement of Laws Regulating Business Transactions and Particularly Anti-Monopoly, Anti-Cartel and Anti-Trust laws.

NEGOTIABLE AND COMMERCIAL INSTRUMENTS
(See also "Business and Corporation Law")

1948 Uniformity in Negotiable Instruments and Similar Documents.

1950 Negotiable Instruments. (Sub-topic under "Conflicts of Laws".)

1952 Committee Report on Commercial Instruments (Discussed in Symposium on Miscellaneous Topics).

PATENTS, COPYRIGHTS AND TRADEMARKS

1948 Principles to be followed in the Protection of Industrial Property.

1950 Trademarks and Patents.

1950 Copyright.

1952 Copyright.

PENAL LAW

1948 International Penal Law.

1950 International Criminal Law (Narcoanalysis; Lie Detector; War Crimes).

1950 Crimes against the Peace and Security of Mankind.

1952 Genocide.
Modern Trends in the Administration of Criminal Justice in America.
Genealogía jurídica de la casación y el amparao mexicano en materia penal.
(Discussed in Symposium on Miscellaneous Topics)

1952 International Penal Law.

PROPERTY RIGHTS (See also "Economic Co-operation")

1948 Restoration of the Law and Property Rights after World War II.

1954 Economic Warfare.

1954 International Aspects of Nationalization.

1956 Proposals for an International Code Regulating the Handling of Property of Enemy Nationals and Residents in Enemy-Occupied Territory.

1958 Protection of Investments Abroad in Time of Peace.

1960 Court and Court Procedure for Protection of Investments Abroad.

1962 Court and Court Procedure for the Protection of Investments Abroad.

1966 (Note: A small committee appointed after the 1962 Edinburgh Conference submitted a report and resolution to the General Meeting at the 1966 Lausanne Conference and a Resolution on "Protection of Investments Abroad" was adopted by the General Meeting, and appears in the Eleventh Conference Report pp. 7-9. The resolution has been sent to the United Nations and to other organizations currently working in this field.)

PROTECTION OF THE INDIVIDUAL

(See also "Human Rights", and "World Habeas Corpus")

1962 Protection of the Individual against the Public Administration:

(a) Comparison of substantive administrative law, of the manner in which the activity of administrative agencies is regulated by law and of the possibilities for the individual to bring court action against an agency for violating his rights in a specific case.

(b) See "Ethics".

1964 Protecting Individual Rights under the Various Laws Governing Administrative Procedure, and Codifying the Basic Procedural Safeguards.

1966 Limits and Restrictions of Public Reporting by the Press of Criminal, Civil and Administrative Court Proceedings.

1968 Proposed Code of Conduct to Inaure Fair Trial and Free Press.

SHIPBUILDING CONTRACTS

1968 Proposed Code of Conduct to Insure Fair Trial and Free Press. Problems in Connection with Finance and Security.

1958 International Shipbuilding Contracts.

(Note: The Council directed that the 1958 Committee Report [pp. 447-465 7th Conference Report] with Draft Convention for the unification of certain rules of law relating to registration of ships under construction be referred to the United Nations and to other organizations currently working in this field.)

SOVEREIGN IMMUNITY

1956 Suggestion for Alleviating Hardships Arising from Sovereign Immunity in Tort and Contract.

(Note: At the 1960 Salzburg Conference, the General Meeting adopted the Resolution Relating to the Immunity of Sovereigns when Engaged in Commercial Activity outside of Their Own Domain — see pp. 8-10, Eighth Conference Report.)

TREATIES (See also "Fiscal Law" re: Treaties on Double Taxation, and various topic headings re: Draft Conventions)

1950 International Treaties.

1964 Legal Aspects and Consequences of the Treaty of Rome (European Common Market), the Treaty of Montevideo (Latin-American Association for Free Trade, ALALC), Alliance for Progress, and Other Regional Programs.

UNIFICATION OF THE LAW (See also "Comparative Law")

1948 Progressive Development in the Field of International Law.

1952 Methods of Unifying the Law.

UNITED NATIONS

1948 United Nations.

1952 Committee Report on Constitutional Structure of the United Nations. (Discussed in Symposium on Miscellaneous Topics)

1954 Constitutional Structure of the United Nations.

WILLS, TRUSTS, ESTATES AND LAWS OF SUCCESSION

1950 Law of Succession. (Sub-topic under "Conflicts of Laws".)

1950 Law of Trusts. (Sub-topic under "Conflicts of Laws".)

1952 Law of Trusts.

1952 La nature juridique de la transmission par décès et la succession des parents légitimes. (Discussed in Symposium on Miscellaneous Topics.)

1956 Administration of Foreign Estates – Problems of Executors and Possible Solutions.

1958 Administration of Foreign Estates.
(Note: The Council directed that the 1958 Committee Report with Draft Convention relating to Administration of Estates [pp. 424-445, Seventh Conference Report] be referred to the United Nations and to other organizations currently working in this field.)

1962 The Form and Legal Effect of Wills Made by the Same Person in Different Countries.

1964 The Form and Legal Effect of Wills Made by the Same Person in Different Countries.

WORLD HABEAS CORPUS

(See also "Human Rights" and "Protection of the Individual")

1964 World Habeas Corpus and International Extradition.

MEMBERS OF THE LEGAL PROFESSION WHO CONTRIBUTED TO THE SUCCESS OF THE DUBLIN CONFERENCE

(P) — Patrons of the IBA.

(S) — Subscribers of the IBA.

(**) — Members of the legal profession not qualified to practice in country of residence.

Note: Members of the legal profession without a symbol after their names are individuals who contributed to the success of the Conference, including Councillors of the IBA, and members of Committees listed in this Report.

ARGENTINA

Practising lawyers in Argentina are usually addressed with "Señor Doctor" or "Sr. Dr." appearing before the name of the individual.

OTTOLENGHI, Sr. Dr. Mauricio A. (S)
Diag. Roque S. Peña 628-7⁰ piso
Dto. P., Buenos Aires

VANOSSI, Sr. Dr. Jorge Reinaldo A. (S)
Juan Mora Fernández No. 2970
suc. 25, Buenos Aires

YURREBASO VIALE,
Sr. Dr. Policarpo A. (S)
Viamonte 885, 2⁰ piso
Buenos Aires

AUSTRALIA

Practising lawyers in Australia are usually addressed with "Esquire" or "Esq." appearing after the full name. Since Australia is a member of the British Commonwealth of Nations, customs of address are generally those appearing under England.

ABBOTT, Esq., Alan Campbell (C)
144 Maitland Street
P. O. Box 198, Narrabri
N. S. W. 2390

AIRD, Esq., Andrew P. (C)
Owen Dixon Chambers
205 William Street
Melbourne, Victoria

AITKEN, Esq., David (C)
234 George Street
Sydney, N. S. W.

ALLEN, Esq., Maurice (S)
10-14 Young Street
Sydney, N. S. W.

ANDERSON, Esq., David R. (C)
89 South George's Tce.
Perth, W. Australia

ARGYLE, Esq., Rory E. S. (S)
c/o Parker & Parker
21 Howard Street
Perth, W. Australia

ATKINS, Esq., Peter H. (C)
Box D 151, G. P. O.
Perth, W. Australia

BAIN, Esq., James Robert (C)
9th Floor, 267 Collins Street
Melbourne, Victoria

BALDOCK, Esq., James O. (C)
180 Phillip Street
Sydney, N. S. W. 2000

BARKER, Esq., Rupert (C)
29 Elizabeth Street
Hobart, Tasmania 7000

BARNARD, Esq., Jan (C)
c/o William Lasica
422 Collins Street
Melbourne, Victoria

BAXTER, Esq., Valentine A. (C)
31 Tintern Avenue
Toorak, Victoria

BINFELD, Esq., John I. (C)
251 George Street
Sydney, N. S. W.

BOWRING, Esq., James Paul (S)
180 Phillip Street
Sydney, N. S. W.

BREWSTER, Esq., Peter R. (C)
127 Phillip Street
Sydney, N. S. W.

BRUCE, Esq., Robert (C)
43 Pentecost Avenue
St. Ives, N. S. W.

BRUXNER, Esq., John M. (C)
Queen's Square
Sydney, N. S. W.

BUBB, Esq., Leslie Albert (C)
P. O. Box 52
Gunnedah, 2380, N. S. W.

BURBANK, Esq., Noel (C)
Owen Dixon Chambers
William Street
Melbourne, Victoria

BUSHBY, Esq., O. B. E., LL. B.
Harold (S) (C)
141-143 Brisbane Street
G. P. O. Launceston, Tasmania

BYRNE, Esq., James R. (C)
171 Queen Street
Brisbane, Queensland

CAMPBELL, Esq., Q. C., W. B.
104 North Quay
Brisbane, Queensland

CARUANA, Esq., Jerome (C)
114 Castlereagh Street
Sydney, N. S. W.

CATER, Esq., Rupert V. (C)
P. O. Box 397
City A. C. T.

CLELAND, Pamela M. (C)
Attorney at Law
Waterfall Gully Road
Beaumont, South Australia

CODD, Esq., Harden (C)
120 Maybe Street
Bombala, N. S. W.

COHEN, Esq., Kenneth (C)
180 Phillip Street
Sydney, 2000, N. S. W.

CONNOLLY, Esq., Peter D. (C)
Inns of Court
107 North Quay
Brisbane, Queensland

CORR, Esq., Vernon M. (C)
290 La Trobe Street
Melbourne, Victoria

COVACEVICH, Esq., Anthony T. (S)
249 Esplanade
P. O. Box 849
Cairns, N. Queensland

CRAMPTON, Esq., John (C)
205 William Street
Melbourne, Victoria

CRAVEN-SMITH-MILNES,
Esq., Herbert (C)
10 Pier Street
Perth, W. Australia

CRESSWELL, Esq., Reginald G. D. (C)
35 Grenfell Street
Adelaide, South Australia

CROCKETT, Esq., William (C)
205 William Street
Melbourne, Victoria

DAWSON, Esq., Frederick (C)
84 William Street
Melbourne, Victoria

DELANEY, Esq., W. K. (C)
77 Queen Street
Brisbane, Queensland

DELANY, Esq., Gerald Edward (S)
London Chambers
452 Lonsdale Street
Melbourne, Victoria

DETHRIDGE, Esq., F. S. (S)
105 King Street
Melbourne, Victoria

DIGNAM, Esq., Clifford (C)
160 Castlereagh Street
Sydney, N. S. W.

DIGNAM, His Hon. Judge William (C)
131 Macquarie Street
Sydney, N. S. W. 2000

DOYLE, Esq., John L. McC. (C)
187 Ryrie Street
Greenlong, Victoria

DUGGAN, Esq., Joseph M. R. (C)
A. C. A. Building
66 King Street
Sydney, N. S. W.

DUGGEN, Josephine (C)
Attorney at Law
443 Little Collins Street
Melbourne, Victoria

DUXBURY, Esq., Gordon W. (C)
T & G Building
Collins & Russell Streets
Melbourne, Victoria

EMMERSON, Esq., Keith McL. (C)
357 Little Collins Street
Melbourne, Victoria

EVATT, Esq., Clive (C)
174 Phillip Street
Sydney, Victoria

FOGARTY, Esq., Michael (C)
Scanlan Building
26 Queen Street
Brisbane, Queensland

FORREST, Esq., Jocelyn (C)
Crown Law Dept.
54 Barrack Street
Perth, W. Australia

FOWLER, Esq., Archibald J. (C)
17 Queen Street
Melbourne, Victoria

FRIEND, Esq., Laurence (C)
64 Queen Street
Warragul, Victoria

GALLEN, Esq., Brian R. (C)
B. M. I. Building
Alinga Street
Canberra City, A. C. T.

GEORGE, Esq., Arthur Thomas (S)
Challis House
10 Martin Place
Sydney, N. S. W.

GILLAN, Esq., Brian T. (C)
Penneys Building
210 Queen Street
Brisbane, Queensland

GILLESPIE, Esq., William Charles (C)
Local Court
Adelaide, South Australia

GLASS, Esq., Harold (C)
174 Phillip Street
Sydney, N. S. W.

GLEESON, Helen (C)
Attorney at Law
151 Clarence Street
Sydney, N. S. W.

GLEESON, Esq., John (C)
9th Floor, 180 Phillip Street
Sydney, N. S. W.

GODDARD, Esq., Andrew (C)
140 Queen Street
Melbourne, Victoria

GOLDMAN, Esq., Philip (C)
26 College Street
Sydney, N. S. W.

GRAHAM, Kathleen (C)
Attorney at Law
119 Phillip Street
Sydney, N. S. W.

GREENING, Esq., Hulbert A. (C)
422 Collins Street
Melbourne, Victoria

HATSATOURIS, Esq., Angelo (C)
10th Floor, 38/40 Martin Place
Sydney, N. S. W.

HEALY, Esq., Michael Desmond (C)
3rd Floor, Wentworth Chambers
180 Phillip Street
Sydney, N. S. W.

HELLMRICH, Esq., John M. (C)
77 Castlereagh Street
Sydney, N. S. W.

HENLEY, Esq., Keith H. (C)
115 Queen Street
Brisbane, Queensland

HICKS, Esq., David S. (C)
Judges Chambers, District Court
Queens Square
Sydney, N. S. W. 2000

HINMAN, Esq., Arthur H. (S)
29 Elizabeth Street
Hobart, Tasmania

HOBAN, Esq., John (C)
441 Law Courts Place
Melbourne, Victoria

HOGAN, Esq., Niell (C)
Lynch Street
Young, N. S. W.

HOOKE, Esq., Murray (C)
P. O. Box 89
Taree

HOYLE, Esq., John R. (C)
10 Martin Place
Sydney, N. S. W.

JOSKE, Esq., Percy Ernest (C)
451 Law Courts Place
Melbourne, Victoria

KENNEDY, Esq., Athol J. (C)
401 Collins Street
Melbourne, Victoria

KENNEDY, Esq., John (C)
199 a Hume Highway
Liverpool, N. S. W.

KENNON, Esq., Edwin C. (C)
83 William Street
Melbourne, Victoria

KERRIGAN, Esq., Alan Bevly (C)
Wentworth Chambers
180 Phillip Street
Sydney, N. S. W.

KING, Esq., W. F. Whitney (S)
108 Queen Street
Melbourne, Victoria

KIRBY, Esq., David (C)
42 Hunter Street
Sydney, N. S. W.

KOTT, Esq., Max (C)
62 Saint George's Terrace
Perth, W. Australia

LAUGHT, Esq., Keith A. (C)
5 Bevington Road
Glenunga, South Australia

LEAHY, Esq., Robert Carter (S)
126 Phillip Street
Sydney, N. S. W.

LEVY, Rose Winstanley (C)
Attorney at Law
Adelaide, South Australia

LIGERTWOOD, Esq., Neil C. (C)
Royal Insurance Building
13 Grenfell Street
Adelaide, South Australia

LOBBAN, Esq., Alan Robert (S)
120 William Street
Melbourne C 1, Victoria

LODGE, Esq., Henry Souttar (S) (C)
164 Saint George's Terrace
Perth, W. Australia

LOUCH, Esq., Thomas S. (C)
20 Howard Street
Perth, W. Australia

LUSHER, Esq., Q. C., Edwin A. (C)
174 Phillip Street
Sydney, N. S. W.

MACQUAIRE, Esq., William McK. (C)
71 Wentworth Street
Port Kembla, N. S. W.

MACREADY, Esq., Hugh T. (C)
34 Hunter Street
Sydney, N. S. W. 2000

MACRIS, Esq., John W. (C)
902 Botany Road
Mascot 2020, N. S. W.

MAGUIRE, Esq., Thomas A. (C)
117 Crown Street
Wollongong, N. S. W.

MANDER-JONES, Esq., David (C)
369 George Street
Sydney, N. S. W.

MARSH, Esq., Robert Robertson (C)
360 Collins Street
Melbourne, Victoria 3000

MARTIN, Esq., Kevin J. (C)
109 Elizabeth Street
Sydney, N. S. W.

MARTIN, Esq., Romuald J. (C)
792 Elizabeth Street
Melbourne, Victoria

MASTERMAN, Esq., George G. (C)
174 Phillip Street
Sydney, N. S. W.

MATTEI, Esq., David (C)
Equity Chambers
472 Bourke Street
Melbourne, Victoria

McCLEMANS, Sheila M. (C)
The Supreme Court
Perth, W. Australia

McCLEMENS, Mr. Justice (S)
Supreme Court
Sydney, N. S. W.

McCoos, Esq., Bernard Joseph (C)
8 Belgrave Street
Manly, N. S. W. 2095

McEWIN, Esq., John N. (C)
18 Leigh Street
Adelaide, South Australia

McKAY, Esq., A. H. (S)
357 Little Collins Street
Melbourne, Victoria

McKENNA, Esq., John
180 Phillip Street
Sydney, N. S. W.

McLELLAND, Esq., Charles (C)
Mena House
Macquarie Street
Sydney, N. S. W.

McPHERSON, Esq., Albert Clifton (S)
26 Rosebery Road
Killara, N. S. W.

MEARES, Esq., Q. C., C. L. D.
180 Phillip Street
Sydney, N. S. W.

MENLOVE, Esq., Neville Vivian (S)
160 Castlereagh Street
Sydney, N. S. W.

MITCHELL, The Hon. Justice
Roma F. (C)
Supreme Court
Adelaide, South Australia

MONT, Esq., John Francis (C)
60 Hunter Street
Sydney, N. S. W.

MOORS, Esq., James D. (C)
70/72 King Street
Sydney, N. S. W. 2000

MORIARTY, Deirdre (C)
450 Little Collins Street
Melbourne, Victoria

MOYNIHAN, Esq., Leonard (C)
144 Adelaide Street
Brisbane, Queensland

MULLETT, Esq., Lyn (C)
470 Bourke Street
Melbourne 3000, Victoria

MURPHY, Esq., Ronald (C)
180 Phillip Street
Sydney, N. S. W.

NEWMAN, Esq., Douglas (C)
12 Ridge Avenue
Myrtle Bank, South Australia

NITSCHKE, Esq., Galva (C)
33 Fitzmaurice Street
Wagga Wagga, N. S. W.

NOSWORTHY, Esq., John R. (C)
163 Adelaide Street
Brisbane, Queensland

O'BRIEN, Esq., Hubert (C)
37 Queen Street
Melbourne 3000, Victoria

O'DONOHUE, Esq., Nicholas (C)
493 Law Courts Place
Melbourne 3000, Victoria

O'DONOHUE, Mrs. Margot Mary (C)
493 Law Courts Place
Melbourne 3000, Victoria

O'KEEFFE, Esq., Justin A. (C)
37 Queen Street
Melbourne 3000, Victoria

O'MEALLY, Esq., John (C)
Wentworth Chambers
180 Phillip Street
Sydney, N. S. W.

O'TOOLE, Margaret A. (C)
Attorney at Law
Forbes Chambers
127 Phillip Street
Sydney, N. S. W.

PALMER, Esq., Richard Oram (S)
120 Lachlan Street
P. O. Box 18
Forbes, N. S. W.

PATTERSON, Esq. Gerald (C)
259 Queen Street
Brisbane, Queensland

PETERSON, Esq., Howarth Adkins (C)
344 Queen Street
Brisbane, Queensland

PIDGEON, Esq., William (C)
P. O. Box 63
Bunbury 6230

PIGGOTT, Esq., C. B. E., J. B.
28 Murray Street
Hobart, Tasmania

PIKE, Esq., Vincent M. (C)
64 Castlereagh Street
Sydney, N. S. W.

PIPER, Esq., Robert William (S)
23 Grenfell Street
Adelaide, South Australia

POLITES, Esq., Peter (C)
150 Queen Street
Melbourne, Victoria

PRENTICE, Gail, Attorney at Law (C)
125 York Street
Sydney, N. S. W.

QUINN, Esq., John (C)
17/19 Bridge Street
Sydney 2000, N. S. W.

REID, The Hon. George Oswald (S)
Attorney General's Dept.
459 Lonsdale Street
Melbourne, Victoria

RICHARDSON, The Hon. Athol (S) (C)
Supreme Court
Sydney 2000, N. S. W.

ROBERTS, Esq., Ivan C. (C)
180 Phillip Street
Sydney, N. S. W.

ROSS-JONES, Esq., Roscoe (C)
67 Castlereagh Street
Sydney, N. S. W.

RUDDY, Esq., Gabriel (C)
6th Floor, M. L. C. Block
Brisbane, Queensland

RUMMERY, Esq., Thomas Edward (S)
54 Woodlark Street
Lismore, N. S. W.

SEWELL, Esq., G. B. (C)
422 Collins Street
Melbourne, Victoria

SIMBLIST, Esq., Samuel (C)
174 Phillip Street
Sydney, N. S. W.

SINCLAIR, Esq., William J. (S)
126 Phillip Street
Sydney, N. S. W.

SKEPPER, Faye (C)
Attorney at Law
414 Lonsdale Street
Melbourne, Victoria

SMALL, Esq., Trevor N. (C)
107 Elizabeth Street
Sydney, N. S. W.

SMITH, Miss Nancy Gordon (S)
c/o Reserve Bank of Australia
Box 3947, G. P. O.
Sydney, N. S. W.

SMITHERS, Esq., Kenneth (C)
210 Pitt Street
Sydney, N. S. W.

SPENDER, Esq., John M. (C)
174 Phillip Street
Sydney, N. S. W.

STAPP, Esq., Michael James (S)
116 Queens Cliff Road
Harbord, Sydney, N. S. W.

STAUNTON, Esq., James Henry (C)
Wentworth Chambers
180 Phillip Street
Sydney, N. S. W.

STEPHENSON, Esq., James Hunter (S)
4 O'Connell Street
Sydney, N. S. W.

STEVENSON, Esq., Andrew (C)
48 Carrington Parade
New Lambton, N. S. W.

STOREY, Esq., Donald W. (C)
346 Church Street
Parramatta, N. S. W.

STOREY, Esq., Geoffrey (C)
33 - 39 Hunter Street
Sydney, N. S. W.

TANNER, Esq., Leon George (C)
Crown Prosecutor's Chambers
Queen's Square, P. O. Box 42
Sydney, N. S. W.

TELTZ, Esq., Richard M. (C)
169 Phillip Street
Sydney, N. S. W.

TEMPLE, Margaret (C)
Attorney at Law
32 Hortense Street
Burwood, Victoria

TESORIERO, Esq., Peter (C)
28 Railway Street
Chatswood, N. S. W.

THOMSON, Esq., John Ebenezer (S)
68 Pitt Street
Sydney, N. S. W.

VAUGHAN, Esq., Bryan Henry (C)
77 Pitt Street
Sydney, N. S. W.

VELIK, Esq., Leon (C)
2 A Merriwee Crescent
Toorak, Victoria

VIRTUE, Esq., John Svenden (C)
Supreme Court
Perth, W. Australia

VOUMARD, Esq., Louis (C)
Equity Chambers
427 Bourke Street
Melbourne, Victoria

WALTERS, Esq., George (C)
Bank of N. S. W. Chambers
Bundaberg, Queensland

WHITE, Esq., Nevin Earl (S)
48 Macquarie Street
Paramatta, N. S. W.

WRIGHT, Esq., Robert (C)
Owen Dixon Chambers
205 William Street
Melbourne, Victoria

ZELLING, Mrs. Sesca (C)
34 Pirie Street
Adelaide, South Australia

ZELLING, Esq., Q. C., Howard E. (C)
24 Wright Street
Adelaide, South Australia

AUSTRIA

Practising lawyers in Austria are addressed "Rechtsanwalt" or "RA". Lawyers who have earned a doctorate are addressed with "Rechtsanwalt Dr." or "RA Dr." before the name.

ASAMER, RA Dr. Kurt (C)
A - 5010 Salzburg G.
Mozart-Platz 4

BRUNEDER, RA Dr. Alois (S)
Landstrasse 16
Linz an der Donau

CZERWENKA, RA Dr. Fritz (C)
Blumelgasse 1
Wien VI

DRAXLER, Dr. Ludwig (S)
Reichsrathsstrasse 11
Wien I

FOGLAR-DEINHHARDSTEIN,
RA Dr. Harald (S) (C)
Plankengasse 7
Wien I

FOGLAR-DEINHHARDSTEIN,
RA Dr. Heinrich (C)
Plankengasse 7
Wien I

JAHODA, RA Dr. Ernst (C)
An der Hulben 1
Wien Lolo

KALTENBÄCK, RA Dr. Leo (S) (C)
Kaiserfeldgasse 15
8011 Graz

KLUG, RA Dr. Carl Josef (S) (C)
Alserstrasse 49
Wien VIII

MICHNER, RA Dr. Herbert (S)
Trattnerhof 2
Wien I

PALLAUF, RA Dr. Ernst (C)
Paris-Lodron-Strasse 16
5020 Salzburg

RINESCH, RA Dr. Gustav (S) (C)
Schwarzenbergplatz 13
Wien IV

SCHIMA, Dr. Dr. h. c. Hans
Weissgerberlande 42
Wien III

SCHINDLER, RA Dr. Johann (S)
Maria-Theresien-Strasse 16
Wien I

SCHÖNHERR, RA Dr. Dr. Fritz
Tegetthoffstrasse 3
1015 Wien

SCHUPPICH, RA Dr. Walter
Falkestrasse 6
1010 Wien

STÖLZLE, RA Dr. Carl
Oppolzergasse 6
Wien I

BAHAMAS

DUPUCH, Esq., Eugene A. P. (C)
P. O. Box 1451
Nassau

SELIGMAN, Esq., Raphael (C)
326 Bay Street
P. O. Box 1241
Nassau

BARBADOS

DEAR, Esq., John (C)
James Street
Bridgetown

BELGIUM

Practising lawyers in Belgium are usually addressed with "Maître" or "Me" appearing before the individual's name.

ABRAHAMS, Me Raymond (S)
18 Rue de Belle-Vue
Brusselles 5

Van den HOUTAN, Dr. J. N. (S)
85 Boulevard de Waterloo
Brusselles

KARL, RA Paul M. (S)
3 Avenue du Manoir d'Anjou
Brusselles 15

BOLIVIA

GUTIERREZ, Dr. Julio A. (S)
Avenida Busch 148
Santa Cruz de la Sierra

BRAZIL

LAIRIHOY, Sr. Dr. don Pedro
Presidente, Instituto dos
Advogados do Rio Grande do Sul
Travessa Acilino Carvalho, 21
Pôrte Alegro, Rio Grande do Sul

RENATO, Sr. Lic. D. Joaquim (S)
Av. Ipirango, 318 A 17 Andar
Sao Paulo

BRITISH HONDURAS

LINDO, Esq., Dean (C)
7 Church Street
Belize City

CANADA

Practising lawyers in Canada are usually addressed with "Esquire" or "Esq." appearing after the full name of the individual, except in the Province of Quebec, where, when writing to a lawyer of French extraction it is proper to use instead "Maître" or "Me" preceding his name. "The Hon." should never be used for a Canadian unless he is strictly entitled to it (e. g. members of the Canadian Privy Council, members of the Senate, member of the Provincial Cabinets, Judges of the Supreme Court of Canada, Judges of the Exchequer Court of Canada, and Judges of the Supreme Court of each of the Provinces). A relatively few Canadians are members of the Imperial Privy Council and as such are entitled to "The Rt. Hon.". A lawyer who is a "Queen's Counsel" is addressed with "Q. C." after his full name and after the "Esq.", but in Quebec if using the French style of address "C. R." is used instead of "Q. C." immediately following his name.

ANDERSON, The Hon. Jacob Carroll (P)
Court House
Judge's Chambers
Belleville, Ontario

BLISS, Esq., Harvey John (P)
100 Adelaide Street W
Toronto, Ontario

BLOOMFIELD, Esq., Q. C., Louis M (P)
930 Royal Bank Building
Place Ville Marie
Montreal 113, Quebec

BRANSON, Esq., Cecil O. D. (P) (C)
505 Yarrow Building
645 Fort Street
Victoria, B. C.

BRAZIER, Esq., Q. C., Charles W. (C)
1403 - 1030 W. Georgia Street
Vancouver, B. C.

CAMPBELL, Esq., Alan T. R. (C)
1400 - 1030 W. Georgia Street
Vancouver, B. C.

COOPER, Hon. Mr. Justice A. Gordon (P) (C)
The Law Courts
Spring Garden Road
Halifax, N. S.

CRAWFORD, Esq., Q. C., Edward Hugh (P)
400 - 208 Edmonton Street
Winnipeg 1, Manitoba

CROSLAND, Esq., Cecil George (C)
1009 7th Avenue, S. W.
Calgary, Alberta

CUTLER, Esq., Phil (C)
Suite 2000, 507 Place d'Armes
Montreal, Quebec

DANSEREAU, Esq., Q. C., Arthur (P)
800 Place Victoria, Suite 2211
Montreal 1, Quebec

DESCHENES, Esq., Q. C., Jules
c/o The Canadian Bar Association
90 Sparks Street
Ottawa 4, Ontario

DIPLOCK, Esq., Q. C., D. Donald
c/o The Canadian Bar Association
90 Sparks Street
Ottawa 4, Ontario

DORFMAN, Esq., Q. C., Irwin
500 Montreal Trust Building
213 Notre Dame Avenue
Winnipeg 2, Manitoba

DUCKWORTH, Esq., Thomas J. (C)
1050 Guinness House
727 7th Avenue S. W.
Calgary 2, Alberta

ELLIOTT, Esq., William McBurney (P)
2236 Albert Street
Regina, Saskatchewan

GILL, Esq., William B. (C)
1220 Calgary House
Calgary, Alberta

GRIFFITHS, Esq., Thomas O. (P)
822 - 470 Granville Street
Vancouver 2, B. C.

HILLAND, Esq., Douglas W. (C)
407 8th Ave. S. W.
Calgary, Alberta

HINDS, Esq., James (P)
142 Elm Street, West
Box 744
Sudbury, Ontario

JAMIESON, Esq., M. B. E., Q. C., LL. D., D. Park (P)
Post Office Box 250
Sarnia, Ontario

KELLY, Miss Miriam (C)
3 McKenzie Avenue
Toronto 5, Ontario

KENNEDY, Esq., John W. (P) (C)
10128 103rd Street
Edmonton, Alberta

KOVACH, Esq., Anthony (C)
1027 Eighth Avenue N. W.
Calgary, Alberta

KOWALSKI, Esq., Mitchell E. (P)
2150 Lakeshore Blvd. West
Toronto, Ontario

LESLIE, Esq., Q. C., LL. D., D. C. L., Everett Clayton (P) (C)
2236 Albert Street
Regina, Saskatchewan

McDONALD, Esq., John A. S. (C)
890 Bentall Building
Calgary 2, Alberta

McDONALD, Esq., Q. C., John G. (P)
Toronto-Dominion Centre
King Street West
Toronto, Ontario

MAGNUS, Esq., John (C)
703 6th Avenue S. W.
Calgary, Alberta

MAIN, Esq., Q. C., Gifford (C)
708 McLeod Building
Edmonton, Alberta

MAYNARD, Esq., Q. C., Lucien (P) (C)
625 Tegler Building
Edmonton, Alberta

MACDONALD, Esq., James C.
100 Adelaide Street West
Toronto 1, Ontario

MERRIAM, Esq., Ronald (C)
Room 320
90 Sparks Street
Ottawa 4, Ontario

MILLARD, Esq., James (C)
505 2nd Street S. W.
Calgary, Alberta

MOORE, Esq., John S. (C)
6th Floor, 407 Eighth Ave. S. W.
Calgary, Alberta

MURPHY, Esq., Angelo J. (C)
Box 479
Vulcan, Alberta

NIELSEN, Esq., Dennis (C)
407 8th Avenue
Calgary, Alberta

O'SULLIVAN, Emily (C)
Family Court
Court House
Calgary, Alberta

OWEN-FLOOD, Esq., Dermod D. (P) (C)
205 - 702 Fort Street
Victoria, B. C.

PHILLIPS, Esq., Neil F. (P)
634 Clarke Avenue
Westmount, Quebec

REID, Esq., Q. C., Robert F. (P)
250 University Avenue
Toronto 1, Ontario

RICHARDS, Esq., Michael J. (C)
10410 - 81 Avenue
Edmonton, Alberta

SAUCIER, Esq., John James, President
The Canadian Bar Association
90 Sparks Street
Ottawa 4, Ontario

SCOTT, Esq., Q. C., Eugene W. (P) (C)
2094 Yonge Street
Toronto 7, Ontario

SHUMIATCHER, Q. C., Dr. Morris C. (P)
2100 Scarth Street
Regina, Saskatchewan

SINNOTT, Esq., Patrick John (P) (C)
201 - 1012 Douglas Street
Victoria, B. C.

SUTHERLAND, Esq., Allan W. (P)
1403 - 1030 West Georgia Street
Vancouver, B. C.

TETLEY, Esq., William (P)
800 Victoria Square
Suite 3400
Montreal 3, Quebec

TURNER, Esq., William O. (C)
Drawerg
Hanna, Alberta

WALKER, Esq., Sydney J. (C)
201 - 5 Birks Building
Saskatoon, Saskatchewan

WARREN, Esq., Ronald Bartlett (P)
45 Elm Street East
Sudbury, Ontario

WEIR, Esq., Q. C., Samuel E. (P)
486 Richmond Street
London, Ontario

WISHERT, Esq., Arthur A. (C)
Office of Attorney General
Parliament Building
Toronto, Ontario

WOLFSON, Esq., Q. C., Charles (P) (C)
1010 St. Catherine Street, West
Suite 300
Montreal, Quebec

CEYLON

WIKRAMANEYARE, Esq., Eric B. (C)
Law Library
Colombo 12

COLOMBIA

Practising lawyers in Colombia are addressed with "Doctor" or "Dr." appearing before the individual's name.

MACKENZIE, Sr. Dr. Mauricio (S)
Apartado Aereo 3447
Bogotá

De la ESPRIELLA, Dr. Eduardo Samek (S)
Apartado Aereo No. 20015
Bogotá 2

VALDERRAMA R., Sr. Dr. Javier (S)
Apartado Aereo No. 58 - 46
Bogotá D. E. (1)

COSTA RICA

FOURNIER, Sr. Lic. D. Fernando (S)
Apartado 1571
San José

DENMARK

Practising lawyers in Denmark are usually addressed "Advokat". Lawyers who have previously acquired the now abolished title "Højesteretssagfører" (barrister to the Supreme Court) or "Landsretssagfører" (barrister to the High Court) are still entitled to use this title. Practising lawyers who have earned a doctorate of laws are addressed "Advokat (Højesteretssagfører, Landsretssagfører), dr. jur.".

ANDERSEN, Advokat Paul H. (S)
13 Badstuestraede
Copenhagen K

BEHRENDT-POULSEN, Højesteretssagfører, P. E.
17 Frederiksgade
Copenhagen K

BUHL, Højesteretssagfører
John Palle (S) (C)
Gl. Torv 18
Copenhagen K

FEDERSPIEL, Advokat
Thomas Holger (S)
109 Gothersgade
Copenhagen K

GERSTED, Højesteretssagfører
Gunnar (C)
Amagertorv 27
Copenhagen K

GRAFF, Advokat Axel (C)
Hovedvejen 87
Glostrup

HJEJLE, Højesteretssagfører
dr. jur. Bernt (S) (C)
Amagertorv 24
Copenhagen K

OPPENHEJM, Advokat Svend (S) (C)
Raadhuspladsen 59
Copenhagen V

ØSTERGAARD, Advokat Poul (C)
Ved Stranden 14
Copenhagen K

PONTOPPIDAN, Landsretssagfører
Ole Jørgen (S) (C)
Frederiksgade 1
Copenhagen K

RASMUSSEN, Advokat Erik
H. C. Andersens Blvd. 40
Copenhagen V

SPANG-HANSSEN, Advokat Aage
Amagertorv 24
Copenhagen K

ECUADOR

GÓMEZ de la TORRE, Sr. Prof.
Lic. Dr. Mario Antonio (S)
(Luis Felipe Borja No. 412)
P. O. Box 1025
Quito

ENGLAND AND WALES

Practising lawyers in England, both barristers and solicitors, are usually addressed with "Esquire" or "Esq." appearing after the full name. In the event that the individual has been Knighted, "Sir" is used instead, before his name; or if he has been elevated to the Peerage, "Lord" or "Baron" without including his Christian name. "The Hon." should never be used for an Englishman unless he is strictly entitled to it (e. g. younger sons of Earls, all sons of Viscounts and Barons, and all High Court Judges). "The Rt. Hon." is part of the title of all Privy Councillors, amongst whom are included all Judges of the Court of Appeal. A barrister who is a "Queen's Counsel" is addressed with "Q. C." after his full name and after the "Esq.".

ALLEN, Esq., Claud Geoffrey (S)
13 King's Bench Walk
Temple
London E. C. 4

ALLEN, Mrs. D. (S)
Pringle & Co.
Bank Chambers
London Road
Redhill, Surrey

ALMOND, Esq., James Pierce (S)
47/48 Hamilton Square
Birkenhead, Cheshire

ANNS, Esq., Bryan
12 King's Bench Walk
Temple
London E. C. 4

ARNOLD, Esq., James Ronald
Matthew (S) (C)
203 Watling Street West
Towcester, Northants

AUGER, Miss Jacqueline
The Law Society's Hall
113 Chancery Lane
London, W. C. 2

BALDWIN, Esq., John Hugh (S)
18 Austin Friars
London, E. C. 2

BART-SMITH, Esq., Herbert (S)
41 A Earl's Avenue
Folkestone, Kent

BECKER, Miss Juliet Angela (S)
66 Queen Street
London, E. C. 4

BECKWITH, Esq., Harvey (S)
72 Market Street
Bradford 1

BERMAN, Mrs. Fay Lillian (S) (C)
3/4 Lincoln's Inn Fields
London, W. C. 2

BLACKWELL, Esq., D. W. (C)
14, Heanton Street
Braunton, N. Devon

BLAIR, Esq., Gordon S. (S)
11 Avenue de Grande Bretagne
Monte Carlo, Monaco

BLATCH, Esq., Cecil Herbert
Spence (S)
48 High Street
Lymington, Hants

BOOTH, Esq., J. Trever (S)
Seaford House, 10 Liverpool Rd.
Walmer, Kent

BOULTON, Esq., William W. (C)
Carpmael Building
Temple
London, E. C. 4

BRANDON, Esq., Michael (S)
1299 Commugny
Vaud, Switzerland

BROWN, Esq., William John (S) (C)
1 Copthall Buildings
London, E. C. 2

BUCKLAND, Esq., John David (S)
13 Prince Albert Street
Brighton, Sussex

BUCKERIDGE, Esq., T. Gordon (S) (C)
59 - 67 Gresham Street
London, E. C. 2

BUDGE, Esq., John Stuart (S)
Messrs. Howes, Percival & Budge
203 Watling Street West
Towcester, Northants

BURGIN, Esq., Patrick Leslie (S)
3 Gray's Inn Place
Gray's Inn
London, W. C. 1

BURROWS, Sir Robert John Formby
(S) (C)
21 Buckingham Gate
London, S. W. 1

BUSFIELD, Kathleen M. (C)
5, New Square
Lincoln's Inn
London, W. C. 2

CAMPBELL, Esq., Q. C., Bruce
Dr. Johnson's Buildings
Temple
London, E. C. 4

CAMSEN, Esq., A. Stephen (C)
The Temple
24 Dale Street
Liverpool 2

CARTER, Esq., William Oscar (S) (C)
Holland Court
The Close
Norwich, Norfolk

CHAPLIN, Esq., Jon Howick (C)
Hilltop Cottage
Greenhills Close
Chorleywood, Herts.

CHORLTON, Miss Margaret G. (C)
9 Albert Square
Manchester 2

CLARK, Esq., George T. (S)
1 Bank Buildings, Princes Street
London, E. C. 2

CLARKE, Esq., Ralph C. G. (S)
18 Austin Friars
London, E. C. 2

COLLINS, Esq., Leon H. (S)
Airedale House
Albion Street
Leeds 1

COOPER, Esq., James William (S)
11 Queen Street
Great Yarmouth, Norfolk

COOPER, Esq., Peter Hilary (C)
30 Kedale Road
Seaford, Sussex

COPE, Esq., John Martin (S)
13 King's Bench Walk
Temple
London, E. C. 4

COUNSELL, Esq., Henry (C)
14 Orchard Street
Bristol 1

COWLING, Esq., Clifford (S)
277 Farnborough Road
Farnborough, Hants.

CREWDSON, Esq., William (S)
4 St. Paul's Churchyard
London, E. C. 4

CRIPPS, Esq., D. S. O., T. D., Q. C.,
Matthew Anthony Leonard (S)
1 Harcourt Buildings
London, E. C. 4

CROWTHER, Esq., Eric John Ronald
(S) (C)
56 Gilpin Ave, East Sheen
London, S. W. 14

CURRIE, Miss Stephanie Ella M. (S)
1 Pump Court
Temple
London, E. C. 4

CURRY, Esq., Kenneth R. (S)
St. Vedast House
150 Cheapside
London, E. C. 2

DAVIS, Esq., Godfrey Mark (S)
19 A Cavendish Square
London, W. 1

DAVIS, Esq., Howard S. (C)
Legal Department
Mobil Oil Co. Ltd.
Mobil House, 54/60 Victoria St.
London, S. W. 1

DEAN, Esq., Wilfred Martin Vernon
(S)
8 Carlos Place
London, W. 1

DENBY, Esq., Richard Kenneth (S)
6 Piccadilly
Bradford 1, Yorks.

dePIRO, Esq., Q. C., Alan (S) (C)
1 Harcourt Building, Temple
London, E. C. 4

DOUGLAS-MANN, Esq., Leslie John (S)
2 Stone Buildings, Lincoln's Inn
London, W. C. 2

DRUMMOND, Esq., David Louis (S)
64 Lincoln's Inn Fields
London, W. C. 2

DUNMORE, Esq., William Sydney (S)
75 Park Lane
Croydon, Surrey

ELLIS, Esq., Harry (S) (C)
Fennbank House
24 Christchurch Road
Bournemouth, Hants.

ELLISON, Esq., Cecil (S)
5 John Dalton Street
Manchester 2

ELLMAN, Esq., Michael (C)
3 Mickleham Hall
Dorking, Surrey

ELLWOOD, Esq., L. A. (S) (C)
1 Watergate
Tudor Street
London, E. C. 4

EVANS, Esq., Anthony
4 Essex Court, Temple
London, E. C. 4

FARMER, Esq., Harold E. (S)
"Golden Broom"
Broom Barn Lane
Great Missenden, Bucks.

FISCH, Esq., Isadore (S) (C)
3rd Floor, Holbeck House
105 Albion Street
Leeds 1

FOULKES, Esq., Brian (C)
5 John Dalton
Manchester 2

FRANKENBURG, Esq., John (C)
65 Davies Street
London, W. 1

GADSEN, Esq., Peter John (C)
5/7 Rowcroft Stroud
Glos.

GARRETT, Esq., Colin (C)
32 Les Pingrouins
Rue Carnot, 54-Vandoeuvre
France

GARRETT, Esq., Geoffrey Elmer (S)
51 Minories
London, E. C. 3

GARSTON, Esq., Eric Michael (S)
6 Wardrobe Place, Carter Lane
London, E. C. 4

GEFFEN, Esq., Ernest Joseph Henry (S)
Africa House 64 - 78, Kingsway
Holborn
London, W. C. 2

GILLETT, Esq., Arthur Douglas Ariel (S)
194 Seabourne Road
West Southbourne, Bournemouth

GILLHAM, Esq., William (S)
5 Botolph Alley
London, E. C. 3

GIRLING, Esq., O. B. E., J. William (S) (C)
19 Cecil Square
Margate, Kent

GLASS, Esq., Harry (C)
16 St. James' Row
Sheffield, 51 IXG

GOODMAN, Esq., Edward (C)
12 High Street
Sutton, Surrey

GREEN, Esq., James (C)
22 Coulson Street
London, S. W. 3

GRIFFITHS, Esq., I. Owen (S)
1 Harcourt Buildings, Temple
London, E. C. 4

GUEDALLA, Esq., T. D., F. Basil (S) (C)
199 Piccadilly
London, W. 1

HEAP, Esq., LL. M., Desmond (C)
Guildhall
London, E. C. 2

HICKS, O. B. E., T. D., D. L., Sir Denys T. (S) (C)
12 Berkeley Square
Bristol 8

HIGHTON, Esq., Cecil Joseph (S)
9 Old Square
Lincoln's Inn
London, W. C. 2

HILTON, Sir Derek Percy (S)
41 John Dalton Street
Manchester 2

HODGINS, Esq., Robert Crossman (S)
Day Whately & Co. Solicitors
Godalming, Surrey

HOLLAND, C. B. E., Q. C., Sir Milner
Chairman, General Council of the Bar
Carpmael Building, Temple
London, E. C. 4

HOLLAND, Esq., Frank Gerrard (S)
Kingsway House
103 Kingsway
London, W. C. 2

HORDERN, Esq., A. C. W. (S)
1 Harcourt Building
Temple
London, E. C. 4

HOPKINS, Esq., David Sime Borrough (S)
Sanderson House
Lower Basinghall Street
Leeds 1

HOSKING, Miss Audrey Kate (S)
18 Churchill Way
Cardiff, Wales

HUGH-JONES, Esq., Vyvyan Derek (S)
6/7 St. John Square
Cardiff, S. Wales

JAMES, Esq., Geoffrey Peter (S)
8 Queen Victoria Road
Coventry

JONES, Esq., Q. C., Kenneth
1 Crown Office Row
Temple
London, E. C. 4

JOWETT, Esq., Malcolm Harry (S)
Caroline House
Bradshawgate
Bolton, Lancs.

KARET, Esq., Jerome I. (C)
11/12 Finsbury Sq.
London, E. C. 2

KEMLO, Esq., Henry Archibald (S)
5 London Wall Buildings
Finsbury Circus
London, E. C. 2

KEOGH, Esq., Paul Engelbert (S)
Caroline House
Bradshawgate
Bolton, Lancs.

KIRK, Esq., Harry
Wareham
Dorset.

KRAMER, Esq., Abraham (S)
40 Portland Place
London, W. 1

LAITNER, Esq., Basil David (S)
26 High Court, High Street
Sheffield

LAUGHLAND, Esq., Graham F. B. (S)
1 Harcourt Buildings
Temple
London, E. C. 4

LEA, Esq., David Geoffrey (S)
Lennox House, Norfolk St. Strand
London, W. C. 2

LEIGH-HOWARD, Esq., Eric (S)
10 New Square, Lincoln's Inn
London, W. C. 2

LEVER, Esq., Jeremy
General Council of the Bar
London, E. C. 2

LEWIS, Esq., Henry Maxwell (S)
28 High Street
Southend-on-Sea, Sussex

LLOYD, Esq., Herbert Mervyn (S)
Port of London Authority
Trinity Square
London, E. C. 3

LOEWENFELD, Dr. Erwin (S)
10 Bulstrode Gardens
Cambridge

LONG, Sir Ronald (S)
Red House
Halstead, Essex

LUND, C. B. E., Sir Thomas (S) (C)
The Law Society
Law Society's Hall
Chancery Lane
London, W. C. 2

LYONS, Esq., Patrick J. M. (S) (C)
16 Baldwin Street
Bristol 1

MACDONALD, Esq., George A. (C)
1 King Street
Emsworth, Hants.

MACWATT, Esq., Robert Edward (S)
10 New Square, Lincoln's Inn
London, W. C. 2

MANGNALL, Esq., Rollo Barratt (S)
Abbey Close
Sherborne, Dorset

MANSON, Esq., Louis Joshua (S)
10 Duke Street, Wigmore Street
London, W. 1

MARSHALL, Esq., Denis A. (C)
3 - 5 Dowgate Hill
London, E. C. 4

MAY, Esq., Q. C., John
2 Temple Gardens
Temple
London, E. C. 4

MCFADYEAN, Esq., Colin (S)
18 Austin Friars
London, E. C. 2

MEARS, Esq., Bernard Sidney (S)
12 High Street
Dartford, Kent

MOLONEY, Sir Joseph (C)
2 Mitre Court Buildings
Temple
London, E. C. 4

MOWER WHITE, Esq., A. P. W. (C)
Harvest House
Felixstowe, Suffolk

MUNRO, Esq., Hector (C)
36 Dale Street
Liverpool 2

MYERSON, Esq., Geoffrey (S)
Midland Chambers
82 London Road
Leicester

NAPLEY, Esq., David (S)
Rolls Chambers
Star Yard, Carey Street
London, W. C. 2

NEW, Esq., John H. S. (C)
Allen & Overy
9/12 Cheapside
London, E. C. 2

NEWMAN, Esq., Gerson (S) (C)
The Temple
Dale Street
Liverpool 2

NEWMAN, Mrs. Phyllis (S) (C)
Solicitor
44 Welbeck Street
London, W. 1

NIMAN, Esq., Philip (S)
137 A Albert Road
Middlesbrough

O'BRIEN, Esq., Francis U. J. (S)
Shell International Petroleum
L. G. L. Shell Centre
London, S. E. 1

O'BRIEN, Miss Kathleen (C)
2 Harcourt Buildings
Temple
London, E. C. 4

PAINES, Esq., Anthony J. C. (C)
Allen & Overy
9/12 Cheapside
London, E. C. 2

PARKINSON, Esq., A. T. (C)
36 Spring Gardens
Manchester 2

PAYNE, Esq., Robert F. (C)
Hanover House
Alfred Gelder Street
Hull

PEARLMAN, Esq., Sidney (S)
2, Stone Buildings, Lincoln's Inn
London, W. C. 2

PEARLMAN, Miss Valerie (S)
Lamb Building, Temple
London, E. C. 4

PENDRIGH, Esq., John R. (C)
15 George Street
Croydon
London CR 9 1 HN

PERKOFF, Esq., Bernard Abraham (S)
2 Harewood Place,
Hanover Square
London, W. 1

PHILPOT, Esq., John Stewart (S)
28, Wide Bargate
Boston, Lincs.

PROTHERO, Esq., Arthur C.
32 Greenwich High Road
London, S. W. 9

RALTON, Esq., Cyril (S)
411 A/413 A Brixton Road
London, S. W. 9

RAPOPORT, Esq., David (C)
192 Lavender Hill
Clapham Junction
London, S. W. 11

RATHBONE, Esq., Brian (S)
3 Essex Court
Temple
London, E. C. 4

REA, Miss Margaret Eveline (S)
Adams & Remers Solicitors
Lewes
Lussesc

ROBERTS, Esq., Arthur B. (C)
15 Gracechurch Street
London, E. C. 3

ROWLAND, Miss Deborah M. (C)
3 Stone Buildings, Lincoln's Inn
London, W. C. 2

RUBENSTEIN, Esq., Alan George (S)
419 Oxford Street
London, W. 1

RUDD, Esq., Brian (S)
Blue House
Washington Co., Durham

RUDOFF, Esq., Theodore (C)
c/o H. M. Land Registry
Lincoln's Inn Fields
London, W. C. 2

RUSK, Dr. Leo Peter (S)
Leara Argyle Walk
Argyle Square
London, W. C. 1

SARGANT, Esq., Henry Edmond
President, The Law Society
Chancery Lane
London, W. C. 2

SCATLIFF, Esq., G. H. M. (S)
64 Skip Street
Brighton, Sussex

SCOTT, Sir Charles Hilary (S) (C)
18 Austin Friars
London, E. C. 2

SHAWCROSS, Q. C.,
The Right Hon. Lord (S)
c/o Shell International Petroleum
Shell Centre
London, S. E. 1

SHEEHAN, Esq., Maurice (C)
28 Station Road
Port Talbot

SHENTON, Esq., David William (S)
1 Serjeants Inn, Fleet Street
London, E. C. 4

SHINGLES, Esq., M. B. E.,
Raymond Edward Laws (S)
Barrington House
59 - 67 Gresham Street
London, E. C. 2

SIMPSON, Esq., K. T. (S)
1 Harcourt Buildings, Temple
London, E. C. 4

SLUZEWSKI, Dr. jur. C. (S) (C)
8 King William Street
London, E. C. 4

SNEATH, Esq., Peter Claude (S) (C)
4 St. Paul's Churchyard
London, E. C. 4

SPARK, Esq., Peter Brownlow (S) (C)
Lawrance, Messer & Co.
16 Coleman St.
London, E. C. 2

TAFFT, Esq., Gilbert Richard (S)
8 Queen Victoria Road
Coventry

TAYLOR, Esq., Walford (S)
The White House,
Highlands Close
Shortheath Road
Farnham, Hants.

THOMAS, Esq., David Brian (S)
6/7 St. John Square
Cardiff, S. Wales

TOLAND, Esq., Brian Edgell (C)
3 Wycliffe Street
Leicester

TURNER, Esq., Harold Horsfall
(S) (C)
The Law Society's Hall
Chancery Lane
London, W. C. 2

TUSON, Esq., Anthony Bryan (S)
117 Old Broad Street
London, E. C. 2

WALKER, Esq., D. J. (S)
1 Hatton Garden
Holborn Circus
London, E. C. 1

WALTERS, Esq., Robert (S)
Regent House, St. Phillips Place
Birmingham 3

WARD, Esq., Robin (S)
10 rue de France
Nice

WAREING, Esq., Charles Hodson (S)
Somerset House, Temple St.
Birmingham 2

WEBB, Esq., Charles J. (C)
60 Uxbridge Road
Shepherds Bush W. 12, London

WEGG-PROSSER, Esq.,
Charles Francis (S) (C)
133 Praed Street, Paddington
London, W. 2

WELLS, Esq., Hugh E. G. (S)
Crossman & Co., Solicitors
Thornbury, Bristol

WHARTON, Esq., M. B. E., T. D., D. L.,
George Anthony (S)
100 Friar Lane
Nottingham

WHITWORTH, Esq., Peter Ernest (S)
5 Paper Buildings, Temple
London, E. C. 4

WIGGIN, Esq., Henry W. (C)
c/o Ryland Martinean & Co.
41 Church Street
Birmingham

WILLIAMS, Esq., John (S)
17 New Road Avenue
Chatham, Kent

WISE, Esq., Reginald Derek (S)
167 rue de l'Université
Paris 7, France

WOOD, Esq., William Peter (S) (C)
29 High Street
Harpenden

WOODHOUSE, Esq., Richard (S)
1 Harcourt Buildings, Temple
London, E. C. 4

FIJI

SHERANI, Esq., Faiz (C)
Box 1004
Suva

FINLAND

There are two forms of address for practising lawyers in Finland; "Asianajaja" for Finnish-speaking lawyers, and "Advokat" for Swedish-speaking lawyers — in both cases, the title to appear before the individual's name. It is suggested that if the language is not known, the Anglo-Saxon form of address for lawyers be used ("Esquire" or "Esq." after the full name).

HAKAPÄÄ, Asianajaja Mauri,
President, Suomen Asianajajaliitto
Unioninkatu 24
Helsinki

HERNBERG, Advokat Olof
Kluuvikatu 3
Helsinki 10

LAGUS, Advokat Klaus (S) (C)
Mikonkatu 13
Helsinki

ROSCHIER-HOLMBERG,
Advokat Ake (S)
Centralgatan 5 A 8
Helsinki

SIPILÄ, Mars. Helvi
Vuorikatu 3
Helsinki 10

FRANCE

Practising lawyers (avocats) in France are usually addressed with "Maître" or "Me" appearing before the individual's name.

BALLEROY, Me Paul (C)
31 Rue la Perouse
Paris 16e

BAUVE, Me Jean-Pierre (C)
46, Rue Ste Anne
Paris 2e

DELMONT, Me Henri, President (C)
Association Nationale des Avocats
30 Rue de Condé
Paris 6e

de RICCI, Me Denis (C)
15 Avenue Matignon
Paris VIIIe

DELVOLVE, Me Jean Louis (C)
4, Ave. Van Dyck
Paris 8e

FABER, Me Gabrielle
26, Rue Champ-la-Garde
Versailles

GASTAMBIDE, Me Philippe (C)
29, Avenue Pierre 1er de Serbie
Paris 16e

GOLDSMITH, Me Jean-Claude (C)
4, Ave. Van Dyck
Paris 8e

JEANTET, Me Fernand Charles
1, Avenue Sylvestre de Sacy
Paris

LASSIER, Me Jacques René Pascal (C)
146 Bld. St. Germain
Paris

MOLIERAC, Me J.-M. (S)
Ancien Batonnier
3, rue Duffour-Dubergier
Bordeaux, Gironde

PADOA, Me Felix Albert (S) (C)
4 Avenue Saint Honore d'Eylau
Paris 16e

PUCCI, Me Roland (S)
P. O. Box 2041
Brazzaville, Congo

SERVOS, Me Joseph (S)
Avocat á La Cour d'Appel
160 Rue Vendome
Lyon

SMYTH, Me John F. (Observer)
Secretariat-General
Council of Europe
67, Strasbourg

VANDON, Me Jean (C)
38 Rue St. Jacques
Marselle

VANULAR, Miss Sonia A. (S)
3 Rue du Départ
Paris 14e

WALRAFEN, Me Eliane
3, rue Charles Dickens
Paris 16e

GERMANY

Practising lawyers in Germany are addressed "Rechtsanwalt" or "RA", with the title appearing before the individual's name. Practising lawyers who have earned a doctorate of laws are addressed "Rechtsanwalt Dr." or "RA Dr. jur." before the name. The title "Bundesrichter" is that of a judge of a Federal Supreme Court of the Federal Republic.

ACKERMANN, RA Dr. Heinrich
Kreuzweg 2
2 Hamburg 1

AHLERS, Dr. Dieter
Hinter dem Schütting/Stintbrücke
28 Bremen

BASEDOW, RA Dr. Klaus (S)
Mohlenhof
2 Hamburg 1

BLOMEYER, RA Dr. Karl (S)
c/o Deutsch-Asiatische Bank
Rathausstraße 7
2 Hamburg 1

BRANGSCH, RA Dr. Heinz (S)
Sievekingplatz 1, Z. 811
2 Hamburg 36

BUNG, RA Dr. Hubertus (S)
Ehinger Straße 334 (EW)
41 Duisburg-Wanheim

BUNGARTZ, RA Dr. Lothar (S) (C)
Kaiser-Friedrich-Ufer 33
5 Köln

BUNZEL, RA Dr. jur. Francis L. (S) (C)
1155 S. Sierra Bonita Ave.
Los Angeles, Calif. 90019, USA

BURCHARD-MOTZ, RA Dr. Heinrich (S) (C)
Poststraße 2, I
2 Hamburg 36

COELER, RA Dr. Gerd (S)
Bei den Mühren 1
2 Hamburg 11

DERINGER, RA Arved (S) (C)
Zitelmannstraße 8
53 Bonn

DOBRING, RA Dr. Eberhard (S)
Rheinstraße 7 - 9
61 Darmstadt

EHLERS, RA Dr. Kurt (S) (C)
Bergstraße 7, IV
2 Hamburg 1

EISENFÜHR, RA Dr. jur. Gottfried W. (S)
Johnsallee 51
2 Hamburg 13

ESSMANN, RA Klaus (S)
Parkstraße 31
4 Düsseldorf

FALKENHAUSEN, RA Dr. Kurt H. Frhr. v. (S)
Am Rasselberg 35
633 Wetzlar

FISCHERHOF, RA Dr. Hans (S)
Grillparzerstraße 41
6 Frankfurt a. M.

FLAD, Dr. Hubert (S) (C)
Westendstraße 84
6 Frankfurt a. M.

FRANZ, RAuN Joachim (S) (C)
Kasseler Straße 30
3505 Gudensberg

FÜNFSTÜCK-FRENZEL, Frau RA Ursula (S)
Hermannstal 97 b
2 Hamburg 34

GERCKE, RA Dr. Egon (C)
Bergstraße 7
2 Hamburg 1

GLEISS, RA Dr. Alfred (S) (C)
Haußmannstraße 46
7 Stuttgart-O

GRIMM, RA Dr. Hermann (C)
Stresemannstraße 13
68 Mannheim

GRUPE, RA Dr. jur. Heinz (S)
Leyboldstraße 9
5 Köln-Marienburg

GÜNTHER, RA Edgar (S)
Meckenheimer Straße 11 a
53 Bonn

HAGEDORN, RA Dr. Jürgen (S)
Martensdamm 2
23 Kiel

HARDOW, RAuN Joachim (S) (C)
Friedrich-Ebert-Straße 1
285 Bremerhaven-G.

HAUSSMANN, RA Dr. Wolfgang (S)
Königstraße 31 B
7 Stuttgart N

HELM, RA Dr. Dieter (S)
Mainzer Landstraße 51
6 Frankfurt am Main

HERRMANN, RA Carl (S)
Kaiser-Wilhelm-Ring 23
5 Köln

HOLSTE, RA Dr. Heinrich (S)
Speicherstraße 11
31 Celle

JUNGE, Assessor Werner (S)
Deutscher Industrie- u. Handelstag
Markt 26 - 32
53 Bonn

KRECKEL, RA Berthold (S)
Johnsallee 51
2 Hamburg 13

LANGEN, RA Dr. Eugen (S)
Inselstraße 2
4 Düsseldorf

LAUTERBACH, RA Wolfgang (C)
Roeckstraße 48
24 Lübeck

LIEBERKNECHT, RA Gottfried (C)
Berliner Allee 2
4 Düsseldorf

MARCETUS, RAuN Dr. Karl (S) (C)
Kaiserdamm 95
1 Berlin 19

MATHY, RA Klaus
An der Burgmauer 10
5 Köln

MERKEL, RA Dr. habil. Hans
Präsident
Deutscher Anwaltverein e. V.
Maximilianstraße 48
89 Augsburg

MIRGEL, RA Dr. Heinrich (S) (C)
Kaiser-Friedrich-Ufer 31
5 Köln

MUELLER, RA Dr. Rudolf (S)
Marienstraße 17
6 Frankfurt a. M.

MULLER-BORNER, RA Dr. Richard (C)
Podbielskiallee 68
1 Berlin 33

OPPENHOFF, RA Michael F. (C)
Burgmauer 10
5 Köln

OPPENHOFF, RA Dr. Walter (S) (C)
Burgmauer 10
5 Köln

OSTEN, RA Dr. Horst von der (S)
Böhmestraße 16
4 Düsseldorf

PAETOW, RA Hans (S)
Neuer Wall 10/II
2 Hamburg 36

PAKUSCHER, LL. M.,
RA Dr. Ernest (S) (C)
Hundekehlestraße 22
1 Berlin 33

PEE, RAuN Dr. Wilhelm (S)
Breite Straße 13, I
24 Lübeck

PINNER, RA Dr. Heinz A. (S) (C)
8105 West Third Street
Los Angeles, Calif. 90048 USA

PLÖTTNER, RA Dr. Eberhard (S)
Zollstraße 11
404 Neuß

POLLZIEN, RA Dr. Götz M. (S) (C)
Dienerstraße 20
8 München 2

PREUSS, RA Ludwig (C)
Damaschkestraße 23
1 Berlin 13

RUNGE, RA Dr. Christian (S)
Zähringerstraße 9
66 Saarbrücken 1

SANDSTEIN, RA Dr. jur. A. (S)
Breite Straße 8
4 Düsseldorf

SCHEFFEN, RA Wilhelm (S)
Postfach 17
5 Köln

SCHLEIFENBAUM, RA Rudolf (S)
Hindenburgstraße 1
59 Siegen

SCHUMACHER, RA Peterjürgen (C)
Arcisstraße 61, I
8 München 13

SCHWARZ, RA Dr. Karl Walter (S)
Podbielskiallee 81
1 Berlin-Dahlem

SIEBEL, RA Dr. Ulf R. (S)
Junghofstraße 5-17
6 Frankfurt a. M.

SILCHER, RA Friedrich (S)
Farbenfabriken Bayer AG
509 Leverkusen-Bayerwerk

SOLMITZ, RA Robert (S)
2128 Veteran Ave.
Los Angeles, Calif. 90025 USA

STEINHAUER, RA Dr. Dieter (S)
Morianstraße 20
56 Wuppertal-Elberfeld

WALTERS, RA Dr. jur. (S)
Ballindamm 25, III
2 Hamburg 1

WILMANNS, RAuN Dr. Hermann (S) (C)
Bahnhofstraße 31 (Postfach 763)
2 Hamburg-Blankenese

WÖLPER, RA Heinrich
Hinter dem Schütting/Stintbrücke
28 Bremen

GHANA

ASARE, Esq., H. E. Theodore (S)
Ambassador of Ghana
P. O. Box 75, Accra
West Africa

GREECE

ECONOMOPOLOUS, Esq., George J. (S)
21, Mavromichali Street
Athens 144

KARATZAS, Advocate Theodoros B. (S)
6, Homirou Street
Athens 133

LEGAKIS, Esq., Kimon Anastasios (S)
14 Nikitaras Street
Athens

LEKKAS, Esq., Spiro D. (S)
72 Tritonos Street
Old Faliron, Athens

VOURVACHIS, Advocate Eleftherios (S)
21 Platia Omonias
Athens

ZEPOS, Esq., Demitros J. (S)
7, Hippocrates Street
Athens 143

ZEPOS, Esq., John D. (S)
7, Hippocrates Street
Athens 143

GUATEMALA

QUIÑONES, Sr. Lic. D. Edmundo
Presidente, Colegio de Abogados
Universidad de San Carlos
de Guatemala

HAITI

Practising lawyers (avocats) in Haiti are usually addressed with "Maître" or "Me" appearing before the individual's name, followed by the title "Avocat".

LIAUTAUD, Maître Pierre L. (S)
P. O. Box 205
Port-au-Prince

HONG KONG

GRIFFITHS, Esq., P. J. (S)
Messrs. Wilkinson & Grist
2, Queen's Road Central

REA, Esq., Dermot (C)
Attorney General's Chambers

VINE, Esq., Peter (C)
Deacons
6th Floor, Union House

IRAN

Practising lawyers in Iran are usually addressed with "Maître" or "Me" appearing before the individual's name.

ABOLGHASSEM, Me Tafazoli (S)
110 Avenue Hoghoughi
Teheran

AGHABABIAN, Dr. Raphael (S)
13, Rue Nowbahar
Avenue Chah
Teheran

AGHAYAN, Prof. Dr. Alexander (S)
Avenue Sevom Esfand
Teheran

AMIR-EBRAHIMI, Me Abdol Majid (C)
4266 Takhte-Djamshid Ave.
Teheran

EHTESHAMI, Me Abdullah
74 Hafiz Ave. 5th Floor
Teheran

FARMAN-FARMAYAN, Dr. A.
Avenue Takhte-Djamshid
Teheran

HOUMAN, Dr. Ahmad, President
Iranian Bar Association
4266 Takhte-Djamshid Ave.
Teheran

KAZEMI, Dr. Parvis (S) (C)
301 Takhte Djamshid 551
Teheran

KHADEM, Dr. Ali (S)
162 Iranshahr Ave.
Teheran

MALEKI, Me Mehdi
Shimram Avenue
Amol Street
Teheran

NARRAGHI, Me Abbass (S)
Crossroads Pahlavi 25
Teheran

TAGHVAII, Dr. Ebrahim
4266 East Takhto-Djamshid Ave.
Teheran

TAJBAKHSH, Mr. Mohamad Bagher
527 Takhte-Djamshid Ave.
Teheran

IRAQ

AL-SAMARRAIE, Me Fayek, President
Iraqi Bar Association
Rashid Street
Baghdad

EL-SINAWI, Advocate Abfullah (S)
Ameen Square - Rasheed Street
Baghdad

MATLOUB, Maître Jamil (S)
Abdul Munim Al-Khudery Bldg.
South Gate
Baghdad

RASSAM, Esq., Noel M.
Iraqi Bar Association
Baghdad

IRELAND

Practising lawyers in Ireland are usually addressed with "Esquire" or "Esq." appearing after the full name. Other forms of address are similar to those appearing under England.

BALLAGH, Esq., T. (C)
Bank of Ireland
College Green
Dublin

BEATTY, Esq., Christopher (C)
68 Fitzwilliam Sq.
Dublin 2

BEATTY, Esq., Walter (C)
68 Fitzwilliam Sq.
Dublin 2

BELL, Esq., David (C)
13 Bachelor's Walk
Dublin 1

BLAKE, Esq., Bruce St. J. (C)
93 Lower Baggot St.
Dublin 2

BOLAND, Esq., John A. (C)
Public Trustee Office
Kingsway, London W. C. 2
England

BURKE, Esq., Francis X. (C)
30 Lr. Ormand Quay
Dublin 1

CARRIGAN, Esq., John (S) (C)
Glengarriff
Thurles Co. Tipperary

CARROLL, Mella (C)
Law Library
Four Courts
Dublin 7

CASSIDY, Miss Agnes (C)
Law Library
Four Courts
Dublin 7

COLLINS, Esq., Anthony (C)
19 Eustace Street
Dublin 2

COLLINS, Esq., Desmond Joseph (S) (C)
19 Eustace Street
Dublin 2

CONDON, Esq., Colm (C)
Government Buildings
Upper Merrion St.
Dublin 2

COYLE, Esq., Geoffrey (C)
Law Library
Four Courts
Dublin 7

DOYLE, Esq., Gerard M. (C)
50 Lower O'Connell St.
Dublin 1

DOYLE, Esq., S. C. Thomas A. (S) (C)
9 Winton Road
Dublin 6

EYRE, Esq., John (C)
Glenbower Park, Churchtown
Dublin 14

FERRELLY, Esq., James M. (C)
1 College Street
Dublin

FINLAY, Esq., Thomas P. (C)
Law Library
Four Courts
Dublin 7

FINLAY, Esq., William O. (C)
Park House
Booterstown Ave.,
Co. Dublin

FRENCH, Esq., Raymond (C)
Ardilea
Westminster Rd., Foxrock
Dublin

GANNON, Esq., Francis J. (C)
Mohill
Co. Leitrim

GANNON, Esq., John M. J. (C)
30 Hollybrook Rd.
Dublin 3

GILMORE, Esq., Dinneen B. (C)
15 St. Stephen's Green
Dublin 2

GOGARTY, Esq., Oliver D. (C)
22 Earlsfort Terrace
Dublin 2

GREEN, Esq., James R. C. (C)
19/20 Lower Baggot St.
Dublin 2

HICKEY, Esq., Gerald D. (C)
26 Shrewsbury Rd.
Dublin

JACKSON, Esq., Thomas (C)
30 Burlington Rd.
Dublin 4

KILLEEN, Miss Carmel (C)
45 Callary Road
Mount Merrion, Co. Dublin

KING, Esq., John P. (C)
13 Anne St. South
Grafton St.
Dublin 2

LANIGAN, Esq., Francis J. (C)
Centaur St.
Carlow

LISTON, S. C., Terence K., Chairman (C)
The General Council of the Bar of Ireland
Law Library, Four Courts
Dublin 7

MACGARRY, Esq., James (C)
34 Lower Abbey St.
Dublin 1

MAHER, Esq., John (C)
20 Westland Row
Dublin 2

MARGETSON, Esq., Ernest (C)
20 Upper Merrion St.
Dublin 2

MCCARROLL, Mary T. (C)
111 Pearse St.
Dublin 2

MCCARRON, Esq., Eunan (C)
9 Upper Mount St.
Dublin 2

MCCARTHY, Esq., Niall (C)
39 Bushy Park Rd.
Dublin 6

MCCORMICK, Esq., Henry W. (S)
37 Molesworth St.
Dublin

MCDONALD, Esq., Alexander J. (C)
21 Earlsfort Terrace
Dublin 2

MCGRATH, Esq., Brendan A. (C)
St. John's Islandbridge
Dublin 8

MCMAHON, Esq., Bryan (C)
Law Faculty
University College, Cork

MOLONEY, Esq., Gerald J.
70 South Mall
Cork County, Cork

MOORE, Esq., Patrick C.
35 South Great George's Street
Dublin 2

MICKS, Esq., S. Christopher (C)
Lurganbrae
Shankhill, Co. Dublin

MORAN, Esq., Desmond (C)
34/35 Lower Ormond Quay
Dublin 1

MORAN, Frances E. (C)
St. James Howth Road
Clontarf, Dublin 3

MULHOLLAND, Esq., Owen (C)
6 Sanford Rd.
Ranelagh, Dublin 6

MURPHY, Esq., Francis (C)
New Quay
Clonmel Co. Tipperary

NASH, Esq., John T. (C)
Templemore
Co. Tipperary

NOLAN, Esq., George A. (C)
83 Quay
Waterford

NOONAN, Esq., LL. B., Patrick (S) (C)
President
The Incorporated Law Society of Ireland
Solicitors Bldg., Four Courts
Dublin 7

O'CONNOR, Esq., Brian (C)
51/52 Fitzwilliam Square
Dublin 2

O'CONNOR, Esq., Daniel J. (C)
42/3 St. Stephen's Green
Dublin 2

O'CONNOR, Esq., Rory (C)
34 Upper Ormond Quay
Dublin 7

O'DALAIGH, The Hon. Cearbhall (C)
Chief Justice, High Court
Four Courts
Dublin 7

O'DONNELL, Esq., Denzil (C)
69/71 St. Stephen's Green
Dublin 2

O'DONNELL, Esq., Patrick T. D. (C)
Dungloe, Co. Donegal

O'DONOVAN, Esq., James W. (C)
53 South Mall
Cork

O'HANLON, Esq., S. C., Roderick (C)
Law Library
Four Courts
Dublin 7

O'KEEFFE, The Hon. Andreas (C)
President of the High Court
Four Courts
Dublin 7

O'SULLIVAN, Esq., Franklin J. (C)
8 Clare St.
Dublin

O'TOOLE-ROWAN, Mrs. Margaret (C)
Law Library
Four Courts
Dublin 7

OSBORNE, Esq., William (C)
Naas, Co. Kildare

OVEREND, Esq., George G. (C)
31 Fitzwilliam Square
Dublin 2

PLUNKETT, Esq., Eric A. (C)
The Incorporated Law Society of Ireland
Solicitors' Building
Four Courts
Dublin 7

PRENTICE, Esq., Peter D. M. (C)
20 Upper Merrion St.
Dublin 2

ROSS, Esq., John N. (C)
20 Upper Merrion St.
Dublin 1

RUSSELL, Esq., Matthew (C)
Law Library
Four Courts
Dublin 7

RYAN, Esq., Edward F. (C)
20 South Mall
Cork

RYAN, Esq., Eoin (C)
4 Winton Road
Dublin 6

RYAN, Esq., Peter P. (C)
Rathdowney
Portlaoise, Laois

SHAW, Esq., Dermot P.
38-40 Parliament Street
Dublin 2

SHEEHAN, Esq., James (C)
1 Clare Street
Dublin 2

SHIOMOIN, Esq., Maire (Nic) (C)
13 Bachelor's Walk
Dublin 1

TAYLOR, Esq., Brian (C)
34/5 Laurence St.
Drogheda, Co. Louth

TAYLOR, Esq., Robert McD. (C)
34/5 Laurence St.
Drogheda, Co. Louth

WALKER, Esq., Ralph J. (C)
15 St. Stephen's Green
Dublin 2

WALSH, The Hon. Mr. Justice Brian (C)
The Supreme Court
Four Courts
Dublin 7

INDIA

Practising lawyers in India are usually addressed with "Mr." appearing before the name and "Advocate" after the name.

N. Venkatarama Ayyar (C)
17, Balakrishna Road
Mylapore, Madras

Jethmalani, Prof. Ram B. (S) (C)
41 Advant Foreshore Rd.
Bombay 1

Singh, Mr. Rajendra (C)
309 Civil Lines North
Jabalpur M. P.

Veeraraghaven, Mr. A. N. (C)
The Bar Council of India
AB/21 Mathura Road
New Delhi 1

ISRAEL

Practising lawyers in Israel are usually addressed with "Esquire" or "Esq." appearing after the full name of the individual. In the event that the lawyer has a doctorate, "Dr." appears before the name, and "Advocate" or "Adv." after the name. Judges are addressed "The Honorable" or "The Hon."

In accordance with the Rules of the Israel Bar recently promulgated, a practising lawyer can — in addition to his academic title — use only the title "Advocate" in English, "Avocat" in French, "Muhami" in Arabic and "Orekhdin" in Hebrew, and the title he acquired, if any, while practising outside Israel as an attorney.

Arazi, Dr. Arye
87 Allenby Road
Tel-Aviv

Fraenkel, Esq., Yehuda (C)
15 Ahad Haam St.
Tel-Aviv

Ganon, Advocate, Mr. I.
47 Haatzmaut Road
Haifa

Katz, Rebecca (C)
Hacalanit St.
Commercial Centre
Kiron

Kennet, Esq., Mordechai (C)
91 Rothschild Bldg.
91, Tel-Aviv

Kister, Mr. Justice Y.
Supreme Court of Israel
Jerusalem

Lipschütz, Esq., Naftali
64 Hameginim Ave.
Haifa

Levi, Esq., Joel (C)
Ahuzat Bayit St., 3
Tel-Aviv

Levy, Esq., Avshalom (C)
10 Lunz Street
Jerusalem

Nahir, Esq., Boas (C)
13 Ahad Haam St.
Tel-Aviv

Rotenstreich, Adv., Dr. Joshua
The Israel Bar
2 Har-Sinai Street
P. O. B. 1881
Tel-Aviv

Salant, Esq., Ephraim (C)
15 Narachasim Street
Ramat-Gan

Shaked, Esq., Barvch (C)
Tel-Aviv 29

Shomer, Esq., Alexander (C)
Agron Street 30

Szatmary, Esq., Moshe (C)
10 Daniel Frisch
Tel-Aviv

Varkonyi, Mrs. Sara Moshkowitz
(S) (C)
Attorney at Law
Palatine Building
28 Achad Haam Street
Tel-Aviv

ITALY

Practising lawyers in Italy are usually addressed with "Avvocato" or "Avv." before the name.

BISCONTI, Avv. Dr. Giuseppe
Via Barberini 3
Rome

ANGELINI ROTA, Avv. Angelo (C)
Rue S. Domenico 20
Rome

BELTRAMO, Avv. Mario (C)
Via Vittorio Veneto 96
Rome

BIAMONTI, Avv. Enrico (C)
Rue Archimede 98
Rome

BRUNO, Avv. Mario (S)
10, Via P. Verri
Milano

CAPRIO, Avv. Salvatore (S) (C)
Via Della Guastalla 15
Milano

CAPUA, Avv. Carlo (S)
Via Venti Settembre 1
Rome

CERNITORI, Avv. Giulio Cesare (S)
7, Via Circo
Milano

DALLA VEDOVA, Avv. Riccardo (S)
Via Varese 12
Rome

d'AMELY MELODIA, Miss Giuseppina (S) (C)
Via Gradisca 7
Rome

DELLA ROCCA, Prof. Avv. Fernando (C)
96 Via Cavour
Rome

EMANUELE, Avv. Turco (S)
Via Bartolomeo Marliano n. 3
Rome 3

FORNARIO, Avv. Carlo (C)
Viale Angelico 92
Rome
(President, de L'Ordre de Rome)

GRAZIADEI, Avv. Ercole (S)
Via Vittorio Veneto 96
Rome

GUERRERI, Avv. Giuseppe (S) (C)
15 Via Quattro Fontane
00184 Rome

NUNZIANTE, Avv. Gianni B. (S) (C)
4, Via del Velabro
Rome

PISANO, Avv. Paulo (C)
4, Via di Porta Pinciana
00187, Rome

PROSPERETTI, Avv. Walter (C)
Via Pier Luigi da Palestrina 19
Rome

ROSSI, Avv. Comm. Paolo Alberto (S)
58, Via S. Angela Merici
Rome

SANTORO, Avv. Rosalbino (S)
Rue Caracciolo 17
Napoli

TULLIO, Avv. Grillo (C)
2/6 Via Pompeo Magno
Rome 00192

UNGARO, On. Avv. Filippo
Piazza della Libertà 13
Rome, 13

UGHI, Avv. Giovanni M. (S)
13, Via San Palol
Milan

VENTURA, Dr. Sergio (S)
10 Rue Joseph Vanderlinden
Brusselles 18, Belgium

JAMAICA

ASHENHEIM, Esq., Leslie E.
President
The Inc. Law Society of Jamaica
11 Duke Street
Kingston

BURKE, Esq., Keith Constantine (S) (C)
47 Duke Street
Kingston

ROBINSON, Esq., Leacroft (C)
16 Duke Street
Kingston

VARMA, Esq., Ashoka K. (S)
42 Duke Street
Kingston

JAPAN

Practising lawyers in Japan are addressed with "Bengoshi Mr." before the name; or, if the individual has a doctorate, "Bengoshi Dr.".

HATTORI, Bengoshi Mr. Sadao (S)
5, Yaesu-4-Chome, Chuo-ku
Tokyo

HIRANO, Bengoshi Mr. Ryuichi (C)
Dept. of Law
Tokyo University
Tokyo

IRIE, Bengoshi Mr. Toshio (C)
Supreme Court of Japan
1-1-4, Kasumigaseki, Chiyoda-ku
Tokyo

KEIZO KANNO, Judge (C)
Supreme Court of Japan
1-1-4, Kasumigaseki, Choyoda-ku
Tokyo

MIKASA, Bengoshi Mr. Teisuke (S)
Toroya Building
Ahasaka 4 chome
Minato-ku, Tokyo

NARITOMI, Bengoshi Dr. Nobuo (S) (C)
Room 408, Yayesu Building
Marunouchi, Chiyoda-ku
Tokyo

NOMURA, Bengoshi Mr. Fuji
118 Kajiya-cho
Kagoshima City
Kagoshima Prefecture

OHTSUKA, Bengoshi Mr. Kiichiro (S)
3-373 Mabashi Suginami-ku
Tokyo

OHYAMA, Bengoshi Mr. Kikuji
President, Japan Fed. of Bar Assoc.
1, 1-chome, Kasumigaseki
Chiyoda-ku, Tokyo

TANIMURA, Bengoshi Mr. Tadaichiro
President, Japan Bar Association
1, 1-chome, Kasumigaseki
Chiyoda-ku, Tokyo

TOICHI, Bengoshi Mr. Noboru
Japan Fed. of Bar Associations
1-1Chome, Kasumigaseki
Chiyoda-ku, Tokyo

YAMANA, Bengoshi Mr. Jyuzo
83 Shimizu-cho
Suginami-ku
Tokyo

KENYA

Le PELLEY, Peter
P. O. Box 14201
Nairobi

KOREA

HAHN, Byun Ho Sa Bok (C)
123 Secondka Namdaemoonro
Chungku
Seoul

KIM, Byun Ho Sa Myong-Yun
290-95 Munwha-Dong
Sungdong-Ku
Seoul

SHIN, Mr. Soon Un, President
Korean Bar Association
38 Seosomoondong
Seodaimoongu
Seoul

WHANG, Byun Ho Sa Sungsoo
Korean Bar Association
38 Seosomoondong
Seodaimoongu
Seoul

KUWAIT

ATTIA, Avocat Dr. Gamal (S)
East Building
Fahd Al-Salem Street
Post Office Box 2857
Kuwait

LEBANON

AKL, Michel (C)
c/o Ordre des Avocats
Beyrouth

ALEM, Maître Youssef
c/o Ordre des Avocats à Beyrouth
Palais de Justice
Beyrouth

GHANZI, Esq., Faouzi
Place de l'Etoile
Banco di Roma Bldg.
Beyrouth

KHOURY, Mr. Amine
Azarieh Building
Mère Gilas Street
Beyrouth

MOBARAK, Jean (C)
c/o Ordre des Avocats
Beyrouth

SHEHADI, Mounir (C)
c/o Ordre des Avocats
Beyrouth

LIBERIA

SIMPSON, Counsellor C. L. (S) (C)
P. O. Box 377
Monrovia

HENRIES, Hon. Richard A., President
Liberian National Bar Association
31 Benson Street
Monrovia

LUXEMBOURG

The titles used for lawyers in Luxembourg are the same as for French lawyers. Practising lawyers are usually addressed with "Maître" or "Me" appearing before the individual's name.

EICHHORN, Me Paul (S)
5 Boulevard Prince-Henri
Luxembourg

LEOSCH, Me Fernand
9 Avenue de la Liberté
Luxembourg

MALAWI

Practising lawyers in Malawi are usually addressed with "Esquire" or "Esq." appearing after the full name. Since Malawi is a member of the British Commonwealth of Nations, customs of address are generally those appearing under England.

Michael Hill Blackwood, Esq. (S) (C)
P. O. Box 9
Blantyre

MALAYSIA

Practising lawyers in Malaysia are usually addressed with "Esquire" or "Esq." appearing after the full name.

CHELLIAH, Esq., Robert (C)
4 Fl. Bangunan Cho Tek
Talan Tuanicu Abdel Rahman
Juala Lumpur

LEE, Kim Yew (C)
10 S. Malacca Street
Singapore I.

SELLAR, Esq., Forbes Keith (S)
64 First Cross Street
Malacca

MALTA

BUSUTTIL, B. A., Professor Edwin (S)
27 Creche Street
Silema

GANADO, Joseph (C)
171 Old Bakery Street
Valletta

MAURITIUS

DAVID, Jean Marc (C)
11 Pope Hennesey St.
Port Louis

MEXICO

Practising lawyers in Mexico are usually addressed with "Senor Licenciado Don" or "Sr. Lic. D." appearing before the name. If the individual has a doctorate, "Dr." is substituted: "Sr. Lic. Dr.".

ARTIGAS, Sr. Lic. D.
Armando Reyes (S)
Av. Morelos No. 98-302
México 1, D. F.

BARROETA, Sr. Lic. D.
Benjamin Flores (S)
Insurgentes Sur 421
Despacho A-506
México, D. F.

BETETA MONSALVE, Sr. Lic. D.
Mario Ramon (S)
Secretaria de Hacienda y
Credito Publico
Palacio Nacional
México 1, D. F.

BREÑA GARDUÑO, Sr. Lic., D.
Francisco (S)
Morelos 110-1002/3
México, D. F.

BUGEDA LANZAS, Sr. Lic. D.
Jesús C. (S)
Morelia 111-306
México 7, D. F.

BUGEDA MUÑOZ, Sr. Lic. Dr.
Jerónimo (S)
Morelia 111-306
México 7, D. F.

CAMPOS LOBO, Sr. Lic. D.
Eduardo (S)
Isabel La Catolica Núm. 43
Despacho 204
México 1, D. F.

CEPEDA V., Sr. Lic. D. Onésimo (S)
P. de la Reforma 76-1502
México 6, D. F.

CHAYET, Sr. Lic. D. Zack V. (S)
6600 East 4th Ave.
Denver, Colorado 80220 USA

COMPEÁN, Sr. Lic. D. Salvador
Lafragua No. 18, 2⁰ piso
México 1, D. F.

DALTON, Sr. Lic. D. Jess N. (S)
Apartado Postal 93 Bis
México, D. F.

DOMINGUEZ AMEZCUA,
Sr. Lic. D. Virgilio (S) (C)
San Juan de Latran 11-204
México 1, D. F.

DÖRING HERMOSILLO,
Sr. Lic. D. Carlos (S)
Paseo de la Reforma No. 355
Apdo. 93-Bis
México, D. F.

ESCOBEDO, Sr. Lic. D. Manuel G. (S) (C)
Avenida Juárez No. 14-803-806
México 1, D. F.

ESCOBEDO, Sr. Lic. D. Miguel S. (S)
Avenida Juárez No. 14-803-806
México 1, D. F.

FÉRNÁNDEZ MARGÁIN, Sr. Lic. D. Adrián (S)
Sullivan 31, 10⁰ piso
México 4, D. F.

FRANCO-GUZMAN, Sr. Lic. D. Ricardo (S)
Liverpool 88-502
México 6, D. F.

GALICIA ALCALÁ, Sr. Lic. D. Manuel (S)
Paseo de la Reforma 51-80
México, D. F.

GAXIOLA III, Sr. Lic. D. Francisco Javier (S)
Reforma 284, 3⁰ piso
México 6, D. F.

GERTZ MANERO, Sr. Lic. D. Federico (S)
Calle de Palma 37
México 1, D. F.

GIORGANA, Sr. Lic. D. Victor (S)
Avenida Juárez 117-109
México, D. F.

GOMEZ CEVALLOS, Sr. Lic. D. Angel (S)
Av. Juárez No. 42, Edificio B, 711
México 1, D. F.

GRAJALES G., Sr. Lic. D. Leopoldo (S)
Medellin 43-801
Plaza Miravalle
México, D. F.

GUAJARDO, Sr. Lic. D. Ignacio A. (S)
Ed. "Lic. A. Guajardo"
Desps. 108-111
Mexicati, B. Cfa.

HALE, Sr. Lic. D. Eduardo (S)
Tabasco 49-101
México 7, D. F.

IBARROLA CERVANTES,
Sr. Lic. don Luis (S)
Venustiano Carranza 69-201
México, D. F.

IBARROLA MURO,
Sr. Lic. don J. Claudio (S)
Venustiano Carranza 69-201
México, D. F.

ITURBIDE,
Sr. Lic. Dr. Francisco Laris (S)
Lucerna 27, Despacho 401
Col. Juárez
México 6, D. F.

LOPEZ ROSADO,
Sr. Lic. D. Felipe (S)
Amargura No. 14
México 20, D. F.

LUNA y PARRA,
Sr. Lic. D. Jorge (S) (C)
Reforma 105-403
México, D. F.

MACEDO, Sr. Lic. D. Miguel (S)
Paseo de la Reforma 185, 6⁰ piso
México 5, D. F.

MACEDO, Sr. Lic. D. Pablo (S)
Paseo de la Reforma 185, 6⁰ piso
México 5, D. F.

MARGÁIN, Excmo. Sr. D. Hugo B. (S)
Embajador de México
2829 16th Street, N. W.
Washington, D. C. 20009 USA

MARTÍNEZ DEL SOBRAL,
Sr. Lic. don Enrique (S) (C)
Paseo de la Reforma No. 95-824
México City

MASSA, Sr. Lic. D. Gil Gil (S)
Banco de México S. A.
Depto de Comercio Exterior
Bolivar 15, 8⁰ piso
México 1, D. F.

MUCHARRAZ SALDAÑA,
Sr. Lic. D. Pedro (S)
Ferrocorril 84
Tlalpam, D. F.

OBREGON, Sr. Lic. D. Juan (S)
16 de Septiembre 38-702
México 1, D. F.

OBREGON, Jr., Sr. Lic. D. Oscar (S)
Reforma 156
17th Floor
México City

OLLIVIER, Sr. Lic. D. Lagos (C)
Paseo de la Reforma 76, 7º
México 6, D. F.

PALACIOS Y BERMÚDEZ DE CASTRO,
Dr. en Derecho Roberto (S)
Av. Juárez No. 42 Edificio C.
México City, D. F.

PÉREZ-VERDÍA, Jr., Sr. Lic. D.
Antonio (S)
Rio Guadiana No. 23
Col. Cuauhtémoc
México 5, D. F.

PÉREZ-VERDIA,
Sr. Lic. D. Enriqua (S) (C)
Gante 15 - Desp. 421-423
México 1, D. F.

PINTADO RIVERO, Sr. Lic. D. Jose (S)
Uruguay No. 55 3º piso
México, D. F.

RAMOS BILDERBECK,
Sr. Lic. D. Eugenio (S)
Liverpool 89, 403-405
México 6, D. F.

RAMOS y RAMOS, Sr. Lic. D.
Augusto Cesar (S)
Av. Morelos No. 98-303
México 1, D. F.

RANGEL MEDINA,
Sr. Lic. D. David (S)
Allende 251
Colonia Clavería
México 16, D. F.

RODRIGUEZ SOLÓRZANO,
Sr. Lic. D. Benito (S)
Balderas No. 68, Despacho 205
México 1, D. F.

SANCHEZ-MEJORADA y VELASCO,
Sr. Lic. D. Carlos (S)
Paseo de la Reforma 122, 10º
México 6, D. F.

SEPÚLVEDA, Sr. Lic. D. César (S)
Tacuba 37-327
México 1, D. F.

DE LA SIERRA, Sr. Lic. D. José (S)
Gante 4-509
México 1, D. F.

SODI ALVAREZ, Sr. Lic. D. Enrique (S)
Parque España 49-4
México 11, D. F.

TERÁN, Sr. Lic. D. Lagos (C)
Paseo de la Reforma 76, 7º piso
México 6, D. F.

VAZQUEZ MENDOZA,
Sr. Lic. D. Rodrigo (S)
Av. Benjamin Franklin 132
México 18, D. F.

DEL VILLAR ARCARAZ,
Sr. Lic. D. Pedro (S)
Gante 9-5º piso
México, D. F.

YLLANES RAMOS,
Sr. Lic. D. Fernando (S)
Av. Juárez No. 76-6º piso
México 1, D. F.

YSITA SEPTIEN,
Sr. Lic. D. Fernando (S)
Av. Juárez No. 88, 3er piso
México 1, D. F.

NETHERLANDS

Practising lawyers in the Netherlands are usually addressed with "Meester" or "Mr." appearing before the name. If the individual has a doctorate, "Dr." is used instead. Jhr — Jonkheer.

BEELAERTS VAN BLOCKLAND,
Mrs. Pieter R. (C)
Herengracht 581
Amsterdam

BERGSMA, Mr. A. C. (S)
Schiedamsesingel 181
Rotterdam

BLOEMSMA, Mr. Marco P. (S)
Koninginnegracht 27
The Hague

BOEKMAN, Miss S.
Parklaan, 5
Haarlem

BREMER, Mr. Theodore R. (S)
Leidsegracht 10
Amsterdam

DIEPHUIS, Dr. J. H. (S)
Carel van Bylandtlaan 30
The Hague

DRIESSEN, Dr. C. F. (S)
Bataafse Int. Petrol. MIJ. N. V.
Carel van Bylandtlaan 30
The Hague

ELLIS, Mr. J. J. A. (S)
Van Ouwenlaan 2
The Hague

VAN DER FELTZ, Dr. Ferdinand baron (S) (C)
Herengracht 499
Amsterdam C

FORTUIJN, Mr. Eduard Droogleever (S)
86 Javastraat
The Hague

FUNKE, Mr. A. Paul (C)
391 Keizersgracht
Amsterdam

GOUDSMIT, Mr. J. W. (S)
J. J. Viottastraat 39
Amsterdam

HARDENBERG, Mr. L. (S)
v. Nijenrodeweg 892
Amsterdam-Buitenveldert

HOOFTMAN, Mr. J. C.
c/o Nederlandse Orde
van Advocaten
Frederik Hendrikplein 23
The Hague

JITTA, Dr. J. W. Josephus (S)
Pr. van Wiedlaan 28
Wassensaar 1

JONKER, Mr. H.
Parklaan, 5
Haarlem

TER KUILE, Mr. H. J. C. (S)
Koninginnegracht 12 B
The Hague

MEIJ, Mr. W. van der
Frederik Hendrikplein 23
The Hague

MOSLER, Mr. Gert (S)
Joh. Vermeerstraat 15
Amsterdam

MULDER, Mr. Jan (S)
Blaak 31
Rotterdam 1

OBERMANN, Mr. Foppe M. (S)
c/o Messrs. A. D. P. V. van Löben
Sels O. H. van Wijk and
F. M. Obermann
Postbox 622 / Nieuve Gracht 60
Haarlem

SPANJAARD, Mr. Eduard (S)
Maliebaan 82
Utrecht

STEINZ, Mr. J. A. (C)
Member Netherlands Bar Assoc.

STRICKER, Mr. Eric (C)
Maselean 38
Olgstgeest

TONNAER, Mr. Antoon A. M. (C)
Burg. v. Rijnsingel 11
Venlo

TONNAER, Mr. Arthur (C)
Burg. v. Rijnsingel 11
Venlo

VELEMA, Mr. J. W. (S)
Montaubanstraat 6
Zeist

VERHAGEN, Mr. Herbert B. A.
10 Leidsegracht
Amsterdam

VOETELINK, Dr. H. M. (S)
Keizersgracht 391
Amsterdam C

VOÛTE, Mr. Jan Reinier (S) (C)
Herengracht 499
Amsterdam C

DE VRIES, Mr. I. S. (S)
de Lairessestraat 107
Amsterdam

WARENDORF, Mr. J. C. S. (S) (C)
93, De Lairessestraat
Amsterdam Z. 07

WETZELS, Dr. Nicolaas J. (S) (C)
Einderstraat 3
Kerkrade

NETHERLANDS ANTILLES

Practising lawyers in the Netherlands Antilles are usually addressed with "Meester" or "Mr." appearing before the name. If the individual has a doctorate, "Dr." is used instead.

HENRIQUEZ, Dr. Ernest Cohen (S)
Kerkstraat 10 A
Curacao

SCHILTKAMP, Dr. J. A. (S)
Kerkstraat 10 A
Curacao

SMEETS, Mr. A. A. G. (S)
Notaris
Handelskade 9 B
Curacao

VAN DE VOORT, Dr. P. P. C. H. (S)
Nassaustraat 68
Oranjestad, Aruba

NEW ZEALAND

Practising lawyers in New Zealand are usually addressed with "Esquire" or "Esq." appearing after the full name of the individual. Since New Zealand is a member of the British Commonwealth of Nations, customs of address are generally those appearing under England.

ANGLAND, Esq., John (C)
P. O. Box 2975
Auckland

BECK, Esq., Lance F. (C)
P. O. Box 40085
Upper Hutt

BISSON, Esq., Gordon Ellis (S)
P. O. Box 715
Napier

BLUNDELL, Esq., E. D.
c/o New Zealand Law Society
P. O. Box 5041
Wellington, C 1

CHAPPELL, Esq., Charles (C)
P. O. Box 39
Taneatua

CLELAND, Esq., Eric A. (C)
P. O. Box 355
Christchurch

CONRADSON, Esq., James M. (C)
c/o James Ward & Co.
P. O. Box 7
Dunedin

DOBSON, Esq., William T. (C)
P. O. Box 349
Napier

EDMONDS, Esq., Charles O. (C)
P. O. Box 3
Te Awamutu

GARLICK, Esq., R. Tonson
Vice President
New Zealand Law Society
26 Waring Taylor Street
Wellington C 1

GREIG, Esq., Alan M. M. (C)
P. O. Box 5121
Auckland

HASLAM, The Hon. Mr.
Justice Alec L. (C)
Judges' Chambers
Supreme Court
Wellington

HEWAT, Esq., Robert P. H. (C)
P. O. Box 11
12-14 Dee Street
Invercargill

HOLLAND, Esq., William S. (C)
Churchill Buildings
Grey Street
Tauranga

INGLIS, Esq., Dr. B. D.
P. O. Box 2621
Wellington

LATHAM, Esq., Fenton (C)
Box 326
Wanganui

MACDONALD, Esq., Morris M. (C)
P. O. Box 253
Invercargill

McLEOD, Esq., William Aeneas (S)
35 Tennyson St.
P. O. Box 151
Napier

McGRATH, Esq., Denis, President
New Zealand Law Society
26 Waring Taylor Street
Wellington C 1

MILES, Esq., Phillip (C)
P. O. Box 184
Feilding

NEIL, Esq., Peter Christison (S)
17 Stirling Street
Remuera
Auckland

O'REGAN, Esq., John B. (C)
Box 946
Wellington

O'REILLY, Esq., James P. (C)
5th Floor
Yorkshire House, Shortland St.
Auckland

ORR, Esq., G. S.
Crown Law Office
P. O. Box 8019
Wellington

O'SHEA, Esq., E. R. (C)
c/o Brookfield, Prendergast,
Schnauer & Smytheman
Box 298
Auckland

PAPPRILL, Esq., Thomas K. (C)
84 Hereford Street
Christchurch

PARKIN, Esq., Frank Lloyd (C)
P. O. Box 927
Wellington

PATTERSON, Esq., Colin I.
Messrs. Watts & Patterson
P. O. Box 764
Wellington

ROSEN, Esq., Harry (C)
Magistrates Court Private Seg.
Auckland 1

SEEMAN, Esq., Gerhard James (C)
New Zealand Law Society
P. O. Box 5041
Wellington

SELLERS, Esq., Edward (C)
151 Rodney Street
P. O. Box 8
Wellford

SMITH, Esq., John F. (C)
Holmden, Horrocks, Kalman & Co.
P. O. Box 1108
Auckland

TWIGG, Esq., Denis Despard (C)
P. O. Box 616
Napier

YOUNG, Esq., Douglas G. (C)
23 Wicksteed Place
Wanganui

NICARAGUA

Practising lawyers in Nicaragua are usually addressed with "Sr. Dr. Don" or "Sr. Abogado Don" appearing before the name of the individual.

ARGÜELLO HURTADO,
Sr. Dr. Don Robert (S)
Apartado No. 173
Managua

GUANDIQUE MARTINEZ,
Sr. Dr. Don Felix E. (S)
5 á Calle N. O. No. 210
Managua

NORTHERN IRELAND

Practising lawyers in Northern Ireland are usually addressed with „Esquire" or "Esq." appearing after the full name of the individual. Other forms of address are those appearing under England.

CAMPBELL, Esq., B. A., Anthony (C)
Bar Library
Royal Courts of Justice (Ulster)
Belfast

COMERTON, Esq., B. A., L. L. M.,
E. Alan
c/o The Inn of Court
of Northern Ireland
The Royal Courts of Justice
(Ulster)
Belfast 1

GREGSON, Esq., Robert V. (C)
Grand's Arcade
Fountain St.
Belfast 1

JEFFERSON, Esq., William John (S)
8/9 Donegall Square North
Belfast 1

MAXWELL, Esq., Patrick, President
The Incorporated Law Society
of Northern Ireland
Royal Courts of Justice (Ulster)
Belfast

MACDERMOTT, The Rt. Hon.
The Lord M. C., LL. D., P. C.
Lord Chief Justice of N. Ireland
The Royal Courts of Justice
(Ulster)
Belfast 1

MURRAY, Esq., Norman H. (C)
Secretary, Incorporated Law
Society of Northern Ireland
Royal Courts of Justice (Ulster)
Belfast 1

O'HARA, Esq., James (C)
92 High Street
Belfast

SHEIL, Hon. Mr. Justice
Charles Leo (C)
Royal Courts of Justice
Chichester St., Belfast

NORWAY

Practising lawyers in Norway are usually addressed with one of the following titles before the individual's name:

"Advokat" is used for a lawyer admitted to the courts of 1st instance and the courts of appeal; and

"Høyesterettsadvokat" or "H. r. advokat" for a lawyer admitted to all courts, the Supreme Court included.

ARNESEN, H. r. advokat Finn (S)
Ø Slottsgate 8
Oslo

ARNTZEN, H. r. advokat Andreas
(S) (C)
Fr. Nansens Plass 9
Oslo

ARNTZEN, H. r. advokat Sven (S) (C)
Fr. Nansens Plass 9
Oslo

BERGER, H. r. advokat Thorleif
(S) (C)
Kr. Augustsgate 12
Oslo

BORGE, H. r. advokat Ole (S)
Kr. Augustsgate 13
Oslo

BRUNSVIG, H. r. advokat Per (S)
Tollbodgaten 27
Oslo 1

BUGGE, H. r. advokat Frederik M. (S)
Haakon VII's gate 2
Oslo 1

CHRISTIANSEN, H. r. advokat
Erling (S)
Grensen 12
Oslo 1

CHRISTOPHERSEN, H. r. advokat Rolf
(C)
Kirkegt. 26
Oslo 1

DAHL, Advokat Einar (S)
Lille Grensegate 7
Oslo 1

DAHL-HANSEN, H. r. advokat
Mathias (S)
Grenson 12
Oslo 1

DEDICHEN, H. r. advokat Lucien (S)
Stortorvet 7
Oslo 1

GJEMS-ONSTAD, M. B. E.,
H. r. advokat Erik (S) (C)
Kongensgate 18
Oslo 1

HAAVIND, H. r. advokat Helge (S)
Ø Slottsgate 8
Oslo 1

HAAVIND, H. r. advokat Kjell (S)
Ø Slottsgate 8
Oslo 1

HÄGG, H. r. advokat Lars Chr. (S)
Markensgaten 6
Kristiansand S.

HAUGE, Advokat Egil Hiis (S)
Strandgaten 4
Bergen

HAUGE, H. r. advokat
Jens Christian (S)
Youngstorget 2
Oslo 1

HJORT, H. r. advokat
Johan Bernhard (S)
Akersgaten 20
Oslo

HJORT, H. r. advokat Johan (S)
Akersgaten 20
Oslo

HOLST, H. r. advokat Peter F. (S)
Akersgaten 20
Oslo

HØYER, Advokat Theis (S)
Kirkegaten 23
Oslo

HVINDEN, Advokat Lars (C)
B. Narvesens Vei 2
Oslo

KARLSRUD, H. r. advokat Rudolf (S)
Tollbodgaten 27
Oslo

KVAMME, Advokat Alfred G. (C)
Strandgaten 1
Bergen

LØCHEN, Advokat Torwald G.
Nedre Vollgate 1
Oslo

LOUS, H. r. advokat Georg (S) (C)
Drammensveien 4
Oslo

MARTENS, H. r. advokat Erik
Torvalm. 4
Bergen

MELLBYE, H. r. advokat Carsten (S)
Tollbodgaten 32
Oslo

MELLBYE, H. r. advokat
Jens Christian (S)
Tollbodgaten 32
Oslo

MYHRE, H. r. advokat Hans B. (C)
Akersgaten 16
Oslo 1

NERGAARD, H. r. advokat Olav
(S) (C)
Tollbodgaten 32
Oslo

NORMAN, H. r. advokat Trygve (S)
Drammensveien 4
Oslo 1

REKVE, H. r. advokat Anders (S)
Klubbgt. 1
Stavanger

RIKHEIM, H. r. advokat Arne (C)
Fjoroveien 75 B
Høvik

RYSSDAL, Høyesterettsadvokat Signe
Marie Stray
Ø Slottsgate 8
Oslo

SUNDE, H. r. advokat Sverre (S)
Stortingsgaten 14
Oslo

SPORCK, Advokat Petter C. (C)
Kirkegaten 21
Oslo

SKOGLY, Advokat Alf (C)
Erik Borresengt. 9
Drammen

SKIRSTAD, Advokat Ole (C)
Thomas Augilla Gt. 8
Trondheim

USTVEDT, H. r. advokat Nils (S)
Tollbodgt. 24
Oslo 1

VALLE, L. L. B., Mrs. Inger
Fornebuveien 45
Lysaker

PERU

Practising lawyers in Peru are usually addressed with "Señor Doctor" or "Sr. Dr." appearing before the individual's name.

ALVARADO ZAÑARTU,
Sr. Dr. Alfonso Arévalo (S)
General Pezet 1648, San Isidro
Lima

CISNEROS, Sr. Lic. D. Maximo (S)
Paseo de la República No. 111
8 piso
Lima

CISNEROS, Sr. Dr. Manuel (S)
Paseo de la República No. 111
8 piso
Lima

GUBBINS FORERO,
Sr. Dr. Guillermo (S)
A. Miro Quesad a 376 - 9 piso
Lima

MANFREDI, Sr. Lic. Dr. Ulises
Montoya
Avda. Nicolás de
Piérola 966/Of. 204
Lima

MONCLOA, D. C., Sr. Dr. Enrique (S)
Av. Tacna 543, Of. 124
Lima

NAVARRO IRVINE, Sr. Lic. Dr. Félix
Colegio de Abogados de Lima
Palacio de Justicia
Lima

VALDEZ, Sr. Dr. Mario Alzamora
President
Colegio de Abogados de Lima
Lima

VARGAS, Sr. Dr. Javier
Carabaya 933, Of. 600
Lima

PHILIPPINES

Practising lawyers in the Philippines are usually addressed with "Attorney" or "Atty." appearing before the individual's name. They may also be addressed with "Esquire" or "Esq." appearing after the full name. Judges of the lower Courts and Courts of First Instance may be addressed as "The Honorable" or "Hon.". Justices of the Court of Appeals and of the Supreme Court may be addressed as "Honorable" or "Justice" appearing before the name. "Dean" is a title indicating that the person to whose name the same is affixed was or is the head of a College in a recognized institution of learning or University. "Senator" or "Congressman", if appropriate, are used for members of the Congress of the Philippines, the first being for Senators and the latter for members of the Lower House or House of Representatives. They may also be addressed simply as "Honorable".

ALAFRIZ, The Hon. Arturo A. (S)
Seventh Floor,
Metropolitan Bank Building
Ayala Avenue
Rizal, Philippines

ARUEGO, Dean Jose M.
Aruego Law Office
Afable Building
Nicanor Teyes Sr. Street
Sampaloc
Manila

BARNES, Dr. Tomas V.
301-3-2 Leyba Building
Dasmarinas St.
Manila

DIOKNO, Senator Jose W.
332 Regina Building
Escolta
Manila

LICHAUCO, Ambassador Marcial P.
6th Floor,
Padilla de los Reyes Building
232 Juan Luna
Manila

MUTUC, The Hon. Amelito R. (C)
51 Tamarind Road
Forbes Park
Makati, Rizal

NUBLA, Prof. Maurice C. (S) (C)
2nd Floor, Pan Asia Building
575 Nueve de Febrero
Mandaluyong, Rizal

OZAETA, Justice Roman, President
Philippine Bar Association
P. O. Box 2084
Manila

TANADA, Senator Lorenzo M.
6th Floor,
Consolidated Mines Building
Azala Avenue
Rizal, Manila

TOLENTINO, Senator Arturo
President
Philippine Lawyers Association
P. O. Box 2051
Manila

VILLANUEVA, Esq., Raymundo I. (S)
Philippine Embassy
12 Via San Valentino
Rome, Italy

PORTUGAL

Practising lawyers in Portugal are usually addressed by the courtesy title of "Doctor" shortened into "Dr.", if they are graduated in law, as, now, they all have to be in order to enter the profession.

However, their official title is "Licenciado". Women lawyers, also "Licenciadas", are called the same in the feminine: "Dra.".

The lawyers that are University Professors and those who have passed the examination of Law Doctorate, are the real "Doctors". Their title is usually given in full and if they are Professors they are addressed as "Professor Doctor".

Besides Lawyers and acting as their helpers are the "solicitadores". They do not need the Law degree and are addressed as "Senhor" ("Mister"). They are chosen by public competition or named "provisionally" by the judges if their panel is not complete.

Judges of the first instance are called "Sr. Juiz" or "Sr. Dr. Juiz". The magistrates on the Appeal Courts have the traditional designation of "Desembargadores" and those of the Supreme Court that of "Conselheiros". But, outside courts, they are all also addressed as "Dr.", this courtesy being extended to everyone having *any University Degree.*

COLACO, Prof. Dra. Isabel de
Magalhaes
Faculdade de Direito
Lisbon 5

DA PALMA CARLOS, Prof. Dr. Adelino
Rua Duque de Palmela, 2-6º
Lisbon 2

GUIMARAES, Dra. Elina
Rua de D. Lourenco
de Almeida 11
Lisbon 3

PITTA, Dr. Pedro, President
Ordem dos Advogados
Largo de S. Domingos, 14
Lisbon

RIBEIRO, Dr. Angelo de Almeida
Largo de S. Carlos, 13-1º
Lisbon 2

PEDROSO RODRIGUES, Dr. Fernando
Rua Ivens, 6, 2º
Lisbon

ZENHA, Dr. Francisco Salgado
Rua Augusta, 281-2º
Lisbon 2

PUERTO RICO

Practising lawyers in Puerto Rico are usually addressed with "Senor Licenciado"; "Don . . . " when the addressee is an older person; "Sr. Lic. D." or "Lic. D." appearing before the name. If the individual has a doctorate, "Dr." is substituted — "Sr. Lic. Dr.".

APONTE GARCIÁ,
Sr. Lic. D. José C. (S)
Departamento de Justicia
San Juan

LOPEZ-PACHECO,
Sr. Lic. Dr. Olaguibeet A. (S)
Apt. Postal 155
Hato Rey

NEGRÓN-FERNÁNDEZ,
The Hon. Luis (S)
Chief Justice, Supreme Court
P. O. Box 2733
San Juan 12

PETRILLI, Sr. Lic. D. Rafael Buono
Apartado de Correos 1900
San Juan

RUIZ DE ROLDÁN,
Sr. Lic. D. Daisy (S)
Apartado 514
Caguas

SANTIAGO, Sr. Lic. D. William F.
President, Colegio de Abogados
de Puérto Rico
Apartado de Correos 1900
San Juan

TEDESCHI-SANT'AGATA,
Sra. Lcda. Leticia (S)
P. O. Box 4588
San Juan

TORO, Sra. Lcda. Fraces H. (S)
General Post Office Box 1884
San Juan

SCOTLAND

Practising lawyers in Scotland are usually addressed with "Esquire" or "Esq." appearing after the full name of the individual. Other customs of address are similar to those appearing under England; except that in Scotland there are advocates and solicitors, instead of barristers and solicitors. All practising solicitors are members of The Law Society of Scotland but some are also members of local Societies or Faculties such as The Society of Writers to the Signet and The Society of Solicitors in the Supreme Courts of Scotland, for which the abbreviations respectively are W. S. and S. S. C.

Scottish Judges are called by a Judicial title of "Lord . . . ", although they are not normally Peers. Their Judicial title is usually the same as their surname, but it may be different.

BELL, Esq., John Robin Sinclair (S)
1 Eton Terrace
Edinburgh

BLAIR, Esq., C. V. O., W. S.;
Alastair Co. (S)
28 Charlotte Square
Edinburgh 2

COOK, Esq., William Allister (S) (C)
105 West George Street
Glasgow, C. 2

DANDIE, Esq., S. S. C.,
James Naughton (S)
4 King Street
Stirling

EDWARD, Esq., D. A. O.
Advocates Library
Edinburgh 1

EMSLIE, Esq., M. B. E., Q. C.; G. C.
Dean of Faculty, Advocats Lib.
11 Parliament Square
Edinburgh 1

FAIR, Esq., James Stuart (S)
11 Whitehall Street
Dundee

FIDDES, Esq., J. R.
25 Herriot Row
Edinburgh 1

GREIG, Esq., K. J. A.
Solicitors Office
St. Andrews House
Edinburgh

GUILD, Esq., W. S., Ivor Reginald (S)
16 Charlotte Square
Edinburgh 2

HORSBURGH, Esq., John
c/o Faculty of Advocates
Advocates' Library
Parliament House
Edinburgh

HUGHES, Esq., Joseph Michael (S)
21 Cairngorm Road
Glasgow, S. 3

KILBRANDON, The Hon. Lord (C)
The Old College
South Bridge
Edinburgh

LAURIE, Esq., O. B. E., W. S.,
Robert Bertram (C)
Law Society's Hall
North Bank Street
Edinburgh

LYONS, Sheriff Hamilton
119 Albert Road
Gourock, Renfrewshire

MACCALMAN, Esq., Hugh T. (S) (C)
170 Hope Street
Glasgow, C. 2

MACFIE, Esq., John (C)
66 Queen Street
Edinburgh

MACKAY, Esq., John (S)
48 Scott Street
Perth

MACROBERT, Esq., J. C. T.
51 Moss Street
Paisley

MAXWELL, Q. C., Peter
Advocates' Library
Faculty of Advocates
Edinburgh 1

MELLICK, Esq., Joseph (S) (C)
160 Hope Street
Glasgow, C. 2

MILLER, Esq., Lawrence S. (C)
16 Heriot Row
Edinburgh 3

QUIGLEY, Esq., John George (S) (C)
402 Sauchiehall Street
Glasgow, C. 2

STEVENSON, Esq., Louis (S)
800 Hinman Avenue
Evanston, Illinois, USA

STEWART, Esq., W. S., James (S)
16 Charlotte Square
Edinburgh 2

STORM, Esq., William James
McDougall (S)
29 Traill Street
Thurso, Caithness

STORM, Esq., W. J. W. (S)
29 Traill Street
Thurso

SUTHERLAND, Esq., James
77 St. Vincent Street
Glasgow, C. 2

WATSON, Esq., LL. B., SS. C., Neil (S)
31 Queen Street
Edinburgh

WILKIE, Esq., Joseph M. (C)
27 Bank Street
Dundee

SOUTH AFRICA

Practising attorneys are usually addressed with "Mr." appearing before, or "Esq." after the full name. If the attorney in question is the holder of a particular academic qualification, e. g. a Doctorate, such qualification would take the place of Mr. before the full name.

ASHMAN, Esq., G. R. (C)
President, The Association of Law
Societies of South Africa
P. O. Box 681
Bloemfontein

COLLINS, Esq., Ramsay Caldwell (S)
P. O. Box 635
Burban, Natal

CONRADIE, Esq., Pieter (C)
c/o Secretary for Justice
Private Bag 81
Pretoria

COOK, Esq., George (C)
P. O. Box 6434
Johannesburg

COSTHUIZEN, Esq., John V. (C)
P. O. Box 205
Durban

ETTLINGER, Esq., Douglas M. (C)
621 Innes Chambers
Pritchard St.
Johannesburg

HARRIS, Dr. S. N.
The Assn. of Law Societies of the Republic of South Africa
Bureau Lane
Pretoria

HORVITCH, Miss Gertie (S)
Attorney at Law
P. O. Box 1811
Johannesburg

LOUW, Esq., Eben
Secretary General
Republic of South Africa
Bureau Lane
Pretoria

LAUWRENS, Esq., Cornelius Julius
P. O. Box 76
Cape Town

SHAW, Esq., Q. C., D. J.
731 West Walk
Smith Street
Durban

SNITCHER, Esq., Q. C., Harry (C)
1 Dorp Street
Cape Town

VAN DER WALT, Esq., Bernardus (C)
Attorney General's Office
Pietermaritzburg, Natal

VENTER, Esq., C. M.
Inc. Law Society of the Transvaal
P. O. Box 1493
Pretoria

VISSER, Esq., Daniel (C)
Deputy State Attorney's Office
7th Floor, Garmor House
Plein Street
Cape Town

VAN RHYN, Prof. J. N. R.
The Assn. of Law Societies of the Republic of South Africa
Bureau Lane
Pretoria

WEBSTER, Esq., G. C.
P. O. Box 454
Pretoria

SPAIN

ALONSO R. RIVAS, Daniel (C)
c/o Sanjurjo No. 3
Leon

ESCOBEDO, Sr. D. Duato M. (C)
Espanoleto 25
Madrid

MARTIN CARRILLO, Sr. D. Antonio (C)
Calle de San Quintin 1, 2⁰
Madrid 13

MAZÓN VERDEJO, Sr. Lic. D. Eugenio (C)
Calle de General Mola, 26
Madrid 1

PABLO-BLANCO, Sr. D. Joaquin
Sagasta, 28
Madrid

PASTOR BOTIJA, Sr. D. Rafael (C)
Avda. Calvo Sotelo, 5
Zaragoza

REYES MORALES, Excmo. Sr. D. Roberto (C)
Avda. Calvo Sotelo 31
Madrid

RODRIGUES SASTRE, Ilmo. Sr. D. A. (S)
Calle del Dr. Fleming, 1
Madrid 16

SANCHEZ TOVAS, Ilmo. Sr. D.
Isidoro (C)
c/o General Mola, 22
Madrid

DEL VALLE ITURRIAGA, Excmo. Sr. D.
Jose Luis (C)
c/o Serrano, 22
Madrid

ZARRALUQUI VILLALBA, Ilmo. Sr. D.
Luis (S)
Serrano, 103
Madrid

ST. KITTS

DAVIS, Esq., Maurice (C)
St. Kitts

SURINAM

VAN DER SCHROEFF, Esq., G. J. C. (S)
Heerenstraat 48
Paramaribo

SWAZILAND

BISSETT, Esq., Colin (C)
Central Chambers
Martins St. (P. O. Box 143)
Manzini

SWEDEN

Practising lawyers in Sweden are usually addressed with "Advokat" appearing before the individual's name.

AHRNBORG, Advokat Bertil (S)
Sveavägen 29
Stockholm C

ALMGREN, Advokat Bengt (C)
Stortorget 29
Malmö C

ALTHIN, Mrs. Margit (C)
Advokat
Hantverkargatan 14
Stockholm K

BAGNER, Advokat Hans (S)
Smalandsgatan 4
Stockholm Ö

BOSTRÖM, Advokat Arthur (S) (C)
Birger Jarlsgatan 15
Stockholm C

BRATTNE, Advokat Gunnar
Box 2235
40314 Göteborg

BYGGE, Advokat Björn (S)
Sveavägen 29
Stockholm C

DREIJER, Advokat Per (S) (C)
Box 2235
40314 Göteborg

ERIKSSON, Advokat Nils (C)
Firman Lagerlof
Strandvagen 7 A
Stockholm

GÄRDE, Advokat Styrbjörn (S)
Karlavägen 73
Stockholm Ö

GOLDIE, Advokat Ormonde (C)
Birger Jarlsgatan 15
11145 Stockholm

HAGBERG, Advokat Lennart (S)
Box 2235
40314 Göteborg

HEDÉN, Advokat Ragnar (S) (C)
Kyrkogatan 20
Göteborg C

HULTGREN, Advokat
Carl Ake Fredrik (S)
Södra Tullgatan 4
Malmö

KÄRRLANDER, Advokat Nils
Malmtorgsgatan 3
Stockholm C

LINDAHL, Advokat Magnus,
President
Sveriges Advokatsamfund
Strandvägen 5 A IV
Stockholm Ö

LUNDEN, Advokat Sven-Olof (C)
Post Box 13
Uppsala

LUNDGREN, Miss Valborg, Advokat
Sveavägen 25-27
Stockholm C

NYQVIST, Advokat Ake (S)
Sturegatan 6
Stockholm Ö

ÖHMAN, Advokat Anders Ragnar (S)
Birger Jarlsgatan 11
Stockholm C

OSVALD, Advokat Per H. (S) (C)
Strandvägen 7 A
Stockholm Ö

PEDERSEN, Advokat Hans (S) (C)
Biblioteksgatan 26
Stockholm

PEHRSSON, Advokat
Wilhelm Ivan (S)
Kungsgatan 36
Stockholm

ROSENLUND, Advokat Johan (C)
Birger Jarlsgatan 15
Stockholm

SANDELL, Advokat Sten (S)
Torggatan 4
Malmö C

SOHLBERG, Advokat Stig (C)
Box 447
75106 Uppsala

WEIBULL, Advokat Eskil (S)
Västra Hamngatan 24
Göteborg C

WICKMAN, Advokat Ove (C)
Stortorget 29
Malmö C

WIKLUND, Advokat Holger
Sveriges Advokatsamfund
Kammakargatan 10
Stockholm C

WISTRAND, Advokat Folke (S) (C)
Kyrkogatan 20
Göteborg C

WISTRAND, Advokat Rolf (S)
Strandvägen 13
Stockholm Ö

SWITZERLAND

Since there are three national languages in Switzerland, if not really four (French, German, Italian and Romanche), there are various titles for practising lawyers. In general, German-speaking Swiss lawyers are doctors of law, and they are called "Dr. . . . " or "Rechtsanwalt", which applies to doctors of law as well as to those who are not. In French Switzerland, whether the avocat is a doctor of law or not, he is addressed "Maître". If he is or has been a Bâtonnier, this is frequently mentioned when addressing him: "Monsieur le Bâtonnier . . . " or "Maître . . . , Ancien Bâtonnier".

BRINER, Maître Robert (C)
25, Grand Rue
1211 Genève 11

BUSSER, Maître Max (C)
Schwanenplatz 8
Lucerne

DE COULON, Maître Philippe (S)
25, Grand' Rue
1211 Genève 11

FEHR, Professor Dr. Conrad
6 Münzgraben
Bern

GLAUSER, Maître Frédéric (S) (C)
16, Rue Voltaire
1201 Genève

GMUER, Rechtsanwalt Dr. Paul (S) (C)
Löwenstrasse 1
Zürich 1

HASSAN, Esq., Salvador (S)
Case Stand No. 215
Genève

HEIZ, Dr. Rudolf (S) (C)
Löwenstrasse 1
8001 Zürich

HOCHSTRASSER, Dr. G., Fürsprecher (S)
Hirschengraben 11
Bern

HOLZACH, Dr. Christopher D. (S) (C)
Magnolienpark 14
CH 4052 Basel

JATON, Dr. Roland, President
Fédération Suisse des Avocats
17 rue Haldimand
1003 Lausanne

JOLIDON, Maître Pierre
Münzgraben 6
Bern

LALIVE, Maître Jean-Flavien (S) (C)
20 rue Senebier
1205 Genève

LANZ, Rechtsanwalt Dr. Gerd (S) (C)
Seefeldstrasse 7
8008 Zürich

LENZ, Maître Raoul (S) (C)
25, Grand' Rue
Genève

MARTIN-ACHARD, Maître Edmond
Ancien Bâtonnier
4 Place Neuve
Genève

MACBRIDE, Esq., Sean, Secretary-General
Internat. Commission of Jurists
2, Quai du Cheval-Blanc
1211 Genève 24

PASCHOUD, Maître Jean-Félix (S) (C)
6, rue de la Grotte
1003 Lausanne

PAYOT, Maître Jean (S)
Ancien Bâtonnier
Avenue Léopold Robert 60
La Chaux-de-Fonds

PESTALOZZI, Rechtsanwalt Dr. Anton (S) (C)
Löwenstrasse 1
Zürich 1

PESTALOZZI, Frau Dr. Regula (S) (C)
Rechtsanwalt
Löwenstrasse 1
Zürich 1

POTULICKI, Dr. Michael (C)
c/o International Commission of the Red Cross
Genève

PLATTNER, Edith (C)
Artherstrasse 6

REICHWEIN, Rechtsanwalt Dr. Heinz (S)
Talacker 41
Zürich 1

RIEDWEG, Rechtsanwalt Dr. Albert (S)
Schwanenplatz 8
Luzern

ROHNER, Rechtsanwalt Dr. Otto Niklaus (S)
Privatbank und Verwaltungsgesellschaft
Barengasse 29
8000 Zürich

SCHLUEP, Maître Martin (S)
Grand' Rue 25
Genève

SONTHEIM, Maître Hubert F. A. (S)
Tradax Genève S. A.
8, Avenue Calas
1211 Genève

STEFFEN, Dr. Robert
Bahnhofstrasse 6
3600 Thun CH

TOMBET, Maître André (S)
Rue de Rive 6
Genève

ZÜBLIN, Rechtsanwalt Dr. Albert E. (S)
Limmatquai 46 / Rüdenplatz 2
Zürich 1

SYRIA

The titles used for lawyers in Syria are the same as for French lawyers. Practising lawyers are usually addressed with "Maître" or "Me" appearing before the individual's name.

EL MIDANI, Maître Zouheir
President, Ordre des Avocats
Ministry of Justice
Damascus

MULKY, Maître Robert (C)
c/o Ordre des Avocats Damas
Ministry of Justice
Damascus

TAIWAN

LING, Esq., Benjamin C. H. (S)
Taipei Bar Association
124, South Chungking Rd., Sec. 1
Taipei

TANGANYIKA

JHAVERI, Kantilal L. (C)
P. O. Box 57
Dar Es Salaas (Tanzania)

THAILAND

Practising lawyers and Judges in Thailand are usually addressed as "Nai", with the title appearing before the name, and this is equivalent to "Mr." in the English language; e. g. "Nai Chamras Kamacharu". However, some of the lawyers and judges are titled personages, equivalent to being "Knighted", and these titles are of five levels viz: Chao Phya, Phya, Pra, Luang and Khun, appearing before the name, e. g. "Phya Prida Naruberrs". Women lawyers are usually addressed as "Nang" if married, or "Nangsao" if unmarried, and "Khun Ying", equivalent to "Lady", if they are given such title.

HUTASINGH, Dr. Jur. Prakab
President, The Thai Bar
Bangkok

KRAICHITTI, Nai Sansern
The Thai Bar
Bangkok

TRINIDAD

JULIEN, Senator M. T. I. (S) (C)
78 Queen Street
Port-of-Spain

TURKEY

Lawyers in Turkey are usually addressed with "Avukat" appearing before the full name.

ARSAL, Dr. Orhan
Bâtonnier d'Istanbul
Palaid de Justice
Istanbul

AGAOGLU, Avukat Sureyya (S)
23, Assikurazyoni Generali Han
Galata, Istanbul

BERKIN, Mrs. Güler, Avukat (C)
Chairman of the Foreign
Relations Committee
Ankara Barosu
Reisligi, Ankara

BÖLÜKBASI, Maître Saffet Nezihi
Ankara Barosu
Reisligi, Ankara

CENANI, Avukat Rasim (S) (C)
Taksim Sarayi 307/308
Taksim, Istanbul

CUBUKGIL, Me Oktay, President
Ankara Barosu
Reisligi, Ankara

ERÜLGEN, Mrs. Sabiha, Avukat (S)
Tünel Meydam Metrohan
Istanbul

INAN, Esq., Nurkut
c/o Ankara Barosu
Ankara

MAGAT, Maître Rahmi
Iskur Han No. 3/10
Ankara

SAV, Avukat Atilâ
c/o Ankara Barosu
Reisligi, Ankara

YESIN, Me Erdogan (C)
No. 47/8
4 uncu Cadde
Bahcelievler, Ankara

UGANDA

BINAISA, Esq., Godfrey L. (C)
Box 2750
Kampala

UNITED ARAB REPUBLIC - EGYPT

The customary method of addressing lawyers in Arabic is to place "El Ostaz" before the name; or, if the lawyer has a doctorate, "El Ostaz Dr.". When the French language is used, "Maître" should appear before the name instead of the above, or in abbreviation "Me".

To address the Bâtonnier of the Bar in Arabic, "Es Ostaz El Nakeeb" is used before the name, which is the equivalent of the French "Monsieur le Bâtonnier".

EL CHIATI, El Ostaz Dr. Ahmed Zaki
13 Place El Tahrir
Alexandria

EL KHAWAGA, El Ostaz, Ahmed,
President, Bar Assoc.
Egyptian Region UAR
51, Rue Ramses
Cairo

EL OTEIFI, Dr. Gamal (C)
10, Hoda Charawi Street
Cairo

IBRAHIM, El Ostaz Kamal Halim (C)
54 Abdel Halek Saroit St.
Cairo

MOHAMED ALI, El Ostaz Maher (C)
16, Adly Street
Cairo

TEWFICK, Maître Kamal
14, Rue Choubrah
Cairo

UNITED STATES OF AMERICA

ALABAMA

ARENDALL, Jr., Esq., Charles B. (P)
Post Office Box 123
Mobile, Alabama 36601

BRADLEY, Jr., Esq., Lee C. (P)
1500 Brown-Marx Building
Birmingham, Alabama 35203

GREAVES, Jr. Esq., Thomas G. (P)
Post Office Box 123
Mobile, Alabama 36601

PIPES III, Esq., Sam W. (P)
P. O. Box 79
Mobile, Alabama 36601

ARIZONA

von AMMON, Esq., Philip E. (P)
900 First National Bank Building
Phoenix, Arizona 85004

BRANDT, Esq., Ralph F. (P)
217 Second Avenue
Yuma, Arizona 85364

CAVANAGH, Esq., Harry J. (P)
1800 First Federal Savings Bldg.
Phoenix, Arizona 85004

CHANDLER, Esq., Thomas (P)
1110 Transamerica Bldg.
Tucson, Arizona 85701

CHRISTENSEN, Esq., Donald J. (P)
P. O. Box 1702
Prescott, Arizona 85714

CRAIG, Esq., J. Early (P)
First National Bank Building
Phoenix, Arizona 85004

CRAIG, The Hon. Walter E. (P) (C)
2020 E. Bethany Home Road
Phoenix, Arizona 85025

DITSCH, Esq., Charles A. (P)
710 First National Bank Bldg.
Phoenix, Arizona 85004

DUECY, Esq., Charles M. (P)
P. O. Box 1605
Scottsdale, Arizona 85252

ELDER, Mrs. Betsy C.
Attorney at Law
2323 N. Central Ave.
Phoenix, Arizona 85004

GRAND, Esq., Richard D. (P)
1005 Phoenix Title Building
Tucson, Arizona 85701

JULIAN, Esq., Vance
101 E. Boca Raton Rd.
Phoenix, Arizona 85022

KINNEY, Esq., Aaron (P)
710 First National Bank Bldg.
Phoenix, Arizona 85004

LOCKE, Esq., George D. (P) (C)
Suite 1734, Townehouse Tower
100 West Clarendon
Phoenix, Arizona 85013

McFALL, Esq., Clifford R. (S) (P)
4th Floor
Valley National Building
Tucson, Arizona 85701

McLELLAND, Esq., David G. (P)
7520 E Camelback Road
Scottsdale, Arizona 85251

McRAE, Esq., William (P)
742 First National Bank Building
Phoenix, Arizona 85004

MANGUM, Esq., H. K. (P)
Post Office Box 10
Flagstaff, Arizona 86001

MUECKE, The Hon.
Charles (Carl) A. (P)
7015 U. S. Courthouse
Phoenix, Arizona 85025

NIETERT, II., Esq., Floyd F. (P)
Post Office Box 1042
Douglas, Arizona 85607

O'CONNOR, Esq., James H. (P) (C)
1800 First Federal Saving Bldg.
Phoenix, Arizona 85002

OTTO, Esq., John P. (P)
2727 North Central Avenue
Suite 100
Phoenix, Arizona 85004

PALMER, Esq., Kenyon T. (P)
P. O. Box 706
Carefree, Arizona 85331

SCHULMAN, Esq., Martin H. (P)
215 North Court Avenue
Tucson, Arizona 85701

SCOVILLE, Esq., Kenneth S. (P)
407 Luhrs Tower
Phoenix, Arizona 85003

SKEENS, Esq., Norman E. (P)
4501 W. Indian School Road
Phoenix, Arizona 85031

SNOWBERGER, Esq., John R. (P)
1712 Guaranty Bank Building
Phoenix, Arizona 85012

TIPTON, Esq., Raymond, J. (P)
710 First National Bank Building
411 North Central Avenue
Phoenix, Arizona 85004

TODD, Esq., Kenneth I. (P)
4307 E. Vernon
Phoenix, Arizona 85008

WALES, Esq., Harold W. (P)
700 Title & Trust Building
Phoenix, Arizona 85003

WESTOVER, Esq., John H. (P)
First Federal Saving Building
Suite 1800
Phoenix, Arizona 85002

WILLIAMS, Esq., Ben. F. (P)
620 Tenth Street
P. O. Box 1078
Douglas, Arizona 85607

ARKANSAS

NEWTON, Esq., R. Lee (P)
P. O. Box 1114
Hot Springs National Park
Arkansas 71902

O'CONNOR, Jr., Esq., J. A. (P)
303 Murphy Building
El Dorado, Arkansas 71730

WILDER, Esq., Franklin (P)
403 Merchants Bank Building
Fort Smith, Arkansas 72901

WRIGHT, Esq., Edward L. (P)
1600 Tower Building
Little Rock, Arkansas 72201

CALIFORNIA

AMES, Esq., C. Hayden (P)
111 Sutter Street
San Francisco, California 94104

ANDERSON, Esq., Paul E. (P)
1600 International Building
San Francisco, California 94108

ANDRE, Esq., Peter R. (P)
210 Sinsheimer Trust Building
San Luis Obispo, California 93401

BACCI, Esq., Leonard S. (P)
5844 Geary Blvd.
San Francisco, California 94121

BALL, Esq., Joseph A. (P)
120 Linden Ave.
Long Beach, California 90802

BARNETT, Dr., Phillip (P)
1000 Chestnut Street
San Francisco, California 94109

BEARDSLEY, Esq., Charles E. (P)
611 W. 6th Street
Suite 2220
Los Angeles, California 90017

BELCHER, Esq., Frank B. (P)
510 South Spring Street
Los Angeles, California 90013

BENNETT, Esq., Eugene D. (P)
225 Bush Street
San Francisco, California 94104

BIRD, Esq., Allan G. (P) (C)
1711 Via El Prado
Redondo Beach, California 90277

BOYLE, Esq., James B. (P)
170 South Euclid Ave.
Pasadena, California 91101

BRONSON, Esq., Roy A. (P)
255 California Street
San Francisco, California 94111

BROWN, Esq., Louis M. (P)
Suite 900 Gateway East Building
Century City
Los Angeles, California 90067

CALHOUN, Jr., Esq., Alexander D. (P)
310 Sansome Street
San Francisco, California 94104

CARMAN, Esq., E. Day (P)
111 West St. John Street
San Jose, California 95113

CARR, The Hon. Charles H. (P)
United States District Court
Room 243-P, Federal Building
312 North Spring Street
Los Angeles, California 90012

CARVELL, Mrs. Mae (P)
Attorney at Law
1631 Buckingham Road
Los Angeles, California 90019

CHOATE, Esq., Joseph (P) (C)
530 West Sixth Street
Suite 701
Los Angeles, California 90014

CHOATE, Jr., Esq., Joseph (P)
450 South Serrano Ave.
Los Angeles, California 90005

COHEN, Esq., George W. (P)
300 South Beverly Drive
Beverly Hills, California 90212

COOPER, Esq., Sheldon G. (P) (C)
44 Montgomery Street
San Francisco, California 94104

COPE, Mrs. Rigmor Barker (P)
Attorney at Law
141 Vista de la Cumbre
Santa Barbara, California 93105

CRANSTON, Esq., John M. (P)
Bank of America Building
14th Floor
San Diego, California 92101

CRONIN, Esq., George T. (P)
111 Sutter Street
San Francisco, California 94104

CROTTY, Esq., Homer D. (P)
634 South Spring Street
Los Angeles, California 90014

CULLINAN, Esq., Vincent (P)
100 Bush Street
San Francisco, California 94104

DANIELSON, Esq., Walter G. (P)
Suite 803
615 South Flower Street
Los Angeles, California

DANNEMEYER, Esq., William E.
(P) (C)
834 North Grandview
Fullerton, California 92631

DEVOR, Esq., George I. (P) (C)
210 West Seventh Street
Los Angeles, California 90014

DITZ, Esq., George A. (P)
916 Bank of America Building
Stockton, California 95202

DOLLE, Esq., Hodge L. (P) (C)
453 South Spring Street
Suite 711
Los Angeles, California 90013

DONNELLEY, Esq. J. A. (P) (C)
2655 Fourth Ave.
San Diego, California 92101

DUNN, Esq., Harry L. (P)
611 W. 6th Street
Los Angeles, California 90017

DUNNELL, Miss, Adey May
Attorney at Law
P. O. Box G
Fairfield, California 94533

DUNNELL, Esq. Leo C. (P)
P. O. Box G
Fairfield, California 94533

DUQUE, Esq., Henry (P)
523 West Sixth Street
Los Angeles, California 90014

ELMORE, Miss, Josephine M. (P) (C)
Attorney at Law
4074 State Bldg.
San Francisco, California 94102

FARRER, Esq., W. M. (P) (C)
445 S. Fiqueroa St.
34th Floor
Los Angeles, California 90017

FORSTER, Esq., Albert Edward (P)
1550 1/2 Diamond Street
San Diego, California 92109

FORSTER, Esq., Richard H. (P)
530 Statler Center
900 Wilshire Blvd.
Los Angeles, California 90017

FULWIDER, Esq., Robert W. (P)
5455 Wilshire Blvd.
Los Angeles, California 90036

GEBHARDT, Esq., H. A. (P)
704 South Spring Street
Los Angeles, California 90014

GOLDBERG, Esq., John J. (P) (C)
111 Sutter Street
San Francisco, California 94104

GRANT, Miss, Isabella Horton
(P) (C), Attorney at Law
2000 Russ Bldg.
San Francisco, California 94104

GREENBERG, Esq., Arthur N. (P)
9720 Wilshire Boulevard
Beverly Hills, California 90212

GUNTHER, Esq., John E. (P)
315 Montgomery Street
San Francisco, California 94104

HAMPTON, Esq., Gordon F. (P)
458 South Spring Street
Los Angeles, California 90013

HANSON, Esq., L. Thaxton (P)
14545 Victory Boulevard
Van Nuys, California 91401

HARNEY, Esq., David M. (P)
650 So. Grand Ave.
Los Angeles, California 90017

HEFNER, Esq., Archie (P) (C)
200 Forum Building
Sacramento, California 95814

HERNEY, Miss Marie M. (P)
Attorney at Law
1700 U. S. National Bank Building
San Diego, California 92101

HIGGS, Esq., De Witt A. (P)
1700 Home Tower
San Diego, California 92101

HUFF, Esq., Carl N. (P)
4937 Gould Ave.
La Canada, California 91010

HUGHES, Esq., R. Bruce (P)
433 California Street
Room 800
San Francisco, California 94104

HURWITZ, Esq., Samuel (P)
100 W. Chapman
Orange, California 92666

JAMES, Esq., W. E. (P)
Haberfelde Bldg. Arcade
Suite 7
Bakersfield, California 93301

JANOFSKY, Esq., Leonard S. (P)
510 South Spring Street
Los Angeles, California 90013

JEWELL, Esq., Stanley (P) (C)
P. O. Box 1831
San Diego, California 92101

JOHNSON, Esq., Gardiner (P)
221 Sansome
San Francisco, California 94104

VON KALINOWSKI, Esq., Julian O. (P)
634 South Spring Street
Los Angeles, California 90014

KAUFMANN, Esq., Kenneth K. (P)
600 South Spring Street
Los Angeles, California 90014

KAY, Esq., Laurence Donald (P)
880 Hinckley Road
P. O. Box 1506
Burlingame, California 94010

KEATINGE, Esq., Richard H. (P)
Suite 120 Rowan Bldg.
458 South Spring Street
Los Angeles, California 90013

KELLY, Esq., Gerald G. (P)
One Wilshire Boulevard
Los Angeles, California 90017

KENNEDY, Esq., Laurence J. (P)
1005 East Street
Redding, California 96001

KIRKHAM, Esq., Francis R. (S) (P)
225 Bush Street
San Francisco, California 94104

KIRTLAND, Esq., Richard Lee (P)
639 South Spring Street
Los Angeles, California 90014

KLUGMAN, Esq., Robert H. (P)
606 South Oliver Street
18th Floor
Los Angeles, California 90017

KNOX, Esq., Wallace W. (P) (C)
1600 Financial Center Bldg.
Oakland, California 94612

KOFORD, Esq., James K. (P)
Financial Center Bldg.
Oakland, California 94612

KRIEGER, Esq., James H. (P)
Box 1028
Riverside, California 92502

KRUEGER, Esq., Robert B. (P)
611 Wilshire Boulevard
Los Angeles, California 90017

LAY, Esq., S. Houston (P)
3902 Lomaland Drive
San Diego, California 92106

LICKER, Esq., David (P)
5455 Wilshire Boulevard
Los Angeles, California 90036

LIPPITT, II, Esq., Henry F. (P) (C)
626 Wilshire Boulevard
Los Angeles, California 90017

LIVERMORE, Esq., Horatio P. (P)
111 Sutter Street
San Francisco, California 94104

LIVINGSTON, Esq., Lawrence (P) (C)
2000 Russ Building
San Francisco, California 94104

LINLEY, Esq., C. Rupert (P)
480 North Magnolia
El Cajon, California 92020

LOPIZICH, Esq., Ivo H. (P)
548 South Spring Street
Suite 835
Los Angeles, California 90013

LYDE, Esq., C. Keith (P)
1453 Huntoon Street
Oroville, California 95965

MADISON, Esq., Marshall P. (P)
225 Bush Street
Standard Oil Building
San Francisco, California 94104

McINNIS, Esq., John W. (P)
1301 U. S. National Bank Bldg.
San Diego, California 92101

McPHARLIN, Esq., Eldon V. (P)
458 South Spring Street
Los Angeles, California 90013

MacKENZIE, Esq., Robert D. (P) (C)
310 Sansome Street
San Francisco, California 94104

MAGAÑA, Esq., Raoul (CP)
Suite 830, Gateway East Bldg.
Century City
1800 Avenue of the Stars
Los Angeles, California 90048

MARTIN, Jr., Esq., William J. (P)
225 Bush Street
San Francisco, California 94104

MAXWELL, Esq., Roland (P)
234 East Colorado, Room 410
Pasadena, California 91101

MINASIAN, Esq., Paul Jackson
(P) (C)
1370 Second Avenue
Oroville, California 95965

MORAN, III, Esq., Hugh A. (P)
880 East Colorado Street
Pasadena, California 91101

MORAN, Esq., Thomas (P) (C)
U. S. National Bank Building
Suite 1325
San Diego, California 92101

MULL, Jr., Esq., Archibald M. (P)
715 Crocker Citizens Bank Bldg.
Sacramento, California 95814

MULLALLY, Esq., Lawrence E. (P) (C)
1005 Central Building
Oakland, California 94612

NORTHCOTE, Esq., Oliver S. (P)
210 West 7th Street
Suite 631
Los Angeles, California 90014

O'BRIEN, Esq., James E. (P)
Standard Oil Building
Room 2066
San Francisco, California 94104

OLDER, Esq., Charles H. (P)
615 South Flower Street
Suite 604
Los Angeles, California 90017

PAINTER, Esq., Howard (P)
811 West Seventh Street
Los Angeles, California 90017

PETERS, Esq., William F. (P)
940 Rowan Building
458 South Spring Street
Los Angeles, California 90013

PHLEGER, Esq., Herman (P)
111 Sutter Street
San Francisco, California 94104

QUINN, Esq., Thomas A. (P)
606 South Oliver Street
18th Floor
Los Angeles, California 90014

REED, Esq., Wallace C. (P)
639 South Spring Street
Los Angeles, California 90014

ROBINSON, Esq., John M. (P)
Suite 2000
One Wilshire Boulevard
Los Angeles, California 90017

RODI, Esq., Karl B. (P)
9777 Wilshire Boulevard
Beverly Hills, California 90212

ROGERS, Esq., Frank L. (P)
480 Cherry Avenue
Long Beach, California 90812

ROGERS, Mrs., Vera Louisa (P)
Attorney at Law
480 Cherry Avenue
Long Beach, California 90812

SCHELL, Esq., Walter O. (P)
458 South Spring Street
Los Angeles, California 90013

SHIFFER, Dr., Harvey A. (P)
Director, Pac. Inst. of Intn'l
and Space Law
448 North Avenue 56
Los Angeles, California 90042

SPROUL, Jr., Esq., Robert G. (P)
111 Sutter Street
San Francisco, California 94104

STANFORD, Esq., Dwight E. (P)
2550 Fifth Avenue
San Diego, California 92103

STICKNEY, Jr., Esq., Jefferson K. (P)
820 Security First Nat. Bank Bldg.
233 "A" Street
San Diego, California 92101

STUTSMAN, Jr., Esq., Carl A. (P)
445 South Figueroa St.
Suite 34
Los Angeles, California 90017

TEMPLETON, Esq., Harry Evans (P)
811 West Seventh Street
Suite 604
Los Angeles, California 90017

VERLEGER, Esq., Philip K. (P)
615 South Flower Street
Suite 1111
Los Angeles, California 90017

VOEGELIN, Esq., Harold (P)
18th Floor
606 South Oliver Street
Los Angeles, California 90014

WELPTON, Jr., Esq., Sherman S. (P)
634 South Spring Street
Los Angeles, California 90014

WILDMAN, Esq., Paul W. (P) (C)
15300 Ventura Boulevard
Suite 203
Sherman Oaks, California 91403

WOLFORD, Esq., Richard H. (P)
c/o Gibson, Dunn & Crutcher
9601 Wilshire Boulevard
Beverly Hills, California 90212

WRIGHT, Esq., Howard W. (P)
210 West 7th Street
Los Angeles, California 90014

WRIGHT, Esq., Loyd (P) (C)
502 Rowan Building
458 South Spring Street
Los Angeles, California 90013

YAGER, The Hon. Thomas C. (P)
Superior Court
Los Angeles, California 90012

YOVINO-YOUNG, Esq., Josef J. (P)
1924 Broadway
Oakland, California 94612

YOUNGER, Esq., Donald (P)
P. O. Drawer 1000
Santa Cruz, California 95060

ZANG, Esq., Robert E. (P) (C)
961 Mills Building
220 Bush Street
San Francisco, California 94104

ZISKIND, Esq., David (P)
756 South Broadway
Room 1205
Los Angeles, California 90014

COLORADO

MILLER, Esq., David J. (P)
Post Office Box 749
Greeley, Colorado 80631

VIGIL, Esq., Charles S. (P)
1804 Security Life Building
1616 Sixteenth Street
Denver, Colorado 80202

CONNECTICUT

BROWN, Esq., Walter L. (P)
5 South Trail
Darien, Connecticut 06820

CROSS, Esq., Samuel S. (P)
500 Summer Street
Stamford, Connecticut 06901

EGINTON, Esq., Warren William (P)
Post Office Box 120
Stamford, Connecticut 06904

FISHER, Esq., Everett (P)
19 West Elm Street
P. O. Box 1158
Greenwich, Connecticut 06830

GEENTY, Esq., William Fox (P)
205 Church Street
New Haven, Connecticut 06510

NEVAS, Esq., Leo (P)
256 East State Street
Westport, Connecticut 06880

PARSELLS, Esq., Norman King (P)
886 Main Street
Bridgeport, Connecticut 06603

PETTENGILL, Esq., Charles W. (P)
Box 1250
Greenwich, Connecticut 06830

REGNIER, Esq., J. Ronald (P)
41 Lewis Street
Hartford, Connecticut 06103

SAVITT, The Hon. Max M. (P) (C)
24 Norwood Road
West Hartford, Connecticut 06117

SCHWARTZ, Esq., Max H. (P)
129 Church Street
New Haven, Connecticut 06510

SMITH, Esq., Allan Kellogg (P)
750 Main Street
Hartford, Connecticut 06103

DELAWARE

COULSON, Esq., George Tyler (P)
3000 Du Pont Building
Wilmington, Delaware 19801

HERRMANN, The Hon. Daniel L. (P)
Court House
Wilmington, Delaware 19801

KILLORAN, Esq., Clair John (SP)
801 Bank of Delaware Building
Wilmington, Delaware 19801

LAYTON, Esq., Rodney M. (P)
4072 Du Pont Building
Wilmington, Delaware 19801

YOUNG, Esq., H. Albert (P) (C)
1401 Bank of Delaware Building
Wilmington, Delaware 19801

WASHINGTON, D. C.

AMRAM, Esq., Philip W. (P) (C)
700 Colorado Building
Washington, D. C., 20005

BARKER, Esq., Richard B. (P)
1700 Pennsylvania Ave., N. W.
Washington, D. C., 20006

BISTLINE, Esq., James A. (P)
Southern Railway Co.
P. O. Box 1808
Washington, D. C., 20013

BRAVERMAN, Esq., A. Marvin (P)
1001 Connecticut Avenue
Suite 638
Washington, D. C., 20036

BRYAN, Mrs., Mildred G. (P)
Attorney at Law
1028 Conn. Avenue, N. W.
Washington, D. C., 20036

CAMPBELL, Esq., Edmund D. (P)
822 Southern Building
15th & H Street, N. W.
Washington, D. C., 20005

CARLSON, Esq., Martin Emilius (P)
Tower Building, N. W.
Suite 601
Washington, D. C., 20005

CARTER, Esq., William Gilbert (P)
3450 Ordway Street, N. W.
Washington, D. C., 20016

COERPER, Esq., Milo G. (P)
700 Federal Bar Building
1815 H Street, N. W.
Washington, D. C., 20006

CONNELLY, Miss, Mary M. (P) (C)
Attorney at Law
1003 Shoreham Building
Washington, D. C., 20005

DOUGHERTY, Esq., Roger M. (P)
1101 - 17th Street, N. W.
Washington, D. C., 20006

DWAN, Esq., Ralph H. (P)
1108 16th Street, N. W.
Washington, D. C., 20036

FARBACH, Esq., Carl F. (P)
1818 H Street, N. W.
Washington, D. C., 20006

FERGUSON, Esq., John H. (P)
1650 30th Street, N. W.
Washington, D. C., 20007

FISHER, Esq., Joel H. (P) (C)
1522 K Street, N. W.
Washington, D. C., 20005

FREEMAN, Esq., Charles William (P)
1748 P Street, N. W.
Washington, D. C., 20036

GALIHER, Esq., Richard W. (P)
1215 19th Street, N. W.
Washington, D. C., 20036

GATES, Esq., Cassius E. (P)
Norton Building
Seattle, Washington, 98104

HOWREY, Esq., Edward F. (P)
1707 H Street, N. W.
Washington, D. C., 20006

JAFFE, Esq., Irving (P) (C)
Civil Division
Department of Justice
Washington, D. C., 20530

JAYCOX, Esq., Warren Cecil (P)
4412 Greenwich Parkway, N. W.
Washington, D. C., 20007

JOELSON, Esq., Mark R. (P)
1000 Federal Bar Building
1815 H Street, N. W.
Washington, D. C., 20006

JUST, Mrs. Carolyn R. (P)
Attorney at Law
Harbour Square
520 N. Street, S. W.
Washington, D. C., 20024

KINTNER, Esq., Earl W. (P)
1100 Federal Bar Building
Washington, D. C., 20006

KÖRNER, III, Prof. Jules G. (P) (C)
700 Brawner Building
Washington, D. C., 20006

KUEHL, Esq., Frank W. (P)
3709 Ingomar Street, N. W.
Washington, D. C., 20015

LESSER, Esq., Lawrence S. (P)
1625 K Street, N. W.
Washington, D. C., 20006

LEVENTHAL, The Hon. Harold (P)
United States Court House
Washington, D. C., 20001

LITTELL, Esq., Norman M. (P)
1826 Jefferson Place, N. W.
Washington, D. C., 20036

LIVINGSTON, Esq., Boynton P. (P)
1730 Rhode Island Ave., N. W.
Washington, D. C., 20036

LUCKEY, Jr., Esq., Albert B. (P)
326 Pennsylvania Building
Washington, D. C., 20004

MANN, Jr., Esq., J. David (P)
1120 Connecticut Ave., N. W.
Washington, D. C., 20036

MARGOLIS, Esq., Daniel H. (P)
888 17th Street, N. W.
Washington, D. C., 20006

MILLER, Jr., Esq., John T. (P)
1001 Connecticut Ave., N. W.
Washington, D. C., 20036

MILLMAN, Esq., Richard M. (P)
1001 Connecticut Ave., N. W.
Washington, D. C., 20036

NAIDEN, Esq., Neil D. (P) (C)
Suite 1100
1140 Connecticut Avenue, N. W.
Washington, D. C., 20036

PURCELL, Esq., Ganson (P)
800 Brawner Building
888 17th Street, N. W.
Washington, D. C., 20006

QUINN, Esq., Arthur Lee (P)
723 Washington Building
Washington, D. C., 20005

REA, Jr., Esq., Bryce (P)
919 Munsey Building
1329 E. Street, N. W.
Washington, D. C., 20004

REASONER, Esq., C. Dean (P)
11th Floor Fleming Building
800 - 17th Street, N. W.
Washington, D. C., 20006

REICH, Esq., David (P) (C)
1815 H Street, N. W.
Washington, D. C., 20006

REIS, Esq., Harold F. (P)
1343 H Street, N. W.
Landmark Building
Washington, D. C., 20005

RHYNE, Esq., Charles S. (P)
400 Hill Building
839 17th Street, N. W.
Washington, D. C., 20006

ROTHWACKS, Esq., Meyer (P)
2480 16th Street, N. W.
Washington, D. C., 20009

ROWE, Esq., Frederick M. (P)
800 World Center Building
Washington, D. C., 20006

SCHLEZINGER, Esq., Julius (P) (C)
1210 18th Street, N. W.
Washington, D. C., 20036

SCHOCH, Miss., M. Magdalena
Attorney at Law
1819 H Street, N. W.
Suite 240
Washington, D. C., 20006

SHEEHY, Esq., Joseph E. (P) (C)
5908 Harwick Road, N. W.
Wood Acres
Washington, D. C., 20016

TIMBERG, Esq., Sigmund (P) (C)
815 15th Street, N. W.
Washington, D. C., 20005

STALEY, Katherine M. (CP) (C)
Attorney at Law
666 Ilth Street, N. W.,
Washington, D. C., 20001

STEADMAN, Esq., Charles W. (P)
1730 K Street, N. W.
Washington, D. C., 20006

SUTTON, The Hon., Leonard v. B. (P) (C)
Office of the Chairman
Foreign Claims Settlement Comm.
Washington, D. C., 20579

UROW, Mrs., Edythe C. (P)
Attorney at Law
1025 15th Street, N. W.
Washington, D. C., 20005

WASHBURN, Esq., John Nelson (P)
1823 Quincy Street
Washington, D. C., 20036

WASSERMAN, Esq., Jack (P)
Warner Building
Washington, D. C., 20004

WEIL, Esq., Frank E. G. (P)
329 I Street, S. W.
Washington, D. C., 20024

WILNER, Esq., Morton H. (P)
Landmark Building
Washington, D. C., 20005

WINSLOW, Esq., John F. (P)
Hispanic Law Division
Law Library
Library of Congress
Washington, D. C., 20540

WOOD, Esq., Laurence T. (P)
777 14th Street, N. W.
Washington, D. C., 20005

FLORIDA

BAYA, Esq., George J. (P)
1328 Du Pont Building
Miami, Florida, 33131

CUTLER, Esq., Edward I. (P)
Post Office Box 3239
Tampa, Florida, 33601

CYPEN, Esq., Irving (P)
825 Arthur Godfrey Road
Miami Beach, Florida, 33140

DEVITT, Esq., James S. (P)
2900 East Oakland Park Blvd.
Fort Lauderdale, Florida, 33306

DUBÉ, Esq., Robert L. (P)
Suite 2105
Biscayne Tower
100 Biscayne Boulevard
Miami, Florida, 33132

FOWLER, Esq., Cody (P)
Post Office Box 1438
Tampa, Florida, 33601

GURNEY, Esq., J. Thomas (P) (C)
Post Office Box 312
Orlando, Florida, 32802

HAMMOND, Esq., Gilman M. (P)
4930 Park Boulevard
Pinellas Park, Florida, 33565

HILL, Jr., Esq., Lewis H. (P)
1014 First National Bank Building
Tampa, Florida, 33602

HOLT, Esq., Parker (P)
Post Office Box 280
Fort Myers, Florida, 33902

JOHNSON, Esq., Thomas McE. (CP)
1600 First National Bank Building
Miami, Florida, 33131

KENT, Esq., Frederick H. (P)
4961 Morven Road
Jacksonville, Florida, 32210

KRIVITSKY, Miss Anna A. (P)
Attorney at Law
12725 Sunshine Lane
Treasure Island
Saint Petersburg, Florida, 33706

LANGER, Esq., Marshall J. (P) (C)
400 City National Bank Building
25 West Flagler Street
Miami, Florida, 33130

LAZONBY, Esq., J. Lance (P)
203 Northeast 1st Street
Post Office Drawer J
Gainesville, Florida, 32601

LEWIS, Esq., John O. (P) (C)
3029 Tyrone Lane
Sarasota, Florida, 33580

LINDEN, Esq., S. Keith (P)
990 S. W. Tamarind Way
Camino Gardens
Boca Raton, Florida, 33432

LUPKA, Esq., Alan R. (P)
251 Alhambra Circle
Coral Gables, Florida, 33134

MALLOY, Esq., John Cyril (P)
169 East Flagler Street
Miami, Florida, 33131

MARKS, Esq., Sam Reynolds (P)
Post Office Box 447
Jacksonville, Florida, 32201

MEHRTENS, William O. (P)
P. O. Box 2379
Miami, Florida, 33101

PAUL, Julia Maddox (P)
Attorney at Law
P. O. Box 301
La Belle, Florida, 33935

PEPPER, Esq., Claude (P)
Washington Federal Building
1701 Meridian Avenue
Miami Beach, Florida, 33139

RANAGAN, Esq., William L. (P)
Post Office Box 549
Pompano Beach, Florida, 35161

REVELS, The Hon., P. B. (P) (C)
Post Office Box 250
Palatka, Florida

ROBERTS, The Hon. B. K. (P) (C)
Chief Justice, Supreme Court
of Florida
Tallahassee, Florida

RUSSELL, Esq., Andrew F. (P)
P. O. Box 21111
Kennedy Space Center
Florida, 32815

SOEHL, Esq., Harold J. (P)
3004 Central Avenue
St. Petersburg, Florida, 33712

STEEL, Esq., William C. (P)
1414 First National Bank Bldg.
Miami, Florida, 33131

STEIN, Esq., Stefan M. (P) (C)
512 Florida Avenue
Tampa, Florida, 33602

STRICKLAND, Delphene (P)
Attorney at Law
Supreme Court of Florida
Tallahassee, Florida

WAHL, Esq., Harold B. (P)
414 Florida Title Building
Jacksonville, Florida, 32202

WECK, Esq., James A. (P)
2641 East Atlantic Boulevard
Pompano Beach, Florida, 33062

WHITE, Esq., Morris E. (P)
1002 Citizens Building
Tampa, Florida, 33602

WURN, Esq., Lonnie (P) (C)
921 Florida Title Building
Jacksonville, Florida, 32202

ZIMMERMAN, Esq., S. Robert (P)
2745 Atlantic Boulevard
Pompano Beach, Florida, 33062

GEORGIA

BROCK, Esq., Pope F. (P)
310 North Avenue, N. W.
Atlanta, Georgia 30313

COHEN, Esq., I. T. (P)
1320 First National Bank Bldg.
Atlanta, Georgia 30308

CLARKE, Esq., Thomas Hal (P) (C)
1610 Atlantic Fed. Saving Bldg.
Atlanta, Georgia 30303

GAMBRELL, Esq., E. Smythe (P)
4000 First National Bank Bldg.
Atlanta, Georgia 30303

JOHNSON, Esq., Herbert (P) (C)
715 Rhodes-Haverty Building
Atlanta, Georgia 30303

KENNEDY, Esq., Harvey J. (P)
217 Zebulon Street
Barnesville, Georgia 30204

KILLORIN, Esq., Edward W. (P) (C)
4000 First National Bank Building
Atlanta, Georgia 30303

KLEINER, Esq., Jack (P) (C)
2222 First National Bank Building
Atlanta, Georgia 30303

MACEY, Esq., Morris W. (P)
64 Pryor Street, N. W.
Atlanta, Georgia 30303

MITCHELL, Esq., Stephens (P)
1610 Atlanta Federal Savings Bldg.
Atlanta, Georgia 30303

PILCHER, Esq., James B. (P) (C)
2614 First National Bank Building
Atlanta, Georgia 30303

SNOW, Esq., Cubbedge (P)
165 Calloway Street
Macon, Georgia 31204

SPANN, Jr., Esq., William B. (P)
1220 Citizens & Southern
National Bank Building
Atlanta, Georgia 30303

HAWAII

ANTHONY, Esq., Joseph Garner (P)
P. O. Box 3199
Honolulu, Hawaii 96801

MIZUHA, Esq., Jack H. (P)
Suite 476, Young Hotel Bldg.
Honolulu, Hawaii 96816

IDAHO

HAWKINS, Esq., William S. (P)
627 Government Way
Goeur D'Alene, Idaho 83814

QUINLAN, Esq., Daniel A. (P)
Weisgerber Building
Lewiston, Idaho

ILLINOIS

APPLEMAN, Miss, Jean (P) (C)
Attorney at Law
1355 North Sandburg Terrace
Chicago, Illinois 60610

AVERY, Esq., William H. (P) (C)
11 South La Salle Street
Chicago, Illinois 60603

BAIRD, Esq., J. Kenneth (P)
2629 Sheridan Road
Zion, Illinois

BAKER, Esq., Russell (P)
1 North La Salle Street
Chicago, Illinois 60602

BANE, Esq., Charles A. (P)
72 West Adams Street
Suite 1700
Chicago, Illinois 60603

BARRETT, Esq., Roger S. (P)
3200 Prudential Plaza
Chicago, Illinois 60601

BARTLETT, Esq., Robert C. (P)
4025 West Peterson Avenue
Chicago, Illinois 60646

BASSIOUNI, Prof., M. Cherif (P)
25 East Jackson Street
Chicago, Illinois 60604

BERNIK, Esq., Joseph M. (P)
14 Street and Sheridan Road
North Chicago, Illinois 60064

CHADWELL, Esq., John T. (P) (C)
135 South La Salle Street
Chicago, Illinois 60603

CLOVIS, Esq., Paul C. (P)
40 South Clinton Street
Chicago, Illinois 60606

CONAGHAN, Esq., Paul R. (P) (C)
208 South La Salle Street
Chicago, Illinois 60604

CRISSEY, Esq., Lachlan (P)
200 North Main Street
Lewistown, Illinois

CULBERTSON, Esq., James G. (P)
1 North La Salle Street
Chicago, Illinois 60602

DORSCHEL, Esq., Querin Peter (P)
231 South La Salle Street
Chicago, Illinois 60604

DUNN, Esq., Leonard J. (P)
115 East Main Street
West Frankfort, Illinois 62896

EDMUNDS, Esq., Palmer D. (CP)
John Marshall Law School
315 Plymouth Court
Chicago, Illinois 60604

EPSTEIN, Esq., Bernard M. (P) (C)
111 West Monroe Street
Chicago, Illinois 60603

EARLY, Esq., Bert H. (P) (C)
American Bar Center
Chicago, Illinois 60637

FLYNN, Esq., David V. (P)
502 James Street
Geneva, Illinois 60134

GERDEN, Esq., Paul (P)
1400 Sheridan Road
North Chicago, Illinois 60064

GIBSON, Esq., Jonathan C. (P)
80 East Jackson Boulevard
Chicago, Illinois 60604

HARRIS, Esq., Ralph W. (P)
Hotel State Suite 22
Marion, Illinois 62959

HODES, Esq., Barnet (P)
1 North La Salle Street
Chicago, Illinois 60602

HOLLEB, Esq., Marshall Maynard (P)
33 North La Salle Street
Chicago, Illinois 60602

JENNER, Jr., Esq., Albert E. (P)
135 South La Salle Street
Chicago, Illinois 60603

JOSEPH, Esq., Jack (P)
69 West Washington Street
Suite 2313
Chicago, Illinois 60602

KENNEDY, Esq., W. McNeil (P)
69 West Washington Street
Chicago, Illinois 60602

KIDSTON, Mrs., Alan R. (P)
Attorney at Law
715 Elmore
Park Ridge, Illinois

KIDSTON, Esq., Alan R. (P)
135 South La Salle Street
Chicago, Illinois 60603

KLASS, Esq., Martin (P)
547 W. Roscoe Street
Chicago, Illinois 60657

KOVEN, Esq., Henry H. (P)
208 South La Salle Street
Chicago, Illinois 60604

KUTNER, Esq., Luis (P)
Bankers Building
105 West Adams Street
Chicago, Illinois 60603

LAURITZEN, II, Esq., Christian (P)
69 West Washington Street
Chicago, Illinois 60602

MACCHESNEY, Prof. Brunson (P)
357 East Chicago Avenue
Chicago, Illinois 60611

MCAULIFFE, Esq., Jeremiah D. (P)
Prudential Plaza
Chicago, Illinois 60601

MCCARTHY, Esq., Hugh J. (P) (C)
111 West Washington Street
Chicago, Illinois 60602

MCDOUGAL, Esq., Edward D. (P) (C)
38 South Dearborn Street
Chicago, Illinois 60603

MCSWAIN, Esq., William A. (P) (C)
38 South Dearborn Street
Chicago, Illinois 60603

McSweeney, Esq., W. Donald (P)
231 South La Salle Street
Chicago, Illinois 60604

Mantynband, Esq., Louis M. (P)
1 North La Salle Street
Chicago, Illinois 60602

Mulroy, Esq., Thomas R. (P) (C)
1 North La Salle Street
Suite 3300
Chicago, Illinois 60602

Nance, Esq., Willis D. (P)
2900 Prudential Plaza
Chicago, Illinois 60601

Oldberg, Esq., Richard S. (P)
111 West Monroe Street
Chicago, Illinois 60603

Propp, Esq., Eugene (P)
134 North La Salle Street
Chicago, Illinois 60602

Rieger, Esq., Mitchell Sheridan (P)
231 South La Salle Street
Chicago, Illinois 60604

Shipman, Esq., David J. (P)
1 North La Salle Street
Room 4600
Chicago, Illinois 60602

Snively, Esq., John R. (P)
401 West State Street
Rockford, Illinois 61101

Snyder, Esq., Erwin P. (P)
135 South La Salle Street
Chicago, Illinois 60603

Stevenson, Esq., Louis (P)
Baker & McKenzie
Prudential Plaza
Chicago, Illinois 60601

Swain, Esq., Timothy W. (P)
912 Central National Bank Bldg.
Peoria, Illinois 61602

Synek, Esq., Henry Thrush (P)
134 South La Salle Street
Chicago, Illinois 60603

Weisbard, Esq., George L. (P) (C)
11 South La Salle Street
Room 800
Chicago, Illinois 60603

Weiss, Esq., Jerome S. (P)
69 West Washington Street
Room 3000
Chicago, Illinois 60602

Wild, Esq., Aribert F. (P)
34 West Palatine Road
Palatine, Illinois 60067

INDIANA

Ainlay, Esq., Charles W. (P)
130 North Main Street
P. O. Box 575
Goshen, Indiana 46526

Berry, Esq., John R. (P)
407 Ben-Hur Building
Crawfordesville, Indiana 47933

Blue, Esq., Sherwood (P) (C)
637 Illinois Building
Indianapolis, Indiana 46204

Fedynskyj, Prof., Jurij (P) (C)
Indiana University
School of Law
Bloomington, Indiana 47401

Harding, Esq., Robert B. (P)
500 Ben-Hur Building
Crawfordsville, Indiana 47933

Orbison, Esq., Telford B. (P)
Union National Bank Building
New Albany, Indiana 47150

Roberts, Janet L. (P) (C)
Attorney at Law
637 Illinois Building
Indianapolis, Indiana 46204

Stipher, Esq., Karl J. (P)
810 Fletcher Trust Building
Indianapolis, Indiana 46204

West, Esq., Everett L. (P) (C)
405 East 6th Street
Fowler, Indiana 49744

IOWA

Peshkin, Esq., S. David (P)
1010 Fleming Building
Des Moines, Iowa 50309

Randall, Esq., John D. (P)
Ten First Avenue East
Cedar Rapids, Iowa 52401

KANSAS

CRANE, Esq., A. Harry (P)
303 New England Building
Topeka, Kansas 66603

KENTUCKY

BRESLIN, Esq., John A. (P) (C)
Courthouse
Maysville, Kentucky 41056

LOUISIANA

BALDWIN, Esq., Cuthbert S. (P)
225 Baronne Street
Suite 2411
New Orleans, Louisiana 70112

BENTON, Sr., Esq., Fred G. (P)
114 St. Louis Street
Baton Rouge, Louisiana 70801

BENTON, Esq., Thomas (P)
144 St. Louis Street
Baton Rouge, Louisiana 70801

BERNSTEIN, Jr., Esq., Harry (P)
1000 Quachita Nat. Bank Bldg.
Monroe, Louisiana 71201

BLANCHE, Esq., Fred A. (P) (C)
P. O. Box 36
Baton Rouge, Louisiana 70821

BROOKS, Esq., Laurance W. (P)
P. O. Box 2471
Baton Rouge, Louisiana 70821

BURKE, Esq., Gibbons (P)
1500 National Bank of
Commerce Building
New Orleans, Louisiana

CANGELOSI, Esq., Robert L. (P)
617 North Boulevard
Baton Rouge, Louisiana 70802

CANGELOSI, Esq., Theodore F. (P)
P. O. Box 3036
Baton Rouge, Louisiana 70821

COLEMAN, Esq., James J. (P)
10th Floor Suite
321 Street, Charles Avenue
New Orleans, Louisiana 70130

DAVIDSON, Jr., Esq., James J. (P)
P. O. Box 3507
Lafayette, Louisiana 70501

DEUTSCH, Esq., Eberhard P. (P)
Hibernia Bank Building
New Orleans, Louisiana 70112

ELLIS, The Hon. Frank B. (P)
2100 St. Charles Avenue
New Orleans, Louisiana 71030

HARDIN, Jr., Esq., Calvin Evans (P)
408 Louisiana Nat. Bank Bldg.
Baton Rouge, Louisiana 70801

DE LA HOUSSAYE, Esq., Malcolm L. (P)
806 Masonic Temple Building
333 St. Charles Avenue
New Orleans, Louisiana 70130

KNIGHT, Jr., Esq., Nat B. (P)
1011 Fourth Street
Gretna, Louisiana 70053

KOLB, Esq., Allison Ray (P)
Post Office Box C
Baton Rouge, Louisiana 70803

LANDRY, Mrs. Frances L. (P)
Attorney at Law
348 Lafayette Street
Baton Rouge, Louisiana 70801

LANDRY, Esq., Jules F. (P)
348 Lafayette Street
Baton Rouge, Louisiana 70801

LEIGH, Esq., Thomas W. (P) (C)
400 South Grand Street
Monroe, Louisiana 71201

MELANCON, Esq., Lloyd Cyril (P)
720 Hibernia Bank Building
New Orleans, Louisiana 70112

MICELI, Esq., Augusto P. (P)
1424 Octavia Street
New Orleans, Louisiana 70115

MILLER, Esq., Ben R. (P) (C)
3125 McCarroll Drive
Baton Rouge, Louisiana 70809

MOORE, Esq., John I. (P)
P. O. Drawer 2471
Baton Rouge, Louisiana

OWEN, Jr., Esq., G. T. (P)
7th Floor Reymond Building
Baton Rouge, Louisiana 70801

PETERS, Esq., Walter C. (P)
P. O. Box 970
Jennings, Louisiana 70546

PORTEOUS, III, Esq., William A. (P)
925 Hibernia Bank Building
New Orleans, Louisiana 70112

PROVOSTY, Esq., Le Doux R. (P)
P. O. Box 1848
Alexandria, Louisiana 71301

RICHARDSON, Esq., E. Leland (P)
P. O. Box 3177
Baton Rouge, Louisiana 70821

SACHSE, Esq., Victor A. (P)
701 Fidelity National Bank Bldg.
Baton Rouge, Louisiana 70801

SARPY, Esq., Leon (P)
1500 National Bank
of Commerce Building
New Orleans, Louisiana 70112

SCHWAB, Esq., John (P)
617 North Boulevard
Baton Rouge, Louisiana 70802

SPAHT, Esq., Carlos G. (P) (C)
P. O. Box 2828
Baton Rouge, Louisiana

STOCKWELL, Esq., Oliver P. (P)
Post Office Box 2900
Lake Charles, Louisiana 70601

THEUS, Esq., John C. (P) (C)
400 South Grand Street
Post Office Drawer 1671
Monroe, Louisiana 71201

VOELKER, Jr., Esq., Richard Louis (P)
424 National Bank
of Commerce Building
New Orleans, Louisiana 70112

WILKINSON, Esq., W. Scott (P)
Post Office Box 1707
Shreveport, Louisiana 71102

WILSON, Esq., Charles W. (P)
P. O. Box 36
Baton Rouge, Louisiana 70821

WILSON, Esq., Maurice J. (P)
701 Fidelity National Bank Bldg.
Baton Rouge, Louisiana 70801

YANCEY, Esq., Clarence L. (P) (C)
Post Office Box 77
Commercial Bank Building
Shreveport, Louisiana 71102

MAINE

BERMAN, Esq., Malcolm Irving (P) (C)
40 Court Street
Houlton, Maine, 04730

MARYLAND

ALLEN, Esq., Joseph (P)
508 Tower Building
Baltimore, Maryland 21202

ANGELOS, Esq., Peter G. (P)
546 Equitable Building
Baltimore, Maryland 21202

BREGEL, Esq., Howard Calvert (P)
1900 One Charles Center
Baltimore, Maryland 21201

CARDIN, Esq., Jacob L. (P)
233 Equitable Building
Baltimore, Maryland 21202

CARDIN, Esq., Jerome S. (P)
233 Equitable Building
Baltimore, Maryland 21202

CARDIN, The Hon. Meyer M. (P) (C)
Associate Judge of Supreme Bench
of Baltimore City
Court House
Baltimore, Maryland 21202

FINCH, Esq., Walter G. (P) (C)
1501 Fidelity Building
Baltimore, Maryland 21201

FLINN, Esq., C. Maurice (P) (C)
Post Office Box 310
La Plata, Maryland 20646

FOSTER, The Hon. Dulany (P)
Court House
Baltimore, Maryland 21202

FRANKEL, Esq., Harold Lee (P)
108 East Lexington Street
Baltimore, Maryland 21202

GALIHER, Mrs. Phyllis S. (P)
Attorney at Law
5816 Highland Drive
Chevy Chase, Maryland 20015

GORDON, Esq., Douglas H. (P) (C)
15 Charlecote Place
Baltimore, Maryland 21218

GREEN, Esq., Walter L. (P) (C)
5303 Baltimore Avenue
Hyattsville, Maryland

HEARNE, Jr., Esq., Charles E. (P)
250 Woodland Road
Salisbury, Maryland 21801

HECHT, Esq., Isaac (P)
10 Light Street
27th Floor
Baltimore, Maryland 21202

MARSHALL, The Hon. Nellie Marie (P)
3 E. Lexington Street
Baltimore, Maryland 21202

McCLURE, Esq., John E. (P)
5325 Chamberlin Avenue
Chevy Chase, Maryland 20015

POE, Jr., Esq., Edgar Allan (P)
Box 1876
Baltimore, Maryland 21203

ROGERS, Esq., Grafton D. (P) (C)
10 Light Street
17th Floor
Baltimore, Maryland 21202

SAGNER, Esq., Louis J. (P)
Suite 440, Tower Building
Baltimore, Maryland 21202

SCHILLER, Esq., Milton S. (P)
10 Light Street
20th Floor, Mathieson Building
Baltimore, Maryland 21202

SHARRETTS, Esq., Douglas N. (P)
603 Munsey Building
Baltimore, Maryland 21202

SKIPP, Esq., Philip J. (P) (C)
Quaker Neck Road
Chestertown, Maryland

SKLAR, The Hon. Albert L. (P)
Court House
Baltimore, Maryland 21202

SLIWKA, Helen A. (P)
Attorney at Law
816 Munsey Building
Baltimore, Maryland 21202

WEINBERG, Esq., Leonard (P)
10 Light Street
20th Floor
Baltimore, Maryland 21202

WIEFERICH, Esq., Robert J. (P)
7913 Kentbury Drive
Bethesda, Maryland 20014

MASSACHUSETTS

BARNES, Prof., William S. (P)
Fletcher School of Law and
Diplomacy
Medford, Mass. 02155

BREWER, Esq., Wm. Conant (P)
53 Beacon Street
Boston, Mass. 02108

CHAPIN, Esq., Melville (P)
84 State Street
Boston, Mass. 02109

COHN, Esq., Haskell (P)
One Center Plaza
Boston, Mass. 02108

DACEY, Miss Kathleen Ryan (P)
Attorney at Law
100 State Street
Boston, Mass.

ECKMAN, Esq., Arthur W. (P)
107 Falmouth Street
Boston, Mass. 02115

ELTON, Esq., Sumner Wilson (P)
390 Main Street
Worcester, Mass. 01608

FOLSOM, Esq., Victor C. (P)
United Fruit Company
Prudential Center
Boston, Mass. 02199

KRUGER, Esq., Joseph (P)
One Federal Street
Boston, Mass. 02110

McCARTHY, Esq., Arthur C. (P)
18 Tremont Street
Boston, Mass. 02108

MOODY, Mrs. Eleanor March (P)
Attorney at Law
80 Federal Street
Boston, Mass. 02110

MUCCI, Esq., Joseph R. (P)
6 Pleasant St.
Malden, Mass. 02148

O'CONNELL, Esq., Lenahan (P)
31 Milk Street
Boston, Mass. 02109

PORTER, Esq., Cedric W. (P)
11 Beacon Street
Boston, Mass. 02108

REARDON, The Hon. Paul C. (P)
Room 1301, Courthouse
Pemberton Square
Boston, Mass.

ROWELL, Esq., George B. (P)
28 State Street
Boston, Mass. 02109

SLOANE, Esq., Christopher (P)
10 Tremont Street
Boston, Mass.

TRUSTMAN, Esq., Benjamin A. (P)
75 Federal Street
Boston, Mass. 02110

VIELE, Esq., Dorr (P)
24 School Street
Boston, Mass. 02108

WILLIAMS, Esq., Burton L. (P)
80 Federal Street
Boston, Mass. 02110

MICHIGAN

COULTER, Esq., Glenn M. (P)
3250 Penobscot Building
Detroit, Michigan 48226

ELSMAN, Esq., James L. (P)
2034 Guardian Building
Detroit, Michigan 48226

GRAWN, Esq., Carl B. (P)
1526-30 Dime Bank Building
Detroit, Michigan 48226

MALONE, Esq., Ross L. (P)
General Counsel
General Motors Corp.
Detroit, Michigan 48226

MARKLE, Esq., James A. (P)
1030 Buhl Building
Detroit, Michigan 48226

OLDS, Esq., Nicholas V. (P)
Asst. Atty. Gen. of Michigan
554 Hollister Building
Lansing, Michigan 48933

TROFF, Esq., Garrett J. (P)
519 South Rose Street
Kalamazoo, Michigan 49007

TURKEL, Mrs. Dorothy G. (P) (C)
Attorney at Law
2760 W. 7 Mile Road
Detroit, Michigan 48221

ZIMMERMAN, Mrs. Mary H. (P)
Attorney at Law
125 Kenwood Road
Grosse Pointe Farms
Michigan 48236

MINNESOTA

ANDERSON, Judge Leslie L. (P)
Court House
Minneapolis, Minnesota 55415

BASSFORD, Esq., Charles A. (P)
1430 Rand Tower
Minneapolis, Minnesota 55402

DEVITT, The Hon. Edward J. (P)
730 Federal Court Building
316 Robert Street
St. Paul, Minnesota 55101

FORSTER, Esq., Reginald Bishop (P)
121 West Franklin
Minneapolis, Minnesota 55404

FOSTER, Esq., Thomas A. (P) (C)
311 Burntside Drive
Minneapolis, Minnesota

GALVIN, Sr., Esq., Michael J. (P)
1000 Minnesota Building
St. Paul, Minnesota 55101

HASSELQUIST, Esq.,
Maynard Burton (P)
2400 First National Bank Building
Minneapolis, Minnesota 55402

HEIDENREICH, Esq., Douglas R. (P)
2100 Summit Avenue
St. Paul, Minnesota 55101

KING, Esq., Warren B. (P)
945 Northwestern Bank Building
Minneapolis, Minnesota 55402

LEVIN, Esq., Donald C. (P)
1200 Cargill Building
Minneapolis, Minnesota 55402

LOCKHART, Esq., Greer E. (P)
1430 Rand Tower
Minneapolis, Minnesota 55402

MCCLOUD, Esq., M. David (P)
West 789 First Nat. Bank Bldg.
St. Paul, Minnesota 55101

MAHONEY, Esq., Richard P. (P)
1300 First National Bank Bldg.
Minneapolis, Minnesota 55402

PLUNKETT, The Hon., Warren F. (P)
309 21st Street, S. W.
Austin, Minnesota 55912

PRIMUS, Esq., Lee B. (P)
432 Midland Bank Building
Minneapolis, Minnesota 55404

SCALLEN, Esq., Raymond (P)
2511 First National Bank Building
Minneapolis, Minnesota 55402

WALSTAD, Esq., Peter F. (P)
904 First National Bank Building
Minneapolis, Minnesota 55402

MISSISSIPPI

CHILL, Esq., Bernard W. N. (P) (C)
1702 Deposit Guaranty Bank Bldg.
Jackson, Mississippi 39201

CLAYTON, Esq., The Hon. Hugh N. (P)
P. O. Box 157
New Albany, Mississippi 38652

COTTRELL, Jr., Esq., David (P) (C)
Box H
Gulfport, Mississippi

DANIEL, Esq., Joe H. (P) (C)
P. O. Box 1084
Jackson, Mississippi

DENT, Esq., Robert Lowry (P) (C)
Post Office Box 789
Vicksburg, Mississippi 39180

GERALD, Miss Martha Wilson
Attorney at Law
Post Office Box 158
Jackson, Mississippi 39205

MORSE, III, Dean Joshua M. (P)
Box 278
University, Mississippi 38677

SATTERFIELD, Esq., John (P)
P. O. Box 466
Yazoo City, Mississippi 39194

WARD, Esq., Mitchell Emmett (P) (C)
P. O. Box 789
Vicksburg, Mississippi 39180

WELLS, Esq., Calvin L. (P)
400 Lamar Life Building
Jackson, Mississippi 39201

WELLS, Esq., W. Calvin (P)
900 Lamar Life Building
P. O. Box 158
Jackson, Mississippi 39201

MISSOURI

HARTMAN, Esq., Erwin C. (P)
Paul Brown Building
818 Olive Street
Saint Louis, Missouri 63101

HENDREN, Esq., John H. (P)
Central Trust Building
Jefferson City, Missouri 65101

JACKSON, Esq., Don M. (P)
820 Home Savings Building
Kansas City, Missouri 64106

KIMBRELL, Esq., Horace W. (P)
Kansas City Life Insurance
3520 Broadway
Kansas City, Missouri 64111

KREAMER, Esq., John H. (P)
1007 Bryant Building
Kansas City, Missouri 64106

LASHLY, Esq., Paul W. (P)
Lashly & Neun, Esq.,
812 Olive Street
Saint Louis, Missouri 63101

LUCAS, Esq., Wilder (P) (C)
2155 Railway Exchange Building
611 Olive Street
Saint Louis, Missouri 63101

McMAHON, Esq., Lee (P) (C)
611 Olive Street
Saint Louis, Missouri 63101

POLLOCK, Esq., T. Hartley (P)
418 Olive Street
Suite 900
Saint Louis, Missouri 63102

RAVA, Esq., Paul B. (P) (C)
818 Olive Street
Saint Louis, Missouri 63101

SPECA, Esq., John M. (P) (C)
University of Missouri
Kansas City, Missouri 64110

STEWART, The Hon. Gladys B.
(CP) (C)
Court House
Ava, Missouri

TABOR, Esq., John T. (P)
121 South Meramec
Saint Louis, Missouri 63105

MONTANA

COLGROVE, Esq., Roland V. (CP) (C)
14 North Ninth Street
Miles City, Montana 59301

NEVADA

FOLEY, Esq., Thomas A. (P) (C)
228 South Fourth Street
Las Vegas, Nevada 89101

POSIN, Esq., Murray (P)
109 South Third Street
Las Vegas, Nevada 89101

NEW HAMPSHIRE

MORRIS, The Hon. Thomas (P)
Washington Road
West Rye, New Hampshire 03891

NIXON, Esq., David L. (P)
489 Canal Street
Manchester, New Hampshire 03101

TOLL, Jr., Esq., Charles H. (P)
95 North Main Street
Concord, New Hampshire 03301

UPTON, Esq., Robert W. (P)
14 Park Street
Concord, New Hampshire 03301

NEW JERSEY

AAROE, Esq., Paul (P)
325 Front Street
Belvidere, New Jersey

BELL, Esq., Robert K. (P) (C)
801 Asbury Avenue
Ocean City, New Jersey 08226

BENNETT, Esq., Richard David (P)
17 Academy Street
Newark, New Jersey 07102

BERRY, Esq., Franklin H. (P) (C)
34 Washington Street
Toms River, New Jersey 08753

CARPENTER, Esq., James D. (P) (C)
744 Broad Street
Newark, New Jersey 07102

CONROY, Esq., Eugene J. (P) (C)
745 Broad Street
Newark, New Jersey 07102

DEBRIER, Esq., Daniel (P)
413 Guarantee Trust Building
Atlantic City, New Jersey

DRESKIN, Esq., Leon (P)
Chamber of Commerce Building
20-24 Branford Place
Newark, New Jersey 07102

EICHLER, Esq., S. Alexander (P)
786 Broad Street
Newark, New Jersey 07102

FOOSANER, Esq., Samuel J. (P)
11 Commerce Street
Newark, New Jersey 07102

FREEMAN, Jr., Esq., Forster W. (P)
26 Hamilton Street
Paterson, New Jersey 07505

GREEN, Esq., David (P)
484 Central Avenue
Newark, New Jersey 07107

GREEN, Esq., Harry (P)
200 Parker Avenue
Deal Park
Deal, New Jersey 07723

HANEMAN, Esq., Vincent S. (P) (C)
215 Guarantee Trust Building
Atlantic City, New Jersey

HARRINGTON, Esq., George W. (P) (C)
215 Broad Street
Elizabeth, New Jersey 07201

HINNEGAN, Esq., Ambrose J. (P) (C)
1010 Diplomat Building
Park View Apts
Collingswood, New Jersey 08107

HOYT, Esq., Malcolm (P)
744 Broad Street
Newark, New Jersey 07102

JUROW, Esq., Irving H. (P) (C)
60 Orange Street
Bloomfield, New Jersey 07003

KELLY, Esq., John R. (P)
26 East Clinton Avenue
Tenafly, New Jersey

KIMMEL, Esq., Arthur (P)
11 North Main Street
New Egypt, New Jersey 08533

KIRKMAN, Esq., Elwood F. (CP) (C)
404 Boardwalk Nat. Bank Bldg.
Atlantic City, New Jersey 08401

KOUVATAS, Esq., Michael N. (P)
1200 Wilson Building
Camden, New Jersey 08102

LEICHTER, Esq., Walter (P)
415 32nd Street
Union City, New Jersey 07087

LILLIE, Jr., Esq., James W. (P)
20 Hibben Road
Princeton, New Jersey

LLOYD, Jr., Esq., John (P) (C)
1421 Atlantic Avenue
Atlantic City, New Jersey 08401

MCGEEHAN, Jr., Esq., John W. (P)
790 Broad Street
Newark, New Jersey 07102

MAX, Esq., Jacob E. (P) (C)
22 Journal Square
Jersey City, New Jersey 07306

MORRISSEY, Esq., Thomas L. (P) (C)
744 Broad Street
Newark, New Jersey 07102

MOSER, Esq., George P. (P)
415 32nd Street
Union City, New Jersey 07087

OSBORN, Esq., Raymond J. (P)
45 N. 5th Street
Camden, New Jersey 08102

PEASLEE, The Hon. Amos J. (SP)
Clarksboro
New Jersey 08020

POPPER, Esq., Norman N. (P)
17 Academy Street
Newark, New Jersey 07102

RAVIN, Esq., David N. (P)
744 Broad Street
Newark, New Jersey 07102

REINERS, Jr., Esq., John Henry (P)
540 Cooper Street
Camden, New Jersey 08102

ROONEY, Dr. Miriam Theresa (P) (C)
66 Myrtle Avenue
Millburn, New Jersey 07041

ROSENTHALL, Esq., Louis P. (P)
91 Highland Avenue
Short Hills, New Jersey 07078

SEIFFERT, Esq., Morgan R. (P)
145 Welton Street
P. O. Box 966
New Brunswick, New Jersey 08903

SMITH, Jr., Esq., Sylvester C. (P)
744 Broad Street
Newark, New Jersey 07102

STAMLER, The Hon. Joseph H. (P)
103 Fernwood Road
Summit, New Jersey 07901

STEEDLE, Esq., Robert H. (P)
1421 Atlantic Avenue
Atlantic City, New Jersey 08401

VAN DUSEN, Esq., Albert E. (P)
25 Woodland Park Drive
Tenafly, New Jersey

WACHENFELD, Esq., William A. (P)
550 Broad Street
Newark, New Jersey 07102

YAUCH, Jr., Esq., John (P)
11 Commerce Street
Newark, New Jersey 07102

NEW MEXICO

BINGHAM, Esq., William J. (P) (C)
712 Simms Building
Albuquerque, New Mexico

HOLT, Esq., Herbert A. (P)
4245 Broadmoor Drive, N. E.
Albuquerque, New Mexico 87108

NEW YORK

ADAMS, Esq., Francis W. H. (P) (C)
277 Park Avenue
New York, New York 10017

ADAMS, II, Esq., Warren S. (P)
717 Fifth Avenue
New York, New York 10022

ALBRECHT, Esq., Ralph G. (P)
520 East 86th Street
New York, New York 10028

ALYEA, Esq., Ethan D. (P)
140 Broadway
New York, New York 10005

ANDERSON, Esq., Roy M. (P)
Box 731
Rye, New York 10580

ANGULO, Esq., Manuel R. (P)
63 Wall Street
New York, New York 10005

ARANOW, Esq., Edward Ross (P)
122 East 42nd Street
New York, New York 10007

ARENSON, Esq., Joseph T. (P) (C)
51 Chambers Street
New York, New York 10007

ARMANI, Esq., Frank H. (P)
4212 West Genesee Street
Syracuse, New York 13219

AVERBACH, Esq., Albert (P)
30 State Street
Seneca Falls, New York 13148

BALAMUT, Esq., George B. (P)
350 Park Avenue
New York, New York 10022

BARKO, Miss Dorothy (P) (C)
Attorney at Law
19 West 44th Street, Suite 1207
New York, New York 10036

BARTON, Esq., Edgar E. (P)
14 Wall Street
New York, New York 10005

BERLE, Esq., Rudolf P. (P)
70 Pine Street
New York, New York 10005

BESHAR, Esq., Robert Peter (P)
26 Broadway
New York, New York 10004

BICKFORD, Esq., Albert C. (P)
120 Broadway
New York, New York 10005

BLACKSTONE, Edward S. (P)
170 Broadway
New York, New York 10038

BLEAKLEY, Esq., Paul L. (P) (C)
30 South Broadway
Yonker, New York 10701

BLISS, Esq., Anthony A. (P)
One Chase Manhattan Plaza
New York, New York 10005

BLUM, Esq., Joseph G. (P) (C)
9 E. 40th Street
New York, New York 10016

BLUMBERG, Esq., Gerald (P)
One Rockefeller Plaza
New York, New York 10020

BOGART, The Hon. Mark A. (P) (C)
99 Park Avenue
New York, New York 10016

BORCHARDT, Esq., Horace W. K. (P)
36 West 44th Street
New York, New York 10036

BOSTON, Esq., Lyon (P)
315 E. 68th Street
New York, New York 10021

BREED, Jr., Esq., William C. (P)
1 Chase Manhattan Plaza
New York, New York 10005

BROME, Esq., Robert H. (P)
16 Wall Street
New York, New York 10005

BROWN, Jr., Esq., Francis C. (P)
520 East 86th Street
New York, New York 10028

BROWN, Esq., Peter Megargee (P)
One Wall Street
New York, New York 10005

BROWN, Esq., Walston S. (P)
1 Chase Manhattan Plaza
New York, New York 10005

BROWNELL, Esq., George R.
10th Floor
360 Lexington Avenue
New York, New York 10017

BROWNELL, Esq., Herbert
25 Broadway
New York, New York 10004

BURNS, Esq., Joseph W. (P)
535 5th Avenue
New York, New York 10017

BURTON, Esq., John R. (P)
2 Rector Street
New York, New York 10006

CAMPBELL, Esq., Matthew M. (P)
Five Hanover Square
New York, New York 10004

CASEY, Esq., William J. (P)
122 East 42 Street
New York, New York 10017

CHOPNICK, Esq., Max (P) (C)
9 E. 46th Street
New York, New York 10017

CLARE, Jr., Esq., William F. (P)
44 Wall Street
New York, New York 10005

CLARK, Frederica Elizabeth (P)
(Mrs. Sidney S. Hein)
Attorney at Law
1600 Central Avenue
Far Rockaway, New York 11691

COHN, Esq., Daniel M. (P)
100 Woodruff Avenue
Brooklyn, New York 11226

COHN, Esq., Roy M. (P)
598 Madison Avenue
New York, New York 10022

CONNELL, Grace H. (P) (C)
Attorney at Law
68 William Street
New York, New York 10005

CONWAY, The Hon. Albert (P)
845 Carroll Street
Brooklyn, New York 11215

COOPER, Esq., Herman E. (P)
655 Madison Avenue
New York, New York 10021

CORNELL, Esq., Ezra (P) (C)
14 Wall Street
New York, New York 10005

CORRIGAN, Esq., Matthew J. (P)
27 William Street
New York, New York 10005

COUDERT, Esq., Alexis C. (P)
200 Park Avenue
New York, New York 10017

COUGHLIN, Esq., George G. (P)
709 Marine Midland Building
Binghamton, New York 13901

COULSON, Esq., Richard (P)
1 Chase Manhattan Plaza
New York, New York 10005

CROAKE, The Hon. Thomas F. (P) (C)
United States District Court
Foley Square
New York, New York 10017

CULKIN, The Hon. Gerald P. (P) (C)
100 Centre Street
New York, New York 10013

DAMIANI, The Hon. Vincent D. (P) (C)
69-78 Street
Brooklyn, New York 11209

DANZIG, Esq., Aaron L. (P)
350 Fifth Avenue
New York, New York 10001

DARRELL, Esq., Norris (P)
48 Wall Street
New York, New York 10005

DARRELL, Jr., Esq., Norris (P)
48 Wall Street
New York, New York 10005

DAUM, Esq., F. Arnold (P)
80 Pine Street
New York, New York 10005

DEBEVOISE, Esq., Eli Whitney (P)
320 Park Avenue
New York, New York 10022

DELATOUR, Esq., Hunter L. (P)
185 Montague Street
Brooklyn, New York 11201

DELSON, Esq., Robert (P)
230 Park Avenue
New York, New York 10017

DEMPSEY, Esq., James (P)
175 Main Street
White Plains, New York 10601

DEPEW, Esq., Franklin M. (P)
205 East 42nd Street
New York, New York 10017

DIGIOVANNA, The Hon. Anthony J. (P)
9 Prospect Park West
Brooklyn, New York 11215

DILLON, Esq., William G. (P)
120 Broadway
New York, New York 10005

DOLAN, Miss Bernadette (P)
Attorney at Law
32 Court Street
Brooklyn, New York 11201

DOMAN, Esq., Nicholas R. (P) (C)
295 Madison Avenue
New York, New York 10017

DONALDSON, The Hon. Dorothea E. (P) (C)
Judge of the Court of Claims
270 Broadway
New York, New York 10007

DORR, Esq., Goldthwaite H. (P)
20 Broad Street
New York, New York 10005

DRABKIN, Esq., Nathaniel (P)
445 Park Avenue
New York, New York 10022

DUBERSTEIN, Miss Maxine K. (P)
Attorney at Law
100 Woodruff Avenue
Brooklyn, New York 11226

DUGGAN, Esq., Stephen P. (P)
120 Broadway
New York, New York 10005

DUNCAN, Esq., John V. (P)
1 Wall Street
New York, New York 10005

DUNDAS, Esq., John A. (P)
1 Rockefeller Plaza, 32nd Floor
New York, New York 10020

DURAND, Esq., Harrison F. (P) (C)
250 Park Avenue
New York, New York 10017

DURHAM, Esq., Hobart N. (P)
80 Pine Street
New York, New York 10005

EATON, Esq., Fredrick M. (P)
20 Exchange Place
New York, New York 10005

EDER, Esq., Phanor J. (CP)
74 Trinity Place
New York, New York 10006

ELLIS, Esq., Eli (P)
26 Broadway
New York, New York 10004

ETTINGER, Esq., Curtis T. (P)
60 East 42nd Street
New York, New York 10017

FARR, Esq., C. Simms (P)
280 Park Avenue
New York, New York 10017

FEINMAN, Esq., Milton (P) (C)
369 Lexington Avenue
New York, New York 10017

FINLEY, Esq., Gerald F. (P)
210 Central Park South
New York, New York 10019

FITZPATRICK, Esq., Bernard H. (P) (C)
393 Seventh Avenue
New York, New York 10001

FITZPATRICK, Esq., William F. (P)
1000 State Tower Building
Syracuse, New York

FOOSHEE, Esq., Malcolm (P)
2 Wall Street
New York, New York 10005

FORD, Jr., Esq., Edwin D. (P)
2 Rector Street
New York, New York 10006

FORROW, Esq., Brian D. (P)
Allied Chemical Corporation
61 Broadway
New York, New York 10006

FOSTER, Jr., Prof. Henry H. (P) (C)
Law School, New York University
40 Washington Square South
New York, New York 10003

FOX, Esq., Littleton (P)
271 Madison Avenue
New York, New York 10016

FOX, Esq., Paul H. (P)
80 Pine Street
New York, New York 10005

FREDEL, Esq., William J. (P) (C)
1095 Ellicott Square Building
Buffalo, New York

FREED, Mrs. Doris Jonas (P) (C)
Attorney at Law
230 Park Avenue
New York, New York 10017

FREEDMAN, Esq., Warren (P)
630 Fifth Avenue
New York, New York 10020

FRIEDMAN, Mrs. Frances M. (P)
Attorney at Law
1016 5th Avenue
New York, New York 10028

FRIEDMAN, Esq., Wilbur H. (P)
300 Park Avenue, Room 2100
New York, New York 10022

FROST, Esq., A. Harold (P)
100 William Street
New York, New York 10038

FRUMER, Esq., Louis R. (P) (C)
Matthew Bender & Co.
New York, New York 10007

GAGE, Esq., William H. (P)
192 Mt. Vernon Road
Snyder, New York 14226

GAIR, Mrs. Harriet E. (P)
Attorney at Law
84 William Street
New York, New York 10038

GAIR, Esq., Harry A. (P)
84 William Street
New York, New York 10038

GALE, Esq., Henry (P) (C)
26 Broadway
New York, New York 10004

GALLAGHER, Miss Alicia E. (P) (C)
Attorney at Law
One Chase Manhattan Plaza
New York, New York 10005

GALLAGHER, Esq., Harold J. (P)
One Chase Manhattan Plaza
New York, New York 10005

GANS, Esq., Hiram S. (P)
405 Lexington Avenue
New York, New York 10017

GATES, Esq., Samuel E. (CP) (C)
320 Park Avenue
New York, New York 10022

GEROME, Esq., Michael (P)
120 Broadway
New York, New York 10005

GILFILLAN, Esq., Andrew B. (P)
516 Erie County Bank Building
Buffalo, New York 14202

GOETZ, Esq., Norman S. (P)
300 Park Avenue
New York, New York 10022

GOLD, The Hon. Samuel M. (P)
975 Park Avenue
New York, New York 10028

GOLDMAN, Esq., Albert E. (P) (C)
909 Wilder Building
Rochester, New York 14614

GOLDSTEIN, Esq., Sidney (P) (C)
The Port of New York Authority
111 8th Avenue
New York, New York 10011

GOODWILLIE, Esq., Eugene W. (P) (C)
63 Wall Street
New York, New York 10005

GUTMAN, Dean Daniel (P) (C)
New York Academy
of the Judiciary
33 Washington Square West
New York, New York 10011

GOULD, Esq., Abbott (P)
295 Madison Avenue
New York, New York 10017

GOULD, Esq., Edward J. (P)
100 East 42nd Street
New York, New York 10017

GRAF, Esq., Karl B. (P)
The Coca-Cola Export Corporation
515 Madison Avenue
New York, New York 10022

GRAY, Esq., Michael C. (P) (C)
233 Broadway
New York, New York 10007

GRAHAM, Esq., William J. (P)
260 Madison Avenue
New York, New York 10016

GREENSPAN, Esq., Benjamin (P)
60 East 42nd Street
New York, New York 10017

HABERMAN, Jr., Esq., Phillip W. (P)
1133 Park Avenue
New York, New York 10028

HACHMANN, Esq., Hans G. (P)
Sinclair Oil Corp.
600 Fifth Avenue
New York, New York 10020

HAIGHT, Esq., G. W. (P)
509 Madison Avenue
New York, New York 10022

HALLEY, Catherine M. (P) (C)
Attorney at Law
40 Central Park South
New York, New York 10019

HALPERN, Esq., Isidore (P)
66 Court Street
Brooklyn, New York 11201

HAMILTON, Jr., Esq., Claude E. (P)
14 Wall Street
New York, New York 10005

HARRISON III, Esq., David A. (P)
120 Broadway
New York, New York 10005

HAYES, James V. (P) (C)
2 Wall Street
New York, New York 10005

HAZARD, Prof., John N. (P)
20 E. 94th Street
New York, New York 10028

HEILMAN, Esq., James M. (P)
501 Fifth Avenue
New York, New York 10017

HENN, Esq., Harry George (P)
Myron Taylor Hall
Ithaca, New York 14850

HESS, Esq., Jerome S. (P)
74 Trinity Place
New York, New York 10006

HEIN, Esq., Sidney S. (P)
1600 Central Avenue
Far Rockaway, New York 11691

HERLIHY, Justice J. Clarence (P)
Warren County Municipal Center
Lake George, New York

HIGHET, Esq., Keith (P)
Curtis, Mallet-Prevost,
Colt & Mosle
63 Wall Street
New York, New York 10005

HINES, Esq., James Irving (P)
c/o Cities Service Co
60 Wall Street
New York, New York 10005

HOUGHTALING, Jr., Esq., Earle H. (P)
3 Bank Street
Waldon, New York 12586

HUGHES, Jr., Esq., Walter T. (P) (C)
380 Madison Avenue
New York, New York 10017

HUMES, Esq., John P. (P)
50 Broadway
New York, New York 10004

ISAACSON, Esq., William J. (P)
425 Park Avenue
New York, New York 10022

JONES, Esq., Richard (CP)
120 Broadway
New York, New York 10005

JORDAN, Jr., Esq., William (P)
26 Broadway
New York, New York 10004

JOSEPH, Esq., Franz M. (P)
60 E. 42nd Street, Suite 3811
New York, New York 10017

KARP, Esq., Walter (P)
19 W. 44th Street, Suite 1011
New York, New York 10036

KIERNAN, Esq., Thomas (P)
14 Wall Street
New York, New York 10005

KIRKPATRICK, Esq., Andrew (CP)
20 Exchange Place
New York, New York 10005

KISSAM, Esq., Leo T. (P)
120 Broadway
New York, New York 10005

KITTELLE, Esq., Sumner S. (P)
1 Chase Manhattan Plaza
New York, New York 10005

KLEIN, Mrs. Fannie J. (P) (C)
40 Washington Square South
New York, New York 10021

KLINE, Esq., Joseph V. (P)
20 Broad Street
New York, New York 10005

KNOX, Jr., Esq., William C. (P)
280 Park Avenue
New York, New York 10017

KOSTELANETZ, Esq., Boris (P) (C)
52 Wall Street
New York, New York 10005

KRAMER, Esq., George P. (P) (C)
20 Exchange Place
New York, New York 10005

KRAUT, Mrs., Rose Baum (P) (C)
Attorney at Law
11 Market Street
Poughkeepsie, New York 12601

KRIPKE, Esq., Homer (P)
N. Y. U. Law School
40 Washington Square South
New York, New York 10003

LAPORTE, Esq., Cloyd (P)
140 Broadway
New York, New York 10005

KUPFERMAN, Esq., Theodore R. (P)
500 Fifth Avenue
New York, New York 10036

LEDERLE, Esq., Nicholas R. (P)
ARAMCO 505 Park Avenue
New York, New York 10022

LEE, Esq., Duncan Chaplin (P)
102 Maiden Lane
New York, New York 10005

LEIBOWITZ, Esq., Ephraim K. (P)
299 Broadway
New York, New York 10007

LEISURE, Esq., George S. (P)
2 Wall Street
New York, New York 10005

LESHER, Esq., Robert S. (P)
1700 Rand Building
Buffalo, New York 14203

LEVET, Esq., William Barlow (P)
c/o I. T. T.
320 Park Avenue
New York, New York 10022

LEVITAN, Esq., Selig J. (P)
630 5th Avenue
New York, New York 10020

LEVY, Esq., Bernard D. (P)
220 Walbridge Building
Buffalo, New York 14202

LEVY, The Hon. Matthew M. (P)
Justice of the Supreme Court
of the State of New York
11 5th Avenue
New York, New York 10003

LIFFLANDER, Esq., Matthew L. (P)
V. P. & Corporate Counsel
660 Madison Avenue
New York, New York 10021

LOEWENTHAL, The Hon. Herbert (P)
U. S. Courthouse
Foley Square
New York, New York 10007

LONGCOPE, Esq., Edwin (P)
26 Broadway
New York, New York 10004

LUCAS, Esq., William D. (P) (C)
155 East 44th Street
New York, New York 10017

LUXEMBURG, Esq., Harold L. (P) (C)
Two Park Avenue
New York, New York 10016

MACLEAN, Esq., Charles C. (P)
40 Wall Street
New York, New York 10005

MCALLISTER, Esq., Breck P. (P)
2 Wall Street
New York, New York 10005

MCCRACKEN, Esq., John E. (P) (C)
150 East 42nd Street
Room 2727
New York, New York 10017

MCDONALD, Esq., Robert J. (P)
48 Wall Street
New York, New York 10005

MCDONALD, Esq., Roy W. (P) (C)
2 Wall Street
New York, New York 10005

MCGLEW, Esq., John J. (P)
28 West 44th Street
New York, New York 10036

MCGRATH, The Hon. Christopher C. (P) (P) (C)
Surrogate's Court, Bronx County
851 Grand Concourse
Bronx, New York 10451

MCMAHON, Esq., Gerald J. (P) (C)
501 5th Avenue
New York, New York 10017

MANNING, Esq., William J. (P)
120 Broadway
New York, New York 10005

MARGULIES, Esq., Irwin (P)
400 Madison Avenue
New York, New York 10017

MARDEN, Esq., Orison (P) (C)
14 Wall Street
New York, New York

MANSFIELD, Esq., Walter R. (P)
2 Wall Street
New York, New York 10005

MARTIN, Esq., William F. (P)
355 Lexington Avenue
New York, New York 10017

MAW, Esq., Carlyle E. (P)
1 Chase Manhattan Plaza
New York, New York 10005

MAWHINNEY, Esq., Donald M. (P)
300 First Trust Building
P. O. Box 1276
Syracuse, New York 13201

MEYER, Esq., Gerald (P)
1501 Broadway
New York, New York 10036

MEYER, Jr., Esq., Martin A. (P) (C)
200 Park Avenue
New York, New York 10017

MEDINA, Jr., Esq., Harold R. (P)
One Chase Manhattan Plaza
New York, New York 10005

MEDINGER, Esq., Frank H. (P)
30 Rockefeller Plaza
New York, New York 10019

MONROE, The Hon. Donald (P) (C)
335 Larchmont Road
Elmira, New York 14905

MOORE, Jr., Capt. Albert W. L. (P)
Box 37
1605th Air Base Wing (MAC)
APO New York, New York 09406

MORONEY, Esq., James C. (P)
Standard Oil Company (N. J.)
30 Rockefeller Plaza
New York, New York 10020

MORRIS, Esq., Eugene J. (P)
1180 Avenue of the Americas
New York, New York 10036

MULDERIG, Esq., Francis J. (P)
102 Maiden Lane
New York, New York 10005

MURPHY, Esq., Gavin P. (P)
Standard Brands, Inc.
625 Madison Avenue
New York, New York 10022

MURPHY, Esq., Grayson M. P. (P)
20 Exchange Place
New York, New York 10005

MUNROE, Jr., Vernon (P) (C)
14 Wall Street
New York, New York 10005

NEUBURGER, Esq., Ralph B. (P)
445 Park Avenue
New York, New York 10022

NEWBURG, Esq., Andre W. G. (P) (C)
Cleary, Gottlieb, Stein
52 Wall Street
New York, New York 10005

NEWMAN, Esq., Milton I. (P)
29 Broadway, 30th Floor
New York, New York 10006

NOVICK, Esq., Bernard (P)
350 Fifth Avenue
New York, New York 10001

O'BRIEN, Esq., T. Stanley (P)
233 Broadway
New York, New York 10007

OLSON, Esq., Carl E. (P)
2 Rector Street
New York, New York 10006

OPTON, Esq., Frank G. (P)
100 Park Avenue
New York, New York 10017

O'NEILL, Esq., J. Ward (P) (C)
80 Broad Street
New York, New York 10009

PAGNUCCO, The Hon. Louis (P)
313 E. 52nd Street
New York, New York 10022

PALEY, Esq., Louis G.
80 Broad Street
New York, New York 10004

PALEY, Esq., Morris A. (P) (C)
80 Broad Street
New York, New York 10004

PARLIN, Jr., Esq., Charles C. (P)
20 Exchange Place
New York, New York 10005

PARRENO, Esq., Albert J. (P) (C)
63 Wall Street
New York, New York 10005

PASTUCHA, Esq., Edward J. (P) (C)
680 Fifth Avenue
New York, New York 10019

PATHY, Esq., Alexander F. (P)
60 East 42nd Street
New York, New York 10017

PAUL, Miss Raymonde I. (P)
Attorney at Law
475 Fifth Avenue
New York, New York 10017

PEASLEE, Jr., Esq., Amos J. (P)
501 5th Avenue
New York, New York 10017

PASZTORY, Esq., Blaise G. A. (P) (C)
25 Broad Street
New York, New York 10004

PECK, The Hon. David W. (P) (C)
48 Wall Street
New York, New York 10005

PENNOYER, Esq., Paul G. (P)
14 Wall Street
New York, New York 10005

PETTE, The Hon. Nicholas M. (P) (C)
166-05 Highland Avenue
Jamaica, New York

PETSCHEK, Esq., Eric K. (P)
Bristol Laboratories
International Corp.
P. O. Box 1235
Syracuse 1, New York 13201

PIEL, Jr., Esq., William (P) (C)
48 Wall Street
New York, New York 10005

PLIMPTON, The Hon. Francis T. P. (P)
320 Park Avenue
New York, New York 10022

POSSES, Esq., Frederick (P)
1 Liberty Street
New York, New York 10005

PRICE, Esq., Harold A. (P)
P. O. Box 84
Morristown, New York 07960

RABIN, The Hon. Benjamin J. (P)
27 Madison Avenue
New York, New York 10010

REEVES, Esq., William Harvey (P)
20 Exchange Place
New York, New York 10005

RAPAPORT, Esq., Henry N. (P) (C)
9 E. 40th Street
New York, New York 10016

RAPHAEL, Esq., Charles G. (P)
750 Third Avenue
New York, New York 10017

RAPP, Esq., Leslie M. (P)
120 Broadway
New York, New York 10005

REVERDIN, Esq., Bernard J. (P)
250 Park Avenue, Room 2000
New York, New York 10017

ROBBINS, Esq., Louis J. (P)
137 East 73th Street
New York, New York 10021

ROBBINS, Esq., Philip (P) (C)
35 Brewster Terrace
New Rochelle, New York 10804

ROBERTS, Esq., Sidney I. (P)
1301 Avenue of Americas
New York, New York 10019

RODGERS, Esq., Churchill (P) (C)
1 Chase Manhattan Plaza
New York, New York 10005

RODRIGUEZ, Esq., V. A. (P)
48 Wall Street
New York, New York 10005

ROGERS, Esq., Hugo E. (P)
80 Broad Street
New York, New York 10004

ROSEN, Esq., Alex L. (P)
225 Broadway
New York, New York 10007

ROSENBLUM, Esq., Jacob J. (P)
180 East 79th Street
New York, New York 10021

ROSENMAN, The Hon. Samuel I. (P)
575 Madison Avenue
New York, New York 10022

ROSS, Esq., I. Arnold (P)
150 Broadway
New York, New York 10038

ROSS, Mrs. Mary Cowell (P)
Attorney at Law
39 E. 79th Street
New York, New York 10021

RUDICK, Esq., Albert J. (P)
103 Park Avenue
New York, New York 10017

RUMMEL, Esq., Edgar F. (P)
DEPE-R
HQ, USAFE
APO New York 09633

SAMUELSON, Esq., Derrick W. (P)
67 Broad Street
New York, New York 10004

SASSOWER, Mrs. Doris L. (P)
Attorney at Law
1049 East 27th Street
Brooklyn, New York 11210

SCHELL, Jr., Esq., Orville H. (CP)
One Wall Street
New York, New York 10005

SCHWARTZ, Esq., Arthur H. (P)
19 East 70 Street
New York, New York 10021

SCHWARTZ, Esq., Marvin (P)
48 Wall Street
New York, New York 10005

SCOTT, Esq., Willard P. (P)
99 Park Avenue
New York, New York 10016

SEGALL, Esq., Arthur A. (P) (C)
230 Park Avenue
New York, New York 10017

SELIGSON, Esq., Charles (P) (C)
1290 Avenue of the Americas
New York, New York 10019

SELLERS, Esq., Charles R. (P) (C)
14 Wall Street
New York, New York 10005

SEMPLE, Jr., Esq., T. Darrington (P)
99 John Street
New York, New York 10038

SEWARD, Esq., George C. (SP) (C)
25 Broad Street
New York, New York 10004

SEYMOUR, Esq., Whitney North (P)
120 Broadway
New York, New York 10038

SHAPIRO, Esq., George M. (P)
1160 Park Avenue
New York, New York 10028

SHAPIRO, Esq., Morris (P)
350 Fifth Avenue
New York, New York 10001

SHEPARD, Esq., Charles (P)
45 Exchange Street
Rochester, New York 14614

SHULL, Brig. General Lewis F. (P) (C)
Judge Advocate, HQ US Army
Europe and Seventh Army
APO New York, New York 09403

SHULTS, Esq., C. Everett (P)
9 Seneca Street
Hornell, New York 14843

SIEGRIST, Esq., Arthur W. (P) (C)
350 Park Avenue
New York, New York 10022

SIMON, The Hon. Caroline K. (P)
227 E. 57th Street
New York, New York 10022

SIMON, Esq., Hermann E. (P)
120 Broadway, Suite 2650
New York, New York 10005

SLOTE, Esq., Edwin M. (P)
475 5th Avenue
New York, New York 10017

SMITH, Jr., Esq., Paul (P)
Socony Mobil Oil Co., Inc.
150 E. 42nd Street
New York, New York 10017

SCOLOW, Esq., A. Walter (P)
580 5th Avenue
New York, New York 10036

SPECTOR, The Hon. Morris E. (P)
Justice of the Supreme Court
State of New York
Supreme Court, 60 Center Street
New York, New York 10007

SPOLIANSKY, Esq., Leon G. R. (P) (C)
63 Wall Street
New York, New York 10005

STARK, Esq., Richard A. (P)
Milbank, Tweed, Hope & Hadley
15 Broad Street
New York, New York 10005

STEEFEL, Esq., Ernest C. (P)
52 Wall Street
New York, New York 10005

STEINBERG, Esq., Harris B. (P)
25 Broad Street
New York, New York 10004

STEPHENS, Jr., Esq., Francis X. (P)
349 East 149 Street
Room 508
Bronx, New York 10451

STOCKER, Esq., Jule E. (P)
1285 Avenue of the Americas
New York, New York 10019

STONE, Esq., Oliver L. (P)
Shell Oil Co.
50 West 50th Street
New York, New York 10020

SULLIVAN, Mrs. Charles (P)
Attorney at Law
2 Woodside Avenue
Northport, New York 11768

SULLIVAN, Esq., Charles Hardin (P)
2 Woodside Avenue
Northport, New York 11768

TARLEAU, Esq., Thomas N. (P)
1 Chase Manhattan Plaza
New York, New York 10005

TEITELBAUM, Esq., David
Two Wall Street
New York, New York 10005

THIESING, Esq., Theodore H. (P)
509 Madison Avenue, Suite 1110
New York, New York 10022

THOMAS, Esq., Milo (P)
223 Alexander Street
Rochester, New York 14607

TENNANT, Esq., John S. (P) (C)
71 Broadway
New York, New York 10006

TILZER, The Hon. George (P) (C)
c/o Supreme Court
Appelate Division
27 Broadway
New York, New York 10010

TONDEL, Jr., Esq., Lyman M. (P)
52 Wall Street
New York, New York 10005

TRACHTMAN, Esq., Joseph (P) (C)
One Wall Street
New York, New York 10005

TRUMBULL, Esq., Allan (P)
One Chase Manhattan Plaza
New York, New York 10005

TWEED, Esq., Harrison (P)
One Chase Manhattan Plaza
New York, New York 10005

TURNER, William H. (P)
475 Fifth Avenue
New York, New York 10017

VAN ORMAN, Esq., Wayne (P) (C)
55 Liberty Street
New York, New York 10005

VERNON, Lillian Malley (P)
Attorney at Law
116 East 66th Street
New York, New York 10021

VERNON, Jr., Esq., Weston (P)
116 East 66th Street
New York, New York 10021

VOGEL, Esq., Harold (P)
633 Third Avenue
New York, New York 10017

WADMOND, Esq., Lowell (P)
14 Wall Street
New York, New York 10005

WALD, Esq., Albert (P)
276 5th Avenue
New York, New York 10001

WALSH, Esq., John B. (P)
70 Niagara Street
Buffalo, New York 14203

WALSH, Esq., Lawrence E. (P) (C)
1 Chase Manhattan Plaza
New York, New York 10005

WEIDEN, Esq., Paul L. (P)
60 East 42nd Street
New York, New York 10017

WERNER, Esq., Victor D. (P)
19 Rector
New York, New York 10006

WHIPPLE, Esq., Taggart (P)
1 Chase Manhattan Plaza, 43 Floor
New York, New York 10005

WHITMAN, Esq., Stewart L. (P)
Room 2815
60 East 42nd Street
New York, New York 10017

WIGGINS, Esq., Platt K. (P)
142 Pierrepont Street
Brooklyn, New York 11201

WILLARD, Esq., Josiah (P)
14 Wall Street
New York, New York 10005

WILLIAMS, Esq., Paul W. (P) (C)
80 Pine Street
New York, New York 10005

WILLIS, Esq., Everett I. (P)
140 Broadway
New York, New York 10005

WILSON, Esq., John A. (P) (C)
20 Exchange Place
New York, New York 10005

WINER, Esq., David E. (P)
445 Park Avenue
New York, New York 10022

WOLF, Esq., Morris (P)
220 5th Avenue
New York, New York 10001

WINTHROP, Esq., Nathaniel T. (P)
20 Exchange Place
New York, New York 10005

WRIGHT, Esq., Stanley R. (P)
25 Broadway
New York, New York 10004

WYNROTH, Esq., Norman C. (P)
104 West 40th Street
New York, New York 10018

YOUNG, Esq., John H. (P) (C)
2 Wall Street
New York, New York 10005

ZUKERMAN, The Hon. Jacob T. (P) (C)
Family Court 283 Adams Street
Brooklyn, New York 11201

NORTH CAROLINA

ADAMS, Jr., Esq., William J. (P)
Box 3463
Greensboro, North Carolina 27402

BLACKWELL, Esq., T. Winfield (P)
P. O. Box 2838
Winston-Salem,
North Carolina 27102

BLOUNT, Esq., Marvin K. (P)
P. O. Box 834
Greenville, North Carolina 27834

Campbell, Esq., Hugh
1626 Queens Road
Charlotte, North Carolina 28207

Clarkson, The Hon. Francis O. (P) (C)
Senior Resident Judge
Twenty-sixth Judicial District
The Superior Court of N. Carolina
Charlotte, North Carolina 28202

DuMont, Esq., Harry (P)
P. O. Box 7526
Court House Station
Asheville, North Carolina

Fairley, Esq., Francis H. (P)
200 Law Building
Charlotte, North Carolina 28202

Frazier, Esq., Robert H. (P) (C)
401-5 Banner Building
Greensboro, North Carolina 27401

Grier, Esq., Joseph W. (P)
1014 Law Building
Charlotte, North Carolina 28202

Hamrick, Jr., Esq., Frederick D. (P)
201-202 Rutherford Drug Building
P. O. Drawer 790
Rutherfordton
North Carolina 28139

Jeffress, Esq., Alonzo Hassell (P) (C)
Post Office Drawer 396
Kinston, North Carolina 28501

Johnson, Esq., Lawrence McN. (P)
P. O. Box 1125
Aberdeen, North Carolina 28215

Leath, Esq., Thomas H. (P)
P. O. Box 1257
Rockingham, North Carolina 28379

Lockhart, Esq., Thomas Ashe (P)
910 N. Carolina Nat. Bank Bldg.
Charlotte, North Carolina 28202

Long, Esq., George A. (P)
1201 West Davis Street
Burlington, North Carolina 27215

McLendon, Jr., Esq., Lennox P. (P)
Post Office Drawer U
Greensboro, North Carolina

Miller, Esq., Garnet Edward (P)
115 S. Fayetteville Street
Asheboro, North Carolina 27203

Moore, Esq., James O. (P)
1600 Johnson Building
Charlotte, North Carolina 28202

Moore, Esq., Beverly C. (P)
Attorney at Law
906 Country Club Drive
Greensboro, North Carolina 27408

Rice, Jr., Esq., Leon L. (P)
P. O. Drawer 84
Winston-Salem,
North Carolina 27102

Rollins, Esq., Clyde T. (P)
604 Southeastern Building
Greensboro, North Carolina

Sapp, Jr., Esq., Armistead Wright (P)
702 Southeastern Building
Greensboro, North Carolina 27403

Smith, Jr., Esq., J. McNeill (P)
Drawer G
Greensboro, North Carolina 27402

Stockton, Jr., Esq., Ralph M. (P)
P. O. Box 2860
Winston-Salem
North Carolina 27102

Thorp, Jr., Esq., William L. (P)
1605 West Thomas Street
Rocky Mount
North Carolina 27801

Wilson, Jr., Esq., J. Kenyon (P)
731 Riverside Avenue
Post Office Box 146
Elizabeth City
North Carolina 27909

Wooten, Jr., Esq., Frank M. (P) (C)
P. O. Box 63
Greenville, North Carolina 27834

NORTH DAKOTA

Bjella, Esq., Arley R. (P)
P. O. Box 1343
Williston, North Dakota 58801

Hjellum, Esq., John (P) (C)
Box 1560
Jamestown, North Dakota 58401

Pringle, Esq., Kenneth G. (P)
P. O. Box 1000
Minot, North Dakota 58701

Traynor, Esq., Mack V. (P)
Devils Lake
North Dakota 58301

OHIO

AUG, Esq., J. Vincent (P)
1005 Atlas Bank Building
Cincinnati, Ohio 45202

BEBOUT, Esq., John W. (P)
Ninth Floor, Toledo Trust Building
Toledo, Ohio 43604

BIESER, Esq., Irvin G. (P)
8 North Main Street
Dayton, Ohio 45402

BOWSHER, Esq., John M. (P)
17 South High Street
Columbus, Ohio 43215

BUCKLEY, Esq., Paul J. (P)
Gem City Savings Building
Suite 820
Dayton, Ohio 45402

CLARK, Esq., C. Kenneth (P)
1200 Mahoning Bank Building
Youngstown, Ohio 44503

COOKSTON, Esq., Raymond E. (P) (C)
540 Union Commerce Building
Cleveland, Ohio 44115

DANAHER, Esq., James B. (P)
Probate Court
Court House
Cleveland, Ohio 44113

DONOHUE, Esq., Charles J. (P)
200 Westview Towers
21010 Center Ridge Road
Rocky River, Ohio 44116

FRASER, Esq., Malcolm (P)
5800 Monroe Street
Sylvania, Ohio 43560

FULLER, Esq., Fred E. (P)
405 Madison Avenue
Toledo, Ohio 43604

GLEASON, Esq., James Arthur (P) (C)
215 Euclid Avenue
Cleveland, Ohio 44114

GOODMAN, Esq., Sol (P)
1016 Fifth-Third Bank Building
Cincinnati, Ohio 45202

HENRY, Esq., Leslie (P)
807 Owens-Illinois Building
Toledo, Ohio 43604

HUGGINS, Esq., William G. (P)
2999 Neil Avenue
Apartment 53 B
Columbus, Ohio 43202

HYDE, Esq., Alan L. (P)
1100 National City Bank Building
Cleveland, Ohio 44114

HYDE, Esq., Howard Linton (P)
1144 E. Market Street
Akron, Ohio 44305

IDDINGS, Esq., Andre S. (SP) (C)
1212 Third National Building
Dayton, Ohio 45402

KENT, Esq., Charles Henry (P)
2550 Henthorne Road
Columbus, Ohio 43221

LARRIMER, Esq., Richard N. (SP)
165 North High Street
Columbus, Ohio 43215

LUMB, Esq., Harold C. (P)
Republic Steel Corp.
1703 Republic Building
Cleveland, Ohio 44115

McDERMOTT, Esq., Thomas J. (P)
1007 Farmers Bank Building
Mansfield, Ohio 44902

McDOWELL, Esq., Thomas J. (P)
300 Republic Building
Cleveland, Ohio 44115

McNEAL, Esq., Harley J. (P)
520 Williamson Building
Cleveland, Ohio 44114

McPHERSON, Jr., Esq., J. W.
134 Sunnyside Street
Hartville, Ohio 44632

MASEK, Esq., Edward Joseph (P) (C)
28500 Gates Mills Blvd.
Pepper Pike, Ohio 44124

MOORE, Esq., Marshall C. (P) (C)
295 Westage At Pearce
Mansfield, Ohio 44906

MORRIS, Esq., Earl F. (P) (C)
37 West Broad Street
Columbus, Ohio

PENNELL, Esq., Miller B. (P)
1656 Union Commerce Building
Cleveland, Ohio 44115

POMERENE, Esq., Warner M. (P)
Coshocton National Bank Bldg.
Coshocton, Ohio 43812

POWELL, Esq., Roger K. (P) (C)
17 South High Street
Columbus, Ohio 43215

REMINGER, Esq., Richard T. (CP)
731 Leader Building
Cleveland, Ohio 44114

ROTH, Esq., Lad J. (P) (C)
320 Superior Avenue East
Cleveland, Ohio 44114

SCHNORF, Sr., Esq., Brandon G. (P)
324 Spitzer Building
Toledo, Ohio 43604

SMITH, Esq., Walter F. (P) (C)
2402 Kroger Building
1014 Vine Street
Cincinnati, Ohio 45202

SPAIN, Esq., John A. (P)
c/o Lindhorst & Dreidame
12th Floor, American Building
Cincinnati, Ohio 45202

STICHTER, Esq., Wayne Edwin (P) (C)
240 Horon Street
Toledo, Ohio 43604

SULLIVAN, Esq., John K. (P) (C)
2187 Overlook Road
Cleveland Heights, Ohio 44106

TEARE, Esq., Albert R. (P)
1114 Terminal Tower
Cleveland, Ohio 44113

TRENKAMP, Esq., Robert H. (P)
1675 Union Commerce Building
Cleveland, Ohio 44115

ZINN, Esq., C. Alfred (P)
305 First National Bank Building
Zanesville, Ohio 43701

OKLAHOMA

BOHANON, Judge, Luther (P)
3001 Federal Building
Oklahoma City, Oklahoma 73101

CHANDLER, The Hon. Stephen S. (P)
United States Court House
Oklahoma City, Oklahoma 73102

ENDICOTT, Miss Margaret (P)
Attorney at Law
1713 Drakestone
Oklahoma City, Oklahoma 73120

FELLERS, Esq., James D. (P) (C)
2700 First National Building
Oklahoma City, Oklahoma 73102

GARRETT, Esq., Douglas (P)
414 Surety Building
Muskogee, Oklahoma 74401

UNGERMAN, Esq., Irvine E. (P)
6th Floor, Wright Building
Tulsa, Oklahoma 74103

WHEATON, Mrs. Norman Frazier (P)
Attorney at Law
810 Franklin Building
Tulsa, Oklahoma 74103

OREGON

BIEREK, Esq., William V. (P)
Suite 108, Lloyd Plaza
1425 N. E. Irving
Portland, Oregon 97232

DEZENDORF, Esq., James C. (P)
800 Pacific Building
Portland, Oregon 97204

EVANS, III, Esq., Walter Howard (P)
560 Leffelle St. South
Salem, Oregon 97302

EVERETT, Miss Gladys M. (P)
Attorney at Law
716 Executive Building
Portland, Oregon 97204

HEFFERNAN, Jr., Esq., Robert D. (P)
P. O. Box 878
Medford, Oregon 97501

JOHNSON, Jr., Esq., Folger (P)
519 U. S. Courthouse
Portland, Oregon 97205

KLIKS, Esq., Bernard B. (P)
410 Pearson Building
418 S. W. Washington Street
Portland, Oregon 97204

MACDONALD, Miss Anne (P)
Attorney at Law
203 North Main Street
Prineville, Oregon 97754

MORRISON, Esq., William H. (P)
17th Floor, Standard Plaza
Portland, Oregon 97204

PHILLIPS, Esq., Clarence D. (P)
807 Electric Building
Portland, Oregon 97205

POZZI, Esq., Frank (P)
808 Standard Plaza Building
Portland, Oregon 97204

SAHLSTROM, Esq., Elmer B. (P)
140 South Park
Eugene, Oregon 97401

WINFREE, Esq., Herbert W. (P)
333 Pacific Building
Portland, Oregon 97204

ZIPPER, Esq., Morris (P) (C)
826 American Bank Building
Portland, Oregon 97205

PENNSYLVANIA

ABRAHAMS, Esq., Robert D. (P)
Land Title Building
17th Floor
Philadelphia, Pennsylvania 19110

ANTOINE, Esq., William C. (P)
1310 Six Penn Center Plaza
Philadelphia, Pennsylvania 19104

ARENSBERG, Esq., Charles F. C. (P)
1404 First National Bank Building
Pittsburgh, Pennsylvania 15222

BATIPPS, Harriette W. (P) (C)
Attorney at Law
23 N. Main Street
Lewistown, Pennsylvania 17044

BERTAS, Miss Helen E. (P) (C)
Attorney at Law
1500 Walnut Street Building
Suite 1401
Philadelphia, Pennsylvania 19102

BIDDLE, Esq., Oliver Caldwell (P)
1035 Land Title Building
Philadelphia, Pennsylvania 19110

BRACKEN, Esq., John P. (CP) (C)
2107 Fidelity-Philadelphia
Trust Building
Philadelphia, Pennsylvania 19109

BROWN, Jr., Esq., Richard P. (P) (C)
2107 Fidelity-Philadelphia
Trust Building
Philadelphia, Pennsylvania 19109

BUTLER, Esq., Thomas R. (P)
16 East Market Street
West Chester, Pennsylvania 19380

CHALLENGER, Jr., Esq., William A. (P)
87 Manito Drive
Mercer, Pennsylvania 16137

COHEN, Esq., M. Barney (P) (C)
1026 Frick Building
Pittsburgh, Pennsylvania 15219

CUSHMAN, Esq., Edward H. (P)
2426 Fidelity-Philadelphia
Trust Building
Philadelphia, Pennsylvania 19109

DUMBAULD, The Hon. Edward (P)
Judge U. S. District Court
911 U. S. Court House
Pittsburgh, Pennsylvania 15219

ERVIN, Esq., Harold L. (P)
Sycamore Mills Road, R. D. 1
Media, Pennsylvania 19063

ESHELMAN, Esq., Joseph F. (P)
1600 Three Penn Center Plaza
Philadelphia, Pennsylvania 19102

FOLEY, Esq., Michael A. (P)
721 Western Saving Fund Building
Philadelphia, Pennsylvania 19107

FREEDMAN, Esq., Abraham E. (P)
1415 Walnut Street
Philadelphia, Pennsylvania 19102

GATZ, Jr., Esq., Arthur D. (P)
1708 Law and Finance Building
Pittsburgh, Pennsylvania 15219

GRAUBART, Ella
(Mrs. Charles F. C. Arensberg)
Attorney at Law
834 Amberson Avenue
Pittsburgh, Pennsylvania 15232

HEADLY, Esq., John F. (P)
1421 Chestnut Street
Philadelphia, Pennsylvania 19102

HILINSKI, Esq., Chester C. (P)
1600 Three Penn Center Plaza
Philadelphia, Pennsylvania 19102

HIRSCH, Esq., Paul Kern (P)
912 Frick Building
Pittsburgh, Pennsylvania 15219

HOGELAND, Esq., Richard Wright (P)
357 Lancaster Avenue
Haverford, Pennsylvania 19041

ISAACSON, Esq., Gerard Harry (P)
Rooms 306-308 Masonic Bldg.
Ebensburg, Pennsylvania 15931

KAIER, Esq., Edward A. (P)
Room 1100
6 Penn Center Plaza
Philadelphia, Pennsylvania 19104

KARET, Esq., Edward (P) (C)
1308 Tyson Avenue
Philadelphia, Pennsylvania 19111

LABRUM, Esq., J. Harry (P)
1500 Seven Penn Center Plaza
Philadelphia, Pennsylvania 19103

LANDY, Rose K. (P) (C)
Attorney at Law
2200 P. S. F. Building
Philadelphia, Pennsylvania 19107

LANDY, Esq., Samuel H. (P) (C)
2220 Phila. Savings Fund Bldg.
12 South 12th Street
Philadelphia, Pennsylvania 19107

LEWIS, Esq., Leroy L. (P) (C)
525 William Penn Pl.
Pittsburgh, Pennsylvania 15219

LITKE, Esq., William (P) (C)
Heverly Building
Bellefonte, Pennsylvania

LITTLETON, Esq., Arthur (P)
2107 Fidelity-Philadelphia
Trust Building
Philadelphia, Pennsylvania 19109

McDONALD, Esq., Henry A. (P) (C)
615 Masonic Building
Erie, Pennsylvania 16501

MACINTOSH, Esq., W. James (P)
2107 Fidelity-Philadelphia
Trust Building
Philadelphia, Pennsylvania 19109

McARDLE, Esq., James P. (P)
606 Frick Building
Pittsburgh, Pennsylvania 15219

McDEVITT, Esq., Vincent P. (P)
1000 Chestnut Street
Philadelphia, Pennsylvania 19107

McMANUS, Esq., Michael C. (P)
555 East City Line Avenue
Bala-Cynwyd, Pennsylvania 19004

McWILLIAMS, Esq., J. Wesly (P)
1500 Morris Building
1421 Chestnut Street
Philadelphia, Pennsylvania 19102

MARKOWITZ, Esq., Arthur (P)
141 East Market Street
York, Pennsylvania 17405

MARKOWITZ, Esq., Lewis H. (P)
Post Office Box 682
141 East Market Street
York, Pennsylvania 17405

MAXWELL, Esq., David F. (P)
1418 Packard Building
Philadelphia, Pennsylvania 19102

MERCER, Esq., H. Fred (P)
1022 Frick Building
Pittsburgh, Pennsylvania 15219

MEYERS, Esq., Morton (P)
910 U. S. National Bank Building
Johnstown, Pennsylvania 15901

O'BRIEN, Esq., David W. (P)
2107 Fidelity-Philadelphia
Trust Building
Philadelphia, Pennsylvania 19109

PINOLA, The Hon. Frank L. (P)
1216 Miners National Bank Bldg.
Wilkes-Barre
Pennsylvania 18701

PRIZER, Esq., John B. (P)
1138 Transportation Center
No. 6 Penn Center Plaza
Philadelphia, Pennsylvania 19104

RUBY, Esq., James K. S. (P)
2101 Duquesne Avenue
McKeesport, Pennsylvania 15132

RUSSELL, Jr., Esq., John (P)
2107 Fidelity-Philadelphia
Trust Building
Philadelphia, Pennsylvania 19109

SCOTT, Esq., John H. (P)
517 Frick Building
Pittsburgh, Pennsylvania 15219

SEGAL, Esq., Bernard G. (P) (C)
1719 Packard Building
Philadelphia, Pennsylvania 19102

SEGAL, Esq., Irving R. (P)
1719 Packard Building
Philadelphia, Pennsylvania 19102

SHAFER, Esq., Morris L. (P)
Dickinson School of Law
College Street
Carlisle, Pennsylvania 17013

SMITH, Esq., Lawrence M. C. (P)
1707 Ben Franklin Parkway
Philadelphia, Pennsylvania 19103

SOLOMON, Esq., Charles M. (P) (C)
1401 Walnut Street
Philadelphia, Pennsylvania 19102

VON STARCK, Esq., Ernest R. (P)
2107 Fidelity-Philadelphia
Trust Building
Philadelphia, Pennsylvania 19109

VOORHEES, Esq., Theodore (P)
1600 Three Penn Center Plaza
Philadelphia, Pennsylvania 19102

WARNER, Jr., Esq., Theodore K. (P)
1334 Transportation Center
6 Penn Center Plaza
Philadelphia, Pennsylvania 19103

WETZEL, Esq., Carroll Robbins (P)
1600 Three Penn Center Plaza
Philadelphia, Pennsylvania 19102

WEXLER, Esq., Morris M. (P)
1 E. Penn Square
Juniper & Market Street
Philadelphia, Pennsylvania 19107

WILDERMAN, Esq., Louis H. (P)
735 P. S. F. S. Building
12 South 12th Street
Philadelphia, Pennsylvania 19107

SOUTH CAROLINA

GRANTHAM, Esq., George L. (P)
P. O. Box 346
Easley, South Carolina 29640

MOZINGO, III, Esq., James P. (P)
P. O. Box 257
Darlington, South Carolina 29532

TENNESSEE

AHLES, Esq., Rodney Victor (P)
201 Lealand Drive
Lebanon, Tennessee 37087

ANDREWS, Esq., Forrest (P)
1108 Knoxville Bank Building
Knoxville, Tennessee 37902

ARMSTRONG, Jr., Esq., Walter P. (P)
15th Floor
Commerce Title Building
Memphis, Tennessee 38103

BRATTON, Esq., Frank N. (P)
P. O. Box 277
First National Bank Building
Athens, Tennessee 37303

CHESHIRE, Esq., J. Ross (P) (C)
Box 6652
Nashville, Tennessee 37215

DOUGHTY, Esq., John H. (P)
Post Office Box 1066
Knoxville, Tennessee 37901

GARNER, Esq., James O. (P)
2103 Sterick Building
Memphis, Tennessee 38103

GLASGOW, Jr., Esq.,
Samuel McPheeters (P)
Court Square Building
300 James Robertson Parkway
Nashville, Tennessee

HARWELL, Esq., Jonathan (P)
401 Court Square Building
Nashville, Tennessee 37201

JENKINS, Esq., Erby L. (P)
Bank of Knoxville Building
Knoxville, Tennessee 37902

KUHN, Esq., Edward W. (P)
150 East Court Ave., Box 123
Memphis, Tennessee 38101

LAWLER, Esq., Edward J. (P)
Suite 1500, First Nat. Bank Bldg.
Memphis, Tennessee 38103

LEE, Esq., J. D. (P)
Box 566
Madisonville, Tennessee 37354

McCONNELL, Esq., Robert M. (P)
Post Office Box 39
Knoxville, Tennessee 37901

UNDERWOOD, The Hon. Shirley B. (P)
Judge, Juvenile Court
401 East Watauga Avenue
Johnson City, Tennessee 37601

WALLER, Esq., William (P)
1200 American Trust Building
Nashville, Tennessee 37201

TEXAS

ATWELL, Esq., Webster (P)
2605 Republic Nat. Bank Tower
Dallas, Texas 75201

BAKER, Esq., Russel M. (P)
1610 Tower Petroleum Building
Dallas, Texas 75201

BOULDIN, Esq., Victor W. (SP)
Vinson, Elkins, Weems & Searis
First City National Bank Building
Houston, Texas 77002

CARRINGTON, Esq., Paul (P)
1900 Mercantile Bank Building
Dallas, Texas 75201

CLEMENS, Esq., Ernest W. (P) (C)
1805 National Bank of
Commerce Building
San Antonio, Texas 78205

COOK, Esq., Cecil N. (P)
1100 Esperson Building
Houston, Texas 77002

DOUGHERTY, Esq., J. Chrys (P)
P. O. Box 98
Austin, Texas 78767

DUNN, Esq., William W. (P)
Ling-Temco-Vought, Inc.
P. O. Box 5003
Dallas, Texas 75222

GARRETT, Esq., Rufus S. (P) (C)
710 Fort Worth
National Bank Building
Fort Worth, Texas 76102

GARRETT, Jr., Esq., Rufus S. (P) (C)
710 Fort Worth
National Bank Building
Fort Worth, Texas 76102

HUDNALL, Mrs. Dulse Lometa Lux
Attorney at Law
1903 South Robertson
Tyler, Texas 75701

JONES, Mrs. Erin Bain
Attorney at Law
P. O. Box 20695
Dallas, Texas 75220

MCCORMICK, Esq., Len G. (P)
Box 1205
Midland, Texas 79701

MACDONALD, Jr., Esq.,
John Alexander (P) (C)
1600 Esperson Building
Houston, Texas 77002

MCWHORTER, Esq., Paul (P)
Box 7633 N. T. Station
Denton, Texas 76201

PARKS, Esq., Fred (P)
1599 Houston Club Building
Houston, Texas 77002

PHILLIPS, Esq., John C. (P) (C)
Box A Capitol Station
Austin, Texas 78711

SHIVERS, Esq., Linward Paul (P)
2207 Windsor Road East
Austin, Texas 78703

SIMPSON, The Hon. Gordon (P)
2300 Rep. National Bank Bldg.
Dallas, Texas 75201

SMITH, Esq., Cyril J. (P) (C)
1811 Houston Natural Gas Bldg.
Houston, Texas 77002

STOREY, Esq., Robert G. (P) (C)
Southwestern Legal Center
Hillcrest at Daniels
Dallas, Texas 75205

THURMOND, Esq., Ray G. (P) (C)
Peoples National Bank Building
Suite 907
Tyler, Texas 75701

UTAH

BEHLE, Esq., Calvin A. (P) (C)
520 Kearns Building
Salt Lake City, Utah 84101

BRAYTON, Esq., Dean F. (P)
1001 Walker Bank Building
Salt Lake City, Utah 84111

OWEN, Jr., Esq., D. Ray (P)
608 El Paso Natural Gas Building
Salt Lake City, Utah 84111

RAWLINGS, Esq., Calvin W. (P)
530 Judge Building
Salt Lake City, Utah 84111

VERMONT

DOLLARD, Elizabeth K. (P) (C)
Attorney at Law
204 Union Street
Bennington, Vermont 05201

RAY, Jr., Esq., George W. (P)
East Thetford Hill
Vermont 05043

VIRGINIA

ANDERSON, Robert N., (P) (C)
2732 North 18th Street
Arlington, Virginia 22201

COOVEL, Miss. Lucile M. (P)
Attorney at Law
1021 Arlington Boulevard
Arlington, Virginia 22209

CRAIG, Esq., William E. (P)
9408 Lakeside Drive
Vienna, Virginia 22180

DAVENPORT, Esq., B. Warwick (P) (C)
Box 1535
Richmond, Virginia

DAWSON, III, Esq., James S. (P)
Sommarbeth
Huntly, Virginia

ELMORE, Esq., E. Whitehead (P)
P. O. Box 1535
Richmond, Virginia 23212

FINE, Esq., Louis B. (CP)
Law Building
147 Granby Street
Norfolk, Virginia 23510

GODDIN, John C. (P)
200 W. Grace Street
Richmond, Virginia 23220

GRAVES, Esq., Edward S. (P) (C)
P. O. Box 958
Lynchburg, Virginia 24505

KELLY, Esq., Robert G. (P)
P. O. Box 553
Charleston, West Virginia 25322

KYLE, Esq., W. E. (P)
333 Federal Building
Norfolk, Virginia 23510

POWELL, Jr., Esq., Lewis F. (P)
1003 Electric Building
Richmond, Virginia 23219

RICHMOND, Esq., Joseph W. (P)
240 Court Square
Charlottesville, Virginia

ROSENBERGER, Jr., Esq., William (P)
P. O. Box 1328
Lynchburg, Virginia 24505

STAKER, Esq., Zane Grey (CP)
National Bank of Commerce Bldg.
Williamson, West Virginia 25661

STEINGOLD, Esq., Israel (P)
Town Point Building
Norfolk, Virginia 23510

STEINGOLD, Esq., Maurice (P)
319 Town Point Building
P. O. Box 3182
Norfolk, Virginia 23510

VIRGIN ISLANDS

MERWIN, The Hon. John D. (P) (C)
P. O. Box 1674
Frederiksted
St. Croix, Virgin Island 00840

WASHINGTON

GREY, Esq., Wheeler (P)
1000 Norton Building
Seattle, Washington 98104

HANLEY, Jr., Esq., Edward B. (P) (C)
853 Olympic National Building
Seattle, Washington 98104

HENRIOT, Esq., James F. (P)
1100 Puget Sound Bank Building
Tacoma, Washington 98402

LEVINSON, Esq., Sam L. (P) (C)
Northern Life Tower
Seattle, Washington 98101

PHILLIPS, Esq., Earl A. (P) (C)
518 Dexter Horton Building
Seattle, Washington 98104

WILLIAMS, Esq., David J. (P)
1804 Washington Building
Seattle, Washington 98101

WISCONSIN

ANDERSON, Esq., Rudolph E. (P)
318 Telegram Building
Superior, Wisconsin 54880

BRUMMUND, Esq., Walter H. (P)
310 River Drive
Appleton, Wisconsin 54911

CHATTERTON, Esq., William A. (P) (C)
321 S. Hamilton Street
Madison, Wisconsin 53703

DOLAN, Mrs. Julia B.
Executive Attorney
Legal Aid Society of Milwaukee
610 North Jackson Street
Milwaukee, Wisconsin 53202

GEFFS, Esq., George S. (P)
Jackman Building
Janesville, Wisconsin 53545

GOLDBERG, Esq., Charles L. (P)
735 North Water Street
Milwaukee, Wisconsin 53202

JOHNSON, Esq., James N. (P)
Vice Pres. Secy., & Gen. Counsel
A. O. Smith Corp.
3333 North 27th Street
Milwaukee, Wisconsin 53216

KROME, Esq., Robert J. (P)
3075 North 35th Street
Milwaukee, Wisconsin 53210

LIPTON, Esq., Paul P. (P)
625 North Milwaukee Street
Milwaukee, Wisconsin 53202

MANDELKER, Esq., Adolph I. (P)
2040 West Wisconsin Avenue
Milwaukee, Wisconsin 53233

MOUAT, Esq., Malcolm P. (P)
Box 546
17 North Franklin Street
Janesville, Wisconsin 53545

SCHLOTTHAUER, Esq., George McD. (P)
20 N. Carroll Street
P. O. Box 750
Madison, Wisconsin 53701

WYOMING

MURANE, Esq., Edward E. (P)
504 Wyoming Nat. Bank Bldg.
Casper, Wyoming 82601

AMERICANS PRACTISING OR LIVING ABROAD

ALEXANDER, Dr., Leon (P) (C)
161 Boulevard Haussmann
Paris 8, France

ANGELO, Esq., Homer G. (P)
284 Avenue de Tervueren
Brussels, Belgium

BAUM, Esq., Axel H. (P) (C)
13 Rue Quentin Bauchart
Paris 8, France

BECKMAN, Miss Gail McKnight (P)
Faculty of Law
University of Glasgow
Glasgow W. 2., Scotland

CAMPBELL, Jr., Esq., Nicholas J. (P)
Esso Europe Inc.
50 Stratton Street
London W. 1., England

COHEN, Esq., Stanley (P)
44 Champs Elysees
Paris 8, France

CRANE, Esq., Benjamin F. (P)
4 Place de la Concorde
Paris 8, France

DIKE, Esq., Norman Staunton (P)
Corsier Port
Geneve, Switzerland

DUPUCH, Esq., Eugene A. P. (P)
P. O. Box 1451
Nassau, Bahamas

EDDLEMAN, Esq., William R. (P)
Cante 15, 421-423
Mexico, 1., D. F.

FARRELL, Esq., Edward F. (P) (C)
Calle de General Mola
17-8⁰ dcha
Madrid 1, Spain

GOTTESMAN, Esq., A. Edward
Coudert Brothers
Aldwych House
Aldwych, London W. C. 2
England

GRAY, III, Esq., Gilson B. (P)
386 Avenue Louise
Brussels, Belgium

HOAGLAND, Jr., Esq., Alexander C. (P)
Av. Juarez 14-802-806
Mexico 1, D. F.

HODGSON, Esq., Patrick H. (P)
54 Gracechurch Street
London, E. C. 3., England

HUNT, Jr., Esq., John T. (P) (C)
4 Place de la Concorde
Paris 8, France

HURLOCK, Esq., James B. (P)
c/o White & Case
96 A Avenue Franklin Roosevelt
Brussels 5, Belgium

JACKSON, Jr., Esq., Roy D. (P)
2 Portman Street
London W. I., England

JAMES, Esq., Thomas S. (P)
c/o Amoco International S. A.
7 rue Versonnex
Geneva, Switzerland

JENSEN, Esq., Norman
C. P. O. Box 1335
Tokyo, Japan

JOLLON, Esq., Alfred J. (P)
Avenida Ipiranga
318-17 andar
Sao Paulo 4, S. P., Brazil

KENTON, Esq., Peter F. (P)
33 rue Eranger
Paris 16, France

LINDZON, Esq., Jerry M. (P) (C)
Villa Santa Maria
Loma de San Pablo
Torremolinos (Malaga), Spain

LOWY, Esq., George T. (P)
4, Place de la Concorde
Paris 8, France

LYMAN, Esq., Albert (P) (C)
Wang Lee Building
297 Suriwongse Road
Bangkok, Thailand

MOORE, Esq., Richard H. (P)
41 Avenue de Friedland
Paris 8, France

NASH, Esq., Paul (P) (C)
2 Place de l'Albertine
Brussels, Belgium

DE PONTET, Esq., Andre B. (P) (C)
Palais Ruscino
14 Quai Antoine 1er
Monaco, Monaco

PISANO, Esq., Paolo
Graham & James
Porta Pinciano
Rome, Italy

RAMSEUR, Jr., Esq., Thomas M. (P)
White and Case
20 Place Vendome
Paris 1, France

REEVES, Esq., H. van Kirk (P)
52 Avenue des Champs-Elysees
Paris 8, France

REZAC, Esq., William Joseph (P)
8, rue de la Paix
Paris, France

SACKMANN, Esq., William Arthur (P)
2 Rue de Lievre
1227 Geneva, Switzerland

STATOPOULOS, Esq., George N. (P)
15 Rue de Crayer
Brussels, Belgium

VON SAHER, Esq., LL. B., Edward (P)
24 Hercules Seghersiaan
Bilthoven, The Netherlands

VENEZUELA

AGUDO FREYTES, Dr. E. (S)
Reducto A Muncipal
Edf. Fonseca No. 5
Caracas

BRICE, Dr. Angel Francisco (S)
Escritorio Brice
Apartado 3416
Caracas

DE LIMA, Dr. Jose Jacinto Faria
President, Colegio de Abogados
del Distrito Federal
Av. Paez - El Paraiso Apart.347
Caracas

MUJICA RODRIGUEZ, Dr. Rafael (S)
Este Edificio Seguros
Oficina 907, Apartado 674
Caracas

PALACIOS BLANCO, Dr. Esteban (S)
Apartado de Correos No. 3857
Caracas

WEST INDIES

McNamara, Esq., Desmond A. (C)
Chambers
Castries, St. Lucia

YUGOSLAVIA

Markovic, Dr. Milivoje (S) (C)
Deligradska 22
Belgrade

ZAMBIA

Care, Esq., Richard Geoffrey (S)
P. O. Box 1544
Ndola

Mitchley, M. A.; A. O. R., President
Law Society of Zambia
P. O. Box 1741
Lusaka

SUBSCRIBING LIBRARIES

American Bar Foundation, Cromwell Library, 1155 East 60th Street, Chicago 60637, USA

Association of the Bar of the City of New York, Library, 42 West 44th Street, New York, N. Y. 10036, USA

California State Library, P. O. Box 2037, Sacramento, California 95809, USA

University of California, School of Law Library, 405 Hilgard Avenue, Los Angeles, California, 90024, USA

University of California, Continuing Education of the Bar Library, Extension Division, 2223 Fulton Street, Berkeley 4, California, USA

The University of Chicago, Law Library, 1121 East 60th Street, Chicago, Illinois 60637, USA

University of Colorado, Law Library, Boulder, Colorado, USA

Columbia University, Law Library, Kent Hall, New York, N. Y. 10027, USA

Cornell Law School, Law Library, Myron Taylor Hall, Ithaca, New York, USA

Deutscher Bundestag, Bibliothek, 53 Bonn, Germany

Duke University, Law Library, Durham, North Carolina, USA

The Ford Foundation, Library, 320 East 43rd Street, New York, N. Y. 10017, USA

Harvard Law School Library, Acquisitions Department, Langdell Hall, Cambridge 38, Mass., USA

University of Houston, Law Library, Cullen Blvd., Houston, Texas 77004, USA

Institut für internationales und ausländisches Recht und Rechtsvergleichung, Freie Universität Berlin, Van't-Hoff-Straße 8, West Berlin, Germany

State University of Iowa, Law Library, Iowa City, Iowa, USA

The Library of Congress, Exchange and Gift Division, Washington, D. C. 20025, USA

Los Angeles County Law Library, 301 West First Street, Los Angeles, California 90012, USA

Louisiana State University, Law Library, University Station, Baton Rouge, La., USA

University of Michigan, Law Library, Ann Arbor, Michigan, USA

University of Minnesota, The Law Library, The Law School, Minneapolis 14, Minn., USA

New York University, Library of the School of Law, Vanderbilt Hall, Washington Square, New York 10003, New York, USA

Northwestern University, School of Law, Elbert H. Gary Library, 357 East Chicago Ave., Chicago, Illinois, 60611, USA

Ohio State University, Law Library, 1659 N. High Street, Columbus 10, Ohio, USA

Oklahoma Department of Libraries, 109 State Capitol, Oklahoma City, Oklahoma, 73105, USA

Palace of Peace, Library, The Hague, The Netherlands

Rutgers University Law Library, 180 Plane Street, Newark, New Jersey, USA

Rutgers University, The State University Law Library, Camden, New Jersey 08102, USA

San Francisco Law Library, 436 City Hall, San Francisco, California, 94102, USA

Southern Methodist University, School of Law, Dallas, Texas, USA

Stanford University, Law Library, Stanford, California, USA

United Nations Library, Acquisition Unit/G & E, New York, N. Y. 10017, USA

United Nations Library, Geneva, Switzerland

Vanderbilt University, Vanderbilt Law Library, Nashville, Tennessee 37203, USA

University of Virginia, Law Library, Charlottesville, Virginia, 22901, USA

University of Washington, Law Library, Seattle, Washington 98105, USA

Wayne State University, Law Library, Detroit, Michigan 48202, USA

Western Reserve University, Law Library, Cleveland, Ohio, USA

University of Wisconsin, Law Library, Madison, Wisconsin 53706, USA

Yale Law School Library, New Haven, Connecticut, USA

Additional material from *Twelfth Conference of the International Bar Association,* ISBN 978-94-017-4549-9, is available at http://extras.springer.com

EXTRA
MATERIALS
extras.springer.com

GPSR Compliance

The European Union's (EU) General Product Safety Regulation (GPSR) is a set of rules that requires consumer products to be safe and our obligations to ensure this.

If you have any concerns about our products, you can contact us on ProductSafety@springernature.com

In case Publisher is established outside the EU, the EU authorized representative is:

Springer Nature Customer Service Center GmbH
Europaplatz 3
69115 Heidelberg, Germany

Batch number: 10830943

Printed by Printforce, the Netherlands